Digital Restoration from Start to Finish

Digital Restoration from Start to Finish

How to Repair Old and Damaged Photographs

Ctein

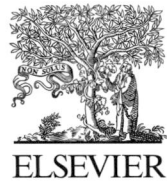

AMSTERDAM • BOSTON • HEIDELBERG • LONDON
NEW YORK • OXFORD • PARIS • SAN DIEGO
SAN FRANCISCO • SINGAPORE • SYDNEY • TOKYO

Focal Press is an imprint of Elsevier

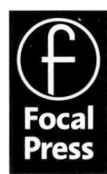

Acquisitions Editor: Diane Heppner
Project Manager: Paul Gottehrer
Assistant Editor: Stephanie Barrett
Marketing Manager: Christine Degon Veroulis
Cover Design: Alisa Andreola

Focal Press is an imprint of Elsevier
30 Corporate Drive, Suite 400, Burlington, MA 01803, USA
Linacre House, Jordan Hill, Oxford OX2 8DP, UK

 Recognizing the importance of preserving what has been written, Elsevier prints its
books on acid-free paper whenever possible.

Library of Congress Cataloging-in-Publication Data
Application submitted

British Library Cataloguing-in-Publication Data
A catalogue record for this book is available from the British Library.

ISBN 13: 978-0-240-80814-7
ISBN 10: 0-240-80814-2

For information on all Focal Press publications
visit our website at www.books.elsevier.com

08 09 10 10 9 8 7 6 5 4 3

Printed in China

Dedication

To Paula Butler and Laurie Toby Edison
with love and admiration—now and always

Contents

CHAPTER 4

Getting the Photo into the Computer   89

CHAPTER 5

Restoring Tone   129

How-To's

Introduction

Why Restore Digitally?

I love reviving old photographs. I get almost as much pleasure from saving someone's cherished, but presumably lost, photograph as from printing a brand new one of my own. I enjoy it so much that I have even started a second business (http://photo-repair.com) just for doing digital photo restoration.

Digital photo restoration is no more magical nor mysterious than ordinary photographic printing . . . and no less. It still feels like a minor miracle has occurred when a lovely photographic print, brand new or restored to life, appears before my eyes. But, whether it happens in the darkroom or at the computer, that miracle is based in established routine, using tools and techniques that anyone can learn. Experience and skill count for a lot, which is why I'm a good printer (and restorer), but it's not a secret art. Anyone can learn to restore photographs, just as anyone can learn to print.

Digital restoration recovers and restores a photograph to its proper glory while leaving the original object unaltered. You can restore almost any type of original photograph—color and B&W; slides, negatives, and prints; sheet film and roll film; and glass plates. You can even reconstruct full-color images from color separation films or plates. The restoration process doesn't involve any physical manipulation of the original photograph beyond making a high-quality scan. All the restorative work takes place in the computer, not on the original photograph, which means there is much less risk of damage to the original than with conventional physical photo restoration.

Digital restoration can work wonders; it usually produces much greater improvements in image quality than conventional physical restoration. It is possible to re-create truly beautiful photographs digitally, something that is often impossible with physical restoration. If restoring the image, not the original photograph, is what's important, then digital restoration is the safest and the best way to resurrect a photograph.

Digital restoration has one other significant advantage over physical restoration: The results are theoretically permanent. A physical restoration of a photograph is subject to physical deterioration, just as the original photograph was. With modern materials and techniques, physical restorations will probably last longer than the original photographs did, but they won't last indefinitely; no physical artwork does. A digital restoration has a potentially unlimited life. As long as proper procedures and precautions are in place, it can be maintained indefinitely in its pristine and original form.

A physical restoration is a unique object, just as the original photograph was. That rarity may be part of its value, but it's also a curse; the restored artifact is just as prone to loss or destruction as it ever was. A digital restoration can be shared with others as prints or images on a screen, it can be duplicated exactly, and it can be stored in multiple places. Once a photograph is digitally restored, its prospects for remaining part of our culture become vastly improved.

Digital restoration can have many goals (see Chapter 1, The Big Picture), but the primary objective is to resurrect the photograph that was originally there. The heart of what I do is not painting, drawing, nor hand-tinting. Restoration is never a matter of mere retouching. The only time I "create" parts of a photograph is when that area in the original is so badly damaged that there is nothing of the image to be recovered.

When you are restoring a photo, you're doing much more than simply performing technical manipulation. Your goal may not even be strict restoration; you may also be reinterpreting the original photograph for different sensibilities and times, as you would when printing any photograph. Always think like a photographer and never forget that you are working on a photograph made by some other photographer. Don't lose sight of this; you want to be "in their head," with the objective of making a beautiful photograph, not just a serviceable rendering.

You won't always know where you're going when you're doing a restoration because originals are often so badly deteriorated that you can't even get a sense of what the photograph must have looked like until you're halfway done. That's different from most crafts, where the skilled artist can pretty well visualize what the final artwork should look like before ever picking up a tool. Nonetheless, when you start out, you'll have some idea in your head of where you want to take the work. Always maintain an aesthetic sensibility about what you are doing and why, and always remember to take that mental step back from the work, look at it, and ask yourself, "Does this photograph look good?"

About This Book

I'm big on workflow. As my friends the Flying Karamazov Brothers put it, "It doesn't matter how you get there if you don't know where you're going." That's why this book is much more than just a compendium of image processing tricks and techniques. I think it's important to understand the entire job of creating a digital restoration from start to finish. The core of restoration is the magic you perform digitally in your favorite image processing program, but that core means little if you don't have a good grasp of the complete work path from getting the deteriorated photograph into the computer to preserving the restored image for the future. I want to make you aware of the context in which you do restoration and how to set up your working environment to do it.

This book mirrors the workflow as much as possible. The first three chapters set the stage on which you'll work. That's where I talk about your objectives and requirements for a restoration job, what computer hardware will best let you meet those goals, and what software is especially valuable for the restorer. I devote the fourth chapter to the subject of converting the photograph to digital form because extracting the maximum useful amount of data from the photograph is the key to achieving a good restoration.

The heart of the restoration process (and of this book) is the digital techniques and tools that actually work the magic of restoration. Chapters 5 through 9 will teach you the "moves." You can read this book as an extended single course in restoration (that's kind of how I wrote it) or you can mine it for particular tricks and techniques you need to solve specific problems. Each chapter starts off with a list of "how to's." Each how to points to a place in the chapter where you can learn how to accomplish a particular task. All of the how to's are listed in their own table of contents (at the end of the regular table of contents) for easy reference.

What comes next is learning how to put those moves together to create a complete "performance." Chapter 10, Examples, presents complete, step-by-step restorations that start with the originals and proceed through to the fully restored images. Chapter 10 sets a very high bar; I'm a perfectionist. Chapter 10 demonstrates the ultimate level of quality I can achieve in a restoration, but you don't have to go that far. Most of the time you'll find that considerably less effort will give you great results. Many of the how to's and examples in the other chapters are sufficient unto themselves. It doesn't take a lot of work to do a very satisfying restoration.

Once the restoration is complete, you'll need to get it back out of the computer. So, I finish the book with chapters on printing and archiving. It's not enough just to make a good print of the photograph you've restored—you should also take steps to ensure that the restoration file endures.

I could no more write a book about digital restoration that didn't focus on Adobe Photoshop than I could write a book on business planning that omitted Microsoft Excel. Photoshop is the big player in digital photography, and I'll be the first to acknowledge that it offers capabilities nothing else does.

I prepared most of the photographs and restorations for this book using Adobe Photoshop CS2 under Windows. Most of the software tools and techniques in this book work just as well under Mac OS (with a few notable exceptions); for the most part, the only difference is certain keystrokes.

Most of my methods work with earlier versions of Photoshop, although the further back you go, the more limitations you'll run into on what tools you can use. To prove that one doesn't need the latest and greatest, Example 3 in Chapter 10 is a restoration I did in the 1990s with Photoshop 5.5 running on a 233-MHz Pentium machine.

Photoshop isn't necessary. There are much less costly alternatives that will let you do restoration work efficiently. My goal is to give you skills and knowledge you can apply to do good restorations with any competent image processing program.

A good alternative for the serious worker who wants to spend under $100 instead of more than $500 (and is using a Windows machine) is Picture Window. I've worked extensively with this program. It's entirely capable and eminently affordable, and I talk more about it in Chapter 3, Software for Restoration.

I use a lot of different third-party plug-ins and software utilities for doing my restoration work. Chapter 3 provides summaries of all of them. If one of these tools catches your interest when you read about me using it, you can learn more about that program there. These tools and the cases where I've applied them are also indexed in the back under "software."

About Other Books

Can you have too many Photoshop and digital printing books? Absolutely! I have a shelf full of excellent books, every one of which has something of value to impart. The problem is that you could spend your whole life reading books like these, and only two things would happen. The first is that you would never get any photographs made and printed, and the second is that eventually your brain would fill up and your head explode.

Some folks are undeniably gurus in this field. I'll read anything that Bruce Fraser or Andrew Rodney cares to write. If you want to understand the underlying principles of Photoshop specifically and digital printing in general, these gentlemen have it nailed. But the single book that I would say you absolutely, positively need to have on your shelf is Martin Evening's *Adobe Photoshop CS2 for Photographers* (also from Focal Press, just like the book you're holding in your hands). I can't think of a better book for telling you how to actually use the program.

I read the current edition before sitting down to write my book. Every time I read something pertinent to this book that I didn't know, I'd forgotten about, or that I'd never had explained to me really clearly before,

I flagged that page with a sticky note. I flagged dozens upon dozens of pages—and it's not as if I'm a beginner; I've been doing electronic (what we called it in the old days) printing for more than 30 years. Point made?

The other book that ought to be on your must-buy list is Katrin Eismann's *Photoshop Restoration & Retouching* from New Riders. Katrin is brilliant, even though she modestly claims otherwise. Her retouching skills are awesome, as is her ability to create entirely missing portions of photographs out of thin air. I'll never be close to her when it comes to wholesale re-creation of absent imagery and fine-art retouching.

If you read and assimilate the two books just discussed and mine, you'll know enough to take over the world.

If you are interested in doing accurate restorations of old prints and want to understand better what they should look like and how they have deteriorated, there is no finer book than *Care and Identification of 19th-Century Photographic Prints* by James M. Reilly. As of this writing, the book seems to be out of print. Normally it would retail for about $30, but the only copies I see available are running $80, an awfully large chunk of change. Recommended, nonetheless, for the dedicated restorer.

Keeping in Touch

Long-time readers know that I'm always happy to answer questions and provide helpful advice whenever I can. If you have any questions about the content of this book or need any assistance in matters photographic, feel free to e-mail me at ctein@pobox.com. Should that e-mail address change, you'll still be able to reach me through my websites, "Ctein's Online Gallery" (http://ctein.com) and "Digital Photo Restoration by Ctein" (http://photo-repair.com).

Photo-repair.com has a "hidden" page devoted to this book at the URL http://photo-repair.com/photobook.htm that contains corrections and updates before they appear in new paper editions of this book. That page also has sample image files from this book for you to work with. The folks who provided their personal photographs for this book have generously given permission for me to put the files online for your private enjoyment. You can download them and practice your restoration techniques on them. These files are for your personal use on your computer only. Please do not redistribute them, publish them, post them on your website, or link to them.

Acknowledgments

First and foremost, I would like to thank my editor, Diane Heppner at Focal Press, who proposed this book, encouraged me to write it, and demonstrated remarkable and gracious patience as it slouched its way toward reality. Paul Gottehrer, my production manager, did a speedy and exemplary job of converting my scribblings into the fine pages you're reading. Paula Butler, Laurie Toby Edison, and Carol Everhart Roper read every last word of the manuscript and corrected my grammar, punctuation, logic, and clarity; their assistance was incalculably valuable.

Finally I would like to thank those wonderful folks who provided the personal and family photographs that serve as examples throughout this book: Dan Becks, Scott Brock, Grace Butler, Tee Corinne, Howard Davidson, Jules Dickinson, Bayla Fine, John Fleshin, Sarah Goodman, Bill Jemison, Ericka Johnson, Stuart Klipper, Laura Majerus, Clyde McConnell, Ron Mowry, Myrna Parmentier, Jane Reber, and Carol Everhart Roper.

About the Author

Ctein is the author of several hundred magazine articles on photographic topics and of *Post Exposure: Advanced Techniques for the Photographic Printer* (Focal Press, 2000). He has been doing darkroom printing for 40 years and is one of the few remaining practitioners of the art of dye transfer printing. He has been making electronic and digital prints for more than 30 years. Ctein resides in Daly City, California, in a house that overlooks the ocean with his companion of 20 years, Paula Butler, along with too many computers, 20,000 books, and two demented psittacines.

CHAPTER 1

The Big Picture

"Where Do You Want to Go Today?"

When I sat down to plan this book, I quickly realized that the ideal photo restoration workflow was an elusive and possibly even mythological creature. Oh yes, in the broadest sense there's a clear-cut pattern. Scan the original photograph into your computer, use the image processing program of your choice to correct the defects, print the finished photograph, and archive the restored digital image file. The organization of this book reflects that flow.

The problem with that facile prescription is that it glosses over the real work that's hidden in the three magic words "correct the defects." The majority of this book is about satisfying that modest phrase. Hanging over that is the larger and more serious question of just what it is you're after. Photo restoration covers a lot of territory. Goals are situational. For example, are you trying to be historically accurate or aiming for the best art? Depends on the job.

So, before diving into photo restoration, think about your situation and contemplate the following questions:

- Who are you, and whose expectations matter?

- Who are you trying to make happy?

- Are you trying to re-create an historically accurate photograph?

- How important is the photograph and how much scrutiny might it be subject to?

- How big will the restoration be?

Of course these are interrelated, but they provide a framework for organizing your thoughts.

Who Are You, and Whose Expectations Matter?

Are you doing a restoration to please yourself or to please a friend, relative, or client? Are you restoring the photograph as a hobby or favor, or are you doing it professionally?

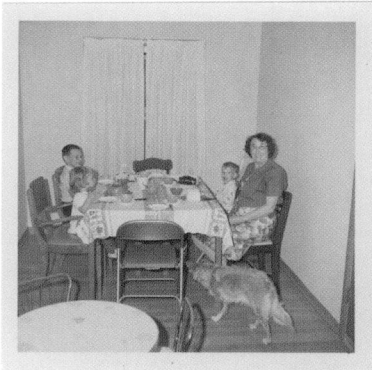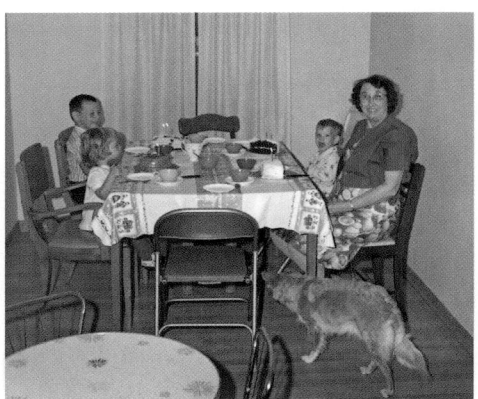

Fig. 1-1 Digital restoration can easily restore a faded family snapshot like the one on the left. Most of the improved tone and color in the restoration on the right results simply from making a good scan, following the principles I present in Chapter 4. A little judicious cropping and burning-in produces a photograph that's even better than the original.

The difference between a professional and a hobbyist in this case is not one of skill or talent. It's that the professional must satisfy a client whose desires come first. Those needs control the kind of work you do.

Who Are You Trying to Make Happy?

Aunt Sarah and Uncle James will most likely be delighted with anything you do to make that family photo look better (Figure 1-1). Their pleasure is more important than perfection. A professional client who is paying you big bucks for a restoration will likely demand considerably more of your skills.

I've written this book from the point of view of the professional and the perfectionist. I like feeling as if I've waved a magic wand that perfectly and invisibly undid the ravages of age. If I can take it one step further and make that photograph into something that's even nicer than the original (Figure 1-2), better still. Making "the best of all possible prints" from the damaged photograph is what makes me happy.

If you master all of the techniques I present in this book, I guarantee you'll be able to do restorations that will please just about anyone. But you may not want nor need to go to the extremes I do. Don't slavishly follow my goals. Figure out what will satisfy you in a restoration, and aim for that. I may take a restoration job from A to Z, but you may feel that stopping at K is entirely satisfactory.

My obsession shouldn't drive you. It's possible to spend unlimited amounts of time playing with a digital photograph, trying to make it absolutely pixel-perfect. If that's what tickles your fancy (it does mine), that's great. But if you're doing professional restorations for clients, they're not going to want to spend unlimited amounts of money, and

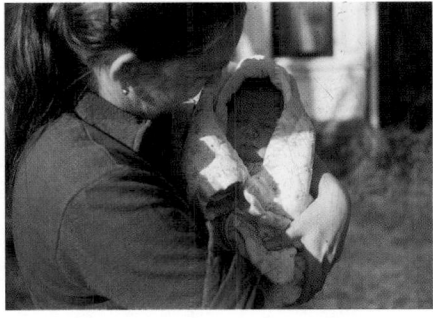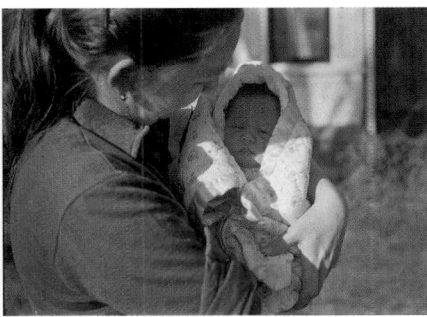

Fig. 1-2 Digital tools can do more than repair damage. The original Kodachrome slide on the left isn't faded at all, although it is badly scratched. Restoration not only removes the scratches, it improves detail in the shadows and highlights. The restoration on the right is a more attractive photograph, overall.

you have to know when to call it quits. And if you're doing restoration for your own enjoyment, never ever forget that it's about having fun. If you reach the point where following still one more recommendation of mine feels more like work than play, then don't! You can achieve good restorations without it.

Are You Trying to Re-Create an Historically Accurate Photograph?

If so, then it's of paramount importance not to introduce any extraneous detail that wasn't there, nor to remove any significant detail from the photograph. That can severely restrict the kind of gross repairs that you can do, especially if entire pieces of the photograph are missing.

In Figure 1-3 there's no important information that would be lost or altered by cropping the photograph or cloning in the lawn to fill in the missing areas. Figure 1-4 is another matter; there's no way to repair the two figures on the right to accurately show what they're doing or even who the rightmost man is. Artistically, we have a free hand in restoring this photograph; historically, most definitely not.

More subtly, does the photo need to be technically accurate? That will rarely be the case, but in Chapter 10, Examples, page 399, where I restore an astronomical plate (Figure 1-5), I had to decide whether I wanted a photograph that looked good or one that remained astronomically accurate. I went for "looking good" and invisibly repaired cracks and gaps with bits of the star field brought in from intact parts of the plate. Consequently, the "restored" image contains a certain number of stars that don't actually exist! Well, it's my photograph, so it's my call. Were I doing this repair for an astronomer or a scientific collection, I would not do that!

If the restoration requires accuracy, then you'll need to know something about what photographs of that type are supposed to look like.

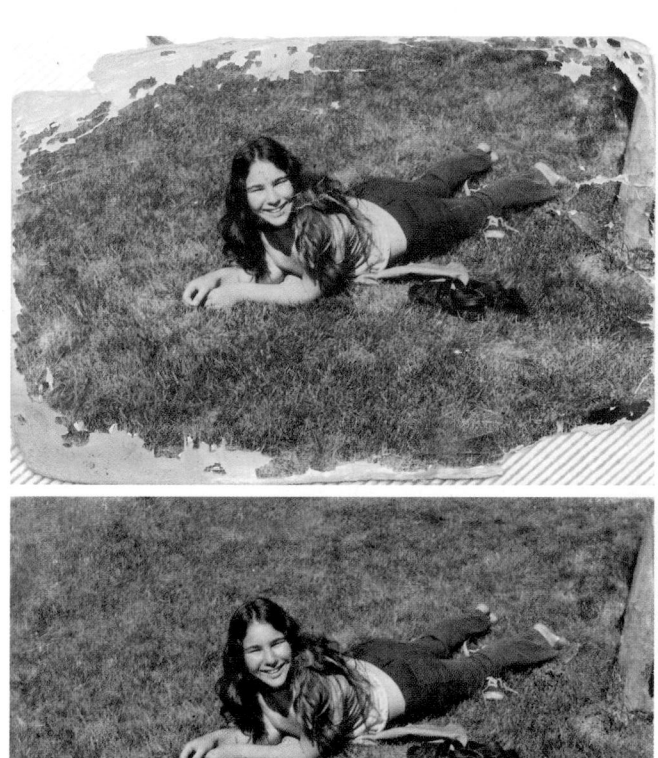

Fig. 1-3 Specialized tools like Image Doctor (see Chapter 3) can fill in missing parts of photographs so perfectly that you can't tell where the original leaves off and the reconstruction begins. It's fine to take such liberties when historical accuracy is unimportant.

James Reilly's book, *Care and Identification of 19th-Century Photographic Prints* (recommended in the Introduction), is a fine reference up through the early part of the 20th century. I don't know of any comparable book for modern color images, so be prepared to do some research on what the color photograph is supposed to look like if you're asked to do an accurate restoration.

Most of the time your goal will be artistic—make the best restoration you can that looks good. This brings me to my next question for you.

How Important Is the Photograph, and How Much Scrutiny Might It Be Subject To?

The ordinary family photograph that Aunt Sarah and Uncle James proudly placed on their mantle is not going to be closely examined nor subject to critical analysis. You can take many liberties in your

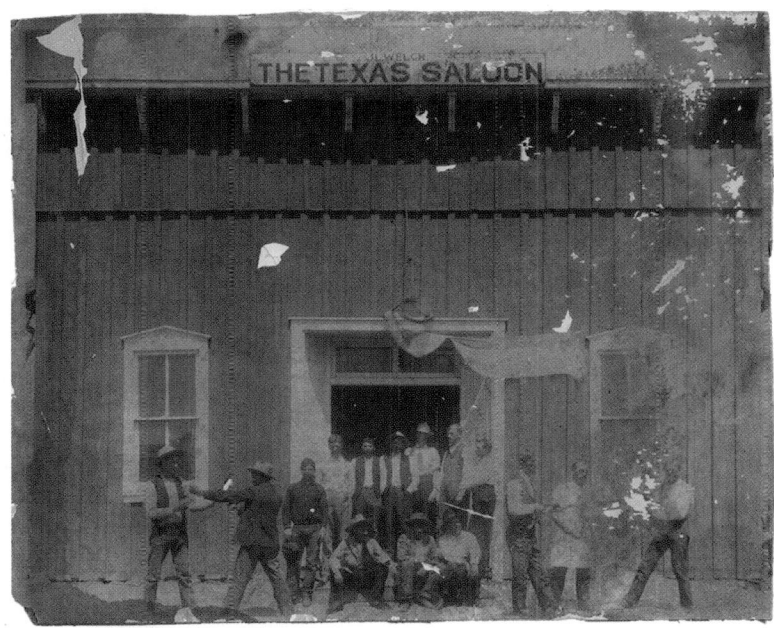

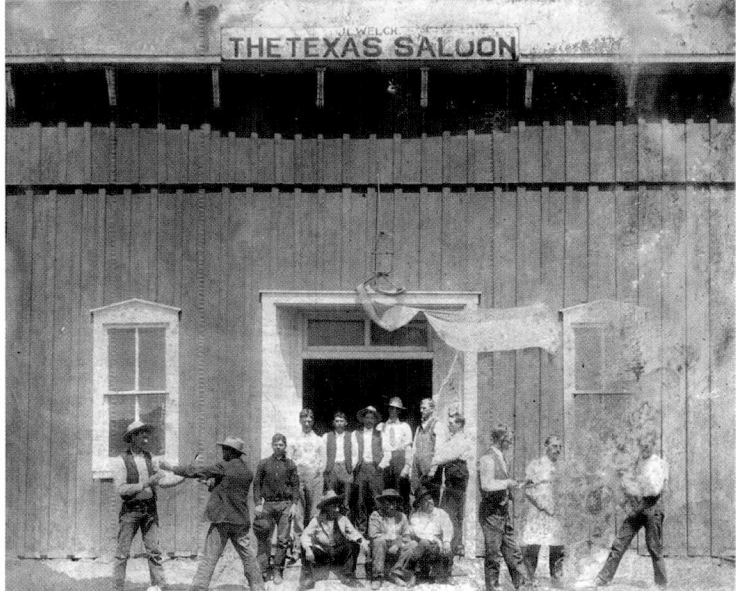

Fig. 1-4 Retouch with caution if historical accuracy matters. Tools like Photoshop's Spot Healing Brush and Image Doctor can make quick work of the missing patches in the original upper photograph. But, as the bottom photograph shows, you can't restore detail that doesn't exist. How you "fix" the half-obliterated man on the right depends on whether you want an artistic restoration or a historically accurate one.

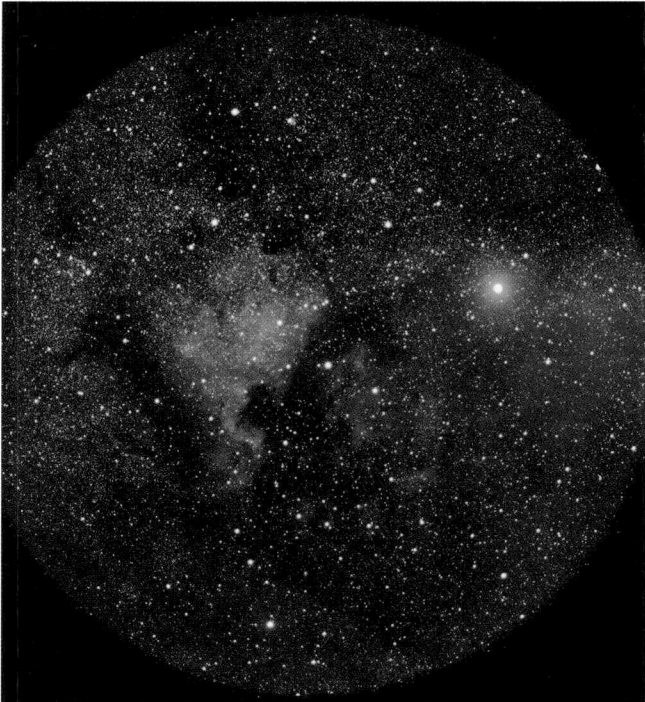

Fig. 1-5 Scientific photographs can be digitally restored. In Chapter 10, I describe, step by step, how this astronomical plate was recreated from eight broken shards of glass.

restoration as long as you remain true to the spirit of the photograph. Slight carelessness in technique will never be noticed.

Photographs of historic events or famous personages as in Figure 1-6 (restored in Chapter 10, page 386), on the other hand, may receive closer examination by future viewers. Minor details matter to the historian; a missing button or frayed collar may tell them something about the financial state of the subject when the photograph was made. Historians look at time sequences of famous personages to gauge their health and guess what effect the strains and joys of life and work may have had on them. Even modest cosmetic retouching of the sort you would do to any ordinary portrait to make the person slightly more attractive can have the effect of distorting history.

How Big Will the Restoration Be?

Most restorations are the same size as the originals or only modestly enlarged. You're not likely to need to make repairs down to the single-pixel level of detail. The more the original photograph is to be magnified in the final print, however, the more detailed and extensive your work has to be, because flaws and unrepaired damage that would never be noticed in a life-sized reproduction will be obvious in a 3× enlargement.

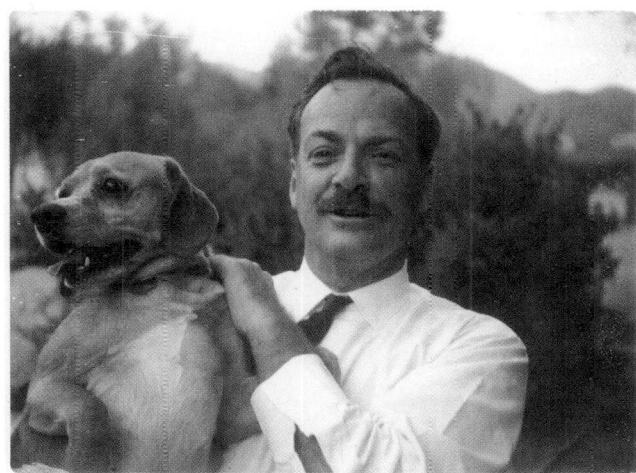

Fig. 1-6 This Polaroid photograph of a mustachioed Dr. Richard P. Feynman has historical importance, so a proper restoration should not change any details of the subject. See Chapter 10 to find out how much digital restoration can do even when subject to such restrictions.

This is not a quiz. You're not going to be graded on your responses. These are only questions to think about before you embark on a new restoration. They'll help you frame the problem in your head as you contemplate the central matter: What restoration challenges will you face?

The Art (and Craft) of Restoration

Most of the work I do to restore a photograph falls into one of the following five categories:

- Restoring tone
- Restoring color
- Fine-detail repairs and cleanup
- Major damage repairs
- Repairing uneven damage.

Restoring Tone

Photographs in need of restoration usually don't have very good tonality. Fading and staining will wash out blacks and make whites dingy and dark. A severely faded photograph will have a very narrow tonal range. A big part of restoration is expanding that compressed set of tones back to its original natural brilliance.

You can accomplish a lot simply by making a good scan of the photograph, and I've devoted Chapter 4, Getting the Photo into the

Computer, to that subject. As you'll discover, the process requires some care and attention to detail, but it's a pretty cut-and-dried one.

Beyond merely getting an acceptable tonal range from black to white, one must refine the tonal placement within the photograph so the highlights have their sparkle, shadow detail is brought out, and overall the print conveys the feeling of a fresh, new photograph. This is where the art and your talent and skill come in. Curves are a powerful tool for achieving great tonality, and once you master them you'll use them a lot. They're not the only tricks in the bag, though. The Shadow/Highlight adjustment in Photoshop and dodging and burn-in adjustment layers (see Chapter 5, Restoring Tone, page 160) go way beyond simple Curves in their power.

Restoring Color

Both B&W and color photographs need their color restored. Some B&W photographs will come to you with a pristine, neutral image, but in most of them, what was originally black and white may now be brown and white, brown and yellow, or even dark brown and not-so-dark brown. Part of the restoration job is getting that photograph back to its original hue. Not all photographs started out as true B&W; many of them were sepia or brown in color. Still, it's a pretty safe bet that the deteriorated photo doesn't have the color it did originally.

Color photographs (prints, slides, and negatives) almost always need color restoration. That's by far the most common reason someone will ask to have a color photograph restored. Only occasionally does one turn up where the color is just fine and there's just physical damage.

Just as with B&W photos, a good scan helps a lot; it's a necessary prerequisite to doing good color restoration. Occasionally a scan will accomplish most of the color restoration all by itself, as Figure 1-1 illustrates (I demonstrate this in Chapter 10, page 354). Most of the time, unfortunately, a good scan will provide the raw data I need but no more than that.

Curves are my constant companion, just as they were for restoring tones, but they're by no means the only tools I depend on for restoring color. Hue and saturation controls are very important; I also make heavy use of specialized plug-ins like Digital ROC.

Fine-Detail Repairs and Cleanup

Old photos invariably need to be cleaned up. They will be dirty and scratched and have fine cracks or crazed surfaces or annoying textures. Every photo you restore will have one or more of these defects to some degree. This kind of fine-structure repair often consumes the majority of the time I spend on a restoration. Much like picking up litter, it's not intellectually or artistically stimulating, and it's tedious to do, but the landscape looks a lot nicer when I'm done. My way of dealing with this is to put some music on so I don't get too bored by the repetitive activity, relax, and go at it.

I cover many tools in Chapter 8, Damage Control, that make this work go faster. The right filters and plug-ins attack the noise and "litter" more than the photographic image I'm trying to recover. I've a collection of masking tricks that select for the garbage, so I can work on it more aggressively (and quickly) without messing up the rest of the photograph. All of these aid the repair efforts, but they're not a replacement for close-in, pixel-by-pixel adjustments. They just make it much more efficient.

Because the cleanup work itself isn't very interesting, I don't dwell on it a lot in the Chapter 10, Examples. It's sufficient to say, "I painted over the scratches with such-and-such a filter with these settings." That tells you everything you need to know about how I did that bit of repair work. That glosses over the important fact that executing that one cleanup step may have taken me more time than all the preceding stages of the restoration.

Major Damage Repairs

Now I'm talking about the big stuff like tears, missing emulsion, and photos in pieces. These types of major repairs require very different tools and approaches than the fine-structure cleanup I just talked about. The damaged or obliterated areas are going to be larger than much of the fine detail in the photograph, so I cannot use mechanical fill-in and erasure tools.

Repairing these problems always requires some degree of re-creation of detail. Sometimes it's as easy as cloning in material from the surrounding area, as in Figure 1-3. Automated patching tools like Image Doctor or healing brushes in Photoshop are a big help to me. Often, though, these repairs require serious retouching and illustration creation skills. I'll be honest and admit that major retouching of this type is what I'm worst at. That's a big reason why I recommend Katrin's book, because she is so good at doing that.

Repairing Uneven Damage

I use the same tools for fixing streaks and stains in a print or tarnished and bleached spots that I use for correcting tone and color overall. The difference is that I have to fix those areas of the photograph separately from the rest. One way to do that is with history brushes or cloning between versions to paint in the corrections just where I want them. A more powerful way to do it, when I can, is to create a special selection or mask that contains only the differently damaged areas.

You've probably noticed that masking cropped up a lot in this list of problems and approaches. That's why I gave all of Chapter 7 over to masking techniques. Masking doesn't let you do much that you couldn't do by hand, but a good mask can save you most of that handwork by automatically placing the corrections where you want them and preventing them from leaking over into other parts of the photograph.

Fooling Around

Figuring out how exactly I'll repair a particular photo is, intellectually, by far the toughest part of the job. Making the corrections may take me a lot of time and work, anywhere from an hour to a day or more, but that part of it doesn't strain my brain. Mapping out the strategy which will get me from "A" (lousy image) to "Z" (great photograph) is the tricky bit.

The very first thing I do when I get a new restoration job is to play with it. I scan in a small version of the photograph. It can either be a low-resolution image or a high-resolution scan of a small portion of the entire photograph; often I do one of each. What I'm after is a small file size, so that I can get it into the computer and mess around with it quickly.

That first scan gives me the lay of the land, to figure out just what I have to work with and how far I might be able to take it. Many of the photographs I restore come to me as unintelligible (and sometimes nearly blank) pieces of paper, like Figure 1-7. I simply can't tell by looking at such photographs with the naked eye how much photographic information is hidden in that *tabula rasa*, let alone how I might fix it.

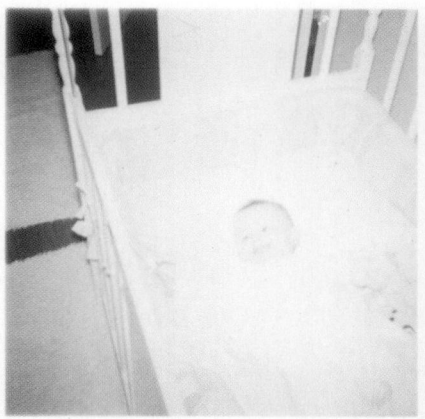 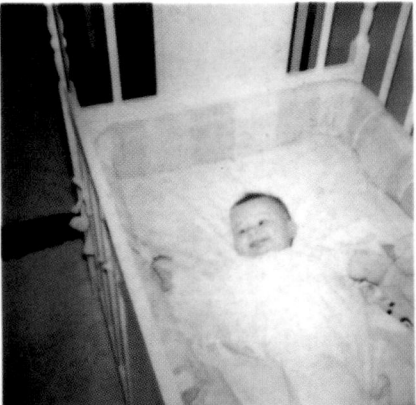

Fig. 1-7 Don't assume a photograph is unrecoverable until you've tried scanning it! A careful scan, using the procedures in Chapter 4, and some clever enhancement tricks (Chapter 5, page 167) can extract amazing amounts of detail from nearly blank photographs. See Chapter 10, Example 8, for the complete restoration process used on this photograph.

Even after years of experience, I am frequently surprised by what's possible. I've learned not to tell clients whether I can give them a good restoration based on my visual examination of the photograph. Too often I'm wrong; I underestimate how much quality photographic data is buried in that seemingly hopeless piece of paper or film and how much my hardware and software and skill can mine it.

Scanners excel at extracting the near-invisible. Using the guiding principles from Chapter 4, I adjust the curves and levels in my scanner software to pull out and emphasize as much of the real photographic information as I can. Looking at that on my screen gives me a pretty good idea of the potential I have to work with.

Once I can see the photograph more clearly, I decide what the biggest and most obvious problems are. Some photographs have great tone and color and lots of physical damage. Others are physically near-perfect but badly stained or faded. Usually it's a mix.

I don't immediately dive into serious restoration. Even though my time is money when I'm working on a job, I very consciously don't "work" with the photograph from the get-go. Instead, I just play, trying out different tools and ideas, noodling around for 30 minutes or so, trying out different approaches to find out what will most effectively fix the photograph's problems. Experience, of course, has given me a good sense of which treatments are likely to be the best remedy for which ills, but every photograph is different and has its little surprises. Hence, the play time.

I try very hard to not be too goal directed. My objective is to figure out where I want to take this photograph by learning what its potentials are and which of my tools and techniques have the most promise for bringing out that potential, not to drive myself in a prejudged direction. I try different sharpening or blurring filters, experiment with different masking tools that I have, explore different color-manipulation plug-ins. When I find something that feels like it might take me someplace interesting, I explore it further. It's exploration for the sake of exploration and the adventure of seeing where a photograph might take me. That's the mind-set I go into this with because, paradoxically, treating this as play makes me more productive by making me more creative. It's valuable because it helps me plan out my strategy and approach to that restoration.

Once I've settled on a course of action, I make a good scan of the photograph and save a copy of it. As I point out in Chapter 4, the kind of scan I make depends on the tools I want to use and the quality of the photograph. Looking at the test scan on the screen, I can see how much fine detail there really is in the photograph and how it relates to the physical damage and defects that I'm going to want to eliminate.

If the photograph isn't very sharp to begin with, I may go with a low-resolution scan that yields me a smaller, easier-to-work-with file. On the other hand, if I think I'm going to do a lot of fine-detail enhancement on the photograph, I scan at higher resolutions than I would if I

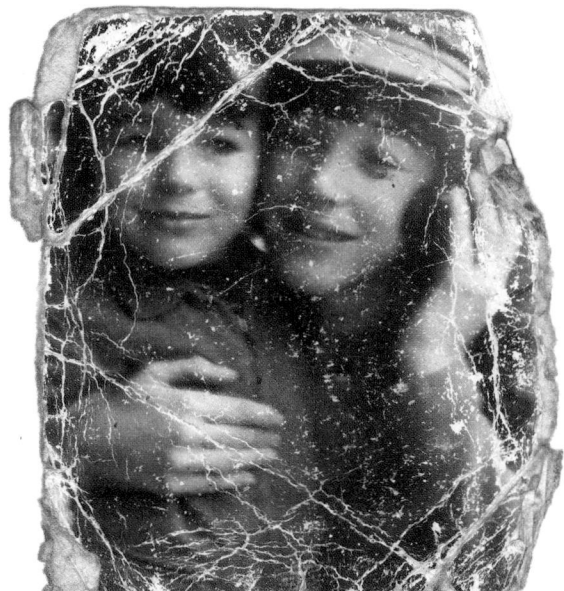

Fig. 1-8 This small photograph is a good candidate for a high-resolution scan, even though the picture isn't very sharp. A scan like that will make it easier to selectively repair the cracks and creases, as demonstrated in Chapter 8.

only wanted to capture the visible detail in the photograph. If a photograph has lots of damage (like cracks all over the surface) that has much finer detail than the actual photographic image does, I may choose to scan at very high resolutions. Then I can use spatial filters (see page 292) to pick out the cracks and crevices for repair without also selecting the true image detail (Figure 1-8).

Don't get the impression, though, that I'm starting out blind each time I get a new photo to restore. Every restoration job, like every photograph, is unique, but it's common for photographs of a similar nature to have similar problems. For example, if someone asks you to restore a mid-1960s color Polaroid print that's been in an album, it's likely that the photograph won't be really badly faded, but the colors will be poorly saturated, with dull and veiled highlights.

Another commonality is that the further you roll back the clock, the more likely the photograph will be physically damaged. There's certainly no shortage of recent photographs that have suffered trauma, and occasionally very old photographs are remarkably well cared for, but the trend is undeniable. Water and mildew damage, even parts of the photograph eaten away by vermin, show up more and more frequently as you go further into the past.

Based on my experience, the next section presents a list of the different categories of photographs you're most often asked to restore, roughly in order of commonness.

A Modest Taxonomy of Restoration

Prints

Amateur snapshots, mid-20th century to present

    B&W

    Color

Commercial and school portraits, mid-20th century to present

    B&W

    Color

Polaroid

    B&W

    Color

        Peel-apart style

        SX-70-style

Old photographs (pre-1930s)

Professional photographs

Slides

Kodachrome

Other slide films

Negatives

Color

B&W

    Film

    Glass plate

Newspaper Clippings

Let's take a look at these various categories.

Prints

B&W amateur snapshots, mid-20th century to present There's a good chance that the photo won't be badly stained or faded, but it will probably be somewhat low in contrast with grayish blacks because that's what the B&W photofinishers usually delivered. The color is often nice and neutral, but cheap albums take their toll, so many older photographs are

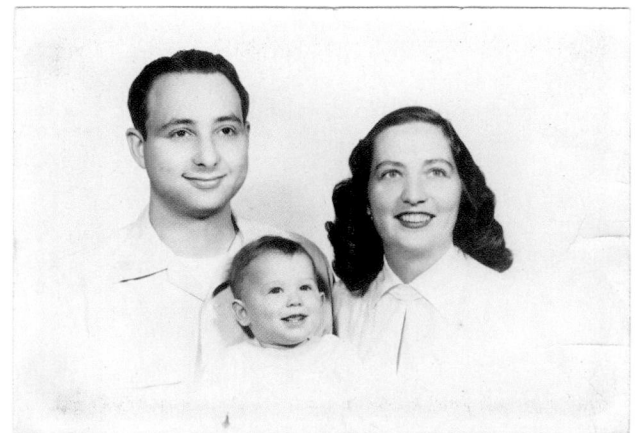

Fig. 1-9 Mid-20th-century B&W photographs may show some yellowing and mild tarnishing, damage that is easy to repair using the techniques from Chapter 9.

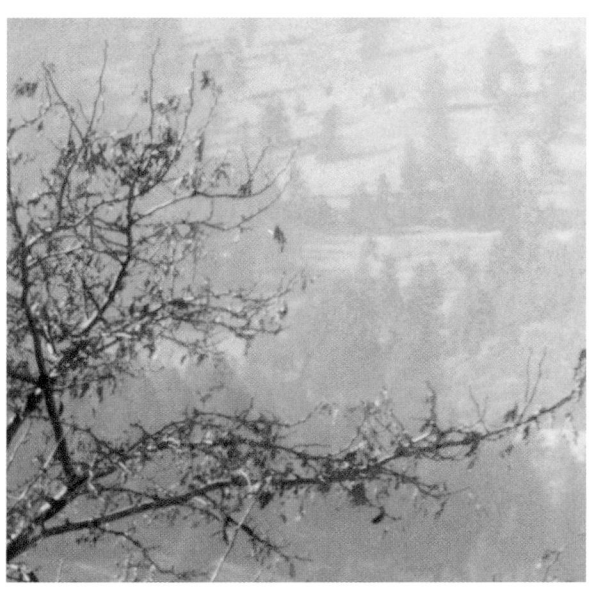

Fig. 1-10 B&W RC prints can suffer serious silvering-out and bronzing problems. The masking techniques in Chapter 7 work well for selecting this kind of damage for repair.

brown or yellow where the silver image has broken down (Figure 1-9).

Prints from the 1950s and 1960s will likely have some cracks from mishandling. Early resin-coated (RC) prints may have lots of fine cracking and crazing due to deterioration of the plastic layer carrying the image. Displayed RC prints may have severe silvering-out and bronzing problems; that is, there will be shiny or yellowish patches on the surface of the print (Figure 1-10). Selective masking of the damaged areas (see Chapter 7, Making Masks, page 244) works great on this.

Color amateur snapshots, mid-20th century to present The more recent the photograph, the better the color will be. If they haven't been on display, prints less than 25 years old won't be too badly faded. They'll have lost some density and saturation, but it won't be hard to bring them back with a good scan. If you get prints that young to restore, it's more likely the restoration is needed because of physical damage than fading.

Older prints will have faded; prints from the early 1970s will mostly be seriously damaged and those from the 1950s and 1960s may appear hopeless at first glance, looking almost blank like Figure 1-7. As you'll learn, it's amazing what good scans and digital techniques can recover even in those "hopeless" cases. Expect to see some uniform highlight stain in all older color prints.

Photographs that have been on display are another problem entirely; by the time they're sent to you, they'll probably be seriously faded. Textured papers, which were very popular in many periods, obscure the image. I discuss some tricks in Chapter 8, page 305, for dealing with them (Figure 1-11).

B&W commercial and school portraits, mid-20th century to present The situation with commercial and school portraits isn't much different than it is for amateur snapshots, but these prints will have better contrast and tonality than their amateur counterparts. The most likely kind of damage you'll see in younger prints will be physical problems such as cracking, tears, and dirt. The further back you go, the more the prints will be stained, but the staining is often uniform and so is easy to correct. Unfortunately, the average quality of older print processing was much poorer. Although quite a few are still in good shape, you see many portraits from the 1930s to early 1950s that have stained and turned brown or even yellow.

Color commercial and school portraits, mid-20th century to present The average quality and problems are no different from those you'll encounter with amateur photographs. Low-cost commercial and school portraiture was very variable in quality. Some school photographs from 30 years ago look surprisingly good; others have changed color in all sorts of bizarre ways (Figure 1-12).

Textured paper was very common, almost ubiquitous, for many years. The more faded the color photograph is, the more intrusive the texture will be after you restore it; the contrast increases you make to restore the color also increase the contrast of the texture pattern. Expect to have all the problems you would restoring an amateur color photograph, plus the paper texture to contend with.

B&W Polaroids Most B&W Polaroid prints needed lacquering to keep the silver image from quickly oxidizing. The condition of old B&W Polaroid prints depends on how well the photographer coated the print

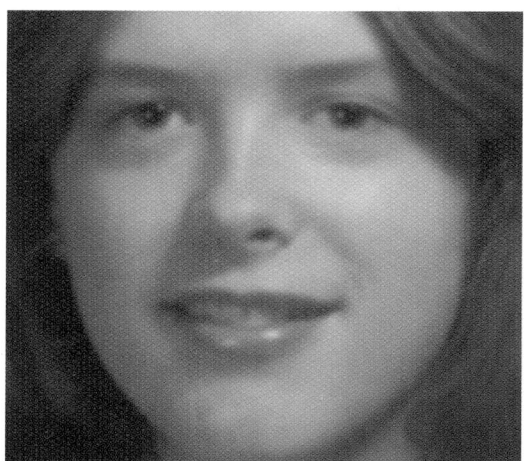

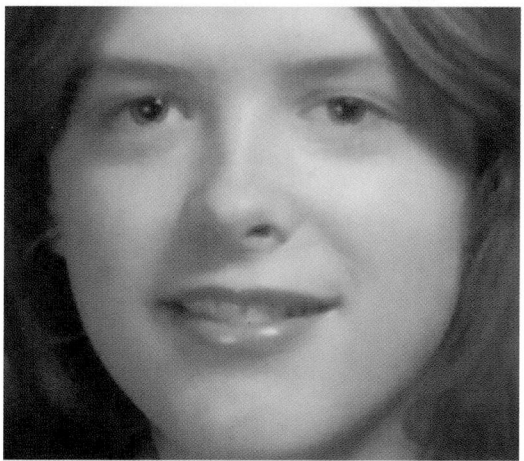

Fig. 1-11 Color portraits are often printed on textured paper that obscures the scanned image. Chapter 8 shows you how to eliminate that textured surface from the restoration.

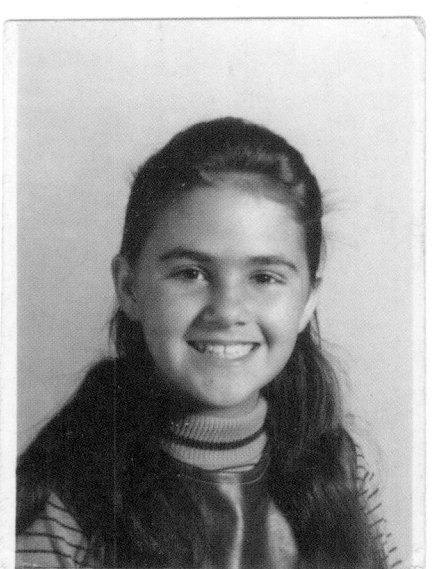

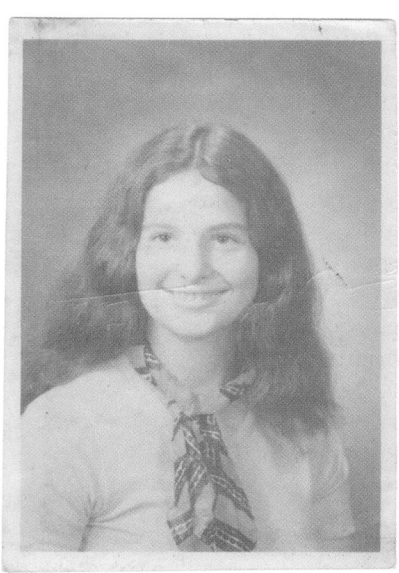

Fig. 1-12 Cheap school portraits come in a variety of (very wrong) colors. Digital restoration, using the methods in Chapter 6, can do a remarkable job of restoring the original color.

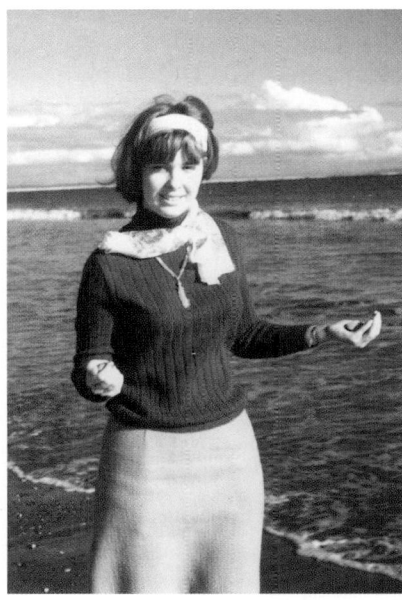
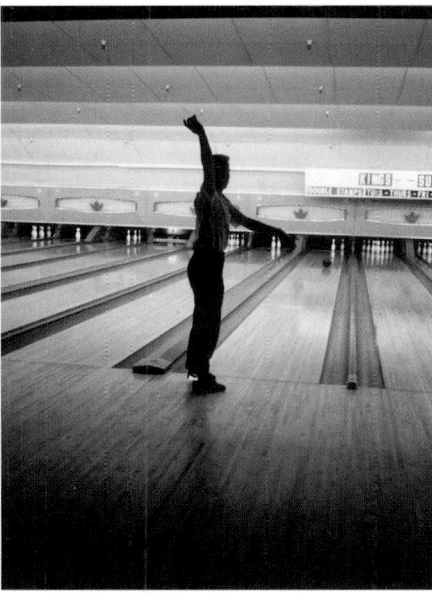

Fig. 1-13 How much B&W Polaroid prints fade depends on how well they were coated. These two prints both date from the same year in the late 1960s and were kept in the same album.

(Figure 1-13). You'll see prints with streaks where the well-lacquered portions still have good neutral B&W tones and the poorly coated streaks have faded to brown or yellow. Selective masking is one way to isolate those areas, but sometimes clever channel mixing will do the trick (see Chapter 7).

I don't know whether it's because of their small size or stiffer paper, but Polaroid prints are usually less cracked or torn than conventional photographs of the same vintage. You'll need to put in more work correcting uneven fading than repairing physical defects.

Color peel-apart Polaroids The peel-apart Polacolor prints have fairly stable dyes when the prints aren't on display. Prints from the 1960s and 1970s have usually faded much less than their conventional color counterparts. Polacolor color and tonal quality was not very good, though, so you'll almost always want to go the extra step in restoring these photographs to make them look better than they originally did (see Chapter 9, Tips, Tricks, and Enhancements). Expect older prints to have a greenish cast to them, especially in the highlights and skin tones, and whites will be far from true white (Figure 1-14). Mostly you'll be repairing physical damage and improving the tone and color quality over what it originally was. Simply making a carefully adjusted scan will often get you pretty good color.

Prints on display are another matter. If they've been exposed to light, Polacolor prints fade just as badly as conventional ones, sometimes worse.

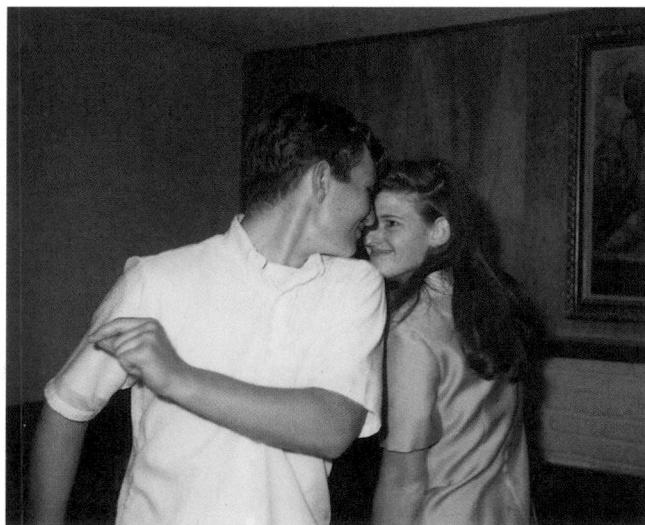

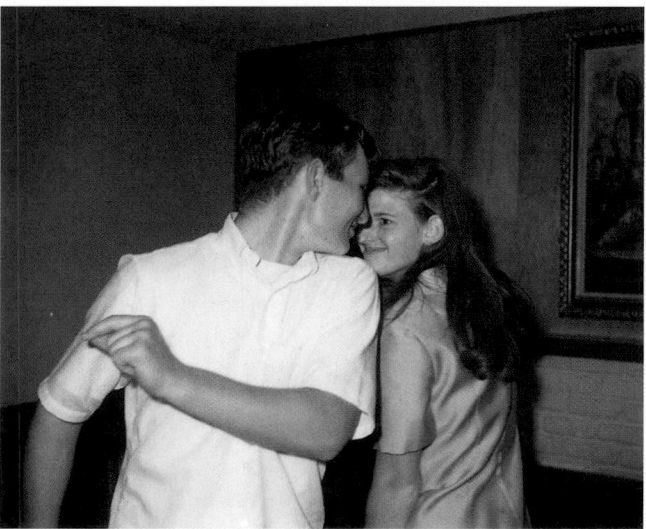

Fig. 1-14 Peel-apart Polacolor prints fade very little when they're kept in albums. The poor color of the original photograph (upper) is normal for this type of print; careful scanning and color adjustment can make them look better than new (lower).

Color SX-70-style Polaroids Just like the peel-apart prints, SX-70-type prints hold up well in the dark, but poorly on display. They acquire a yellowish highlight stain pretty quickly under all conditions, but it's usually uniform. Color improved with each successive generation of these materials, but it was never as good as conventional color prints, so my comments about improving the color of Polaroid prints apply here.

Because of their sturdy protective shell, these photographs usually won't be cracked, torn, or dirty, but they are subject to internal damage. Some older SX-70-style prints develop internal cracks, crazing, or a fine frost-like pattern that obscures the image (Figure 1-15).

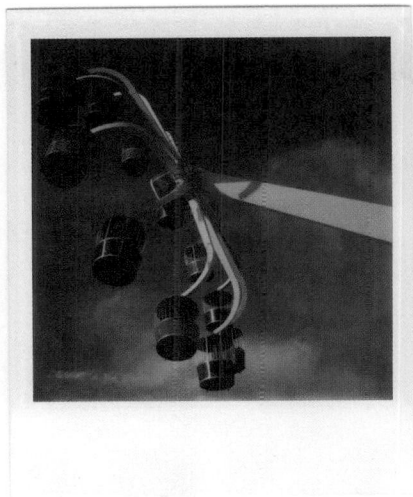 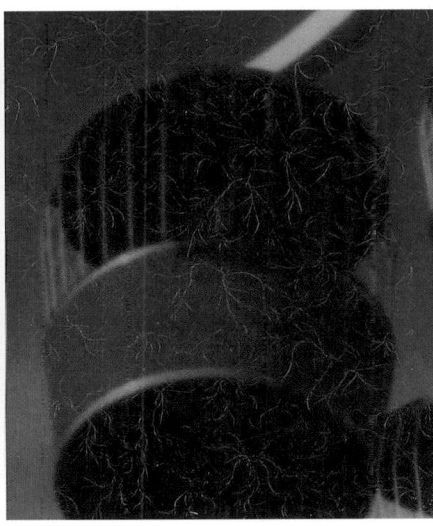

Fig. 1-15 Some Polaroid SX-70 prints have suffered internal damage. Repair them the same way you would a photograph with fine cracks or scratches on it (see Chapter 8).

Old photographs (pre-1930s) These "vintage" photographs will almost always be B&Ws. The whites invariably darken and turned anywhere from pale tan to dark brown. The image itself may be faded, so the overall contrast can be extremely low. The damage is often very non-uniform, so you'll have to make local corrections to the tones as well as overall ones. Dodging and burning masks (see Chapter 5, Restoring Tone) are of considerable help.

All of the photos will have some degree of physical damage (Figure 1-16). Restoring the tonal range of a low-contrast photo exaggerates the flaws; in extreme cases you'll be dealing with "noise" that is almost as strong as the "signal." Very old photographs are often missing pieces of the emulsion that will need to be re-created to make the photograph look good again.

Many of the photographs will have "tarnished out"; there will be shiny metallic-looking bronze or silver patches on the surface of the photograph, especially in higher density areas (Figure 1-17). You'll do best to attack those with selective masking (Chapter 7, Making Masks, page 244) so that you can correct those problems separately from the rest of the photograph. Chapter 8, Damage Control, page 298, tells you how to repair tarnish.

You'll see a fair number of hand-tinted B&W portraits. They will present you with challenging questions, not technical in nature, but artistic. If the goal is to produce a good-looking, hand-tinted portrait, modern tastes and sensibilities around such work are very different from those of 50 to 100 years ago. By today's standards, you may get a more pleasing photograph by eliminating the tinting entirely (not difficult) and turning it into a straight B&W photograph.

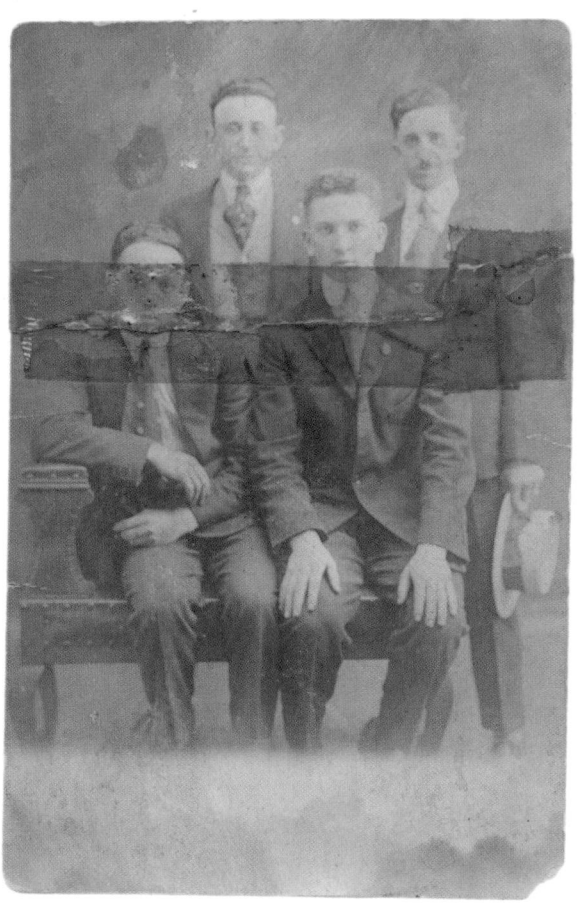

Fig. 1-16 The older the photograph, the more likely it is to be physically damaged. At the very least there will be dust, dirt, and scratches; in many cases there will be cracks and tears.

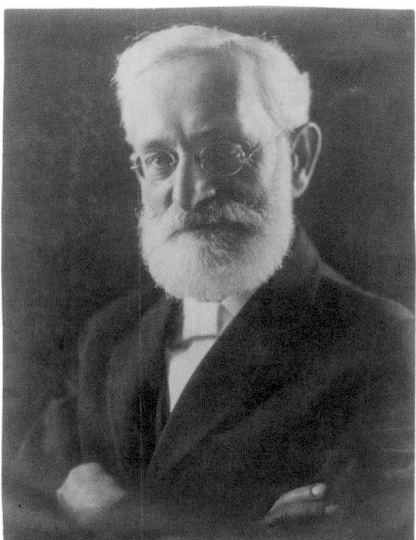
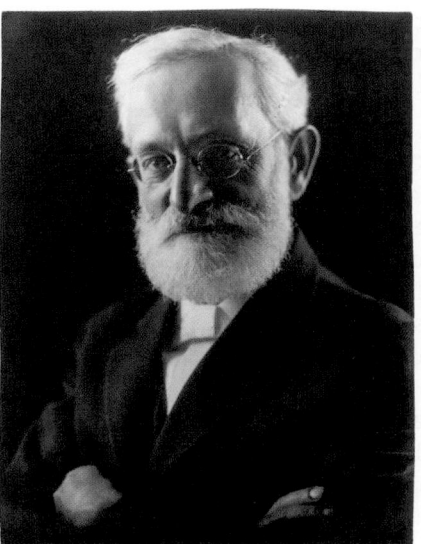

Fig. 1-17 Severe cases of tarnish can be quickly and effectively repaired. Chapter 8 explains how.

If your objective is to produce an historically accurate restoration, then you'll need to know a lot about the tools and techniques, not to mention the aesthetics, of the era when the photograph was made. The tints you see in the damaged photograph will not be representative of the original hues, and anything that you do to restore proper tone and contrast and eliminate stain and yellowing will alter the colors in ways you can't predict.

Professional photographs Professional photographers usually took better care of their photographs than amateurs, and the photographs were usually made with more care and processed better. Until we get back into the "vintage" era, professional photographs for the most part look better than comparable amateur ones. The most notable exception is that color prints will fade regardless of how well they were processed (although the cheap processing of many cheap commercial portraits significantly accelerated their fading), so old professional color prints may look just as bad as amateur ones of the same era. Except for color dye fading, though, you're more likely to get a modern professional photograph to restore because it's suffered physical damage than because it's badly in need of tone and color correction.

Slides

Kodachrome I've never seen a badly faded Kodachrome slide, and neither will you, unless it's one that has been projected a lot. Kodachrome dyes are extremely stable in the dark, although they fade rapidly in the light. If you get a Kodachrome slide to restore, it will probably need very little tone or color correction (Figure 1-2). More probably you'll be asked to restore it because it is physically damaged. Water and mildew damage repair are common restoration jobs; occasionally a slide will get mis-handled and badly scratched.

Other slide films Recent non-Kodachrome slide films are pretty stable. As with Kodachromes, you are more likely to be doing restoration work to correct physical damage than fading. Go back to the 1960s and it's a different matter; just as with color prints, you'll be looking at slides that have faded or stained. Slides from the 1950s will be in extremely poor shape. If they aren't brick-red (Figure 1-18), they will be very badly darkened and stained.

In either case, color correction tools like Digital ROC can work miracles. The hard part will be getting a good scan. Most of the slides will have one or more dye layers that have faded very little, so the overall density range in the slide can be quite high. See Chapter 4 and Chapter 9 for ways to deal with this.

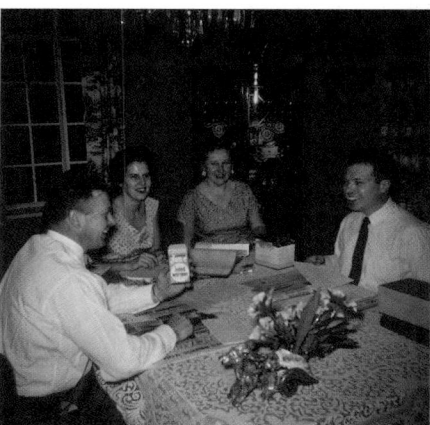 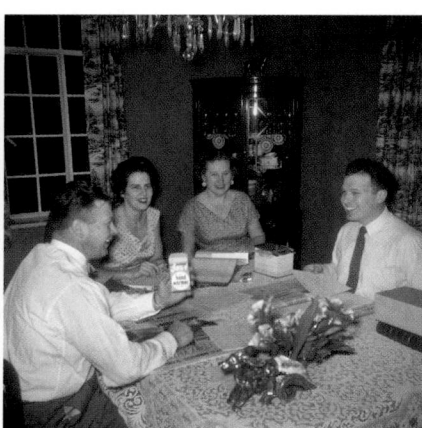

Fig. 1-18 Excellent restorations are possible from severely faded slides, such as this Ektachrome from the early 1950s. See Chapter 10, page 372, for the step-by-step details of how I completely restored this photograph.

Negatives

Even though the majority of photographs made in the last 50 years has been negatives, most of the time you'll work on a deteriorated print. Usually that will be because the client doesn't have the negative, but it never hurts to ask. Original negatives, B&W or color, almost always permit better restoration than the prints made from them.

Color negatives This is not to say that negatives don't deteriorate. In fact, color negative films are among the least stable of all types of films, and older ones were especially bad. Physically, the color negatives are likely to be in pretty good shape; they've probably never come out of their folders and sleeves since they came back from the photofinisher. You won't have unusual numbers of scratches and dirt specks to clean up.

The most common physical damage I see in old color negatives is due to poor processing. There may be long scratches down the film or water spots; sometimes there are surge or flow marks where the developing chemicals didn't bathe the negative evenly. Mildew damage is a less common occurrence.

Most of the time you will be faced with a clean but uniformly faded negative. Your task will be to figure out the major tone and color adjustments needed to produce a correct-looking print. There will be serious dye loss; the fading will be at least as bad as with very old color slide films. Color correction will be a major challenge.

What makes it possible to do good restorations from old color negatives is that they recorded a lot more information than ever gets conveyed in a print. Most of that information can get lost through fading and still leave you with plenty for producing an excellent photograph. As with slides, special color correction tools can automate a lot of this color and tone restoration for you. Unlike slides, you won't encounter

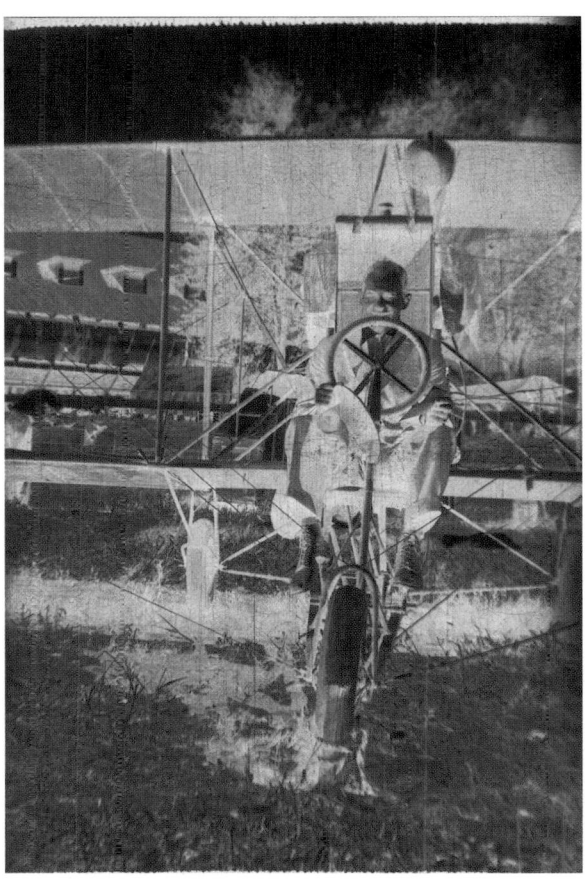

Fig. 1-19 Old B&W negatives, like this cellulose nitrate negative from the early 20th century, are usually very contrasty. That makes them hard to scan, but Chapter 9, page 316, tells you how to do it well.

color negatives with extremely high densities, so scanning will be much less tricky than it is with slides and old B&W negatives.

B&W film negatives Modern acetate-based B&W negatives don't usually present a lot of fading problems. Properly processed B&W negatives are extremely stable, but they may not have been stored properly or washed well when they were processed. Physical damage is the most likely reason someone will send you a B&W negative, so you'll mostly be cleaning up dust, scratches, and tears and correcting for a little bit of unevenness in density.

Before acetate "safety" film, there were nitrate-based B&W films. Those negatives will all have some degree of staining and yellowing, from modest to severe. The silver image densities will usually be pretty good, even if they've turned brown (Figure 1-19). In fact, these old films had so much contrast to begin with that scanning them will be difficult. A somewhat faded negative may actually prove easier to work with. (*Caution:* these negatives can be brittle with age, so handle with care!)

B&W glass plate negatives   Glass plate negatives, like vintage B&W prints, turn up in all kinds of condition, often in pieces! Fortunately, reassembly on the computer is much simpler than in real life (see Chapter 10, Examples). Really old plates may have bleached out almost to the point of invisibility; others will not have faded at all. In the least-faded photographs, the long density ranges of these old materials will make getting a good scan challenging. Other than fixing broken plates, restoring glass negatives is no different from restoring film ones.

Newspaper Clippings

As long as the paper isn't so brittle and fragile that you dare not handle it, the condition of newspaper clippings and halftone photographs doesn't matter a lot. The nature of the printing inks used means that they will rarely be faded even if the paper is badly stained or discolored. You can expect good contrast between the halftone ink dots and the paper. Since the paper is supposed to be white, and the ink dots are supposed to be black, and there aren't any tones in between, scanning halftones is easy (see Chapter 4, Getting the Photo into the Computer).

What you will find challenging about working with a halftone is eliminating (or at least minimizing) the screen pattern—a good percentage of your clients will want to know if you can turn the halftone into a "nice photograph." Very often the answer is yes. The trick is to do this without blurring out much of the photographic detail (Figure 1-20). I provide some software techniques for that in Chapter 9, Tips, Tricks, and Enhancements, page 320.

Take Your Time

If you're new to photo restoration or even digital print making, don't be in a hurry to do great work. You won't achieve a wonderful result the first time you restore a photo. I don't think it's so much that the learning curve is steep as that doing digital work well requires knowing a great deal of information.

That's true of any craft, including wet darkroom printing. But with material crafts it takes a while to physically master the tools and become proficient in their handling. I haven't found printing on the computer to be more conceptually difficult than darkroom printing, but the darkroom forced me to ease into the knowledge because there was so much physicality to get under control. The computer lets you jump right into the deep end of the pool.

For example, you don't have to learn any more about masking to do good tonal control on the computer than you do in the darkroom. But it will take you days or even weeks to master darkroom techniques for making masks, during which time you mentally assimilate the concepts. On the computer you can learn the technique in a matter of minutes

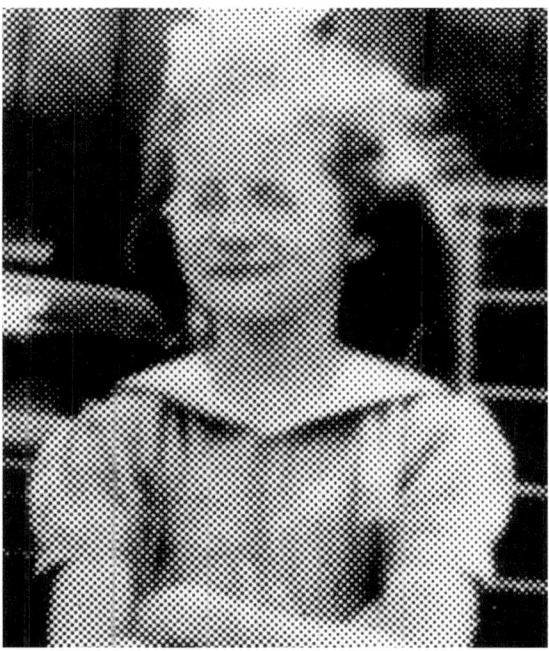

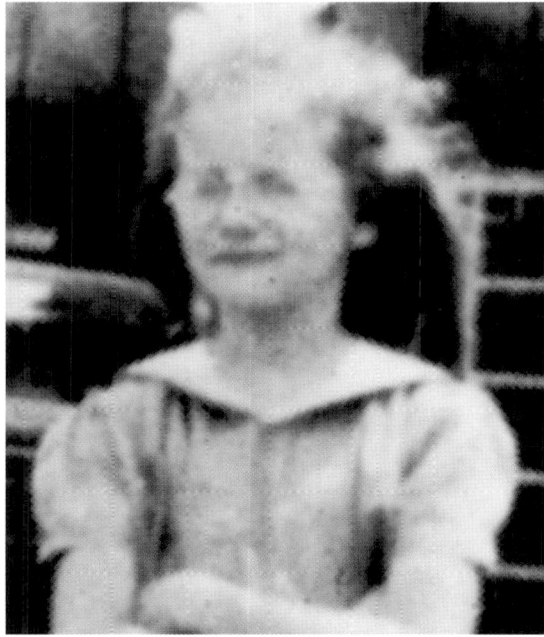

Fig. 1-20 Even screened newspaper photographs can be restored and turned into acceptable photographs. Chapter 9 presents several ways to clean them up.

and make technically perfect masks with a couple of mouse clicks. Then you discover it's still going to take you weeks to internalize the knowledge.

Subjectively this makes it seem as if the computer stuff is much harder. It's only that it takes time to digest the knowledge. Even if you can push the buttons on the computer in 5 seconds, you can't (so to speak) push the buttons in your brain that fast.

One thing I have learned is that it's very difficult is to spend "an idle half hour" doing digital photographic work. It's just as hard as spending only 30 minutes doing serious printing in the darkroom. It takes time to get your head into the right place, think about what you're doing, and do it well. Once you've really internalized the techniques, you can do productive work quickly. While you're learning what you are doing, you need to allow yourself several hours at a time so that you can play with the tools and controls and feel comfortable and not be distracted by watching the clock. You need to take the time to experiment enough to get a feel for how different changes have different effects. Don't be utterly goal directed; explore different paths and ideas, try different techniques and settings. That's what Undo commands and the original scan file that you saved are for: to let you explore without being committed. Digital restoration is a process of exploration. No two damaged photos are quite alike, and there's no completely fixed routine for handling them. Learn to play.

CHAPTER 2

Hardware for Restoration

The "Bottom" Line

Here's the short form: The most important thing is to have lots of memory, as much as you can afford. Next comes plenty of hard-disk space and media to archive data off site (external or removable hard drives or CDs). Spend your money on these priorities instead of buying a faster computer.

For your display, get either a CRT (TV-type tube) or a good liquid crystal display (LCD). Don't get an inexpensive LCD. For scanning prints in and printing out your finished restorations, you don't need to spend more than $250 to $500 apiece on a flat-bed scanner or printer.

The rest of this chapter goes into more technical detail about computer hardware—more detail than most people need to do good restorations. If you're interested in the whys and wherefores of my recommendations, read on. Otherwise, just read the sidebar on page 48, and you're ready for the next chapter.

The Computer

Just about any computer bought since about 2001 can handle digital restoration. A newer machine is likely to make the work go faster, but it won't make it any better. I work on a several-year-old Athlon XP 2400+ system with 2 gigabytes (GB) of RAM, 360 GB of hard-drive storage, and a 19-inch Hitachi RasterOps CRT monitor. You could put together a comparable system today for under $1000.

While I have my personal preferences, I can't come up with many objective reasons for deciding between a Mac or Windows machine. I really like Macs; I prefer the interface and the way it handles color management more than Windows. On the other hand, the low-cost image processing program I think the most highly of, Picture Window, only runs under Windows. If you have an older Mac, you can run Picture Window under Virtual PC, but don't expect it to be fast. I write a bit more about that in the next chapter. The Intel-based Macs can natively run Windows as well as Mac OS; they may offer the best of both worlds in one machine.

If you're thinking about buying a new computer to replace an older one, keep in mind that most software manufacturers don't offer very good bargains for cross-platform software purchases, if they offer them at all. Switching from Mac to PC or vice versa can cost you far more in replacement software than you paid for the computer. By historical accident, most of my graphics software is for Windows. It would be too costly and inconvenient to switch over. That is why, despite having a moderate preference for Macs, I prepared all the photographs in this book under Windows.

I recommend your computer have both FireWire and USB 2 ports. Macs do; PCs often don't. If your computer didn't come with both, buy an I/O board with extra USB 2 and FireWire ports. They're very cheap. The reason I recommend this is that a lot of professional digital equipment uses FireWire. For example, my medium-format film scanner, a Minolta DiMAGE Scan Multi Pro, has ultrawide SCSI and FireWire interfaces but no USB interface. There are some technical arguments about which kind of interface performs better for which kind of tasks, but for most of you this will be less important than simply being able to run the peripheral devices you want to use. Keeping your machine versatile gives you more options.

These days I don't think you need SCSI ports. Hardly any new devices I know of have only SCSI interfaces. Even fast external hard-drive arrays, the last great bastion of SCSI, are being challenged by FireWire arrays. On the other hand, if you want to invest in older hardware (charmingly referred to as "legacy" technology), you may need a SCSI card. My fine Umax Powerlook III flat-bed scanner, for example, only has SCSI I/O, as do some of my older external storage devices.

Memory

More important than a fast CPU and hard drive is buying as much memory (RAM) as you can afford. Digital scans can get extremely large. A color photograph scanned at 16 bits per channel produces 6 bytes of data per pixel. If you're scanning at 600 pixels per inch (ppi), you're collecting 2 megabytes (MB) of image data per square inch of original print. That's more than 50 MB for a mere 4-inch by 6-inch print and more than 150 MB for an 8-inch by 10-inch print.

If you scan your original at 8 bits per channel, that cuts the file size in half, but if your original needs to be scanned at 1200 ppi instead of 600, the file size quadruples! For example, an 8-bit-per-channel scan at 1200 ppi of that 4-inch by 6-inch print will saddle you with a 100-MB file (Table 2-1).

Programs like Photoshop and Picture Window eat up memory very, very quickly. The old rule about needing an amount of RAM equal to

Table 2-1 Scan Sizes

	File Sizes of Color Scans (MB)							
	300 ppi 8 bits	300 ppi 16 bits	600 ppi 8 bits	600 ppi 16 bits	1200 ppi 8 bits	1200 ppi 16 bits	2400 ppi 8 bits	2400 ppi 16 bits
2″ × 3″	1.6	3.2	6.5	13	26	52	105	205
4″ × 5″	5.4	11	22	43	85	175	345	690
5″ × 8″	11	22	43	85	175	345	690	1350
8″ × 10″	22	43	85	175	345	690	1350	2750

three to five times the file size doesn't work any longer. If you have less than 10 times the file size in available RAM, your program is going to end up writing scratch files to the hard drive. Doing really fancy work in Photoshop might push that up to 20 times.

What does that mean for performance? Everything in the world! Reading and writing data to the fastest hard drive is 10 times slower than handling that same data in RAM. Your image processing program will slow down by three to five times the instant that hard-drive access light comes on and stays on. When it comes to real-world performance, you'll almost always be better off buying a machine with a slower processor and more RAM.

How much RAM is enough? Get at least 2 GB. More is good. This is one area where Macs currently have it over Windows machines; they handle large amounts of RAM (over 2 GB) more gracefully. That will change with the release of 64-bit Windows, but for the present if you want a machine that supports really large amounts of RAM, your best bet is a dual-processor Mac.

It's not easy calculating your total memory requirements. Usually you find out you don't have enough memory when something goes wrong. Figuring out your needs is difficult because different operations may all fight for the same memory, but they're not all operating all the time, so you may not realize you don't have enough RAM to satisfy them all.

For photo restoration work there are four main consumers of memory: the operating system, the image processing software, plug-ins for that software, and the printer driver and print spooler. Those last two categories of memory consumers are what most people don't plan for.

A program like Photoshop lets you set how much of the available RAM it will use. It's common on systems with plenty of RAM to give Photoshop 80% of what's available. On my Windows 2000 machine with 2 GB of RAM, for example, that would leave 400 MB for the operating system. I can check the Task Manager to see what the OS is routinely consuming; it's almost always below 250 MB. It would seem, then, that

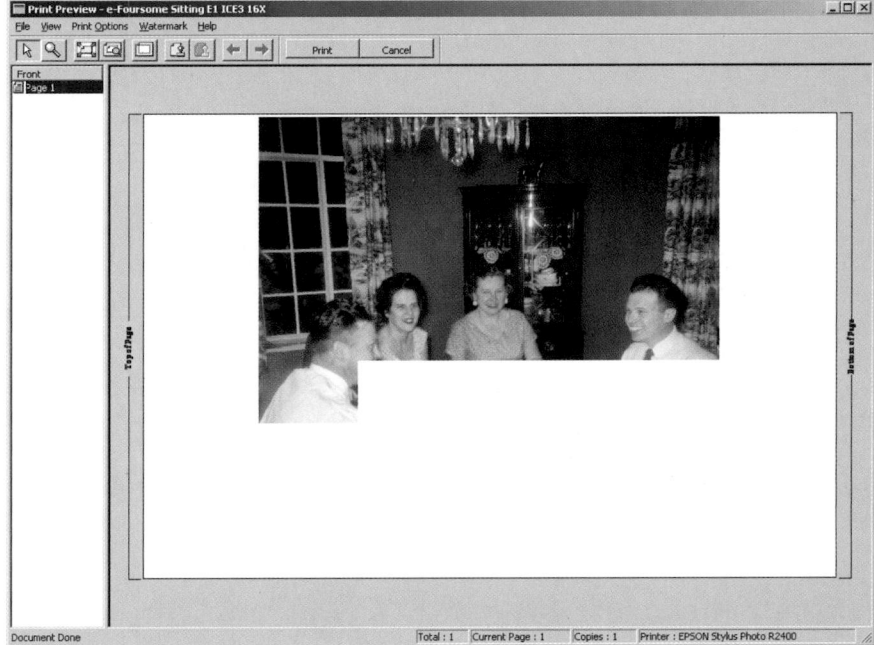

Fig. 2-1 It takes considerable memory to print out large files. If your print preview shows a truncated picture like this one, it means you don't have enough free RAM available to the system. Reduce by 10% the amount of RAM assigned to Photoshop in its memory preferences, and try printing again.

I'd be safe with the 80%-for-Photoshop setting and have plenty of RAM left over for momentary demands.

It doesn't work that way. If I try to print out my largest photographs, which are 20 to 30 million pixels in size, I run out of memory with Photoshop set for 80% RAM consumption. I don't get a warning that I'm out of memory, but the printer preview window shows a truncated photograph with some lower part of it missing (Figure 2-1). That is not an artifact of the preview; if I print the photograph, it'll be truncated.

Why? The software that converts the photograph to printer data uses a lot of RAM while it's creating that printer file. If it runs out of RAM before it has fully rendered the file, it doesn't abort the process; instead it sends off an incomplete photograph. The fix is easy: Decrease the amount of RAM that's given dedicated to Photoshop so the operating system has more. Setting it down to 70% usually works; setting it down to 60% always works.

In that case, why not just leave Photoshop using only 60% of RAM or even less, just to be safe? One reason is that when Photoshop runs out of RAM, it starts swapping to disk. It'll keep running, but it runs *much* more slowly. A more serious problem is that third-party plug-ins generally have to use the same RAM that Photoshop does, but they can't use a scratch disk as Photoshop can. If I open up a large file with Photoshop set for only 50% or 60% of RAM, some of my plug-ins will report that they can't function because they've run out of RAM. So, it's back up to 80% for Photoshop, at least until I need to print again. Getting this all to behave well on your computer is a trial-and-error process.

Simply adding more RAM doesn't necessarily solve the problem. Above 2 GB of RAM, some software can't take advantage of the extra memory. Some functions need to work in the lower 2 GB of RAM. If there's insufficient memory available to satisfy those functions, additional RAM above the 2-GB limit won't help.

The reason I'm bringing up such examples is that I've seen many photographers run into these RAM limits and be confused by the erratic and peculiar behavior of their computers. If you see unusual behavior by your program, or if it fails to complete an operation or does it only halfway, the first place to check is the amount of RAM that's available for the program. That's especially true when plug-ins abort or printers fail to print out complete photographs.

The Monitor

A good LCD monitor will serve you just as well as the traditional "glass onion." CRTs have an edge when it comes to contrast range and the gamut of colors they can display, unless you've got many thousands of dollars to spend, but in my opinion the differences aren't great enough to matter for restoration work. In either case a good monitor profile will have a bigger effect on how accurately you can work (see Chapter 3, Software for Restoration, page 52).

A good LCD is more expensive than a CRT of comparable quality. Although you can buy very inexpensive LCD panels, these are not suitable for serious photographic work. Lesser quality LCDs don't display a uniform image over the entire screen; there are large variations in brightness and gamma with the vertical viewing angle.

You can observe this on the LCD display of any laptop computer by bringing up an image that has a lot of dark tones in it. (It's hard to see this problem looking at bright colors and light grays and whites.) Tilt the screen toward and away from you, and observe how drastically the darker tones and the blacks change in appearance as the angle of the screen changes (Figure 2-2).

Even after you rigidly fix the angle at which you view a cheap LCD, you will still have viewing-angle problems from the top to the bottom of the screen. This is readily seen by looking at a large and uniform dark gray image. You can create one in your image processing program by opening up a new image window, setting the foreground color to a gray value of about 65, and filling the window with the paint bucket. The image should look uniformly charcoal gray over the entire screen. On a poor LCD monitor. it will look much darker at the top of the screen than at the bottom (Figure 2-3). This variation makes it impossible to do accurate photographic work. The more expensive LCD panels, starting in the high hundreds of dollars, don't have this problem.

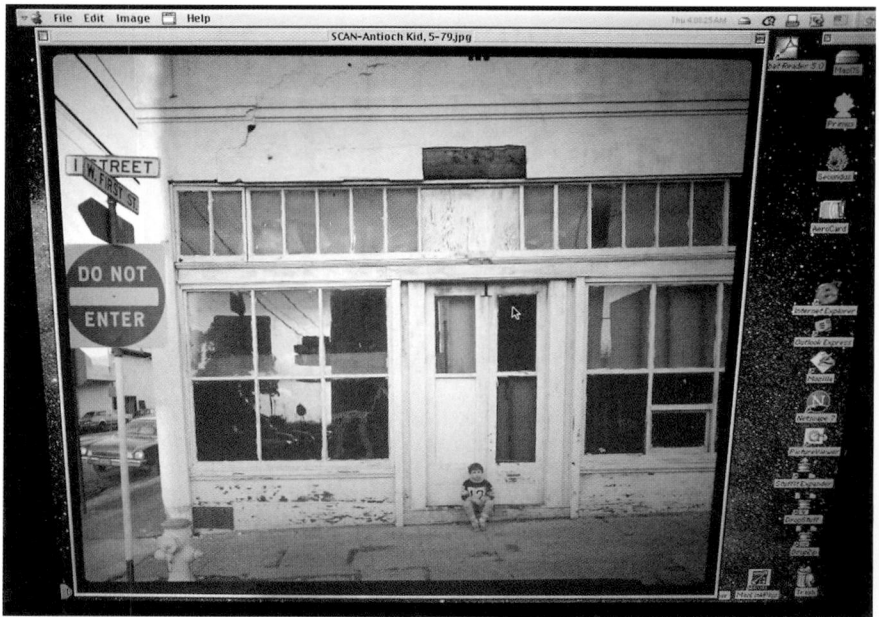

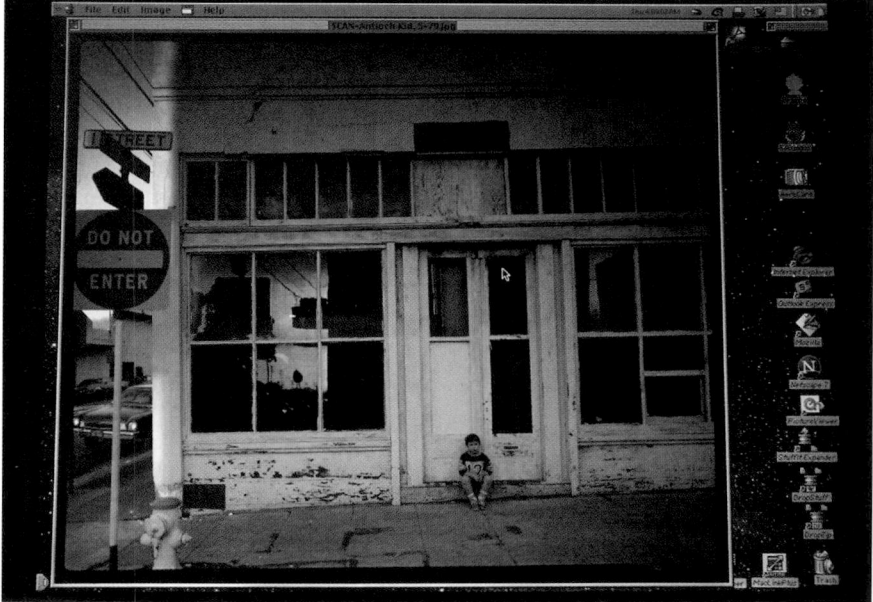

Fig. 2-2 Don't buy an LCD monitor whose gamma (midrange brightness) changes like this one when you tilt the screen toward or away from you. Cheap desktop monitors (and laptop displays) have this problem; more expensive displays show you a consistent image over a wide range of viewing angles.

Fig. 2-3 This is a photograph of a laptop LCD screen that is displaying a uniform gray image with a value of 65. The difference in brightness from top to bottom is caused by changes in gamma with viewing angle. You can't use a display like this for precision photographic work!

When you go shopping for an LCD monitor, check it out by viewing a dark image and tilting the screen toward and away from you, top to bottom. If you see large brightness changes when you do that, don't buy that monitor. Shop around until you find one that looks the same over a wide range of vertical viewing angles. It will be fine for serious photographic work.

If you're not a games player, just about any professional-grade video card will be fine for doing photo restoration. The Matrox G650 sells for around $150, and I've got no complaints about its performance. If you're heavily into computer games, you'll probably have to spend more money to get a stable card that's also a good games performer. Today's state-of-the-art games want lots of RAM and powerful hardware graphics rendering.

Make sure your video card uses hardware "color look-up tables" (CLUTs) if you want to do monitor color management. I think you'd be hard pressed to find a decent video card today that doesn't have this, but if you have any doubts, query the manufacturer before purchasing. You can download a utility from Digital Light & Color (http://www.dl-c.com) that will test your existing card for hardware CLUT support.

Storage and Backup

When we contemplate data storage for computers, we normally think in the short term. Our first concern is the immediate one: How much hard-drive space to buy. Then we think about how we back up our system in case the operating system crashes or a hard drive fails.

The more prudent among us think about off-site backups, ensuring that a copy of the data on our hard drives is stored someplace other than the home or office where our computer is. That way a major disaster at at the computer's location results in a loss of only hardware, which is easily replaceable. Still, this is thinking about the short term; backups go out of date pretty fast.

Restoring photographs engages us in a whole new concept of time. Months and years are minor matters; it's decades and possibly even centuries that concern us. The photographs we restore may be as young as 15 years or as old as 150 years, but we're restoring them because they're important to us and didn't last. One of the great promises of digital restoration is that in principle the restored photographs can last indefinitely.

The last chapter of this book, Archiving and Permanence (Chapter 12), covers this in detail. As I argue there, currently the two best ways to store your files are CDs and hard drives. In terms of convenience, durability, and cost per bit, both media are excellent. One advantage of storing your files on CDs is that this approach doesn't require much additional money; your machine probably already has a CD burner. High-quality CD blanks are inexpensive. The (relatively!) small capacity and low price of CDs can be handy, especially if you want to distribute work to several people.

Removable hard-drive storage requires a bit more of an investment, but the cost per bit becomes very competitive when your storage requirements mount up into the hundreds of gigabytes. Hard drives have gotten incredibly cheap; they cost no more per gigabyte than high-quality CD blanks. You have to buy your storage in chunks that cost tens of dollars instead of tens of pennies, but it's hard to beat the convenience and compactness of a hard drive.

For as little as $20, you can buy a removable hard-drive *bay* or *drawer* for your computer that lets you use standard IDE hard drives as removable media (Figure 2-4). A hard-drive bay is a hollow shell into which

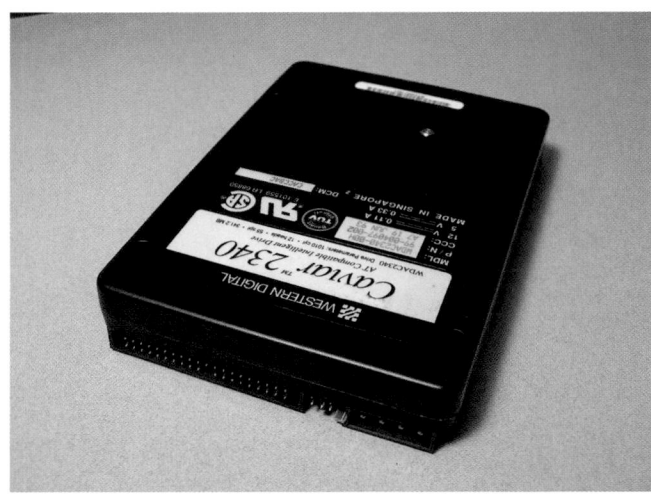

Fig. 2-4 Ordinary IDE hard drives, installed in removable hard-drive trays, are great for external and off-site file storage. They are as cheap per gigabyte as CDs, and they're much faster than any other storage medium.

you plug *trays* or *caddies* that contain ordinary internal hard drives. The bay is attached to the data bus of your computer; it has internal connectors that mate with the tray to connect the hard drive to the computer. You install a drive in a caddy, plug the caddy into the bay, and read and write data to it just as if it were a regular hard drive inside your computer. There's no muss. no fuss, and you don't need special software, as when burning CDs. Because of the interface circuitry, these bays are sometimes not quite as fast as hard drives installed directly on your machine, but they will still be much, much faster than reading and writing data to CDs.

With hard-drive caddies, a year's worth of work can fit on a single drive and go into your safe deposit box for safekeeping and security. A hard-drive bay also means you'll likely never run out of internal hard-disk storage. You can reserve your internal hard drives for the critical stuff like your applications, scratch files, and those files and documents you really need to have on your machine all the time. Everything else can go on removables.

Removable drive units come in all sorts of flavors. CompUSA sells $20 IDE hard-drive drawers that sit in one of the normal drive slots in your desktop computer. At that price the very first hard drive you set up this way will save you money over buying a self-contained external drive.

Disadvantages of this least-expensive solution are that the bay takes up one of your physical slots and uses up one of the four IDE ports. In addition, IDE bay drives are usually not hot-swappable. That means that you have to shut down your computer when you want to change hard-drive cartridges. If you try to change cartridges while the computer is on, the least that will happen is that your operating system will be very confused and unable to recognize the new cartridge until you reboot. The worst is that you can destroy data on your drives.

For more money, you can get hot-swappable bays that connect through your USB 2 or FireWire port. The trays still use those inexpensive internal IDE drives; the bay contains "glue" circuitry that couples the drive's IDE bus to the USB or FireWire. You don't have to worry about it; just plug the drive in and let the electronics take care of the interfacing. These bays are considerably more expensive, but they let you treat the hard-drive tray like any other removable storage medium. You can insert and remove hard-drive cartridges without having to power down and reboot. If you're maintaining duplicate backups—as you should when archiving—that's a big convenience factor.

Drive bays are also available as external devices, usually for more money. They're good if you don't have a spare slot in your computer case or if you want to move the bay between different computers. One source (among many) for external bays and USB and FireWire bays is Weibetech. They're not inexpensive, but they're well regarded.

Scanners

Flat-bed scanners that cost no more than several hundred dollars will do quite well for restoration work. They are limited in their ability to capture very high densities and extremely fine detail. Fortunately, you'll find that 99% of the time the print to be restored isn't very contrasty; sometimes it's so faded as to be almost invisible (Figure 2-5). Being able to capture high densities with the scanner just isn't very important. Similarly, resolution won't be a major worry; you'll hardly ever find an old photo that you need to scan at more than 1200 ppi.

On the other hand, being able to capture at 16-bit depth is critical. You won't always need to scan your originals at 16 bits per channel, but some originals will be so badly faded or distorted in tone and color that you'll need to capture the most subtle differences if you want to get a good-looking restoration. These days my habit is to scan everything at 16-bit depth and decide later whether I need to keep all those bits or downconvert to 8-bit color. Mostly, I hang on to all the data.

Based on these considerations, just about any midrange flat-bed scanner you can buy today will do for restoring prints. One feature to consider, if your budget permits, is a film adapter for the flat-bed scanner. Usually these take the form of a special lid that includes a light source so that the original can be illuminated from the back instead of from the front as you would with a reflection print (Figure 2-6). In some scanners there's a separate tray for loading film into the scanner.

The advantage of a flat-bed scanner is that it does not cost a great deal of money to get the capability of scanning 5-inch by 7-inch and 8-inch by 10-inch films and glass plates. Dedicated film scanners for anything larger than 120 roll film format are extremely expensive. Old film that is not the same size as modern standard formats (and much of it isn't) is sometimes physically difficult to scan with a dedicated film scanner, which may have film carriers that can only accommodate specific formats.

Be aware that older films and glass plates, unlike prints, frequently have extremely high density ranges, even when they are damaged and faded. They can also have lots of fine detail that will require scanning at high resolutions to capture. If you're going to be regularly scanning old B&W sheet film or glass plates, you'll probably have to spend $1000+ on a high-quality, flat-bed scanner. For occasional use, a lot less'll do you.

A film adapter for a flat-bed scanner is not a substitute for a dedicated film scanner for smaller formats; such a scanner will almost always capture the film with much better resolution, more accuracy, and a longer density range. If you plan to work from roll film or 35-mm originals, seriously consider buying a high-quality film scanner. The quality you will get from a film scanner will almost always run rings around flat-bed scans.

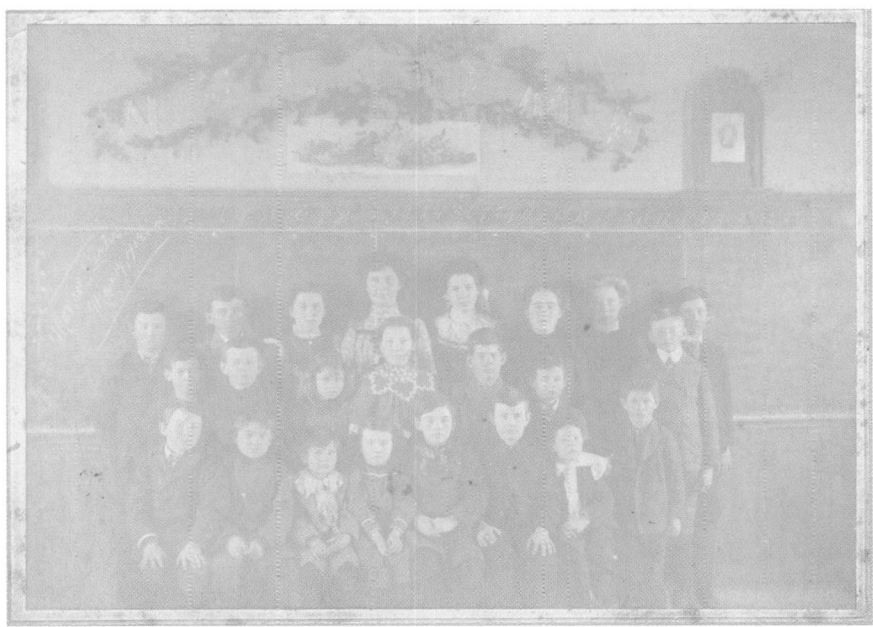

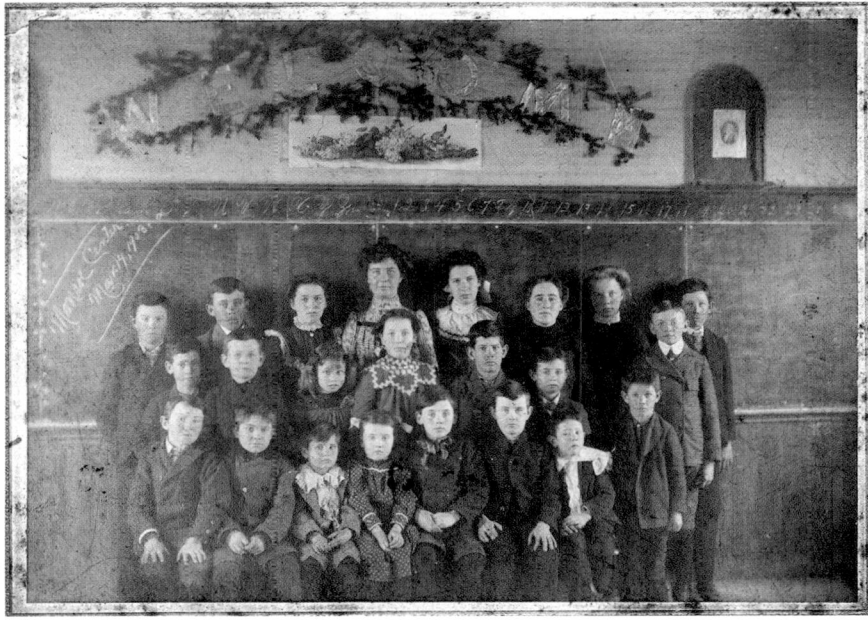

Fig. 2-5 Old photographs (upper) often look hopelessly faded to the naked eye. A good scanner, used properly (see Chapter 4), can recover an amazing amount of detail that's nearly invisible to us (lower).

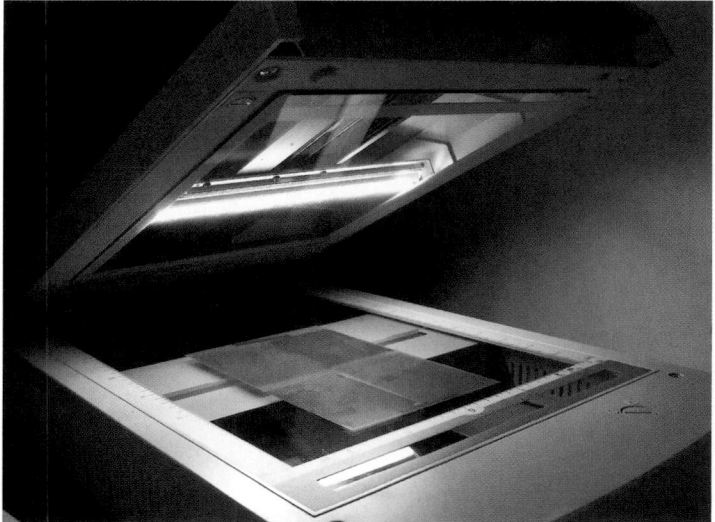

Fig. 2-6 Get a scanner with a film-scanning lid like this one. Then you'll be able scan prints, sheet film, and glass plates for restoration. A dedicated film scanner, though, will serve you better for scanning roll and 35-mm films.

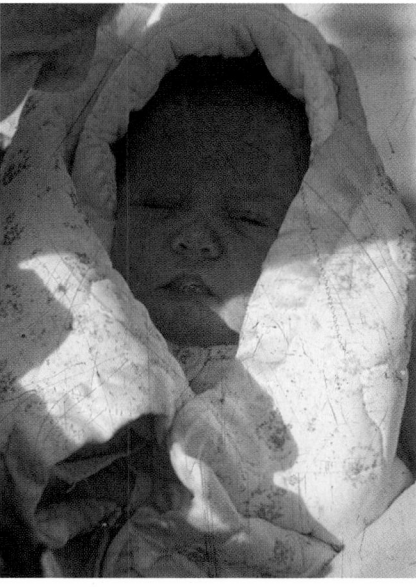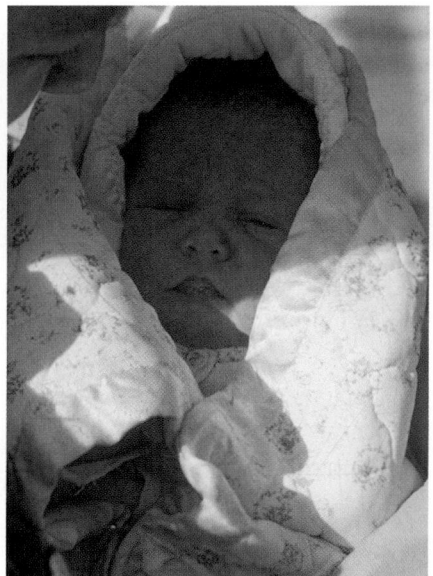

Fig. 2-7 DIGITAL ICE, built into many film scanners as part of the DIGITAL ICE³ package, is the first line of defense against dust and scratches. This Kodachrome slide was scanned without (left) and with (right) DIGITAL ICE. DIGITAL ICE sometimes doesn't work well on Kodachrome slides, but it worked fine with this one.

Make sure you get a film scanner that includes DIGITAL ICE³. DIGITAL ICE³ scanner software has three tools: DIGITAL ICE, DIGITAL GEM, and DIGITAL ROC. DIGITAL ICE removes scratches and dirt from color scans amazingly well (Figure 2-7). It does not work with silver-based B&W films (although it will work fine with chromogenic ones like Ilford XP2), and sometimes it won't work for Kodachrome slides. In all other cases, it does a vastly better job of eliminating dirt and scratches than any post-scanning software can.

DIGITAL ROC (which restores color) and GEM (which reduces noise and grain) have plug-in counterparts (page 61), so it's not absolutely necessary to have them built into your scanner, but I still think it's a good idea. The scanner versions work differently from the plug-ins, and the capabilities of the two versions complement each other. In addition, the scanner versions have access to the raw scanner data, and sometimes this can make a big difference in the quality of the results. For example, the scanner's DIGITAL ROC does a really good job with contrasty originals because it works on the raw scanner data before the regular scanner software "corrects" brightness and contrast. In Chapter 10, Examples, the only way I could capture the entire range of the slide in Example 4 in a single scan was by using DIGITAL ROC (Figure 2-8), and it did the job beautifully.

Printers

As little as 5 years ago I would've gone on at some length about just what kind of printer you ought to buy. I'd have discussed the pros and cons of inkjet versus dye sublimation printers and the differing characteristics of the pigment-based and dye-based ink sets. I'd have spent a lot of time talking about comparative print longevity, tonality, color gamut, and overall print quality.

My considered opinion is that this is all now water under the bridge. Spend several hundred dollars, and you will get a printer capable of making excellent and long-lived prints. It doesn't matter whether you're buying a current, top-tier Epson, Canon, HP, Kodak, or Olympus printer. Prints right out of the box are going to look very good; prints made with a custom profile (see Chapter 11, Printing Tips) are going to look excellent. Meaningfully distinguishing between printers requires full-length reviews of each one, just the sort of articles I write for the photography magazines that run several thousand words. I don't think you bought this book to read 20,000 words worth of printer reviews. It used to be true that one could make important statements about print longevity and color gamuts that were true across all printers of a particular class. That's not the case any longer. If one has faith in the accelerated tests, on average, pigment-based inkjet prints will have a longer life than dye-based inkjet prints, but some brands of dye-based prints have longer lives than some of the pigment-based prints.

Besides, any of these printers produces prints that will last on display for many decades and in albums and storage for considerably longer. Overall, these new digital prints are likely to prove much more stable than the original photographs on which they were based.

Personally, I take published longevity numbers with a big grain of salt; there's still a lot we don't know about these new media. But that doesn't give me any reason to favor one class of print over the other. Uncertainty applies across the board, and all we can do is take the numbers at face value and keep our fingers crossed.

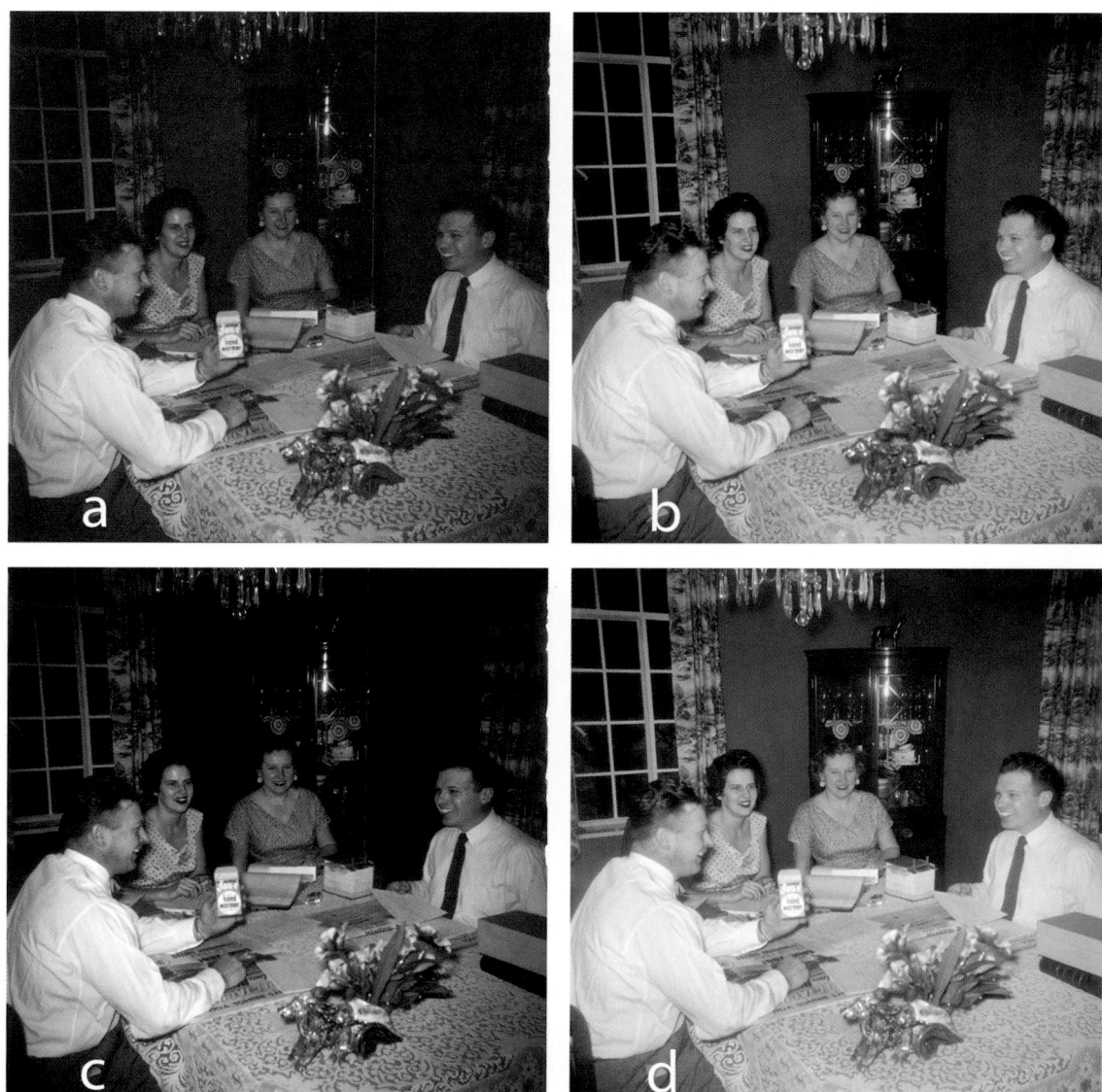

Fig. 2-8 DIGITAL ROC is available as part of the DIGITAL ICE[3] scanner software and as a Photoshop plug-in. (a) This Ektachrome E-1 slide from the early 1950s is badly faded and too dark. (b) The same slide scanned with DIGITAL ROC turned on. Great color and good tonality, automatically! (c) The green channel (magenta dye image) from part (a). Without DIGITAL ROC the scanner was unable to pull out any shadow detail. (d) The green channel recovered by DIGITAL ROC, from part (b).

The prints won't all look alike. I definitely have my personal preferences, and so does every other fine printer I know, but those preferences are completely personal and subjective. I can tell you that I use an Epson 2200 printer and like it a lot, but that's no assurance that you would like it is much as I do or that it would be your best choice. Continuing in this vein, I see less and less difference every year in the kind of print densities and color gamuts produced by pigment-based and dyed-based inks. Again, on average, dye-based ink prints will have higher maximum densities and larger color gamuts than pigment-based prints. But just as with longevity, this is merely an average for which there are notable exceptions; some of the kinds of pigment-based prints are definitely superior in all respects to some of the dye-based prints. Even the average quality difference is becoming less significant; pigment inks have been getting better faster than dye inks.

Another nonissue is printer resolution. By that I mean the "dpi" that's given in the printer manufacturer's specs. That droplet-per-inch value is now so high that it's been years since I tested any printer where the individual droplets were visible at a normal viewing distance. More ink drops are only loosely connected to the actual resolution of the printer (see the sidebar for an explanation of how dpi and ppi have gotten confused). I realize this doesn't give you very much specific information to go on when selecting a printer. Sometimes, though, it can be very valuable knowing what *not* to pay attention to.

What would I get? Well, if money and office space were no object, there's no one printer I'd get. I'd buy three (as of early 2006): an Epson Stylus Photo R2400 (Figure 2-9), a Canon i9900 (Figure 2-10), and an HP Designjet 130 (Figure 2-11). All of them produce great-looking, long-lived prints. Each of them does something the others don't. Your printing

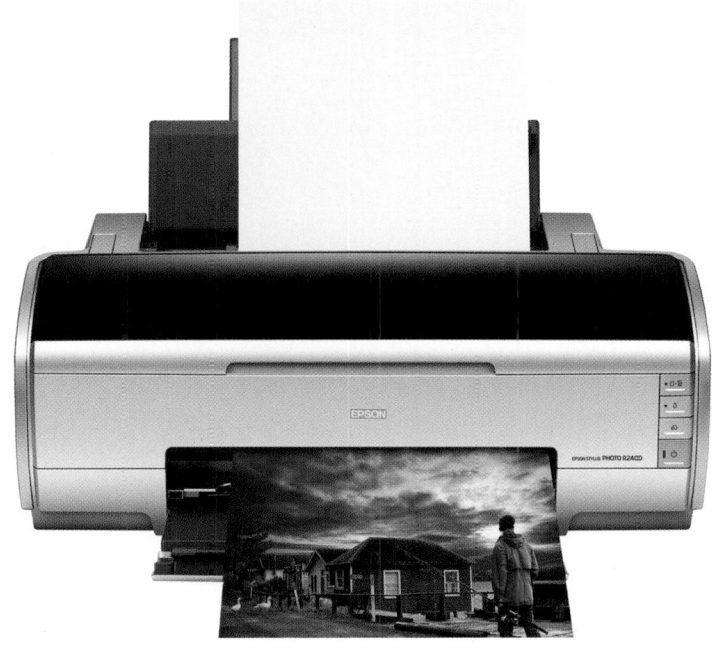

Fig. 2-9 The Epson R2400 printer produces really great-looking and long-lived matte finish prints, up to 13 inches wide. It's got some especially nice B&W printing software.

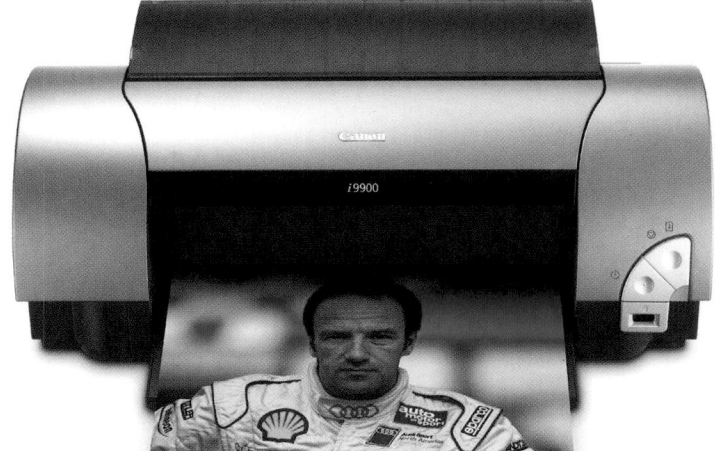

Fig. 2-10 The Canon i9900 printer is fast, and its glossy color prints have exceptional sharpness and an unusually large color gamut. It also prints up to 13 inches wide.

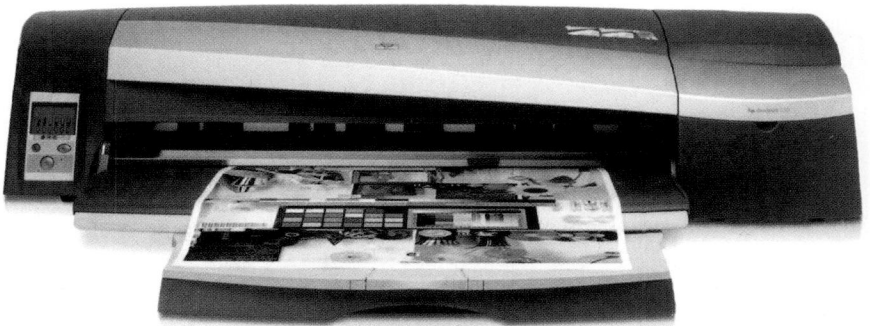

Fig. 2-11 The HP Designjet 130 printer produces good-looking color and B&W prints up to 24 inches wide. HP has the best-looking semigloss paper I've seen; it looks just like a nonglossy photographic print.

needs and priorities won't be the same as mine. That's why I won't tell you what to buy.

That's it for hardware shopping. Next you'll need some software to make that hardware useful, so it's on to Chapter 3, Software for Restoration.

PPI, DPI, Resolution: What's the Diff? "Dpi" has become a much misused and overused term. Image processing programs adopted this traditional printing term in order to make things less confusing for the graphic arts business. It has not quite worked out that way! Originally "dpi" meant halftone dots per inch when talking press reproduction with screened plates, like those used for magazines and newspapers.

Today, "dpi" is also used to mean ink droplets per inch (for inkjet printers) or pixels per inch (for image files and full-color devices like displays, photographic output devices, and dye sublimation printers). In other words, it doesn't refer to a single standard unit of measure. This is a seriously confusing situation for lots of people.

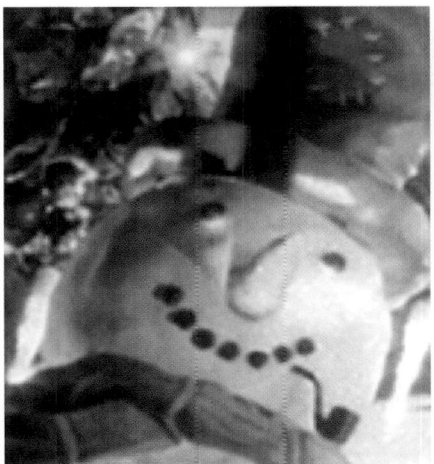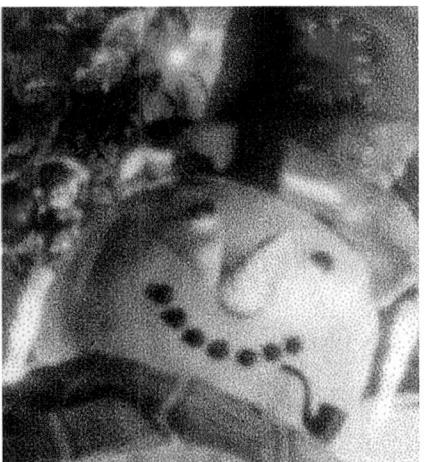

Fig. 2-12 The print on the left is made up of full-color pixels; it's a scan from a dye-sublimation print. The print on the right is made up of ink droplets. Its resolution and tonality are similar to that of the dye sublimation print, but it uses many ink droplets to make a single pixel. Don't get pixels, dots, and ink droplets confused; they're all different!

To begin with, image files don't come in dots, they come in pixels. Pixels and halftone dots aren't the same thing. most software requires somewhat more than one pixel to generate one sharp halftone dot. The correct measure of digital image resolution is pixels per inch, no matter what your software says. That's why I use "ppi" instead of "dpi" when I'm actually talking about image pixels, and it's a habit you might want to try to get into yourself.

Your inkjet printer is not rated in ppi. In fact it isn't even rated in "dots per inch." An inkjet printer's "dpi" really means "ink droplets per inch." A droplet isn't a pixel or a halftone "dot." It's just a blob of ink. The key difference is that a single pixel or halftone dot can convey the range of tones from black to white. Inkjet printers can make droplets in at most a few different sizes. The printer uses a fine spray of droplets of each color to build up continuous tone, with more droplets to produce higher densities (Figure 2-12). It takes several ink droplets of each color to make up a full-color, full-tone pixel. So the actual resolution of the printer when you're printing out continuous-tone color is considerably less than the printer's official dpi. That's why you need a printer with a much higher dpi than your file's ppi in order to get good tonal reproduction.

How many is "several drops?" It depends on the printer's *dpi* (droplets per inch) in combination with how it creates the spray pattern of droplets that make continuous tones. The program that does that (called a *dither algorithm*) is built into the printer and the driver. Dithers are complicated. There's no easy way to calculate the real resolution (in pixels per inch) that a printer can portray. You find that out by printing a series of real-world images with increasing ppi's and seeing when the prints stop getting sharper. The Epson 2200 can make use of at least 400 to 600 ppi of image detail. You don't have to use that much to get a decent-looking print—300 ppi is enough to look nice and sharp. But if you have the same image in both 300 and 600 ppi and print them out and put them next to each other, the 600-ppi one will look a bit sharper.

CHAPTER 3

Software for Restoration

Profile Mechanic Monitor

Photoshop CS2

Picture Window Pro v4

DIGITAL ROC Pro

DIGITAL GEM Pro

DIGITAL GEM Airbrush Pro

Color Mechanic

Image Doctor

Focus Magic

Asiva Selection

Mask Pro

CurveMeister2

PixelGenius PhotoKit

PixelGenius PhotoKit Sharpener

Neat Image Pro+

Color Management

Color management software is at the top of my software list, because without good color management, everything else becomes much harder. You need to manage your system's color if you want to get quality results.

Why should color management matter? Walk into any consumer electronics store and look at the wall of TVs they have for sale. They're all tuned to the same program, but no two of them look alike. Identical inputs, different outputs—that's the problem. No equipment displays or reproduces color perfectly, and that's true of your computer monitor and printer.

Minimize monitor errors, and you'll be a lot closer to seeing your photograph's true tones and colors. Reduce printer errors, and you'll get better-looking prints than you ever did before, and you'll get them more easily. Your operating system must support color management for you to get good control over your photographs. All recent flavors of Mac OS Classic and OS X work. If you're running Windows, upgrade to Windows 2000 or XP.

Color management uses data files called *profiles* to fix color rendering problems. Profiles don't alter your image file. The profile is a little translator that adjusts the electronic data before it goes to your monitor or printer to cancel the errors that the monitor or printer introduces. It works behind the scenes to make sure that "what you see" is closer to "what you get."

Profiling your printer is most important for quality results, and I cover that in Chapter 11, Printing Tips. If you don't spend any other money to get into digital restoration, do spend the money for a custom printer profile. It's really worth it.

You don't really need a calibrated monitor to do good digital printing, but working without one slows the work. You'll have to do more mental translation from what you see into what you think you'll get, and you'll waste more time and money on tests.

Don't worry about scanner profiling. For normal digital photographic work, you'd also want a good profile for your scanner to ensure that your scans have maximum fidelity. In restoration work this is not even desirable. As I explain in Chapter 4, Getting the Photo into the Computer, it's unlikely you'll want to make a scan that faithfully reproduces the damaged photograph in its deteriorated state.

Profile Mechanic Monitor (http://www.dl-c.com)

Your monitor probably has controls to correct the overall color temperature, brightness, and contrast. Tools like Adobe Gamma work with that and only ensure that on average your monitor is operating properly; there will still be errors in how colors and tones are displayed. A monitor profile corrects all of those individual color errors.

For example, your monitor may reproduce a middle gray just fine but portray fire-engine red as being a little too bright and a little too yellow. A custom profile won't alter the grays, but it will make the red a little darker and a little bluer to compensate, just enough to balance out the distortion of the monitor.

To profile your monitor, you need special hardware and software that measures and analyzes the colors being displayed. Profile Mechanic Monitor ($180) from Digital Light & Color is inexpensive as monitor-profiling packages go (Figure 3-1). To use it, your video board must

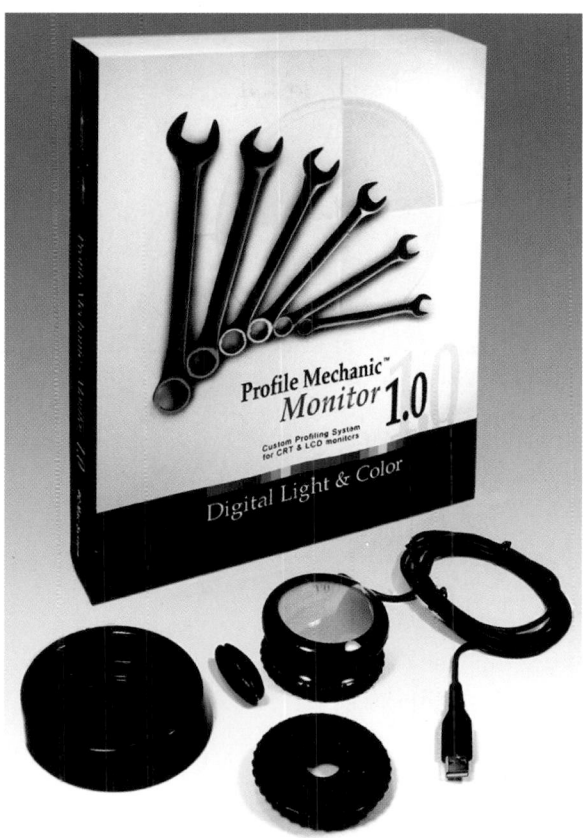

Fig. 3-1 Unlike your printer, it's not absolutely necessary that your monitor be calibrated to produce the best restorations. However, calibrating your monitor using a package like Profile Mechanic Monitor will make sure that what you see on the screen looks a lot more like what you'll get in the print. That lets you work faster and easier, with fewer wasted test prints.

support hardware color look-up tables (CLUTs). Just about all modern video chip sets do.

Profile Mechanic Monitor includes a USB "hockey-puck" photosensor that directly measures the light and color produced by your screen. You position the sensor over a box displayed on the screen, and the software flashes a series of differently colored squares. In the initial trial-and-error manual stage, you must adjust the controls on your monitor to make the brightness and contrast match a displayed ideal brightness curve. After that, profile creation is an entirely automatic process.

A monitor can be set up in any of several different standard ways. You have a choice of color temperatures of 5000 kelvins (D50), 6500 kelvins (D65), or 7500 kelvins (D75) and of gammas of 1.8 or 2.2. (Gamma is a measure of how light the middle gray tones look.) There's no one right configuration. Many standardize on D65 and gamma 2.2 as a good compromise between adequate monitor brightness and correct color rendition. D50 and gamma 1.8 is often recommended for work that is going to a press.

I like D50 and gamma 2.2. D50 is bright enough for me, and it's a close match to standard daylight viewing conditions. It is also better than D65 for work that will be viewed under incandescent lights. My experience is that gamma 2.2 produces a closer brightness match to the prints that come off modern inkjet printers than gamma 1.8.

By the way, this is true whether you're running a Mac or PC. The old rule that the Mac gamma should be set to 1.8 is based on ancient and obsolete technology. It's got no more bearing on current equipment than 72 dpi does on actual monitor resolution.

You don't have to agree with my preferences. Experiment! I made profiles for all six combinations of color temperature and gamma and looked at them to decide which ones worked best for me.

Monitors age and drift in brightness and color with time. It's a good idea make a new profile every couple of months to ensure that your display is still producing the quality it ought to.

Image Processing Software

Photoshop CS2

In this book I use the latest version of Photoshop, CS2, but older versions are quite serviceable. Some of my techniques work on versions as far back as Photoshop 5.5. If you're running an older version of Windows or Mac OS 9 Classic, as I am on one of my computers, the latest version of Photoshop you'll be able to run is Photoshop 7. Many of Photoshop 7's most valuable tools and filters are 16-bit capable, as is the all-important History Brush tool, but it only supports layers and adjustment layers in 8-bit mode.

If you think Photoshop is your cup of tea and you can't afford (or can't run) the latest version, search around and you may find legitimate individual copies of Photoshop 7 for sale for under $100. If you buy a used copy, make sure that the seller transfers the serial number to you; Adobe has an established procedure for doing that. Also look for copies that are "upgradable," meaning that the original owner hasn't already upgraded to a later version of Photoshop. That gets you into the Photoshop food chain, where upgrades are much, much cheaper than full packages.

One big warning: Beware of vendors that claim to sell you "OEM" versions of Photoshop and websites that say you can download it from them. Photoshop has never been legally distributed that way. A vendor who seems to have unlimited copies of Photoshop at supercheap prices is selling counterfeit or pirated goods. Don't get taken in, and please don't support the crooks!

If you're a registered student, Adobe often has educational packages that save you considerable money over the list price. Look into this before paying regular prices for Photoshop.

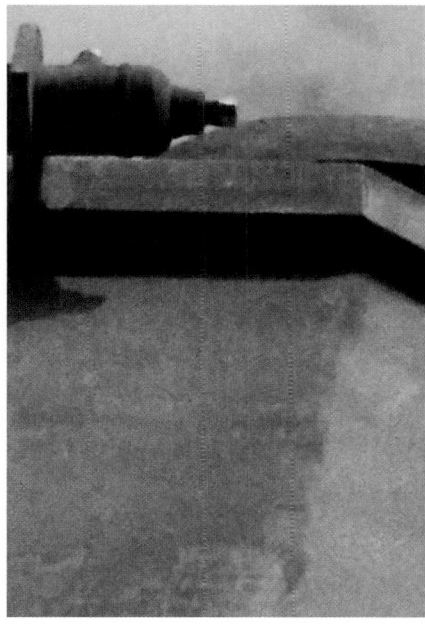 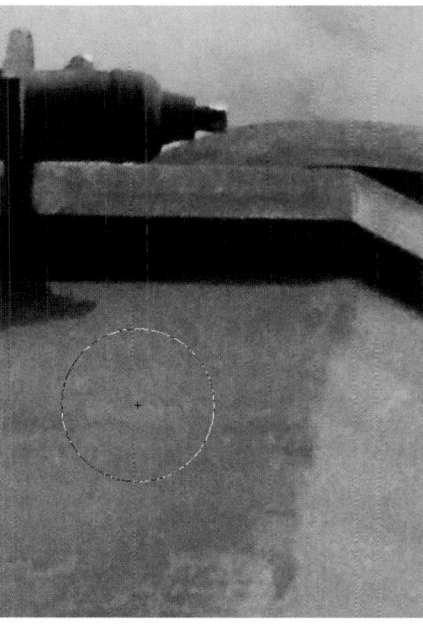

Fig. 3-2 Photoshop CS2 has a new cursor, and it's worth the price of the upgrade all by itself. The photograph on the left shows a circular brush cursor in Photoshop CS. It pretty much disappears against middle tones. The new CS2 cursor (right) never disappears, and you can add a crosshair to the middle for precision work.

Why do I think CS2 is worth the upgrade? For a start, you'll be able to use more memory (as much as 3.5 GB of RAM), but you'll need to be running on a 64-bit CPU with a 64-bit OS, like Windows Server or Mac OS X.

The tool cursor is changed for the better! In the past, it faded into invisibility over midtones. The new cursor is *always* clearly visible, regardless of the background (Figure 3-2). A new preference adds central crosshairs to a brush tip cursor. Now I can see the area a tool is affecting and precisely maneuver it at the same time, which is really useful when I'm trying to do precision cloning. I can assign the mouse scroll wheel to zoom in or out of the image. I do a lot of bit-twiddling and fine work when doing restorations; zooming in and out without touching the keyboard is just great.

These "minor" changes save me lots of time and eyestrain. I swear I'd upgrade to CS2 just for these.

The new Spot Healing Brush is a big improvement over the old Healing Brush. I didn't find myself using the original Healing Brush very much, because I thought there were better ways to fix problems. The new Spot Healing Brush is easier to use and works a lot better.

Smart Sharpen goes way beyond Unsharp Masking. There's a new blur algorithm I prefer; Lens Blur doesn't produce as much bright haloing around edges or grain/noise enhancement as Gaussian Blur does. Shadow and Highlight controls let you define how much sharpening gets applied to light and dark tones. For example, you can suppress shadow sharpening in film scans and underexposed digital photos that suffer from a lot of shadow noise.

The Reduce Noise filter also has a very nice range of controls; I can choose how much noise reduction to apply to each channel and select to preserve and even enhance certain levels of detail while reducing overall noise (Figure 3-3).

One unpleasant change: The progress bar now only pops up (in mid-screen) if an operation is taking longer than 8 seconds, a very long time to wait. Worse, the behavior is unpredictable: Sometimes it pops up after 2 seconds; other times it doesn't show after a dozen seconds or more. It's maddening. A Windows registry patch named ForceProgress_ON. reg, in the Goodies\Optional Plug-Ins\Photoshop Only\Optional Extensions folder of the CD, will force the bar to appear any time an operation is going to take more than a fraction of a second. This is worse than the old, unobtrusive progress bar, but it's better than the erratic default behavior. I don't know what Mac OS users can do.

Picture Window Pro v4 (http://www.dl-c.com)

Picture Window Pro (Figure 3-4) is an impressive and, at $90, inexpensive digital darkroom program. Published by Digital Light & Color, this program is fully 16-bit native, offers multiple undos, supports color management and device calibration better than Photoshop, has color correction and advanced sharpening tools that outdo Photoshop's, and takes up only 5 MB of your hard drive. A bonus: Picture Window has no annoying activation schemes, like Photoshop. (*Note:* The nonpro version only supports 8-bit images and lacks some of the best tools of Picture Window Pro.)

If you don't already own Photoshop, Picture Window Pro will give you a lot more bang per buck. You can download a free trial that is fully functional for 30 days. Picture Window Pro only runs under Windows. I run the program under Virtual PC on a Mac, so (non-Intel) Mac lovers aren't entirely out of luck, but it will run much slower. Picture Window Pro understands 8- and 16-bit TIFF, so Picture Window Pro and Photoshop share a common file format, but Picture Window Pro will not read nor write PSD files. If you like using Photoshop's special PSD-related features, you won't be able to easily go back and forth between the two programs.

Picture Window Pro is a deceptively simple-looking program. I've known people to dismiss it simply because it's not Photoshop and doesn't include some of the tools they expect to find. What such cursory examination fails to reveal is that Picture Window Pro comes well equipped with its own unique tools and methodologies.

Picture Window Pro's interface is not Photoshop's. Personally, I don't consider that a bad thing, as I've never been a big fan of the Photoshop

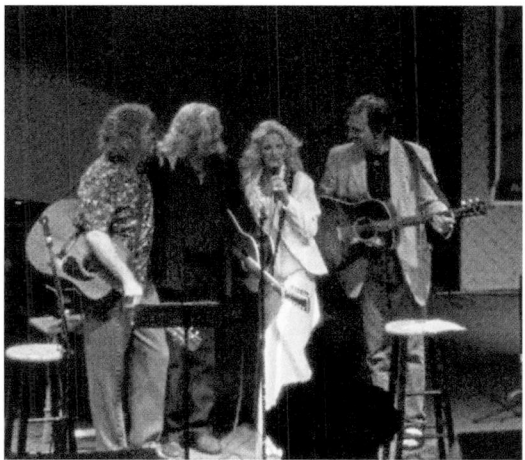

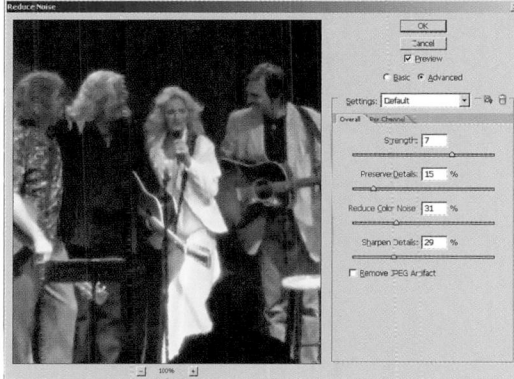

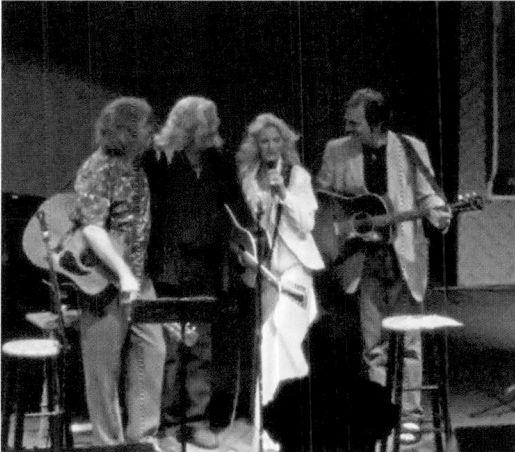

Fig. 3-3 The new Reduce Noise filter in Photoshop CS2 is a good tool for cleaning up noisy scans. Slider adjustments control strength, sharpness, detail preservation, and color noise elimination. The latter comes in especially handy when you're cleaning up film scans, as I did here. The filtered bottom photograph is a lot better than the raw photograph at the top.

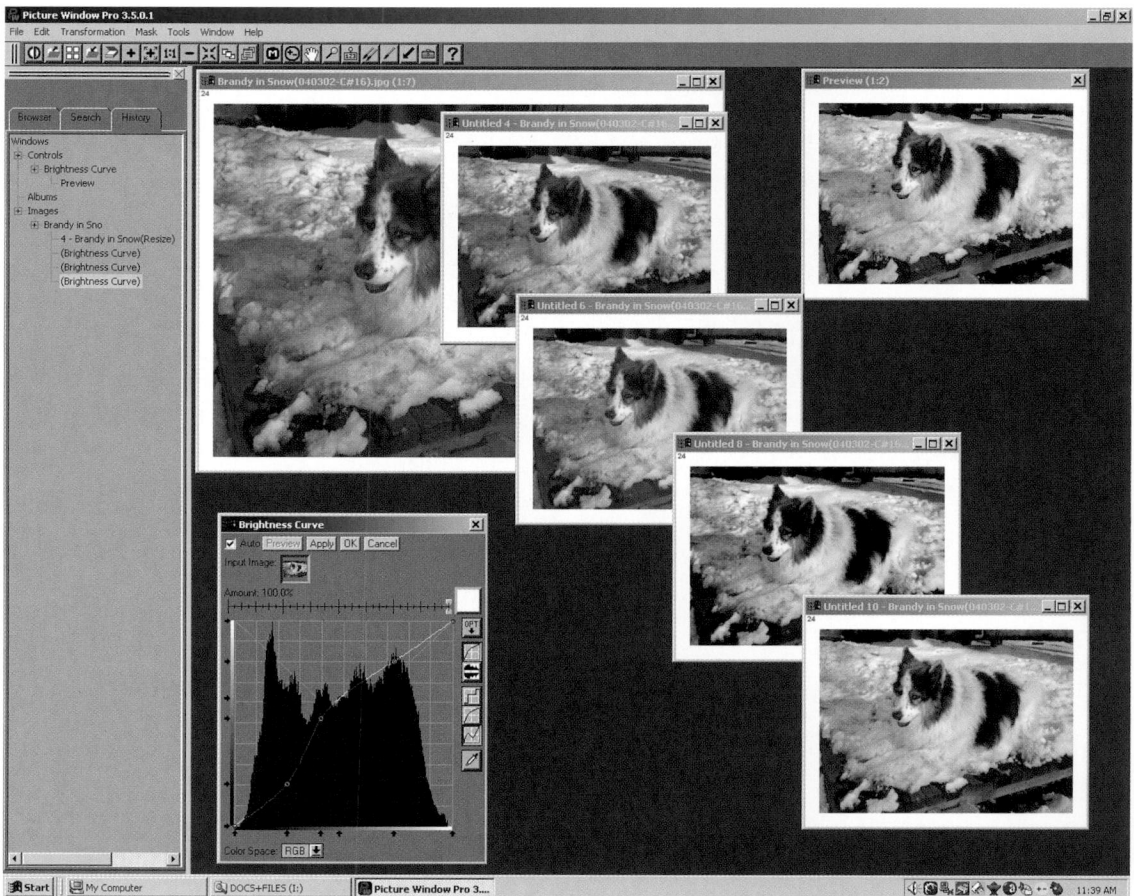

Fig. 3-4 Picture Window, from Digital Light & Color, works like a real digital darkroom. Each time you change a photograph, you create a new print. This screenshot shows me using the Brightness Curve Transformation to produce four different versions of the original photograph in the upper left background. I can save as many of these "prints" as I choose. I can also work on each print with other tools, and so follow parallel, independent paths of development for the same original photograph.

interface. To use Picture Window Pro effectively, you'll need to unlearn some Adobe ideas and acquire new ones.

Each time you perform an operation in Picture Window Pro, you create a new copy of the photo in a new window (hence, the program's name). I can't overstate how different this is from Photoshop, where operations change the original image. It's more like darkroom printing, where printing a photo differently doesn't erase previous prints, except that these are live files. You can go back and work with each one, taking it down its own artistic path.

For example, when the brightness curve control panel appears, so does a copy of the photo in a new preview window. As you adjust the curves, changes are reflected in the preview window. Press the Apply button, and a third window opens up containing the transformed image. Your original image remains unaltered in its own window, and the preview window and the control panel remain open; you can try other curve settings and every time you press Apply, a new window with a new modified image appears.

These image windows all exist independently of each other, and you can modify any of them using other transformations. PW's browser provides a tree diagram showing the genealogy of all of your image windows, so you can track and manage your workflow.

You can pull off some interesting tricks, once you wrap your head around this. For instance, each image in Picture Window Pro is similar to a snapshot in Photoshop, except it has its own independent existence. Using the clone tool between different image windows is a credible alternative to Photoshop's History Brush. Cloning isn't quite as convenient nor does it have as many options, but you can use it between any two images in PW, without worrying about the chronology of history states. You can "brush" backward or forward in time, even sideways between parallel branches of development.

Picture Window Pro includes some wonderful tools. The color correction controls emulate CC, Wratten, and color temperature correction photographic filters. These feel familiar to traditional photographic printers. Picture Window Pro's color correction transformation (also available as a separate Photoshop plug-in called Color Mechanic, described later in this chapter) is extraordinarily powerful and intuitive and unlike any other color correction tool you've ever used. If you already own Photoshop and have no desire to add Picture Window Pro to your ensemble, purchase that plug-in; you won't regret it.

Picture Window Pro offers resampling with sharpening using advanced sharpening options that do a better job of enhancing fine detail than Photoshop. For the ultimate in preservation of detail, there's PW's advanced sharpen transformation. It's actually a three-part affair: a noise reduction stage, a speck removal stage, and finally a sharpen stage. The first two stages are most useful by themselves for cleaning up photographs, whether or not you need to enhance their sharpness.

I use Picture Window Pro's powerful mask selection methods even when working primarily in Photoshop (masks are just grayscale images, so you can create them with one program and use them with another). You can define masks with hue, saturation, and value ranges, a la Asiva Select (described later in this chapter), with a Mask Brightness Curve (Figure 3-5), and with mask-painting brushes that can find edges and select pixels of similar color (see Chapter 7, Making Masks, page 234). While PW is very speedy at opening and saving files (even faster than Photoshop), most of its comparable transformations run slower. Assume operations like Curves and sharpen or blur filters will take two to three times as long in PW as in Photoshop.

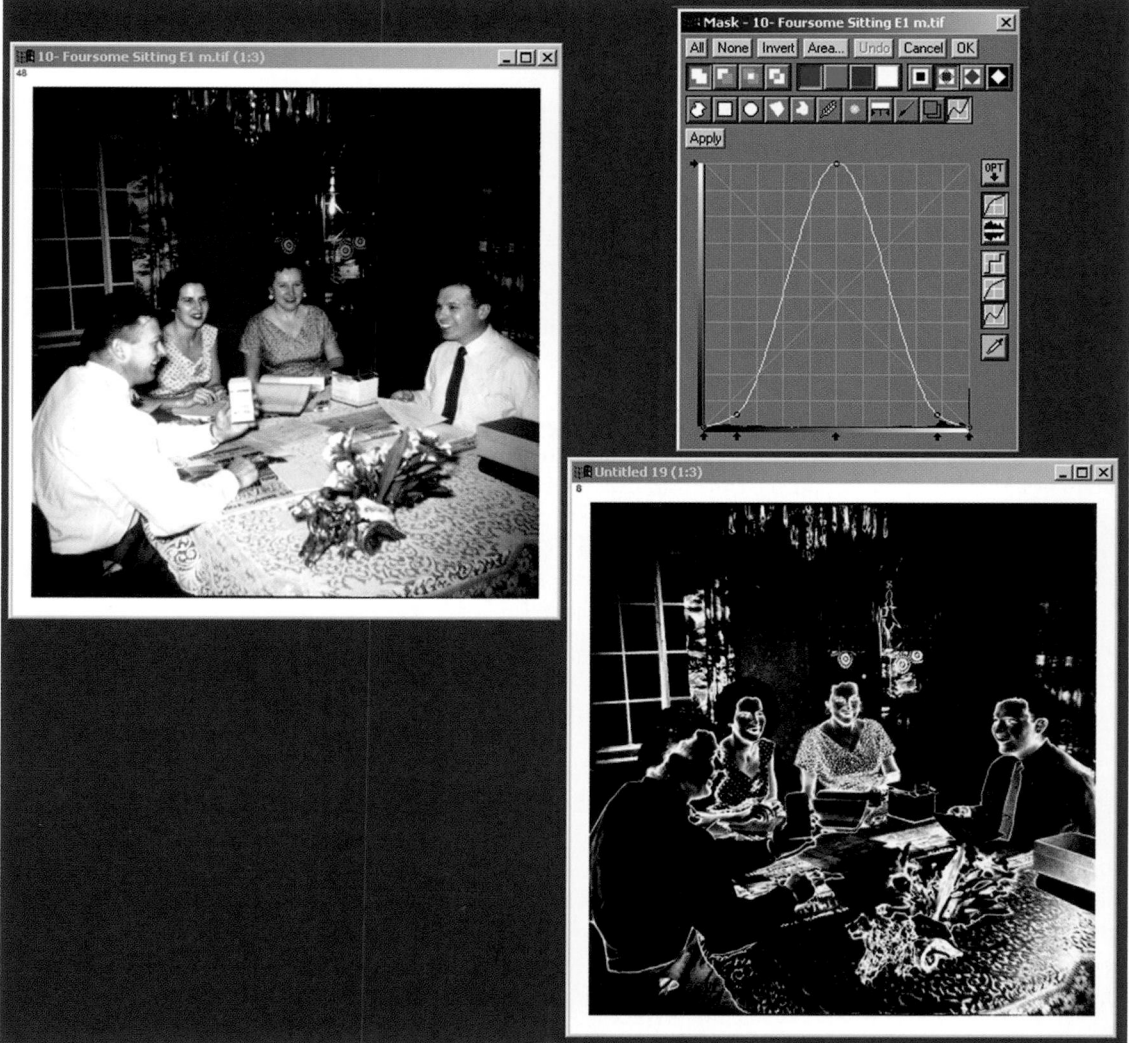

Fig. 3-5 Picture Window has some very powerful mask-making tools. The Mask Brightness Curve, for example, is much more flexible and useful than Photoshop's crude Color Range tool. Here I used the Curve to create a mask (lower right) that selected the midtones of the photograph in the upper left and smoothly faded out toward the whites and blacks. You can create very complex masks by using several of the masking tools in combination.

Plug-Ins

Plug-ins let me work much more efficiently, saving me much time and effort. Many plug-ins produce higher quality results than I could ever achieve by hand, no matter how much time I might spend. In the remainder of this chapter I introduce you to plug-ins that aid my restoration work. These are by no means tutorials nor even complete descriptions of their capabilities. Throughout the book I use these plug-ins in my examples of how to fix various kinds of problems. That will give you some sense of their worth and how to apply them. All of them have trial downloads, so you can check them out thoroughly.

You don't necessarily need Photoshop to run plug-ins; most plug-ins will run in Adobe Photoshop Elements, Adobe PhotoDeluxe, and Corel Paint Shop Pro, but each plug-in maker decides which programs their plug-ins will be compatible with and what OS they'll run under. A few, for example, only work under Windows (noted below), and several may require a more recent version of Windows or Mac OS than you're running. Check the plug-in publisher's website to find out which environments their plug-in will run in.

Plug-ins come with a cost, and I don't just mean their purchase price. Plug-ins are frequently memory hogs, because they're performing very complicated calculations. See my remarks on RAM usage in Chapter 2, page 34. As a rule plug-ins need to use a piece of the RAM that is available to Photoshop. As long as you've got at least twice as much RAM assigned to Photoshop as the size of the file you're opening, bare-bones Photoshop will usually run. It will run slowly, because as soon as you start doing anything it will start writing scratch files to the disk, but it will perform.

Not so for plug-ins. They need to work in real RAM, and sometimes their RAM demands are large. For example, DIGITAL ROC and DIGITAL GEM need additional RAM that's equal to about two and a half times the size of the image file you're working on. DIGITAL GEM Airbrush needs almost seven times the file size!

Some plug-ins perform extraordinarily elaborate computations and take a long time to run even on a very fast machine. It can truly try one's patience waiting for some of them to finish executing. Still, what I get in return for that time can be incredibly valuable. So, as the seconds (and sometimes minutes) tick away, I try to remind myself that if I were doing this manually, it would take me 10 times as long, and it wouldn't look half as good.

Remember that you can use plug-ins with masks, history brushes, and layers that you can blend into the original image in different ways. Don't just take what a plug-in hands you; shape it to your needs.

DIGITAL ROC Pro and GEM Pro (http://www.asf.com)

DIGITAL ROC and DIGITAL GEM are built into some scanners as part of the DIGITAL ICE^3 package. Applied Science Fiction, now known as the Eastman Kodak Austin Development Center, has turned them into plug-ins.

I strongly recommend these two plug-ins even if you have a scanner that's equipped with ICE^3. The plug-ins work differently from the scanner software and have advantages that the scanner software doesn't.

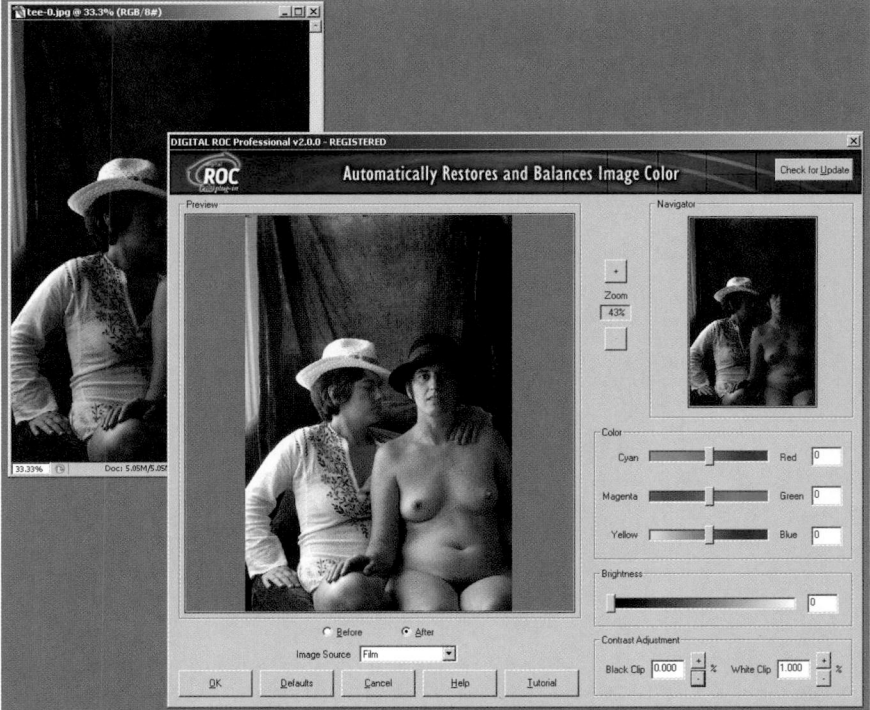

Fig. 3-6 The DIGITAL ROC plug-in for Photoshop does things that the version built into DIGITAL ICE³ cannot. The plug-in version lets you adjust color balance, brightness, and contrast for optimal results. This screenshot shows DIGITAL ROC correcting a badly faded slide from the late 1970s.

Although the scanner plug-ins get to work on the raw scanner data before it gets to your computer and consequently often do the most effective job of repairing flaws, they aren't very flexible. They have fewer adjustments and controls than do the plug-in versions. Furthermore you can't use masking techniques or layers to selectively control where and how the scanner software works its magic. Controlled application of DIGITAL ROC and GEM is a very powerful tool.

These plug-ins come in regular and professional versions. Buy the professional versions, even though they cost twice as much ($100 apiece) because they work on 16-bit as well as 8-bit images, but more importantly they include a number of adjustment controls that aren't available on the regular versions. I find these controls absolutely essential to getting really good results.

ROC stands for *restoration of color*. DIGITAL ROC Pro (Figure 3-6) analyzes the color gamut of the original file to adjust, expand, and normalize each color channel. Think of it as kind of an automatic graphic equalizer for color instead of sound. The plug-in is not as effective as the version incorporated into scanners, because it doesn't have access to the raw scan data, but it's the next best thing.

Just about any color rendition problem can be fixed using Photoshop's standard tools, but it can take a lot of work and expertise to do

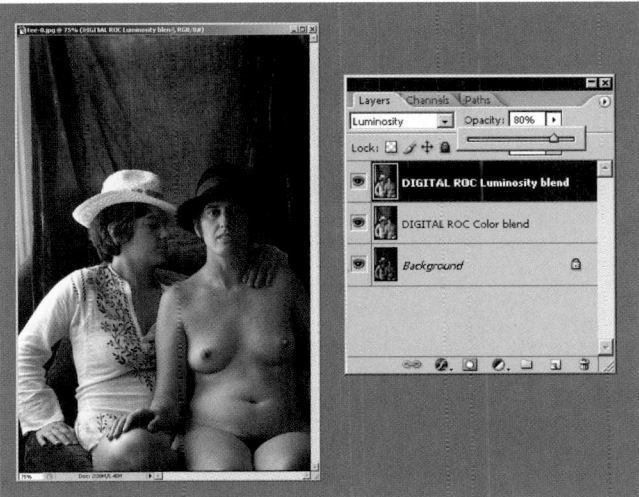

Fig. 3-7 By itself, DIGITAL ROC produces great color, but the results are often too contrasty, with extreme highlight and shadow detail clipped. A great way to control this plug-in's contrast is to make two duplicate layers of the original photograph and apply DIGITAL ROC to both of the duplicates. Set the first duplicate layer to Color blend and the second to Luminosity blend. Adjust the opacity of the Luminosity-blended layer down from 100% to reduce the contrast of the photograph to the desired level. If you keep this as a layered file instead of flattening it, you can go back at any later time and alter the opacity settings to change the way the photograph looks.

so. DIGITAL ROC will do 50% to 75% of the job all by itself in one pass. It's that good. Don't confuse what DIGITAL ROC does with a simple Auto Levels or Auto Color adjustment in Photoshop. DIGITAL ROC really does restore color, coming up with credible tones and hues from extremely faded, nearly monochrome originals. It probably doesn't do anything that I can't do manually in Photoshop, but it does it automatically and swiftly.

Sometimes DIGITAL ROC can be too contrasty and saturated, with a tendency to blow out the highlights. Normally I set the brightness level much lower than the default of 25; sometimes I take it all the way down to 0. I also usually set the black clip at 0%. Setting the white clip to 0% sometimes produces obviously distorted results, but typing a value between 0.1% and 1% works well.

I often apply DIGITAL ROC to duplicate layers of the photograph and blend them into the base layer with luminosity and color blends (see Chapter 6, Restoring Color, page 193). That lets me modulate the strength of the color and contrast changes separately (Figure 3-7). See Chapter 9, page 336, for a complete restoration of this photo.

DIGITAL GEM (Figure 3-8) reduces grain and noise without significantly affecting fine detail. GEM is a special kind of noise filter that is designed for film grain, but I have found it extremely useful for dealing with any kind of fine random noise. I use it primarily to reduce the grain

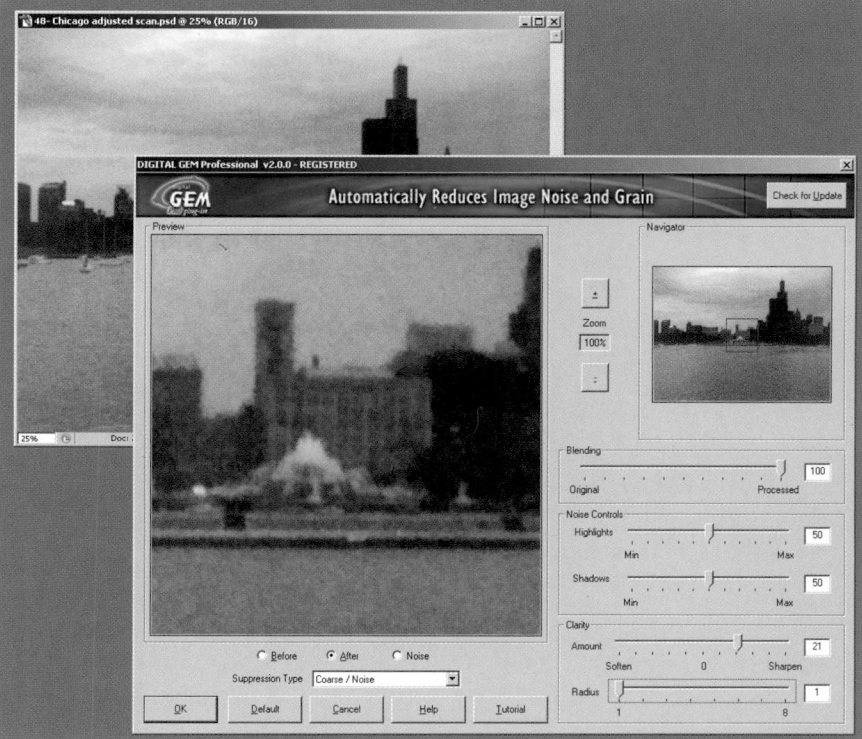

Fig. 3-8 The DIGITAL GEM plug-in for Photoshop does things that the version built into DIGITAL ICE[3] doesn't. The plug-in lets you choose whether to suppress coarse or fine noise, emphasize highlight or shadow noise suppression, and sharpen up the photograph after noise reduction. I used DIGITAL GEM with the settings shown here to improve the photograph in Figure 3-9.

in my restorations, especially with very low-contrast originals that will have their contrast increased during restoration (Figure 3-9). Whenever I have a vexing noise problem, whether it is due to paper surface texture, cracking or grazing, or dirt on the original, I experiment with GEM to see if it will improve the situation more than Photoshop's standard filters.

GEM's controls are rather complex and take some practice to master. DIGITAL GEM has two different filter types, a *coarse* mode and a *fine-grain* mode, with different sets of controls. In the coarse mode, noise control sliders control how much the filter reduces grain noise in the highlights and shadows. Moving a slider toward maximum tends to decrease image detail for those tones, while moving it toward minimum preserves fine detail but removes less of the noise.

In the fine-grain, mode the noise controls change to a *suppression* slider and a *detail sensitivity* slider. The suppression slider controls the strength of the operation; as you push the slider toward maximum, it more aggressively filters out grain and noise. The detail sensitivity slider determines how much image detail the filter preserves versus how much grain it suppresses. Increasing the value in this slider preserves more fine detail but may leave more grain behind.

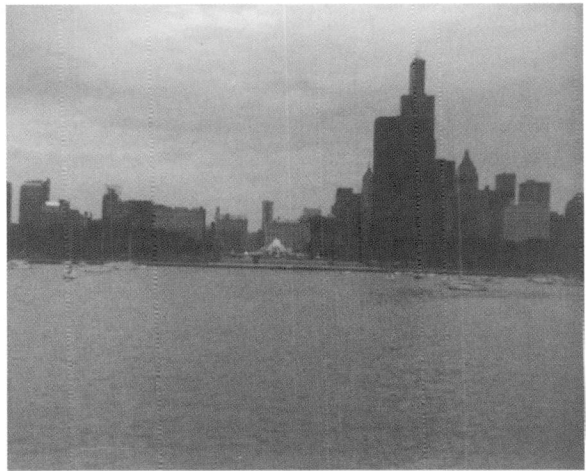

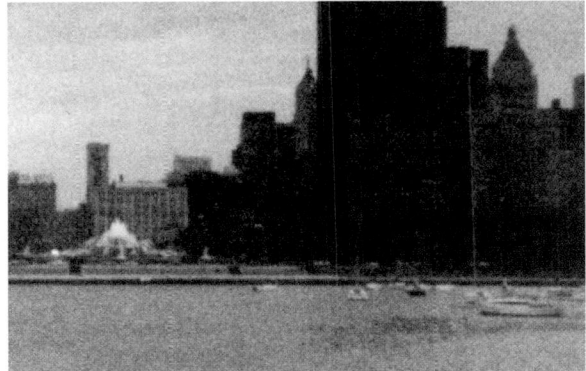

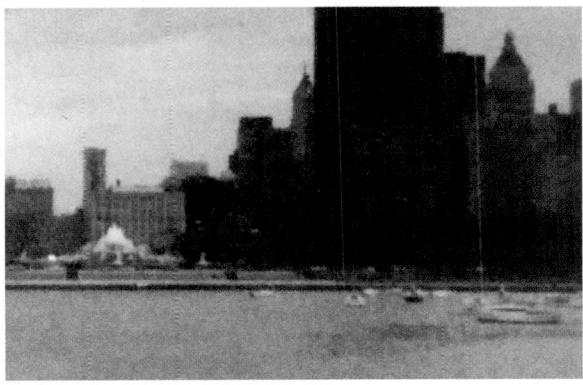

Fig. 3-9 Low-contrast and faded originals may become very grainy when they're restored because the increased contrast emphasizes the grain along with everything else. The restoration of the top photograph (enlarged in the middle photo) demonstrates this problem. The color and tone are fine, but the grain dominates the photograph. Applying DIGITAL GEM with the settings shown in Figure 3-8 produced a much nicer photograph, seen at the bottom.

Because grain suppression is almost always somewhat destructive of fine detail no matter how cleverly done, I often use this with the History Brush, so that I can apply grain reduction exactly where I want at a controllable strength.

When I need to use DIGITAL ROC, I usually apply it before doing anything else, to bring the photograph into some semblance of correct

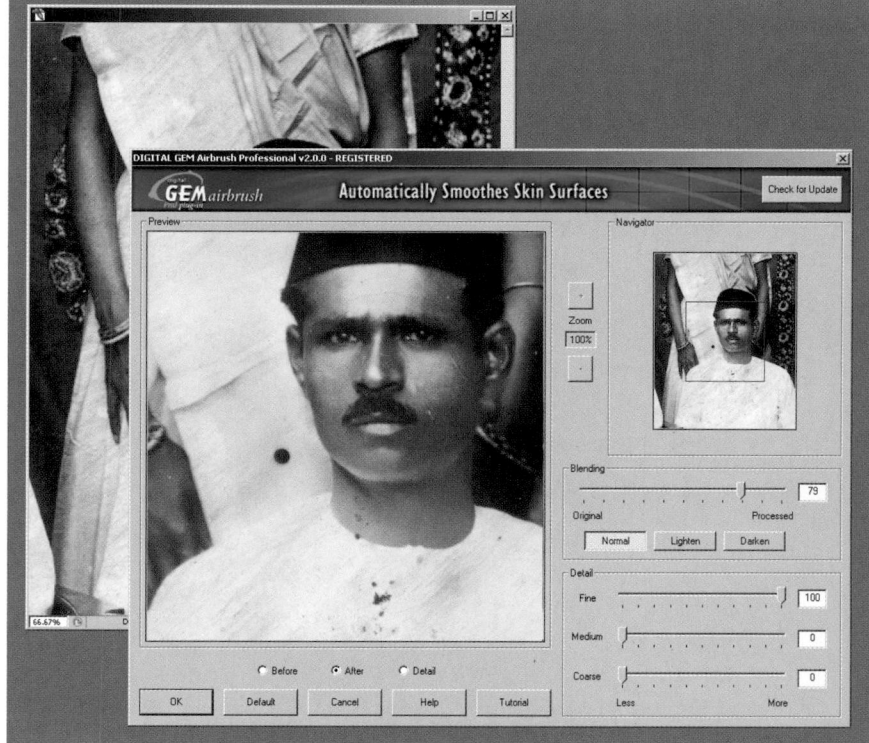

Fig. 3-10 DIGITAL GEM Airbrush, as its name and title bar suggest, is primarily a retouching tool that produces smoother and more attractive skin tones. Nonetheless, it can be a very effective tool for reducing fine, overall damage, like the pervasive small scratches that obscure this photograph.

tonality and color. There are times, though, when I find it better to apply DIGITAL GEM first to reduce the noise in the image. DIGITAL ROC can be confused by very high noise levels; GEM lightly applied can clean up scans so that DIGITAL ROC does a better job.

DIGITAL GEM Airbrush Pro (http://www.asf.com)

DIGITAL GEM Airbrush Pro (Figure 3-10) is a more specialized kind of grain and noise reduction tool than DIGITAL GEM. As its name suggests, it's meant as more of a retouching tool, to soften blemishes, creases, and lines in people's hands and faces. If your restoration objectives include "prettifying" the subject, this plug-in makes that work go much faster.

I have found, however, that GEM Airbrush has uses beyond the mere cosmetic. Many old-time portraits had rather heavy-handed retouching done to them. Faces will show obvious cross-hatching or stippling marks that to the modern eye look more like disfigurement than enhancement. GEM Airbrush sees them as not much different from facial wrinkles, and it can help eliminate them. GEM Airbrush can also suppress fine scratches and scuff marks (Figure 3-11).

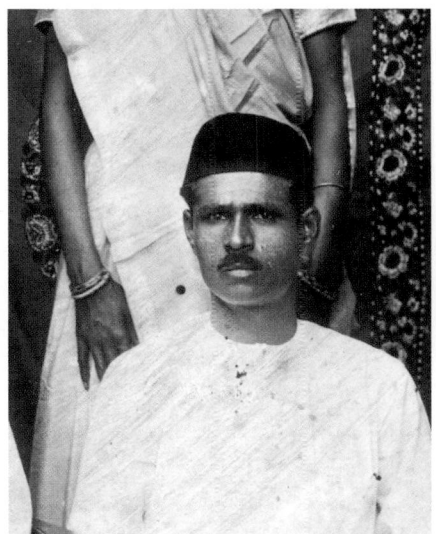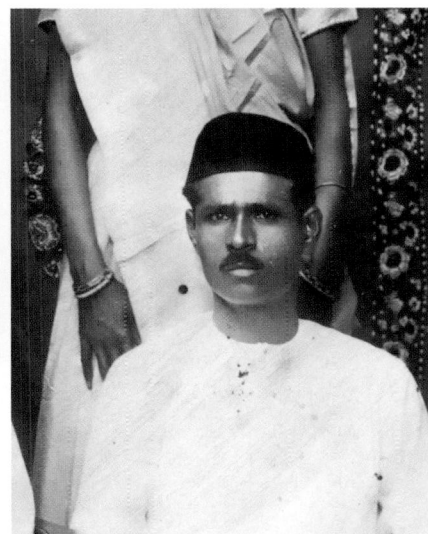

Fig. 3-11 The photograph on the left is covered with fine scratches. Applying DIGITAL GEM Airbrush, with the settings shown in Figure 3-10, eliminated most of the scratches (right photograph). Normally, you should apply this filter with a History Brush so that you can avoid altering areas with important fine detail that might be damaged by the filter.

This plug-in tends to destroy moderate and fine detail, so you want to apply it carefully. There are three detail-controlling sliders for fine, medium, and coarse detail. Increasing the adjustment from 0 to 100 increases the amount of that kind of detail that is retained in the filtered photograph.

GEM Airbrush is a tricky tool to learn to use well; its behavior isn't exactly intuitive. Still, I have found that its unique noise-filtering abilities make it worth one's while to spend the time to understand it. I think it's best used with masks or the History Brush, so that its effect can be applied only where desired.

Color Mechanic (http://www.colormechanic.com)

Color Mechanic (Figure 3-12), from Digital Light & Color is derived from the incredibly useful Color Correction Transformation in Picture Window. That's good news for Mac users, since Color Mechanic plays happily with Mac versions of programs like Photoshop.

Color Mechanic comes in a regular ($30) and a pro ($50) version; the pro version supports 16-bit files and has some additional controls I find valuable. Digital Light & Color also allows one to upgrade from the regular to professional version for an additional $30, so you won't lose much money if you decide to get the regular version and later decide you need the professional.

Color Mechanic takes advantage of the way we naturally think about color correction. We can look at a photo and immediately identify the colors and tones that are off, but Photoshop lacks an intuitive way to correct them. We can't simply tell Photoshop, "That skin tone is too pink

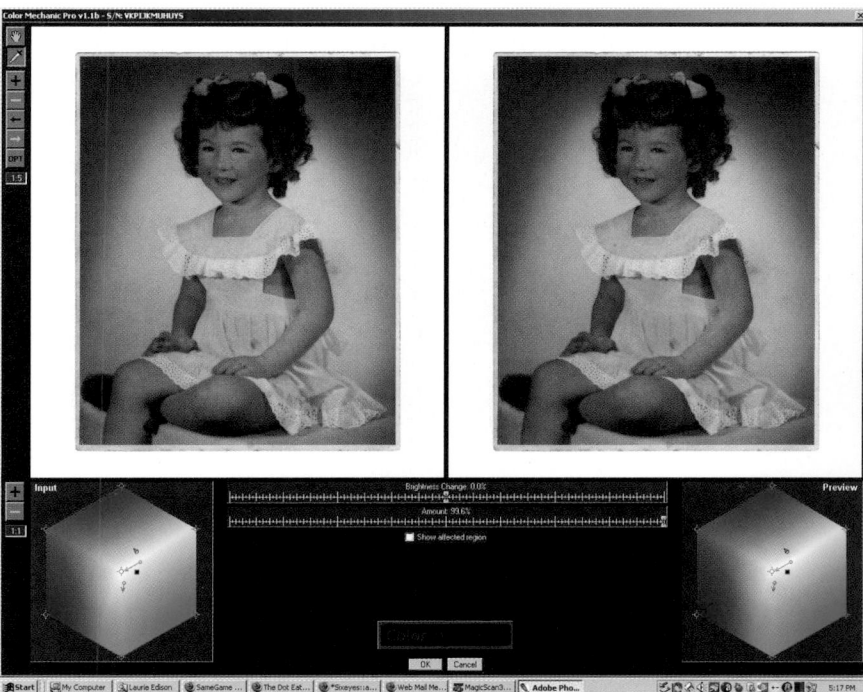

Fig. 3-12 Color Mechanic is a most remarkable and unique Photoshop plug-in for manipulating colors in a photograph. Clicking the eyedropper on the "before" photograph (left) sets control points in the color-space hexagon at the lower left. Dragging those points to new locations changes the original colors to new ones. Nearby colors warp smoothly, so there are no abrupt and unnatural-looking color changes. The resulting photograph and color-space hexagon are shown on the right. Figure 3-13 shows an expanded view of the color space for this adjustment.

and that gray too blue; fix it." Color Mechanic comes close to doing just that with a remarkably simple way to correct color. It presents you with a view of your file and a color-space hexagon. Click on a point in the image, and the corresponding color is selected within the color hexagon. You can drag that color into any other place in the color space. The color space warps smoothly around that change, as if it were a rubber sheet change, so related colors adjust to fit; greatly different colors aren't affected at all (Figure 3-13). Changes are immediately reflected in the "after" image and the color hexagon. There are also sliders to control the brightness and (in the pro version) the strength of the color changes.

You can do this to as many color points as you like, custom-tuning the color palette to fit the photo. You can lock down colors so that they don't change by adding a correction point and not dragging it to a new location. That pins the color at its original value, no matter what other warps you make to the color space.

Restoring the color in a badly faded photograph is often a process of approximations. Some fine adjustment is usually needed to get the colors to look exactly right. Color Mechanic's great for that, especially for correcting slight color casts in neutrals and skin tones without introducing unwanted side effects. That can be extremely difficult with Photoshop's standard tools, even with plug-ins like DIGITAL ROC. See Chapter 6, Restoring Color, page 227, for more about using this wonderful plug-in.

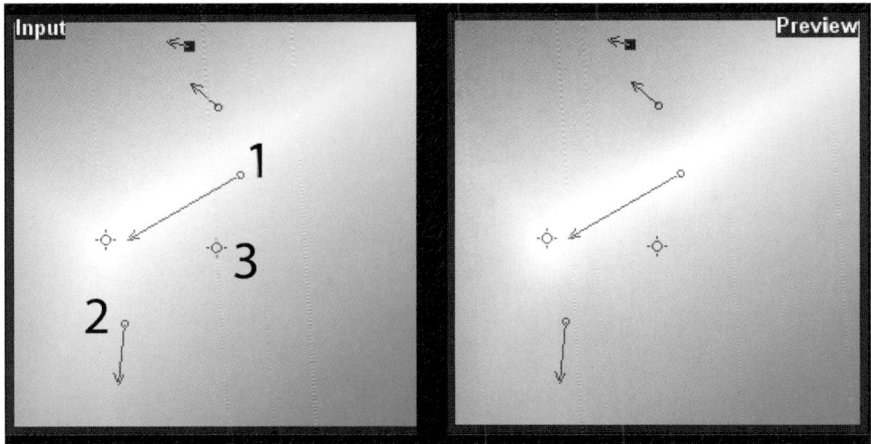

Fig. 3-13 These are enlarged views of the color-space adjustments I made in Figure 3-12. The numbered points demonstrate the different kinds of changes that Color Mechanic can make. I dragged Point 1 toward the neutral center point to desaturate the background of the photograph. The Preview color space shows that white has "bled" from the head of the arrow back to the control point. Point 2 was dragged away from the center and from the green hues. That increased the saturation in the dress and shifted the hue slightly to the blue. I used Point 3 as a lock-down point; since I didn't draw an arrow from it, the input and preview colors will be the same. It preserves those yellow-green hues in the color space unchanged.

Image Doctor (http//www.alienskin.com)

Image Doctor ($130) from Alien Skin Software is a plug-in that I recommend with qualifiers. Image Doctor contains four tools; the ones that will most interest restorers are Smart Fill (Figure 3-14) and Spot Lifter (Figure 3-15).

Smart Fill is an extremely powerful image repair utility. Smart Fill serves a function similar to that of Photoshop CS2's Patch Tool, but it is more sophisticated (and more difficult to use). It can fill in large gaps in a photograph with surrounding tones and complex textures so adroitly that it's difficult to tell that any repair work has been done (Figure 3-16).

Image Doctor is brilliant when applied to simple selections but not good on complex ones. It's sometimes easy to create a selection mask that isolates the missing parts of a photograph or a network of cracks (see Chapter 7, Making Masks), so that you can work on restoring those without messing up the remaining photograph. You'd think Image Doctor would be the perfect tool for filling in networks of cracks or crazing in a photograph and for quickly restoring missing chunks of image. The problem is that the amount of computation that Image Doctor has to do increases with the complexity and size of the selection (obviously very high for networks of cracks). Image Doctor creates a sampling box for re-creating the missing detail based on the expanse of the

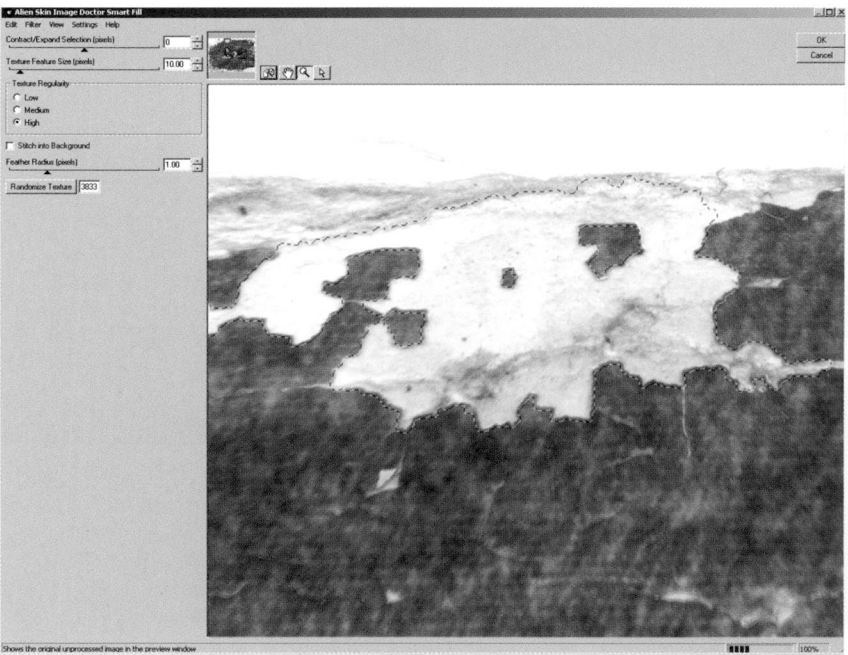

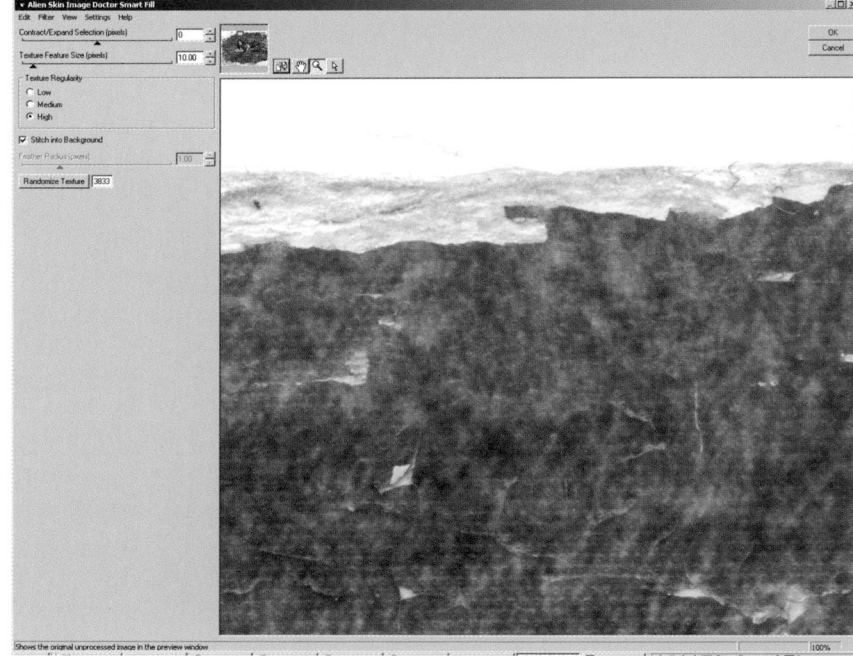

Fig. 3-14 Image Doctor is an efficient plug-in for doing the first level of repair on damaged originals. Its Smart Fill function repaired the selected area in the top photograph, producing the bottom photo (this is a close-up of the photograph in Figure 1-3). Smart Fill can't perfectly interpolate detail that isn't there, but it does a good enough job of reestablishing tones and textures to substantially reduce the amount of manual labor needed to completely fix the missing pieces.

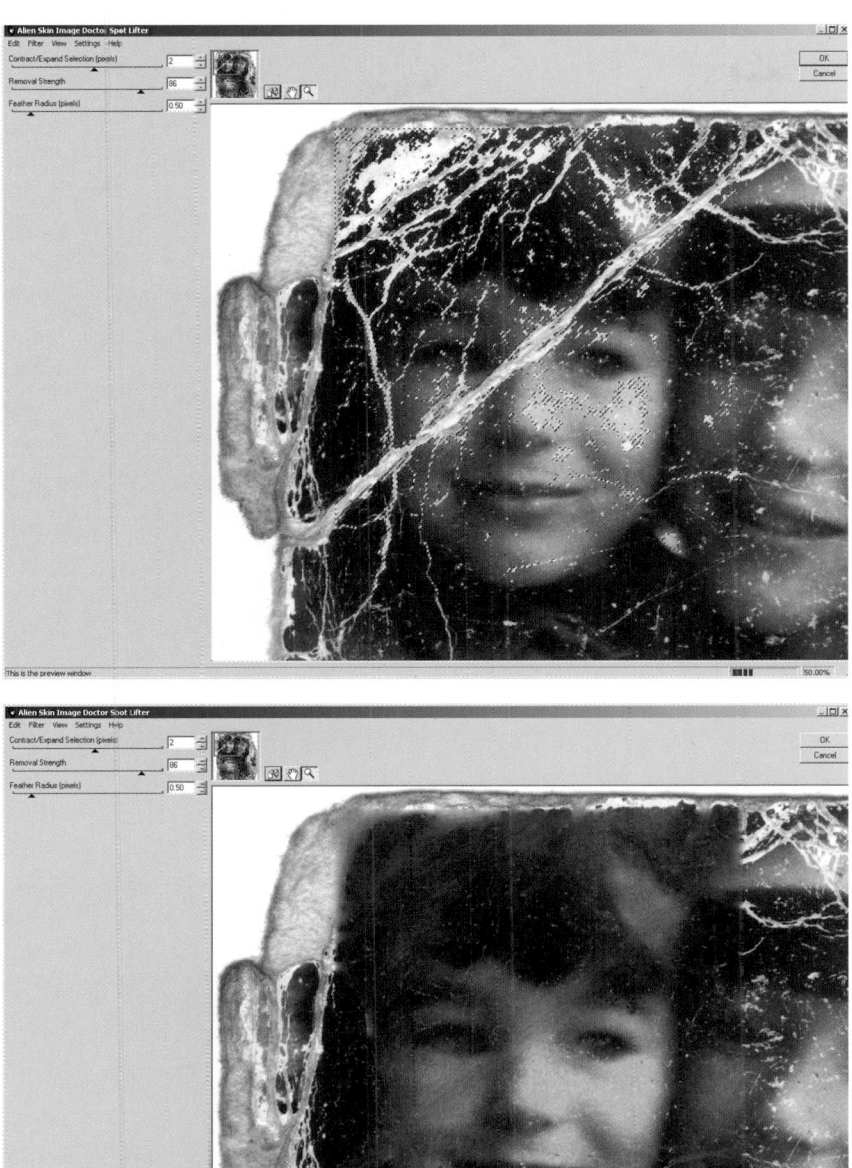

Fig. 3-15 Image Doctor's Spot Lifter works rapidly on complex selections (upper photo), but it doesn't create brand-new textures like Smart Fill does. It did a very good job of filling in the cracks in this portion of Figure 1-8, once I had created a selection for them (see Chapter 7).

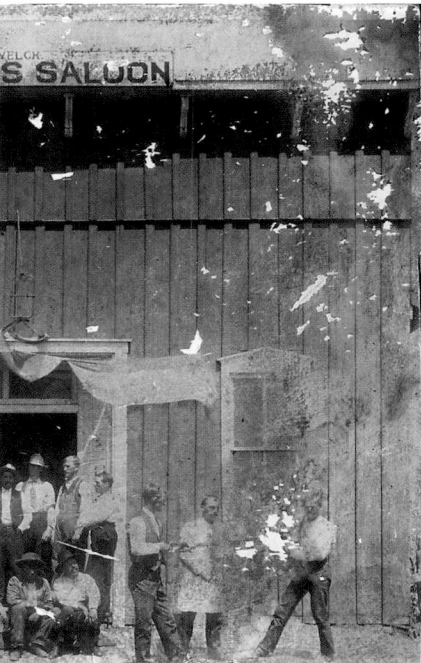 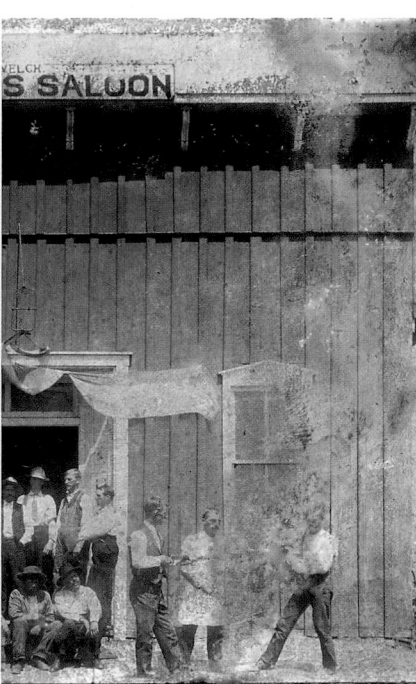

Fig. 3-16 Smart Fill can repair multiple areas in one pass, as it did in the photograph on the right, but you'll need a very fast computer and patience. It's still a lot faster, however, than doing the repair work by hand!

selected areas; for damage scattered across an entire photograph, Image Doctor attempts to analyze the entire photograph for all of the regions that need repair. The result is exponentially increasing processing time. I can readily come up with selections that take Image Doctor the better part of an hour to process. Image Doctor will tax the fastest CPU you can throw at it.

Image Doctor is so useful, though, that it's worth figuring out some work-arounds. The following work principles tame Image Doctor enough to make it a useful tool:

- Divide the photograph into small regions, and work on them separately. Image Doctor will take much less time to fill in many voids that fall within a region that's only 5% of the total area of the photograph than it will to fill in a handful of voids scattered across the entire image.

- The more complex the shape of the selected regions to be filled in, the longer it seems to take Image Doctor to do its job. Smooth masks to keep the edges and contours of the selections as simple and uncomplicated as possible.

Spot Lifter is Smart Fill's simpler sibling. It's faster and easier to use, but it doesn't do anywhere near as clever a job of replicating surroundings, because it doesn't attempt to duplicate textures. It doesn't work well when the void it's filling is surrounded by areas with lots of detail. Spot Lifter will work on much larger regions and more complex selections without taking insanely long amounts of time. Spot Lifter usually doesn't do an invisible repair job, but it often suppresses damage to the point that it is no longer a distraction in the printed photograph.

Image Doctor also includes a highly effective JPEG Repair tool. You won't need this when working on scans you've done yourself, but on occasion you may have to do restoration from a file someone sends you because they don't have the original any longer. It's possible to do decent restorations from such files, and in those circumstances you'll find JPEG Repair valuable for cleaning up compression artifacts. It does a much better job than Remove JPEG Artifact in Photoshop's Reduce Noise filter.

Focus Magic (htpp://www.focusmagic.com)

Focus Magic ($45) is a remarkable piece of software. It's an honest-to-God real sharpening algorithm that works as a stand-alone program or a Photoshop plug-in. I'll spare you the math about how it works. What's important is that this is not a mere edge-enhancement routine like most so-called sharpening filters; this one actually undoes the blur.

Focus Magic can remove motion blur as well as out-of-focus blur (Figure 3-17). Sometimes its improvements are astonishing It cannot work true miracles; I'd estimate that usually it's limited to about a factor of two gain in real fine detail and sharpness; that's often enough to take a lousy photo and turn it into an acceptable one or make a borderline photograph really sharp.

The cleaner and more noise/grain-free a photograph is, the better Focus Magic will work; it indiscriminately sharpens noise and grain just as much as image detail. This can produce objectionable artifacts, especially in areas that demand smooth tonality, like faces. Focus Magic has settings that will minimize these artifacts at the expense of some efficacy. Its default source setting is *Digital Camera*, which requires a very noise-free original. Unless your photograph has almost no grain, dirt, and noise, the *Grainy Image* source setting will work a lot better. That may give sharpened photographs a slightly plastic look, with sharpened edges but smoothed-out continuous tones.

I use Focus Magic to help deal with textured photographs. especially those printed on that annoying "honeycomb" paper surface that used to be so popular and creates so much trouble when I scan it. It's not hard to get rid of that texture with one or another of the noise or blur filters in Photoshop, but that almost always degrades the fine detail in the photograph. An adroit use of a filter to remove the paper texture followed by an application of Focus Magic often eliminates the paper texture with little or no loss of any actual image detail (Chapter 8, page 307).

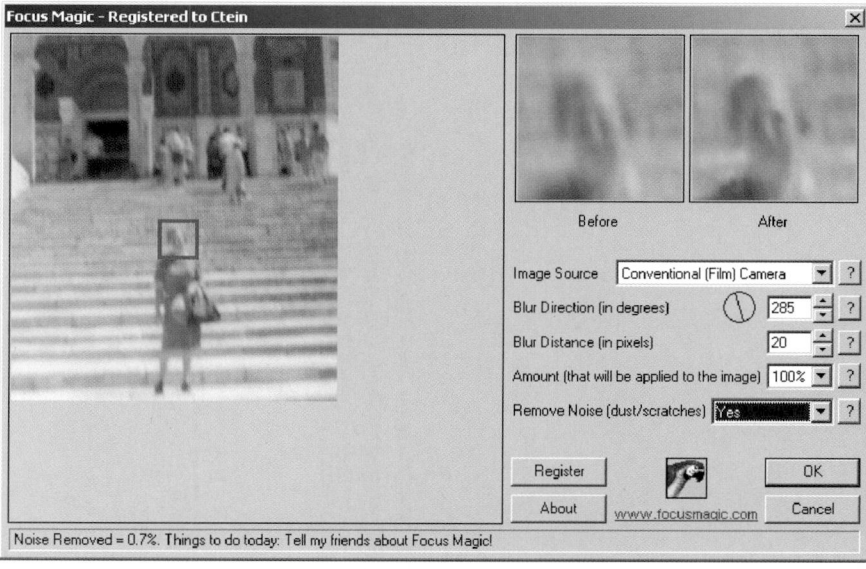

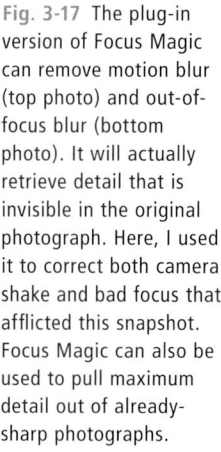

Fig. 3-17 The plug-in version of Focus Magic can remove motion blur (top photo) and out-of-focus blur (bottom photo). It will actually retrieve detail that is invisible in the original photograph. Here, I used it to correct both camera shake and bad focus that afflicted this snapshot. Focus Magic can also be used to pull maximum detail out of already-sharp photographs.

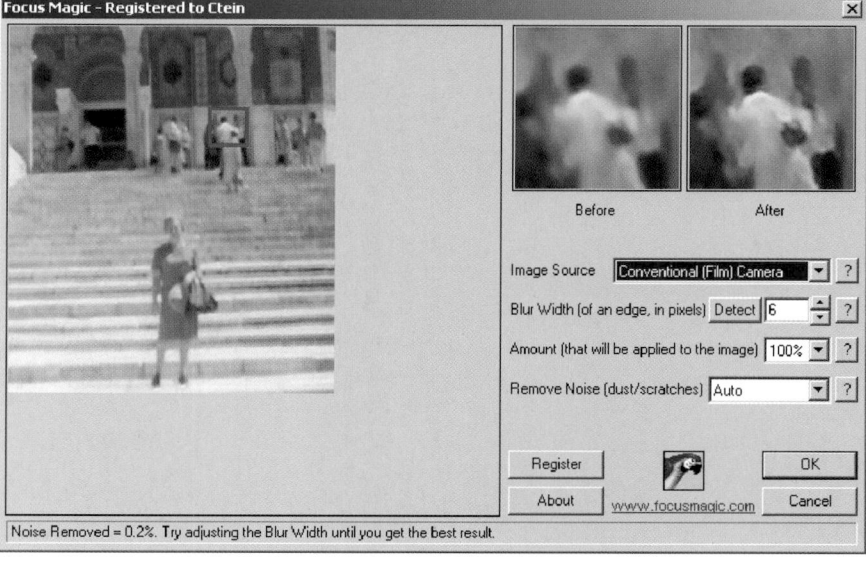

Given that many of the photos we get to restore aren't really sharp, this tool is great to have. With a low-noise photo, the results can border on the unbelievable (Figure 3-18). I apply Focus Magic in some fashion or another to many photographs I restore. Even when working with high-quality scans from my own original photographs, I often apply Focus Magic with a one-pixel radius setting to subtly enhance fine detail and kick up the edge sharpness a bit.

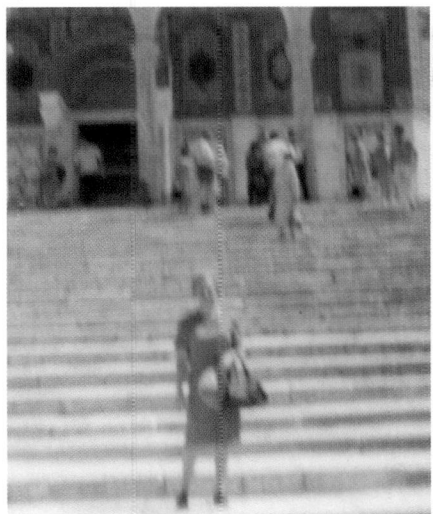 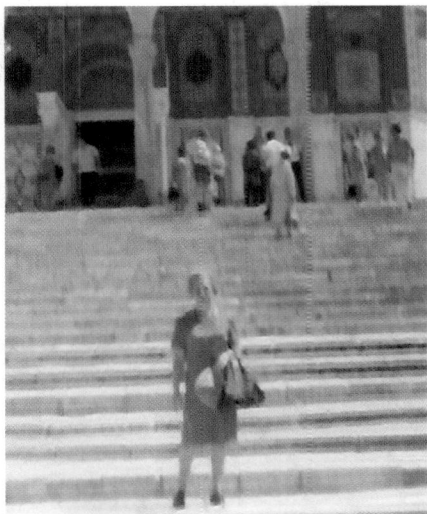

Fig. 3-18 On the left, the snapshot before Focus Magic. On the right, the improvements Focus Magic wrought. The plug-in turned an unusable photograph into an acceptable one. With a better original, Focus Magic can make a marginal photograph excellent.

As a stand-alone program, Focus Magic has some features that aren't available through the plug-in. The *despeckle* filter does a very good job of descreening scans of halftone photographs. It minimizes the halftone dots and extracts the maximum amount of real image detail at the same time (see Chapter 9, Tips, Tricks, and Enhancements, page 320, for other good ways to descreen halftones). It's fast, too. The big disadvantage of the stand-alone program is that it can only open and save JPEG files. The plug-in works on any file that can be opened in Photoshop.

Asiva Selection (http://www.asiva.com)

Asiva Selection ($40) is a plug-in that creates masks. Asiva's novel selection method uses hue, saturation, and intensity (HSI) to isolate different parts of the photograph (Figure 3-19). Hue corresponds to spectral color: red, orange, yellow, etc. Saturation (or chroma) is how pure the color is; for example, primary yellow and red have high saturation, and pastels have low saturation. Intensity (or value or luminance or brightness) is how light or dark the tone is, white being maximum and black minimum. Regardless of what color-space your images are using in Photoshop, Asiva Selection works with HSI values automatically. Three curve windows in the Asiva Selection interface control the range of hues, intensities, and saturation that will be selected.

Learning how to set these curves well takes some practice, even if you're familiar with HSI space. Fortunately, a save option lets you preserve settings and reload them later, so you can experiment with different ones. There are also useful preset *quick curves*. A drop-down menu loads selection curves for a variety of subjects, including multiethnic skin tones, water and sky, and primary colors.

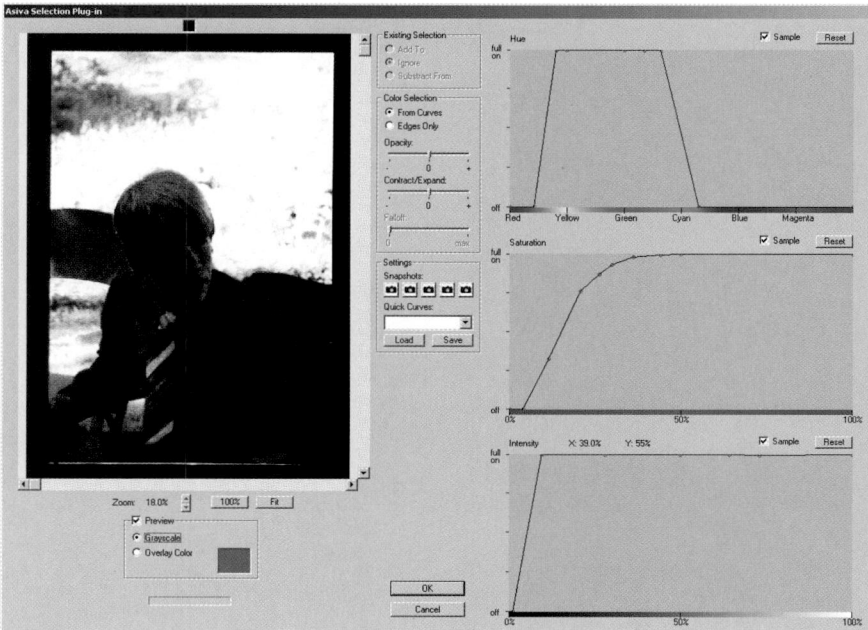

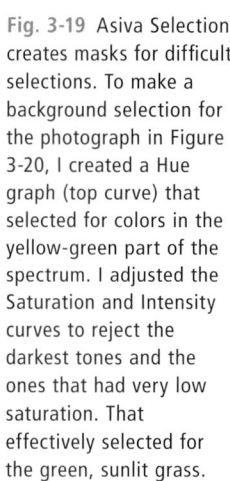

Fig. 3-19 Asiva Selection creates masks for difficult selections. To make a background selection for the photograph in Figure 3-20, I created a Hue graph (top curve) that selected for colors in the yellow-green part of the spectrum. I adjusted the Saturation and Intensity curves to reject the darkest tones and the ones that had very low saturation. That effectively selected for the green, sunlit grass.

You can manually create a selection in one of three ways. The first is to draw in the hue, saturation, and intensity curves directly. Click on the curve to add a control point to it, which can be dragged up or down and left or right. You can see the results of your manipulations in the preview window, either as a grayscale image or as a color overlay on the original photograph.

The second way is to click on a point in the preview window with the eyedropper, and the values near that pixel are fed directly into the selection graphs. You can then modify those curves by hand. You can choose which of the selection graphs are affected by the eyedropper by checking or unchecking the sample option above each graph.

The third and most useful way to specify a selection is to drag the eyedropper tool diagonally across the preview window, which samples all the pixels in a rectangular box. You can use adjustment sliders to expand or contract your selection and to fade its edges. The finished mask can be used with any other Photoshop tools. In Figure 3-20, I used the mask from Figure 3-19 to soften and tone down the background.

Mask Pro (http://www.ononesoftware.com)

Mask Pro is an elaborate and expensive ($200) masking plug-in. It actually incorporates three related tools. The Mask Pro filter extracts portions of the image, Mask Pro Select defines a mask that you may use with other Photoshop filters and tools, and Mask Pro Work Path converts

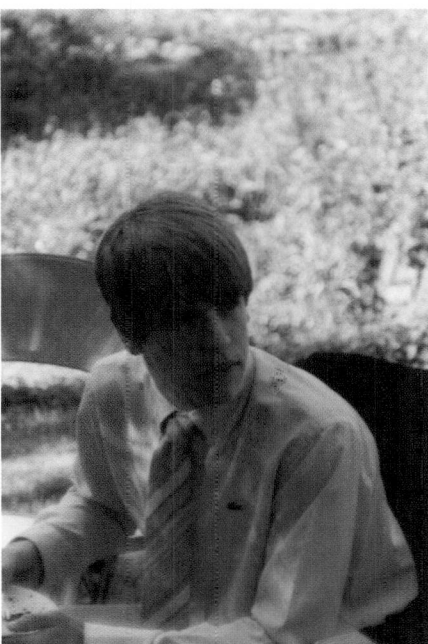 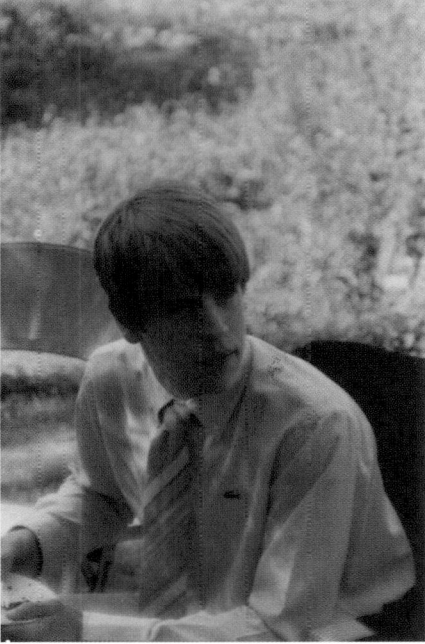

Fig. 3-20 The original photograph is shown at left. To produce the photograph on the right, I applied the selection created in Figure 3-19 and used the Curves and Saturation tools to darken and soften the background. Even though I made a very substantial change to those areas, there's no visible evidence of masking; the boundary between the foreground and background still looks natural and clean.

a channel or selection into a work path. I primarily use Mask Pro Select.

Peculiarly, this "professional" plug-in is limited to working on 8-bit files. That's inconvenient, but masks are portable, so there's a work-around. If I want to create a mask with Mask Pro for a 16-bit image, I duplicate that image, convert it to 8 bits, create my mask, save it in a channel, and then copy that channel back over to the original 16-bit file.

The two tools I use most often for creating masks are the Highlighters and Eyedroppers (Figure 3-21). Highlighters are good and fast when there are large areas to mask that have relatively simple geometries. Run the Keep Highlighter tool around the inside of the perimeter of the area to be selected. Run the Drop Highlighter tool around the perimeter of areas to be excluded. You don't have to be terribly accurate; what Mask Pro does is analyze the range of tones and colors in your "keep" and "drop" selections and use those to find the edges of the regions you want to mask.

The Keep and Drop Eyedroppers sample many points in the photograph to build up a palette of colors and tones that you want to include (Figure 3-22). The Eyedroppers are vital when you're trying to isolate poorly distinguished areas like wisps of hair or similar colors.

Usually, once you've made these selections, you'll activate Mask Pro's Magic Brush tool and tell Mask Pro to apply it to the entire image. That creates the whole mask based on your criteria at once. If you need to be

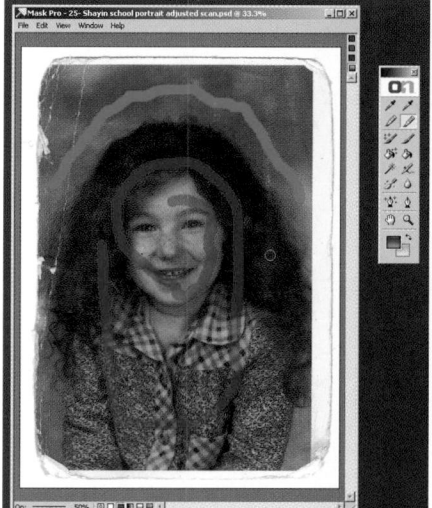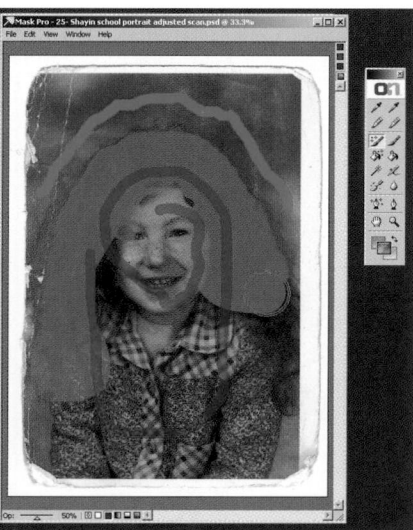

Fig. 3-21 The Mask Pro plug-in for Photoshop has extremely sophisticated selection tools. I used the Keep and Drop Highlighter tools to tell Mask Pro which colors I want to select (the green squiggle) and which colors I want to mask (the red squiggle) in the figure on the left. I activated the Magic Brush tool (green cursor circle on the right) and painted it over the photograph. Mask Pro automatically generated the mask, shown in tan. Mask Pro does a good job masking along complex and diffuse edges, such as the boundary between the girl's hair and the background.

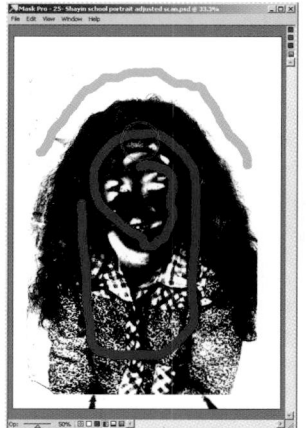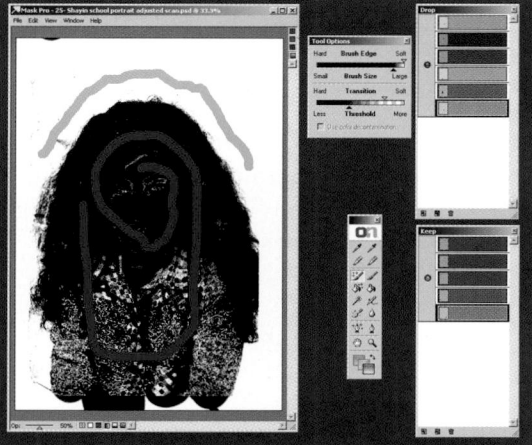

Fig. 3-22 Mask Pro's Keep and Drop Eyedropper tools let me refine the mask selection. I repeatedly clicked the Eyedroppers on the photograph to create palettes of colors that I wanted to keep and drop (shown on the right). Then I applied those choices to the whole image. The mask on the left is the one that I generated using just the Highlighter tools. The mask on the right is the one I created with the help of the Eyedropper tools.

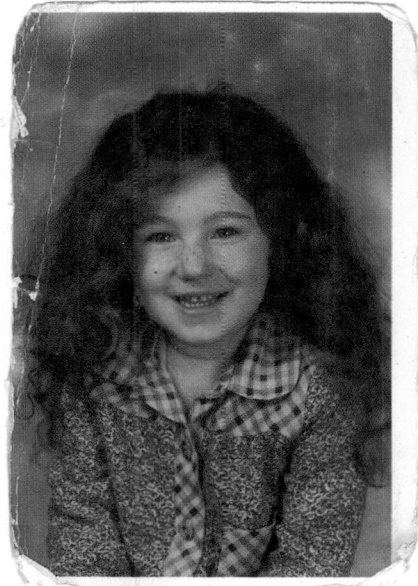 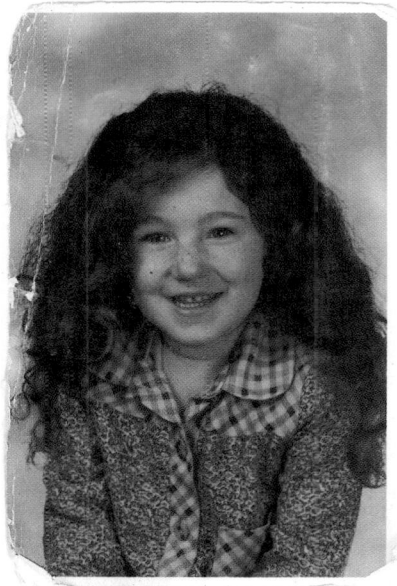

Fig. 3-23 I applied the mask I generated with Mask Pro in Figure 3-22 to the photograph on the left. I used the Curves tool to substantially lighten the background and shift it to a more attractive shade of blue. This demonstrates how well Mask Pro works when faced with complex selections and convoluted boundaries.

more selective and fine-tune what you're doing, you can use the Magic Brush to paint in the mask manually. You can create very elaborate masks, altering the "draw" and "keep" selections and palettes on the fly to use one set of criteria for masking one part of the image and another set for another part. You can also vary the strength and threshold settings for the mask brush as you work to control how "aggressive" your masking will be.

Unlike Photoshop's Extract tool, Mask Pro can analyze the entire image based on the inclusion data and create a very elaborate mask with multiple regions that need not be contiguous (Figure 3-23). Mask Pro isn't the least bit fazed by complicated mask criteria and geometries. Mask Pro is much more flexible and versatile in applying its functions and does a better and more sophisticated job of analyzing what is to be selected than does Photoshop's Color Select. Mask Pro is less confused by noisy originals; its selections are much cleaner and require less touching up.

A unique Mask Pro tool is the Chisel. It shaves off or adds pixels at the edge of a selection, based on your selection criteria; it doesn't just mechanically alter masks like "expand" or "contract." Chisel always smoothly follows the perimeter of the selection, so you can't accidentally take a big gouge out of your selection.

CurveMeister2 (http://www.curvemeister.com)

I will admit that it took me a while to warm up to CurveMeister2 (Windows only, $80). The reason it's making my recommended plug-in

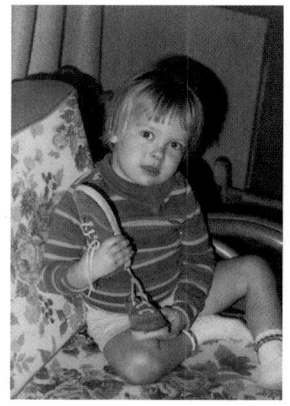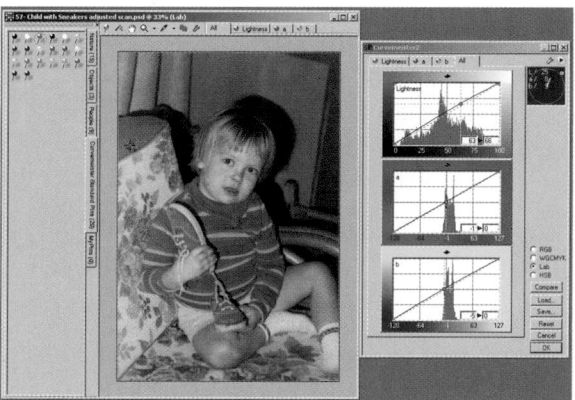

Fig. 3-24 The photograph is too blue. The CurveMeister 2 plug-in has several clever tools for correcting color and lets you choose different color spaces to try them out in. Yet, you don't need a sophisticated knowledge of Curves to make corrections with this plug-in—that's its whole reason for existence. To fix this photograph, I used pushpins. I selected the gray-color pushpin (upper left) and placed it on the back of the cushion in the photograph. CurveMeister 2 instantly created a set of curves that corrected the overall color of the photograph quite well.

list is that I think many readers will appreciate its value much more readily.

The Curves tool is the heart and soul of fine image control in Photoshop (see Chapter 5, Restoring Tone, page 134). If you haven't mastered curve corrections, you can't precisely manipulate tone and color rendition in your photographs. Unfortunately, curves are not a natural nor familiar concept for many photographers, and so they tend to avoid them. This is a mistake.

CurveMeister2 hands photographers powerful and intelligible ways to adjust curves. For a start, the CurveMeister2 interface (Figure 3-24) is much more agreeable than Photoshop's. You can see and work with the curves for all the channels simultaneously. The curves have histograms superimposed on them, which makes it a lot easier to match the range of values in your photograph with points on the curve.

CurveMeister2 lets you work simultaneously in four different color spaces. You can experiment with curve adjustments in each color space and compare the results in the plug-in preview window before committing yourself to applying the curve adjustments in one particular space. There's much to be said for noodling around; often playing with curves leads to a better result than going into them with a certainty of exactly what adjustments you need to make. CurveMeister2 encourages such useful playfulness.

CurveMeister2 adds a bunch of special controls to the curves windows that make standard adjustments easier to do, such as increasing contrast or saturation without altering overall color balance or midrange values. CurveMeister2 has several ways to assign pixels in the image to points on the curves to set highlight or shadow points or maintain overall neutrality. The "floating neutral" point in particular is a fast and clear way to alter brightness levels with minimum alteration of colors.

Pushpins are a clever idea! Pushpins are predefined colors that you can assign to points in your photograph. CurveMeister2 comes with a set of standard pins, and additional sets can be downloaded from the author's website. For instance, CurveMeister2 comes with a collection of pushpins for skin tones from a deep ebony to pale Nordic. You can add intermediate skin tones of your own to the existing set. Stick one of these pins into the skin of a person in your photograph, and the curves will adjust themselves to make the subject's skin tone and color match the pin's. By pinning key colors this way, you can quickly bring a badly color-distorted photograph into approximate compliance with reality.

CurveMeister2 is of minimal value to me because it's not layer-savvy. When you apply most adjustments and filter plug-ins in Photoshop to the base layer of an image, you see the results as they will look after they're filtered through any overlying layers. The preview window in CurveMeister2 completely ignores those layers; all you see is the layer that you're working on and the effect that CurveMeister2 will have on it. This means that the actual effect of applying CurveMeister2 to a multilayer image file looks entirely different from what the preview shows.

I would not normally recommend a tool with this flaw, except that I do know how much trouble controlling curves gives many otherwise-skilled photographers. The best way to figure out if CurveMeister2 is for you is to download the trial version of the plug-in and thoroughly and carefully read the extensive help manual. There are lots of worthwhile gems buried in this application that won't be obvious to you until you do.

PixelGenius PhotoKit (http://www.pixelgenius.com)

PixelGenius PhotoKit ($50) is a nice finishing tool for photographs. It's a collection of special effects such as dodges and burns, contrast and brightness changes, modest sharpening and noise reduction, and B&W toning. PhotoKit is actually a bundle of scripts that appears under the File/Automate menu. There's little in the way of user interface; selecting PhotoKit brings up a simple dialog box with drop-down menus from which you select the effect you want (Figure 3-25).

PhotoKit creates a new layer with a modified image in it that lets you alter or discard changes you make with no damage to the original, using any of the usual layer options. You can stack multiple PhotoKit effects because each time you apply it, it creates a new layer.

The effects have deceptively simple titles. In truth they are visually sophisticated adjustments, designed with great finesse and subtlety. Do

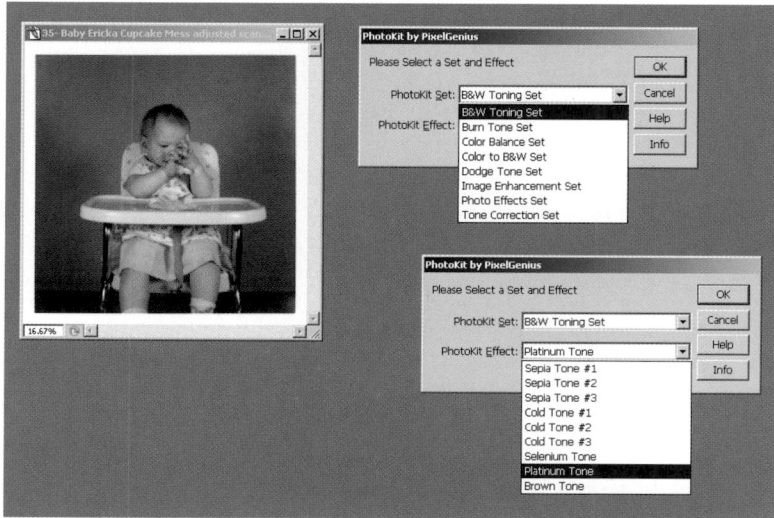

Fig. 3-25 PixelGenius PhotoKit is a collection of automated scripts for Photoshop. The B&W Toning Set, pictured here, is a good way to digitally tone photographs before printing them out. Shown here are the drop-down menus for selecting B&W Toning (upper right) and the type of toning (lower right). Note that I'm applying this script to a color photograph; PhotoKit will create a B&W photo automatically.

not mistake them for ordinary curves or color adjustments; I can't do anywhere near as good a job myself of replicating the looks of various kinds of darkroom prints as PhotoKit can.

The B&W Toning Set is the one I find most useful in photo restoration because it very closely replicates the look of many conventional B&W photographic images (see Chapter 11, Printing Tips, page 440). Platinum tone, for example, does a spectacular job of creating the look and feel of a platinum print from any B&W or color photograph (Figure 3-26). Similarly, selenium and brown toning realistically emulates toned darkroom prints.

The dodges and burns, image sharpening, and noise reduction effects are equally clever; mundane names belie their complexity. Not all of you will feel the need for the finishing touches that this plug-in can provide, but I strongly recommend downloading the trial version to get a feel for yourself of the aesthetic quality of these scripts.

PixelGenius PhotoKit Sharpener (http://www.pixelgenius.com)

Photoshop's sharpening tools are pretty primitive and not terribly sophisticated. (Picture Window has smarter sharpening tools.) Filters like Unsharp Masking in Photoshop are convenient, but many scripts and actions have been written to try to make them work better; in other words, to do more of the kind of sharpening we want with fewer of the artifacts we don't want.

PhotoKit Sharpener ($100) is the logical outgrowth of many of these hacks. Like PhotoKit, it is a collection of scripts. PhotoKit Sharpener has four collections of effects. The first two collections deal with sharpening the captured image (Figure 3-27). The third applies creative sharpening

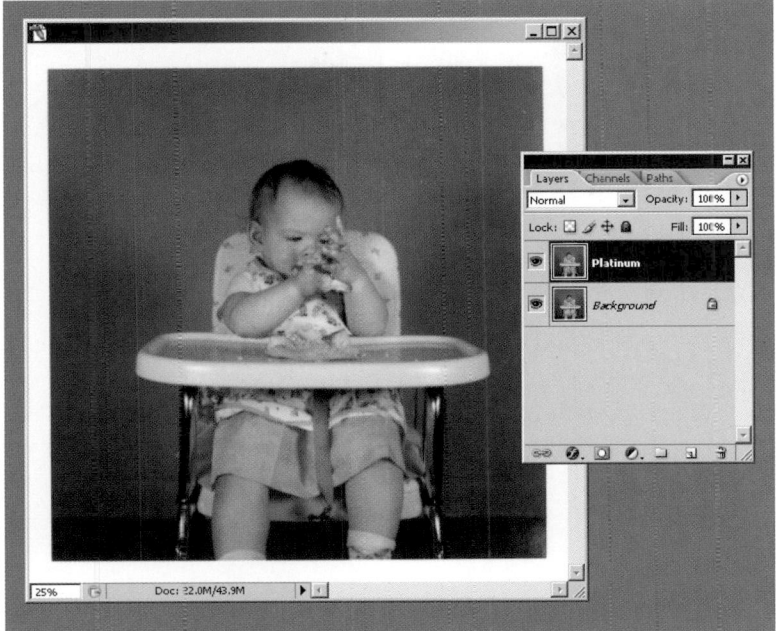

Fig. 3-26 Here are the results of applying PhotoKit Platinum Tone to the color photograph in Figure 3-25. PhotoKit has created a beautiful platinum look that would require considerable skill to create by hand. The "platinum" image is in its own layer; the original photograph hasn't been irrevocably changed the way it would be if you used Photoshop's Duotone controls to tone this photograph.

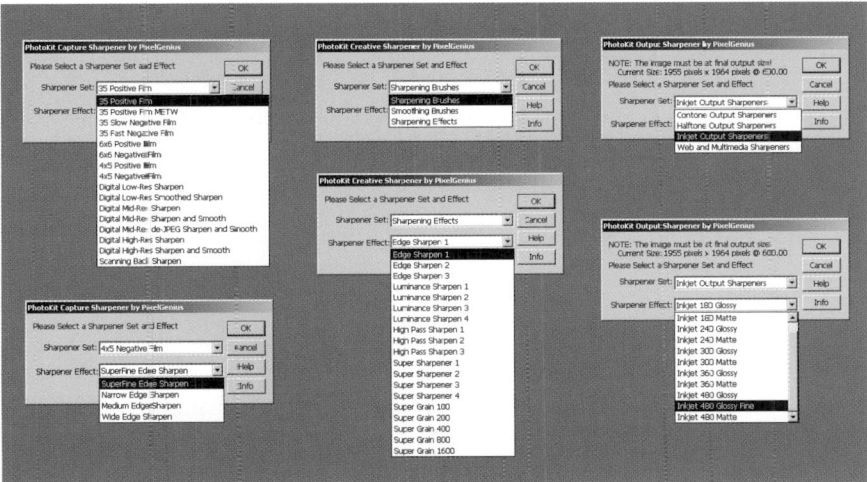

Fig. 3-27 PhotoKit Sharpener has an almost bewildering collection of sharpening options and methods. The Capture Sharpener collection (left) lets you choose the input medium and an effect to apply to that medium. Creative Sharpener (center) has three different tools, each with its own large collection of sharpening effects. Output Sharpener (right) lets you select how the image will be printed out and optimize the sharpening effect for different devices within that category.

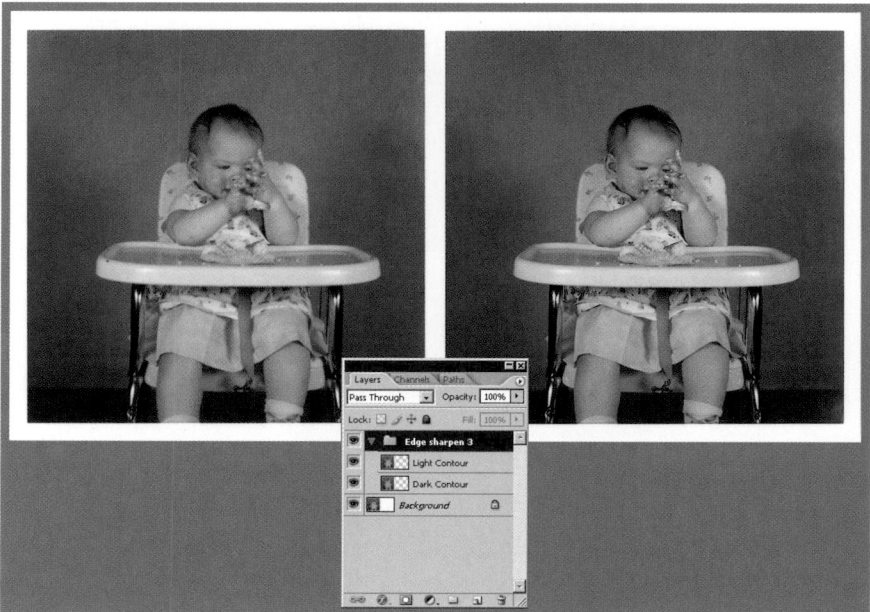

Fig. 3-28 Applying PhotoKit Sharpener's Edge Sharpen 3 option to the photograph on the left produces the one on the right. As the Layers window shows, PhotoKit Sharpener applies its changes in layers. With light and dark edges enhanced separately, you can control the influence of each using the Opacity slider. The original photograph remains unaltered in the background layer.

to enhance an image's edges and fine detail. Last, the output sharpening collection tweaks the image just enough to compensate for the softening effects of various kinds of printers and print settings.

The capture sharpening scripts address the modest losses in sharpness that can occur during scanning. Ideally, one would like to restore those losses without exaggerating noise at the same time (difficult for true sharpening algorithms like Focus Magic). PhotoKit Sharpener provides a bunch of preset sharpening routines for different kinds of input conditions. The plug-in was designed with film scanners and cameras in mind, not print scanning, but many of the algorithms work well for scans of faded prints. The manual clearly explains the purpose of each scanning choice, so you can intelligently decide what will work best with your print scan. For example, the negative film scan settings do more to minimize grain enhancement than positive film scan settings, so they'd be preferable for working with noisy print scans.

The sharpening is applied in separate layers for highlight and shadow sharpening and each layer's sharpening selection masks are preserved (Figure 3-28). You can change the strength of the sharpening by adjusting the opacity of the layer, and you can control where it's applied to the scan by modifying the layer mask. For example, if you want a stronger edge effect and less sharpening in broad tonal areas, a simple Curves adjustment to the mask will do the job.

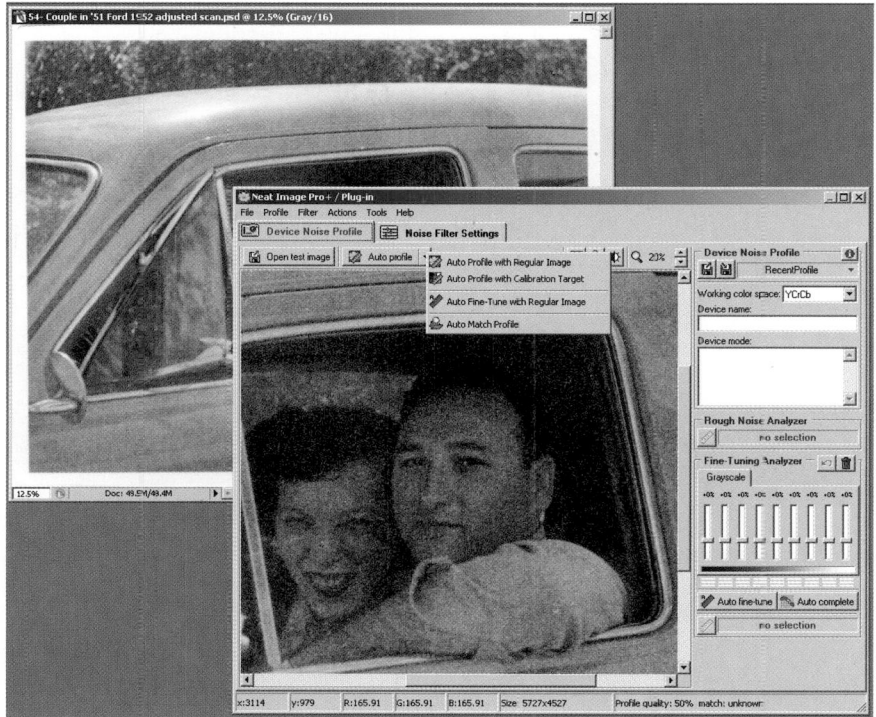

Fig. 3-29 Neat Image is an extremely sophisticated noise filter that profiles the noise in an image, builds a custom filter from that, and lets you control exactly how that filter gets applied to eliminate noise from the photograph. In this screenshot I'm using Neat Image to Auto Profile the noise in the photograph.

Different printers soften image detail in different ways, so PhotoKit Sharpener has many preset sharpening routines to optimize the quality of the output for just about any kind of printing device. Like CurveMeister, this package doesn't really do anything that you can't do by hand. What it does is turn the sharpening expertise of some really talented people into automated scripts, so you don't have to reinvent a wheel that's already been perfected.

Neat Image Pro+ (http://www.neatimage.com)

Neat Image is an extraordinarily versatile noise- and grain-reduction program. Hand it any image with undesirable grain or texture in it, and Neat Image will analyze the characteristics of the photograph and construct a custom profile tailored to the noise in the photograph (Figure 3-29). Neat Image subdues ordinary film grain or scan noise, paper textures (see Chapter 8, Damage Control, page 307), and even halftone screens.

Neat Image runs under Mac OS X or Windows 98 and up, as either a stand-alone program or a Photoshop plug-in. Several different flavors

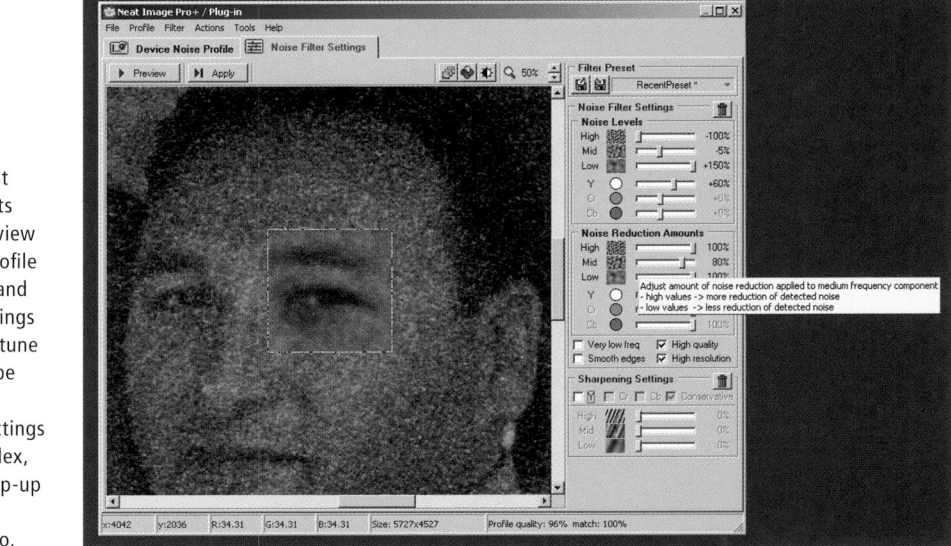

Fig. 3-30 Once Neat Image has created its profile, you can preview the effect of that profile on the photograph and adjust the filter settings on the right to fine-tune how that filter will be applied to the photograph. The settings are many and complex, but they all have pop-up help windows that explain what they do.

of Neat Image are available, ranging from a free download with useful but limited capabilities to Pro+, which is 16-bit capable and includes both the stand-alone and Photoshop plug-in versions of the program. Pro+ runs $75; if you don't need Photoshop compatibility, then Pro provides all the same capabilities for $15 less.

Neat Image was surprisingly easy to use, considering how versatile it is and how many control settings there are to play with. I barely had to glance at the quick-start instructions before diving in. That's not an argument against reading the 60-page manual; you'll get a lot more out of the program if you do. It's a compliment on how well Neat Image is designed. Controls even have pop-up windows (Figure 3-30) that give quick instructions in how to use them when you mouse over them.

Neat Image cleanup is a three-step process. First, generate the noise profile. Neat Image analyzes a small portion of the image that is free from true subject detail to determine the grain and noise characteristics. It will automatically select that region, but if you don't like its choice, you can move the selection box anywhere in the image that you think is more appropriate. Second, preview the profile's effects and alter the filter settings to tailor the noise reduction to your needs. Finally, apply your filter settings to the photograph.

You can save the noise profile and settings if you want to use them on a series of similar photographs or experiment with a bunch of different settings to see which ones give you the most attractive final result. I used Neat Image on an intractably noisy photograph that my other noise reduction tools were incapable of dealing with (Figure 3-31). The

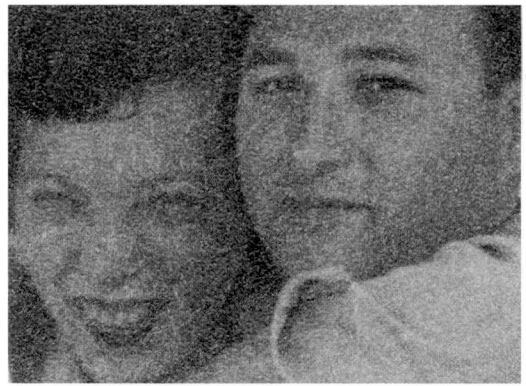

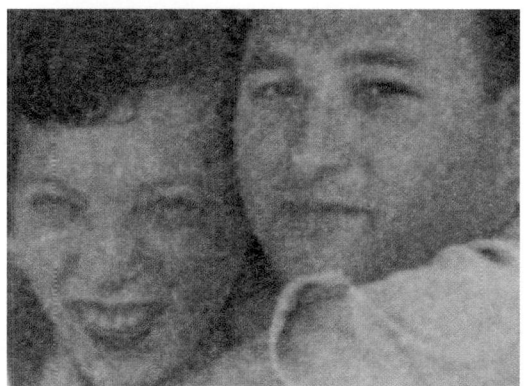

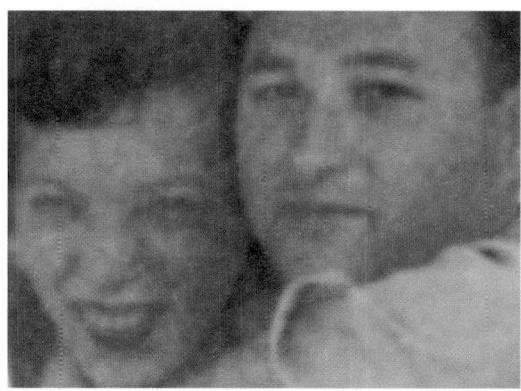

Fig. 3-31 Changing the filter settings in Neat Image changes its effect on a photograph. The top figure is the original noisy photo. The middle and bottom figures are the same photograph after being filtered by Neat Image. The filter profile is the same in both of these photos, but varying the filter settings greatly altered the results.

top illustration shows the original photograph, while the middle corresponds to the filter settings in Figure 3-30, which I think looks pretty good. The bottom illustration shows what happens when I turn the filter settings up to maximum strength. Even with maximum noise reduction, there's surprisingly little loss of real image detail, given the amount of grain suppression that's going on. Neat Image is one amazing program.

CHAPTER 4

Getting the Photo into the Computer

How-To's in This Chapter

How to unmount a s ide
How to scan a faded B&W print
How to scan a dark B&W print
How to scan a magazine or newspaper illustration
How to improve color with a good scan
How to inspect very dark parts of a scan
How to scan color negatives
How to scan very dense or faded color film
How to determine what resolution to scan at
How to photograph tarnished prints

Before you can digitally restore a photograph, you have to get it into the computer. Most likely you'll be doing this by scanning the photograph on a flat-bed or film scanner (although, as I'll explain on page 126, sometimes you're better off rephotographing it).

The closer you can come to working with the original source photograph, the better your restoration will be. You often have no choice in this matter, but when you do, exercise it. When a client sends you a print for restoration, ask if the original negative or transparency is available. In almost every circumstance, you'll be able to do a better restoration by scanning the original film than scanning a print derived from it (Figure 4-1).

It is possible for the original film to be so badly deteriorated, or the print so heavily retouched, that restoring from a scan of the print is the better option, but it's very unusual. Don't let having to re-create modest amounts of print retouching dissuade you. Physical retouching is, frankly, cruder than what you can do on the computer; you can almost always re-create the retouching work better than the original. Read Katrin

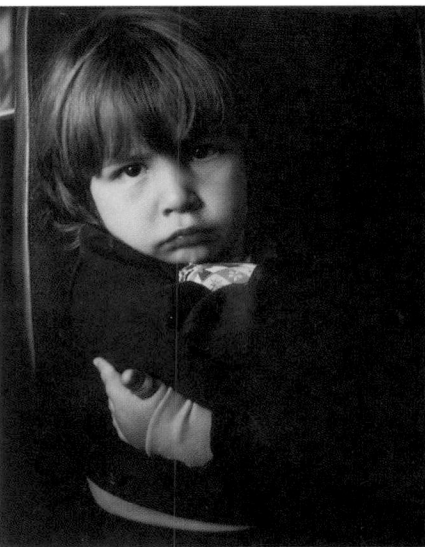
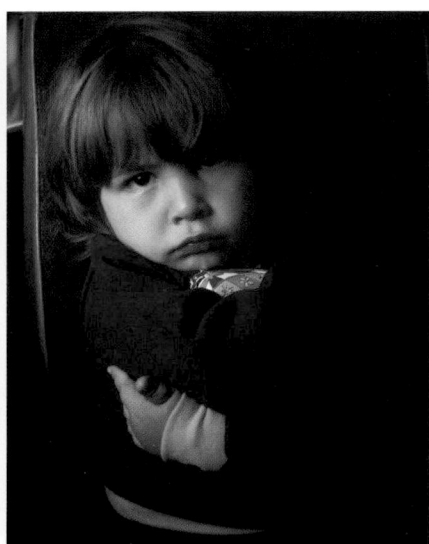

Fig. 4-1 The photograph on the left is a print made from the slide on the right. The print has faded substantially, but the slide is in nearly pristine condition. It's usually true that original film will be less deteriorated than any prints that have been made from it.

Eismann's book, *Photoshop Restoration & Retouching,* which I recommended in the Introduction. She's a retouching wizard.

Half the job of doing a good restoration is making a good scan. Scanning a deteriorated original is not the same as scanning a high-quality photograph. Usually, you won't want to make a scan that faithfully reproduces the photograph in its damaged state. As you'll learn, that is more likely to lead to inferior results; at best, it will require you to do much more work in your image processing program to produce a good restoration.

Getting a good scan for restoration is not difficult if you follow the guidelines in this chapter, but this is not knowledge that any of us was born with. Making a good scan for restoration is a learned skill, and for that reason you're better off doing the restoration from a scan you do yourself than one provided by the client unless that client is *very* good at this kind of work. If you have·no choice, you can create a good restoration from scans sent to you by others, but if they provide you with poor scans it will make your life harder.

Some originals are so valuable or fragile that the owners will very sensibly not let them out of their possession. In that situation the best you can do is carefully instruct the owner about what constitutes a good scan and hope for the best. Don't be discouraged if you can't get original source material. Although the results get better the closer to the original you can get, I've done good restorations from lousy scans and mediocre, highly compressed JPEG files that people have e-mailed me (Figure 4-2).

No matter what the source of your image file is, never work on the original file when doing your restoration. Save it, and set the saved file's

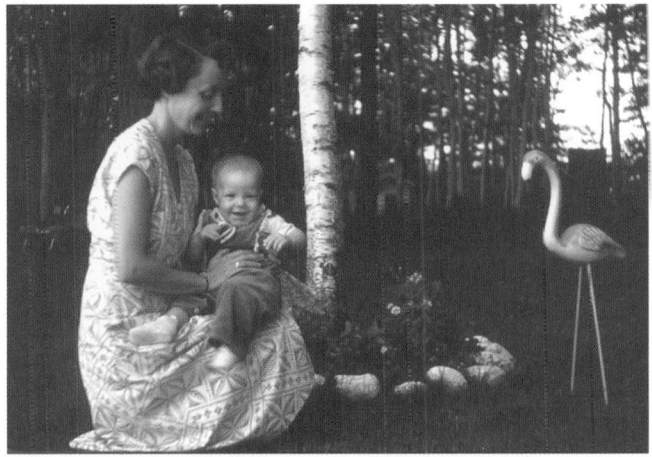

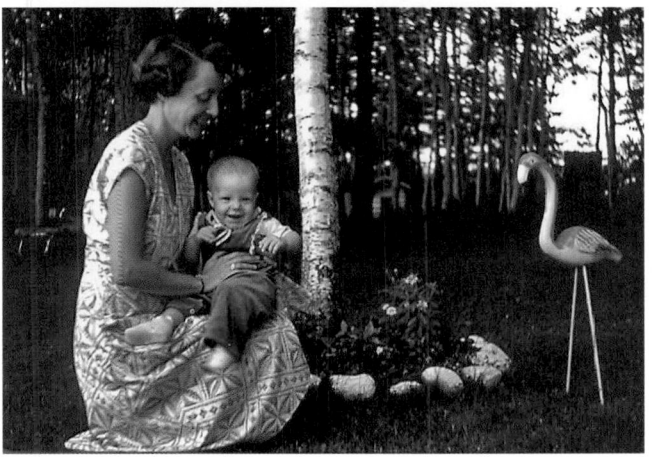

Fig. 4-2 This is a restoration done from a JPEG (top) the clients sent to me of a scan they did. It's better to get the original photograph and scan it yourself, but don't give up hope if all you can get is a mediocre JPEG. You still may be able to produce great results (bottom).

permission to read-only. Work only on duplicates of the file; that way if you need to start over, you don't have to rescan the photograph (or ask the client for replacement scans). Save intermediate results often, in case you decide to backtrack and try a different approach.

Preparation and Cleaning

One very important way in which scanning damaged photographs differs from scanning ones in good condition is how you prepare the photographs for scanning. Old photographs are often fragile, so you want to stress them as little as possible. If the print you are going to scan is taped or glued to an album page or mounting board, do not attempt to remove it or peel the tape away from the photograph. You will surely damage the photograph. Leave it where it is, and scan it on the page.

Be careful with photographs that are in those horrid "magic" adhesive photo albums. The gum on the page that is supposed to let you easily remove or reposition the photograph hardens with time into a rigid adhesive. Don't try to pry the photograph away from the adhesive board; you'll crack it. Fold back the page's plastic cover sheet, and scan the photograph on the album page.

On the other hand, 35-mm slides ought to be removed from their mounts before scanning. I recommend that you do this because most film scanners will not produce tack-sharp results unless the film is sandwiched between glass to hold it flat. Even though many scanners are sold without a glass film carrier as standard equipment, you need it for getting good scans of slides or negatives. Even if the carrier is deep enough to accommodate the mount, leaving the slide in its mount just prevents the glass from doing its job.

HOW TO UNMOUNT
A SLIDE

Plastic slide mounts open pretty easily. Many are designed to be opened, and the rest can be snapped apart by prying up on one face of the mount at the edge with a blade until the spot welds that hold the two halves together break. It won't take a lot of force.

Cardboard mounts are more of a pain. You'll need a sharp thin blade, like a single-edge razor blade or X-Acto knife, and a steady hand. Don't try to cut directly through the cardboard near the slide to free it; unless you are very experienced at this, there's too much of a risk that your hand will slip and you will cut the slide. There's a safer way.

Look closely at the edges of the mount, and you will usually see fine perforations along one edge. Carefully cut through those perforations and try to peel the cardboard apart. If there aren't any perforations, cut the edge where the seam is most obvious (Figure 4-3). The cardboard is glued together, but don't worry about damaging it. Do make sure it's the cardboard that you're bending, though, and not the slide when you do this.

If you're fortunate, the mount will split right along the center window, and you'll be able to lift the slide out of the mount. If the mount didn't split at exactly the right point, there will be only a thin layer of paper covering the edges of the slide and preventing you from removing it. You can easily cut away that paper to get to the slide. Sometimes the slide is spot-glued along one or both perforated edges to the cardboard. Slip the tip of the blade (carefully!) between the slide and the cardboard to break those glue points (Figure 4-4).

Scanners are notoriously good at exaggerating every little defect and flaw; it's virtually impossible to produce a perfectly clean scan regardless of the state of the original. If we start with a dirty original, the time and effort involved in cleaning it up on the computer is horrendous. Normally, we take fairly aggressive steps to eliminate every bit of dirt and dust before we make the scan in order to reduce the time and tedium of retouching an inordinate number of spot and specks in the computer.

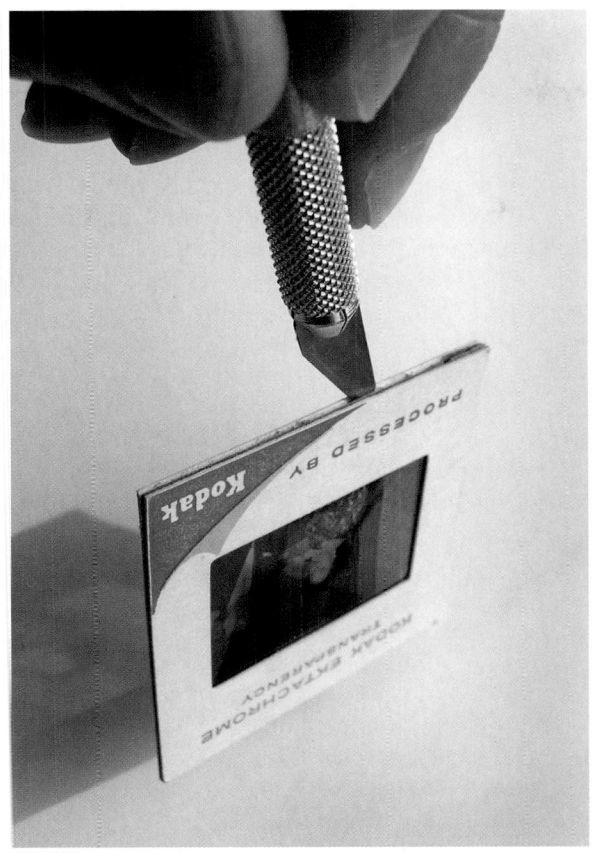

Fig. 4-3 Slides are best scanned when they're unmounted. To split open a cardboard slide mount, carefully slice around the edges with a sharp, narrow blade. Observe the position of the blade between the two halves of the cardboard sandwich.

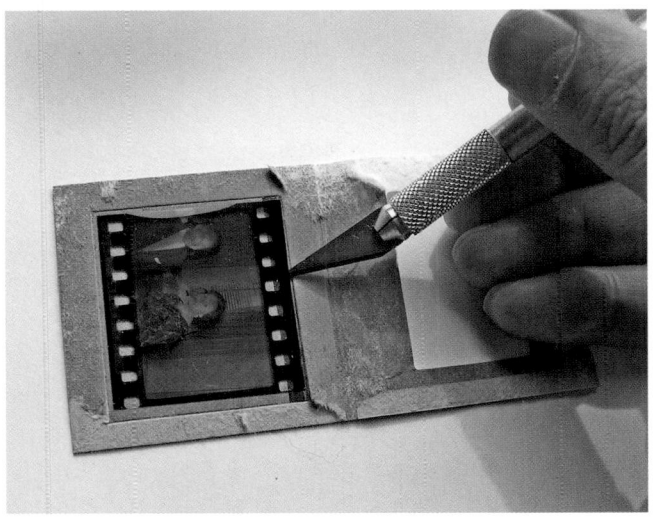

Fig. 4-4 Once you've sliced the edges of the mount, you should be able to pry the halves apart. The slide will probably be glued to one-half of the mount along one or both edges. Carefully slip the blade of the knife between the slide and the cardboard to slice through this bond.

I always clean my regular photographs (that is, the ones in good condition) with PEC-12 and PEC Pads, dust them off with an anti-static brush, and give them a solid blast of compressed air to remove any lingering specks. I've become almost obsessive about cleanliness. It's a kind of conditioned response; whenever I slack off, I end up with a scan that takes me hours to tidy up, and that shock to my system provides powerful negative reinforcement for any sloppy cleaning techniques.

But . . . this is not the approach you want to take when performing a restoration. Deteriorated images are frequently in a very fragile physical state. Bits of emulsion may just be waiting to flake off at a too-firm touch. Any kind of wet cleaning is an especially bad idea. Water is an absolute no-no. In the case of prints, it can wash away important retouching or cause it to bleed and leave you with a complete mess on your hands. Water may also mobilize damaging chemicals locked in the paper base and actually hasten the further deterioration of the photograph. In the case of color films and older prints, the final processing step usually involves a stabilizing chemical; dilute that and you compromise image permanence even more.

Mold or mildew actually makes emulsions soluble in water! The little bugs gobbling away at the photo damage the gelatin enough so that it will dissolve if you get it wet. Inorganic chemicals can attack emulsions in similar ways; spots and stains on the photograph may turn out to be places where the image can dissolve. If you apply a water-based cleaner, you'll remove the entire image in those areas.

Even solvent-based cleaners like PEC-12 are not to be trusted with older originals. PEC-12, for example, will dissolve unhardened gelatin and albumen emulsions, and it should not be used on photographs that have suffered biological or chemical damage. The manufacturer, Photographic Solutions (photosol.com), makes no secret of this and warns that PEC-12 should never be applied to a photograph of unknown characteristics.

Many cleaners carry no such warnings; that does not make them safer. You can do irreparable harm by attempting any sort of wet cleaning of deteriorated photographs. Because deterioration is often not uniform over the entire photograph (chemical spots and mildew stains being prime examples), a spot test at one corner of a photograph that goes well is no assurance that the entire image will survive cleaners. This is not even considering the other kinds of physical damage you might easily do. If the photograph's surface is delicate, even the most careful wet cleaning runs the serious risk of scratching the surface with bits of dust and dirt picked up by the cleaning pad as it's wiping down the photograph.

Wet cleaning should be left to knowledgeable professionals. It's a very risky process never to be undertaken by amateur conservators. The only wet cleaning I ever do is to the glass side of a glass plate. Glass is hard and inert enough that it's safe to clean dirt and grime from it. Be careful not to use so much cleaning solution that any can leak onto the emulsion side of the plate. Just dampen the cleaning pad, don't saturate it.

Never use cotton swabs such as Q-tips. I mention this because they're a common tool used by photographers and retouchers, but they are really very abrasive. In my tests of several different cleaning aids, cotton swabs scratched even worse than ordinary kitchen paper towels or facial tissues. They will mar an original more readily than just about anything else you might use.

The least abrasive materials I've tested are the PEC Pads made by Photographic Solutions, the folks who make PEC-12. But even PEC Pads are not perfectly nonabrasive; nothing is. That's why I recommend avoiding as much physical contact with the original as possible.

So, how do I clean originals before restoration? Minimally. A very light and delicate dusting with a very soft anti-static brush. Then careful bursts of compressed air. If a dust speck or bit of lint doesn't want to move, I leave it. I do everything in my power to stifle my justifiably obsessive cleaning impulses. It is simply not worth the risk of damaging an irreplaceable original to save myself some spotting time on the computer.

Scanning Prints—Maximize Your Information by Getting the Tones Right

A good photograph almost always has a full range of tones from black (or nearly black) to white (or nearly white). See Chapter 5, Restoring Tone, for more elaboration on this point, but for the time being take it as gospel.

Correspondingly, a good scan of a deteriorated photograph spans most of the range of values from near-black to near-white. It doesn't throw away any of the intermediate tones in the photograph by forcing them to pure white or pure black. This is true for color as well as B&W photographs. A good scan's histogram looks like the middle one in Figure 4-5; you don't want it to look like the top or bottom histograms. The former makes poor use of the range of available values, while the latter clips some of the near-whites and near-blacks.

It's usually a bad idea to make a scan that faithfully reproduces a deteriorated photograph. The upper photo in Figure 4-6 is a straight, uncorrected 8-bit scan from a faded B&W print. This is not a good basis for a restoration. The upper histogram in Figure 4-7 shows why. Only half the total range of values available is actually being used in this scan. I can expand the tonal range of the scan in Photoshop to restore the photograph to a full-valued, neutral-colored image, but if I do that I get one of those unwelcome "picket fence" histograms (Figure 4-7, bottom). There are many gaps in the tonal scale that will show up as discontinuous-tone steps in the print (Figure 4-8, left). The bottom photo in Figure

✓ HOW TO SCAN A
FADED B&W PRINT

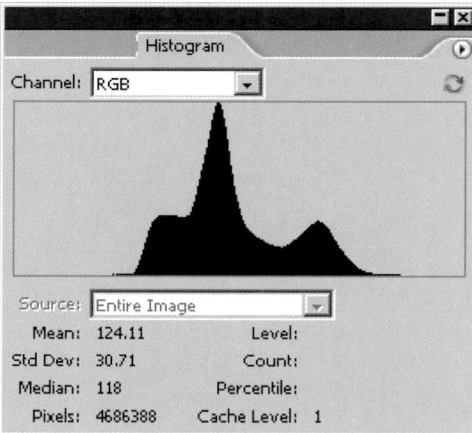

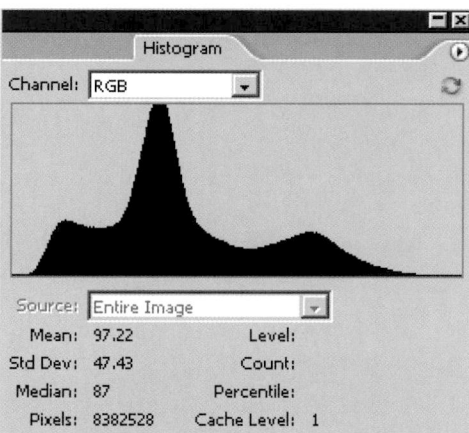

Fig. 4-5 A good scan uses most of the range of tonal values available. The histogram at the top is from a scan that is too low in contrast; barely half of the full range of 256 values is being used. The middle histogram shows an ideal scan; most of the values have some data, but no information is being clipped off. The histogram at the bottom shows a scan that is too contrasty. There are big spikes at values of 0 and 255, which means that some light and dark tones have been forced to pure B&W. That highlight and shadow information is lost forever; avoid that in your scans.

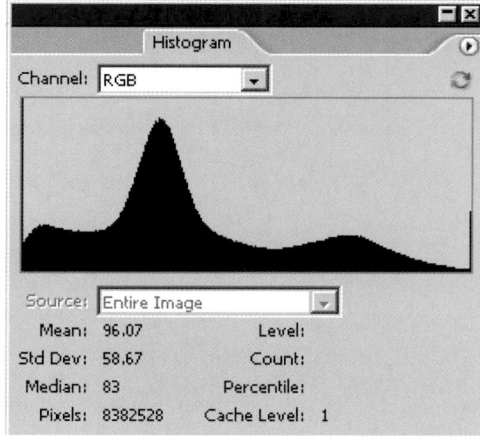

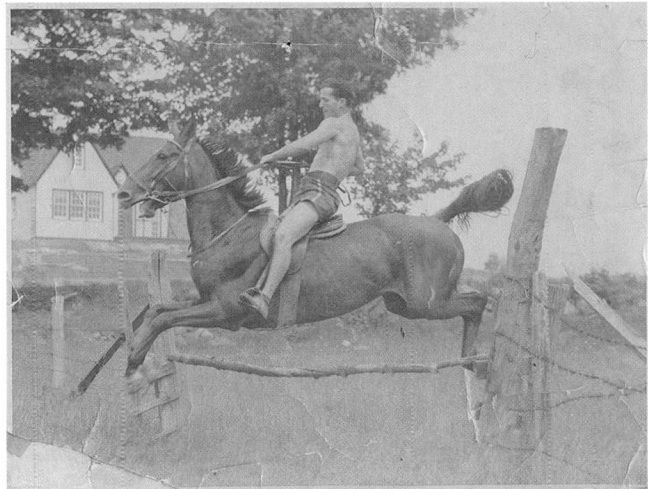

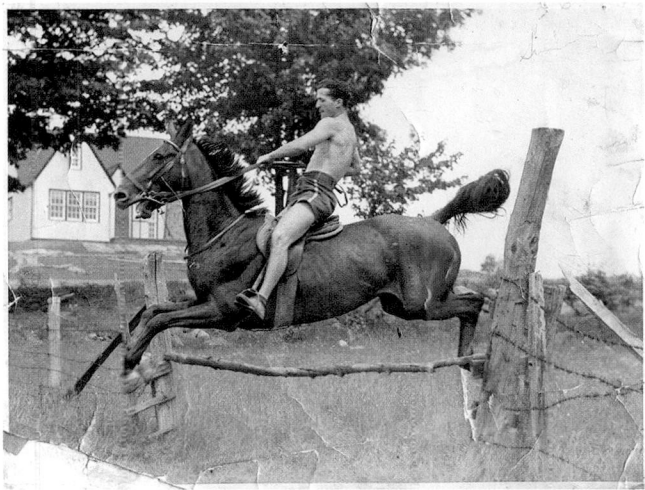

Fig. 4-6 A good scan is vitally important to doing a good restoration. The upper photo is a straight 8-bit scan from a badly faded original, similar in appearance to the original photograph. It is a very poor place to start from because it doesn't take advantage of the full range of tonal values that are available in the scan. I adjusted the scanner software's curves and levels controls in each color channel in the scanner software to produce a good range of tones for all three colors. (I also desaturated the image in Photoshop to eliminate a small amount of lingering color cast.) That produced the good 8-bit scan in the bottom photograph; it has a histogram like the middle one in Figure 4-5.

4-6 is from a good scan, one where I adjusted the curves and levels controls in the scanner software to produce an image that had a much more complete and neutral range of tones. When I use that as the basis for my restoration, I get results like that in Figure 4-8, right; here, there is good, continuous tonal quality.

Any time you use your image-processing software to expand the range of tones that you have in the scan, you're going to get some gaps in the gray scale. That's normal, and a few gaps in the histograms really won't be visible in a print. Don't be obsessed by the histogram. Some folks feel that if there are any gaps at all in their photograph's histogram, the quality of the output will be terribly compromised. That's an extreme exaggeration; a moderate number of gaps are almost never visible in the print. The examples I'm presenting here *are* extreme so that I can make ▼

HOW TO SCAN A FADED B&W PRINT (continued)

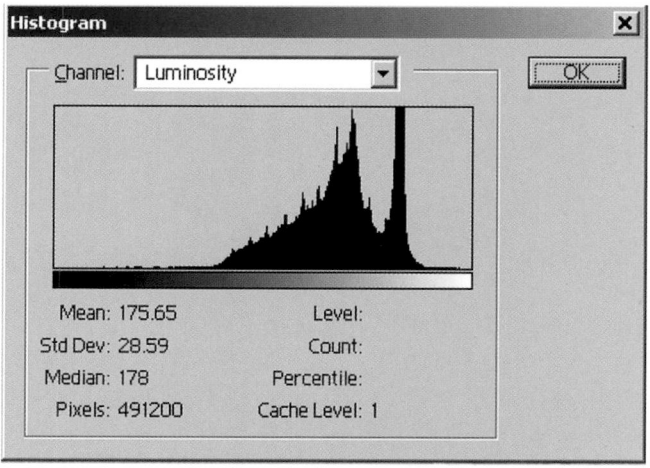

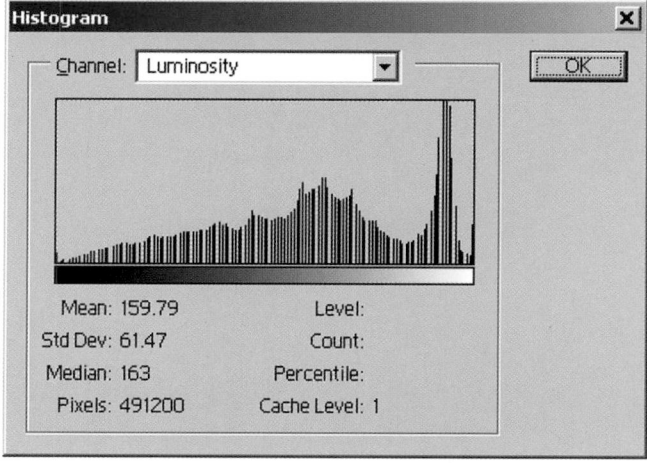

Fig. 4-7 These histograms show the problems that a poor 8-bit scan will cause. The top histogram is from the top scan in Figure 4-6. The bottom histogram shows what happens when I attempt to restore that scan in Photoshop to produce a photograph with a full range of tones from black to white. There are many gaps in the histogram because there aren't enough distinct gray levels to fill them in. This "picket fence" problem degrades the quality of the restoration.

HOW TO SCAN A
FADED B&W PRINT
(continued)

it clear that many gaps are not a good thing, but you can have a pretty ratty-looking histogram and still see excellent tonality in the final print. Unless I'll be expanding or compressing the tonal scale by more than 25% when I work on the file, I don't worry about gaps.

There are two routes to better, fuller histograms. The first is to do all your scanning in 16-bit mode. There is much to be said for this, and it's my normal working habit. Even when the original has a very narrow tonal range, as in Figure 4-6, a 16-bit scan will usually capture enough gray levels to produce a fully populated histogram when the tonal scale is expanded to produce a normal range of densities from black to white. That produces much better tonality in the finished restoration.

The other way to avoid the picket fence histogram is to adjust the levels and curves controls in the scanner software to produce a good range of data in the scan. All scanners collect data internally to more

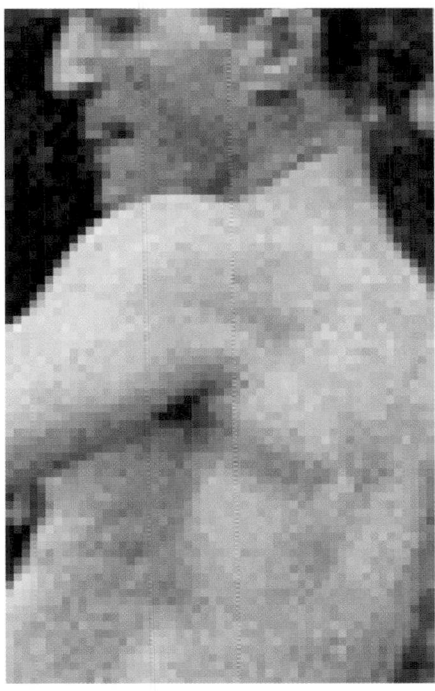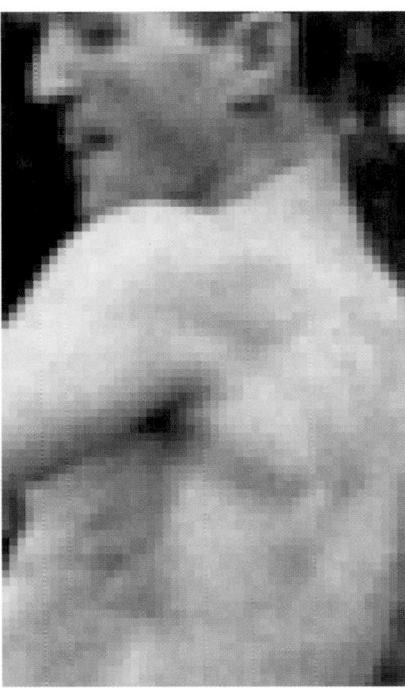

Fig. 4-8 Enlarged portions of finished restorations from the straight (left) and optimized scans (right) in Figure 4-6. The "picket fence" effect degrades the tonal quality of the left restoration. Only about half the normal number of gray levels is available in the scan. The skin tones look sandy instead of smooth because there are intermediates tones missing. The restoration from the optimized scan shows very smooth tonality because it uses almost all the available tonal levels.

than 8 bits even if you've set the controls to output an 8-bit scan. The scanner has plenty of extra value levels available to fill in any holes, just as you do when you work on a 16-bit file in the computer. That means you can greatly expand or compress parts of the tonal range in the scanner settings without producing tonal gaps in an 8-bit output.

By the way, it's true that most scanners (and digital cameras, for that matter) don't produce true 16-bit files. That is, they don't actually produce 2^{16} (65,000) distinct gray levels for each color channel. More commonly they produce 10 or 12 bits worth of clean and distinct tonal information. The really good ones may produce 14. But that's plenty! Even 10 bits of clean data is 1000 gray levels—there will be four gray levels in this file for every one that you'd have in an 8-bit scan. That means you could expand portions of the tonal range by a factor of four before you would start to see gaps in the histogram. I expanded the range of tones in Figure 4-7 by only half that much (a factor of two), and that was a major adjustment. Expanding the tonal scale by a factor of four is enough to correct the most seriously faded photograph. So, even a few extra bits of data in each pixel are sufficient to give you full histograms with few gaps, no matter how much you manipulate the photograph.

Here's how making the scanner adjustment works in practice. The B&W print in Figure 4-9 has a very limited range of tones because of fading and staining. A straight 8-bit scan with no special corrections

HOW TO SCAN A
FADED B&W PRINT
(continued)

✓ HOW TO SCAN A
DARK B&W PRINT
▼

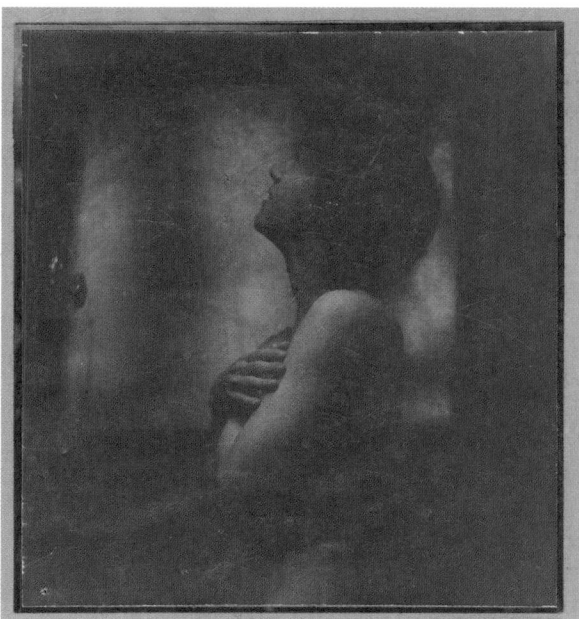

Fig. 4-9 This photograph is very dark and low in contrast. In all probability it was printed poorly to begin with, but that's fixable with digital restoration.

HOW TO SCAN A
DARK B&W PRINT
(continued)

produces the upper histogram in Figure 4-10. You can see that this doesn't come close to taking advantage of the full number of levels available in Photoshop.

Figure 4-12 shows the Levels adjustments I made in my scanner software. Observe how I've pulled in the "white" and "black" sliders so that they more closely bracket the range of tones in the print. Allow yourself some safety margin. Keep the darkest pixels in the scan at values of 10 to 20 and the lightest pixels around 240. That way you'll avoid accidentally clipping the highlights or shadows. If you need a pure white or a pure black in the finished restoration, you can adjust the range in your computer without visibly compromising tonal quality.

The results of this adjusted scan are clearly much better both visually and data-wise (Figure 4-11). The histogram looks much fuller (Figure 4-10, lower). This would be a good starting point for restoration in either an 8-bit or a 16-bit scan.

Even though I'm working with a "B&W" original, I scanned it in full-color mode. A scanner's "B&W" mode usually uses only one channel (green) of data. That yields noisier scans than scanning in full-color mode and combining the channels in your image processing program. It's easy enough to convert the image to monochrome once it's in your computer, and the quality will be much better.

Don't worry about the exact image color when you're scanning monochrome originals. Once you've got the scan in the computer, you'll desaturate it and neutralize any color casts. When you print the restored image, you can adjust the color to replicate the look of an original, pristine print. I tell you several ways to do that in Chapter 11, Printing Tips.

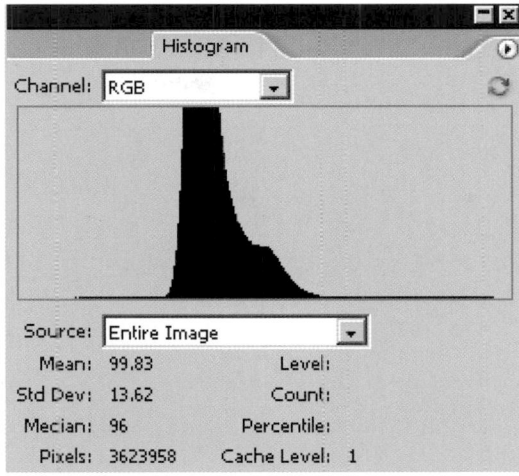

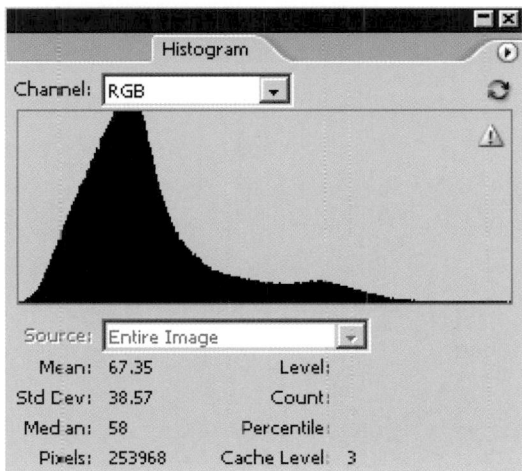

Fig. 4-10 The top histogram shows how little tonal information there is in Figure 4-9. Barely one-third of the histogram bins contain any data. The bottom histogram represents Figure 4-11, which was made using the scanner levels settings shown in Figure 4-12. This is a much better populated histogram than that of the straight scan.

The PhotoKit plug-in I (Chapter 3, Software for Restoration, page 81) has some very nice presets for antique print looks.

Color is a valuable tool for restoring B&W photographs. Differences in color in different parts of the photograph are evidence of damage or deterioration. Color is a distinguishing factor you can use when creating masks that select especially damaged areas for restorative work (see Chapter 7, Making Masks, page 244). You can also use that differential color information to fix the damaged parts of the photograph (Chapter 8, Damage Control, page 278). There are even advantages to scanning monochrome photographs with exaggerated and unrealistic color. Exaggerated hues in the photograph can be most useful for creating masks that isolate areas of tarnish, tape marks, and stains (Figure 4-13). Once selectively masked, you can apply corrections to those areas separate from the rest of the image. This is an extremely effective way of elimi-

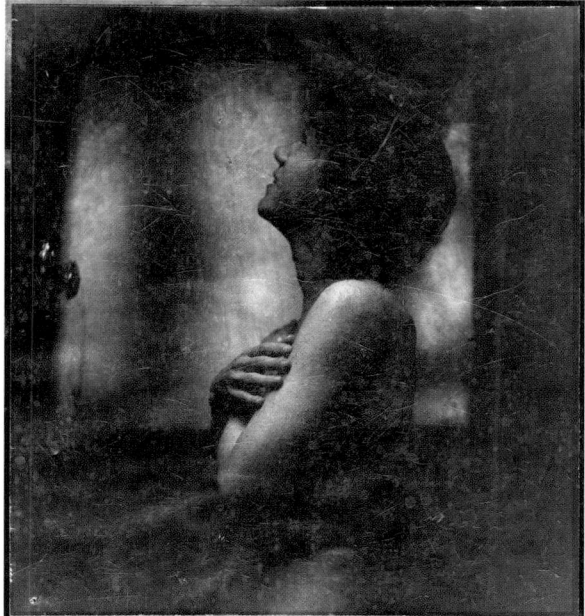

Fig. 4-11 This is a much better scan of the photograph in Figure 4-9. The scanner's Input Levels settings in Figure 4-11 expanded the tonal range to something more normal and attractive (and revealed a great deal of physical damage in the photograph).

Fig. 4-12 These scanner level settings turned Figure 4-9 into Figure 4-11. Observe how the B&W set points are positioned just outside the range of populated bins in the histogram. Such a setting ensures that no shadow or highlight detail gets clipped.

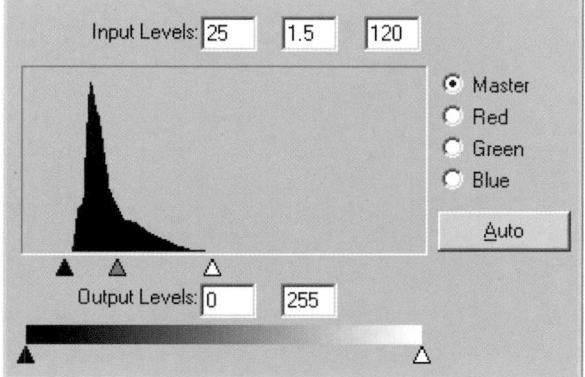

nating surface tarnish and silvering-out. You can read about a full restoration of the photo from Figure 4-13 in Chapter 8, page 298.

Here's another reason for not scanning your prints in B&W mode: The color channel the scanner uses for B&W scanning is not necessarily the best one to use for a restoration. That's a choice you, not an unthinking piece of hardware, need to make. In Figure 4-14 the red channel is by far the most useful for performing a clean restoration. The damage to the original photograph is substantially less visible in this channel because the stains are primarily orange-yellow in color.

When I'm ready to convert the scan of a monochrome photograph to grayscale, I almost never use the Desaturate adjustment or grayscale

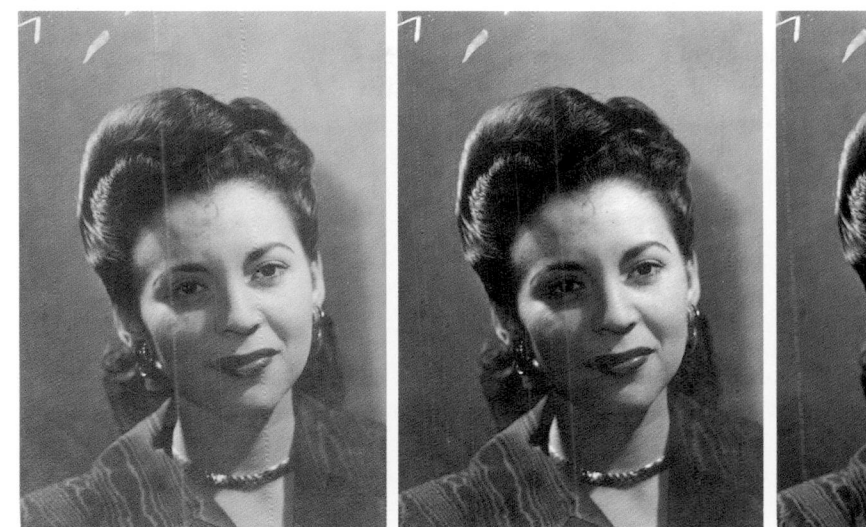

Fig. 4-13 The figure on the left is the original, tarnished photograph. I exaggerated the color saturation in the scan I made (middle) so that the tarnish would stand out clearly. I used that exaggerated color difference to make a mask that selected for the tarnish, making it much easier to correct the damage and restore the photograph (right).

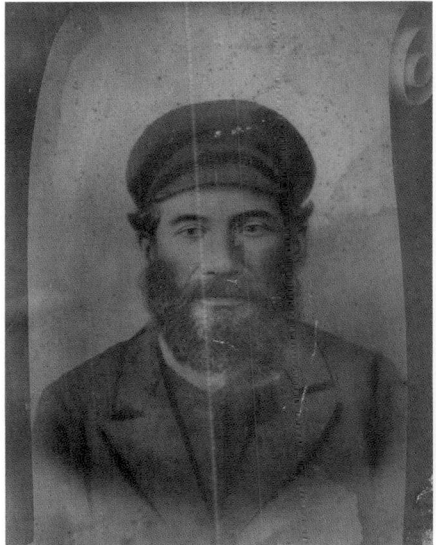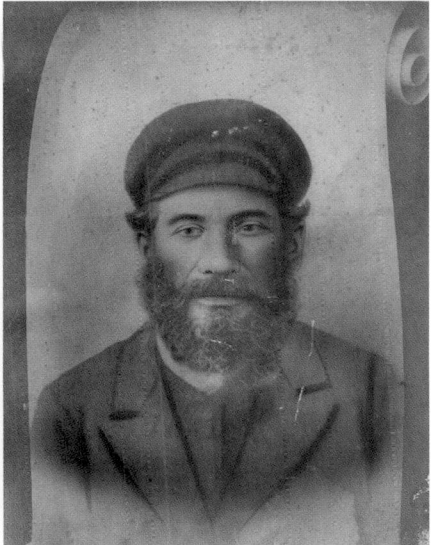

Fig. 4-14 Most B&W photographs will show less damage in one color channel than in the others. This photograph is very badly stained and faded (left). Most of the stains, though, are orange-yellow in color, which means that they hardly show up at all in the red channel of the scan (right). That's the channel to use as the basis for a good B&W restoration.

mode conversion. Instead, I use the Channel Mixer with the monochrome option selected.

Why? It's about control. Desaturate simply mixes equal amounts of all three color channels. It's a good choice when all three channels in your scan are of equal quality, with none significantly noisier nor showing more dirt and stains than the others. Torn or cracked photographs that otherwise are clean and unfaded may have these qualities, but badly deteriorated B&W photographs usually don't.

Automatic grayscale conversion does a weighted mix of the three channels, about 60% green, 30% red, and 10% blue. This will hardly ever be the optimum mix for converting a scan. Channel Mixer, however, lets me specify how much of each color channel goes into the grayscale version of the photograph. Sometimes one channel is obviously superior to the others, such as in Figure 4-14, in which case I'll use 100% of that channel. At other times one channel may be significantly worse than the other two, so I'll use none of that channel and some weighted mix of the other two (it doesn't have to be 50%–50%).

So, you see that how you do the conversion to monochrome (assuming that's what you want to do) depends on the characteristics of the photograph and exactly how you plan to restore it. A conversion that eliminates one or more color channels of data because they emphasize defects is a good place to start a restoration. Conversely, a conversion that emphasizes the channels that show damage most clearly will be useful for constructing selections and masks to isolate the damaged areas for repair (Chapter 7, page 246).

For these reasons, don't gratuitously throw away information. Even if you're sure that the final photograph will be reconstructed from only one color channel, save the other two. You may find that they contain information that's going to help you in other ways.

Scanning Halftones

You may not know the term *halftone,* but most of the photographs you see are halftone reproductions. Newspaper and magazine reproductions are halftones. The photograph is made up of a pattern of black (or colored) dots on white paper (Figure 4-15). The illusion of continuous tone is created by variations in the size of the dots to produce more or less ink coverage of the paper, but there really aren't any intermediate tones.

HOW TO SCAN A
MAGAZINE OR
NEWSPAPER
ILLUSTRATION

A good scan of a halftone print has very different characteristics than a good scan of a regular, continuous-tone photograph. When scanning a regular photograph, it's important not to push the extreme tones all the way to pure white or pure black, lest you accidentally lose some highlight or shadow detail. The best scan of a halftone, though, will almost always be one that makes the majority of the ink dots come out close to a true black and most of the un-inked paper close to true white. That means setting the white and black level points in your scanner software (Figure

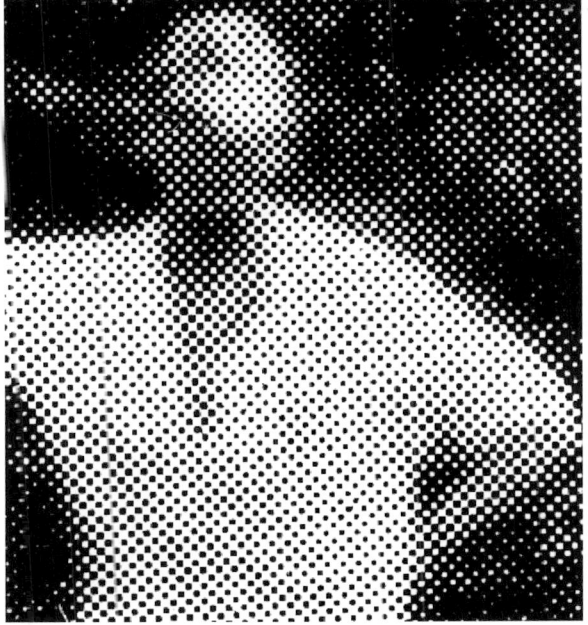

Fig. 4-15 This is a highly magnified view of a B&W newspaper print. There are no intermediate tones in the image, just black dots of varying size that simulate the appearance of different shades of gray.

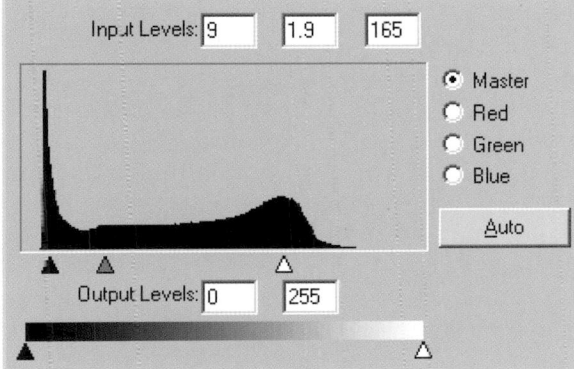

Fig. 4-16 These are the scanner software levels settings I used to create Figure 4-15. Notice how I set the black and white end points inside the range of tones seen by the scanner. That makes the ink blacker and the paper whiter, minimizing or eliminating stains and faded spots in the halftone. That makes it much easier to restore this photograph.

4-16) well within the range of tones in the photograph. The correct white and black level points are the ones that come closest to achieving this without obliterating the very smallest dots. The histogram you see in the finished scan should look something like that of Figure 4-17.

Figure 4-17 is very different from a good histogram for a continuous-tone photograph, where you don't want the scan to force any of the tones

HOW TO SCAN A
MAGAZINE OR
NEWSPAPER
ILLUSTRATION
(continued)

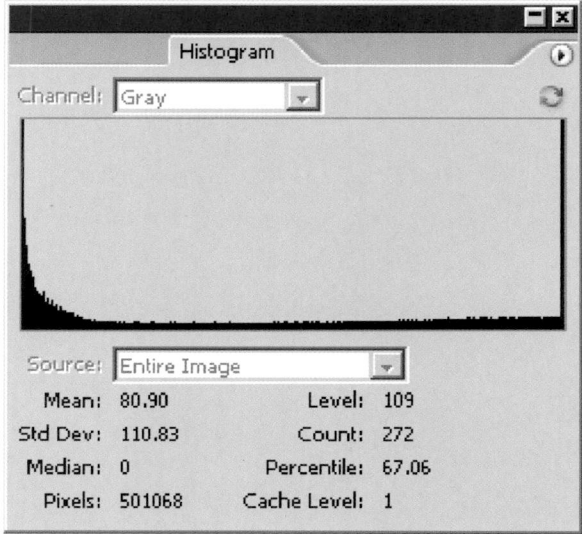

Fig. 4-17 This is the histogram for the halftone scan in Figure 4-15. Unlike a good scan of a continuous-tone photograph, a good halftone scan will have lots of pixels that are pure white and pure black.

HOW TO SCAN A MAGAZINE OR NEWSPAPER ILLUSTRATION (continued)

in the photograph to pure white and pure black. Also, because you don't care about having lots of continuous-tone information in a halftone scan, there's no need to scan in 16-bit mode. Eight-bit mode works just as well for halftone scans, and you'll get files that will be only half as big and will process twice as quickly.

In Chapter 9, Tips, Tricks, and Enhancements, page 320, I show you some ways to get rid of the dot pattern (a process known as "descreening"). A high-resolution scan, which shows the size and shapes of the dots clearly, works best for this. I scan a halftone at four to eight times the dot spacing. Newspaper photographs will be reproduced with somewhere between 65 and 100 dots per inch (this, by the way, is the actual and correct use of dpi as a unit of measurement). Magazine illustrations can be anywhere between 125 and 200 dpi. I never scan at less than 600 ppi and sometimes I go to 1200.

Pulling in the Color

The same overall principles that work for scanning B&W prints apply to scanning color prints (and for that matter, slides, but not color negatives). It's usually a safe bet to assume the print originally had a complete range of tones from paper-white to maximum black. Unless you know that the original had a limited range of tones in one or more channels, strive for a scan that makes best use of the full range of values available and looks similar in overall color balance to your desired result.

HOW TO IMPROVE COLOR WITH A GOOD SCAN

Adjust the levels or curves in the scanner software the same way you would if you were scanning B&W prints (Figure 4-18). Frequently this will give you a very good start on a proper restoration (Figure 4-19). In Chapter 10, Examples (page 354), I can take the scan from Figure 4-19

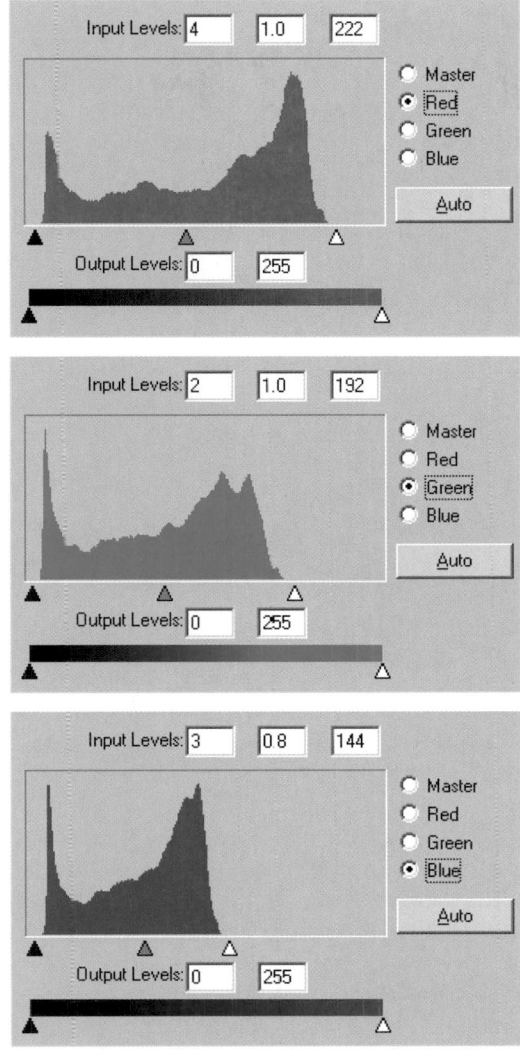

Fig. 4-18 The rules for making a good color scan are no different than those for making a good B&W one. The only difference is that you have three channels to correct instead of one. This figure shows the scanner software levels settings I used to make a good scan of the photograph in Figure 4-19. In each of the three color channels, I adjusted the black and white end points so that they bracketed the full range of tonal information in that channel without clipping any of it. I made a slight overall color correction by adjusting the gray midpoint for the blue channel from 1.0 to 0.8 (that is, I moved the gray slider triangle to the right). That made the scan a bit more yellow, eliminating a blue cast.

and turn it into a fully restored photograph by making just a handful of further corrections.

You may find that even when you make these adjustments the resulting scan has an overall color cast. You can correct much of that in the scan by shifting the midtone sliders in each channel's levels adjustment until the average color looks good. This can make a substantial difference in the quality of the scan and get you well on the way to a complete restoration. The "corrected" scan of the photograph in Figure 4-19 originally had a blue color cast. I adjusted the midpoint in the levels control for the blue channel (bottom histogram in Figure 4-18) to make the scan more yellow.

HOW TO IMPROVE
COLOR WITH A
GOOD SCAN
(continued)

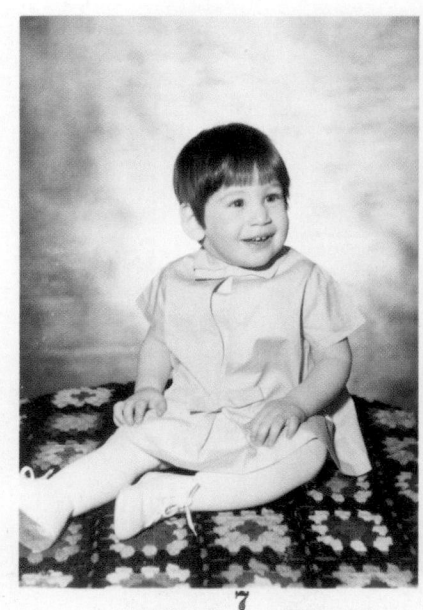 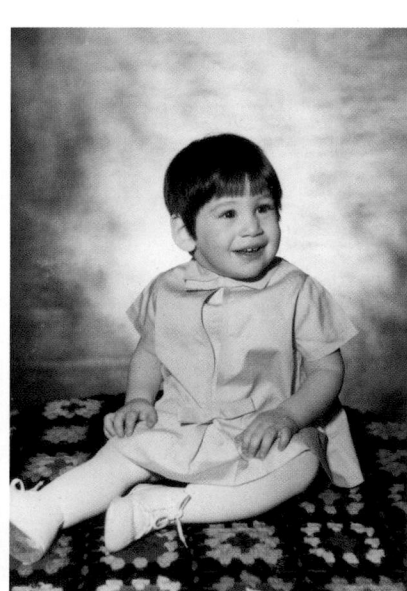

Fig. 4-19 The figure on the left is the original photograph. I scanned it using the scanner software levels settings shown in Figure 4-18. Those settings produced the photo on the right, which is well on its way to having completely restored color.

It can take a while to become proficient at scanning, and some trial-and-error time will always be involved. Scanning badly deteriorated prints is a bit of an interpretive art. I find that I usually make three or four different scans of a print before I settle on the one that I'm most happy with.

If you plan on using tools like the DIGITAL ROC Photoshop plug-in to restore the photograph's color, don't go overboard on messing with the scanner curves. DIGITAL ROC is surprisingly insensitive to the quality of a scan. It produces results almost as good from a straight scan that looks just like the faded photograph as from one with the B&W levels carefully normalized to produce a full range of tones.

Moreover, if you distort the curve shapes substantially in trying to fine-tune the color by eye, it can confuse DIGITAL ROC, which works its magic by analyzing the distribution of tones and colors in the photograph. The recovered color in that case may actually be worse than it would be if you didn't refine the scan as much—yet another reason why I usually fiddle with several different scans before settling on the one that will work best for my restoration.

Not so incidentally, don't worry about profiling your scanner (or camera) for accurate color and tonal rendition. The originals you're scanning will have badly distorted colors and tones, and you're going to end up substantially modifying those. As I've said for B&W, capturing values exactly the way they are in the original not only doesn't matter—it's often counterproductive.

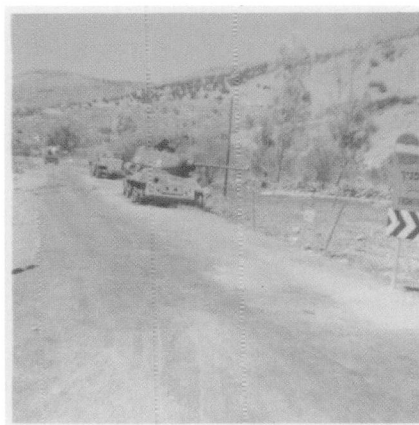 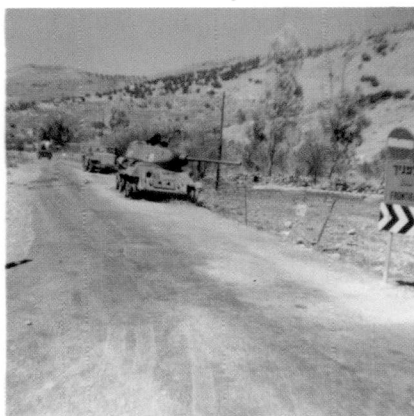

Fig. 4-20 The figure on the left shows the original photograph, captured as a 16-bit scan, with no effort made to correct the tonal color during scanning. This is an accurate representation of the original photograph. On the right is the same scan after I crudely corrected the color using the curves in Figure 4-22. Having 16 bits of data per color channel makes it possible to do extreme corrections like this and still get a photograph of good quality.

Is 16 Bits Really Necessary?

I prefer to scan in 16-bit mode. I've found that the ideal way to produce scans and extract maximum formation from the original photograph is to optimize the curves and levels settings in the scanner software *and* do a 16-bit scan. I usually do this because ultimately it saves me work time. Truth be told, in 16-bit mode I can be rather sloppy about the levels and curves in the scanner settings, just not so much that I'm likely to lose any data by overdoing it. I can scan batches of photographs in 16-bit mode using similar scanner settings with less trial-and-error and repeated scans that otherwise eat up considerable time. None of the scans will be perfect when done this way, but with 16 bits of tonal depth to play with, there's plenty of data for me to fix everything in the computer.

Figures 4-20 through 4-22 show how flexible 16-bit data is. The left-hand photograph (Figure 4-20) and histograms (Figure 4-21) come from a straight scan of a snapshot with no corrections. Because the photograph is so faded, less than half of the range of tonal values is actually used; the spikes at the right side of the histograms are just from the white paper border. I crudely corrected the range of tones and colors with the curves settings shown in Figure 4-22 to get the much better looking photograph on the right side of Figure 4-20.

These are very extreme corrections! Even so, the histograms in the right side of Figure 4-21 show that I did not get the dreaded "picket fence" effect that is so obvious in Figure 4-7. I have a well-populated histogram that will produce good, continuous-tone quality in the finished restoration. I would never recommend accepting a scan this bad,

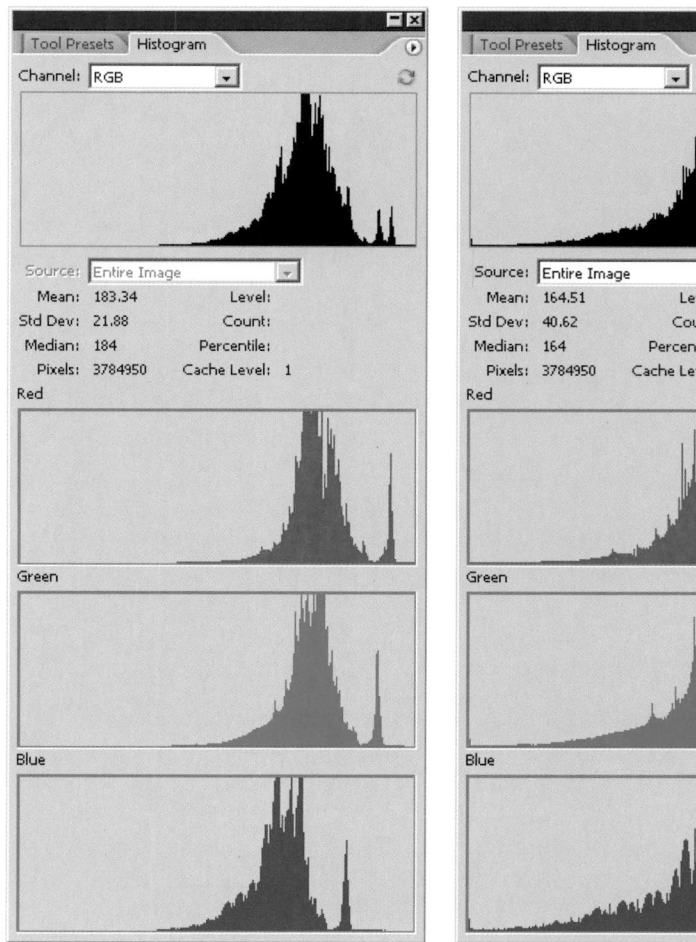

Fig. 4-21 The histogram on the left belongs to the left-hand photograph in Figure 4-20. Each color channel in the scan has only a narrow range of tones (the big spike on the right in each histogram channel corresponds to the "white" paper border). The histogram on the right shows what the tones look like after applying the curves in Figure 4-22, which produced the right-hand side of Figure 4-20. Notice that there is no "picket fence" effect, with gaps in the histogram, as we saw in Figure 4-7.

even in 16-bit mode. It demonstrates, though, the considerable robustness of a 16-bit scan.

You may find that a practical limitation on doing 16-bit scans will be the power of your computer. It's not just that computations take twice as long. I pointed out in Chapter 2, page 34, that an 8-inch by 10-inch print scanned at 600 ppi in 16-bit mode is going to produce a 175-MB file. Start adding layers to that in Photoshop, or working with multiple generations in Picture Window, and in short order you're swapping scratch files to disk. Your performance crashes dramatically. It's something to keep in mind when you're deciding on your scan depth. It may seem that scanning in 8-bit mode and consequently having to really fine-tune your scanner settings will slow down your work, but that's not going to be the case if doing a 16-bit scan means that your image processing program goes running to the hard drive every time you perform an operation on the file.

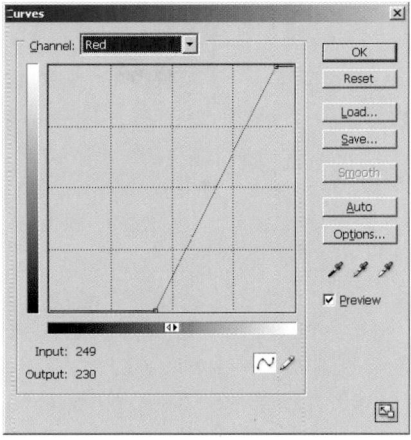

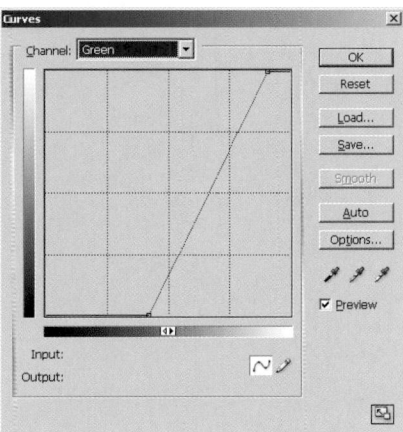

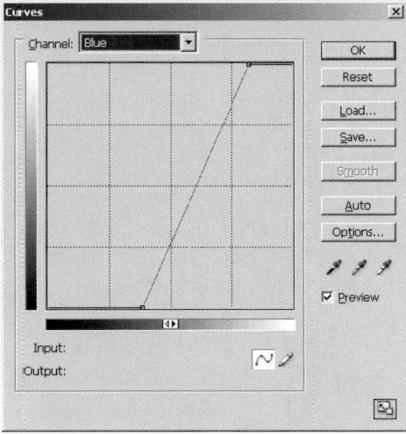

Fig. 4-22 These are the curves I used to correct Figure 4-20. The contrast change in each channel is extreme, expanding the tonal range by a factor of two to three. This would have produced visible image degradation in an 8-bit scan; a 16-bit scan, however, has enough extra data to handle it.

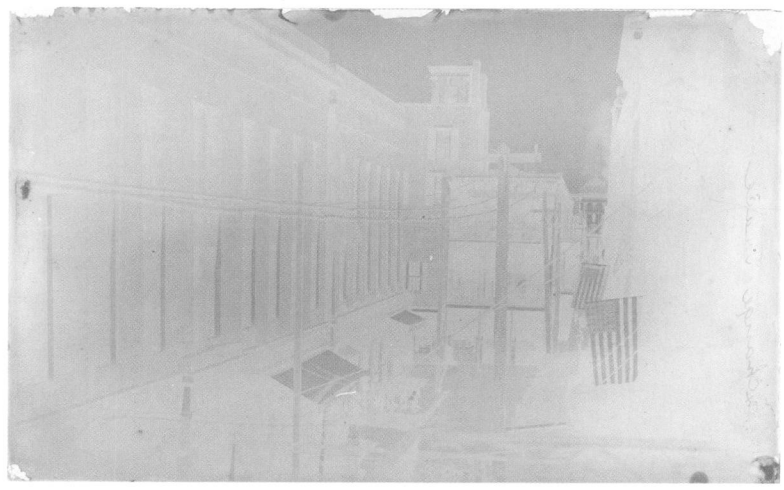

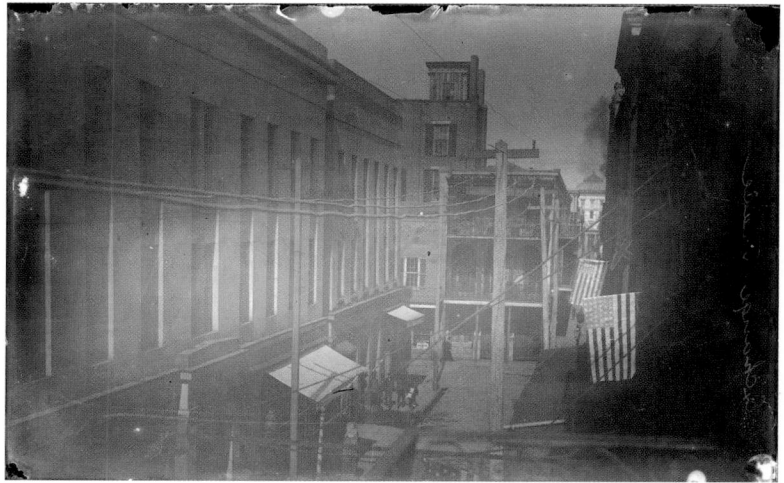

Fig. 4-23 The upper figure shows a very badly faded glass plate. I scanned it and inverted the tones, producing the photograph in the lower figure. There's plenty of information here to do a restoration from, but the density and contrast vary so much in different parts of the plate that it would be impossible to do a good restoration from an 8-bit scan, even with carefully adjusted scanner software settings. This is a case where 16-bit scans are a must for good results.

Back when I only had 512 MB or 1 GB of RAM in my machines, I did my best to avoid working on 16-bit files unless the originals were quite small. Now that I have 2 GB, I'm inclined to scan in 16-bit mode, if for no other reason than to reassure myself that I really captured all of the data in the photograph.

Sometimes 16-bit data is going to be a must. When the condition of the original is so uneven that no overall set of corrections in scanning is going to produce good results, you'll need those extra bits. I'm currently restoring a severely degraded glass plate (Figure 4-23) that is almost entirely bleached out, and the scanned density isn't anything close to even. Until I can manipulate the file into a uniform-looking image, I need to work in 16 bits so that I can do different strong corrections on different parts of the scan and still have well-filled histograms of data.

If your computer really isn't up to working on 16-bit files for the whole restoration process, I recommend a compromise. Do your scans and as much of the gross color and tone correction as you can in 16-bit mode. Then convert the file to 8-bit mode. That will minimize the image-quality problems of working with 8-bit files. Don't worry about doing damage repair and cleaning up dust, scratches, and cracks before you convert. You can do that work as invisibly in 8-bit mode as in 16-bit mode.

The closer you get to the finished restoration, the less having 16-bit data will matter. When you get to the output stage, 16-bit color may not make any difference. Today's printer drivers don't take advantage of 16-bit data. For example, if you converted your finished 16-bit file to 8-bit just before printing, you would see absolutely no difference in the print quality. Also, while Photoshop and TIFF file formats preserve 16-bit data, JPEG doesn't. If your clients wants the finished image in JPEG form, you will be sending them 8-bit color, no matter what you were working on in the computer.

How to Scan B&W Film and Glass Plates

If you're working from roll film originals, a high-quality film scanner is in order; if you're trying to scan old B&W sheet film or glass plates, a very good flat-bed scanner is going to be necessary. Old glass plates and sheet film are especially challenging to scan well. Old-style photographic emulsions were typically much more contrasty than modern films. The older the photograph, the more likely it is to place severe demands on your scanner's ability to capture detail in the highlights, the densest parts of the negative (Figure 4-24). In Chapter 10, Examples, page 341, I do a complete repair and restoration on the photograph shown in Figure 4-24.

The situation is made worse because the grains of silver that make up the image are more likely to scatter light out of the optical path than

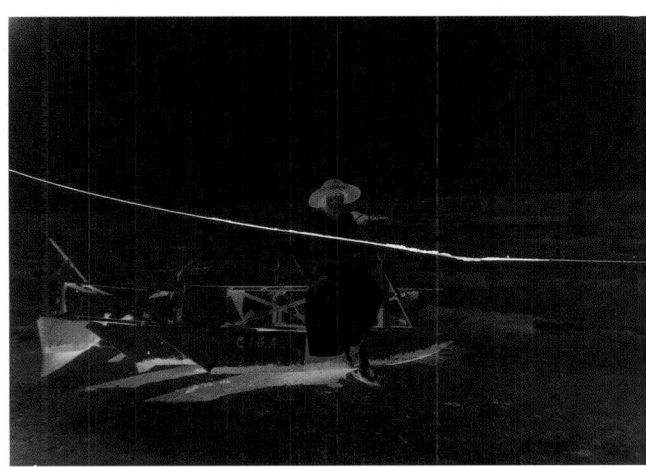

Fig. 4-24 Old B&W films and glass plates are often very dense and contrasty. They demand a lot from your scanner. I was just barely able to capture a good scan of this cracked glass plate negative on my professional flat-bed scanner.

back into it. Consequently, most scanners read B&W silver emulsion densities as being much higher than what you would measure on a densitometer and than the equivalent density in a dye-based (color or B&W chromogenic) photographic image. For example, my Minolta DiMAGE Multi Pro film scanner can handle about 4.2 density units (d.u.) in color film and chromogenic B&W film like Ilford XP2, but it's limited to silver-based B&W densities of 2.7 to 3.0 d.u.

That's a lot, by modern darkroom standards, but unfortunately not by early photographic standards; the printing materials they used then had extremely long exposure ranges. Adding to the difficulties are early photographers' predilections for generous exposures. Emulsion making and exposure determination were nowhere near the precise crafts that they are today. It was far better to have to "print through" some extra and unneeded density than to underexpose and be saddled with an unprintably thin or mostly blank negative, so the majority of old films and plates are dense.

The only times when you're not likely to see high B&W densities are when the original is severely faded or bleached, as in Figure 4-23. That doesn't make repairs any easier! Such damage is rarely uniform across the photograph, and a very narrow contrast range in the negative only serves to exaggerate the impact of dirt and scratches.

Whenever you scan contrasty and high-density originals, regardless of the film format or type, be sure to mask off the unexposed areas at the edges of the film, film sprocket holes, and the clear parts of the film carrier or platen. The unattenuated white light blasting through those clear areas will cause flare that degrades the quality of the scan if you don't block it (Figures 4-25 and 4-26). Good film scanners come with masks for different formats, so you shouldn't have to worry about this. When scanning dense film or plates on my flat-bed scanner, I just mask off the surrounding area with strips of black construction paper. It's simple, even primitive, but it's most effective.

Scanning old B&W plates and films is best done in 16-bit mode, using whatever scanner settings will let you capture the maximum density range. Finding out what that is for your scanner will take some experimentation. In some scanners, 16-bit mode automatically captures a longer density range; in others (my Minolta DiMAGE, for example) there may be a separate mode with a name like "16-bit linear" that captures the longest density range.

Even though you are scanning a B&W negative, you'll probably find that you can capture the longest density range if you tell the scanner software that you're working with a color transparency. Frequently scanner software tries to be "helpful" and scan for normal-contrast results. The software boosts contrast and restricts the range of densities you capture if you scan the film as a negative instead of as a transparency because modern negatives, B&W and color, have lower density ranges and less contrast than slide films.

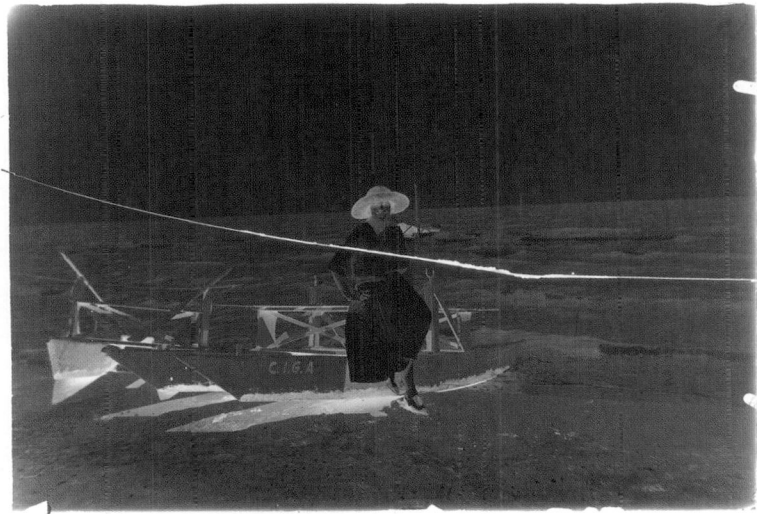

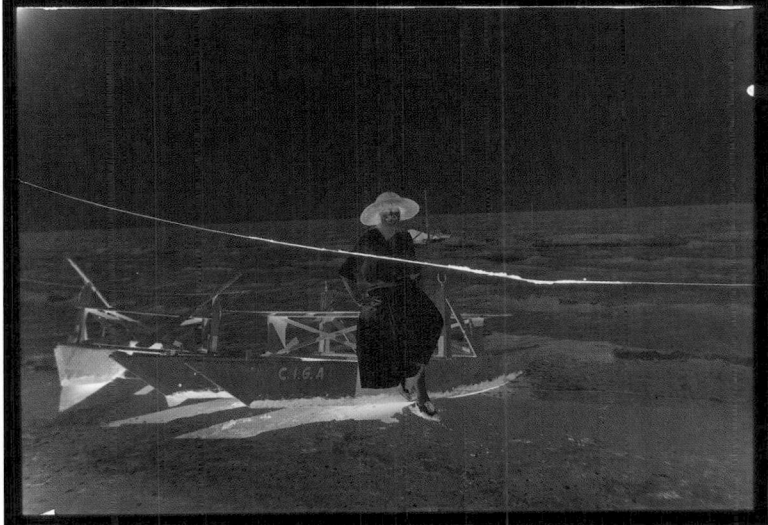

Fig. 4-25 Clear areas around the image must be masked off when scanning a dense negative. The upper figure shows the scan I made of this glass plate on my flat-bed scanner when I didn't mask off the clear areas of the platen. The lower figure shows the scan made with exactly the same settings, but this time I used black paper to mask off the region outside of the image. Figure 4-26 shows what a difference this made in the quality of the highlights (densest parts) of the negative.

You are going to need to run some experiments to find out what combination of these settings works best with your equipment. Don't worry about what gets captured in the shadows (the thin parts of the negative); they will take care of themselves. Open up the scan files in your image processing program, and look at how much information you capture in the densest highlight areas (Figure 4-27). Use the Curves tool to exaggerate the highlight detail, making it easier to compare quality between the scans (Figure 4-28). Find the scanning mode that gets you the maximum amount of highlight information, and stick with it for all your scans unless the original is severely faded.

✓ HOW TO INSPECT VERY DARK PARTS OF A SCAN

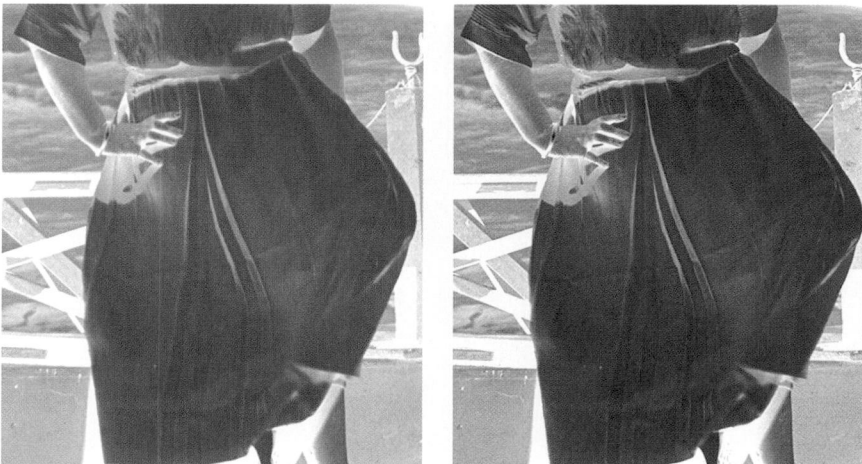

Fig. 4-26 Here's an enlarged portion of the unmasked (left) and masked (right) scans of Figure 4-25. I lightened the scans and increased their contrast to make more visible the highlight detail (the dense parts of the negative). Even though this area is in the very center of the plate, far from the unmasked edges, flare has crept in and lightened the high-density areas. It also reduced contrast; the folds and ripples in the white dress aren't as clear in the unmasked scan as the masked one. The masked scan has much better highlight detail and contrast.

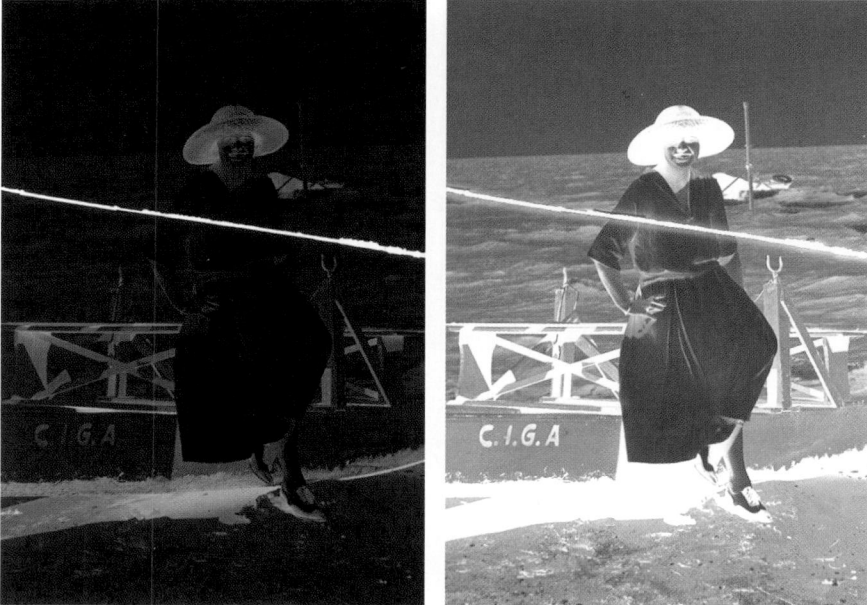

Fig. 4-27 An easy way to check whether you've got good highlight detail in the scan of a very dense negative is to increase its brightness and contrast using the curve in Figure 4-28. The photo on the left shows the scan viewed normally. The photograph on the right shows the same scan after I applied the enhancing curve in Photoshop.

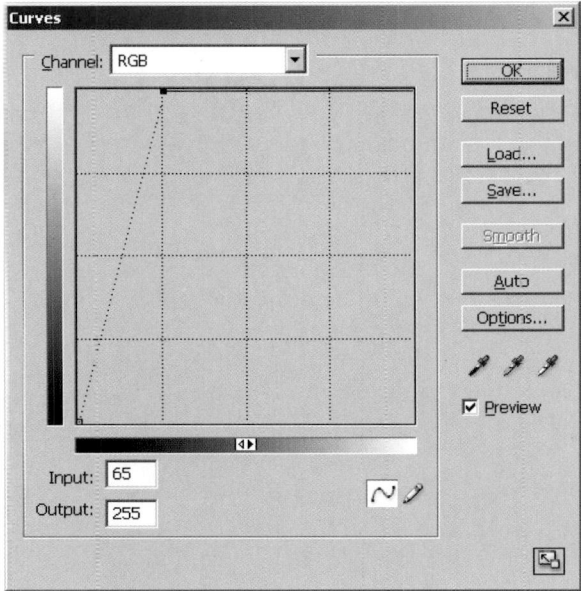

Fig. 4-28 This curve increases the contrast in a negative's highlights fourfold. It makes it possible to clearly see the quality of the highlight detail in scans of very dark negatives.

When you are working with extremely contrasty originals, consider making two scans with very different exposures, one for the highlights and one for the shadows. In Photoshop CS2, you can use the "Merge to HDR" automation to combine several differently exposed 16- or 8-bit files into a single, extended-range image. Picture Window has a simple tutorial explaining how to do this using its Stack Image operation. This operation is a lot more intuitive than Photoshop's automation, and I like Picture Window's results much better. I give you detailed instructions on using it in Chapter 9 on page 316.

Depending on the capabilities of your scanner, combining multiple scans may not capture a longer density range than a single scan could. But it will get you much higher quality data in the extreme highlights and shadows, with less noise and better tonal separation.

Be aware that, just like point-source enlargers, most film scanners also really exaggerate scratches and dust and dirt. There are software tools that will help reduce that, but using them without compromising sharpness is tricky. Hardware-based scratch and dust suppression, such as the DIGITAL ICE found in dedicated film scanners, won't work with silver-based images. Resign yourself to the fact that a certain amount of "spotting" is necessary with any scan.

Scanning Color Film

Scanning old color negative film is usually more of an aesthetic than technical challenge. Old color film does not have much higher densities than modern film. Unless you're scanning a relatively recent photograph that has only suffered physical damage that needs repair, you'll be dealing with color emulsions that have faded with time, so their maximum densities are even lower. Most scanners should have no trouble capturing the full range of densities in a negative.

HOW TO SCAN COLOR NEGATIVES

I strongly recommend capturing negatives in 16-bit mode, especially 16-bit linear mode if it's available. Because a negative's contrast is naturally low, it gets boosted substantially when it's printed, even more so if the negative is faded. If you start with a mere 8-bit scan, you will run the risk of getting a "picket fence" histogram that's bad enough to degrade the quality of the restored photograph, the same way you would with a straight scan of a badly faded print (Figure 4-8).

I recommend 16-bit linear mode for scanning color negatives because most scanner software assumes that when you scan a negative you want a positive image of "normal" contrast and color saturation. Usually it will not capture the full density range of the negative, only a partial range that produces what the software thinks will make the best-looking print.

These are not decisions you want your software making for you. You want a scan that contains as much information from the negative as possible. Linear mode capture usually accomplishes this; it's intended to pass on the data collected by the scanner with the minimum amount of software interpretation. That's left up to you, as it should be.

If your scanner doesn't offer a linear mode, and your negative scans are clipping either the highlight or shadow detail, try scanning the negative as if it were a slide, since scanner software is designed to retain a greater density range when scanning slides. The image you see on your screen will then, of course, be a negative, but a simple inversion operation will give you a positive image.

Don't expect the image you see to look anything like a good photograph. The color will be wrong, the contrast will be flat, and it may appear much lighter or darker than you would want a good-looking photograph to be. That's all correctable. Not correctable are highlights and shadows that are entirely lost because your software threw away some of the detail in the photograph.

Using 16-bit scanning mode is less critical for scanning slides if they're not severely faded, but it's still a good idea. A lot can be done to improve the quality of chromes, especially old ones. The original slide in Figure 4-29 was a badly scratched Kodachrome that had never been projected. Kodachrome slides are very stable in the dark. Consequently, once the scratches were all repaired, the tone and color were in like-new condition. Typical of slides, it has very contrasty midrange tones and flat highlights and shadows.

Some photographers intentionally took advantage of the harsh characteristics of their films, but far more often they only tolerated it as the best that could be done at the time. This may be a look you want to

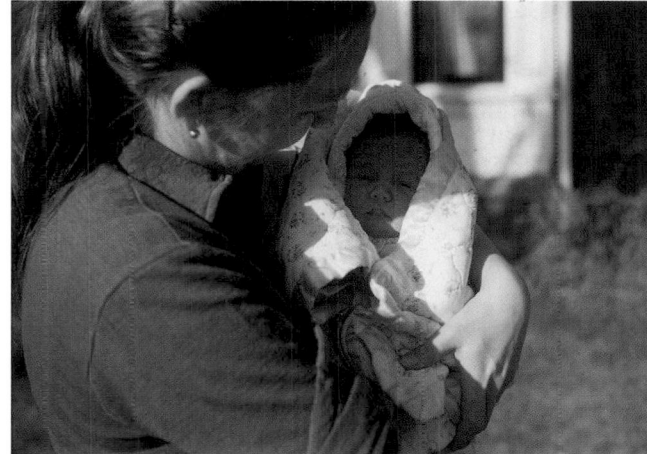

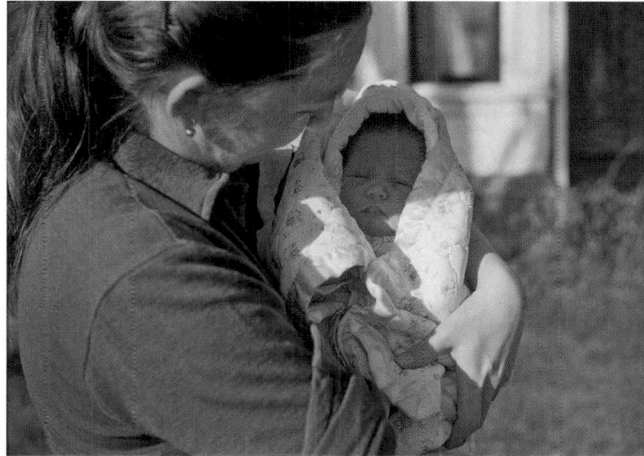

Fig. 4-29 This Kodachrome slide (top figure) has like-new tone and color because Kodachrome is very stable in the dark and this slide was rarely, if ever, projected. That does not mean it can't be improved. I produced the photograph in the lower figure using Photoshop's Shadow/Highlight, Hue/Saturation, Dodge, and Burn tools. The bottom photograph has better highlight detail and improved color, and it shows the mother and child more clearly and better focuses the viewer's attention on them.

preserve, but more often than not the client will be thrilled if you can do something to improve the tonal quality (see Chapter 9, page 335). Scanning the chrome in 16-bit mode ensures that you have plenty of well-discriminated tonal information in the highlights and shadows, so that you won't see posterization and banding when you improve the overall contrast characteristics of the photograph.

Faded slides can be particularly tricky to scan. Often one dye layer is hardly faded at all, while at the same time there is an overall buildup of stain. The result is that even though the slide looks pale and washed out to the eye (and sometimes to the scanner's exposure control), it may actually have higher-than-normal density in one or more channels. Despite the best efforts of your scanner, the darker areas in that channel may go solid "black" in the scan, eliminating any possibility of good color correction in those portions of the photograph.

HOW TO SCAN VERY DENSE OR FADED COLOR FILM

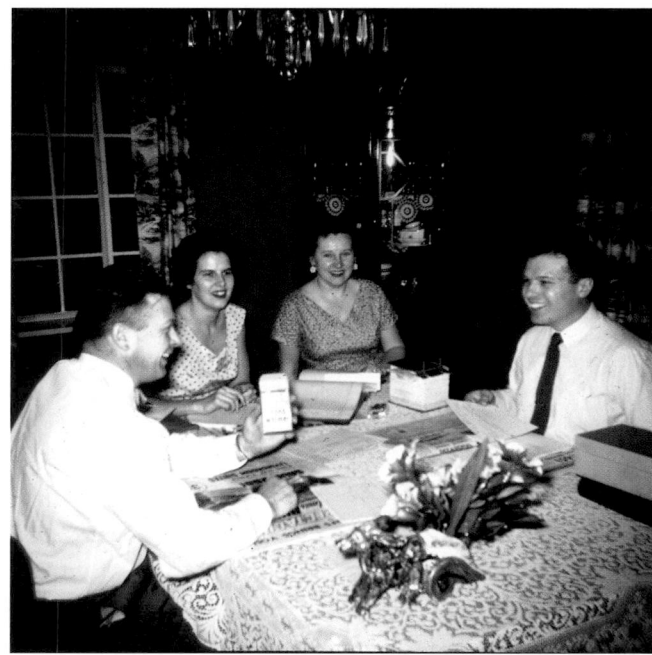

Fig. 4-30 This early 1950s E-1 slide is very contrasty. Even after color and tone correction (shown here) a single 16-bit scan can't encompass the full range of detail that was in the slide, from highlights to shadows.

HOW TO SCAN VERY DENSE OR FADED COLOR FILM (continued)

Scanning using your film scanner's 16-bit linear mode may bring in that extra-high-density data. However, you'll encounter cases in which even that won't be enough (Figure 4-30). When that happens, the answer is to make two or even three scans at very different exposure settings and combine them as in Figure 4-31 (Chapter 9, page 316).

Resolution Decisions

Usually you won't have to scan prints at extremely high resolutions. It's rare to find an old print that has 1200-ppi worth of fine detail. For 8-inch by 10-inch and larger originals there usually won't be even 600-ppi worth of detail in the photograph. Often a mere 300-ppi scan can capture all of the real detail to be had. This is true even of contact prints from glass plates and large-format film negatives.

HOW TO DETERMINE WHAT RESOLUTION TO SCAN AT

If you believe that a particular photo merits a high-resolution scan, do some test scans of a small section of it at different resolutions: 300, 600, 1200 ppi, and so on (Figure 4-32). Compare the scans on your monitor at 100% scale, at least. If you find that the pixelation in the lower resolution scans makes it difficult for you to compare the amount of image detail with the higher resolution scans, resample all of the files to the same ppi (Figure 4-33). Use this to determine the point where increasing the scan resolution further doesn't get you any more picture detail.

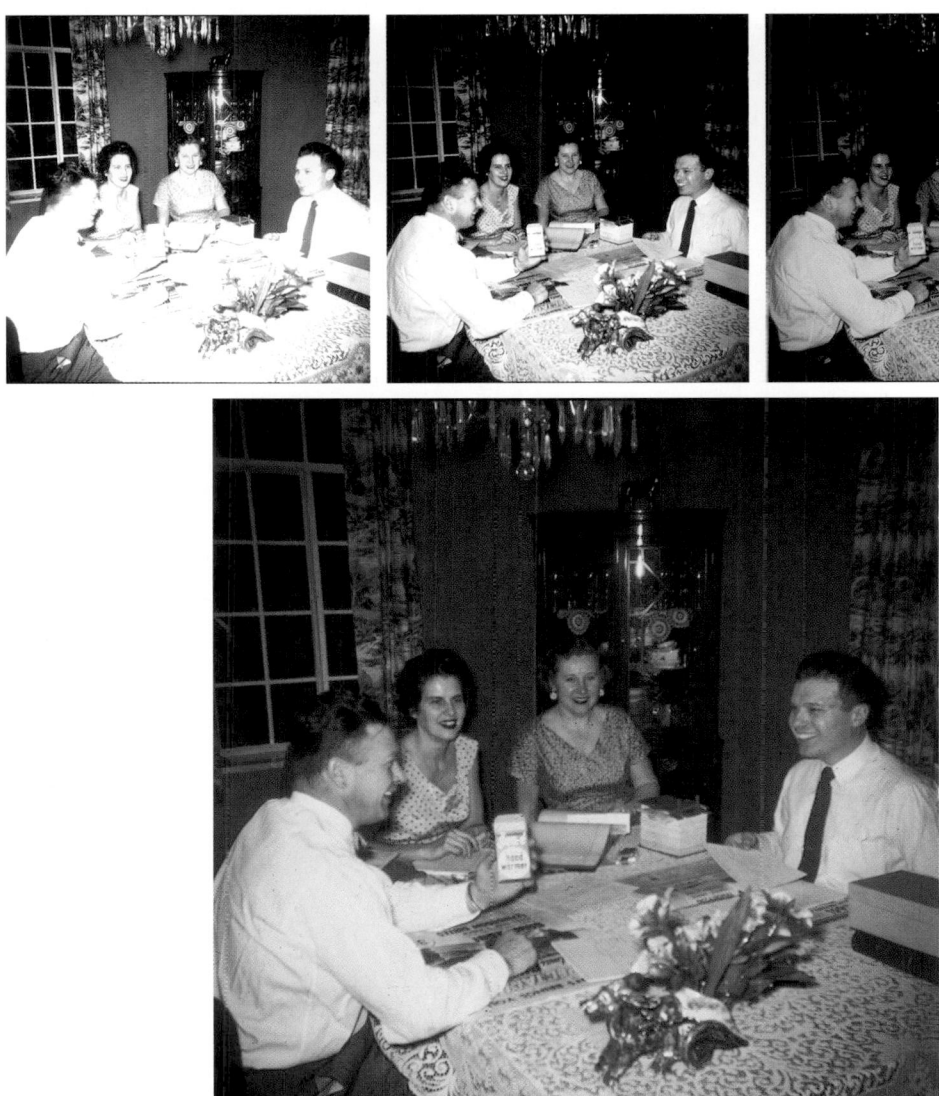

Fig. 4-31 You can create an extended-range scan from several individual scans made with different exposures by using Picture Window's Stack Images Transform operation. I used that transform to create the large composite photograph here from the three individual scars at the top of the figure. Compare the vastly improved highlight and shadow detail with that of the photograph in Figure 4-30.

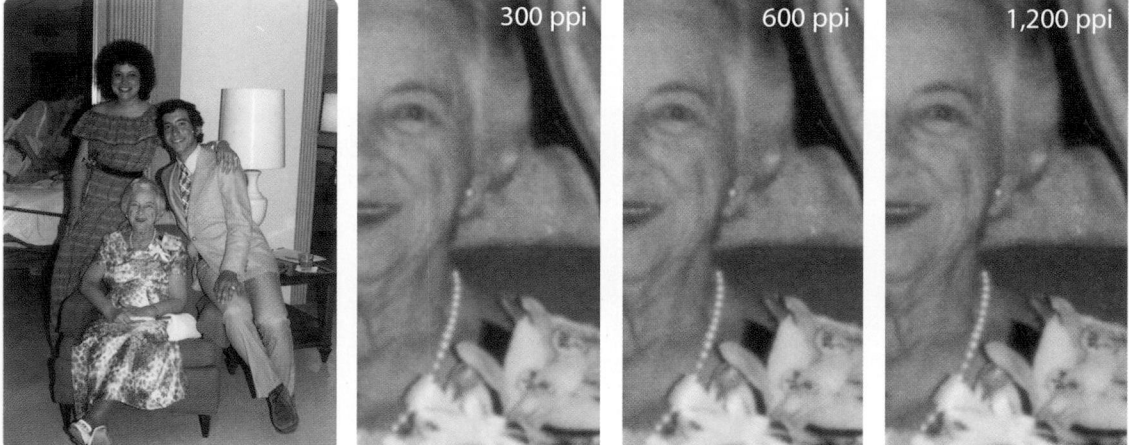

300 ppi   600 ppi   1,200 ppi

Fig. 4-32 I scanned a small portion of the snapshot on the left at 300-, 600-, and 1200-ppi resolutions to see how fine a scan was needed to capture all of the detail in the photograph. The 600-ppi scan is a little sharper than the 300-ppi one. The pearls and the flowers in the corsage have a little more detail at 600 ppi. There's no difference between the 600- and 1200-ppi scans. This tells me that I don't need to scan this photograph at a higher resolution than 600 ppi.

Fig. 4-33 Here's how to resample a lower resolution scan to higher resolution when comparing different scans, as in Figure 4-32. The upper control panel shows the settings for the 300-ppi scan. To make it match the 600-ppi scan in scale, change the Resolution to 600 (lower panel) and make sure that Resample Image: Bicubic is selected.

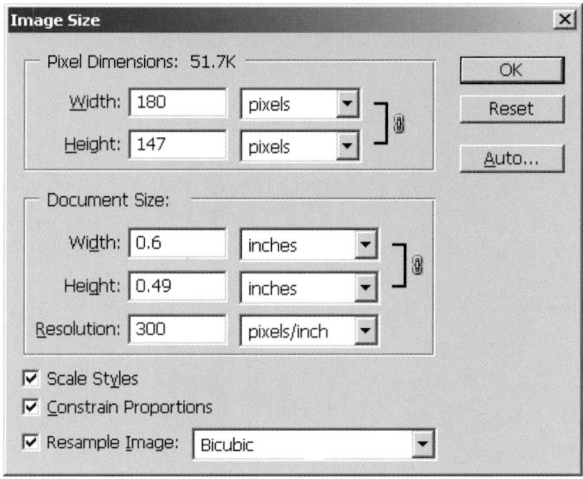

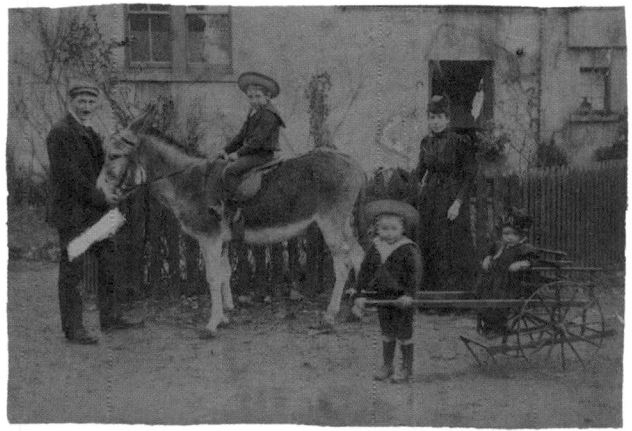

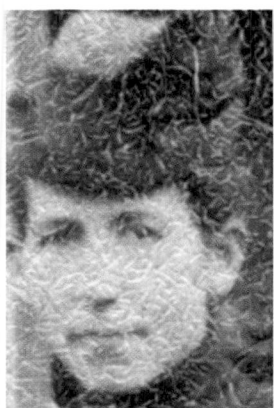 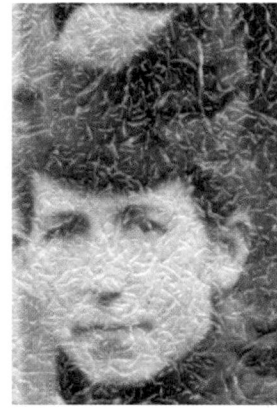

Fig. 4-34 Sometimes it's a good idea to scan at very high resolutions. This photograph is covered with a network of fine cracks. The 600-ppi scan (lower left) records as much photographic detail as the 1200-ppi scan (lower right), but the cracks are much sharper and better defined in the 1200-ppi scan. That will make it easier to create a mask that selects just the cracks for repair (see Chapter 7).

There's no harm in scanning at unnecessarily higher resolutions, but it expands your file size dramatically. The size of the image file you get goes up as the square of the scan resolution: A 600-ppi scan will be four times as large as a 300-ppi scan, and a 1200-ppi scan will be 16 times as large.

High-resolution scans of low-resolution prints can be useful when there's physical damage with sharply defined, clear edges (Figure 4-34). Scanning at higher resolutions spreads out real image detail over many more pixels, while the edges of damaged areas remain pixel-sharp. This makes it easier to use edge-finding filters and similar tools in your image processing program to extract the boundaries of the damaged areas. When a damaged region's edges and the finest image details are both only 1 or 2 pixels wide, it's hard for software to distinguish between them. When an edge is 1 or 2 pixels wide while the finest photographic detail is 5 to 10 pixels wide, you can do a pretty good job of masking that selects for the sharp damage. I apply this technique to the photo in Figure 4-34 in Chapter 7, Making Masks. page 240.

Masks can be resized the same way image files can, so you aren't stuck with a monstrous, ultra-high-resolution file to work with. If you need to scan at, say, 2400 ppi to create a good mask, don't be afraid to do so. Once you've made that mask and saved it, you can resample both the mask and the image file down to something more workable, like 600 ppi, and perform your restoration on much smaller files.

When you're scanning film, be aware that scanning usually increases grain, no matter what type of film was used. That's because a "grain" in a digital file can be no smaller than a single pixel. Even coarse-grained B&W film has film grains smaller than most scanners' pixels. Consequently, grain is magnified in scans. Good software tools exist for reducing the impact of grain (notably DIGITAL GEM, which is part of the DIGITAL ICE[3] software package incorporated in many film scanners and is also available as a plug-in for Photoshop), but it's hard to make it go away entirely. The best way to minimize grain in a digital scan is to scan at the very highest true (not interpolated) resolution you can. That will make the grain finer and more like it was in the original negative and more like it would be in a wet darkroom print.

Low-resolution scans don't solve the grain problem until you get to *very* low resolutions. Film grain, unfortunately, acts like random noise, which means it doesn't blur out as much as you'd expect when you make the pixels bigger (for the mathematically inclined, grain contrast only goes down as the square root of the size of the pixel). Figure 4-35 shows highly enlarged sections of a photograph scanned, top to bottom, at 4800, 2400, and 1200 ppi. As the resolution drops, the film grain gets larger and mushier, but it still hasn't gone away even at 1200 ppi. The random noise effect of grain leaves its imprint on individual pixels even after fine detail is blurred out.

Putting aside grain problems, the older the original, the less likely you are to need a high-resolution scan of it. By and large, old-time photographs get their wonderful sharpness and rich tonal qualities from the large size of the films and plates of the time. However, although old-style emulsions were often very fine grained and sharp, the same cannot be said for the camera lenses. The techniques of the photographers of the time didn't usually lend themselves to ultra-sharp photographs. On average, a photograph made by a casual 35-mm camera user in the late 20th century has much finer detail than a professional photograph made a century earlier.

One important tip for scanning smaller negatives: Always scan film in a glass carrier! No glassless flat film carrier made holds the film well enough to give you an edge-to-edge sharp scan, no matter what the manufacturers may foist off on you as a standard carrier for your scanner. Pay for a glass carrier when you buy your scanner, even if it costs you extra.

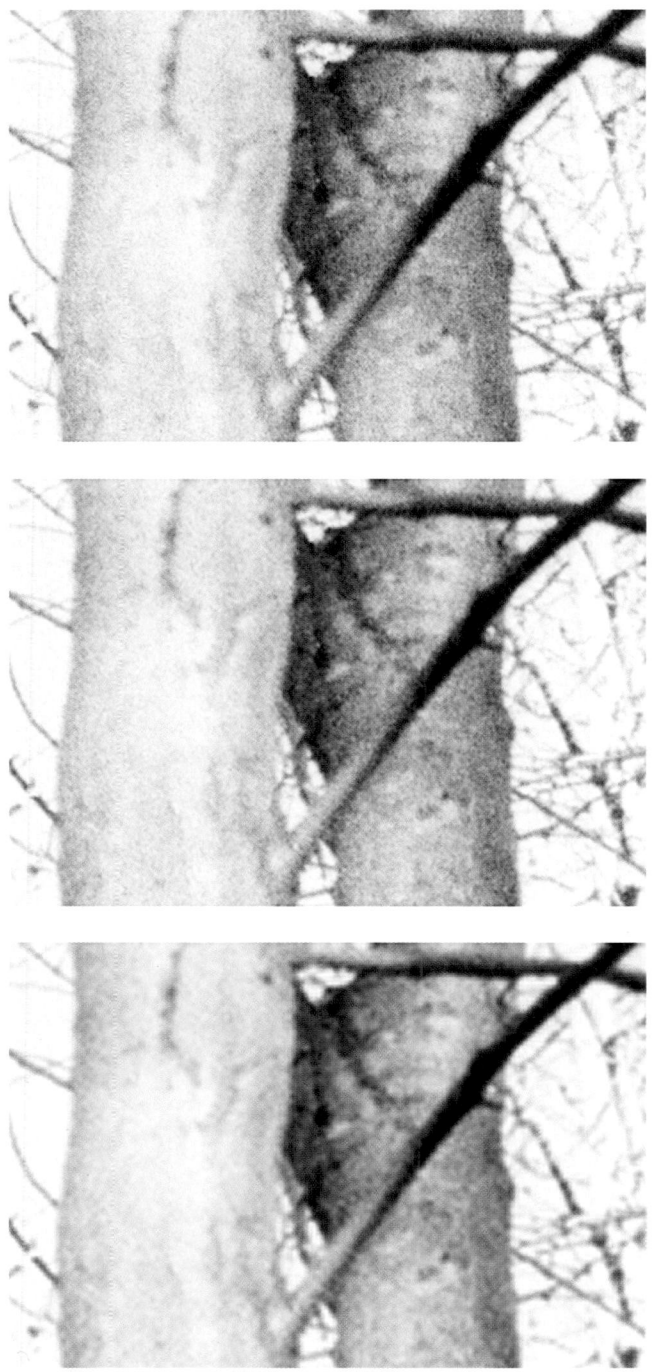

Fig. 4-35 Reducing scan resolution is not a good way to suppress noise and grain. Th s B&W negative was scanned at 480J, 2400, and 1200 ppi (top to bottom). The film grain gets mushier as scan resolution drops, but it doesn't go away, and much fine detail is lost.

Rephotography

If you're trying to restore prints that have lots of fine cracks or a really heavy surface texture, you may be better off rephotographing the print with a good digital single-lens reflex (SLR) camera. Flat-bed scanners use highly directional light that accentuates surface flaws and brings out textures. Defects that are hardly visible under normal diffuse light viewing can dominate a scan. Taking the more conventional photographic route on a copy stand lets you use all the clever lighting tools that had been developed over the years for minimizing surface blemishes: light tents, double crossed polarizers, careful off-axis placement of lamps—the whole bag of tricks. Used properly, this approach can save you many hours of work on the computer.

Copy photography is a specialized skill that isn't difficult to learn but does involve techniques you're not likely to have encountered while doing regular photography. In particular, the trick of using crossed polarizers to suppress textures and reflections is something every good copy photographer knows, but there's almost never a reason to have learned it outside of that discipline.

A good instructional book on copy photography is the 1984 Eastman Kodak publication *Copying and Duplicating in Black-and-White and Color*. An online search will turn up numerous sources for this book. Even though it's 20 years old and so is entirely film oriented, it's timely. Many of the copying techniques are just as applicable to modern digital photography as they were to film photography. You'll even see some nice examples of photo restorations done using film and filters instead of scanners and computers. Be sure to study the section on the use of polarizers carefully.

HOW TO PHOTOGRAPH TARNISHED PRINTS

Prints that have silvered out (developed shiny metallic spots on the surface) can be difficult to scan because the metallic surface of the print bounces light directly into the scanner sensor. This is a problem that you may be able to fix when you restore the image with some more clever masking tricks, as in Figure 4-13, but sometimes it's easier to avoid it in the first place. Copying that same photograph with crossed polarizers over the lights and the camera lens suppresses reflections from the tarnish spots and the paper texture to provide a much cleaner image to work with (Figure 4-36).

Recapturing a photograph with a camera has two disadvantages. The first is density range; your digital camera may not capture the full range of the print in a single exposure. In that case you'll need to make two exposures, one for the highlights and one for the shadows, and merge them in your image processing program (see Chapter 9, page 316). Regardless, you will want to do your captures in 16-bit TIFF or RAW mode.

The other handicap is resolution. Don't expect digital photography to be as sharp as scanning. The actual resolving power of most digital SLRs is in the range of 1500- by 1500-pixels worth of fine detail. The

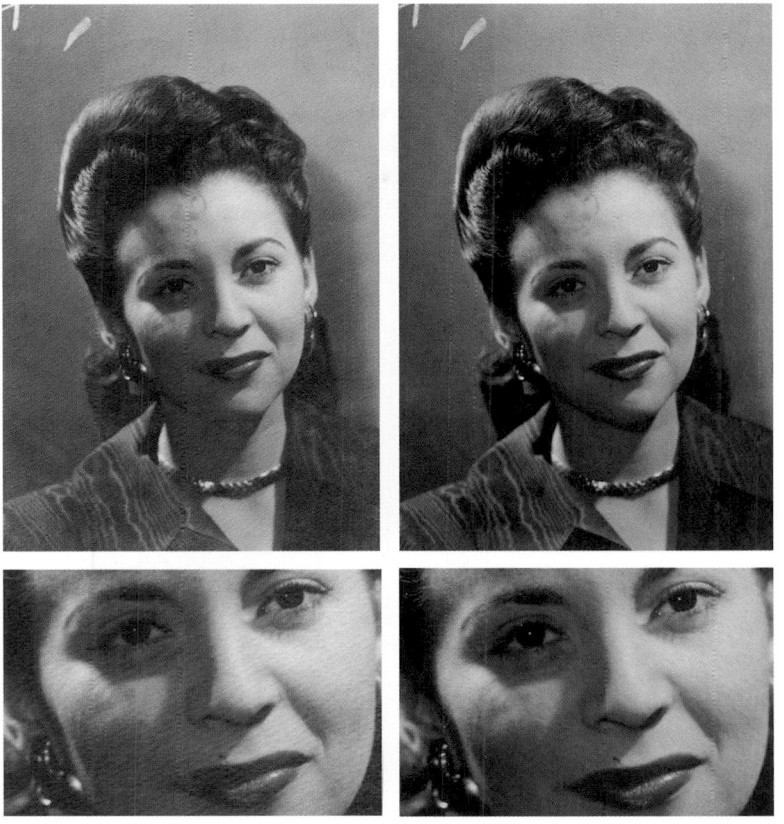

Fig. 4-36 The original photograph on the left has an intrusive paper texture and considerable tarnish. A flat-bed scanner captures these flaws along with the underlying image I want to restore. I made the figure on the right by rephotographing the original print on a copy stand with a digital camera. I used two floodlights set at 45-degree angles to the print so the paper texture wouldn't cast shadows. I covered the floodlights and the camera lens with polarizers rotated at right angles to each other. That killed the specular reflections from the tarnish, making them almost invisible.

most expensive ones get up to more than 3000 by 3000 pixels. I'm not talking about the file size in pixels but the actual amount of fine detail that is there. Put another way, a sharp 600-ppi scan of a 4-inch by 6-inch print will record as much fine image detail as even a very good digital SLR. In many cases, though, the digital photograph will be more than good enough, especially for the advantages it offers in suppressing cracks, textures, and silvering out.

Some digital cameras have a problem with lateral chromatic aberration (color fringing toward the edges of the frame). You can fix that in Photoshop, but I much prefer Picture Window's tool for correcting this problem. See Chapter 6, Restoring Color, page 219, for instructions.

CHAPTER 5

Restoring Tone

How-To's in This Chapter

How to evaluate contrast with a histogram
How to change overall brightness and contrast with Curves
How to add contrast to midtones with Curves
How to use sample points with Curves
How to make a print look more brilliant and snappier with Curves
How to lighten or darken a print with Curves
How to bring out shadow tones with Curves
How to improve a copy print with Curves
How to improve snapshots with the Shadow/Highlight adjustment
How to improve a copy print with the Curves and Shadow/Highlight adjustments
How to correct uneven exposure with a Curves adjustment layer
How to do dodging and burning-in with masked Curves adjustment layers
How to scan a nearly blank photograph
How to recover a nearly blank photograph with Curves adjustment layers and
   "multiply" blends
How to improve contrast without making colors too saturated
How to fix harsh shadows on faces
How to retouch faces with a masked Curves adjustment layer

What Makes a Good Print?

Let's talk a bit about what a good print looks like.

The First Rule of Good Tonality is that a good photograph almost always has a range of tones that run from near-white to near-black. This is true even of high-key and low-key photographs. This is partly a result of the inherent nature of real-world subjects, which usually have highlights and shadows, even if they are a very small part of the photograph. It is also partly a result of the limited exposure range of most photographic films. Whatever the reason, this dictum holds so often that the exceptions to the rule are, well, exceptional. If you assume the

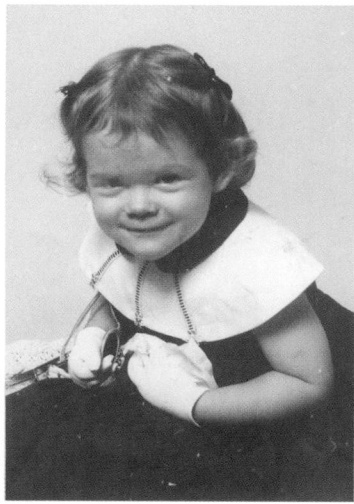 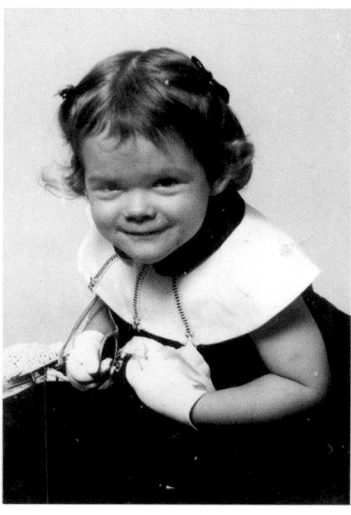 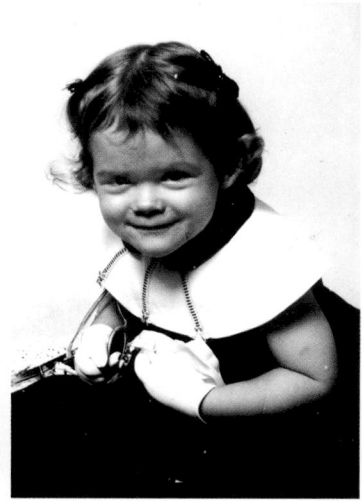

Fig. 5-1 A good-looking B&W photograph almost always has a full range of tones from black to white. The photograph on the left is too low in contrast; it looks muddy and flat. The photograph on the right has too much contrast; midtones are harsh, and some important highlight and shadow detail has been pushed to pure blacks and whites. The photograph in the middle is just right!

photograph you are restoring is supposed have a full range of tones, you will almost never be wrong.

Conversely, a good photograph usually doesn't have large areas that are pure white or solid black without there having been a specific aesthetic reason to make it that way. This is not as universal a truth as my First Rule, but it's true more often than not.

HOW TO EVALUATE
CONTRAST WITH A
HISTOGRAM

The classic error that the neophyte printer makes in the darkroom is getting the overall contrast wrong. Flat prints with muddy blacks and grayish whites are what I most commonly see. Occasionally someone will err the other way and produce prints that are way too contrasty, with lots of solid blacks and pure whites where there should be continuous tone and delicate gradation (Figure 5-1).

That potential for error still exists when printing digitally, but fortunately we have a tool that makes it much easier to tell when we're going astray. It's the histogram (Figure 5-2). A good histogram spans most of the range of values from black to white. A smattering of pixels may be pure whites and blacks in the finished photograph, but for restoration work we want to minimize that until we get to the very last stages of image preparation for printing.

You'll recall from Chapter 4 (and you'll see in later examples) that I strive when scanning a photograph to get tones that fill most of the range of the histogram. I don't do that just because it maximizes the amount of data I have to work with in the restoration, although that would be

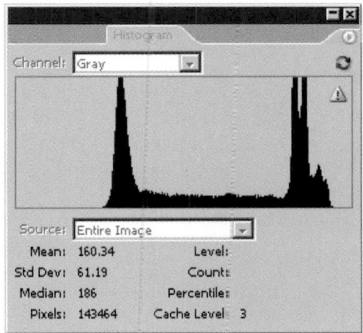 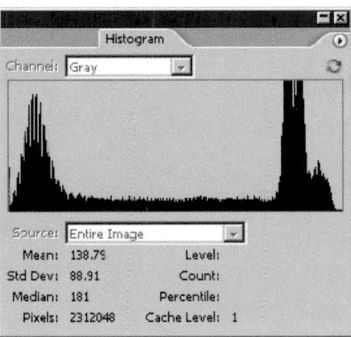 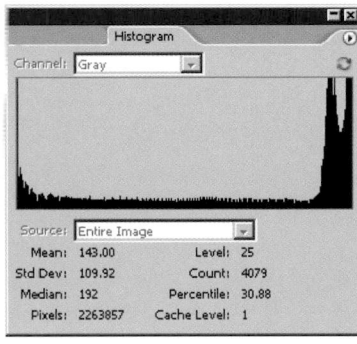

Fig. 5-2 These are the histograms of the photographs in Figure 5-1. The low-contrast photograph (left) doesn't make good use of the full range of tones available; there's no data below a value of about 70. The high-contrast photograph (right) has forced a lot of pixels to pure black or white (values of 0 or 255). Highlight and shadow detail is missing, and the photograph is unattractive. The middle histogram makes good use of the tonal scale without clipping off highlight or shadow detail.

reason enough. I do it because it also gets me much closer to a photograph with good tonality.

The First Rule is almost an absolute law for original slides and prints made from slides. Slide film has an extremely short exposure range; hardly ever do slides lack a true white and a true black somewhere in the scene. This is usually, but not always, true for color negatives and prints made from them. Professional portraits may lack a true white and a true black, especially if they were supposed to be soft "flattering" portraits made with diffusion filters. Amateur portraits are a different matter; the First Rule likely applies. The color print processes were not as good as today; while films tended to be contrasty, prints were often low in saturation and lacked a really good black. Almost all color prints from that era are severely faded and stained.

Many old B&W photographs were not black and white to begin with; they were brown or sepia in color. But you should treat them as if they were true B&W. Because of the staining and fading that afflict old photographs, you will normally eliminate all vestiges of hue during the restoration process. At the last stage, once the restoration is complete, you can digitally "tone" the print to give it the hue you want (see Chapter 11, Printing Tips, page 429).

Moreover, most amateur photographs from the mid-20th century were terrible prints to begin with. Photofinishing back then was poor, and people's expectations were lower. Well-preserved B&W snapshots from that era (Figure 5-1, left) are more often gray and white rather than black and white. Such originals would not qualify as a good photograph by my rules. But we can improve them, unless the goal is a strict historically accurate restoration. As part of the restoration process, we can turn those gray-and-white snapshots and prints with washed-out color into full-toned photographs that will be much more lovely than

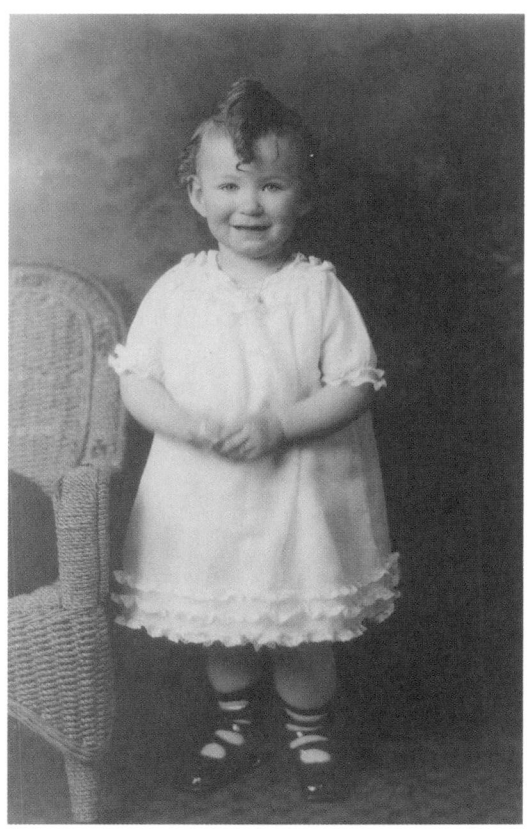

Fig. 5-3 Another flat photograph with grays where there should be blacks and whites. The histogram in Figure 5-4 tells the tale.

the original ever was. It's always a good idea to check with the client to make sure this is acceptable; in the majority of cases they will be both delighted and amazed that you can actually improve on the original.

Now that I've laid down some guidelines, how do we get to that good-looking print? Consider the photograph in Figure 5-3 and its histogram in Figure 5-4. It's easy to see what needs to be done; the whites are too dark and the blacks very washed out. The photograph needs to be brighter and more contrasty overall.

Well, whatever you do don't use the Brightness/Contrast adjustment to fix this! It is the tool of amateurs and is way too blunt an instrument for doing good work. Furthermore, although I find levels adjustments useful for controlling the scan quality (see Chapter 4), I don't make much use of the Levels tool in Photoshop itself (Figure 5-5). Levels adjustments lack fine control and subtlety; you're limited to setting the end points for the pure black and white tones and a single midrange point that controls how light or dark the middle grays are. Levels definitely improves the photograph (Figure 5-6), but truly fine control over tonal placement isn't possible with this tool.

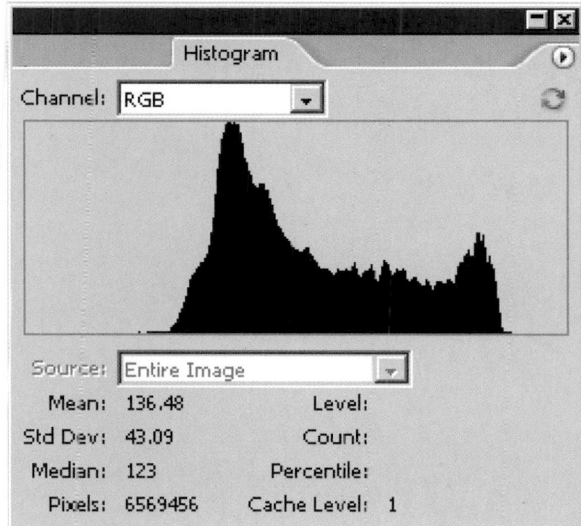

Fig. 5-4 This histogram shows why the photograph in Figure 5-3 looks so bad. None of the tones comes anywhere close to black—there is nothing darker than a dark gray. At the highlight end of the scale, the white dress is being rendered as a dishwater gray.

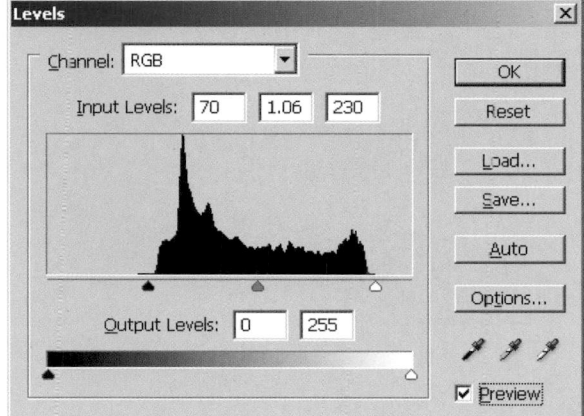

Fig. 5-5 Photoshop's Levels tool can crudely correct the tones and contrast of Figure 5-3. The B&W sliders are positioned just outside the range of tones portrayed in the photograph. The black slider is moved in much further than the white slider, so the picture is going to become darker, overall. To compensate, the midtone gray slider is shifted slightly to the left (a value of 1.06) to brighten up the middle grays a bit.

Level's limited flexibility is, in fact, why I like using such adjustments in my scanner software. As long as I've got a good range of values in the scan, I want the data to be pretty linear and unmassaged. I'd rather do that work myself and not have it locked into the original scan. Some plug-ins I use are happier working with linear tones than with heavily manipulated ones. But what makes Levels just right for scanner settings makes it mostly wrong for real restoration work. If I'm not recommending you use the Brightness/Contrast or Levels tools, what's the alternative?

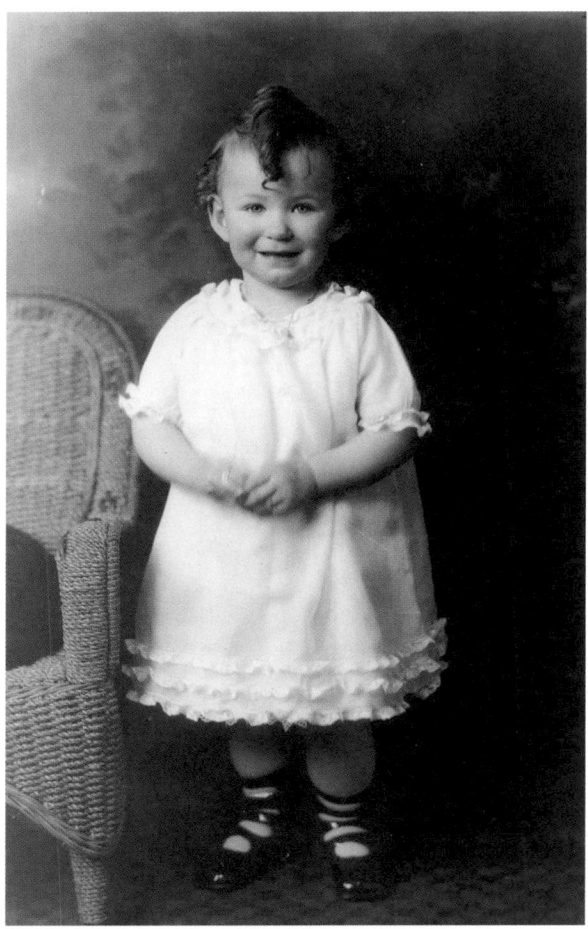

Fig. 5-6 This is the same photograph as Figure 5-3 after the Levels settings in Figure 5-5 are applied. Levels is not a tool for making sophisticated tonal corrections, but it still produces photographs with more natural-looking and attractive tones and more normal contrast.

Curves

HOW TO CHANGE
OVERALL
BRIGHTNESS AND
CONTRAST WITH
CURVES

The Curves tool does everything that the Brightness/Contrast and Levels tools can do for you, and it does much more. A Brightness tool increase of +32, for example, becomes this in the Curves tool in Figure 5-7. A contrast increase of +16 looks like Figure 5-8. The Levels adjustment in Figure 5-5 is just the same as the Curves adjustment in Figure 5-9.

What makes Curves the tool of choice is that it does so much more. You can attach a multitude of control points to a curve and shape it your will. This is the secret to getting good tonality in B&W restoration, and it's absolutely essential for color. Careful Curves adjustments in color (see Chapter 6) are often the only way to produce exactly the right color corrections. If you want to do great restoration work, you must become completely comfortable with and master Curves. Read Chapter 10 to see how much I depend on manipulating Curves to make my color and tone corrections and even to repair damage.

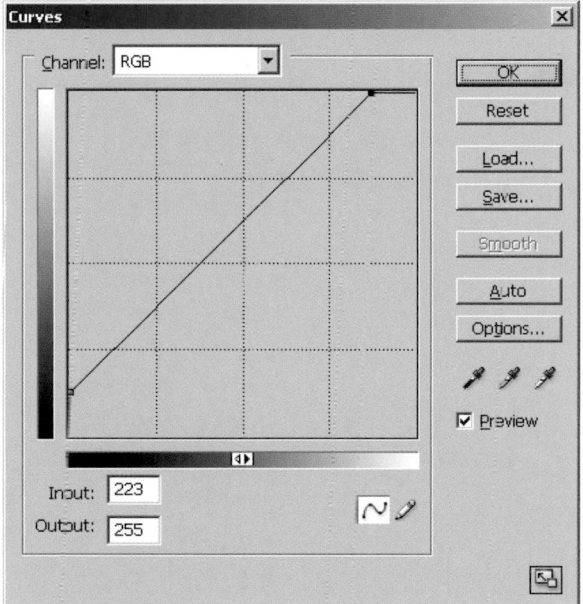
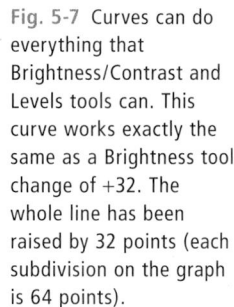

Fig. 5-7 Curves can do everything that Brightness/Contrast and Levels tools can. This curve works exactly the same as a Brightness tool change of +32. The whole line has been raised by 32 points (each subdivision on the graph is 64 points).

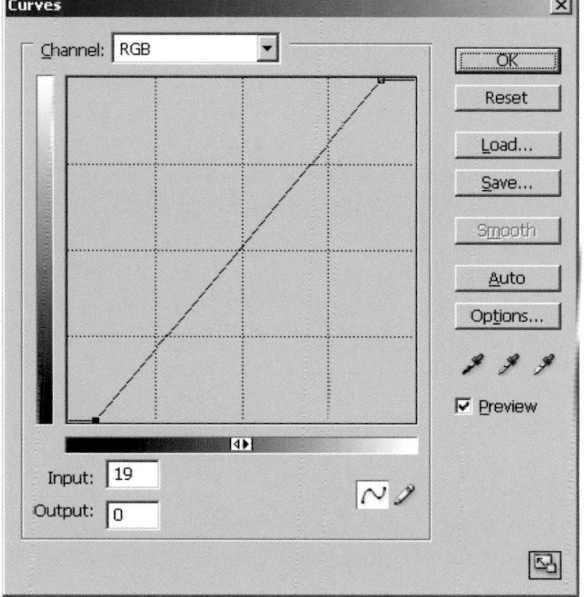

Fig. 5-8 This curve corresponds to a Contrast tool increase of +16. The black and white end points of the curve have been dragged inward, making the curve steeper.

Curves are not the only way to manipulate the tonality of a print; later in this chapter I'll bring up some very powerful techniques that don't depend on the Curves tool at all to greatly improve the tonal qualities of a photograph. But curves are going to end up doing most of your heavy lifting, tone-wise. All of the clever tricks in this book won't get you a good restoration without the assistance of Curves. Contrariwise,

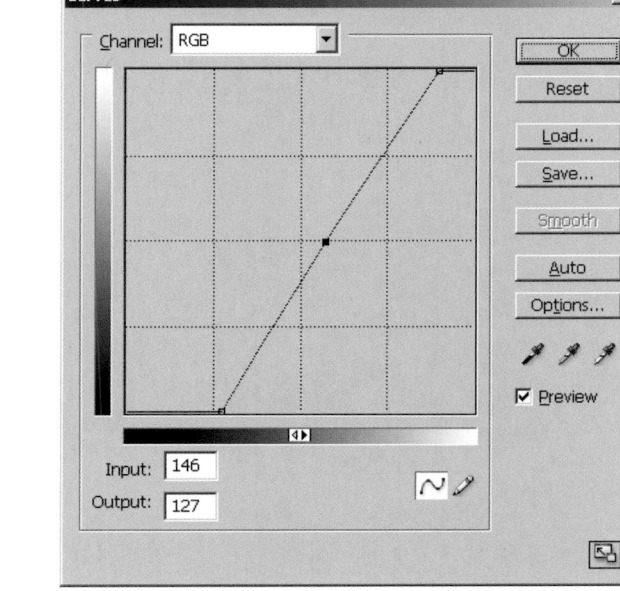

Fig. 5-9 This curve has precisely the same effect as the Levels tool in Figure 5-5. The black and white end points of the curve are dragged in to match the positions of the black and white sliders in the Levels tool. The midpoint of the curve is moved slightly upward to make the middle grays lighter.

as Example 3 in Chapter 10 demonstrates, you can use primitive tools and ancient software and do fabulous restoration work if you know how to bend (literally!) those curves to your will. Consequently, I spend most of this chapter talking about ways to use Curves to improve tonality. I appreciate that many newcomers to the world of digital work find Curves a tough row to hoe, so I'll take some time to get you more comfortable with this tool.

HOW TO ADD CONTRAST TO MIDTONES WITH CURVES

As an example of the power of Curves, the simple S-shaped curve in Figure 5-10 markedly increases midrange contrast and the overall sense of brightness and contrast. It turns Figure 5-11 into Figure 5-12 without altering the values rendered as pure whites and pure blacks. This scan started out with pretty good whites and blacks. Had I tried to achieve the same level of tonal improvement with the Levels or (worst of all) Brightness/Contrast tool, I would have clipped some of the highlight or shadow tones and entirely eliminated that detail from the photograph (Figures 5-13 and 5-14).

Although the woman looks almost identical in Figures 5-12 and 5-14, Curves retains delicate highlight detail in the water and the background that cruder tools wipe out. This one set of tone corrections is enough to make a very satisfactory restoration.

Obviously curves are potent tools. As you'll see in the rest of this book, I use them more often than any other adjustment, by themselves, in adjustment layers, and in combination with masks. Unfortunately, many photographers understandably have trouble warming up to the

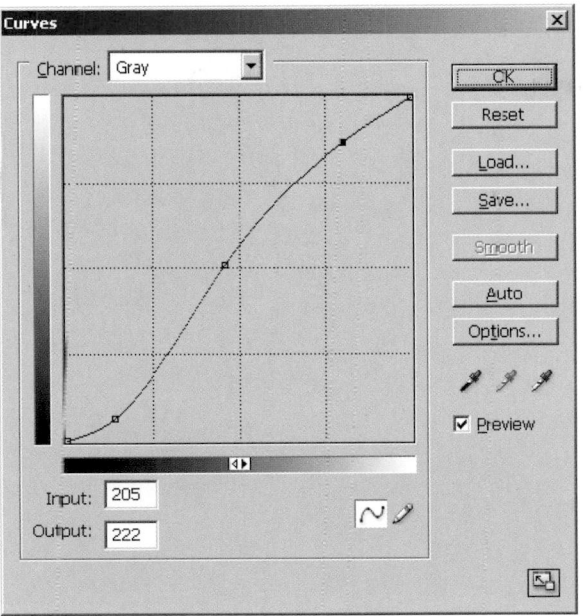

Fig. 5-10 A curve like this one substantially increases contrast and sparkle in midtones without throwing away any highlight or shadow detail. Highlights are lightened and shadows are darkened, but since the end points of the curve remain at 0 and 255, the total tonal range is unchanged.

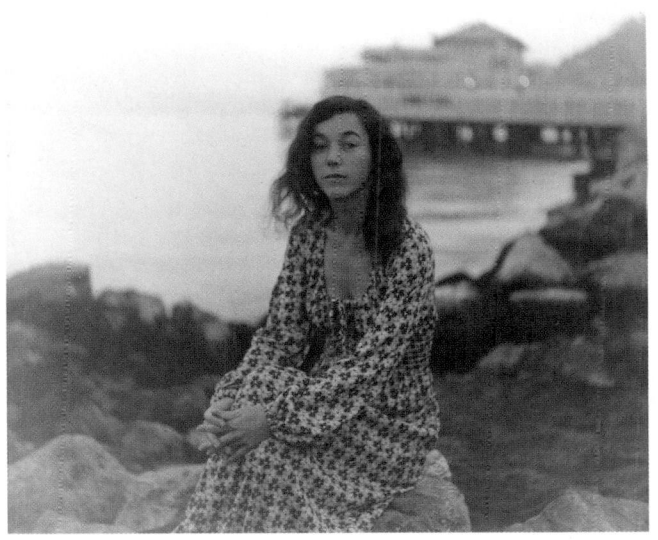

Fig. 5-11 This photograph has a full range of tones from black to white, but it looks dull and lifeless because there isn't much contrast to the midtones. Midtone contrast is what puts "snap" in a print. The curve in Figure 5-10 can fix this problem.

Fig. 5-12 This is what Figure 5-11 becomes after applying the curve in Figure 5-10. The extreme white and black points haven't changed, but the photograph looks brighter and more alive and contrasty as a result of using that S-shaped curve.

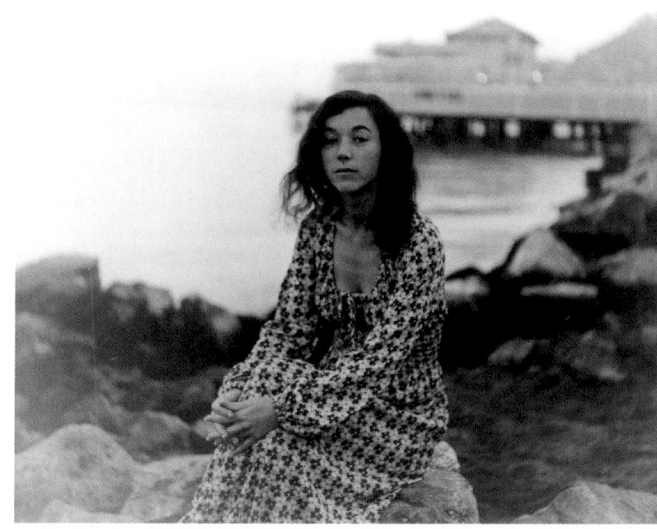

Fig. 5-13 The Levels tool can simulate the tonal changes produced by the curve in Figure 5-10 for the midrange tones, but it can only do this by sacrificing highlight and shadow detail. Curves is a much better tool for doing sophisticated adjustments of tonality than Levels.

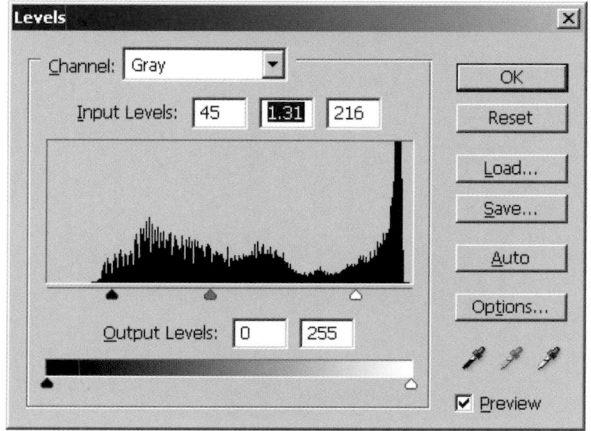

Curves tool. Relating levels of brightness in a photograph to numbers on a graph doesn't always come naturally.

HOW TO USE SAMPLE POINTS WITH CURVES

Photoshop includes several features that help to make this less forbidding. When a Curves window is open, clicking the cursor (now an eyedropper) anywhere on the photograph places an open-circle indicator on the curve at the tonal value of that point in the photograph (Figure 5-15). Numerical readouts below the graph report what the exact value is at that point (Input) and what it will change to when the curve is

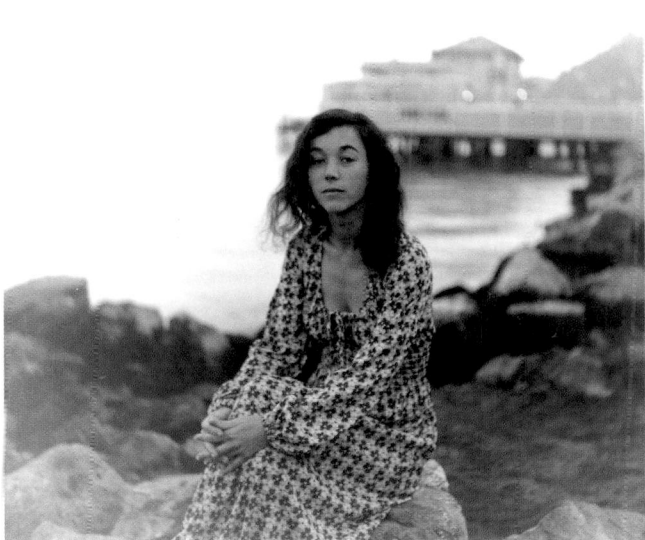

Fig. 5-14 This is the result of applying the Levels adjustment in Figure 5-13 to Figure 5-11. Compare this to Figure 5-12, which was created using Curves. The midtones are not much different in the two photographs, but the Levels-adjusted photograph, here, has lost highlight detail in the water and shadow detail in the rocks. The seated woman looks similar in both photographs, but the background looks much harsher in this one.

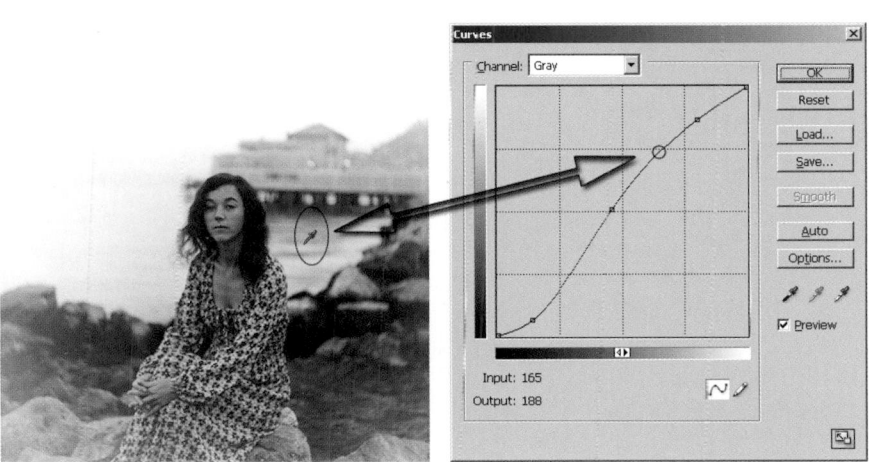

Fig. 5-15 Use the cursor to match tones in a photograph with points on the Curves tool. In this figure, I'm sampling the water in the background by clicking the cursor (the eyecropper in the oval) on the photo. That creates a corresponding circle in the Curves panel (right) whose input value matches the tone in the photograph. The Input readout at the bottom of the Curves panel says that this point has a tonal value of 165. The Output readout reports that this will become a lighter value of 188 when the curve is applied to the photograph.

HOW TO USE SAMPLE
POINTS WITH CURVES
(continued)

applied (Output). You can move the cursor around with the Shift key held down and watch the indicator slide up and down the curve and the numbers change as you pass over bright and dark parts of the photograph. This is a good way to learn how the tones in the photograph correspond to values on the curve. Photoshop's Info window, shown in Figure 5-16, will also tell you the numerical values for the photograph under your cursor; that data's available with any tool, not just when you have Curves opened up.

You can set adjustment points on the curve by control-clicking on the tone in the photograph that you want to modify. Once you set a point, you can drag it up or down and to the left or right to alter the tones. That way you don't have to guess what value that tone corresponds to on the curve or pay attention to the numerical values.

Once you get comfortable with the numbers, you can use the eyedropper tool to monitor several different points in the photograph while working on it. If you shift-click on a point in the photograph with the eyedropper, it adds a readout point to the photograph; the numerical values for that point appear in the Info window (Figure 5-16). You can place up to four separate readouts in the photograph that will always tell you what the values are at those points, regardless of where your cursor is or what you're doing.

Learn to use of all these tricks; it will help you internalize the relationship between numerical values and tones in the image. The more that becomes instinctive to you, the easier you will find Curves.

Let's now turn to some more basic curve manipulations that you'll use to improve the tonality in a photograph. Usually you'll use them in combination; think of them as individual seasonings you might add to a dish in different combinations to give it exactly the flavor you want.

HOW TO MAKE A
PRINT LOOK MORE
BRILLIANT AND
SNAPPIER WITH
CURVES

As with Figure 5-11, you can do a lot with Curves to change the tonality of a print without throwing away any of the highlight or shadow detail. The sense of brilliance in a photograph is primarily controlled by the contrast in the midtones. You can have two photographs that encompass exactly the same range of tones from white to black (Figure 5-17), but one has a lot more "snap" than the other. The difference lies in the shape of the curves. Making the curve slightly S-shaped increases the contrast in the middle tones and adds brilliance (Figure 5-18), although if you take it too far it will make a photograph look harsh. You'll use this kind of adjustment frequently in restorations. It keeps your final prints from having that flat, "this is a copy" look. A really good restoration doesn't look like a copy; it looks like an original photograph.

HOW TO LIGHTEN OR
DARKEN A PRINT
WITH CURVES

Adding a single midpoint to a curve and raising or lowering it, as in Figure 5-19, will alter the overall brightness or darkness of the photograph. This also doesn't change the black or white points (Figure 5-20). It does substantially alter the contrast in the highlights and the shadows. Raising the midpoint compresses the highlights, lowering their contrast and tonal separation. At the same time it increases shadow contrast and

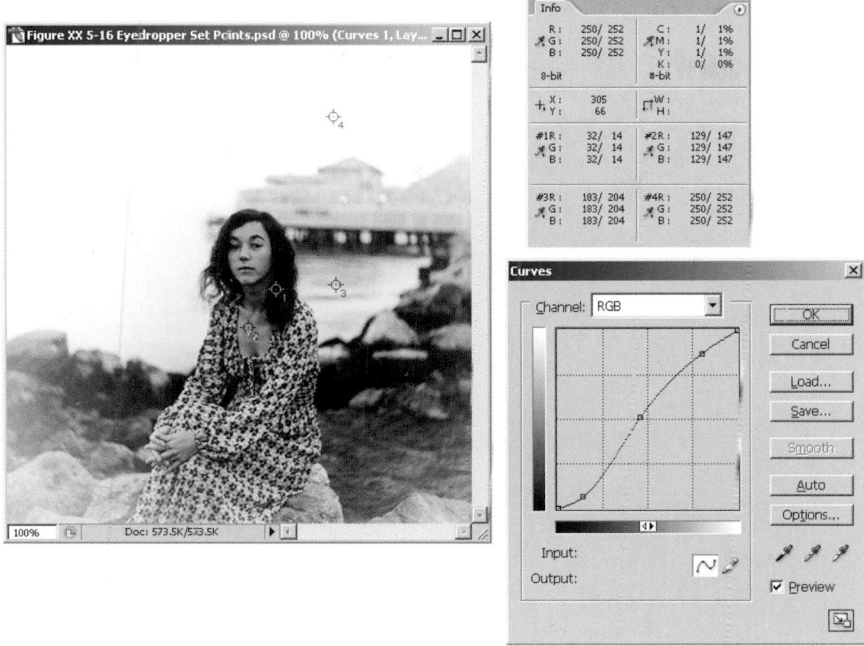

Fig. 5-16 To monitor the values at several points in a photograph, shift-click the Eyedropper tool on the photograph. That will create new RGB readouts in the Info window (upper right). I've placed four monitoring points in the photograph—in the woman's hair, on her neck, in the water, and in the sky. Those readouts will report the effects of Curves and other adjustments on those points no matter where I move the cursor. Each readout is showing the tonal values at its corresponding point in the original photograph and what those values will become after the Curves adjustment at the lower right.

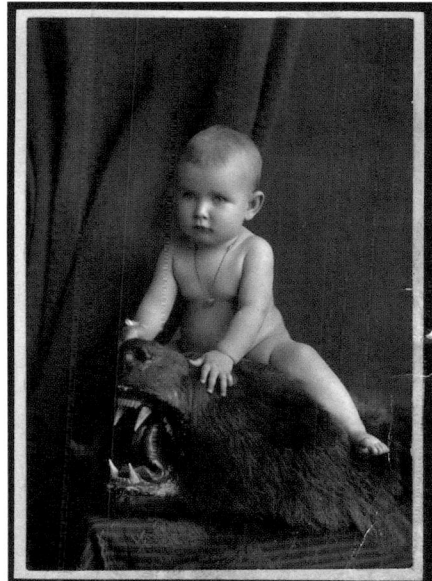 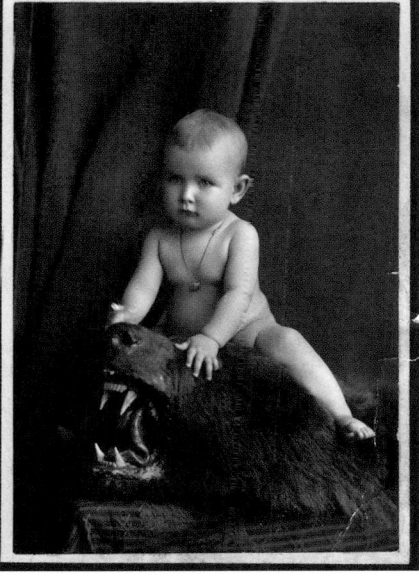

Fig. 5-17 These two photographs contained exactly the same total range of tones; the tones are just distributed a little differently between them. The photograph on the right looks more brilliant and contrasty because of the application of the Curves settings in Figure 5-18.

Fig. 5-18 This curve changes the photograph on the left in Figure 5-17 into the photo on the right. Notice that there's no change in the black and white end points, so the total tonal range portrayed in the two photographs is the same. I've added control points at the values 64 and 192 and adjusted those to reduce contrast a little bit in the highlights and shadows and increase contrast by about 20% in the midtones. What a difference that makes!

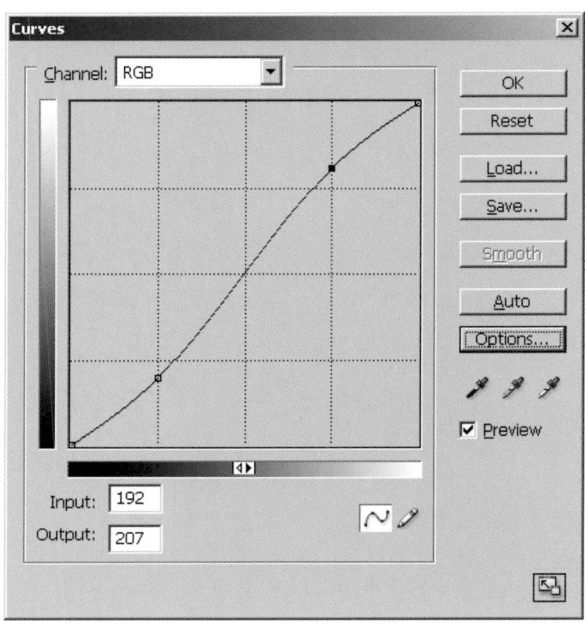

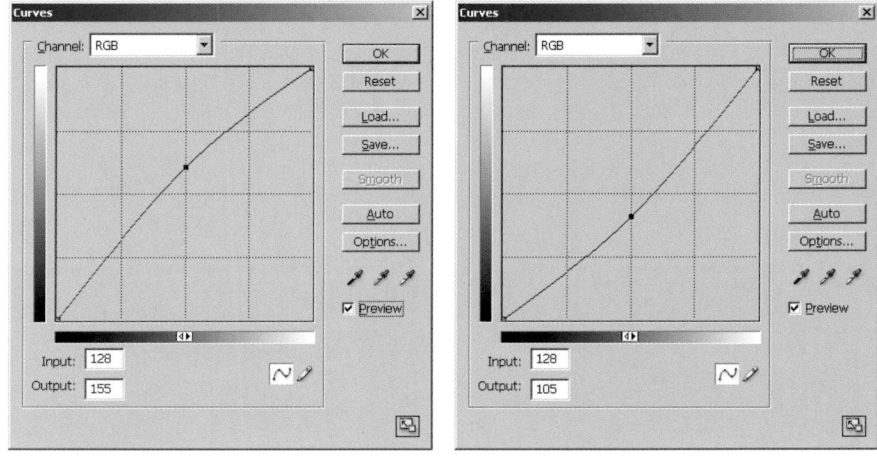

Fig. 5-19 Curves like these don't change the overall contrast or tonal range of a photograph, but they make it look markedly lighter or darker. Raising the midpoint of the curve (left) produces a much lighter, more open-looking photograph. Dropping the midpoint (right) makes the photograph darker and more somber in appearance. Figure 5-20 shows how both of these curves affect the original photograph in Figure 5-17.

HOW TO LIGHTEN OR DARKEN A PRINT WITH CURVES (continued)

makes those tones more clearly visible and distinguishable. Lowering the midpoint has exactly the opposite effect, increasing highlight contrast at the expense of shadow separation.

Sometimes you *will* want to change the black or white points. Remember how I told you to pull back a little bit on the scan and not make it too contrasty so you didn't accidentally clip off tones? That means that initially your blacks won't really be black but will be a very, very dark

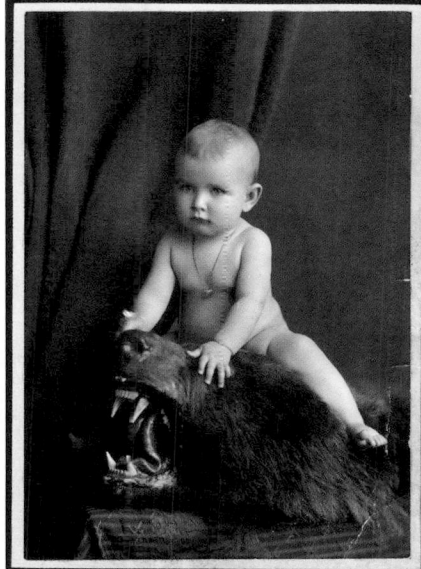
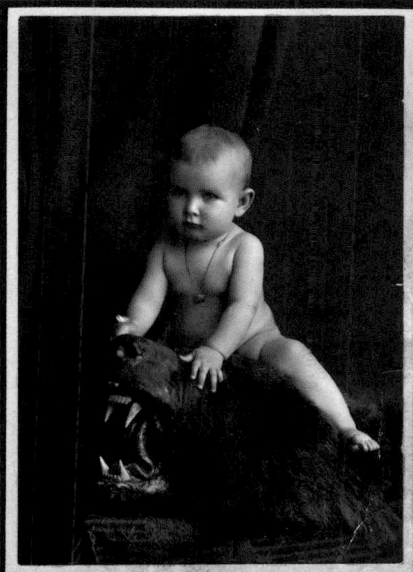

Fig. 5-20 The left photograph in this figure takes the leftmost photograph from Figure 5-17 and modifies it using the Curves settings in Figure 5-19, left. This opens up midtones and creates a more light, airy feel. Applying the Curves from Figure 5-19, right, instead increases the drama of the photograph on the right and gives it a more intense and "theatrical" look.

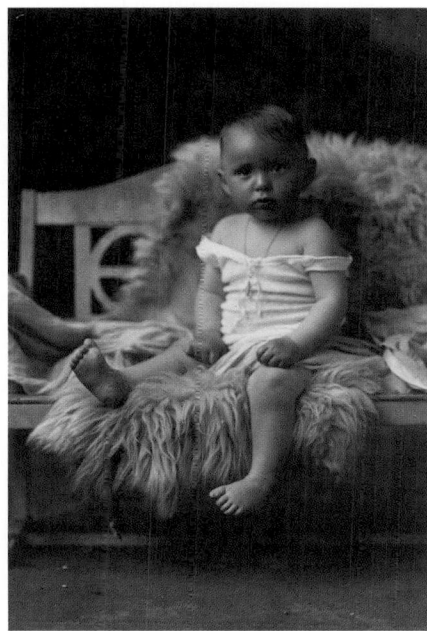
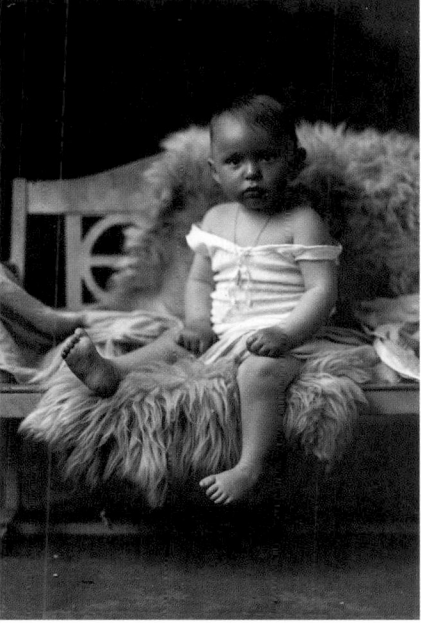

Fig. 5-21 The photograph on the left is too dark and too dull. The Curves adjustment in Figure 5-22 turned it into the photograph on the right. The histograms for the before and after photographs are also shown in Figure 5-22, on the right.

gray, and your whites will be fogged (Figure 5-21). At some point in the restoration process you'll fix them to place the "blacks" and "whites" exactly where you want them to be for a good-looking print. Curves can take care of that (Figure 5-22).

Sneak up on those end points cautiously. You don't want to throw away highlight or shadow detail that you'll need later. It's best to leave

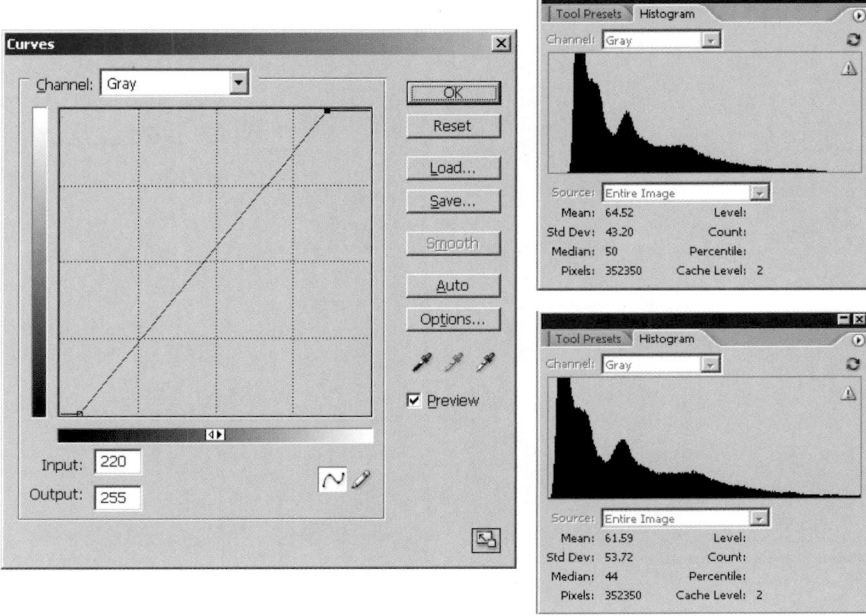

Fig. 5-22 This Curves adjustment increases both contrast and brightness. Moving the end points of the curve in raises the contrast. Adjusting those so that the midpoint of the curve is above the center point of the graph makes the photo lighter. This produces exactly the same result as could be obtained with a combination of Brightness and Levels tools. The histograms on the right represent the photograph before and after applying this Curves adjustment. The adjusted photograph makes much better use of the available tonal range than the unadjusted one.

the photograph a little too flat and grayish up until just before you want to print it out. Then you can adjust the end points of the curve to place the black and white values exactly where they need to be to give you a full-range print.

HOW TO BRING OUT SHADOW TONES WITH CURVES

Many faded prints have very poor contrast in the shadows. Even when you restore the overall contrast range of the print you may not have a good tonal separation in the darker areas. The curve in Figure 5-23 fixes that. I restricted the lightening effect by adding adjustment points along the curve to keep it from arcing upward overall, as did the curve in Figure 5-19, left. Locking down values near the highlights ensured that they didn't lose any contrast at all. It increases the contrast a lot in the shadows and sacrifices a little contrast in the other tones. It also makes the prints somewhat lighter overall (Figure 5-24).

HOW TO IMPROVE A COPY PRINT WITH CURVES

Heavily stained and copy prints (Figure 5-25) usually have poor highlight tone separation (you'll also see that in a very severely faded photograph). The curve in Figure 5-26 takes care of those problems. I've also applied other control points a la Figure 5-23 so that the rest of the

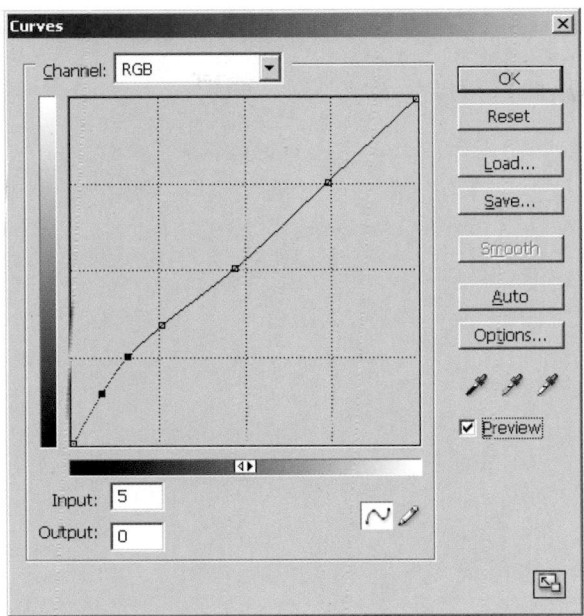

Fig. 5-23 This Curves adjustment greatly increases the contrast in the deepest shadows and lightens them up to bring out more detail, as shown in Figure 5-24. It does not affect the tonal range of the print, its overall contrast, or the brightness of the highlights. Note the multiple control points in the middle of the curve that keep the midtones and highlights close to their original values.

photograph doesn't become too much darker. I've darkened the middle-highlight tones considerably and at the same time dragged in the white point to restore the sparkle to the whites. The result is livelier and looks more like an original than a copy print.

HOW TO IMPROVE A COPY PRINT WITH CURVES (continued)

Now that we've covered some of the basic moves with Curves, let's look at some nifty tricks for improving tone. There's a lot more I can do to improve this copy photograph, and I cover that on page 151. First, I want to introduce a very powerful Photoshop tool for improving tonality.

The Shadow/Highlight Adjustment

This may well be the most underrated feature in Photoshop. The Shadow/Highlight adjustment is an amazing (and complicated) control that improves the contrast and visibility of detail in both highlights and shadows. What makes it amazing is that it can do that without destroying midtone contrast.

Problems can arise when you want to improve both shadows and highlights at the same time. You'd do that with a curve like the one shown in Figure 5-27. This kind of curve shape, called a "reverse-S," expands the contrast in the highlights and shadows but compresses tones and contrast in the midrange.

Subtle adjustments like this work well. I used a much less aggressive version of this kind of curve to improve Figure 1-2. That photograph

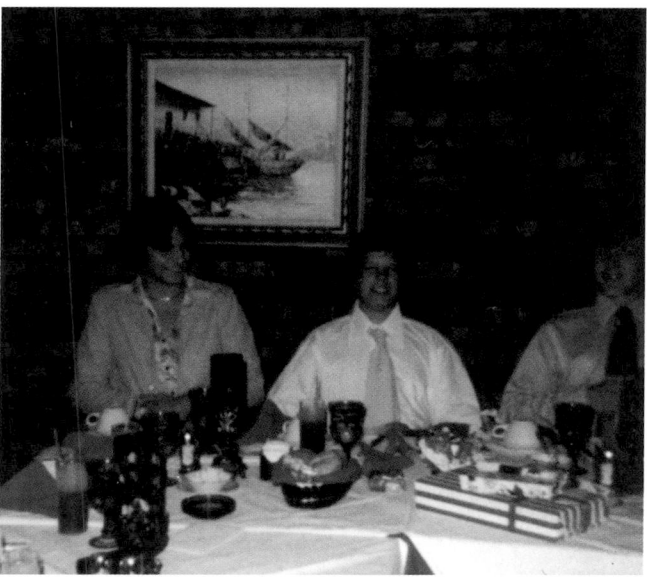

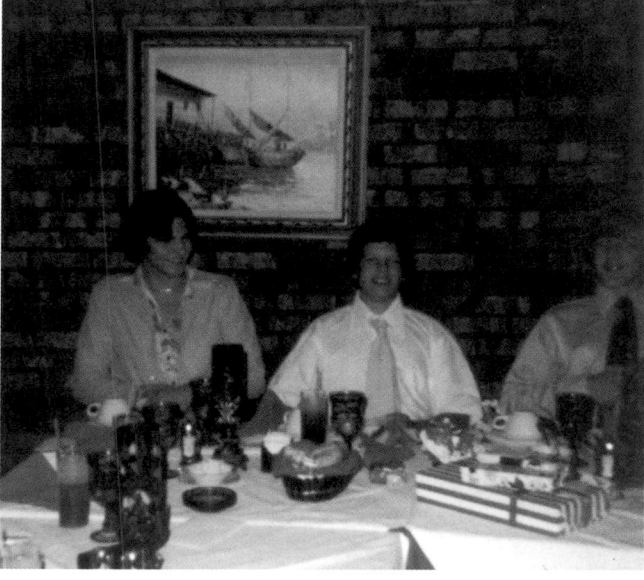

Fig. 5-24 The original photograph (top) has a lot of important subject detail buried in the shadows. The middle-to-dark tones are a little too contrasty; this is most obvious in the subjects' faces. The Curves adjustment in Figure 5-23 created the lower photograph. A lot more shadow detail is visible, and contrast in the darker midtones is greatly improved.

is typical of amateur photographs; there's a lot of midrange contrast, and the tones in the highlights and the shadows are pushed toward black and white. Consequently, highlight and shadow detail is obscured. Almost every amateur photograph suffers this to some degree; somewhat blown-out highlights and blocked-up shadows are practically hallmarks of the snapshot.

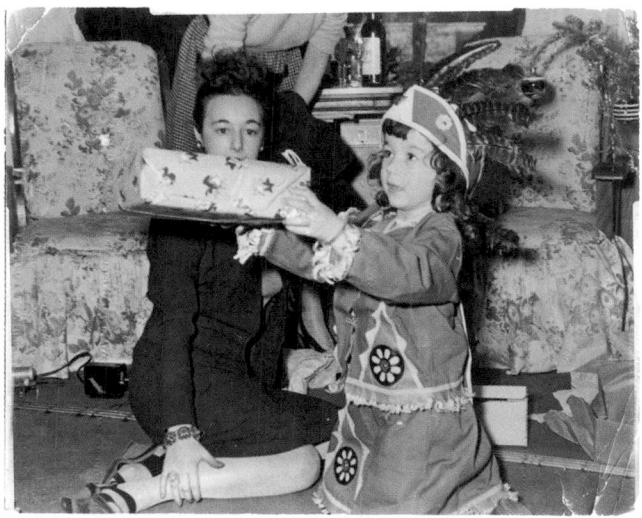

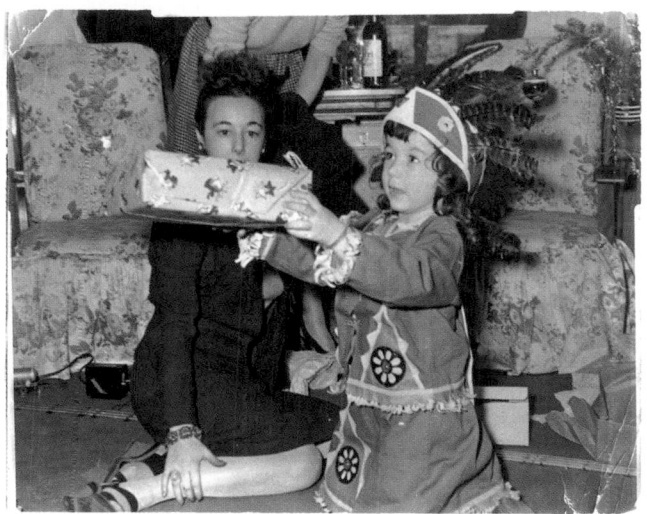

Fig. 5-25 Copy prints, like the upper photograph, usually have flat, dull highlights, with poor contrast and grayish whites. The Curves adjustment in Figure 5-26 improves these quite a bit (bottom photograph).

Copy photographs also have especially bad tonal separation in the highlights and shadows, where the contrast will be extremely low. It may take strong changes to bring out good shadow and highlight detail. But strong changes like those of Figure 5-27 don't usually produce attractive results. The midtones become so compressed and low in contrast that the print looks flat and lifeless.

By way of example, I applied this Curves adjustment to the slide restoration I did in Example 4 of Chapter 10. When I did that restoration, I chose not to change the overall tonality of the photograph because I wanted to preserve the original "amateur" quality of on-camera flash in

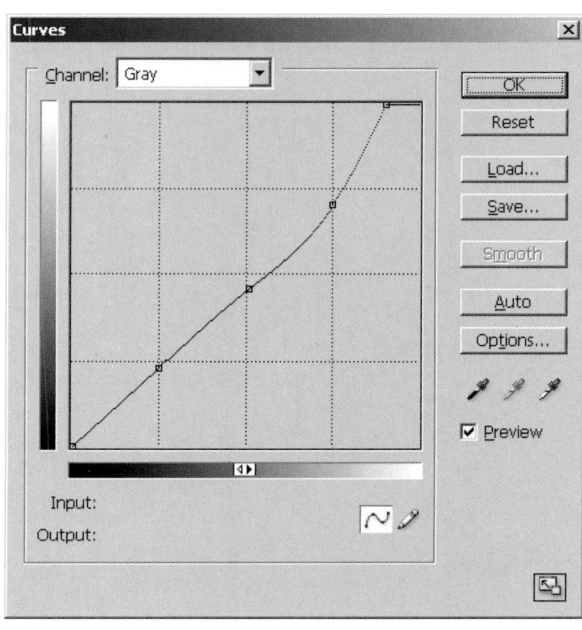

Fig. 5-26 This curve increases contrast in the highlights and restores the whites, without having much effect on the midtones and shadows. As with Figure 5-23, I've used multiple control points to minimize changes to those tones (in the shadows) that I want unchanged.

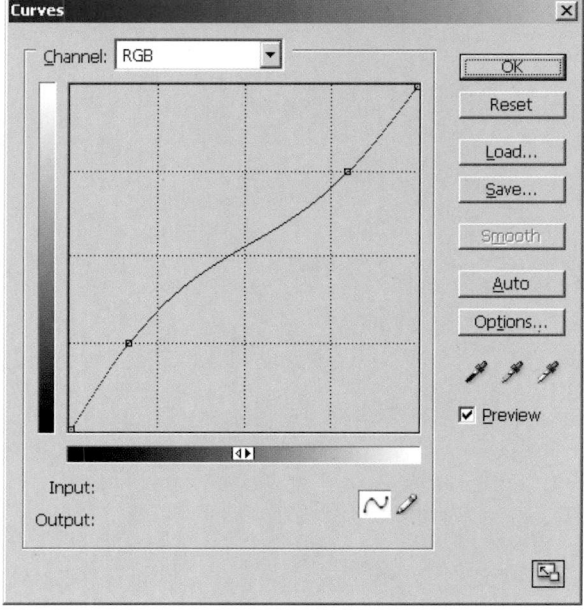

Fig. 5-27 This Curves adjustments doesn't alter the total tonal range of the photo, but it increases contrast and separation in both the highlights and the shadows at the same time. In consequence, midtone contrast is reduced. That can make a print look lifeless, as shown in Figure 5-28, so use adjustments like this carefully.

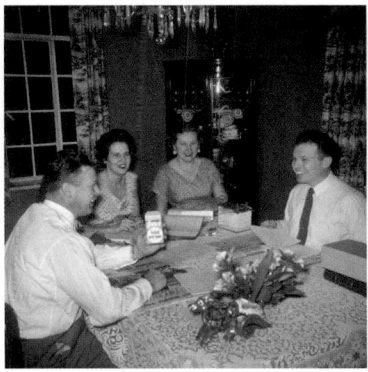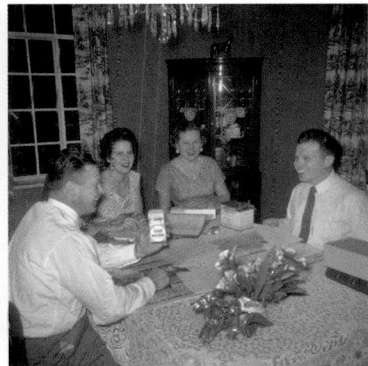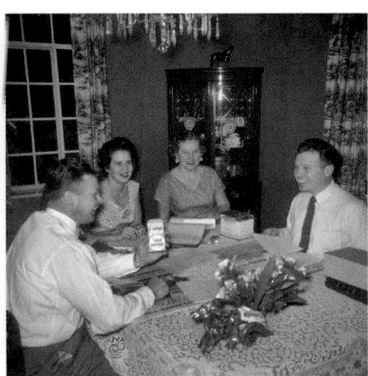

Fig. 5-28 This figure shows how the reverse-S Curves adjustment in Figure 5-27 and the Shadow/Highlight tool improve shadow and highlight detail. The photograph on the left is the unaltered version. The photograph in the middle shows the effect of the Curves adjustment. You see better detail in the highlights and shadows, but the midtones look unnaturally flat. The Shadow/Highlight adjustment from Figure 5-29 does a much better job of bringing in highlight and shadow detail without ruining the midtones (right).

the 1950s (Figure 5-28, left). That was an artistic choice and a completely arbitrary one; I could have just as well decided to give the photograph a more professional look. That would require toning the harsh highlights down and bringing out the details that were lost in the shadows. Curves can do that (Figure 5-28, middle), but look at what happens to the midtones, most obviously in the tablecloth and in the people's faces. They look very flat and artificial, as if someone just painted the tones and colors onto the photograph.

Figure 5-28, right, shows what miracles Shadow/Highlight can work. The highlights have more details, and the shadows are more open with better color and saturation than in the Curves-altered version, without destroying the midtones. The faces and the tablecloth look just as lifelike and natural as they did in the original version, yet somehow the overall contrast of the photographs is moderated. It almost looks like it was lit professionally.

The Shadow/Highlight adjustment can do this because it doesn't blindly apply curves changes to the entire photograph. It analyzes the tones present in the photograph and selectively works on areas of highlights and of shadows but leaves midtone areas alone. Figure 5-29 shows the adjustment with the settings I used. Separate sets of sliders are used for adjusting the shadows, adjusting the highlights, and maintaining midtone contrast and color saturation.

As I said, this is a complicated control. I'll describe what the sliders do in the next several paragraphs, but don't be surprised if this description is very confusing. The way to understand what this tool does is to play with it and look at how the preview changes when you move the sliders around. The explanation I'll provide will help you figure out *why*

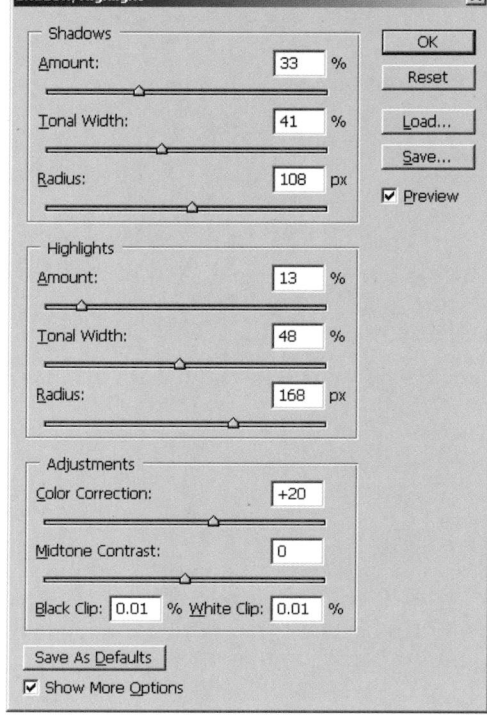

Fig. 5-29 Photoshop's Shadow/Highlight tool does an excellent job of improving tones and enhancing detail in highlights and shadows, almost like dodging and burning in a print in the darkroom. This adjustment was applied to the photograph in Figure 5-28, right. See the main text for an explanation of what the different control settings do.

moving a slider has the effect it does, but messing around with this adjustment on your computer is the only way to understand it.

Starting at the top of the Shadows section, there's a slider for Amount. That controls the strength of the adjustment, with 0% being no effect on the shadows at all. In this case I applied a moderate 33% effect to bring out the background detail. The next slider, Tonal Width, controls the range of tones over which the effect is applied. Set it near 0%, and only the tones very close to the darkest ones will be affected. Set it near 100%, and almost all the tones in the photograph will be lightened.

The last Shadows slider, Radius, controls how wide an area the adjustment samples to determine what range of tones to correct. This is the part that is smart enough to figure out how to leave the mid-tones alone. The adjustment takes into account all the tones within a radius to find out which ones are the shadow tones that should be adjusted.

The Highlights sliders work the same way. The only difference is that the highlight tone width is measured starting from white and working down, instead of from black and working up. Most often you'll apply only a very small amount of highlight correction. The 13% I used results in a pretty potent effect.

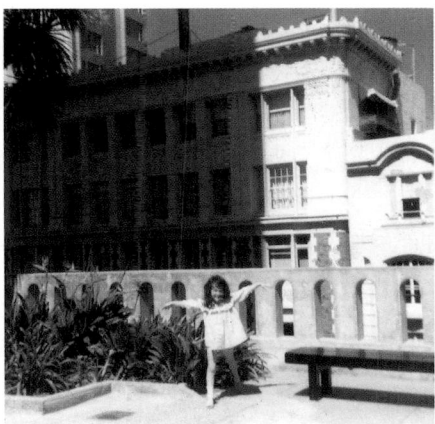 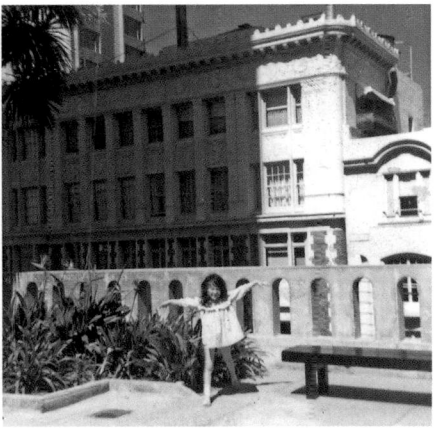

Fig. 5-30 Amateur snapshots are often contrasty, with poor detail in the highlights and shadows. The Shadow/Highlight adjustment from Figure 5-31 greatly improves this photo's tonality (right).

The last set of controls ensures that the shadow and highlight adjustments don't make the image look too dull. The Color Correction slider controls the saturation in the areas being altered. It doesn't have any effect if you're working on a B&W photograph. Midtone Contrast does about what you'd think—it's a way to control how snappy the print looks in the midrange. To some degree, it counteracts the effect of the Shadows and Highlights adjustments, so use it sparingly. If you get good at setting the Shadows and Highlights sliders, you'll need to make only very slight midtone contrast corrections. The Midtone Contrast slider is very useful for fine-tuning the look of the photograph after you've set the shadow and highlight corrections.

Figure 5-30 shows a more typical use for the Shadow/Highlight adjustment to correct this snapshot from 1970. The settings I used are shown in Figure 5-31; I circled the three settings that are different from Photoshop's default settings. Because I was primarily interested in improving the highlight detail, I pulled back the shadow amount to 17% and turned the highlight amount up to 15%. I boosted the contrast in the midtones by nine points so they have a little more clarity. That's how little it took to produce the marked improvement you can see in this photograph. This level of improvement in family snapshots would make many clients very happy.

✓ HOW TO IMPROVE SNAPSHOTS WITH THE SHADOW/ HIGHLIGHT ADJUSTMENT

How to Improve a Copy Print

Let's return to the copy photograph from Figure 5-25, reproduced in Figure 5-32a. Ignoring the matter of repairing the physical damage, what will most improve this photograph? The histogram in Figure 5-33 shows that the print lacks good whites and blacks. Looking at the print itself, it's very clear that tonal separation is weak in both the highlights and the shadows.

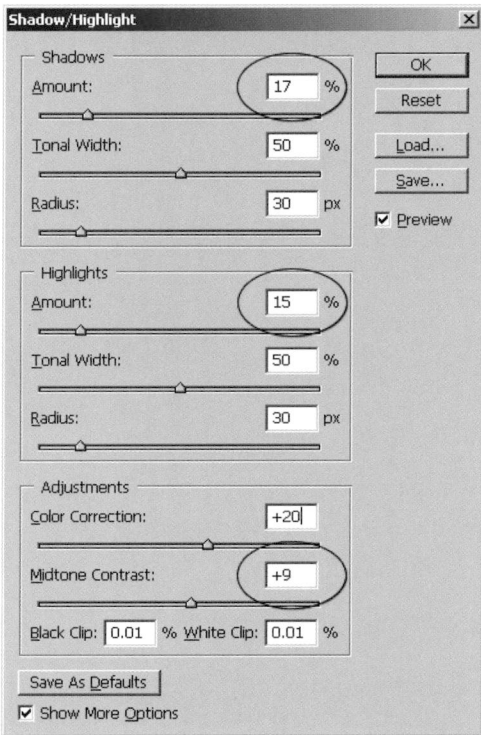

Fig. 5-31 This Shadow/Highlight adjustment was used to improve the photograph in Figure 5-30. All of the control settings are the default ones except for those that are circled. Their function is explained in the main text.

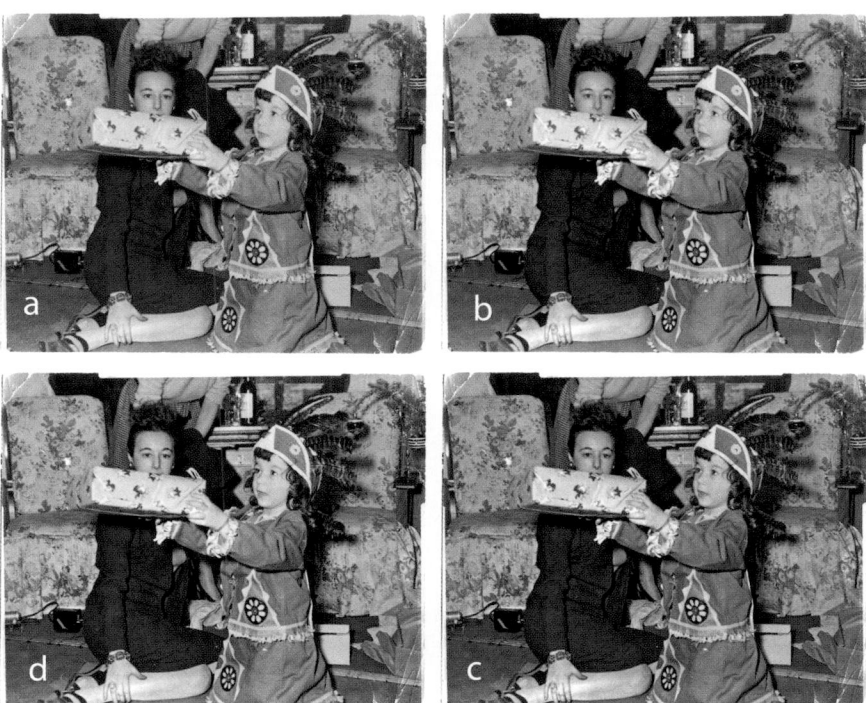

Fig. 5-32 There are several ways to improve a copy photograph, like the one in figure (a). You can use Curves (b), the Shadows/Highlight tool (c), or a combination of the two (d). My personal favorite is (d), but they're all good.

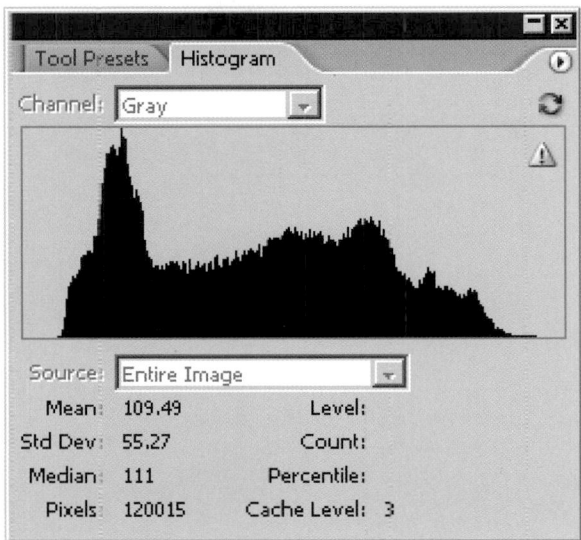

Fig. 5-33 This is the histogram for Figure 5-32a. The blacks should be a little darker, and there's a very pronounced lack of bright highlight detail.

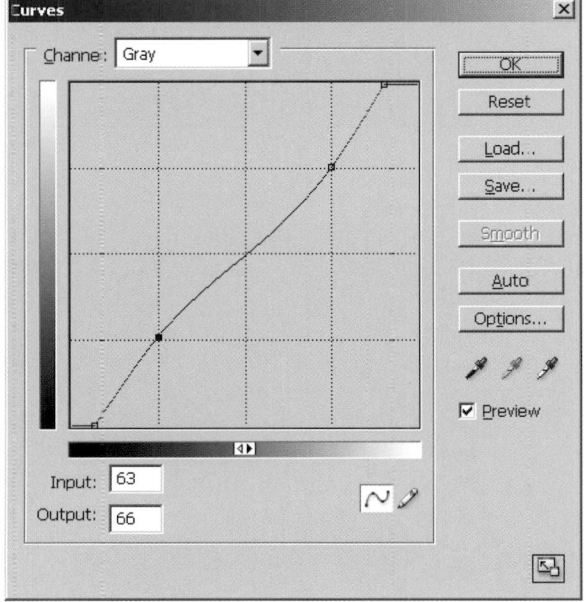

Fig. 5-34 This Curves adjustments produced Figure 5-32b. I pulled in the end points of the curve to make the blacks blacker and the whites whiter, increasing the overall contrast of the photograph. The two other control points on the curve increase the contrast of the highlight and shadow detail at the same time that they bring the midrange contrast back to normal. This curve adds a lot of tonal separation to the highlights and shadows without making the print look too harsh overall.

The curve in Figure 5-34 is the most straightforward fix. I've pulled in the white and black points so that the photograph has some true whites and blacks. Then I added control points that gave the curve a reverse-S shape that increased contrast in the highlights and shadows in exchange for some midtone contrast. That produced Figure 5-32b, which is much improved over the original. Still, I wouldn't mind opening up the shadows more and restoring some of the lost midtone contrast.

✓ HOW TO IMPROVE A COPY PRINT WITH THE CURVES AND SHADOW/HIGHLIGHT ADJUSTMENTS

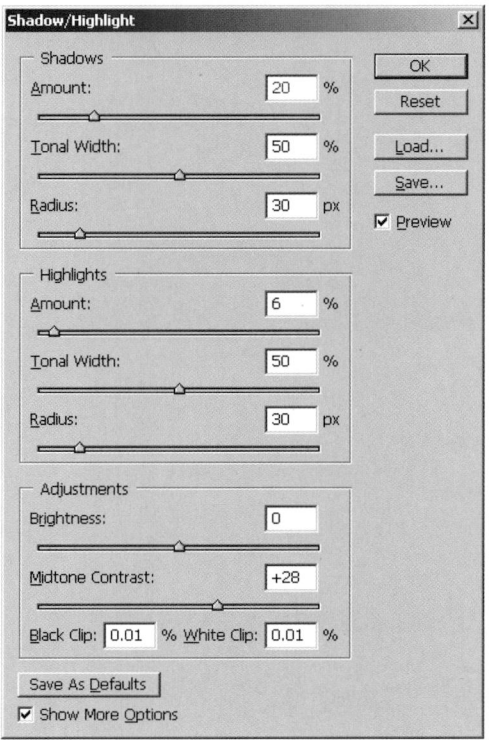

Fig. 5-35 This Shadow/ Highlight adjustment produced Figure 5-32c. The overall tonality is not a lot different, but there's a better sense of separation and detail throughout the tonal range, even in the midtones. Note the hefty boost to Midtone Contrast (+28 points) in the control settings; that's what keeps the snap in the midtones.

HOW TO IMPROVE A COPY PRINT WITH THE CURVES AND SHADOW/HIGHLIGHT ADJUSTMENTS (continued)

That's a job for the Shadow/Highlight adjustment (Figure 5-35). I throttled back the shadow amount to 20%, added a 6% highlight amount to keep them from getting blown out, and increased the midtone contrast by a substantial 28 points. That took me to Figure 5-32c.

There are ways in which I like that a lot better, but overall the photograph now feels "busy" to me; it has lost too much visual focus. Maybe I did too good a job of equalizing contrast over the entire tonal range. So I tried a less aggressive tack for equalizing contrast. Starting with the original, I applied the curves from Figure 5-36. This is just a straight overall contrast increase; I pulled in the white and black points to increase the density range in the photograph, but I didn't reshape the curve to alter the relative contrast of the highlights, midtones, and shadows. Then I applied the Shadow/Highlight adjustment shown in Figure 5-37. This opened up the shadows and toned down highlights just a little bit. Since I hadn't flattened out the midtones with the curves, I didn't need to increase their contrast very much. The result is Figure 5-32d. Personally, this is my favorite of the three improved versions. There's room for further refinements, but for many clients, you could stop right here; this is a good-looking photograph.

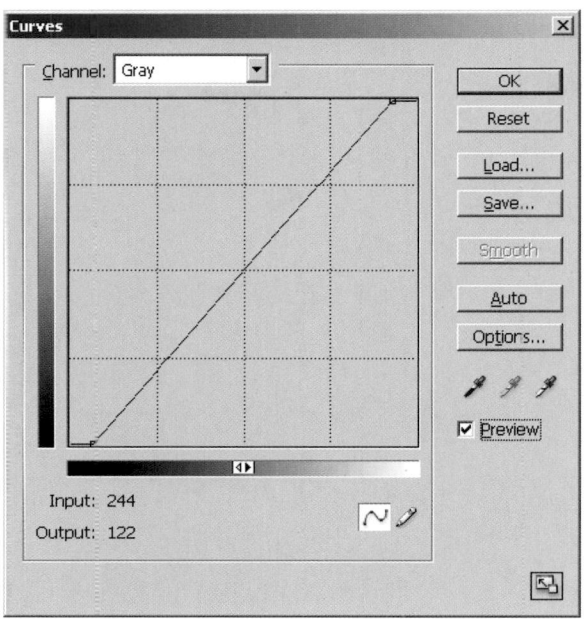

Fig. 5-36 I applied this Curves adjustment to Figure 5-32a as the first stage in producing Figure 5-32d. This curve causes a modest contrast increase and makes the blacks a little darker and the highlights a little whiter.

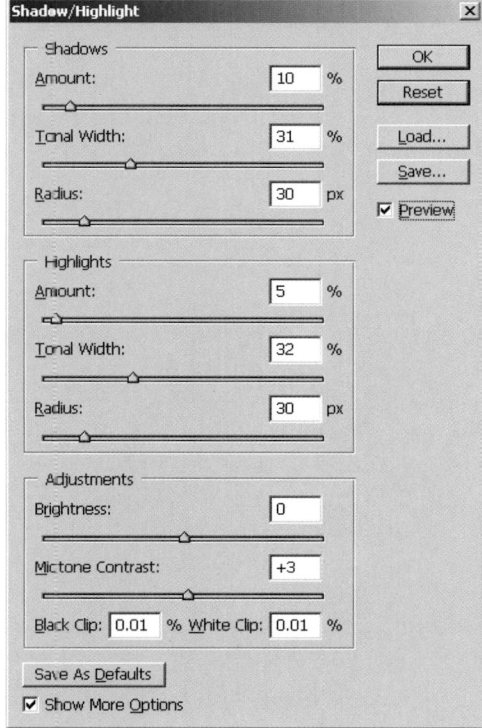

Fig. 5-37 This Shadow/Highlight adjustment takes the photograph that resulted from the Curves adjustments made by Figure 5-36 and yields Figure 5-32d. Notice that there's only a slight Midtone Contrast increase; that's because the previous Curves adjustment took care of most of the overall contrast change needed. The Shadow/Highlight adjustment kicks up the detail in the highlights and shadows just enough to make the resulting photograph look like an original print instead of a copy print.

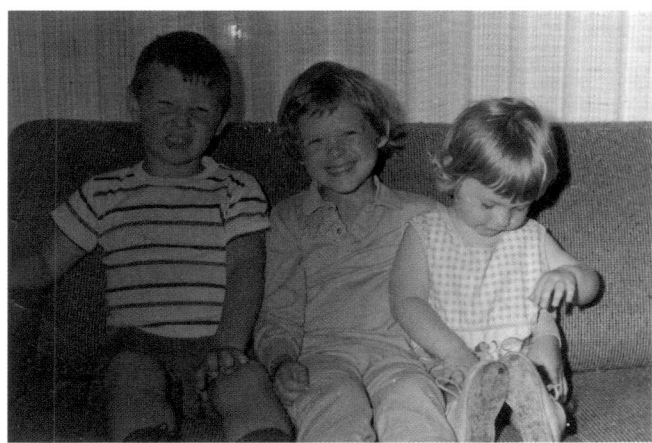

Fig. 5-38 This photograph is an amateur blunder: The camera's flash sync was incorrect, so only the right side of the photograph got a full flash exposure. I can fix this with a masked Curves adjustment layer.

Why did I bother including the other two versions if this is the one I like best? Because, they're all good; they just appeal to different tastes. This harks back to points I made in Chapter 1. First, good restoration is about art and aesthetics, about constructing the image that looks like a *good* photograph to you, not just mechanically correcting errors. Second, there's value in playing around. Trying out different settings and controls to see what they get you is the best way to get to the photograph you really like. Single-mindedness is not a virtue.

How to Correct Uneven Exposure

The photograph in Figure 5-38 is not badly faded, but it was very badly made! Aside from the usual low-contrast printing typical of B&W photofinishing in the mid-20th century, it was improperly exposed. The flash sync on the camera was set incorrectly, so only the right side of the picture got good flash exposure.

HOW TO CORRECT
UNEVEN EXPOSURE
WITH A CURVES
ADJUSTMENT LAYER

The easiest and best way to correct uneven exposure like this is with a Curves adjustment layer combined with a mask to control what parts of the picture are altered. You create an adjustment layer by going to the Layer menu, selecting "New Adjustment Layer" from the drop-down menu, and picking the kind of layer you want to create (Curves, in this case).

While creating the Curves adjustment layer, I didn't make any curve changes. When the Curves tool opened up, I merely clicked "OK." I did that because I wanted to first create a mask for that layer so that the properly exposed part of the picture wouldn't be changed. That way, when I experiment with different curve settings to correct the left side of the photograph I can see how well I'm matching the right side.

I set my foreground and background colors to white and black and selected the Gradient tool (Figure 5-39). I chose "Foreground to Back-

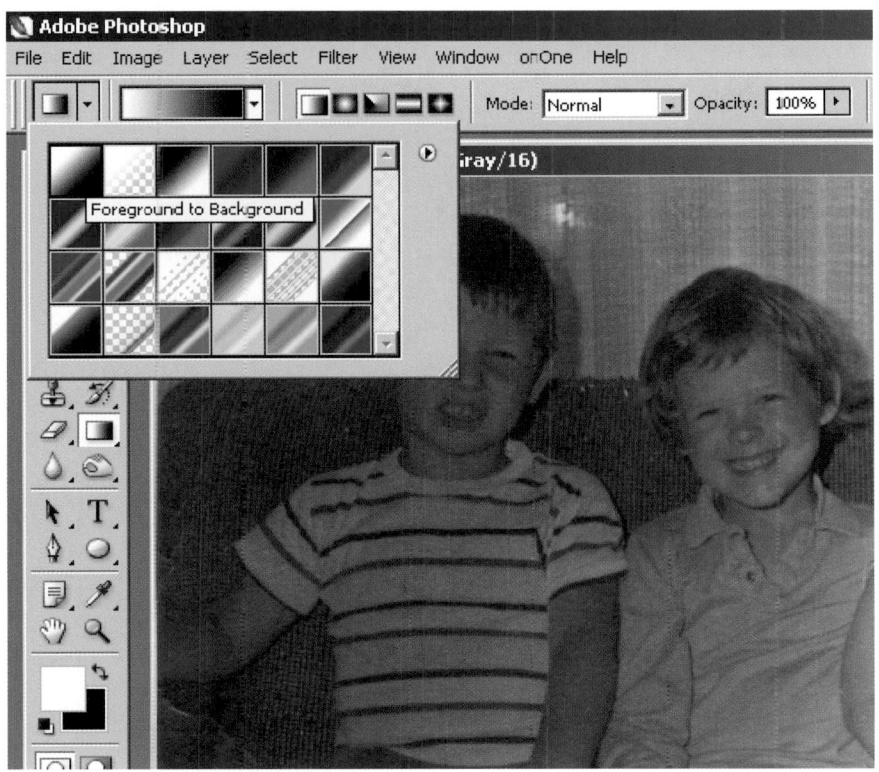

**HOW TO CORRECT
UNEVEN EXPOSURE
WITH A CURVES
ADJUSTMENT LAYER**
(continued)

Fig. 5-39 Making a gradient mask for the adjustment layer for Figure 5-38 isn't difficult. Set the foreground and background colors to white and black, select "Foreground to Background" from the gradient options, and draw a line with the gradient tool across the photograph from where you want the gradient to start to where you want it to end (Figure 5-40).

ground" as the gradient type, made sure that the linear gradient button was pressed, and left the mode normal and the opacity 100%. I created the gradient by drawing a horizontal gradient line from left to right, starting under the baby girl's nose and extending almost to the boy's arm. That was my best guess of where the exposure fall-off began and ended (Figure 5-40). The black area on the right side of the gradient is completely masked off; there the adjustment layer has no effect. As the gradient fades to white, the effect of the adjustment layer increases until it becomes 100% for the left portion of the picture.

The advantage of doing this with an adjustment layer and a mask is that I don't have to get this correct on the first try; I just have to make a usefully close guess. If I discover that this won't give me the uniform exposure correction I'm after, I can modify or replace the gradient in the Curves mask channel. Now I'm ready to correct the exposure.

I didn't do anything fancy to come up with the adjustment layer's curve in Figure 5-41. I just moved in the white point until the highlights looked about the same on both sides of the photograph in the preview. Then I dragged in the black point until the shadows looked similarly dark. That left the midtones on the left side a little too dark, so I added ▼

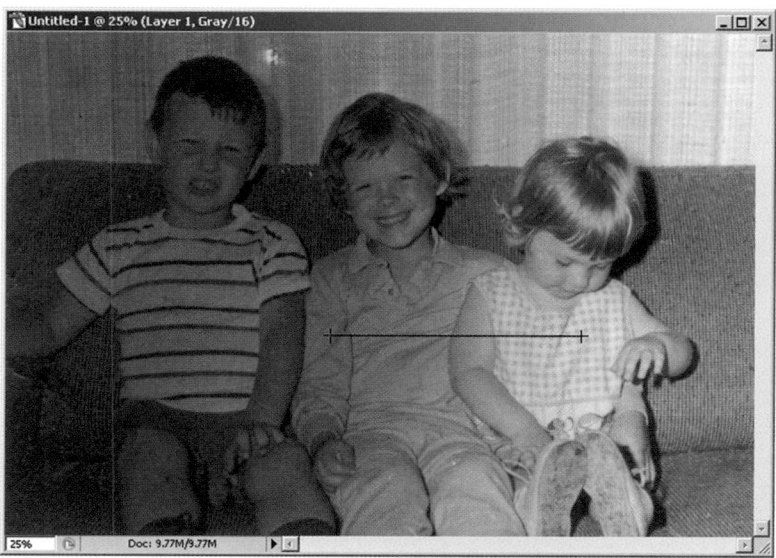

Fig. 5-40 I estimate that the flash fade-out starts just under the littlest girl's nose and ends on the right side of the older girl. Drawing a line with the gradient tool from left to right between those points produces the gradient mask shown underneath the photograph.

HOW TO CORRECT UNEVEN EXPOSURE WITH A CURVES ADJUSTMENT LAYER (continued)

a center point to the curve and raised it up a bit to lighten those tones so that they matched on both sides of the photograph.

Figure 5-42 shows the results of my efforts. My first attempt at a gradient mask turned out to be pretty good. There's a slightly darkened band between the two girls where the Curves adjustment wasn't quite strong enough. I fixed that by lightening up the mask along a vertical band in that area. I just painted a stripe down the mask with a wide-radius white airbrush set to 5% opacity, nothing fancier than that.

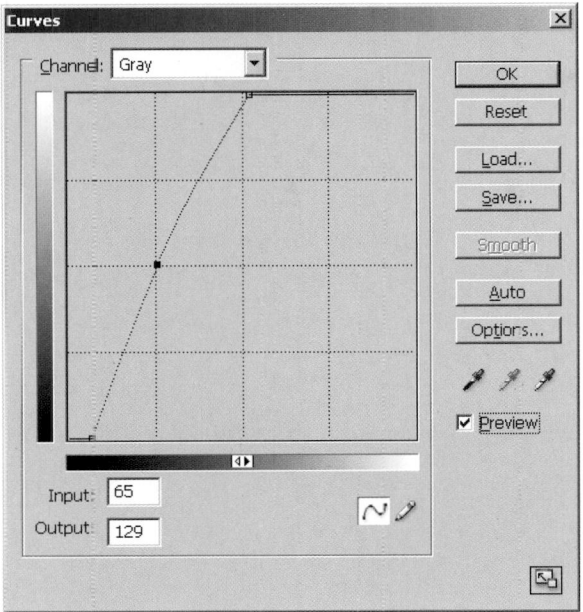

Fig. 5-41 This adjustment layer curve turns Figure 5-38 into Figure 5-42. It greatly increases the contrast in the underexposed parts of the photograph and changes the dim grays into light highlights.

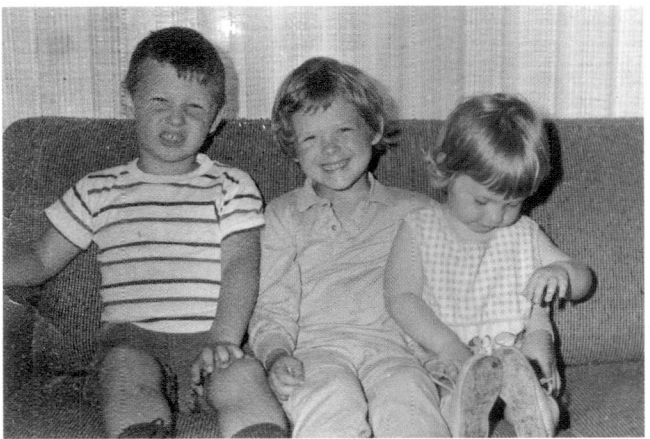

Fig. 5-42 Here's Figure 5-38 after I've added the masked Curves adjustment layer to it. The illumination is much more even; there is still a bit of a darker band between the two girls.

It was only a slight correction; Figure 5-43 shows the original gradient mask in the top half and the airbrushed mask in the bottom half. The alteration is so subtle, in fact, that I'm not attempting to reproduce the difference it made to the photograph in the pages of this book. I bring it up only to illustrate the level of refinement that's easily achievable when you use these kinds of masks.

Figure 5-42 isn't anywhere close to being a finished restoration. Overall the tonality is bad and the huge contrast increase I did to the left side of the photograph enhanced defects like paper texture and

Fig. 5-43 Masks are modifiable! To get rid of the dark band between the two girls in Figure 5-42, I dodged the mask to lighten it up in that region. That increased the strength of the adjustment layer there, which eliminated the dark band.

cracks. Considerable work would be needed to turn this into a good restoration, but evening out the exposure was the critical first step.

By the way, this is a good example of a photograph that must be scanned in 16-bit mode. The contrast adjustment I made to the left side of the photograph threw away almost two-thirds of the value range. Expanding an 8-bit image's contrast by a factor of three would produce very visible and unacceptable contours.

Repairing Uneven Density: Dodge and Burn with Masked Adjustment Layers

It's not much of a conceptual leap from using gradient masks to control local photograph densities to using any kind of mask, including hand-painted ones.

Hand-painted masks are uniquely valuable because they let you apply correction effects exactly where you want them. The effect can be as broad as half a photograph or as narrow as a single pixel; it's just a matter of what radius brush you use to paint the mask with.

You can apply any kind of Curves alteration you want this way, but I'm going to concentrate on the two most useful ones. I call them "dodging" and "burning-in" masks (and layers) because they produce effects a lot like those of dodging and burning-in when doing darkroom printing. Unlike darkroom printing, however, you can have as many different dodge and burn-in effects going on as you want by creating a new adjustment layer for each particular flavor of alteration you want to make.

Even better, any dodging or burning-in you do is reversible. If you find you've overdone the correction at some point, just paint over that part of the mask with a black brush to reduce or eliminate the change there. In other words, this requires no painterly skills. The better you

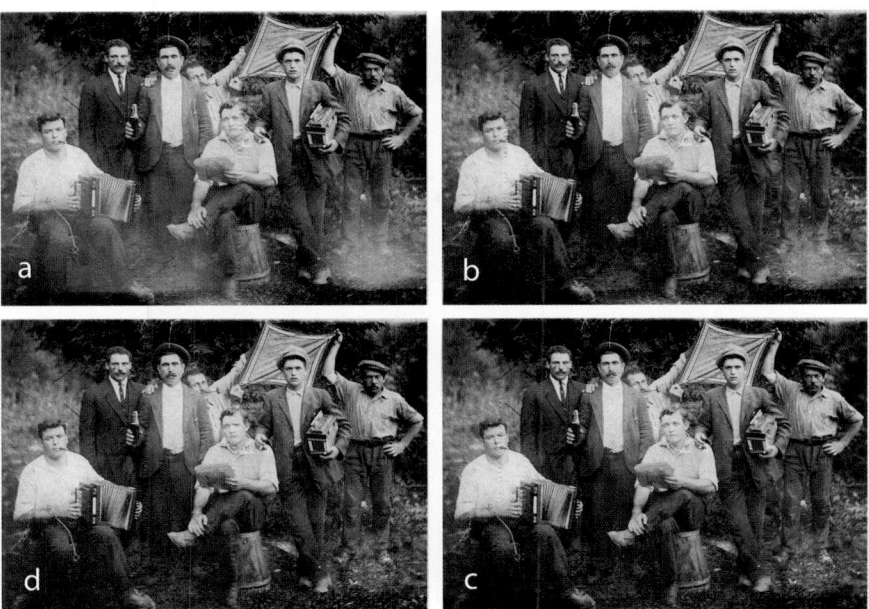

Fig. 5-44 Figure (a) shows a scan of a poor photograph I received from a client. The original negative suffered from some light leaks during exposure, so this photograph has large washed-out spots in the lower half that reduce contrast and ruin the shadows. Dodging and burning-in Curves adjustment layers, explained in the main text, are the keys to repairing this damage. Figure (b) was created by a burn-in adjustment layer that used the Curves and mask shown in Figures 5-45 and 5-46, respectively. Figure (c) added a second burn-in adjustment layer that used Figures 5-47 and 5-48. Figure (d) incorporated a dodging adjustment layer using Figures 5-49 and 5-50.

are with wielding a (digital) brush, the more efficiently you'll be able to do this, but you can erase or rework any mistakes you make, so you'll always be able to get there bit by refined bit.

Good dodging and burning-in curves are hugely exaggerated versions of the kinds of basic curve corrections I talked about earlier in this chapter. They're intentionally super-strong so that you can paint them into the layer mask with a low-opacity brush, building up the changes you want stroke by stroke in a controllable way.

The photograph in Figure 5-44a is a good candidate for burning-in and dodging. The original negative was apparently light-fogged. Large parts of the lower half of the photograph are washed out and pale, although low-contrast detail is visible in those areas.

For the first round of repairs on this image I created a Curves adjustment layer with the curve shown in Figure 5-45. This extreme correction greatly increases the contrast and density of any tones below light gray. I designed this curve to produce such a strong change that it could fix the flare problem in all but the worst spots. It doesn't matter that it's too strong for most of the photograph because I'll be painting in the adjustment only where I want it at the strength I want.

✓ HOW TO DO DODGING AND BURNING-IN WITH MASKED CURVES ADJUSTMENT LAYERS

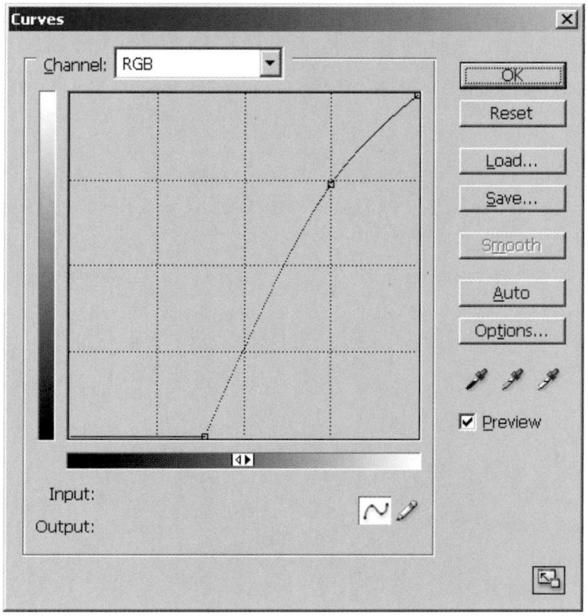

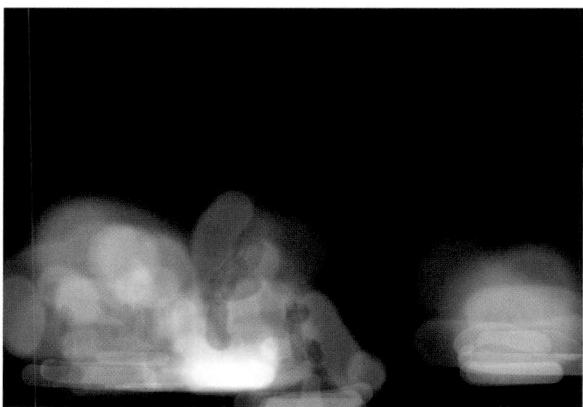

Fig. 5-45 This Curves adjustment has little effect on the highlights but substantially darkens everything else. It's strong enough to correct the near-worst of the flare when applied at 100%.

Fig. 5-46 This is what the burn-in mask looks like for the Curves adjustment layer I created from Figure 5-45. It eliminates almost all of the flare on the left and about half the flare on the right in Figure 5-44b.

HOW TO DO DODGING AND BURNING-IN WITH MASKED CURVES ADJUSTMENT LAYERS (continued)

Next, I inverted the layer mask to make it black instead of white. I selected the Brush tool and gave it a radius about two-thirds the size of the largest areas I wanted to burn in. I set the opacity of the brush to 12%; I've found that values between 8% and 15% work best for doing dodging or burning-in. I did not turn on the mask layer visibility. There's no need to see what the mask layer looks like, only the effect of the brush on the photograph.

I made a couple of passes at the mask layer with the large-radius brush to dampen the overall flare. Then I switched to a smaller radius brush and started filling in the places the large radius brush had missed.

When that was close to correct, I switched to an even smaller radius brush to touch up the areas that still needed to be toned down. If I went too far and made an area too dark, I switched the brush from white to black and painted some of the mask back in to reduce the overadjustment in that area.

I find that working back and forth between black and white brushes like this and shrinking the radius of the brush as I refine the adjustments is a very efficient way to do this kind of painting. I think this is just my style, though. If you want to take a different approach to painting in the mask, do whatever feels most comfortable and efficient for you.

Only a few minutes' work got the photograph to Figure 5-44b. The burn-in mask is shown in Figure 5-46. It looks strange, doesn't it! Still, it does the job and does it well.

I created a second burn-in adjustment layer to deal with the flare patches that the first layer didn't entirely fix, mainly a flare spot at the lower right corner of the photograph. I assigned that layer the curve in Figure 5-47. It darkens most of the tones but also greatly increases contrast in the lighter areas, so it could make the flare spots both darker and more contrasty and even improve the whites a bit. The burn-in mask in Figure 5-48 got me to Figure 5-44c.

Next, I needed to do some dodging along the lower edge of the photograph where there was a very dark strip. I created a third adjustment layer with the curve in Figure 5-49. This curve leaves the black point unchanged but extremely lightens everything else. When I was done dodging the dark areas that needed correction, shown in the mask in Figure 5-50, I had Figure 5-44d.

That finished the technical correction I set out to make. I still saw room for improvement. Dodging and burning-in layers are useful for artistic work as well, just as dodging and burning-in in the darkroom are. They're a much better tool for artistic control than the simple, crude Dodge and Burn tools built into Photoshop, as my final corrections demonstrate.

In Figure 5-44d. I felt that several of the faces and the white clothing were too washed out. I wanted to increase their contrast and make them darker, but I didn't want the highlights to go gray. In fact, I wanted the highlights to be a little brighter.

I created my final masked correction layer with the curve in Figure 5-51. Although I instinctively tend to think of this as burning-in, because overall it makes the faces look darker, it really is unlike ordinary burning-in. Most of the tones are darkened, it's true, but the near-whites are substantially brightened because I dragged the white point in from a value of 255 to 227. So, at the same time that I'm burning in the highlights, I'm also improving their contrast and preserving whites. That's impossible to do with the Photoshop Burn tool; its midtone range setting has little effect on highlights, and the highlight setting grays out everything, including whites.

HOW TO DO DODGING AND BURNING-IN WITH MASKED CURVES ADJUSTMENT LAYERS (continued)

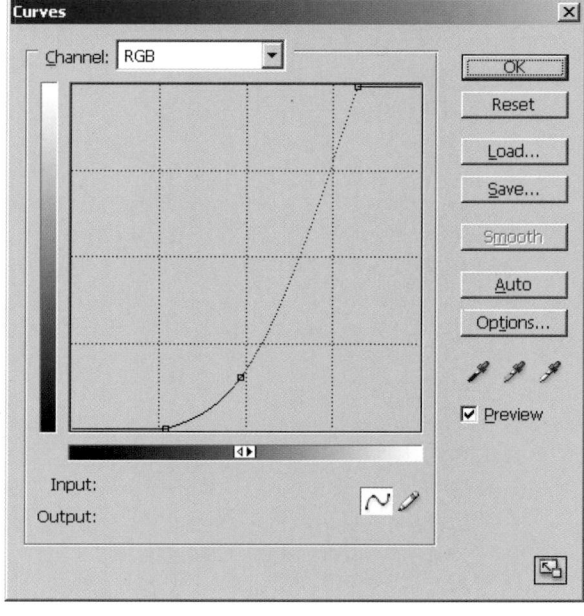

Fig. 5-47 This is the Curves adjustment for the second burn-in layer. It works much like the first burn-in layer, except that the lighter tones have been pushed toward white to increase the contrast everywhere in the tonal scale.

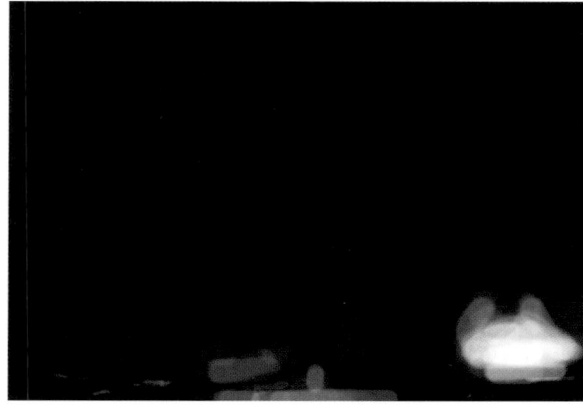

Fig. 5-48 This burn-in mask uses the Curves adjustment in Fig. 5-47 to produce Figure 5-44c. It corrects the flare and light leaks that remained after applying the first burn-in layer.

HOW TO DO DODGING AND BURNING-IN WITH MASKED CURVES ADJUSTMENT LAYERS (continued)

After another few minutes' work, I had the mask shown in Figure 5-52 and the corrected photograph shown in Figure 5-53. The dodging and burning-in layers have completely corrected all the unevenness in the original photograph. This is not a fully restored photograph, by my perfectionist standards. The overall tonal and contrast characteristics are not exactly what I would want in a perfect print. But I can assure you that many clients would be delighted to have a restoration of this quality.

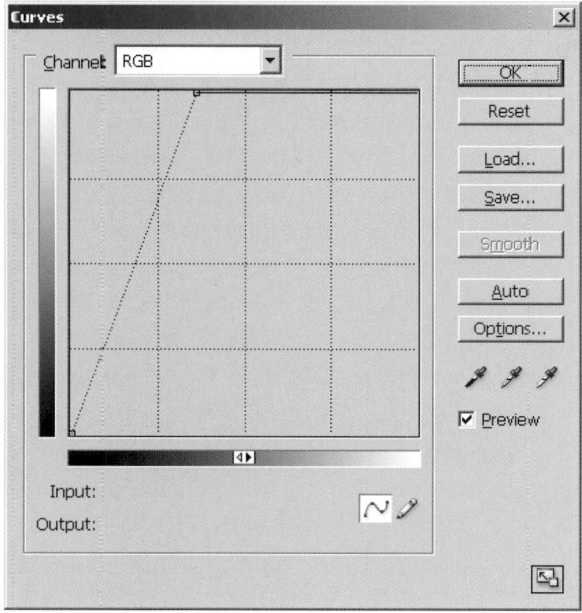

Fig. 5-49 This is the Curves adjustment for the dodging layer that I used to correct a band of underexposure at the bottom of the photograph. It increases the brightness of all tones by a factor of three.

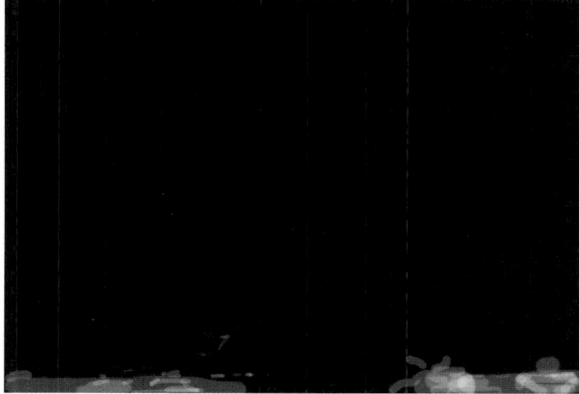

Fig. 5-50 I used this dodging mask with the Curves adjustment in Fig. 5-49 to touch up small parts of the bottom of the photograph and eliminate the band of darker exposure there. The result is Figure 5-44d.

How to Enhance Almost-Blank Photos

The half-century-old color print shown in Figure 5-54 is the most badly faded photograph I've ever worked on. Although there is considerable shadow density, the midtones and highlights have almost completely disappeared. This is also apparent in the scanner software histograms (Figure 5-55), which show that most of the tones fall into a huge peak near the highlights.

The first step in recovering information from a photograph like this is making the scan. Because I'll need to make truly radical changes to the tonal distribution to produce a good restoration of this photograph,

✓ HOW TO SCAN A NEARLY BLANK PHOTOGRAPH ▼

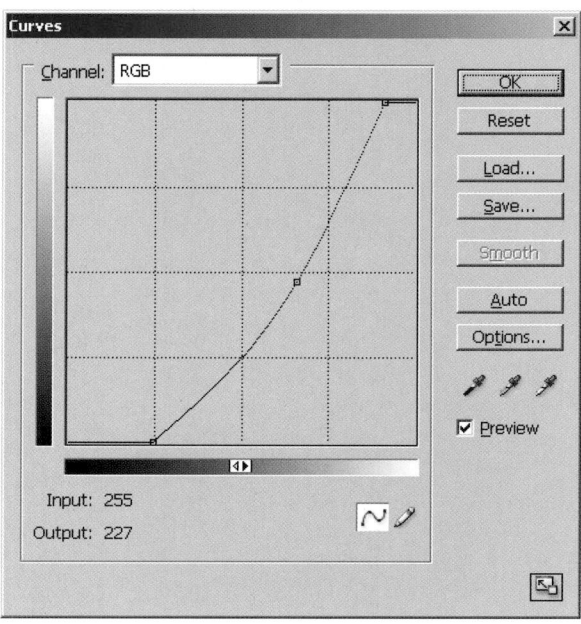

Fig. 5-51 This curve controlled the mask adjustment layer I created to produce Figure 5-53. It performs several corrections at once: It increases the contrast in the faces, darkens the shadows on them, and increases separation and modeling in their highlights.

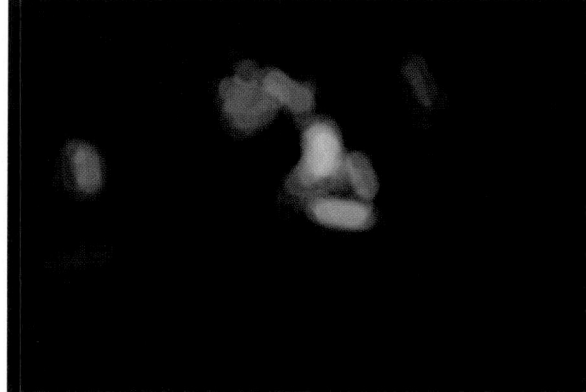

Fig. 5-52 Here's the mask for the final adjustment layer, using the Curves adjustment in Figure 5-51.

HOW TO SCAN A NEARLY BLANK PHOTOGRAPH (continued)

a 16-bit scan is a must. I set the levels controls in my scanner software to maximize the range of values in the file, which got me Figure 5-56. It's still bad, but now at least I could make out some more detail in the baby and the crib. Because tones were so lacking and badly distorted, I felt it necessary to do some color correction before I made major changes in the tonal distribution or I'd risk losing data from the most badly faded red channel. Running the photo through DIGITAL ROC (see Chapter 6, Restoring Color) got me to Figure 5-57. Neutrality was restored, but the photograph was still extremely faint.

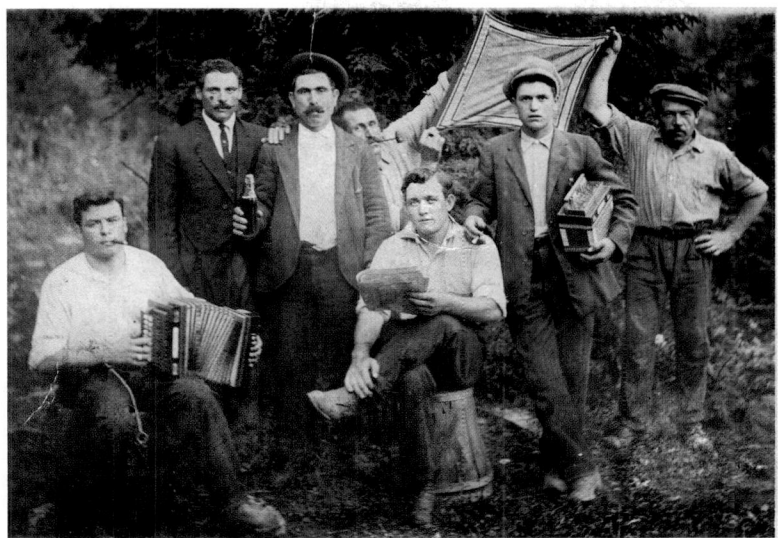

Fig. 5-53 The photograph after complete tonal correction with four dodging and burning-in adjustment layers. The light leak and exposure problems are almost completely repaired; you can hardly tell that the bottom half of the original photograph was badly fogged. This job is nearly ready for damage repair.

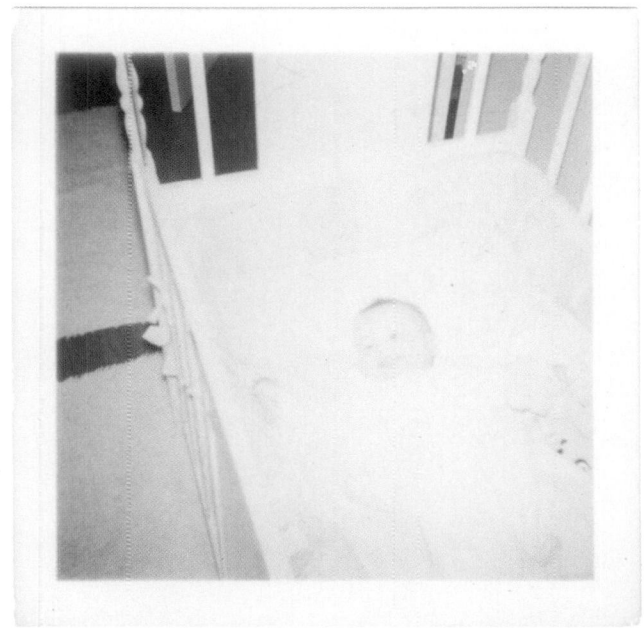

Fig. 5-54 This 55-year-old color snapshot is yellowed and faded to the point of near-invisibility.

I've two approaches for handling images like this. The first is, as usual, Curves. I created the curve in Figure 5-58 for this photograph. It's an unusual curve for photo restoration; I gave three-quarters of the darker tones very low contrast so that I could greatly exaggerate the density range in highlight tones. I moved the white point in a bit to eliminate the residual highlight stain.

HOW TO SCAN A NEARLY BLANK PHOTOGRAPH (continued)

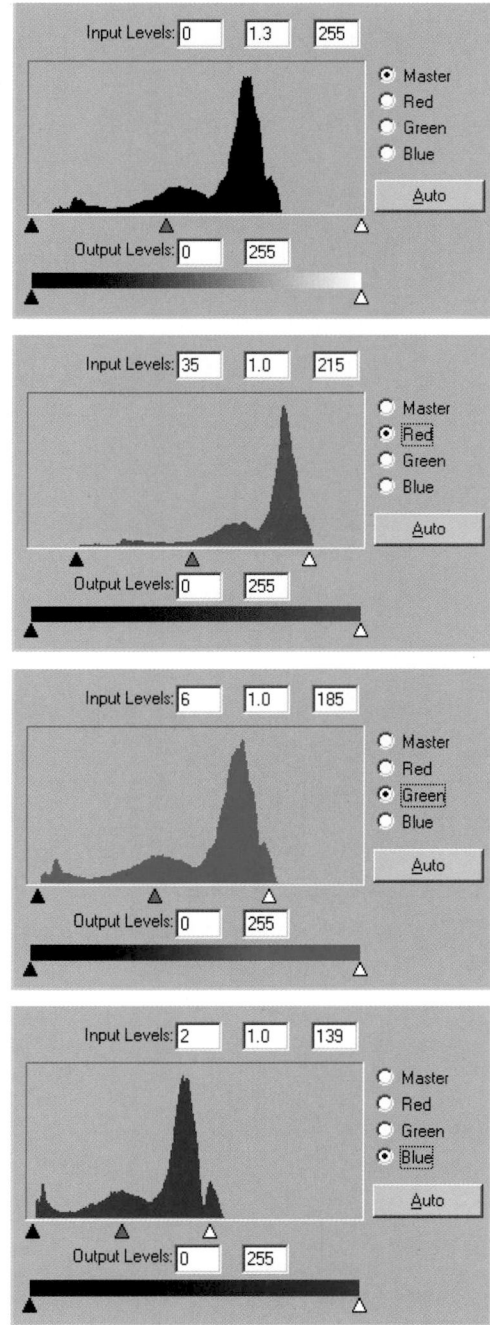

Fig. 5-55 The scanner software histograms for Figure 5-54 confirm the overall fading problem but indicate that there is still information in the faded areas, as shown by the broadened peaks to the right in the histograms.

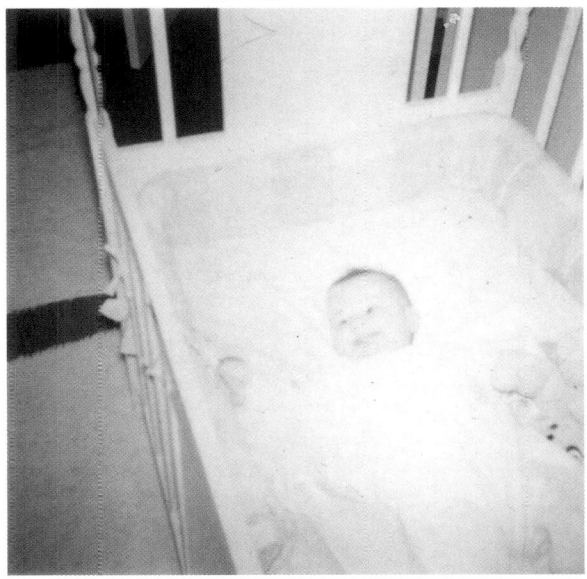

Fig. 5-56 A new scan of the snapshot using the levels settings from Figure 5-55 shows much more detail in the baby and the crib. This photograph may not be a hopeless case.

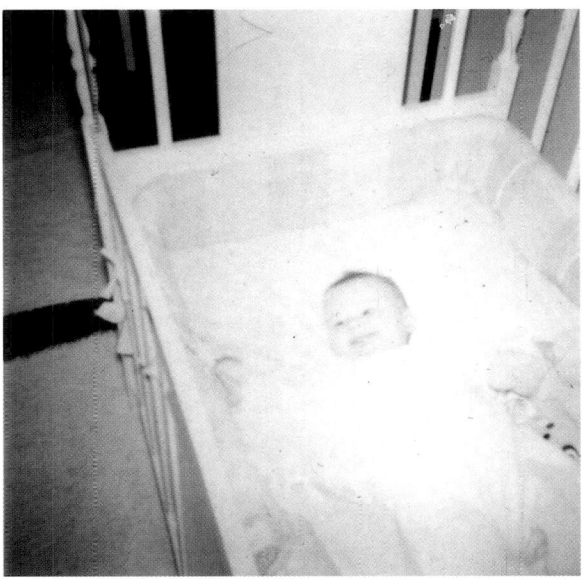

Fig. 5-57 Running the photograph in Figure 5-56 through the DIGITAL ROC plug-in restores even more detail and brings the faint beginnings of correct color to this photograph.

The resulting photograph, in Figure 5-59a, could not remotely be considered a good photograph. A lot of work needs to be done to turn this into an acceptable restoration; see Chapter 10, Examples, page 413, for a description of how I completely restored this photo. What's important, though, is that a good scan and a serious dose of Curves were sufficient to turn nearly blank photographic paper into a recognizable, acceptably detailed image.

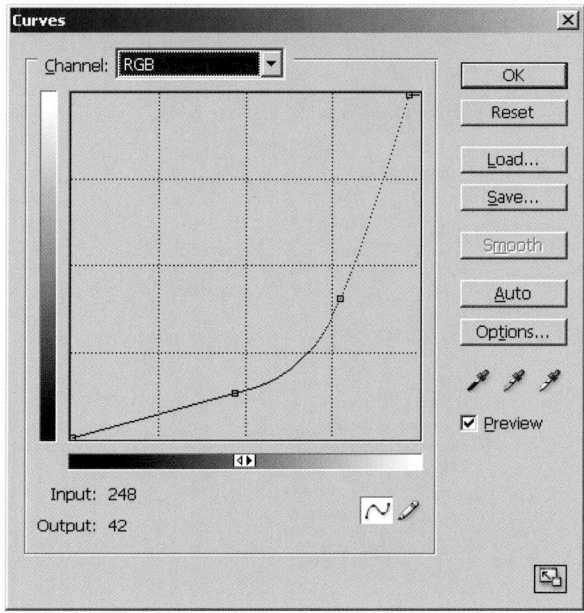

Fig. 5-58 This Curves adjustment turns Figure 5-57 into Figure 5-59a. The curve drastically darkens the highlights and midtones, and it increases contrast in those tones by a factor of four.

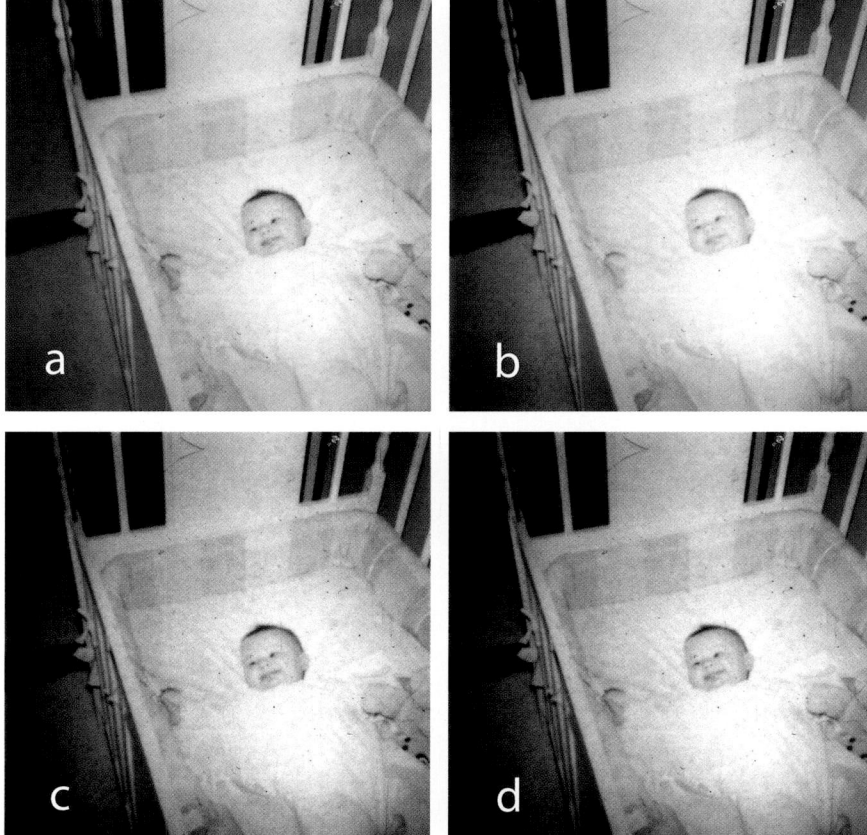

Fig. 5-59 There are many ways to intensify detail in a faded photograph. All the photographs here are derived from Figure 5-57. Figure (a) is the result of applying the Curves adjustment in Figure 5-58. To create (b) I took Figure 5-57, duplicated the background layer, and blended it in using the Multiply mode. I produced (c) by making two duplicate layers and blending them both in using Multiply. Figure (d) is the same as (c), except that I desaturated the second duplicate layer, so that I was multiplying luminosity but not color.

Good scans and Curves are techniques you can use with any image processing software, but Photoshop provides another way to enhance faint images. It's the "multiply" blend mode. Take an image, duplicate the layer, and set the new layer's blend mode to "Multiply." You'll see a marked increase in contrast and density.

I did this to the photograph from Figure 5-57 and got Figure 5-59b. In some ways it's not quite as good as Figure 5-59a. Multiplication didn't produce as much enhancement of the highlight detail. On the other hand, there is less color distortion in the multiplied version, especially in the midtones and shadows.

✓ HOW TO RECOVER A NEARLY BLANK PHOTOGRAPH WITH CURVES ADJUSTMENT LAYERS AND "MULTIPLY" BLENDS

For extreme highlight recovery, multiply more than two layers together. I took Figure 5-59b, duplicated the base layer again, and blended it in multiply mode. That produced Figure 5-59c. Now there's a decent range of densities, but color distortions, noise, and defects are similarly amplified. It will take a lot of work to clean up this photograph.

Here's a very useful variant on the last trick. I kept the new layer as a multiply blend, but I desaturated that layer. In effect, that only multiplied the luminosity. That eliminated some of the color distortions at the cost of reduced saturation (Figure 5-59d). Sometimes this would be an acceptable trade-off. Luminosity multiplication is a good technique to remember when you want to exaggerate or enhance the tonal scale without doing the same to the color values.

How to Make Extreme Tone Changes without Distorting Colors

RGB (red-green-blue) color space is the normal working mode for digital photographers and printers. It is so universally used, in fact, that this book takes it for granted that you'll be doing your work in RGB space. Tone corrections in RGB space, though, can have unwanted side effects when you're working on color photographs.

Problems show up because there's no such thing as pure "brightness" in RGB space—light and dark tones are made up of combinations of red, green, and blue. When you alter brightness, contrast, and tonal placements by manipulating the RGB curve, you're really manipulating those individual color values. Because of this, extreme changes in tonal placement and contrast will distort the colors in your photograph. Increases in contrast also increase color saturation; decreases in contrast reduce color saturation.

Figure 5-60a shows a photograph that was very low in contrast but still had reasonable amounts of color. I applied the RGB curve in Figure 5-61 to improve the tonal scale and return some true whites and blacks to the photograph. The result, Figure 5-60b, has good contrast but very unpleasant color. The great increase in contrast I desired resulted in a very undesirable increase in color saturation, to the point of garishness.

✓ HOW TO IMPROVE CONTRAST WITHOUT MAKING COLORS TOO SATURATED

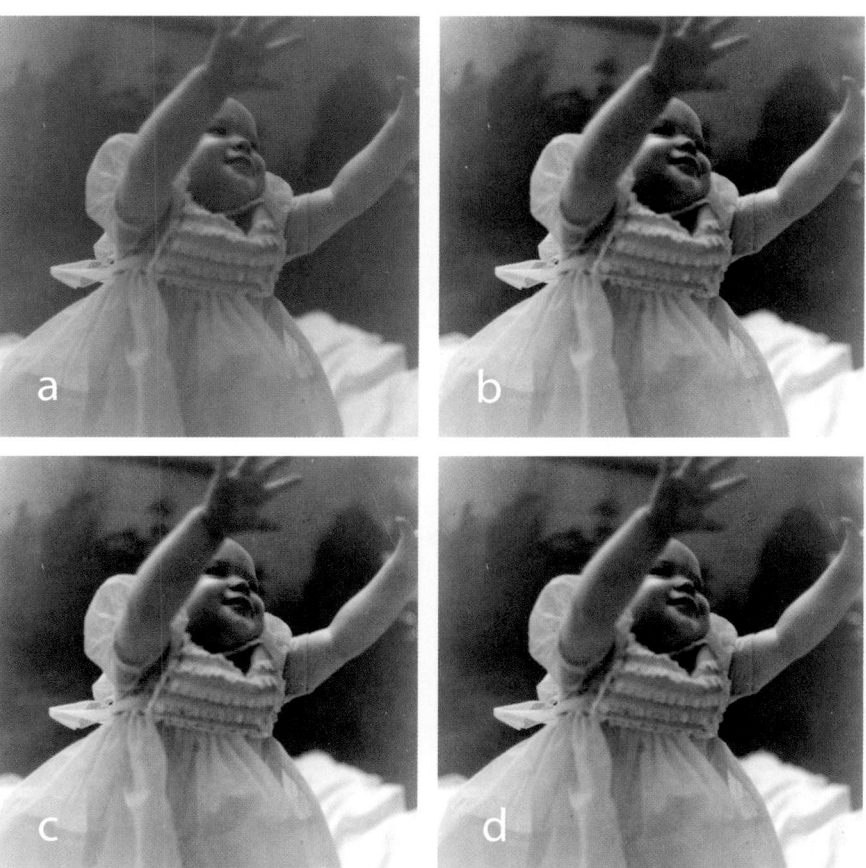

Fig. 5-60 Increased contrast usually means increased color saturation, but there are ways to control it. Figure (a) has pretty good color but very low contrast. (b) The Curves adjustment in Figure 5-61 satisfactorily increases the contrast, but it makes the colors garish. (c) To increase contrast but not saturation, use the Edit/Fade command after applying Curves. Change the Fade Mode to Luminosity, as in Figure 5-62. (d) Use the Hue/Saturation tool to produce the degree of saturation you want, as in Figure 5-63, after you've made a Curves Luminosity Fade adjustment.

HOW TO IMPROVE CONTRAST WITHOUT MAKING COLORS TOO SATURATED (continued)

If you convert the photograph to Lab space, you can work on the Lightness channel (that's what the L in "Lab" stands for; I discuss Lab space in more detail in Chapter 6) with Curves and other tools without altering colors. Unfortunately, that space isn't an intuitive working space for most photographers, so there's not much that you're likely to want to do there, but it's occasionally useful. See Chapter 6, Restoring Color, page 222, for more information about using Lab space. The Curve-Meister2 plug-in I described in Chapter 3, page 79, lets you do manipulations in a number of different color spaces, including Lab, and it makes dealing with these nonintuitive spaces easier.

Photoshop offers two techniques for getting some of the benefit of Lab space without having to deal with it directly. The first way is to do your Curves correction in an adjustment layer and set the blending mode to Luminosity. That behaves almost the same as making the corrections in Lab space. You can make extreme curve adjustments that radically change brightness and contrast but have little effect on colors.

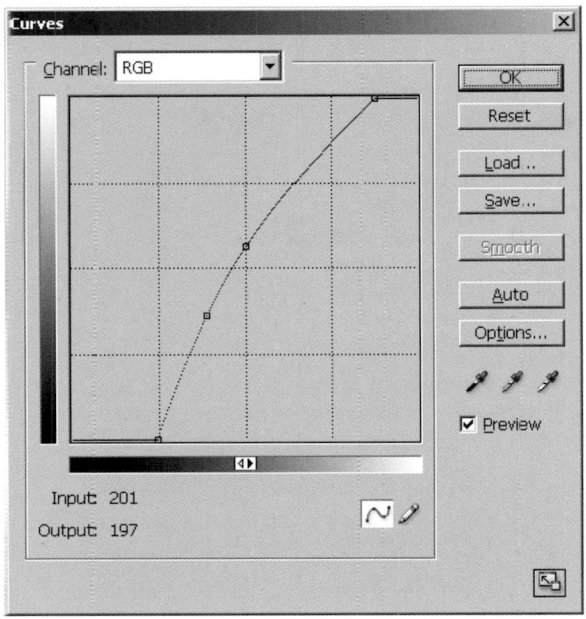

Fig. 5-61 This Curves adjustment produces good tonality in Figure 5-60b. I've moved the end points in to increase overall contrast and create some good whites and blacks. Control points in the middle raise the curve and make the midtones lighter. This curve also undesirably increases the saturation in the photograph.

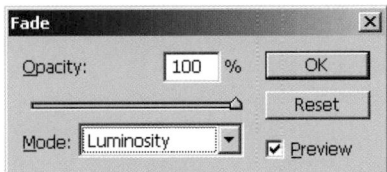

Fig. 5-62 The Edit/Fade command can be used to change the blending mode of adjustments you make. Here I used it to change the Curves adjustment in Figure 5-60 to a pure Luminosity adjustment, so that it increases the contrast but doesn't change the saturation of Figure 5-60c.

The second way to do this is to use the "Fade" command that's under the Edit menu. That lets you alter the strength of the most recent operation you did. It's useful for scaling back a change if you found you went a little too far. The Fade Control Panel contains a Mode box (Figure 5-62) that has a drop-down menu just like the blending options for adjustment layers. I turned Figure 5-60b into Figure 5-60c by using the Fade command with the Opacity strength left at 100% but the Mode changed to Luminosity. That converted the effect of the curve from its normal one to only affecting brightness.

Figure 5-60c had good tonal values, but I felt it was a little bit too undersaturated. I corrected that with the Hue/Saturation control (Figure 5-63), which increased saturation by 14 points. That got me Figure 5-60d, which is a nice combination of greatly improved contrast and moderately increased saturation.

HOW TO IMPROVE
CONTRAST WITHOUT
MAKING COLORS
TOO SATURATED
(continued)

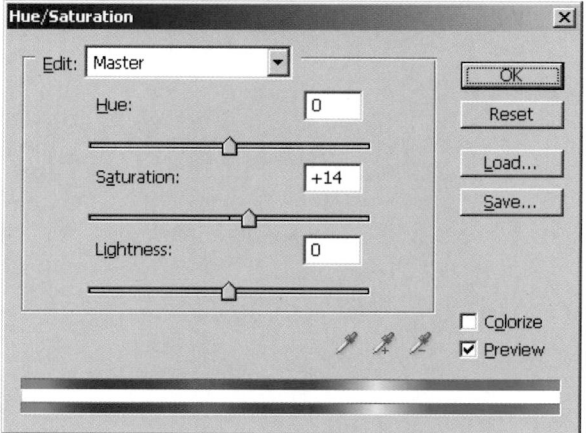

Fig. 5-63 This Hue/
Saturation adjustment
adds just the right
amount of color emphasis
to Figure 5-60d.

How to Fix Harsh Shadows on Faces

Most photo restoration requires increasing the contrast of the photograph. Unfortunately, that usually doesn't flatter people's faces. The
original photograph, especially if it was an amateur snapshot, may have
had pretty harsh contrast to begin with. If it was also printed poorly, as
many old photos were, restoring the blacks and whites to their full richness will produce some very harsh skin tones. They will need corrective
surgery before you'll be able to make an attractive print.

HOW TO FIX HARSH
SHADOWS ON FACES

Figure 5-64a was a commercial portrait that wasn't badly faded; the
print was badly made, so it was very low in contrast to begin with. The
good news is that, because the print densities were undamaged, all it
took to get a full-range photograph were careful scan settings (Figure
5-65) and a small amount of Curves adjustment in Photoshop. That
yielded Figure 5-64b, which has a nice range of tones from black to
white.

Technically it's quite satisfactory, but it's not particularly attractive.
The original lighting in the photograph was too directional and came
from too high an angle. When the child leaned forward, the shadows
fell harshly on her face. Happily, there are many ways to improve this.

I applied the Shadow/Highlight adjustment (Figure 5-66) to the corrected photograph to get Figure 5-67a. Because I didn't increase the
midtone contrast in the adjustment, it softened those tones. In combination with slightly opening up the shadows and substantially reining in
the highlights, this adjustment improved the face quite a bit.

Another way to fix the face is the good old Dodge tool. It only takes
a few strokes to turn Figure 5-64b into Figure 5-67b. I set the radius of
the tool to about the width of the child's lips with the hardness at 30%
(a fairly soft edge). I set the range for midtones and the exposure to
12%. Anywhere there was a dark shadow on the child's face I dodged

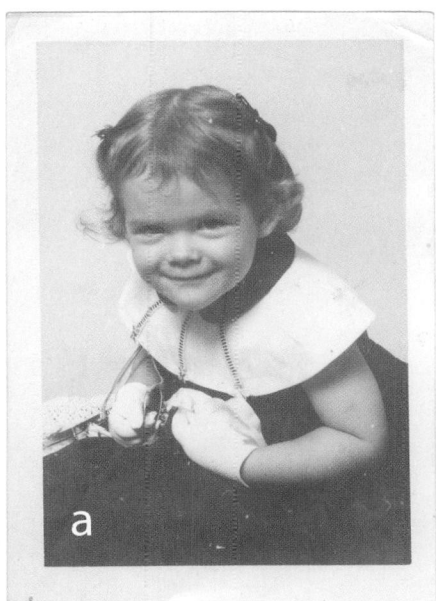
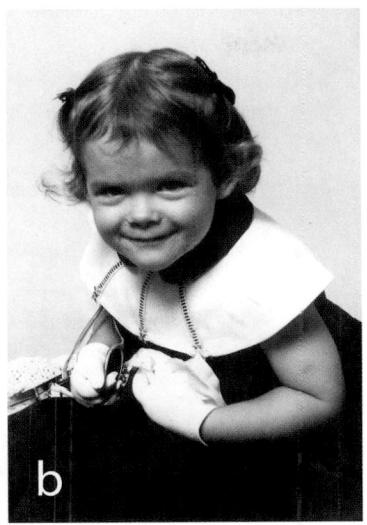

Fig. 5-64 (a) This early-1960s portrait was printed badly, so it is very flat and lacking in contrast. A good scan (b), using the scanner settings in Figure 5-65, restores a full range of tones to this photograph.

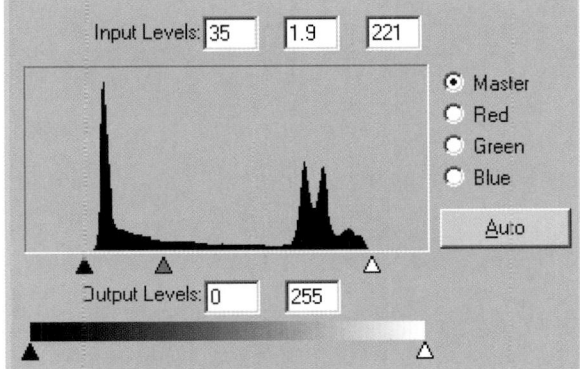

Fig. 5-65 The scanner software histogram and Levels settings for Figure 5-64. I set the black and white end point sliders to tightly bracket the range of tones in the histogram, producing good blacks and whites. I adjusted the midtone slider way to the left (a value of 1.9) to lighten up the skin tones and bring out more detail in the shadows.

it with this brush. Specifically, I ran the brush under her eyebrows and across the bridge of her nose, over her eye sockets, and along the bags under her eyes. I also clicked the brush a couple of times in the whites of her eyes on either side of the pupils to bring them out a bit more.

Next I ran the brush over the "muzzle lines" running from her nose down to the corners of her mouth. I dodged just under her lower lip and along the darkest shadows under her cheeks to soften them up. That's

HOW TO FIX HARSH
SHADOWS ON FACES
(continued)

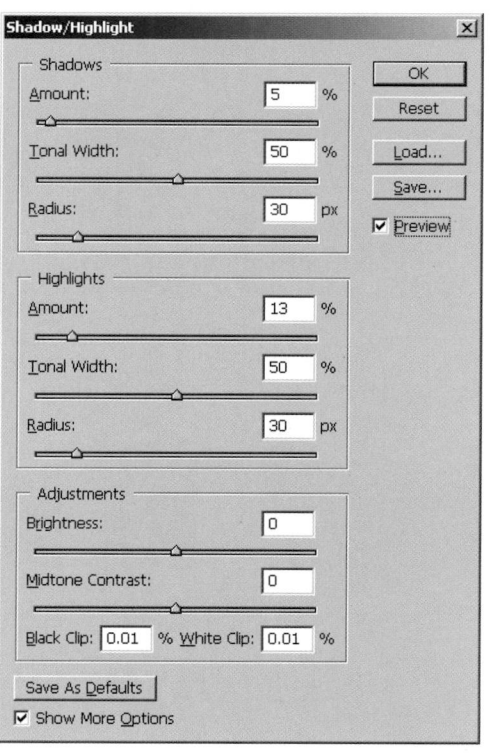

Fig. 5-66 The Shadow/Highlight tool does a great job on Figure 5-64b, producing 5-67a. I set the Shadows Amount to 5%, which brought out a bit more detail in the hair and the dark dress. I set the Highlights Amount to 13%, which toned down the highlights a lot and created much more detail. I left the Midtone Contrast alone, which softened the skin tones and made the light on the girl's face less harsh.

HOW TO FIX HARSH
SHADOWS ON FACES
(continued)

everything; it's not much! You don't have to completely rework a face to soften its look; just tackle the darkest and most contrasty spots, and you'll see a big improvement.

When the dodging tool seems too crude and unresponsive, there's a better way: Use the History Brush as a customized dodging tool. I applied the curve shown in Figure 5-68 to the portrait and got Figure 5-67c. All those harsh shadows have been grayed out (along with everything else in the photograph). I assigned that state to the History Brush and reverted to the original portrait. Now I could use the History Brush to paint in that softening effect.

I set the brush to an opacity of 9% so that I could work the effect in controllably, with each stroke of the brush slightly lightening the shadows. I worked over the same areas with the History Brush that I had with the dodging tool to get Figure 5-67d.

The advantage of using the History Brush is that it's easy to customize the effect of the brush to alter tones exactly as you wish. For example, if the portrait had also had harsh, blown-out highlights, I could have pulled down the white point on the curve to a light gray and had a brush that would both lighten shadows and darken highlights automatically.

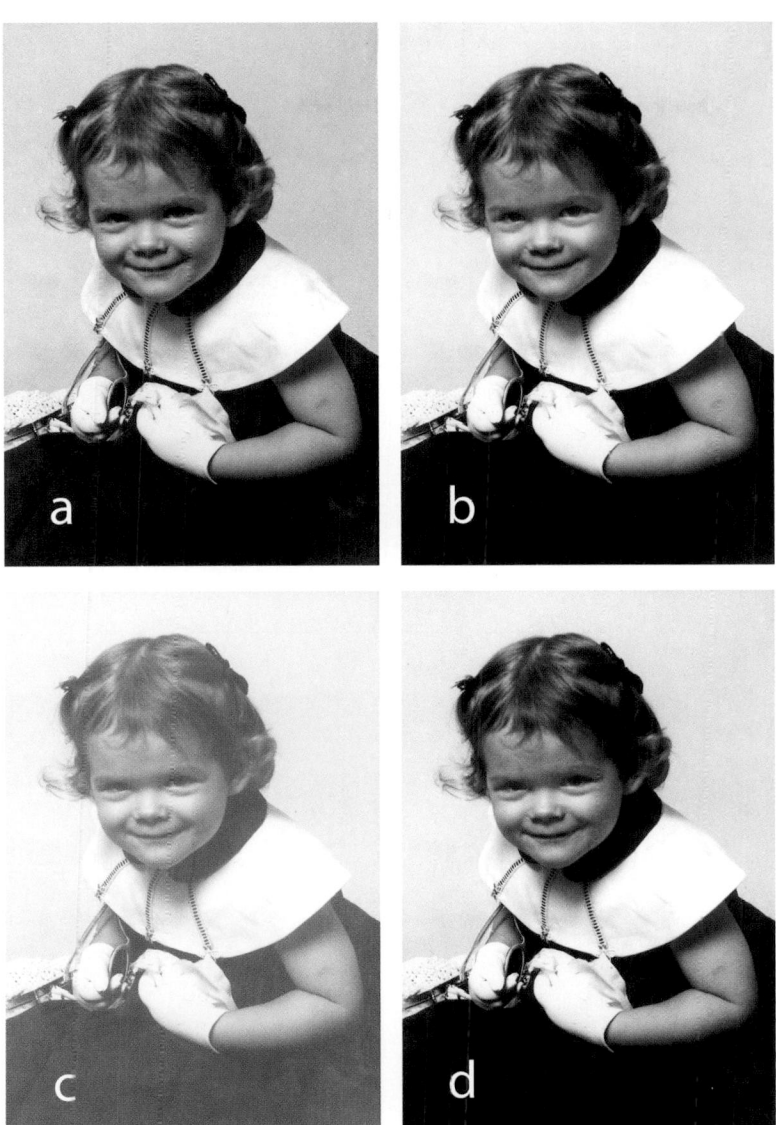

Fig. 5-67 (a) Applying the Shadow/Highlight adjustment in Figure 5-66 to Figure 5-64b produces a much more attractive photograph, with better shadow and highlight detail and more flattering skin tones. (b) The Dodge tool does a good job of removing harsh shadows and lines from faces and opening up eye sockets and brightening eyes. A few minutes work with that tool turned Figure 5-64b into this photograph. (c) I made this "dodging print" (see the main text for details) using the Curves adjustment in Figure 5-68. (d) I assigned the History Brush to the "dodging print" and used it to paint out the harsh shadows in the photograph. This is a more versatile approach than using the simple Dodge tool.

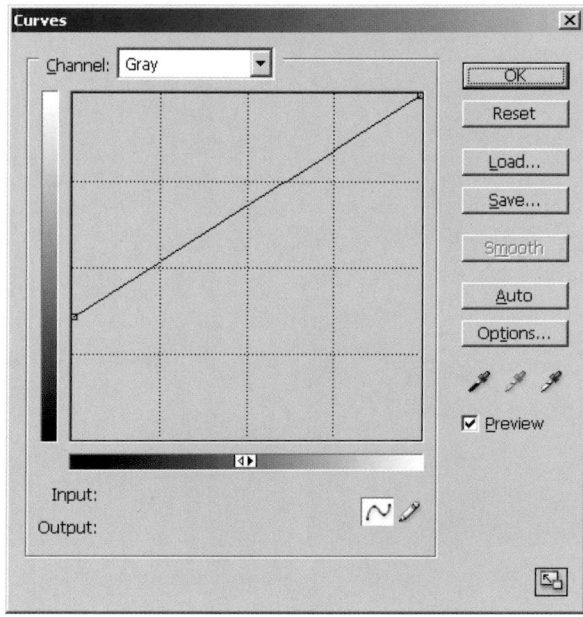

Fig. 5-68 This Curves adjustment created the "dodging print" in Figure 5-67c. I also used it in a Curves adjustment layer in Figure 5-69 that I used as a dodging adjustment layer to improve the portrait.

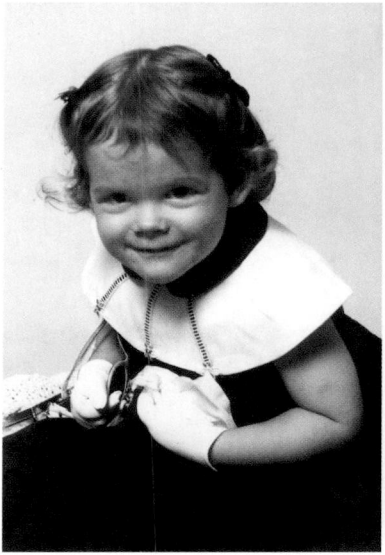

Fig. 5-69 The original portrait, from Figure 5-64b, after correction with a dodging adjustment layer that used the Curves adjustment from Figure 5-68. The dodging mask I created is shown in the right half of the figure. The lighter the mask, the more dodging that gets applied to the portrait at that point.

Using the History Brush as a dodging tool also lets you previsualize what the effect will be. Before reverting the history state to its pre-Curves condition, you can duplicate the modified image and keep it on your desktop as a reference. That way, when you're working with the History Brush, you can always see which direction it will be pushing the tones and how far it can push them.

For maximum control, use a masked dodging layer, as I explained ✓ | HOW TO RETOUCH FACES WITH A MASKED CURVES ADJUSTMENT LAYER

earlier in this chapter. Instead of applying the curves in Figure 5-68 directly to the portrait, I used them in a Curves adjustment layer. I inverted the layer mask to make it black, which zeroed out the effect of the layer. Now I could paint in the Curves adjustment just where I wanted by using a white brush to paint over the mask. Just as when using the dodging and History Brush tools, I used a small radius brush set to very low opacity.

This method has all the advantages of using the History Brush along with being completely reversible. If you make a mistake and dodge somewhere you didn't mean to or overdo it, just change the brush from white to black and paint over your mistake. You can switch back and forth between white and black brushes any time you like, so that you can rework the mask as much as you need. This is a great method for beginners, as well as advanced workers, because you never have to worry about doing anything irreversibly wrong. You can see my results, along with the layer mask I ended up with, in Figure 5-69.

CHAPTER 6

Restoring Color

How-To's in This Chapter

How to make a scan that produces good color
How to correct color with the midtone eyedropper
How to correct color with Picture Window Color Balance
How to correct color using Auto Color options
How to correct color with DIGITAL ROC
How to use layers to correct color and luminosity separately
How to improve color with Curves and Hue/Saturation adjustment layers
How to make skin tones smoother with Curves adjustment layers
How to retouch skin tones with an airbrush layer
How to fix a faded school portrait with airbrush layers
How to hand-tint a photograph with masked layers
How to remove color fringes from a photograph
How to remove developer marks from a photograph
How to improve color with Color Mechanic

What Makes a Good Print?

After reading Chapters 4 and 5, you've likely figured out that the qualities that make for good color in a photograph are a lot like the ones that give a photograph good tonality. A photograph with good color usually has a rich range of values from near-white to near-black; this is what I called the First Rule of Good Tonality in Chapter 5. Somewhere in that color print you'll find a bit of deep shadow that approaches black and a bit of a highlight glint that approaches white. They aren't necessarily large or important parts of the photograph, but they're usually there.

Look through this book at before and after illustrations of color photo restorations like the one shown in Figure 6-1 and its accompanying histograms (Figure 6-2). Almost always what distinguishes the restored photograph from the degraded original is this richness of tones. The faded-color original won't have any clean whites or blacks. It's very much the same situation we saw with faded B&W prints. Color is not as

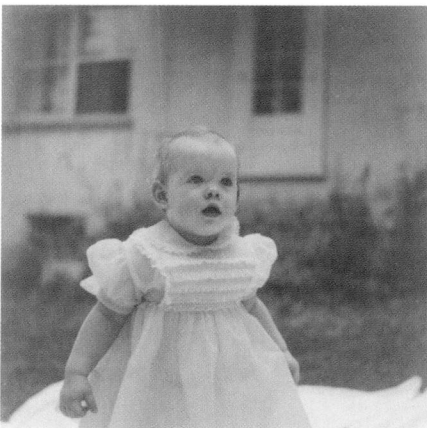
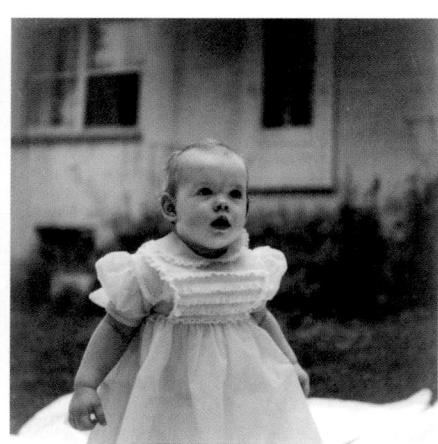

Fig. 6-1 The faded photograph on the left has a narrow range of tones, shown in the histogram in Figure 6-2. Each of the three color channels has a restricted tonal scale. In contrast, the photograph on the right with good color has color channel histograms that use most of the tonal range.

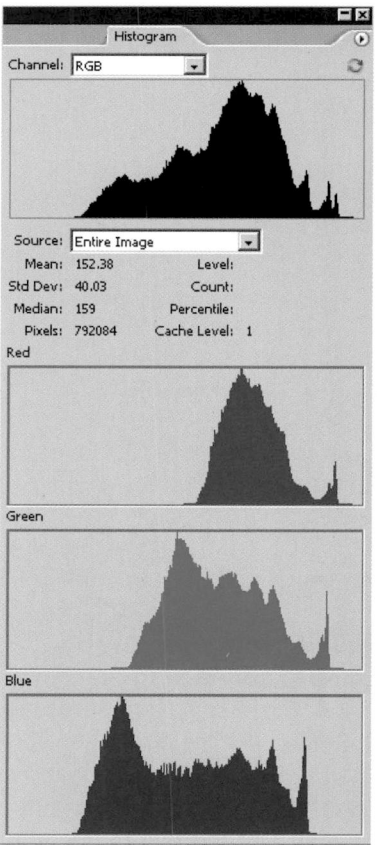
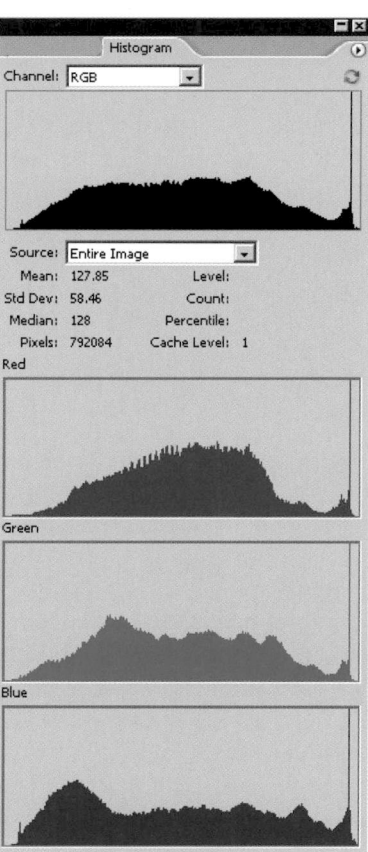

Fig. 6-2 These are the histograms for the faded (left) and color-corrected (right) photographs in Figure 6-1. Each color channel in the faded photograph looks similar to what you'd see in a faded B&W photograph—no clean whites and no tones anywhere near maximum color density. The color-corrected photograph has broad, well-populated histograms in each color channel.

different as you might think, but let's now concentrate on those differences.

B&W has only one channel of tonality: gray. It's easy for people to understand B&W tonality: As the value rises from 0 to 255, the gray tone changes from black to white. Color has three dimensions to it: red values, green values, and blue values (known in shorthand as *RGB*). Each of those channels behaves like the gray channel in a B&W photograph, but the color we perceive is the combination of all three and not the component values.

To get really good color in a photograph, we have to be able to adjust each of those channels individually with as much finesse as we adjusted the tonality in a B&W photograph. This is much more difficult to do, but fortunately many software tools will help us.

There aren't really any deep secrets to getting good color, but there are some smart rules you may not have thought of. They turn out to be true so often that you may consider them to be very reliable guides to good color restoration. Remember the First Rule of Good Tonality that I said only "usually" applies to color photographs at the beginning of this chapter? Well, it is much more true when you examine each color channel separately. The photograph may not have any true whites or true blacks, but somewhere in the photograph there will almost always be pixels that will have values near 0 or 255 for one of the individual colors. This is an idea that takes some getting used to, so here's a concrete example. The purest, most saturated yellow will have a blue value of 0 and red and green values of 255. You don't need a white or black pixel to get extreme values in the individual color channels of a color photograph; any pure color will have some component color values near black or white.

It's true that some color photographs won't have pure colors in them, just as it's true that some won't have true blacks and true whites. But the number of photographs that have no whites, no blacks, and no fairly saturated colors is awfully small. That means we do have a good general rule for good color photographs: Each of the individual color channels will have a broad set of tones spanning most of the range from black to white. This is not the only requirement for good color, but it is one of them. That's why, when I talked about what made a good scan in Chapter 4, I put such emphasis on adjusting the levels for the color channels to produce histograms that span most of the range from 0 to 255 for each color (Figure 6-3). It's about more than just having a lot of good data to work with; it gets me a lot closer to the color I actually want, as Figure 6-4 shows. Observe the difference in the Photoshop histograms (Figure 6-5) for the unadjusted and adjusted scans of Figure 6-4. In Chapter 10, Examples, page 354, I do a complete restoration on this photograph, starting from this adjusted scan.

✓ HOW TO MAKE A SCAN THAT PRODUCES GOOD COLOR

A second guiding principle is that tone and color are closely connected. Changing the lightness of a photograph changes its color: rich

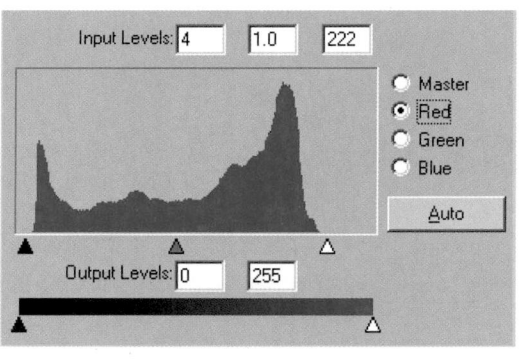

Input Levels: 4 | 1.0 | 222
○ Master ● Red ○ Green ○ Blue
Auto
Output Levels: 0 | 255

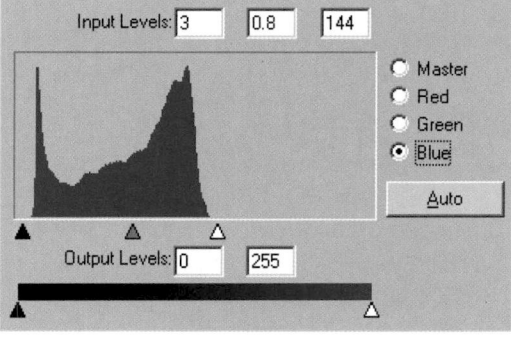

Input Levels: 2 | 1.0 | 192
○ Master ○ Red ● Green ○ Blue
Auto
Output Levels: 0 | 255

Input Levels: 3 | 0.8 | 144
○ Master ○ Red ○ Green ● Blue
Auto
Output Levels: 0 | 255

Fig. 6-3 These are the scanner software histogram and Levels settings for the photograph in Figure 6-4, left. The blacks aren't bad in this photograph, but there's serious staining and loss of midtone dye densities. The Levels settings that produce a good scan closely bracket the range of tones in each channel, just as they would for making a good B&W scan. The blue midtone slider is shifted to the right (a value of 0.8) to eliminate excess blue from the scan.

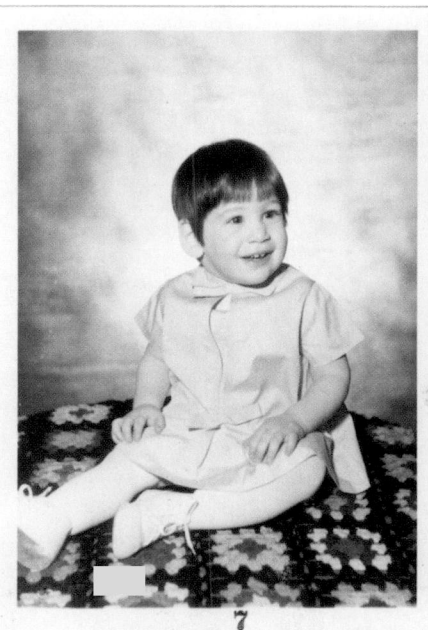

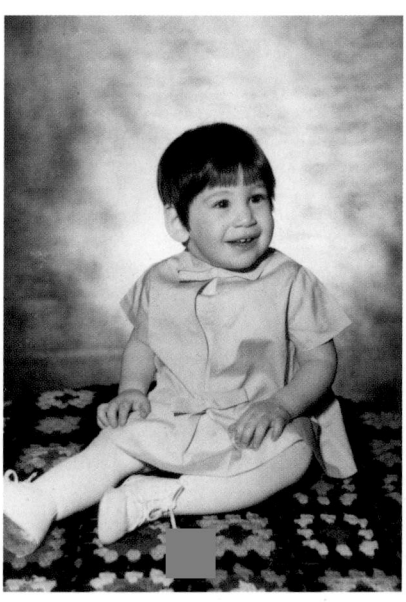

Fig. 6-4 The original photograph (left) is in good physical condition, but it's faded and very badly stained. The vastly improved version on the right is simply the result of making a good scan, using the settings in Figure 6-3.

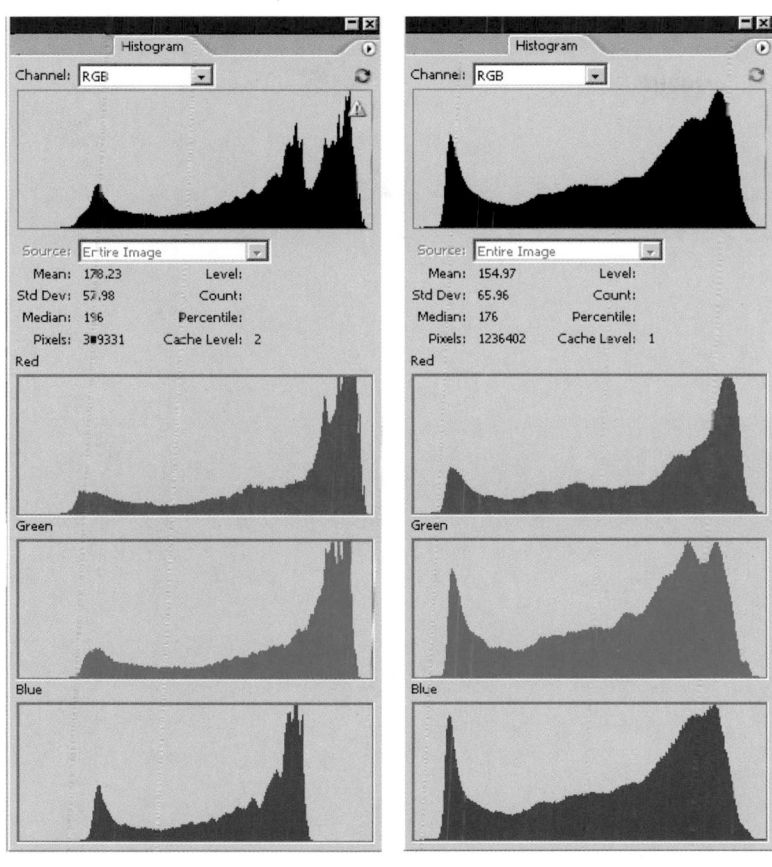

Fig. 6-5 Here are the histograms for the photographs in Figure 6-4. A good scan, using the levels settings in Figure 6-3, takes the unevenly balanced histograms in each channel of the faded photograph (left) and normalizes them. All three histograms now cover about the same range of tones and make good use of the available tonal scale.

colors are usually associated with dark values, and pastels with light values. You cannot alter tone without altering color and vice versa.

Most importantly, contrast and color intensity (saturation) are intimately intertwined. When you increase the contrast of an RGB image, you increase its color saturation; when you decrease its contrast, you decrease the color saturation (Figure 6-6). It's important for you to get the overall contrast of the photograph approximately right before trying to fix the saturation. A common mistake is to look at a photograph that is too low in contrast, decide that the color is undersaturated, and boost the saturation. When you kick up contrast to the proper level, the colors become garish because of the additional increase in saturation.

Consequently, I usually try to correct the tonality and contrast as much as I can before fine-tuning the color. Still, color and tonality are a two-way street. If I have a photograph that is wildly off in color, I can't evaluate and correct its tonality accurately on the first pass. I will crudely correct the tonality and contrast; then I'll approximately correct the color and saturation. Once the color is roughly correct, I can go back

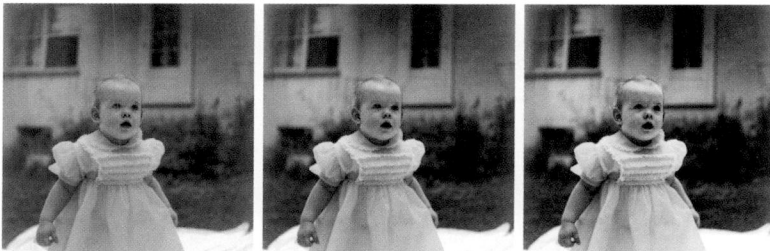

Fig. 6-6 Contrast and color saturation are closely linked. These three photographs are identical, except that I used Curves to increase the contrast from left to right. As the contrast increases, so does the color saturation.

Fig. 6-7 Correcting a single midtone gray using Curves will do a lot to correct the overall color balance of a photograph. On the left is the original color-restored photograph with a sample point (#1) added to the background. Figure 6-8 shows the Info window with the values at the sample point and the red and blue curves that I used to color correct that point and make it neutral (point #2). That results in the photograph on the right.

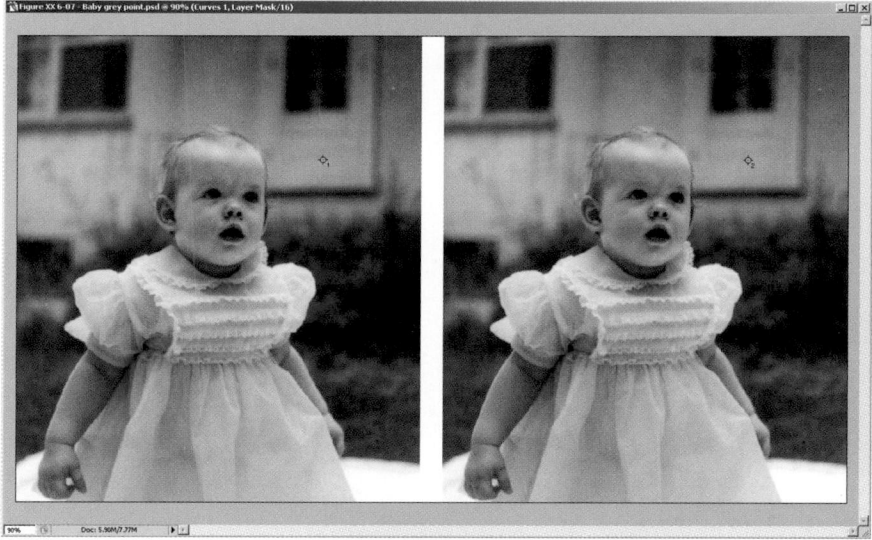

and evaluate the tone and contrast much more accurately and fine-tune them. Then it's back to the color to refine it, working back and forth until I've got the tonality and color just where I want them.

Adjustment layers are a *really* good way of doing this. As I warned, it's easy to overshoot your mark by confusing low contrast with low saturation, or the converse. Adjustment layers allow you to adjust the colors and tonal values without locking yourself into a fixed result.

HOW TO CORRECT COLOR WITH THE MIDTONE EYEDROPPER

One last guideline: If you get the blacks, whites, and middle grays correct, the rest of the colors will follow. Like the other guiding principles in this section, this is not an absolute law of nature. Even when you have the whites, blacks, and grays just where you want them, the color may still be off. But most of the time it's amazing how close it will be to what you want.

I inserted two eyedropper sample points in Figure 6-7 using the methods I presented in Chapter 5, Restoring Tone, page 140. Figure 6-8

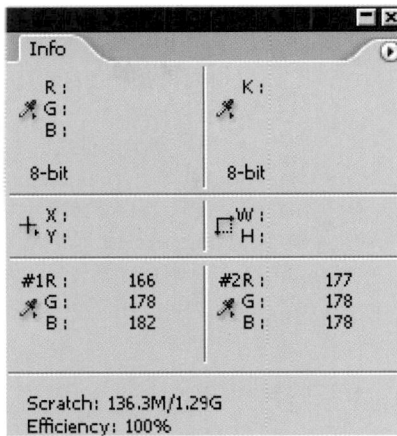

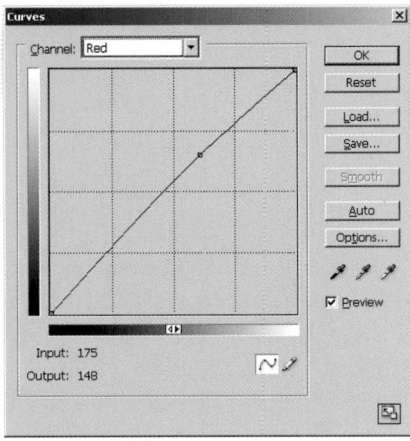

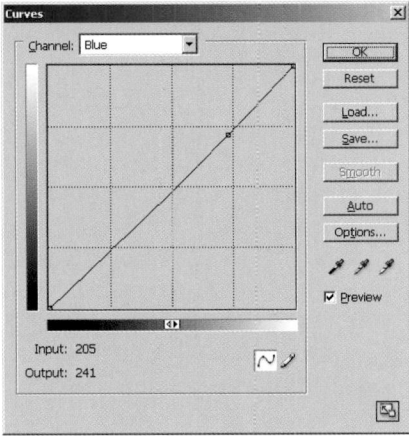

Fig. 6-8 Sample points #1 and #2 in the Info window correspond to a point in the background before and after color correction. Knowing that the house was neutral, I added correction points to the red and blue channels and raised and lowered them, respectively, until the value of the sample point was about the same for all three channels (178). That eliminated the overall bluish-green cast in the photograph.

shows the RGB values at the eyedropper sample point before (point #1) and after (point #2) I applied the red and blue correction curves shown. The color isn't perfect, but it's much closer to being correct.

A big part of successful color restoration is getting yourself in the neighborhood. RGB color space is a big place; it's a lot easier to fine-tune the aesthetics of your photograph when you're close to having decent color than when you're floundering around out in the hinterlands of RGB space, lost and trying to figure out how to get to where you want to be. The software tools in the next section are no substitute for manually correcting color, but they can get you into the ballpark. It's up to you to polish it up and do the finishing touches.

Getting the Color Right (Semi-)Automatically

Picture Window's Color Balance tool lets you do some pretty sophisticated color correction without having to mess directly with Curves or Levels. It's a very visually oriented tool. Figure 6-9 will give you some idea of what you can do with it. This is a screenshot from Picture Window of color balancing in progress. The photograph in the upper left is the original uncorrected photograph. In the upper right is a preview photograph showing what the color balance settings will do when they are applied. At the lower left is the Color Balance main control panel.

Although the Color Balance tool includes a set of RGB curves that you can manipulate directly, you rarely need to involve yourself with them. You can do what you need to with probes and aimpoint adjustments. Here's how it works:

On the left side of the Color Balance control panel, you'll see a column labeled "Remove" and another one labeled "Add." The rows in each column correspond to highlight, shadow, and midtone values. The Remove column shows the highlight, shadow, and midtone target points that are going to be corrected. You can change those target points by double-clicking on the color rectangle and opening Picture Window's version of a color picker, but there's an easier way. Set the probe to the value you want to correct (highlight, shadow, or midtone) and then click the cursor on an appropriate point in the original photograph. Picture Window will assign that hue to the "Remove" box.

Do that for all three values, click Apply, and you'll get a result that looks like the second photograph from the upper left in Figure 6-9. The color balance is pretty good, but the picture is very flat. Why is that? Because the default settings for the Color Balance tool change the color but not the brightness; Color Balance is correcting color but not luminosity.

You have manual control over brightness values. Click one of the boxes in the Add column. That opens up a new window in which you can set the brightness and fine-tune the color (if you need to). I opened

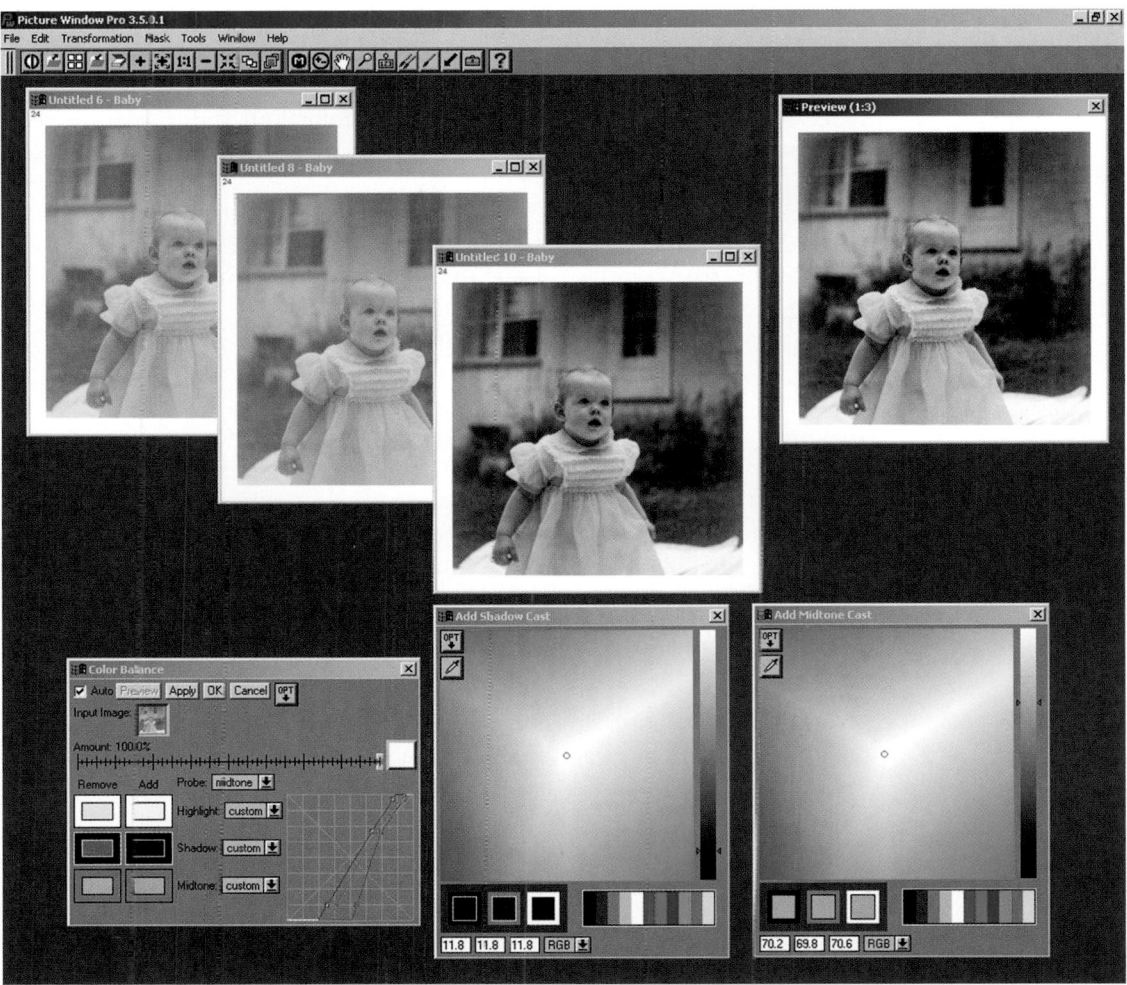

Fig. 6-9 Picture Window's Color Balance transformation is a nice, visually oriented way to do color correction. The original photograph is in the upper left of this screenshot, the Color Balance control panel lower left, and the Preview window upper right. Clicking on points in the photograph assigns them to Highlight, Shadow, or Midtone values. You can correct the colors and values of those points using color picker windows, lower right. Picture Window takes care of manipulating the curves for you. Two color-corrected versions of the original photograph are shown midscreen.

windows for the shadows and the midtones. These are the two rainbow-filled windows in the lower right of Figure 6-9. The grayscale slider on the right side of each window changes the brightness of the adjustment point. The little circle in the rainbow field lets you choose the color for that point. For the highlights and shadows, you usually just want to adjust the grayscale slider up or down. You'll often use the color selector to refine the color balance of the midtone point, especially if there isn't a point in your picture that corresponds to a proper neutral gray.

HOW TO CORRECT COLOR WITH PICTURE WINDOW COLOR BALANCE (continued)

HOW TO CORRECT
COLOR WITH
PICTURE WINDOW
COLOR BALANCE
(continued)

The preview window changes as you move the color point and gray-scale slider around, so you can see what your adjustments are accomplishing. It's a simple, intuitive way to get the photograph into the neighborhood of correct color. I used the color and slider settings seen here to produce the second corrected version of the photograph in the middle of Figure 6-9.

Remember that Picture Window keeps multiple versions of the photographs open; every time you hit the Apply button, you generate a new photograph from your color balance settings. If you can't settle on the best version just by looking at the Preview window, you can create as many variations as you like (I created two in this example) and decide which one you most prefer later.

Even if you work mostly in Photoshop, this is still a great tool for getting your color roughly corrected, because this kind of tone and color adjustment is one of the first things you want to do to your scan. Save your scan file as a TIFF document, open it up in Picture Window, correct it and save it, and do the remainder of your work in Photoshop.

Photoshop's Auto Color adjustment can do a great deal to improve the color of even a very bad original (or scan). In its default mode (the command directly under the Image/Adjustments menu), it's not very good. The trick to making it work well is to call up its semi-hidden options; then it can turn out some pretty fine results.

HOW TO CORRECT
COLOR USING AUTO
COLOR OPTIONS

Figure 6-10 is an intentionally poor scan. It's very faithful to the original, faded photograph—precisely the kind of scan I said not to make back in Chapter 4. But it could be the kind of scan you'd be stuck working with if your client provided the file to be restored.

Here's how to semi-automatically correct color. Under Image/Adjustments, click the Levels command. In the Levels control panel, click the Options button. In the Correction Options control panel, select "Find Dark & Light Colors" and "Snap Neutral Midtones" (Figure 6-11). That does most of the color correction for us.

We've one more adjustment to make. The default shadow and highlight tones are 0% and 100%, which is likely to clip some highlight or shadow detail that we want to preserve. Click the Shadows (black) box, and the Color Picker window opens. Set B (brightness) to 10% and close the Color Picker (Figure 6-12). Then click the Highlights (white) box and set B to 90%.

Click OK to close the Auto Color Correction Options, click Auto in the Levels control panel, and click OK to close the Levels control panel. When Photoshop asks if you want to save the new target colors as defaults, click Yes. You'll find the 10% and 90% end points much more useful than Photoshop's original 0% and 100% default values.

That takes us to Figure 6-13. The color is improved, but the tones are very bad because the large white areas threw off the automatic adjustments. I could've made a mask that excluded them; then the Auto Color tool would've done a satisfactory job of restoring tone, but I'll show you

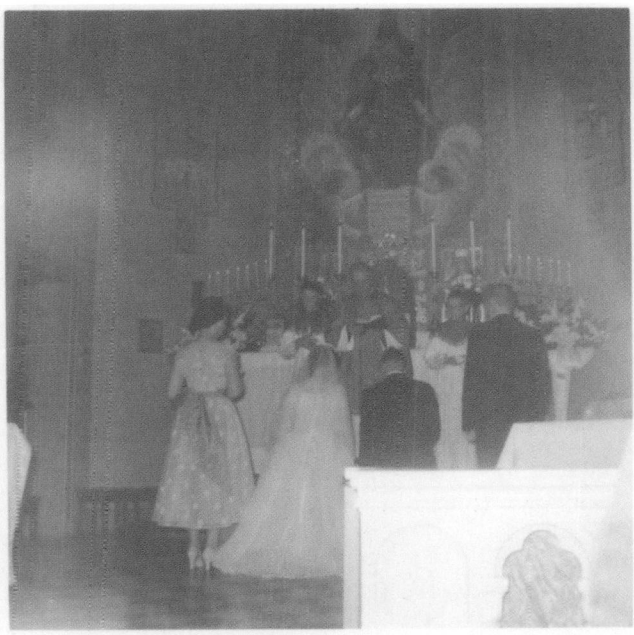

Fig. 6-10 This old wedding photograph has faded to brownish-orange. The Auto Color settings in Figures 6-11 and 6-12 can restore much of the missing color.

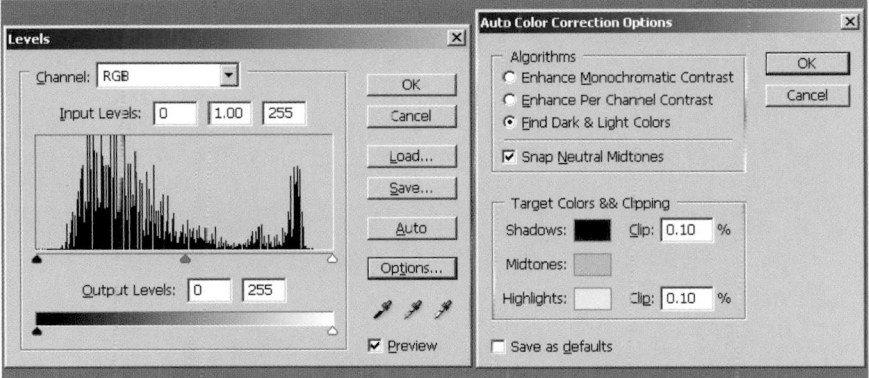

Fig. 6-11 The key to using Auto Color effectively is taking advantage of its options. You can use these to tell Auto Color to find appropriate light and dark colors and to automatically make midtones neutral. The Correction Options also let you control the target colors, to avoid forcing intermediate tones to pure black and white (see Figure 6-12).

a different, better way to handle this with blended layers in the next section, Color Correcting with Layers.

My third and favorite way to do automatic color correction is with the DIGITAL ROC plug-in (Figure 6-14), which I introduced in Chapter 3. It gives a lot of control without being excessively time consuming, and the results are usually better than either Picture Window's Color Balance or Photoshop's Auto Color.

✓ HOW TO CORRECT COLOR WITH DIGITAL ROC

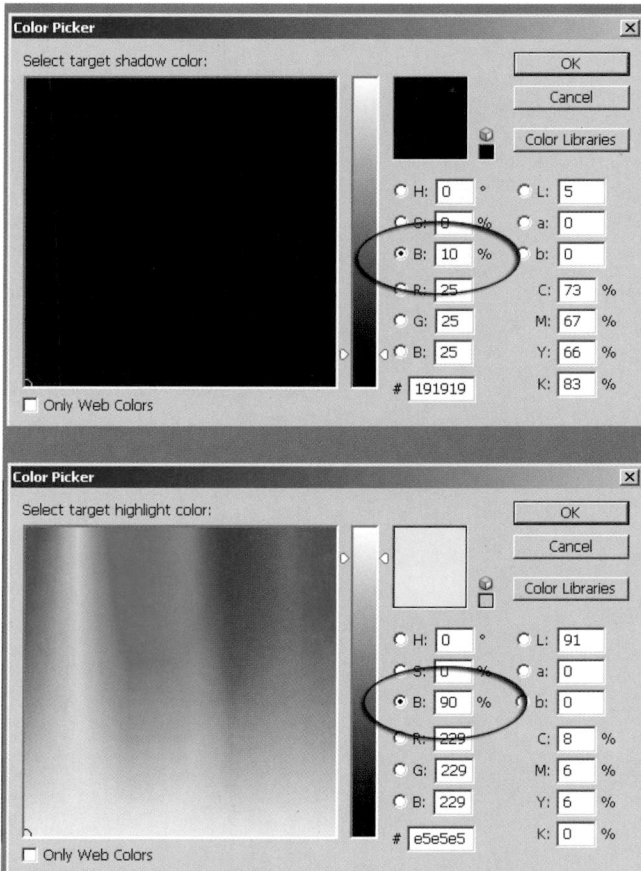

Fig. 6-12 The Color Picker options for the target colors let you avoid clipping important tonal information in the photograph. I always set my black and white points to 10% black and 90% black, respectively. That makes acceptable use of the full tonal range available for working on the photograph, but it ensures that no detail in the photograph is accidentally eliminated.

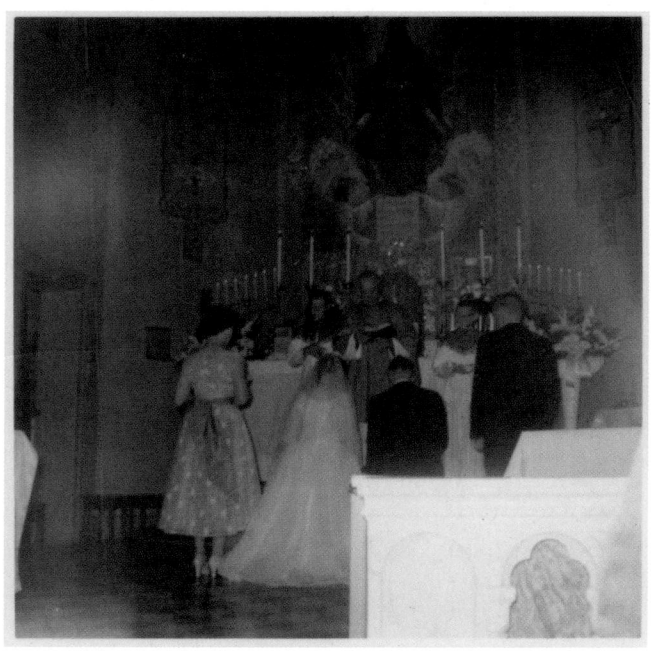

Fig. 6-13 This is what Figure 6-10 looks like after applying Auto Color. The tones in most of the photograph are too dark because the large overexposed area in the lower right threw off Auto Color's corrections, but the colors are much improved. This is a big step toward a successful restoration.

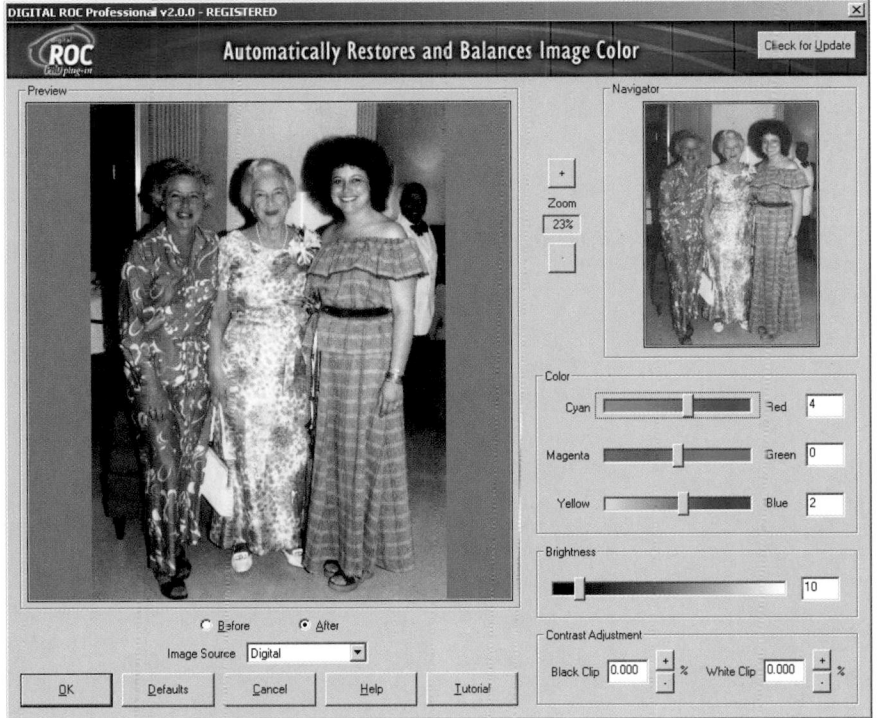

Fig. 6-14 The DIGITAL ROC plug-in is my favorite way to correct color in faded photographs. It does an amazing job of extracting useful color information from badly faded photographs. The plug-in version of this utility (which is built into the DIGITAL ICE[3] scanner software) has capabilities the scanner software lacks; it gives you control over color, brightness, and contrast balance. You can selectively apply color correction with masks, layers, and the History Brush.

Figure 6-15 compares all three methods. Starting clockwise from the upper left, it shows the original, badly faded color print, Picture Window's Color Balance transformation, Photoshop's Auto Color correction, and DIGITAL ROC's correction. All three improved versions are good starts on full-color correction, but DIGITAL ROC did the best job (which is most evident in the color of the clothing, according to the owner of the photograph). All of these photos, however, share two problems: low saturation and poor tonality, especially too much contrast. We can fix all that with layers.

HOW TO CORRECT COLOR WITH DIGITAL ROC (continued)

Color Correcting in Layers

As Figures 6-13 and 6-15 showed us, automatic color correction often produces undesirable tones. It would be nice to be able to get color improvements without unwanted tonal changes. Photoshop layers are a versatile tool for separating color from tone control.

Let's start with Figure 6-13. I like what Auto Color did for the overall color balance, but the main subject area of the photograph is much too dark and too flat. Here's how I fixed that. First, I made another copy of the original scan (remember, always work on copies, never

✓ HOW TO USE LAYERS TO CORRECT COLOR AND LUMINOSITY SEPARATELY ▼

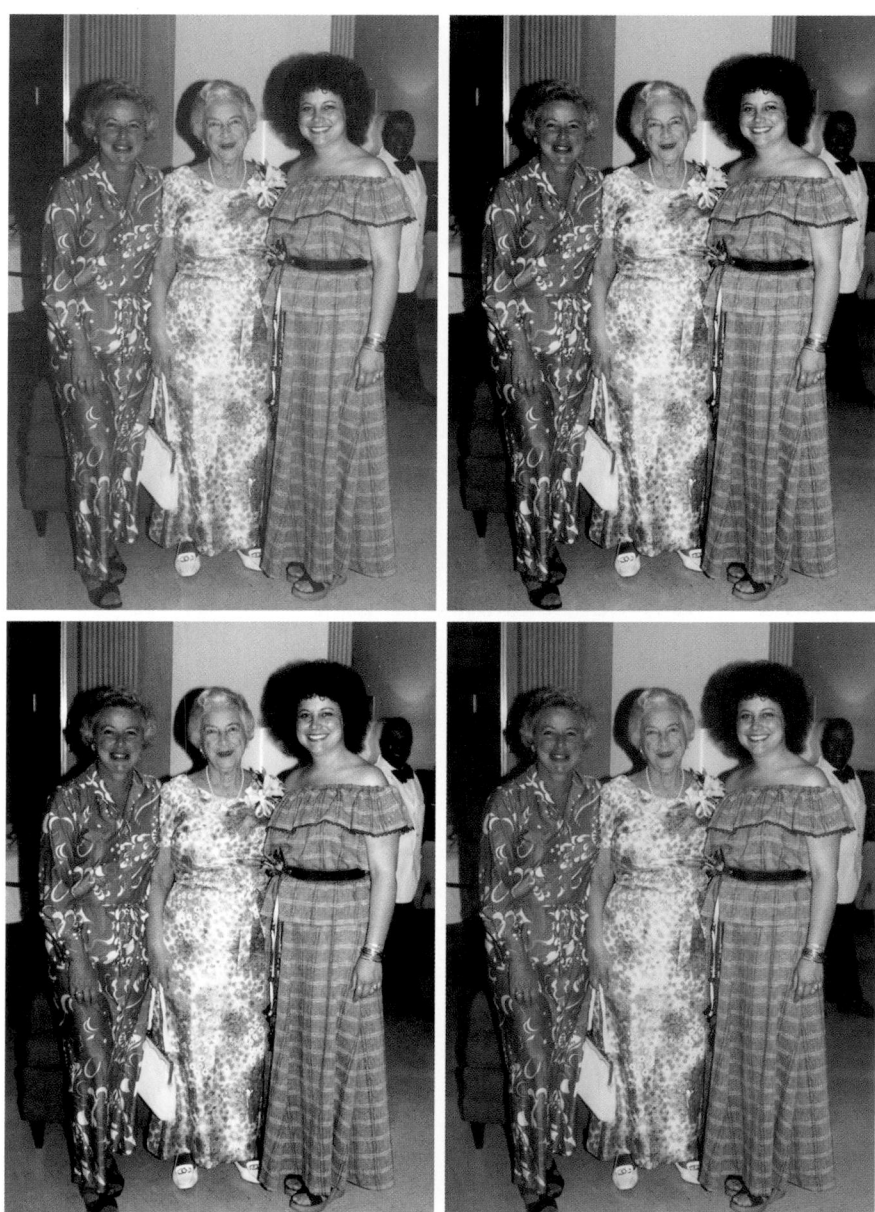

Fig. 6-15 Color correction three different ways. The original, faded photograph is in the upper left. I used Picture Window's Color Balance transformation to create the photograph at the upper right. Photoshop's Auto Color produced the lower right photograph, and DIGITAL ROC got me the photograph at lower left.

HOW TO USE LAYERS TO CORRECT COLOR AND LUMINOSITY SEPARATELY (continued)

on the original files) and I pasted the Auto Color image from Figure 6-13 into it. That made the original scan the background layer and the Auto Color version Layer 1. I set Layer 1's blend option to Color. That superimposed the color changes onto the original but threw away the tonal changes, giving me Figure 6-16. The composite is now very washed out, like the original, but I can fix this with a Curves adjustment

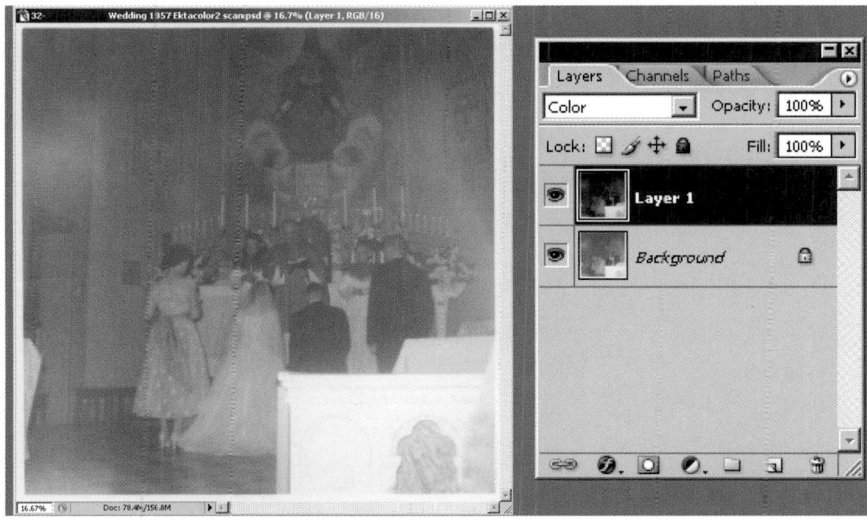

Fig. 6-16 Layers is a great tool for controlling color and tonality separately. This photograph is based on Figure 6-13. Auto Color does a good job of bringing back some of the color to that photograph, but it produces a photograph that's far too dark. In this photograph, I've copied Figure 6-13 into a new layer on top of the original photograph. Setting the blend mode for that layer to Color applies the color changes wrought by Auto Color, but not the brightness and contrast changes.

HOW TO USE LAYERS
TO CORRECT COLOR
AND LUMINOSITY
SEPARATELY
(continued)

layer (Figure 6-17). The settings for that layer are shown in Figure 6-18.

The most important change is the huge contrast boost in the RGB curve, where I pulled the black end point way in to produce a much wider range of tones in the photograph. I also made moderate adjustments to the red, green, and blue curves to get more neutral whites and blacks. This is a much better result than I got from Auto Color alone, and it's a vast improvement over Figure 6-10. Figure 6-19 shows the before and after histograms for this heavily modified image. Even though the photograph has undergone drastic changes, there are no major gaps in the new histograms. That's the benefit of working with 16-bit color files instead of 8-bit.

Similar tricks improved the photograph I corrected with DIGITAL ROC in Figure 6-15. I began with the uncorrected image as the background layer and pasted in two copies of the DIGITAL ROC-altered photograph (Figure 6-20) as Layers 1 and 2. I set the blend mode on Layer 1 to Color. I changed the blend mode on Layer 2 to Luminosity and dropped its opacity to 32%. These layers retained all the color alterations that DIGITAL ROC had made to the original photograph, but only about one-third of the tone and brightness changes. That suppressed the excessive contrast produced by DIGITAL ROC and gave me the photograph on the left in Figure 6-21.

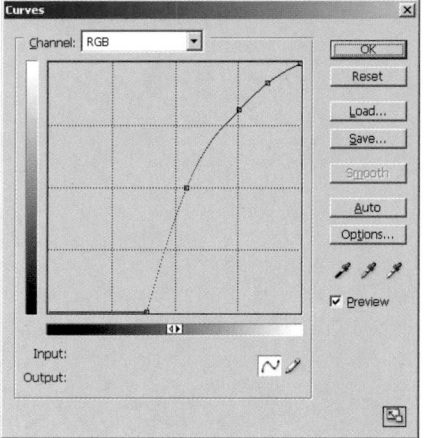

Fig. 6-17 A Curves adjustment layer improves Figure 6-16. Note that this layer is above the other two layers, because I want it to work its changes on the photograph after the Auto Color corrections have been applied. The Curves settings are shown in Figure 6-18.

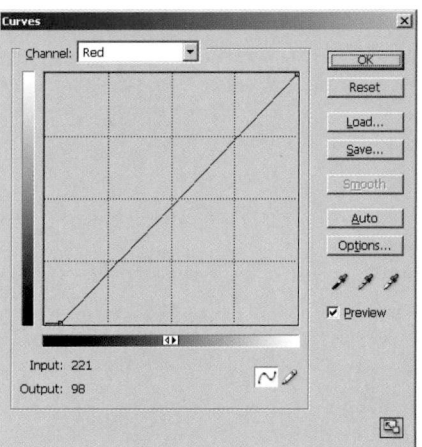

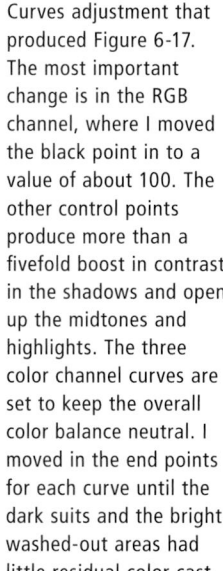

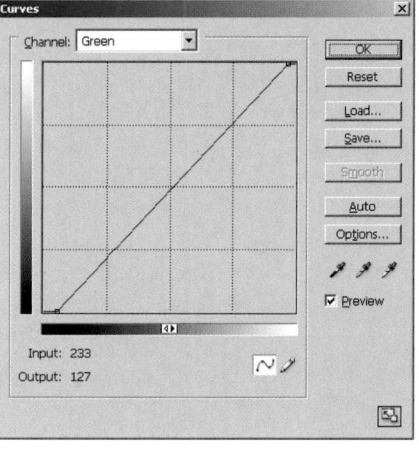

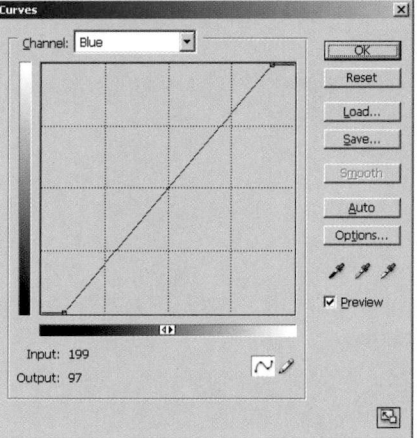

Fig. 6-18 This is the Curves adjustment that produced Figure 6-17. The most important change is in the RGB channel, where I moved the black point in to a value of about 100. The other control points produce more than a fivefold boost in contrast in the shadows and open up the midtones and highlights. The three color channel curves are set to keep the overall color balance neutral. I moved in the end points for each curve until the dark suits and the bright washed-out areas had little residual color cast.

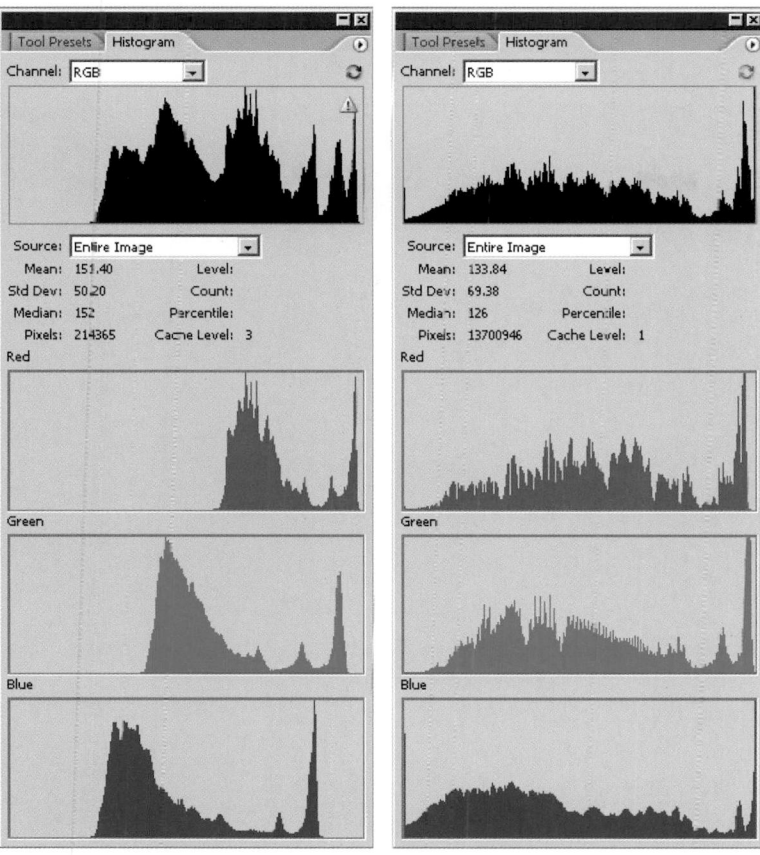

Fig. 6-19 The histogram on the left corresponds to Figure 6-10. The tonal distributions in each color channel are narrow, and they're displaced horizontally with respect to each other. That says that the photograph is low in contrast and has a pronounced color cast. The histogram on the right represents Figure 6-17; it shows the beneficial effects that Auto Color and a Curves adjustment layer have on this photograph's tone and color distribution.

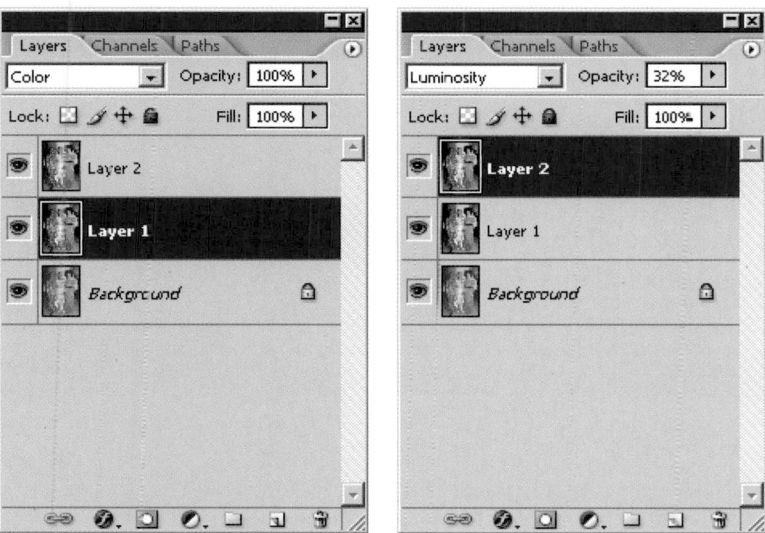

Fig. 6-20 Layers make DIGITAL ROC work a lot better. ROC does a great job of restoring color, but it tends to increase contrast too much, blowing out the near-whites and near-blacks in a photograph. I fix that by applying ROC to two duplicate layers instead of the original background layer. I set Layer 1 to Color blend and leave the opacity at 100%, so I get the full benefit of the color correction. I set Layer to Luminosity blend and drop the opacity on that layer until the contrast looks right, as shown in Figure 6-21, left. This has the same color as Figure 6-15, lower left, but the layered version has much better contrast and doesn't look anywhere as harsh.

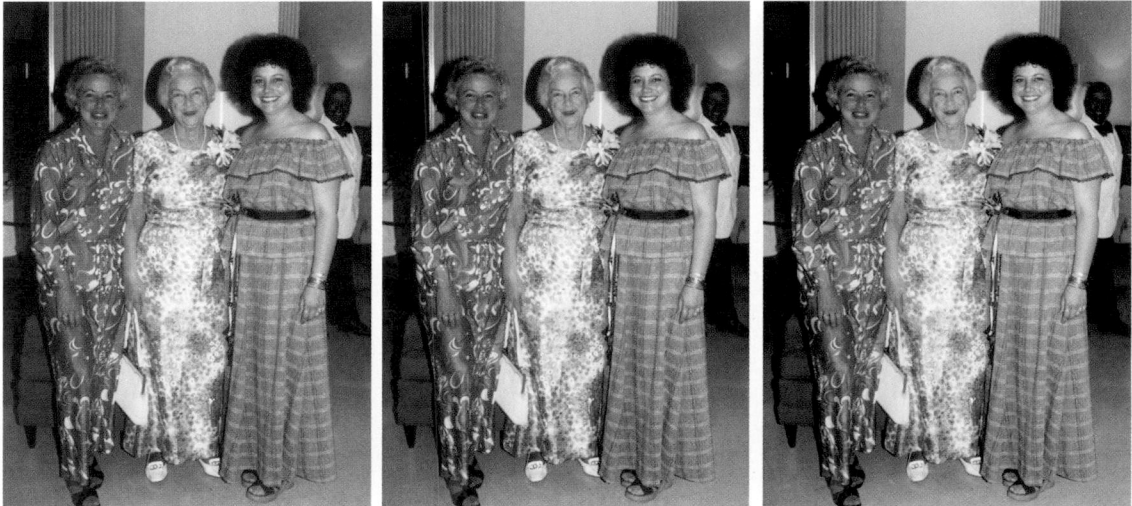

Fig. 6-21 The photograph on the left shows how DIGITAL ROC, applied in Color and Luminosity layers, substantially improves on the original photograph. The middle figure shows the photograph after applying the Hue/Saturation adjustment layer shown in Figure 6-22. The figure on the right has better shadows and blacks because I inserted a Curves adjustment layer into the layers stack, as I've shown in Figure 6-23.

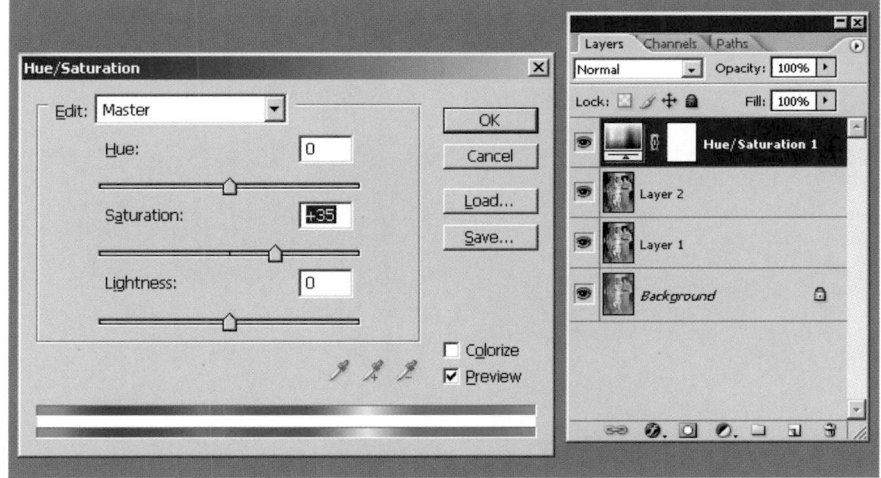

Fig. 6-22 This Hue/Saturation adjustment layer substantially boosts the saturation in Figure 6-21, center.

HOW TO IMPROVE COLOR WITH CURVES AND HUE/SATURATION ADJUSTMENT LAYERS

This photograph is undersaturated, so I added a Hue/Saturation adjustment layer (Figure 6-22) and set the saturation level to +35. That got me to the middle photograph in Figure 6-21. I felt the tonality could use some further improvement: The midtones and highlights were too harsh and contrasty, while the shadows were washed out. So I created a Curves adjustment layer between Layer 2 and the Hue/Saturation

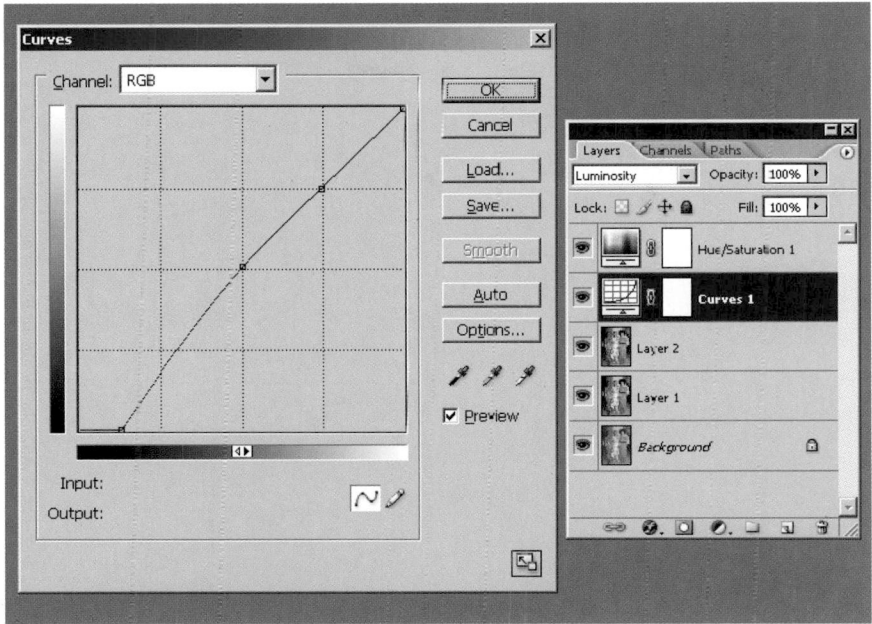

Fig. 6-23 This Curves adjustment layer produced Figure 6-21, right. It creates better blacks without altering the midtones and highlights. The blend mode is set to Luminosity so that it doesn't alter the saturation of the photograph; that's the job of the Hue/Saturation layer above it.

adjustment layer (Figure 6-23). I set the blend mode to Luminosity so that it would alter the tones but not the colors. The curve increased the contrast in the shadows and made the darkest tones much closer to true black, while slightly lightening and lowering the contrast in the mid-tones and highlights. That produced the right-hand photograph in Figure 6-21.

We're well on our way, but this photograph needs a lot more work before it will be a good restoration. Some color distortions should be corrected—the highlights are pink, while the shadows have gone a bit cyan. The skin tones aren't pleasant, mostly because there's way too much contrast in the faces. While that was probably a result of the on-camera flash and may be an entirely "accurate" restoration, it's not attractive!

Fixing the overall color isn't hard. In Figure 6-24 I added two eye-dropper readouts to the photograph to show the color errors in the highlights and the shadows that I talked about. I opened up the Curves tool (Figure 6-25) and adjusted the end points for the red and blue curves to make the highlight and shadow readouts neutral.

That greatly improved the overall color, which is now considerably more accurate in the clothes and the room furnishings. The shadows and highlights no longer have a bad color cast. Unfortunately, this has made the skin tones look even worse (Figure 6-26, left). Fortunately there's a solution.

HOW TO IMPROVE COLOR WITH CURVES AND HUE/ SATURATION ADJUSTMENT LAYERS (continued)

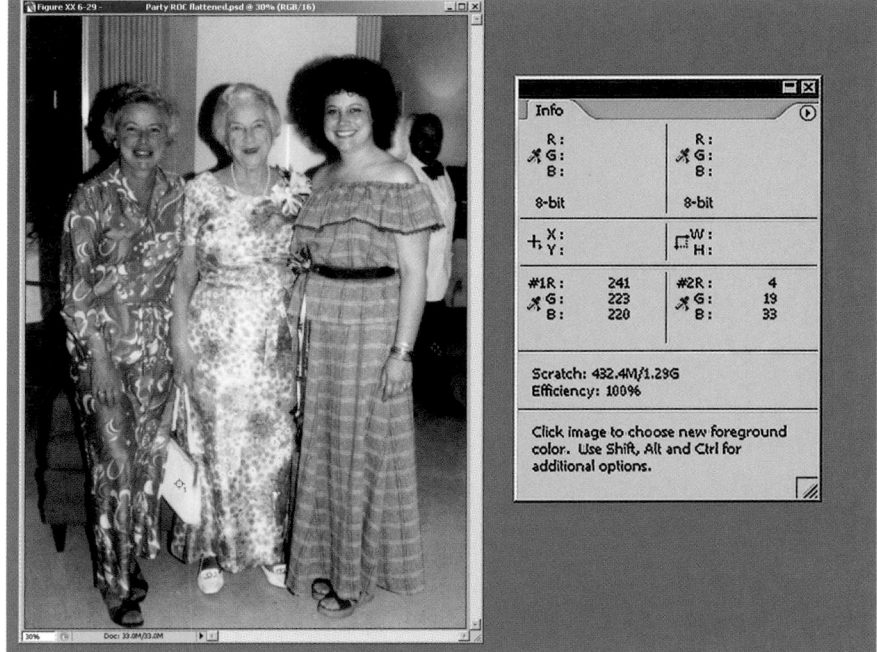

Fig. 6-24 This photograph still needs some color correction, so I've added two sample points by shift-clicking with the eyedropper on the photograph. Those sample points, in the white purse and the black pants of the waiter, will guide me as I adjust the curves of a Curves adjustment layer in Figure 6-25.

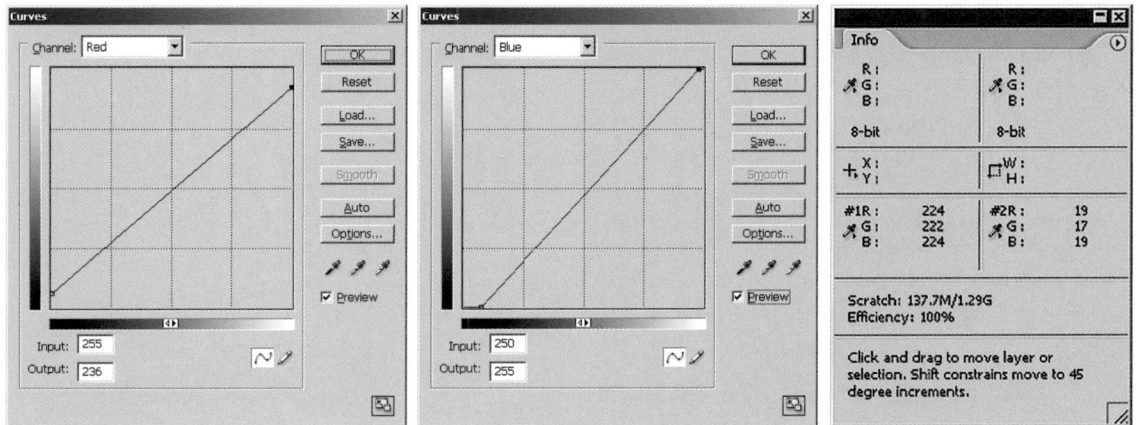

Fig. 6-25 To make the sample points in Figure 6-24 neutral, I adjusted the end points on the red curve to darken the whites and lighten the "blacks," so that the red values in the sample points matched the green values (Info window on right). I made similar adjustments to the end points of the blue curve, so that all three values were approximately the same, resulting in neutral blacks and whites. This Curves adjustment layer produces better and more accurate colors in most of the photograph, but the skin tones lost their healthy richness (Figure 6-26, left).

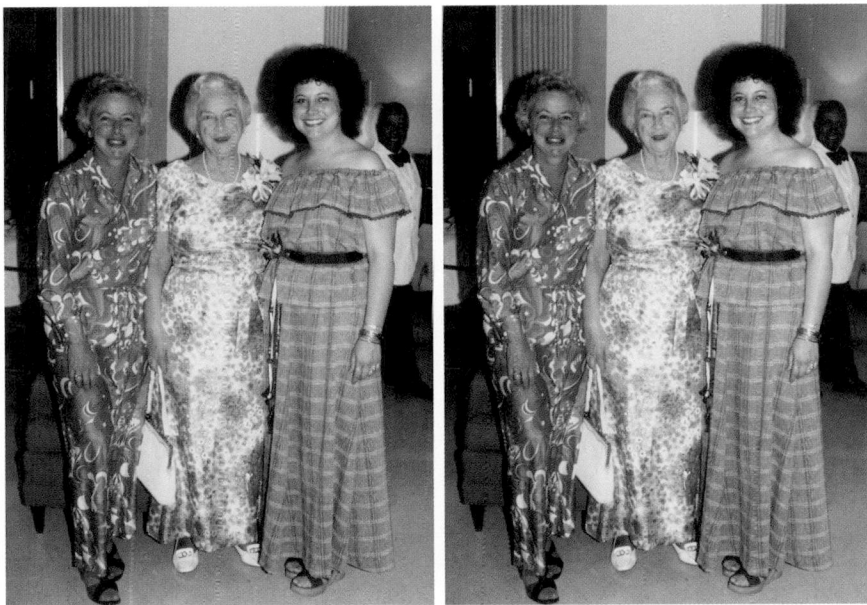

Fig. 6-26 The photograph on the left, the result of applying a Curves adjustment ayer with the curves shown in Figure 6-25, has a more correct overall color balance, but the skin tones were better without this adjustment. To fix that, I created a mask for the adjustment layer (Figure 6-27) which blocks the effect of the adjustment layer on the women's skin. The result, right, combines the good skin tones of the earlier version with the more neutral and correct overall color produced by the Curves adjustment layer.

Getting Better Skin Tones

The Layered Approach

I had applied the curves in Figure 6-25 as a Curves adjustment layer. Because of that, I can now alter where those curves get applied to the photograph by adding a mask. In this case, I decided to paint the mask in by hand because the areas that needed to be masked were pretty simple. I could just as easily have used a tool such as Mask Pro, and for a more complex masking job that's what I would do.

There are no irreversible mistakes when creating a layer mask. I started off with a large-radius black brush and painted over the faces and arms of the women. Then I shrank the radius of the brush and filled in the edges. If I painted out too far, I switched the brush to white and corrected my errors. Pressing the "Q" key turns the Quickmask view on and off in Photoshop, so I could inspect the mask directly while cleaning it up. I checked it frequently to make sure I didn't miss a spot.

In about half an hour, I had the mask shown in Figure 6-27. That mask blocked the effect of the Curves adjustment on the faces and arms, producing the photograph in Figure 6-26, right.

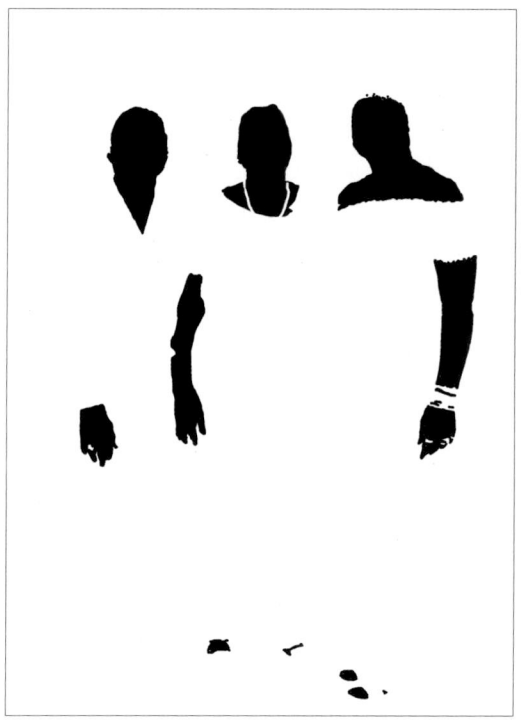

Fig. 6-27 This mask separates the skin tones from everything else in the photograph. By using this mask (and its inverse) I can create adjustment layers for the photograph that worked separately on the skin tones and the rest of the photograph, as I do in Figures 6-26 and 6-29.

I'm not finished with that mask. Masks are just grayscale images and they can be copied and pasted and modified with all the usual Photoshop tools. Inverted, this mask would help me correct the skin tones.

Skin tones in old color photographs commonly have two problems. The first is high overall contrast: Tones are usually too harsh, and highlights tend to be blown out, with lines and shadows accentuated. The second problem is blotchy color; high contrast in each of the individual color channels exaggerates what should be more subtle differences in skin hues. Instead of having a healthy range of colors, you see faces with some patches that look flushed and others that look jaundiced.

I can fix problems like these with adjustment layers or with careful hand work. First, I'll show you the adjustment layer approach. In this example I apply the same corrections to all three women's faces, which won't be optimal for any of them. For high-quality work, I'd make individual masks for each woman and correct each one's skin tones separately.

I copied the mask from Figure 6-27, inverted it, and used it to create a Curves adjustment layer (Figure 6-28). I set the blend mode on that layer to Luminosity so that it would alter tonal values but not colors. What that curve did was reduce contrast in the midtones and highlights and drop the maximum density in the highlights.

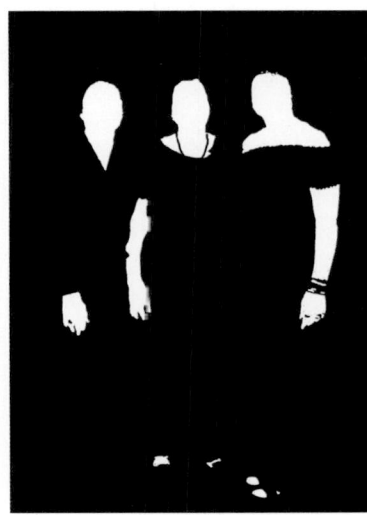

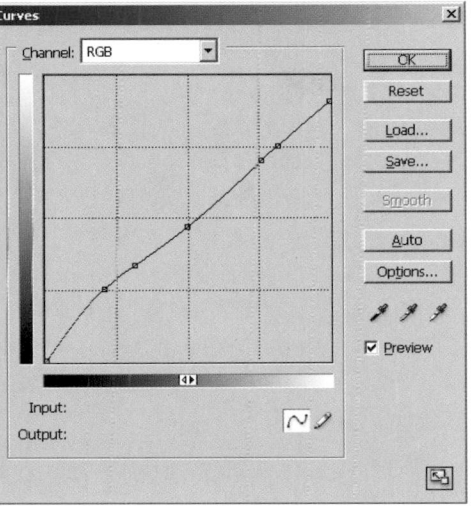

Fig. 6-28 This is the basis for another Curves adjustment layer to be used with Luminosity blend. The mask for this layer, at left, restricts the adjustment to working only on the skin tones. The RGB curve reduces contrast and substantially tones down the bright hot spots in the women's complexions caused by the on-camera flash.

Figure 6-29 shows successive improvements I made to the women's complexions. Figure 6-29a is the same as in Figure 6-26, just repeated here for easy comparison. The second photo (Figure 6-29b) shows the effect of the luminosity Curves adjustment layer I just created. There's no change in the color balance, but the harsh effects of the on-camera flash are tamed.

With lower contrast, it's easier to see the blotchy color problem I described. To understand what's behind that, look at Figure 6-30. From top to bottom, this shows the red, green, and blue channels of the aforementioned photograph. The red channel looks great. The contrast in the faces in the green channel (the magenta hues) is a little bit high, and the contrast in the blue channel (corresponding to yellow) looks very harsh. It's that excess contrast in the magenta and especially the yellow hues that causes the blotchy skin colors.

I described in Chapter 5 how to use an inverted-S curve to tame midtone contrast. That's just what I did here. Figure 6-31 shows green and blue curves that will substantially soften those problematic colors. I created a second Curves adjustment layer using the mask for the women, this time with the blend mode set to color. I applied the curves from Figure 6-31, which produced Figure 6-29c.

HOW TO MAKE SKIN TONES SMOOTHER WITH CURVES ADJUSTMENT LAYERS

The skin tones here looked pretty natural, but I felt they were a little bit under-saturated. There's a flat and pasty quality to them, typical of insufficient saturation. So, I created a third masked adjustment layer, this time for Hue/Saturation, and applied the settings in Figure 6-32. That produced Figure 6-29d. The complete stack of layers for these corrections is shown in Figure 6-32, right.

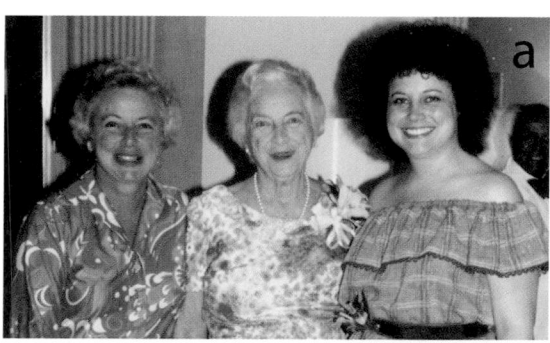

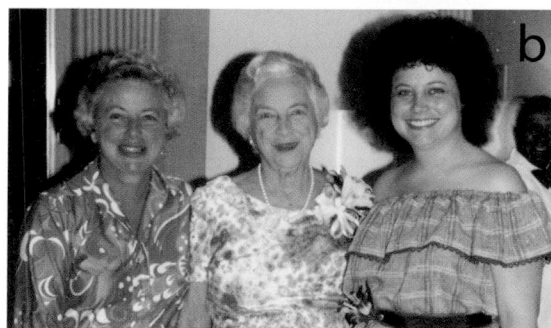

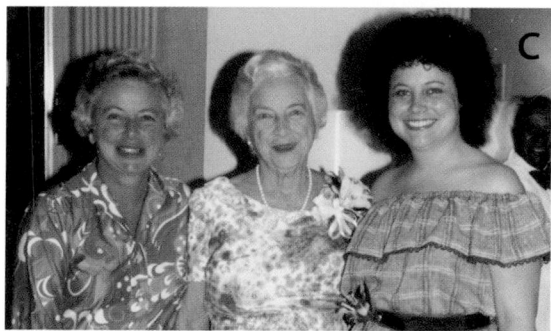

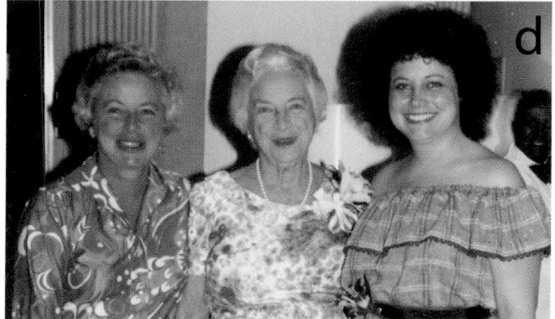

Fig. 6-29 Masked adjustment layers make a big improvement in skin tones. Figure (a) is a section from Figure 6-26, right. It shows the background image with DIGITAL ROC applied in a masked layer. This photograph corresponds to the bottom two layers, "background" and "ROC," in the layer stack shown later in Figure 6-32. Figure (b) shows how the harsh highlights are softened by the Curves adjustment layer from Figure 6-28 (the "Women 0" layer in Figure 6-32). (c) Skin tones still look blotchy, with uneven yellowish and pinkish patches. Another Curves adjustment layer, "Women 1," using the settings in Figure 6-31, fixes that. Finally, a Hue / Saturation layer using the settings in Figure 6-32 improves the saturation and refines the brightness to produce the natural-looking results in Figure (d).

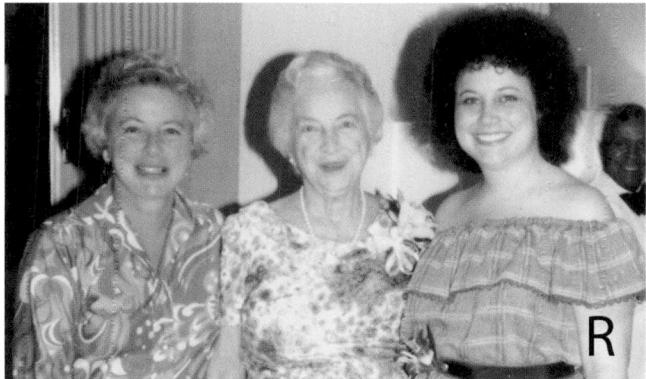

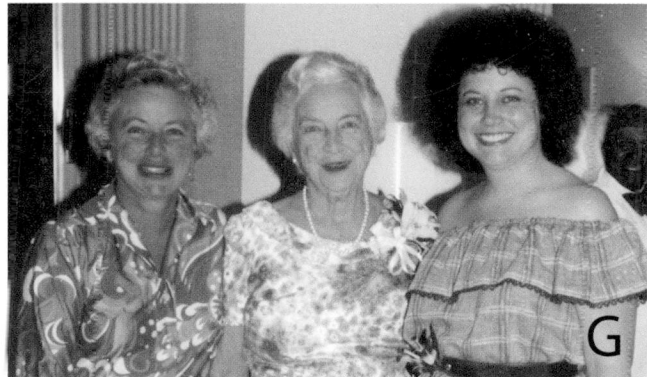

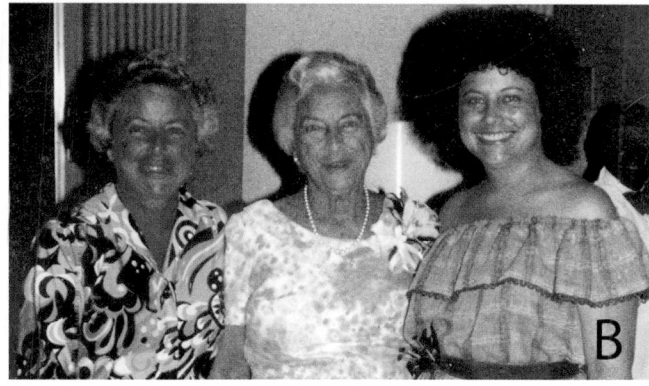

Fig. 6-30 These individual channel images show why the skin tones in Figure 6-29b look blotchy. The red channel (R) has smooth, low contrast, but the green channel (G) is harsher, and the blue channel (B) shows large variations in brightness in the skin areas. The curves in Figure 6-31 fix this.

The Airbrushed Layers Approach

When a photograph has too much contrast in the faces but the color is pretty good, a little handwork often does the trick. Consider Figure 6-33. The original photograph is on the left, my improved scan on the right. I used the scan Levels settings in Figure 6-34 to get reasonably neutral highlights and shadows. The other colors and tones pretty much fell into line.

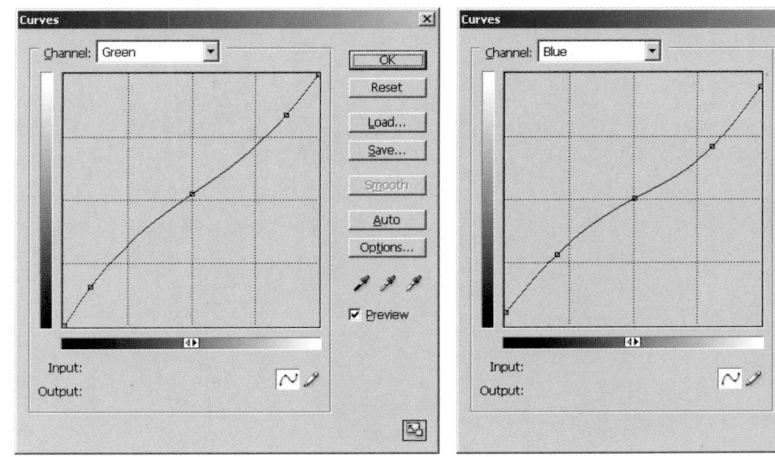

Fig. 6-31 These inverted-S curves, applied in the masked adjustment layer "Women 1," even out the skin color because they reduce the contrast in the midtones of the green and blue channels. Lower contrast means smaller color differences, so excessive variations in skin color are suppressed.

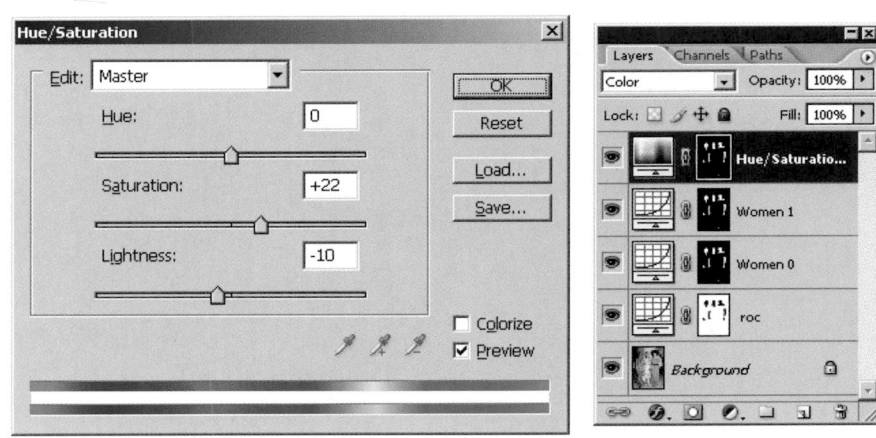

Fig. 6-32 A Hue/Saturation adjustment layer completes the layer stack that fixes the skin tones in Figure 6-29d. Increasing the saturation removes the pasty look from the faces, and darkening the tones a little bit makes them blend in better with the rest of the photograph. Like the two underlying Curves layers, this layer uses the mask from Figure 6-28.

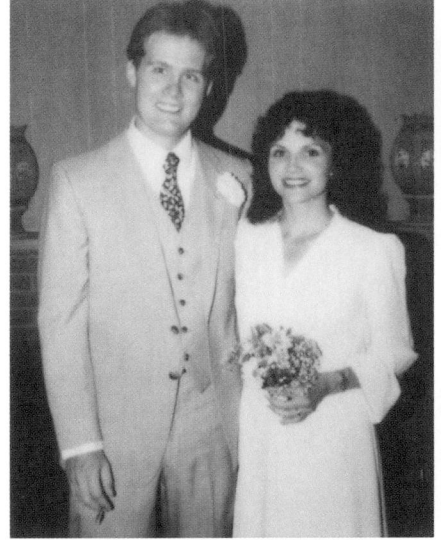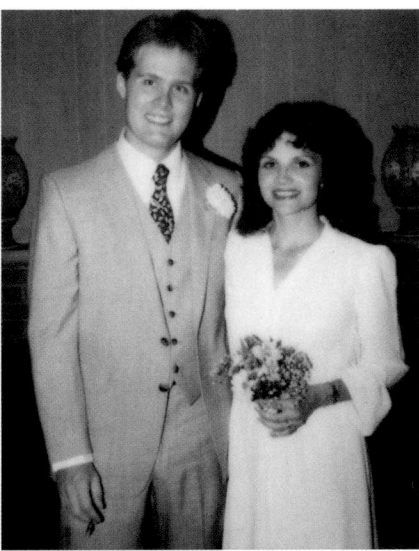

Fig. 6-33 The original photograph (left) is moderately faded and stained, but a good scan fixes most of that (right).

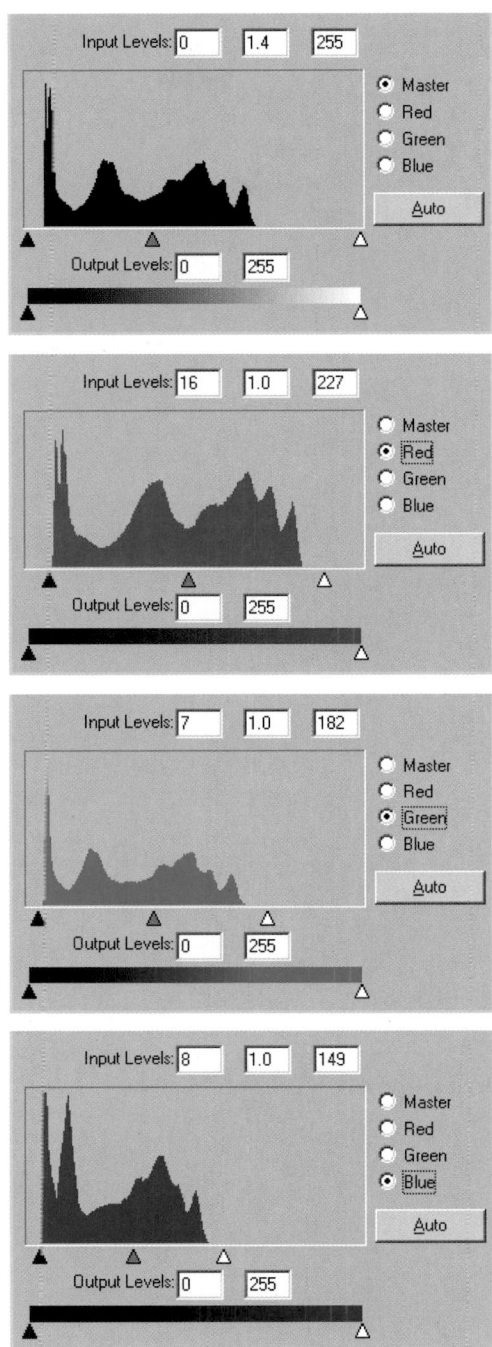

Fig. 6-34 The scanner software histograms and levels adjustments for Figure 6-33. As is typically the case, bracketing the range of tones in the histograms with the black and white Levels sliders produces a much-improved photograph.

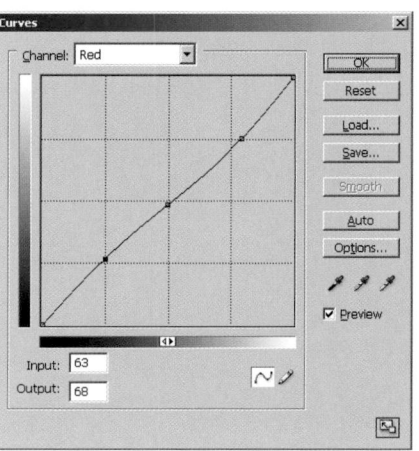
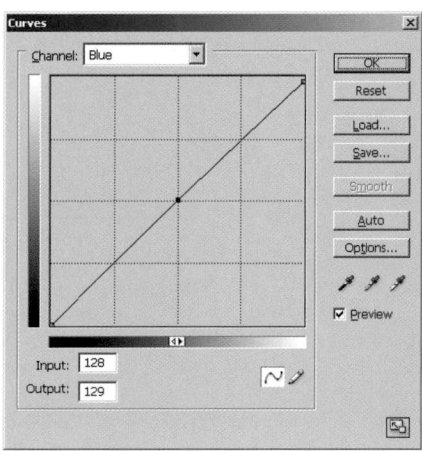

Fig. 6-35 The white dress and gray suit in Figure 6-33 made color correction much easier; they gave me a wide range of neutral tones to aim for. These red and blue curves make the clothes come out neutral (Figure 6-36, left). I applied these curves in a Curves adjustment layer named "Curves 1," as shown in Figure 6-37.

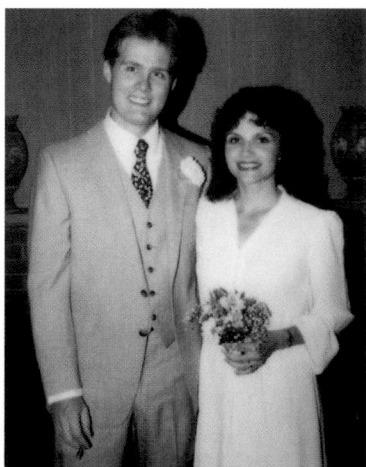
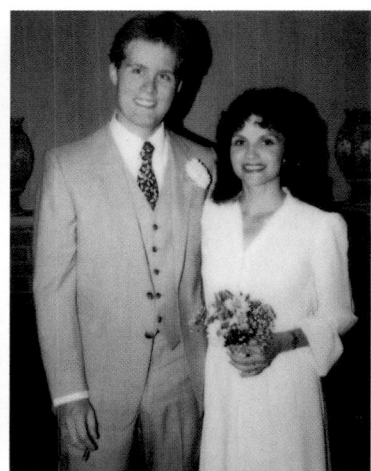
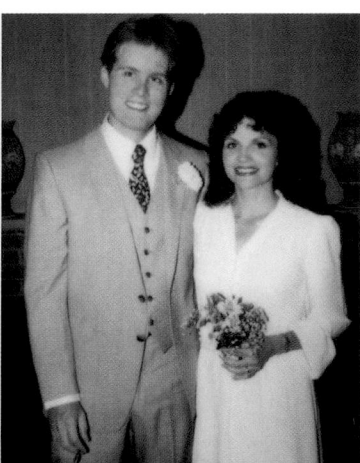

Fig. 6-36 The photograph on the left shows how the Curves adjustment layer from Figure 6-35 improves this photograph. Although the color is quite good, the skin tones have that harsh, "on-flash" look. The middle photograph shows how an airbrush darkening layer eliminates the hot spots on the couple's faces. A lightening airbrush layer softens the shadows on their faces and hands (right). The lighting in the photograph now looks much more professional and natural than it did in the original.

There's a little bit of color crossover, with the highlights being too pink and the shadows too cyan, but the man's suit made it really easy to correct this by eye. All I needed to do was use the eyedropper to look at the colors in various tones in his suit and shirt, by clicking/sampling different places on the suit and shirt, and adjust some of the curves so that they came out neutral. The curve settings I used are in Figure 6-35. That got me to Figure 6-36, left.

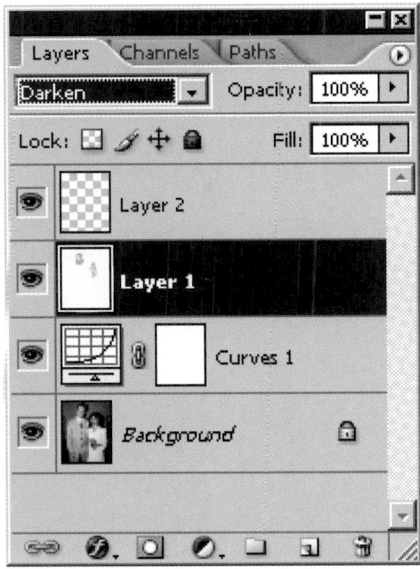

Fig. 6-37 The layer stack that fixes Figure 6-36. Layer 1 is an airbrush layer set to Darken blend, and it removes the hot spots from the photograph. Layer 2 is set to Lighten blend; airbrushing in that layer opens up the shadows.

✓ HOW TO RETOUCH SKIN TONES WITH AN AIRBRUSH LAYER

I was happy with the color balance, but not with the contrast; there were lots of blown-out highlights in the faces, and the shadows were pretty harsh. I decided to airbrush away these problems. Instead of attacking the problems directly, though, I created some special retouching layers to make the work much easier and less error prone. I added two layers to the photograph (Figure 6-37) and set Layer 1 to Darken blend and Layer 2 to Lighten blend. Note that these are not adjustment layers; they're ordinary image layers.

Next I selected the airbrush tool and set its opacity to a very low level: 9%. I activated Layer 1, sampled the color in the man's face next to the highlight on his forehead, and started airbrushing over his forehead. Because I had the opacity set to such a low level, I could build up tone very, very gradually and blend it in smoothly with the surrounding skin tones.

With this layer set to Darken mode and such a light tone in the airbrush, I didn't have to worry about accidentally airbrushing over any of the other parts of his face. Sloppy brushwork won't mess up tones that I don't want to change. Should I slip with the brush and run it across his hair or a darker midtone, it would have no effect on the blended image, because the color I was painting with would be lighter than those background layer colors. When I did occasionally overextend my retouching, I airbrushed away the excess retouching by switching the color of the brush to white. Alternately, I could've used a white eraser to remove my mistakes from the layer.

I airbrushed any part of his face where I thought the highlights were too bright and shiny. Wherever I airbrushed a highlight, I used color ▼

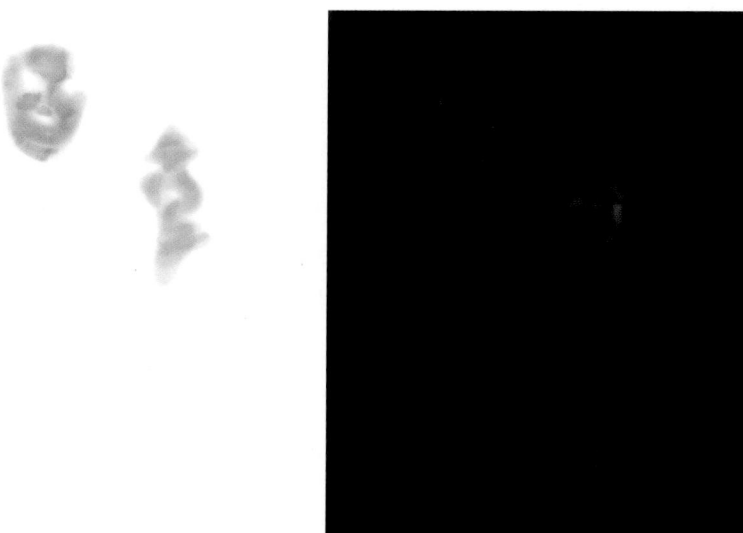

Fig. 6-38 Here's what I painted into the airbrush layers of Figure 6-36. The figure on the left shows the Darken airbrush work that reduces glare and reflections from the skin tones. The mostly black figure on the right represents the contents of the lightening airbrush layer; this is what softens the shadows. This layer is actually mostly transparent; I made the background black for clarity's sake.

HOW TO RETOUCH
SKIN TONES WITH AN
AIRBRUSH LAYER
(continued)

sampled from a nearby area. For example, when I airbrushed his cheeks I sampled a spot of color right under his eye. When I was toning down the highlight on his chin, I sampled the color between his lower lip and the chin. This kind of retouching is really easy; it took me longer to write this that it did to do the work. You'll probably find that it's much simpler to do it than to understand my explanation of it.

The darkening retouching I did is shown in Figure 6-38, left. As you can see, I didn't follow the outlines of the face or highlights very closely at all. The results, shown in Figure 6-36, center, look entirely professional. Blending in light-toned airbrushing like this really does produce a seamless-looking photograph.

To deal with the shadows, especially those in the woman's face and hand, I switched to Layer 2, which was set to Lighten blend. I worked the same way I had in Layer 1, using the airbrush at very low opacity and setting its color to one that was adjacent to the shadows I wanted to lighten.

I didn't try to remove much of the shadowing; shadows define the shape and three-dimensional structure of the faces and hand. Flatten out those tones too much, and you'll get a very strange look, as if people were wearing flat cardboard masks with pictures of their faces on them. You don't want to go that far! The shadow work that I did is shown in the right half of Figure 6-38. I made the background black in this illustration so that the airbrushing would be visible as lighter brush strokes against the background. The background of that layer is actually transparent, but that makes it too hard to see the airbrush work, which is pretty subtle. The combined highlight and shadow retouching produced the photograph in Figure 6-36, right.

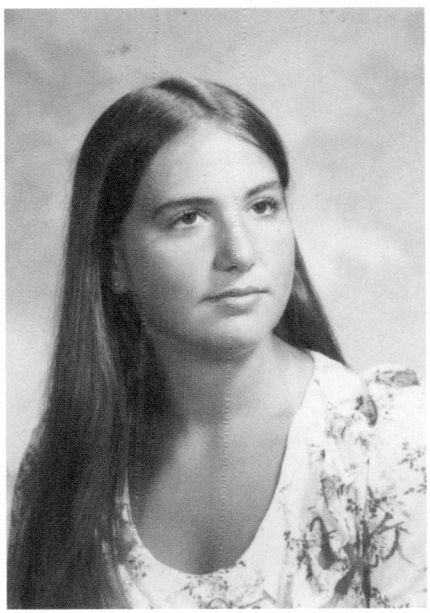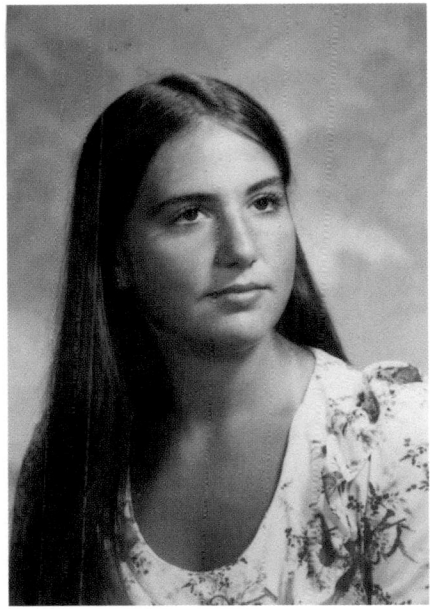

Fig. 6-39 This old school portrait (left) is very badly faded, with little color apparent save for pale greens and purples. A good scan (right) reveals a lot more detail in the photograph, but the color is still extremely anemic.

In truth, I overdid the retouching in this example to make sure the changes would show up clearly in the illustration for this book. But my efforts weren't wasted. A nice thing about having done this work in layers is that I can dial back the strength of my retouching. Dropping the opacity in the two retouching layers to a strength of about 60% gets me a photograph that looks great as a finished print.

The Color Airbrushing Approach

A nice, painterly tool for correcting blotchy skin colors is the color airbrush. In fact, the color airbrush is good for correcting all kinds of color aberrations when pleasing color is more important than technically accurate results. Like the previously described airbrush techniques, it's fast, flexible, reversible, and it doesn't require you to be a great artist to use it effectively.

The school portrait in Figure 6-39, left, was extremely faded. To the eye, it seemed to have only two colors—a washed out green and a reddish purple. I made a good scan of the print, following the methods I've used with the other color photos, carefully bracketing the tones in the scanner software color histograms with the black and white Levels sliders. This scan (Figure 6-39, right) showed there was more to the photo, but it was in very bad shape.

✓ HOW TO FIX A FADED SCHOOL PORTRAIT WITH AIRBRUSH LAYERS

The very first thing I did was to substantially increase the saturation (Figure 6-40) because there was so little color differentiation between ▼

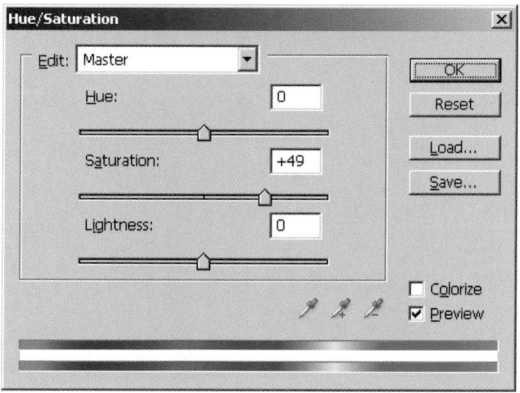

Fig. 6-40 A substantial (+49) increase in Saturation makes a big difference to the photograph in Figure 6-39. The results, in Figure 6-41a, show that better color is possible for this photograph.

HOW TO FIX A
FADED SCHOOL
PORTRAIT WITH
AIRBRUSH LAYERS
(continued)

the parts of the photograph. That produced Figure 6-41a. Now I needed to do something about the overall color. I made the curve changes shown in Figure 6-42. They are pretty complex, so I'll spend a little time describing what they do.

The RGB curve leaves the whites untouched, but it darkens the midtones and highlights and increases their contrast and detail. I left the moderate shadow tones alone, but I made the very darkest tones darker and closer to true black, which also increased the contrast in the deep shadows, bringing out their detail. The highlights were a little bit reddish, but the rest of the tones had a cyan cast. I lowered the maximum value of the red curve but added an adjustment point that raised all the other values, thereby adding a bit of cyan to the highlights but removing it from everything else. The shadows had a very strong magenta/purple cast to them, so I raised the shadow values in the green curve (subtracting magenta) and lowered them in the blue curve (adding yellow). I also removed a little bit of magenta and added a little bit of yellow to the midtones, but I made sure that the highlights didn't change because they were pretty neutral.

That got me to Figure 6-41b. That was good enough for me to start working with color airbrushing. I added a new, empty layer to the photograph and set the blend mode to Color—anything I painted into that layer would alter the color of the underlying photograph, but it wouldn't change its brightness or tonality.

I set the opacity of the Brush to 15%. Note that I used the tool in its Normal mode: The layer blend setting is taking care of how the airbrushing gets merged. If I wanted to paint directly on the original photograph, I'd select Color as the airbrush mode, but then I wouldn't have the ability to easily revise my work.

Figure 6-43 shows successive stages of color airbrushing from start to finish. First, I decided to remove the cyan cast that was still present in the highlights on the face and neck. I set the airbrush color to the

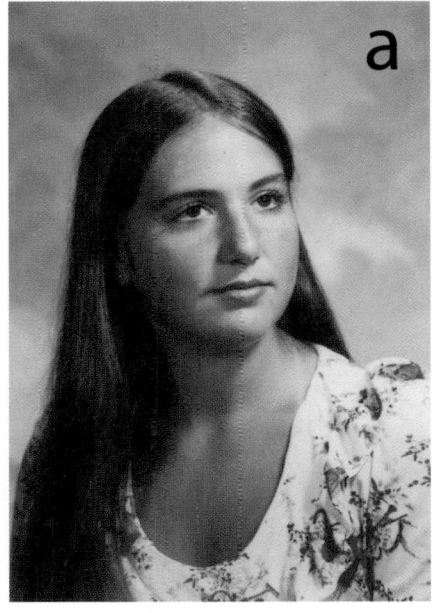
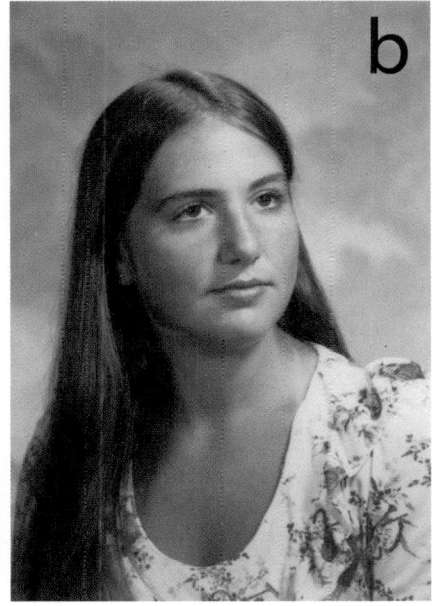
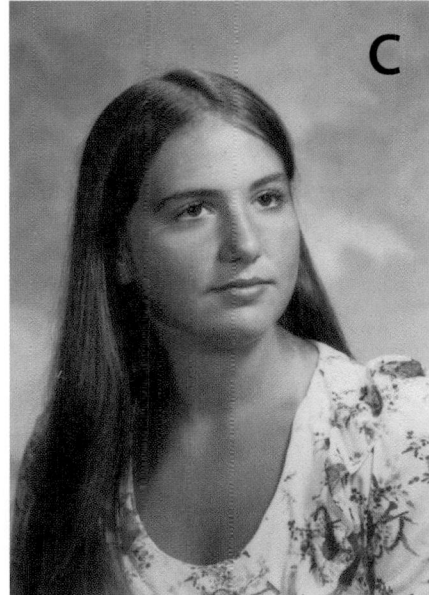
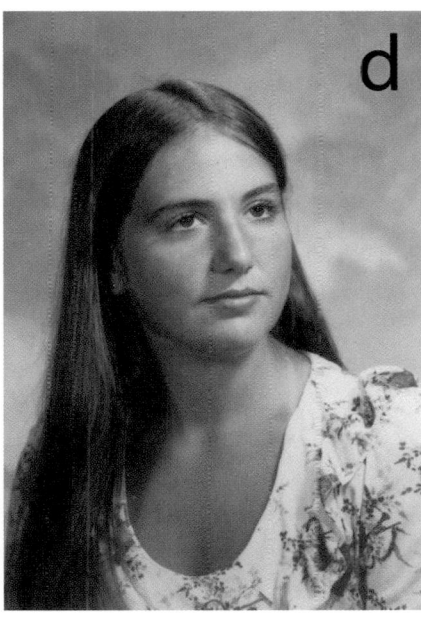

Fig. 6-41 Figure (a) is the result of applying the Hue/Saturation correction from Figure 6-40 to Figure 6-39. The color balance is poor, but at least there is color. (b) The curves in Figure 6-42 restored the overall color balance but leave many details to be corrected. (c) The same photograph after skin colors are repaired by the color airbrushing in Figure 6-43c, applied via a layer set for Color blend mode. See the main text for a full description of this technique. (d) This photograph now looks excellent after the complete color airbrushing shown in Figure 6-43f.

pink hue of the cheek and brushed over the woman's forehead, around her eye sockets, across the bridge of her nose and her upper lip and chin, and along her neck (Figure 6-43a). Her skin was now more uniform in color but too pink. I used a broad airbrush at very low opacity, selected some brown from her hair, and ran the brush over her skin to produce a flesh tone that I liked (Figure 6-43b).

HOW TO FIX A
FADED SCHOOL
PORTRAIT WITH
AIRBRUSH LAYERS
(continued)

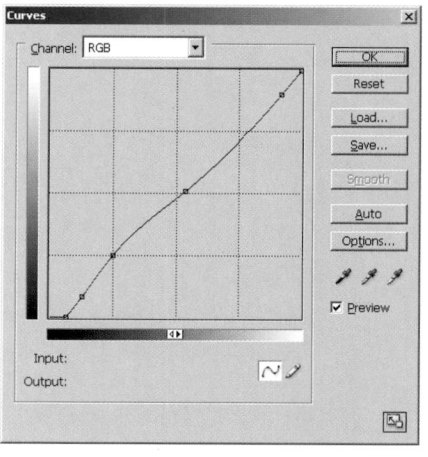
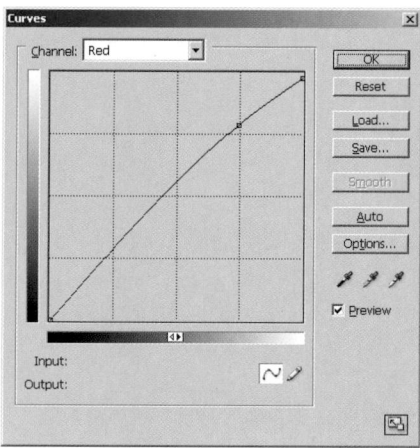
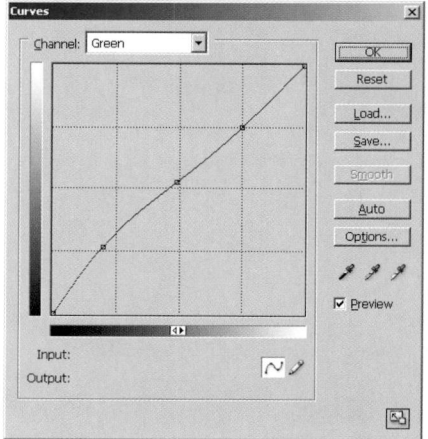
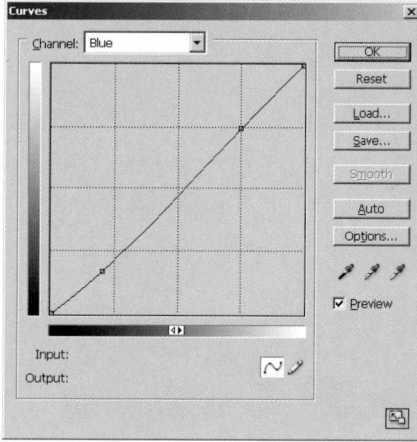

Fig. 6-42 These curves correct the overall color and tonality in Figure 6-41a, producing Figure 6-41b. See the main text for an explanation of how each curve affects the photograph.

The shadows on the woman's neck and hair were very magenta, so I selected a yellow-brown tone from her hair and painted over her neck at moderate strength and her hair at high strength to correct those colors (Figures 6-43c and d). That gave me the photograph in Figure 6-41c. Her hair and skin color now looked very good, with the magenta shadows obliterated and the cyan highlights converted to healthier skin tones.

The upper left part of the photograph was stained yellow, so I sampled the background on the right and used the airbrush at about 50% strength to change the color of the stained areas to match the rest of the background (Figure 6-43e). That got me almost to where I wanted to be.

The whites of her eyes and the folds of her dress were too cyan. I sampled a gray tone and used a small-radius brush at 30% opacity to dot in the whites of her eyes, erasing the cyan there. I then ran the brush over the folds of her dress, taking care to avoid the red pattern, making the folds in the fabric much more realistically neutral. The finished color

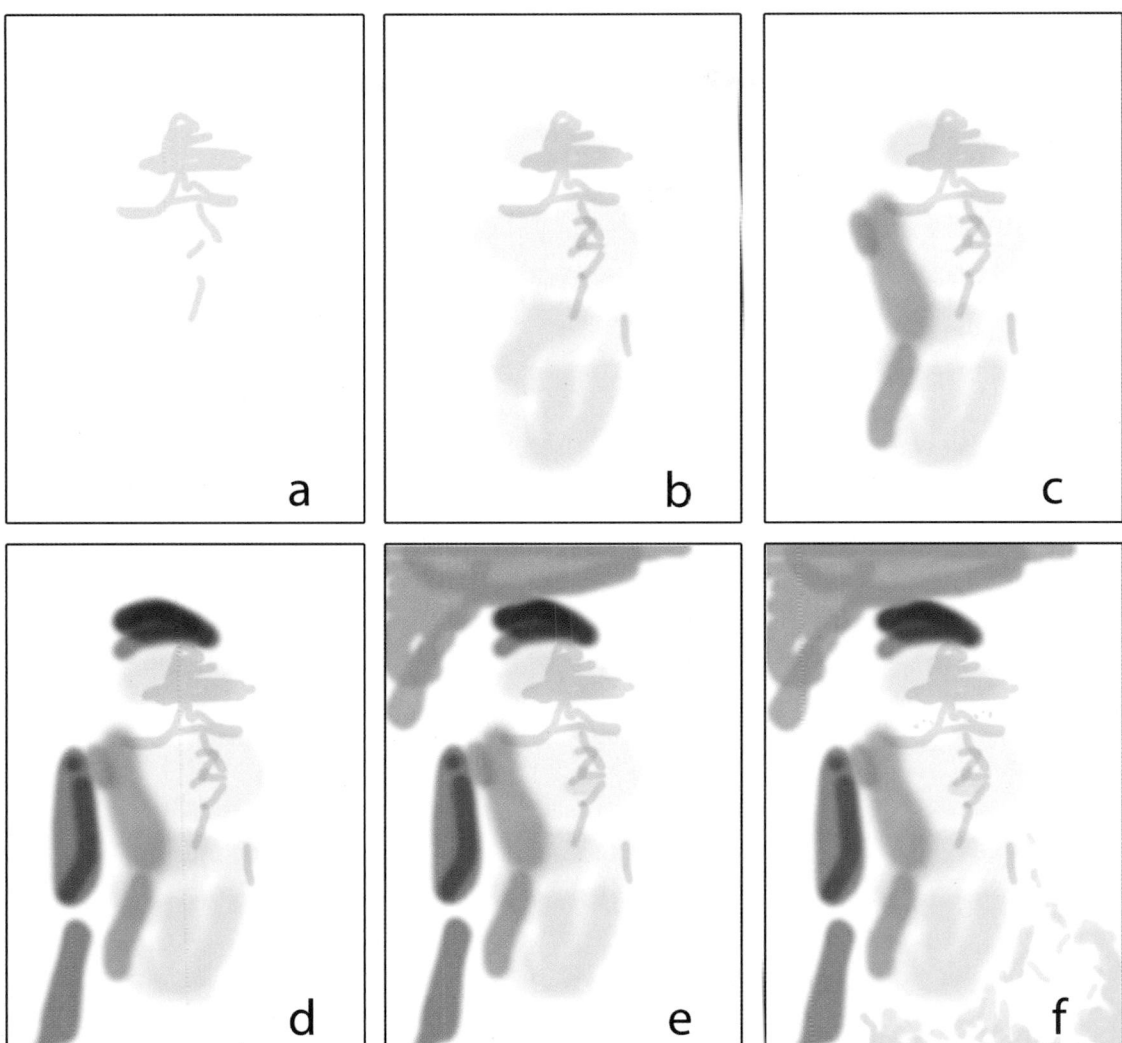

Fig. 6-43 Color airbrushing is done by painting into an empty layer whose blend mode has been set to Color. This shifts the hue of the underlying layers without altering their density or contrast. The frames here show successive stages in the process of airbrushing Figure 6-41. Restoration starts with airbrushing the highlights in the woman's face to eliminate their cyan cast. The airbrushing in frames (b) and (c) evens out the skin color over the rest of her face and eliminates greenish highlights on her hair. The effect of this intermediate stage of airbrushing is shown in Figure 6-41c. Frame (d) corrects the color in the woman's hair, and frame (e) removes the yellow stains from the background. Frame (f) makes the excessively cyan shadows and folds in her blouse more neutral, with the finished result shown in Figure 6-41d.

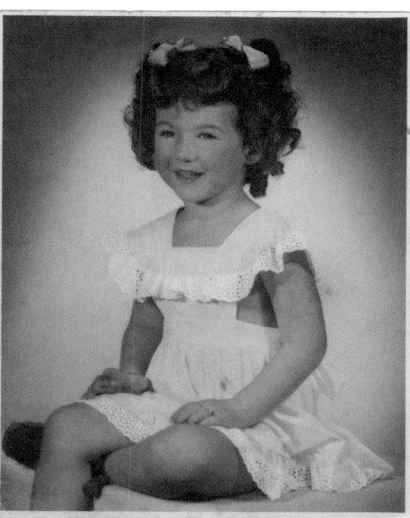 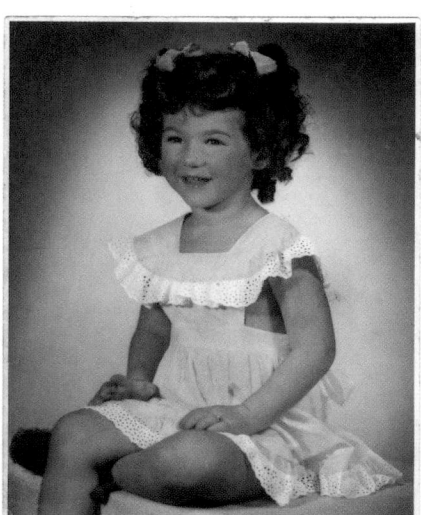

Fig. 6-44 On the left is a faded and stained hand-tinted photograph. On the right is the scan I made from it. The goal of the scan was only to get a full range of tones from black to white. The color balance of the scan isn't too important because I'm going to retint the photograph.

airbrush layer is shown in Figure 6-43f. That layer gave me the photograph in Figure 6-41d.

Using Masked Layers to Hand-Tint Photographs

Adjustment layers are a great way to repair hand-tinted B&W photographs. Figure 6-44 shows a 60-year-old photograph that has turned brown and faded. It also has a little bit of physical damage, some cracks and stains, but mostly it's the poor tonality and color that's the problem.

As with any restoration, the first step is making a good scan. The scan I made is shown on the right in Figure 6-44. The purpose of the scan was not to produce good color, but to get a good range of tones from near-black to near-white. The color was something I'd take care of with the adjustment layers.

HOW TO HAND-TINT A PHOTOGRAPH WITH MASKED LAYERS

I constructed a set of masks, one for each area that was to be tinted (see Chapter 7, Making Masks, page 257, for details). You can create such masks with the magic wand in Photoshop; the mask range selection tools in Picture Window; any of the masking plug-ins I recommended in Chapter 3, such as Asiva Select or Mask Pro; or you can draw the selection by hand with the Lasso or edge-selection tool. It doesn't really matter which method you use in a situation like this. It's not critical that the mask be perfect, because you can rework the masks at any time, adding or subtracting from them with the Brush tool.

I made masks for the dress, the background, the bare skin, the shoes, the hair ribbons, and the hair. I saved each selection in a separate channel and named it (Figure 6-45, left). Then I created Hue/Saturation

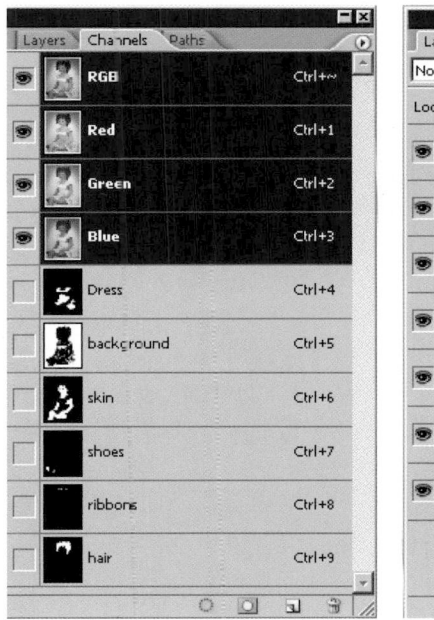 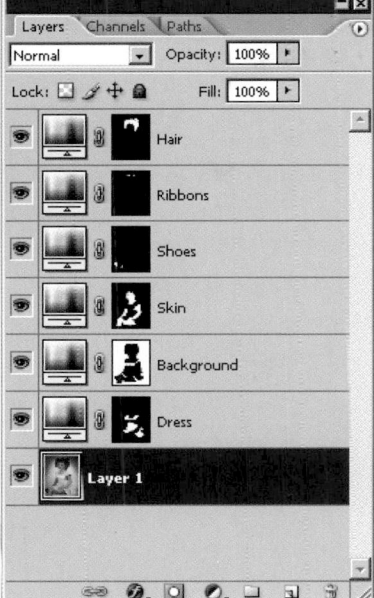

Fig. 6-45 On the left are the masking channels I created to hand-tint the photograph. See Chapter 7 for techniques for making these masks. On the right is the stack of Hue/Saturation adjustment layers I created from those masks. Each layer corrects the tint in a different part of the photograph.

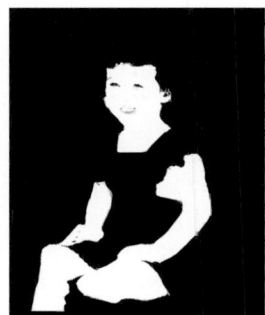 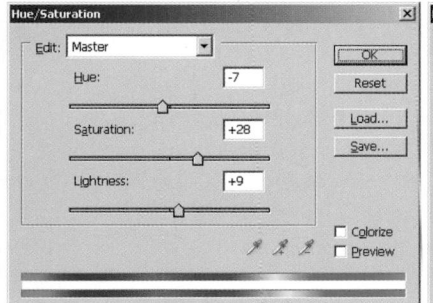 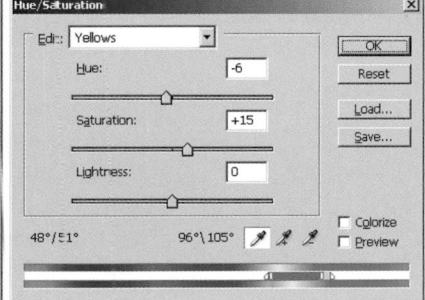

Fig. 6-46 These are the adjustments in the Skin adjustment layer. On the left is the mask for the layer, which restricts its effect to bare skin only. The Master Hue/Saturation adjustment (center) increases the saturation and lightness of those tones and makes them redder because I've shifted the Hue by −7 points. I also modified "Yellows," shifting their Hue even further toward the red and increasing saturation by +15 points. This layer converts the scan in Figure 6-44 to the photograph in Figure 6-47, left. Observe how this changes the rainbow scale at the bottom of the control panel.

adjustment layers using each of those masks (Figure 6-45, right). Adjusting the settings in each layer let me custom-tint the selected area without altering the base image.

Figure 6-46 shows the mask for the skin adjustment layer along with the Hue/Saturation settings that I used. In the master channel, I entered −7 for the hue to make the skin tones more pink (notice how the rainbow scale at the bottom of the control panel shifted). I increased the

HOW TO HAND-TINT A PHOTOGRAPH WITH MASKED LAYERS (continued)

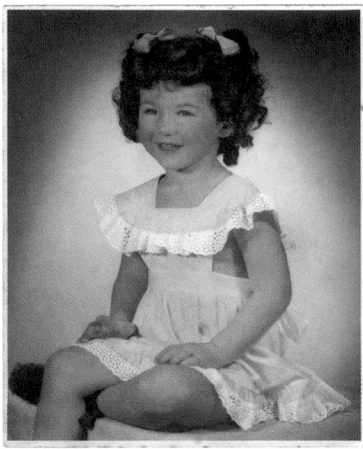 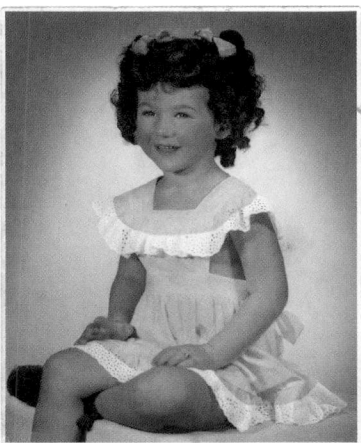 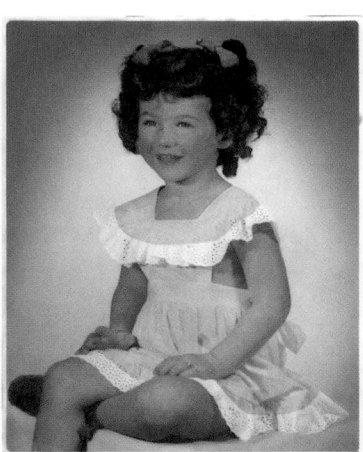

Fig. 6-47 Successive stages of hand-tinting. The figure on the left shows the changes produced by the Skin adjustment layer only. The middle figure shows how the photograph changes after I tinted the background, using the settings in Figure 6-48. The figure on the right shows the finished, retinted photograph. See the main text for full details.

HOW TO HAND-TINT
A PHOTOGRAPH
WITH MASKED
LAYERS (continued)

saturation significantly and also lightened the tones until they looked right to my eye. The shadowed areas in the skin tones were still sallow, so I went to the yellow channel, shifted the yellows toward the red, and increased their saturation. That warmed up the shadows sufficiently to give me the skin tones in Figure 6-47, left.

Next, I corrected the background adjustment layer, using the mask and Hue/Saturation settings given in Figure 6-48. The adjustments I made improved the whites, lightened the background, and gave it a slightly warm tone (Figure 6-47, center). I made comparable corrections, judging by eye and my taste, to all the Hue/Saturation adjustment layers. Because everything was being corrected in layers, if I decided I didn't like an earlier adjustment, I could go back and correct it by changing the settings in that layer's control panel.

I discovered in many cases that my masks weren't perfect. For example, the skin mask overlapped the background in a couple of places. Fixing that was easy. I highlighted the skin adjustment layer, which automatically activated the mask in that layer, set the Brush tool to a small radius, and painted with black or white to add or subtract from the mask. Mask changes were instantly reflected in the photograph's tone and color, so it was very easy for me to fix up the masks by eye. Periodically, I turned on the Quickmask (Q) view to make sure I had not missed any spots.

Once I was completely happy with the colors, I went back to the base layer to clean up the stains and damage. That's another good thing about layers; I can repair physical damage without messing up any of the color corrections I've done.

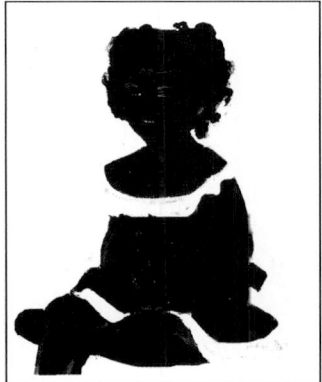
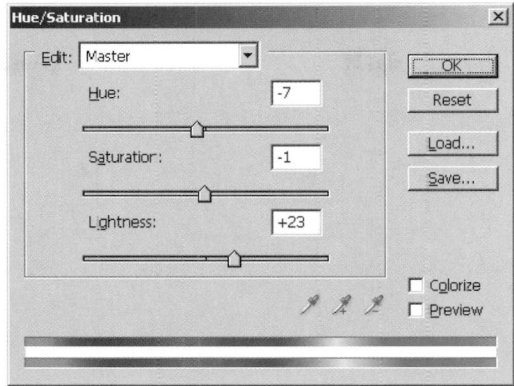

Fig. 6-48 The adjustments for the Background adjustment layer. On the left is the mask that selects the background and the white trim on the dress. The Hue/Saturation adjustment shifts the Hue by −7 points, eliminating the greenish cast, and lightens the tones by a substantial +23 points. That whitens the lace on the dress and makes the shadows in the background softer and more attractive. The result is shown as the middle photograph in Figure 6-47.

I used the Dust & Scratches filter and the Clone tool to clean up the stains and cracks in the background, and I blurred the background overall to smooth out the tones. The finished result is shown in Figure 6-47, right.

This is not a very sophisticated job of tinting, because the original hand-tinting was crude and hastily done. Look along the border between the blue dress and white lace; the studio didn't even make much of an effort to follow the contours of the dress and lace. It would have been easy for me to do a much nicer job of hand-tinting, but I wanted to preserve the charm of the original.

On the other hand, should I change my mind about this, my options are preserved in the channels and adjustment layers. I can go back and refine the masks, even add new selections and masks if I want to do more detailed tinting and color corrections; there's really no limit. My decision to stop here is not irrevocable.

HOW TO HAND-TINT A PHOTOGRAPH WITH MASKED LAYERS (continued)

Fixing Chromatic Aberration with Picture Window

Old amateur color photographs frequently suffer from a bit of lateral chromatic aberration (color fringing at the edges of the photograph) because the lenses on the cameras weren't very good. Some modern digital cameras also have this problem, so you may see color fringing if you're rephotographing the original instead of scanning it. Chromatic aberration isn't a big deal, but it is so easy to fix that it's worth repairing. If you're working on a small photograph that is going to be enlarged, eliminating it helps the enlargement look sharp.

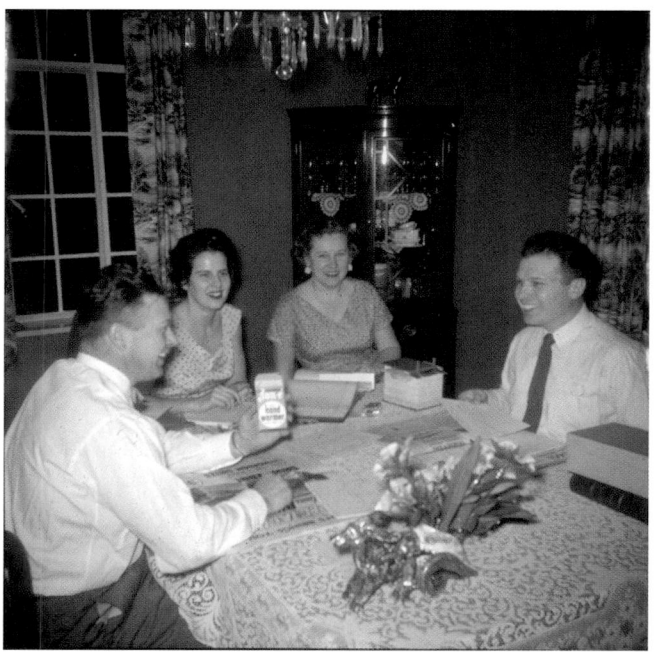

Fig. 6-49 Lateral chromatic aberration (color fringing at the edges of a photograph) frequently shows up in old amateur color photographs because lenses weren't very good. It's not a serious problem, and it's easy to fix, and doing so makes the photograph sharper.

Figure 6-49 is a typical 1950s photograph with a case of chromatic aberration. Photoshop has a tool for eliminating it (the Lens Correction filter), but I don't like it very much. It's a coarse adjustment that is too hard to use precisely. Whenever I need to eliminate chromatic aberration, I use Picture Window.

HOW TO REMOVE COLOR FRINGES FROM A PHOTOGRAPH

Figure 6-50 shows how Picture Window corrects chromatic aberrations. The window in the upper left displays a 300% view of the corner of the photograph that I corrected. Chromatic aberration gets stronger the further you get from the center of the photograph, so a corner or edge with sharp detail like this is where to look to judge your corrections.

The window at the upper right shows what the corrected photograph will look like. The long rectangular window at the bottom is the Chromatic Aberration correction control panel. Picture Window lets me change the size and shape of the control panel, so I stretched it out horizontally to expand the correction scales. That way I could make very fine adjustments.

I moved the red shift slider back and forth until I minimized the cyan and red fringes around the fine detail in the preview window. Then I did the same for the blue shift slider. It's harder to see the blue correction, because the fringing will be yellow versus blue, which doesn't have very good visual contrast. One does the best one can. Once I had the sliders set, I clicked Apply to create a new, corrected photograph.

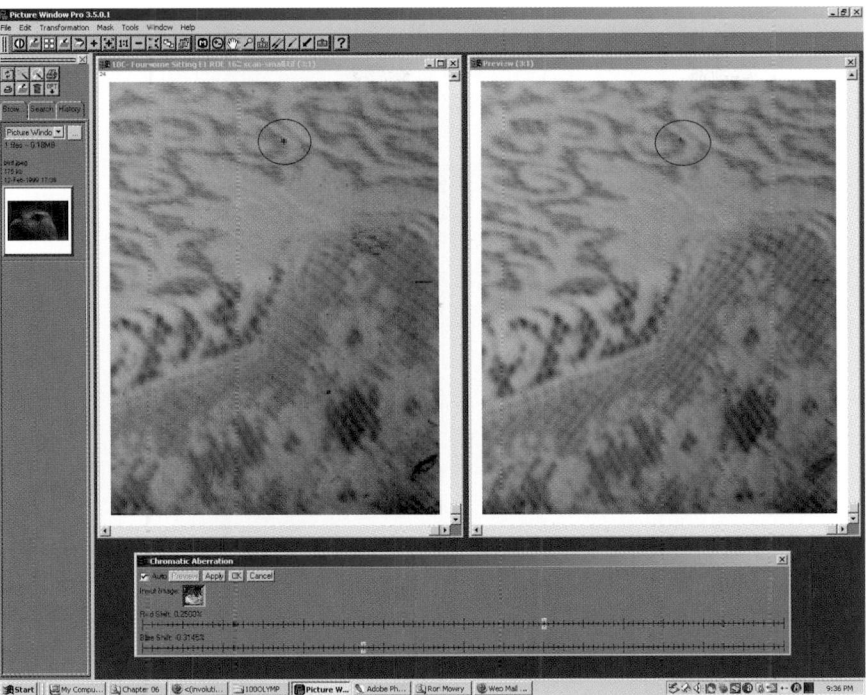

Fig. 6-50 The Chromatic Aberration transformation in Picture Window does a more controllable and precise job of fixing this problem than the Lens Correction filter in Photoshop. This screenshot shows the transformation at work. The window on the left shows the lower right corner of the photograph from Figure 6-49 at 3× magnification. The color fringing is quite clear at this scale. At the bottom is the Chromatic Aberration control panel stretched out horizontally to give me very precise control over the position of the Red Shift and Blue Shift sliders. On the right is the Preview window showing how the transformation will change the image.

HOW TO REMOVE
COLOR FRINGES
FROM A
PHOTOGRAPH
(continued)

If you're unsure whether you've gotten the degree of correction just right, reposition the sliders and click Apply again. Each time you do this, you'll create a new window with the new version of the corrected photograph. Once you're finished, click OK and you can pick the version that looks best and save it.

Repairing chromatic aberration should be the second thing that you do in the restoration process. The very first thing is to clean up the scan, eliminating all dust, dirt, and physical damage from the photograph. I didn't do that in this case, to illustrate why it's necessary. Look at the circled area with the dirt speck in the before and after photographs, enlarged in Figure 6-51. Because dirt's not part of the image, it doesn't have any color fringes. Correcting the chromatic aberration for the photograph smears out the speck into a rainbow smear that will be a lot harder to retouch. That's why you want to do all your cleanup first.

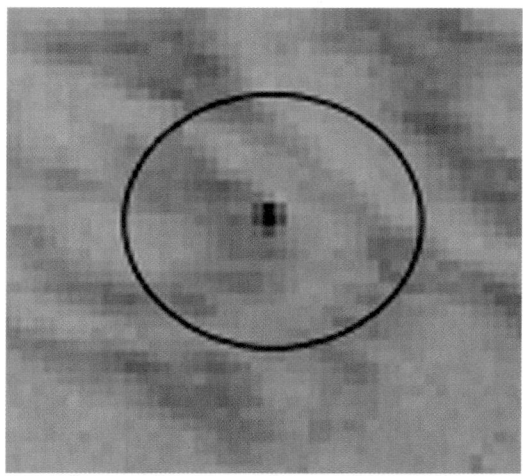

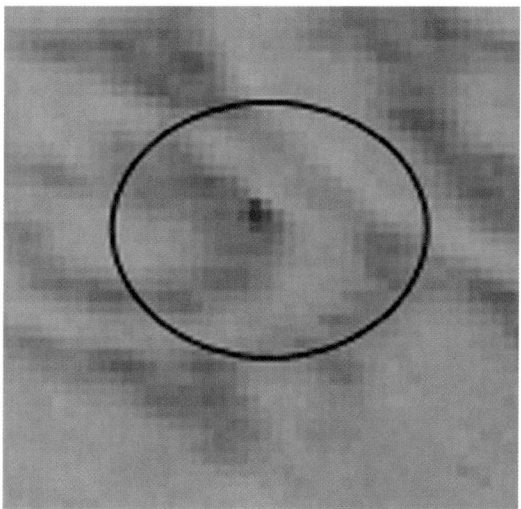

Fig. 6-51 This is a greatly magnified dust speck, showing what happens to it after chromatic aberration correction. Because the speck didn't have any color fringes to begin with, the correction turns it into a rainbow-colored smear. This will be much harder to clean up than the original sharp speck. Make sure you repair all dust, dirt, and physical damage before correcting chromatic aberration in a photographic image.

Fixing Color Stains and Development Marks

Sometimes photofinishers misprocess film. Figure 6-52 shows a photograph from a 35-mm negative that received improper agitation. There are pink and green bands along the edges where the developer flowed unevenly around the sprocket holes in the film. This ruined an otherwise good-looking photograph. Fortunately, I can fix that digitally.

HOW TO REMOVE DEVELOPER MARKS FROM A PHOTOGRAPH

Often the best way to tackle a color stain problem like this is to convert the photograph from RGB to Lab color. Lab has three channels, like RGB, but they're quite different. The first channel is a Lightness (or Luminosity, L) channel that holds the information about how bright and dark the photograph is (Figure 6-53). The second channel, the "a" channel, represents how green or magenta the color is. The closer the

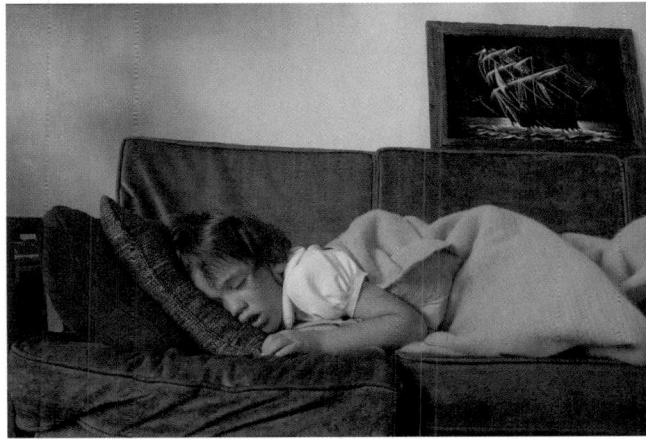

Fig. 6-52 This color negative was poorly processed by the photofinisher; the pink and green bands at the top were caused by uneven developer flow around the film's sprocket holes.

tone is to white in that channel, the more magenta; the closer to black, the more green. Middle gray is neutral. The last channel, the "*b*" channel, represents how yellow or blue the color is, white being pure yellow and black pure blue.

You can see why Lab space is good for correcting this problem. The surge marks are almost invisible in the Lightness and *b* channels; the problem is mostly with the *a* channel. Fix that channel, and the photograph will look much better.

The Brush works well for this. I sampled the color midway between a pink and green band. The circle in Figure 6-54 shows a good sample point. Then I clicked the *a* channel to activate it and turn off the other two channels. I painted over the bands with the airbrush. The bands were almost eliminated, as you can see in the *a* channel and full-color images of Figure 6-55.

The wall didn't come out perfectly. Although the worst of the color banding is eliminated, you'll notice some fainter pink and green splotches caused by the uneven development. It was easy to paint those away by sampling the color midway between them. I dialed back the opacity on the Brush to about 30% so that I could paint over the variations in the *a* channel with more control, blending the "light" and "dark" areas into each other. After I finished cleaning up the color, I switched to the Luminosity channel and used the dodging tool to soften the harsh shadows on the wall (Figure 6-56).

This was easy staining to fix because the wall was pretty uniform. In most photographs the bands and stains cross a variety of tones and colors. To correct those, you have to use more than one color with the airbrush, sampling between each pair of bands to get the right color for that part of the picture. The concept is the same; it just takes more work.

HOW TO REMOVE
DEVELOPER MARKS
FROM A
PHOTOGRAPH
(continued)

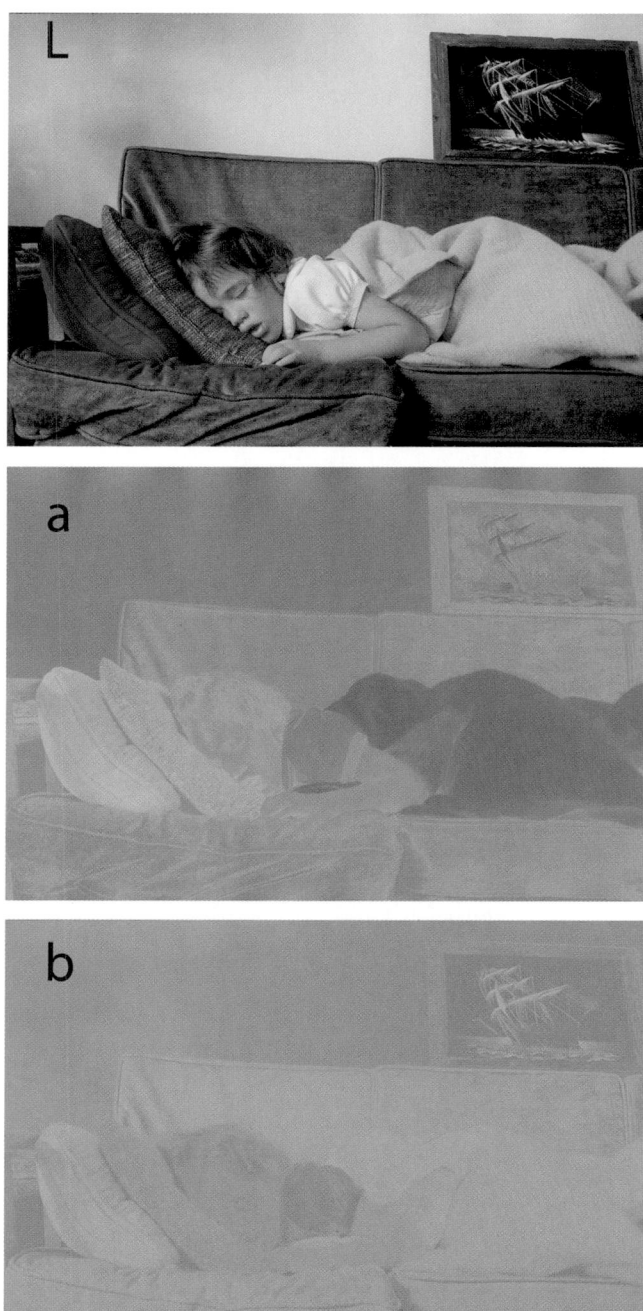

Fig. 6-53 The individual channels of Figure 6-52 in Lab space. Almost all of the development damage is in the *a* channel; it's hardly visible in the *L* or *b* channels. See the main text for an explanation of what Lab space is.

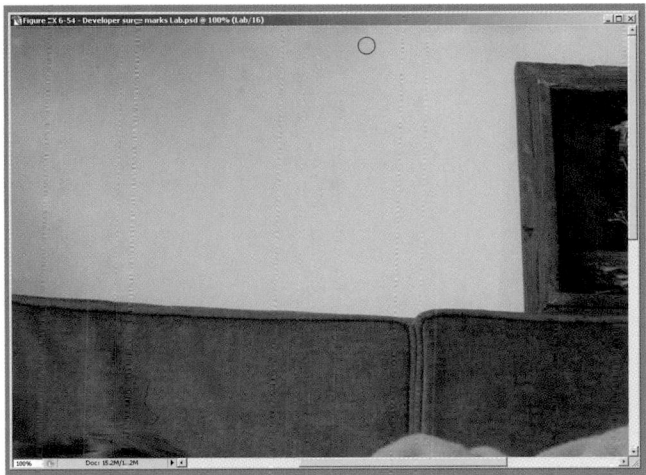

Fig. 6-54 This screenshot shows the appropriate point to sample for the correct average color to repair the development bands—it's midway between the pink and green bands.

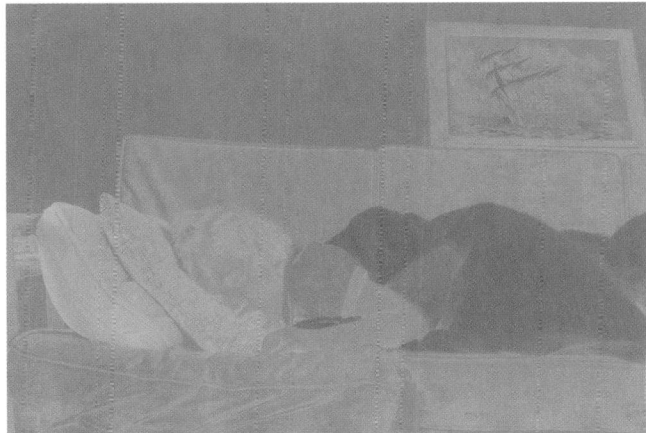

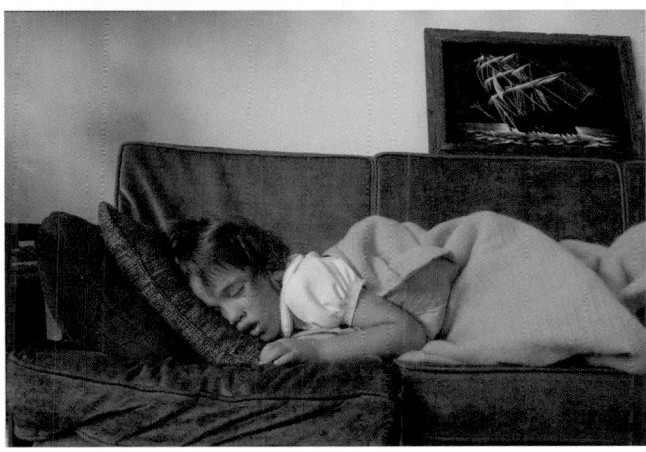

Fig. 6-55 The upper figure is the *a* channel after airbrushing; the lower figure is the full-color photograph, showing how much of the developer bands has been removed by this single correction.

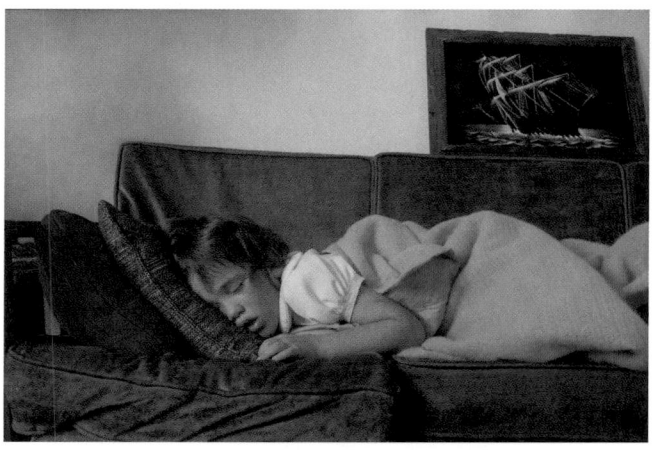

Fig. 6-56 After further airbrushing of the *a* channel and some dodging of the shadows in the *L* channel, the wall in the background looks much smoother, and the distracting shadows are suppressed.

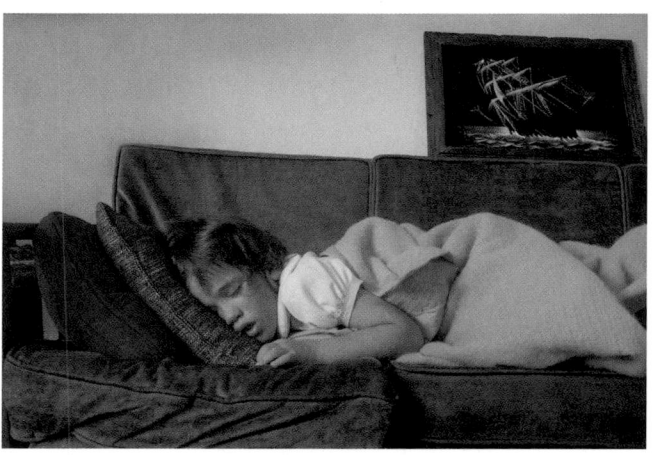

Fig. 6-57 The photograph from Figure 6-56 after applying the Curves adjustment from Figure 6-58. Overall color balance is restored by those curves, and this photograph is now ready for the finishing touches that will make the color perfect.

When you're done cleaning up the *a* channel, you can convert the photograph back to RGB color to continue your restoration. That was what I did to finish up the photograph in Figure 6-57. I blurred the wall to smooth out the distracting shadows and made Curves adjustments to correct the tone and color (Figure 6-58).

Plugged-In Color Correction

It's not difficult to see what's wrong with Figure 6-56 just by looking at it. The walls are an unlikely shade of green, the sleeve isn't white, the girl's hair looks too red, and her skin tones are sallow. Being able to correct all of that with just a handful of Curves adjustment points, as I did, is another matter. Years of experience and a certain amount of intuition guided my hand. It's not a skill I can teach you in

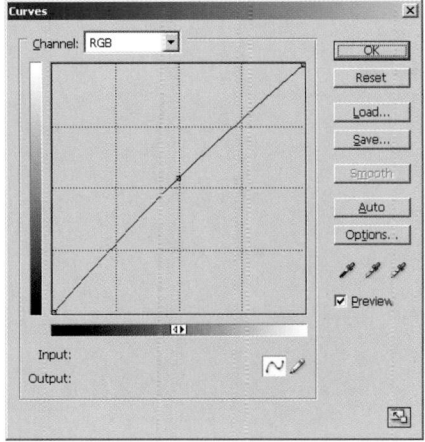
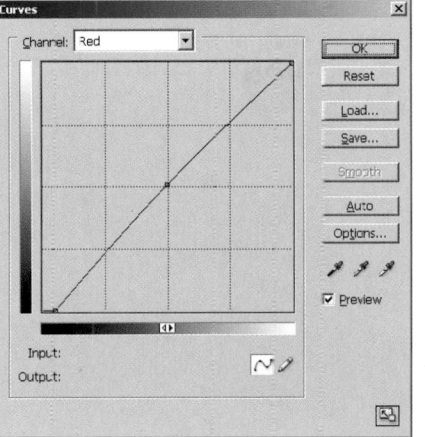
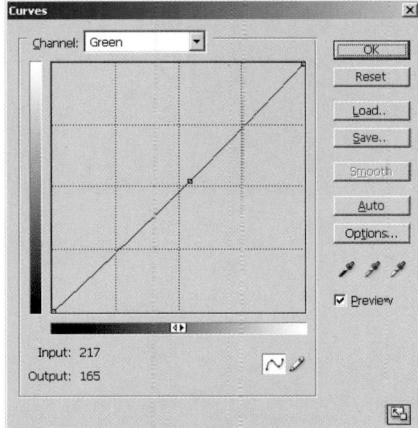
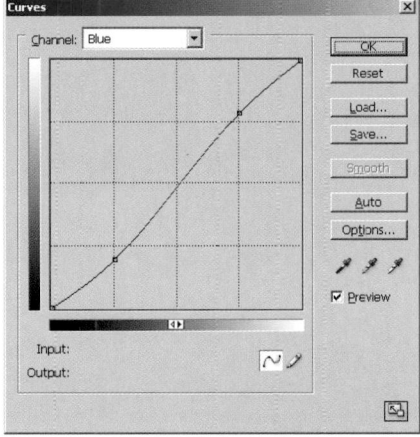

Fig. 6-58 These curves correct the color and tonality of Figure 6-57. The RGB curve slightly lightens the photograph. The red curve fixes some minor color crossover, eliminating a cyan cast from the highlights and taking excess red out of the shadows. The green curve makes the photograph overall more neutral by adding magenta (reducing green). The blue curve eliminates a substantial amount of color crossover, making the shadows considerably more yellow and highlights significantly bluer.

a couple of pages; it's something you'll develop on your own after much practice.

Fortunately, there's another way to correct the color that is a lot more artistically intuitive. The Color Mechanic plug-in that I introduced in Chapter 3, Software for Restoration, did an even better job than my curve corrections (Color Mechanic is also built into Picture Window). I'm going to walk you through the corrections I made using that tool.

Figure 6-59 shows the full control panel for Color Mechanic with my first correction. I wanted to make that wall neutral, so I clicked on it, which set the light green control point in the color map at the lower left. I dragged the arrow from that point to just slightly on the warm side of the neutral center marker. The Preview window in the upper right shows what happened to the color; the color map on the lower right shows how all the colors were altered to accommodate this adjustment.

✓ HOW TO IMPROVE COLOR WITH COLOR MECHANIC

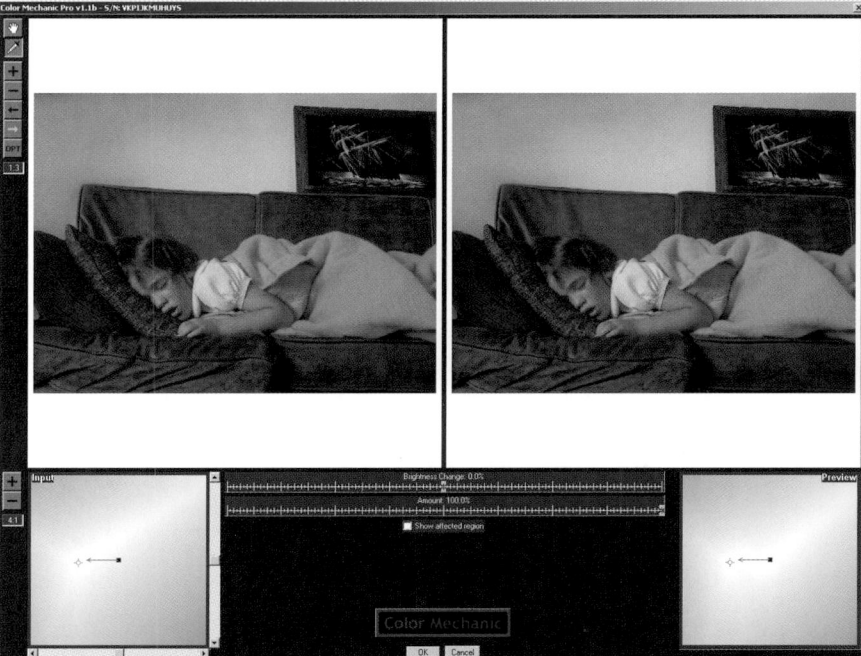

Fig. 6-59 The Color Mechanic plug-in is another way to correct the color of Figure 6-56. In the first step, pictured in this screenshot, I selected a point on the wall and dragged it toward the neutral center point, clearing out much of the overall greenish color cast of the photograph.

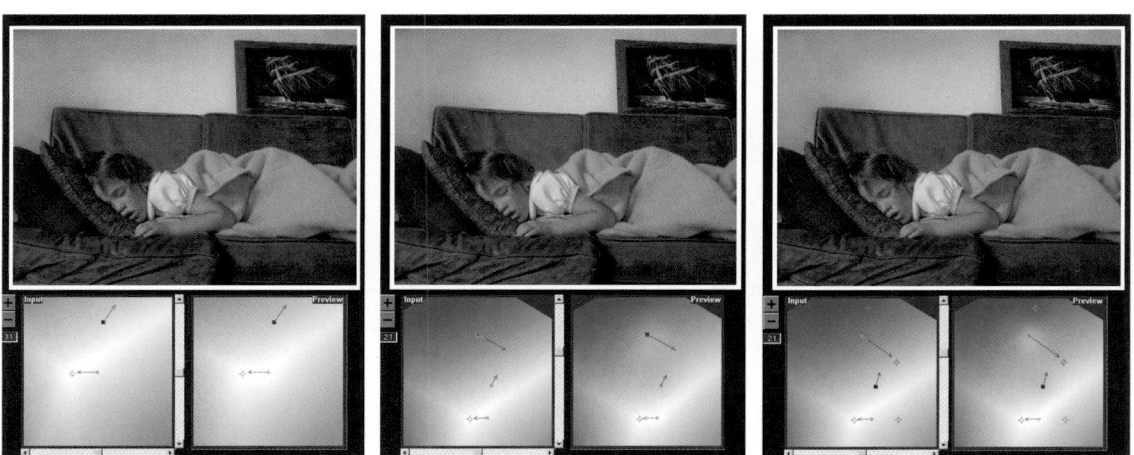

Fig. 6-60 Successive stages of Color Mechanic correction. On the left, I've set a control point in the little girl's skin and dragged it to a more saturated, slightly pink hue. The center figure corrects the color of the girl's hair, eliminating an unlikely pinkish tinge by making it yellower (browner). In the final adjustments on the right, I added fixed control points for the green blanket, red pillow, and brown sofa to lock those colors to their original hues.

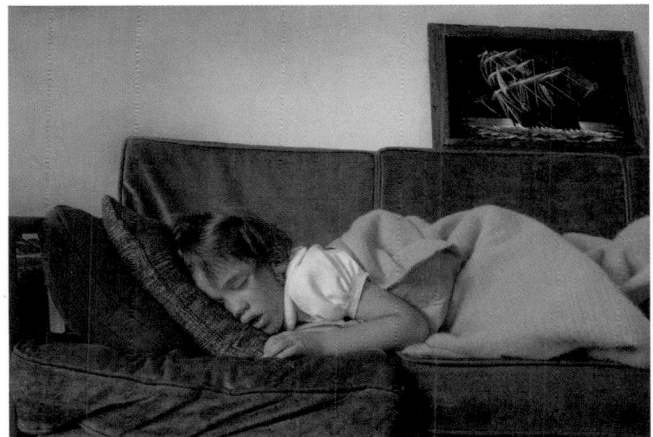

Fig. 6-61 This is the photograph from Figure 6-56, as corrected with Color Mechanic. This is even better than the Curves-corrected version in Figure 6-57. Of course, there's nothing to keep you from using both of these tools on the same photograph.

The wall and the sleeve were now neutral, and I wanted to fix the skin tones next, so I clicked on the girl's arm. I dragged the new control point's arrow away from the center and a little toward the red, which warmed the color and increased its saturation (Figure 6-60, left). I removed the excess red from her hair by clicking on a highlight in it to create the red control point shown in Figure 6-60, center. I dragged that arrow toward the yellow, which made the hair browner.

I added three more control points by clicking on the green blanket, the bright red pillow, and the brown sofa. The new red, green, and orange points in Figure 6-60, right, pinned those colors to their original values. I also made slight refinements to the control arrows for the girl's skin and hair. This got me the final version of the photograph you can see in Figure 6-61.

HOW TO IMPROVE
COLOR WITH COLOR
MECHANIC
(continued)

CHAPTER 7

Making Masks

How-To's in This Chapter

How to eliminate tarnish from a photograph
How to select cracks with the Find Edges filter
How to select cracks with the Picture Window Edge tool
How to enhance cracks for selection
How to select tarnished parts of a photograph
How to select scratches and dirt by color
How to create masks for hand-tinting photographs
How to select cellophane tape damage for correction

Why Mask?

You can do restoration without masks, but mask making is an essential skill if you want to do *really* good restoration work. Masks let you apply changes to parts of photographs, so that you can control precisely where and how strongly an adjustment changes the photo. A mask has no direct effect on a photograph, it merely governs the adjustment. In other words, a mask is a means to an end, not an end in itself.

A mask is merely a grayscale image that is the same size as the photograph. Black areas in the mask completely block whatever change you're making to the photograph: white parts of the mask permit the change to work at 100% strength. Gray values in a mask produce intermediate-strength changes—the lighter the tone in the mask, the stronger the effect on the photograph of your adjustment.

Masks are portable. You can save masks as stand-alone grayscale image files, as Alpha channels in a Photoshop layer, or as separate layers. You can copy a mask from one image to another; you can even make masks with one application and use them in a different one. For example, I use some of the mask-making tools in Picture Window to create masks for use in Photoshop.

Saving and using masks is very simple. Once you've composed the grayscale mask image, create a new channel in the photo you'll be

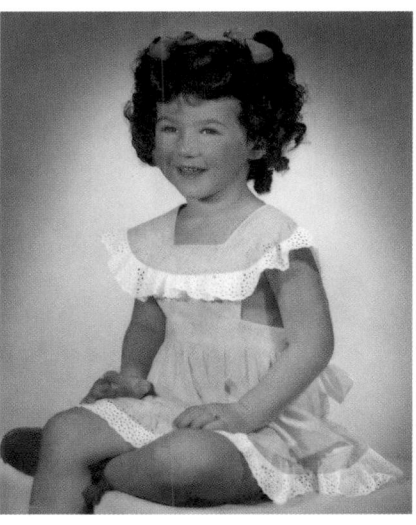
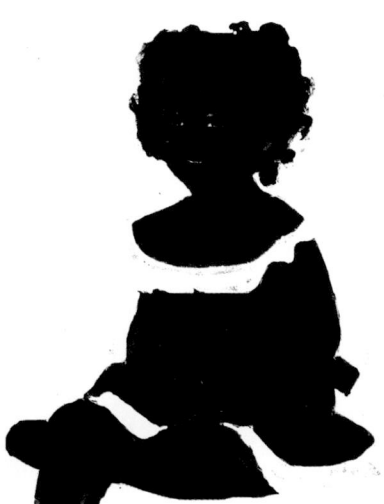

Fig. 7-1 A mask is nothing more than a grayscale image that is the same size as the photograph that you want to mask. It can be a simple B&W silhouette, as shown here. This mask selects for the background and the white lace trim on the little girl's dress and blocks everything else.

masking, copy the mask image, and paste it into that channel. When you want to use the mask as a selection, go to Select/Load Selection, pick that channel and click OK. The mask becomes a selection.

A mask can be as simple as a B&W outline or silhouette, like the ones I used for hand-tinting a photograph in Chapter 6, Restoring Color, page 216, one of which is reproduced here (Figure 7-1). Near the end of this chapter, I show you how to make these masks.

Every adjustment layer in Photoshop automatically has a mask. Much of the time you don't pay attention to it because the mask is, by default, white everywhere. In that case the layer adjustments change the whole photograph uniformly at full strength. Modifying that white adjustment-layer mask is a very useful way of controlling how the photograph looks.

HOW TO ELIMINATE
TARNISH FROM A
PHOTOGRAPH

For example, for the photograph in Figure 7-2 I created the continuous-tone mask shown to select for the tarnished areas in the photograph (see page 244 to find out how I made this mask). I used that mask in a Curves adjustment layer with the settings shown in Figure 7-3 to eliminate the tarnish in a single operation. That's the power of a good mask!

A mask doesn't even have to portray the content of the photograph. I use such masks to manually control the strength of an alteration and where it gets applied to the photograph. In Chapter 5, page 156, I used a gradient mask (Figure 5-40) in a Curves adjustment layer to correct uneven exposure and contrast in the photograph shown in Figure 5-38. For the photograph shown in Figure 5-44, page 161, I used hand-painted masks in Figures 5-46 through 5-52 to burn in parts of the photograph to correct tones and repair the damage caused by light fog in the original negative. In Figure 5-69, page 178, I used a very simple hand-painted

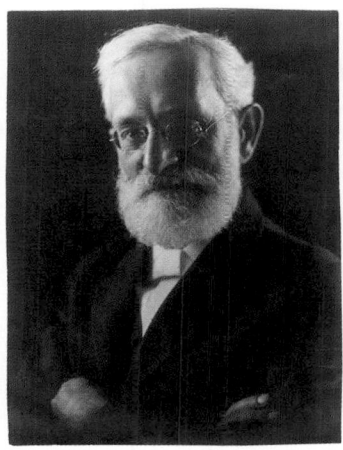 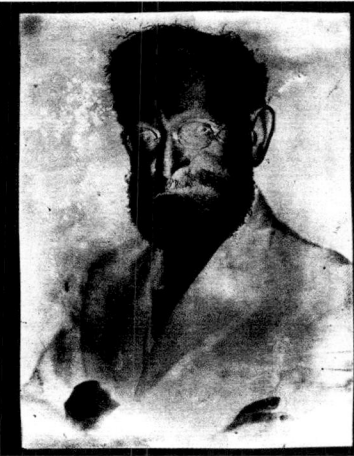 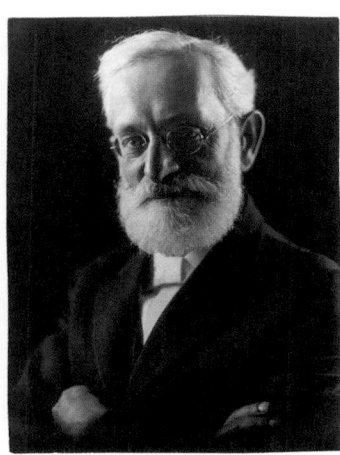

Fig. 7-2 Continuous-tone masks are powerful correction aids. The photograph on the left is badly tarnished. The mask in the middle, made using techniques explained later in this chapter, selects for that tarnish. When that mask is used in combination with the Curves adjustment in Figure 7-3, the tarnish is almost completely eliminated in a single step.

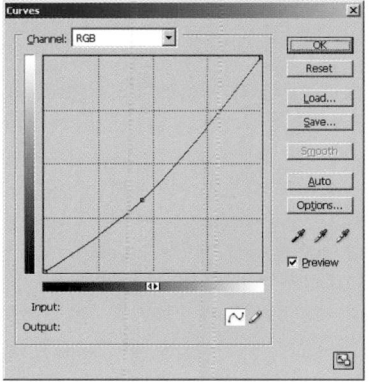 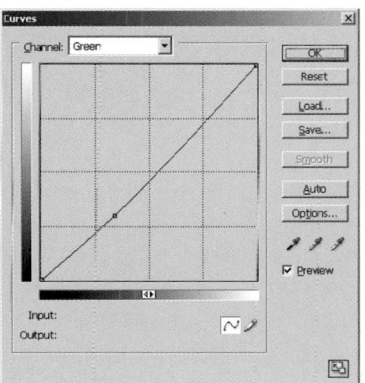 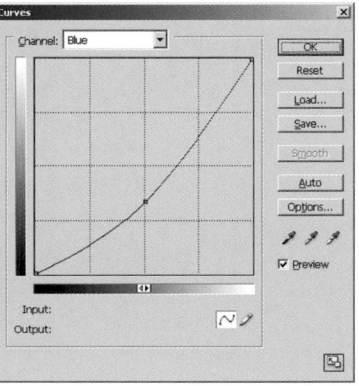

Fig. 7-3 This Curves adjustment, used in conjunction with the mask from Figure 7-2, repairs the pale-blue tarnish. The RGB curve makes the tones darker, the green curve makes them more magenta, and the blue curve makes them much more yellow. This is an extremely effective tarnish-repair technique.

mask to dodge and retouch a face, eliminating hard shadows and lines.

Many Ways to the Same Goal

Just as there are many kinds of masks, there are many ways to create them. At the end of this chapter, I show you five different ways to mask the same photograph. Different masking tools appeal to different people and have different strengths and weaknesses. Simple masks can simply be drawn or painted in, as I did with the photograph of the three women in Figure 6-26, page 201. In most situations, though, manually constructing a mask is very time consuming and tedious. I much prefer tools and techniques that let the software do the work for me. I use a lot of different tools for making masks. I discuss my favorite tools in the following paragraphs.

The simplest tool is the Magic Wand in Photoshop. I know a lot of professionals who think it's too crude a tool to be very useful, but I'm pretty fond of it. I use it a lot when I need to make a purely black-and-white mask. The key to using it with some precision is to keep the tolerance low and use the wand in "Add" mode, so that you can build up your selection from carefully selected colors and tones. If I select too much, then the "Subtract" mode comes in handy, along with "Undo" and history reversions. The big limitation of this tool is that it's no good for creating a continuous-tone grayscale mask, which is important for most masking work.

Conversely, I know professionals who are very fond of the Color Range Select tool in Photoshop, but I've had trouble warming up to it. I think it's great for selecting highlights and pretty good for selecting shadows, but when it comes to using it in the "Sampled Colors" mode, I usually have difficulty getting exactly what I want. On the other hand, it does generate a continuous-tone mask.

Back in Chapter 3, I described two Photoshop plug-ins that I'm fond of: Mask Pro and Asiva Selection. The former is especially useful when I need to construct a complicated mask and I don't have strong image characteristics like contrasting tone or color that easily define a mask. When I can define a mask in terms of tone, saturation, and color, Asiva can create it for me very quickly.

Picture Window has several mask tools that work well for me. The one I like best of all is the Paint tool with the "Similar Pixels" option selected. Figure 7-4 shows a mask under construction (the bright green areas are selected areas) that uses the brush settings of Figure 7-5. The brush makes the pixel values at its center point the selection reference; it selects any other pixels within its radius that are similar to the target pixel. As you paint with the brush, it finds such pixels and adds them to the selection.

This is a great tool for masking complicated and subtle boundaries. Paint along the perimeter of the area you want to mask, keeping the center of the brush in the selected area. The brush will automatically include the pixels that are similar and mask out the pixels on the other side of the border because they're different. You can set the threshold to be as narrow or inclusive as you like, so you can mask some very subtle boundaries automatically. I used a tight threshold in Figure 7-4, and I was able to selectively mask the legs of the high chair without masking the background. In the photograph I can barely tell them apart visually, but the low-threshold masking brush picked up on the difference. With

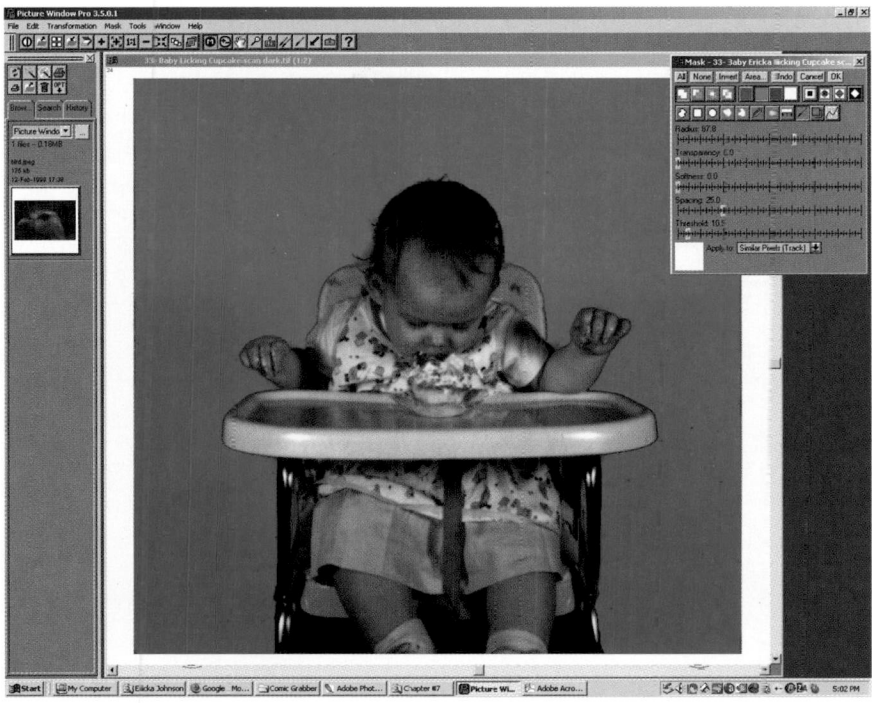

Fig. 7-4 This screenshot shows how well Picture Window's masking tools work to find edges (the unmasked photograph can be seen in Figure 7-6). The bright green area is the selected area. I painted in that selection using the Mask Paint tool, set to track "Similar Pixels." Painting that tool along the border between the baby and the background selects pixels in the background but rejects those in the baby and high chair.

Add, Subtract, and Difference options available for the masking tools, plus an Undo button, it's not difficult to refine a selection.

Figure 7-6 shows the original photograph and the mask I created this way. It's still a crude mask: There are lots pinholes in the white areas because of the tight threshold I used, and the baby and high chair aren't masked off perfectly in a few places. Since the mask is just a grayscale image, I can use the normal Brush and Eraser tools to clean up those mistakes. Meanwhile, creating the basic mask took me only a couple of minutes to get 95% of what I need.

Picture Window also has a Brightness Curve tool at the right end of the row of masking tools. The Color Range Select tool in Photoshop works like a crude version of that, when you choose the Highlights, Midtones, or Shadows range for masking. In Picture Window's tool, you can control in detail which brightness values get masked by drawing a curve. You can select a broad or narrow range of tones or even a complicated combination of light and dark tones. Whatever you can draw in a curve, you can mask for.

How do I decide which tool to use in a particular situation? I look at the photograph to figure out what is distinctive about the area that I want to mask. That's the key to masking: All of these tools work by finding some difference between the part of the photo you want to mask and the part you don't. The areas I want to mask might differ from the

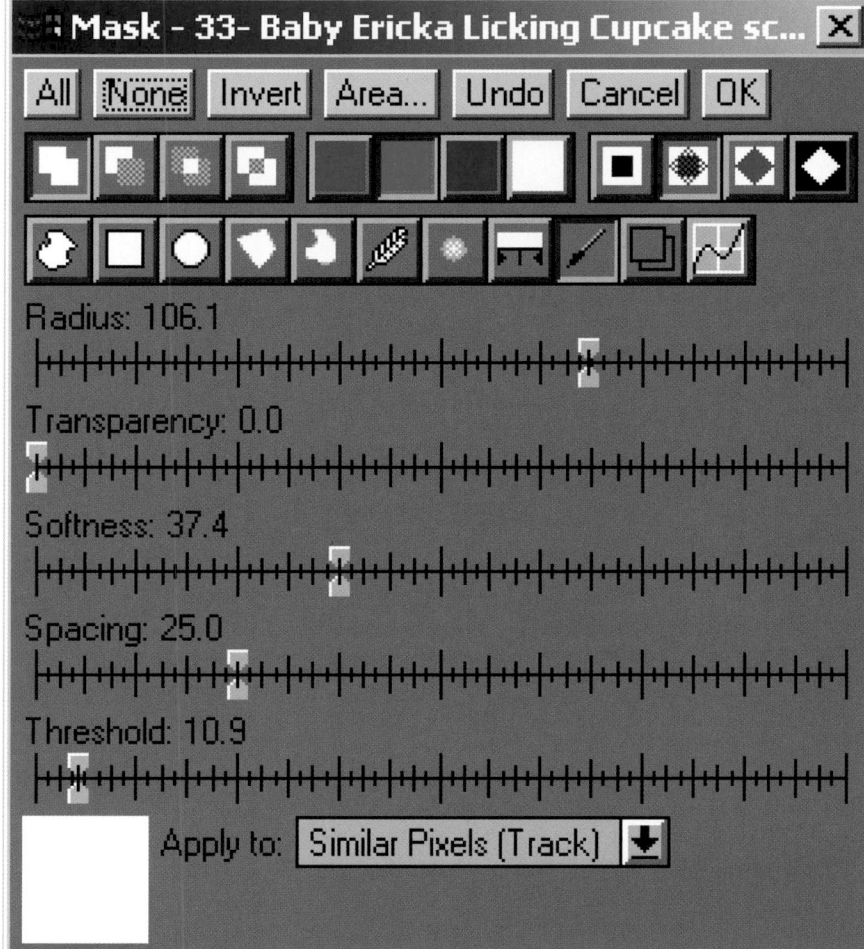

Fig. 7-5 A close-up of the Mask tool control panel in Picture Window. The Paint tool is selected; note the large number of controls at one's disposal for this tool. Other tools include Color Range and Brightness Curve selection tools as well as an assortment of geometric shapes and spines, plus combinatorial tools for adding and subtracting from mask selections.

ones I don't in brightness, in color, or in sharpness. The approach I use to getting a good mask is to emphasize the difference that best defines my intended selection and then pick the masking tool that works best with that kind of a difference. Let's look at some examples of how that works.

Isolating Cracks

You may not have thought of masking according to sharpness, because none of the tools you normally use for masking distinguishes between sharp and unsharp parts of the photograph. Photoshop and Picture Window, though, have filters that can do just that.

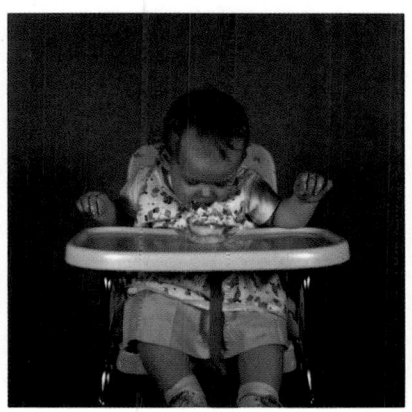 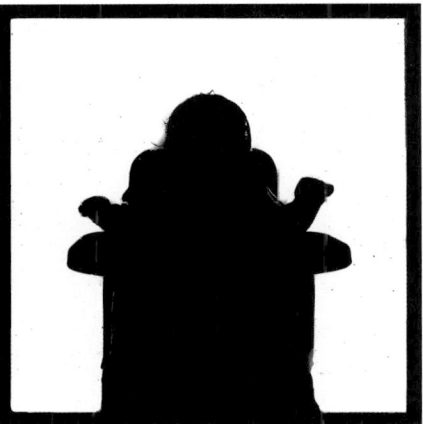

Fig. 7-6 The unmasked photograph of the baby and the mask created with the "Similar Pixels" Paint tool in Picture Window. The mask needs cleaning up and refinement, but the Paint tool has done a remarkable job of automatically finding the boundaries between the foreground and the background.

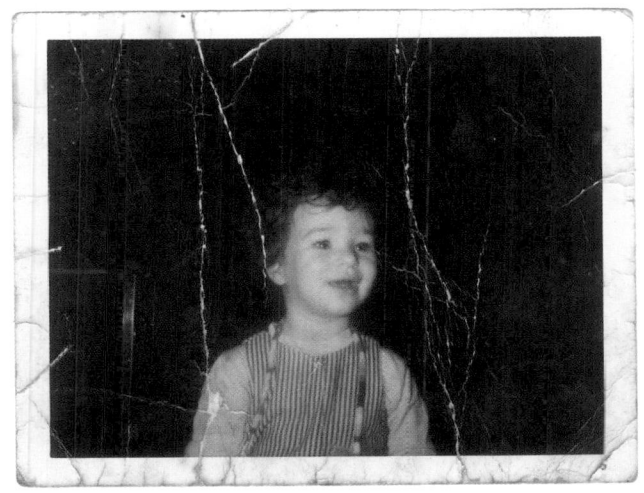

Fig. 7-7 This 35-year-old color photograph is badly cracked and creased. Manual damage repair would work just fine, but a mask that selects the damaged areas will make repairs go much faster.

Figure 7-7 is in surprisingly good shape, color-wise, for a 35-year-old color photograph. The problem is one of physical damage—it's riddled with cracks, creases, and missing chunks of emulsion, as the close-up view in Figure 7-8, left, shows. Frankly, I could paint the whole background charcoal gray, and nobody would notice. Instead, let's treat it as a challenge: What can I do to clean up that damage without changing anything else in the photograph? The answer is to create a clever mask that selects only the damaged areas.

I scanned this 3-inch by 4-inch photograph at very high resolution: ✓ HOW TO SELECT
1200 ppi. As you can see in Figure 7-8, the photograph isn't anywhere CRACKS WITH THE
near sharp enough to justify that detailed a scan. I did it because I FIND EDGES FILTER
wanted to make the physical damage as sharp and distinct from the
photographic image as possible.

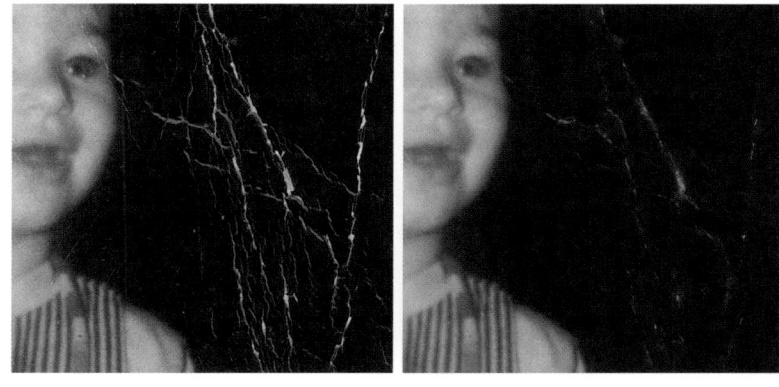

Fig. 7-8 A close-up of Figure 7-7 shows just how extensive the cracking is. The much-improved photograph on the right is a close-up of Figure 7-12, the result of the masking and repair methods shown in the next four figures.

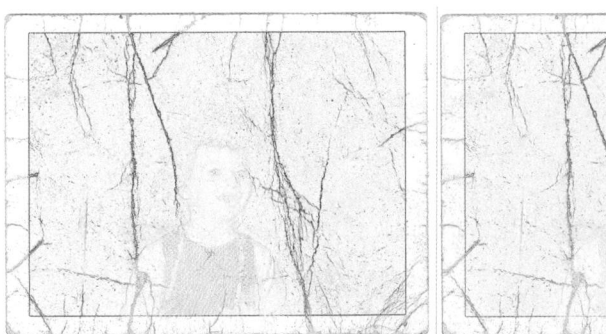

Fig. 7-9 The Find Edges filter in Photoshop can pick out fine cracks. The figure on the left shows the full-color image produced by applying this filter to a copy of Figure 7-7. The photograph on the right shows the blue channel only, which does the best job of picking up the cracks while ignoring the real photographic detail.

HOW TO SELECT
CRACKS WITH THE
FIND EDGES FILTER
(continued)

I made a copy of the scan and ran the Find Edges filter on it. That produced Figure 7-9, left. The blue channel did the best job of showing the cracks without showing the photographic detail, so I copied that as a grayscale image and discarded the other channels (Figure 7-9, right).

Next, I manipulated that filtered image to turn it into an effective mask. A highly enlarged section of the blue channel appears in Figure 7-10, upper left, with successive alterations shown clockwise. First I applied a Gaussian Blur to the mask, to widen the edges, and then I used Curves to make the features much darker and more contrasty. The blur and curve settings are in Figure 7-11. Lastly, I inverted the mask so that it would select for the cracks instead of everything else.

I copied the mask into an Alpha channel in the original photograph (Figure 7-12, bottom) and loaded it as a selection, using Photoshop's Select/Load Selection command. I applied a Median filter with a 20-pixel radius, which got me Figure 7-12, top. The enlargement in Figure 7-8, right, shows how much garbage I eliminated in a single operation by using this mask.

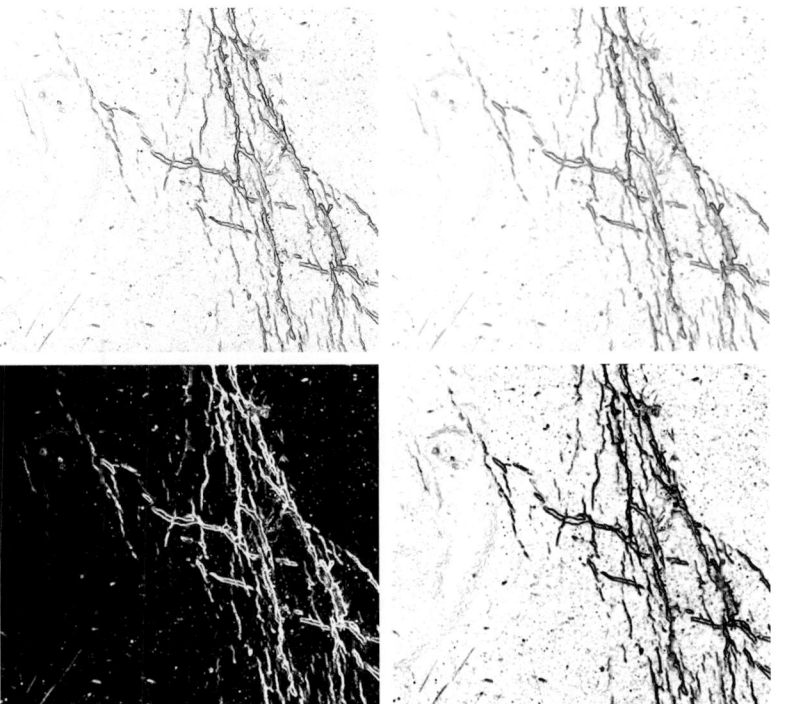

Fig. 7-10 Successive stages in making a crack-selection mask. Clockwise from the upper left, this is an enlarged view of the blue channel from Figure 7-9. I applied a Gaussian Blur to that channel to broaden the edges of the cracks. Then I used the Curves tool to increase contrast and make the cracks much blacker. The settings for these adjustments are shown in Figure 7-11. Lastly, I inverted the image so that the cracks were selected (white).

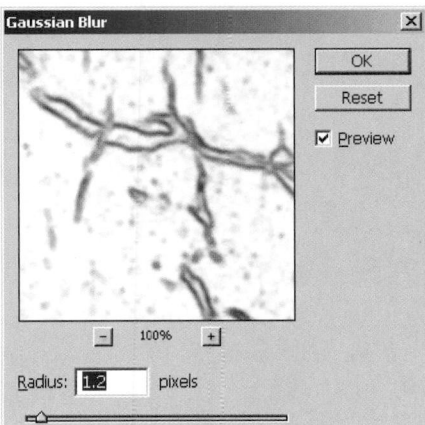

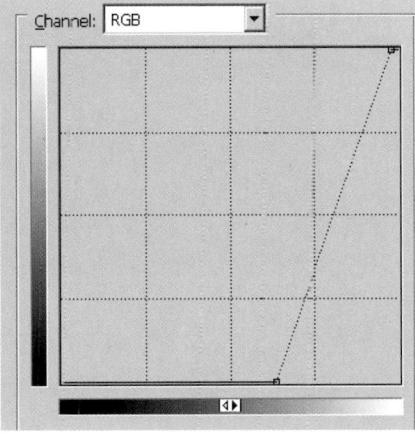

Fig. 7-11 A Gaussian Blur with a 1.2-pixel radius broadens the edges of the cracks and smooths them out. The Curves adjustment makes the background white and the crack edges solid black, so that the mask strongly distinguishes between them. This makes a much better mask for doing crack repair.

If you're intrigued by this technique but would like more flexibility when creating your edge masks, consider using Picture Window's Edge transformation tool (Figure 7-13). This tool has three different mathematical methods for finding edges that produce different results. It also has adjustable strength and two special Action modes: Darken and Lighten.

✓ HOW TO SELECT CRACKS WITH THE PICTURE WINDOW EDGE TOOL

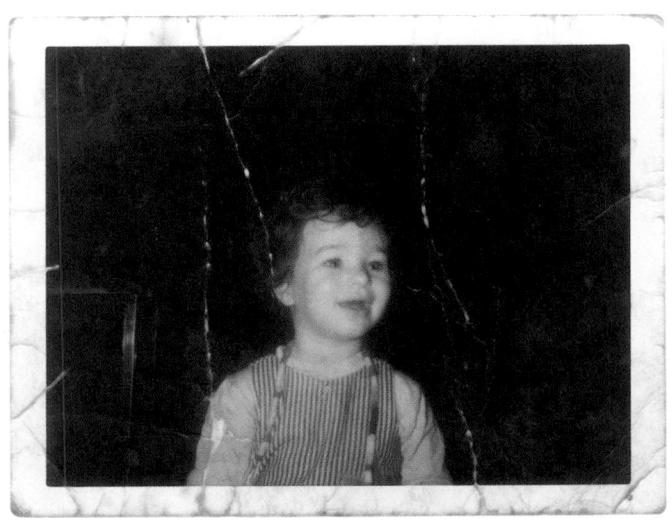

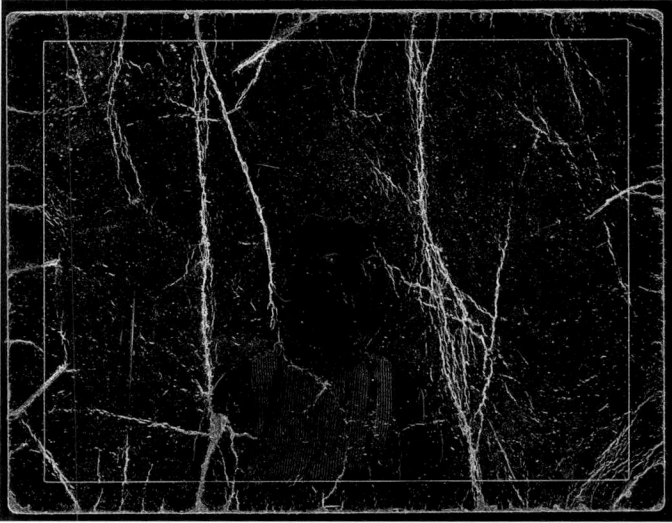

Fig. 7-12 The full mask from Figure 7-10 is shown at the bottom. Above it is the photograph after being filtered with a Median filter with a 20-pixel radius. The mask limits the effect of the filter to the crack edges, so it eliminates a majority of them while having very little effect on the photographic image. An enlarged section of this photograph appears in Figure 7-8, right.

HOW TO SELECT CRACKS WITH THE PICTURE WINDOW EDGE TOOL (continued)

HOW TO ENHANCE CRACKS FOR SELECTION

The Darken action can minimize a lot of damage directly, as you can see in Figure 7-14, right. You can set how much it darkens the edges with an adjustment slider. Lighten (Figure 7-14, center) makes cracks and light spots stand out even more strongly. This mode is not something you would use for repairing cracks directly, but emphasizing them can make it easier to select them using other masking tools.

While I'm on the subject of emphasizing features to make them easier to mask, here's another way to make it easier to select fine cracks and other damage for repair. Sharpen a copy of the photograph to enhance the edges of the cracks before using the Find Edges filter or Picture Window's Edge tool. Figure 7-15a shows a portion of a photograph that

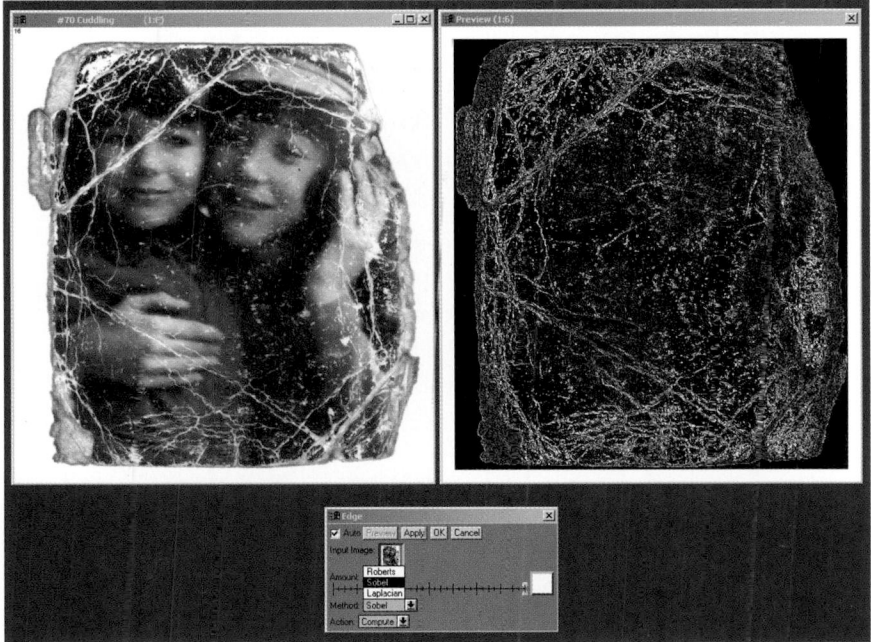

Fig. 7-13 Picture Window's Edge tool has several different mathematical methods for computing edges that produce different results. This screenshot shows the Sobel method.

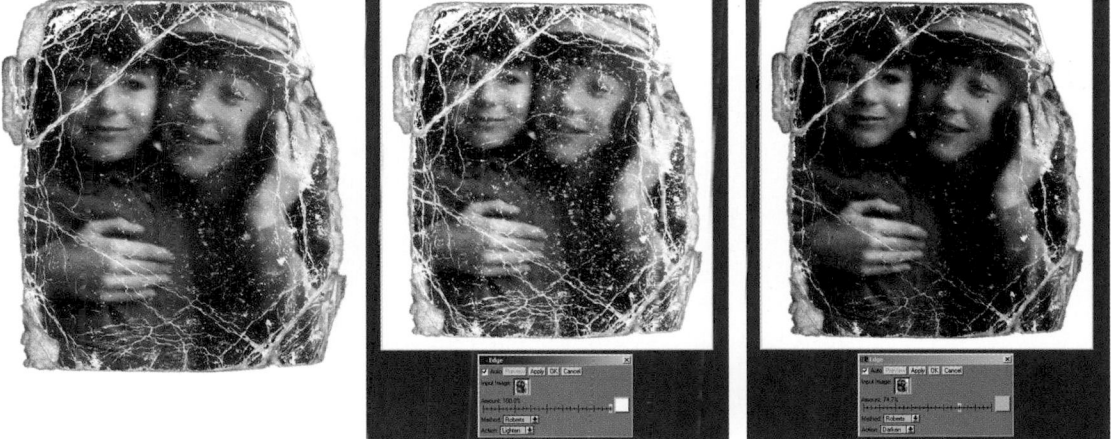

Fig. 7-14 The Picture Window Edge tool has options for lightening or darkening the edges it finds. You can use this to enhance cracks (center) to make it easier to make masks from them, or to suppress cracks (right) to repair damage.

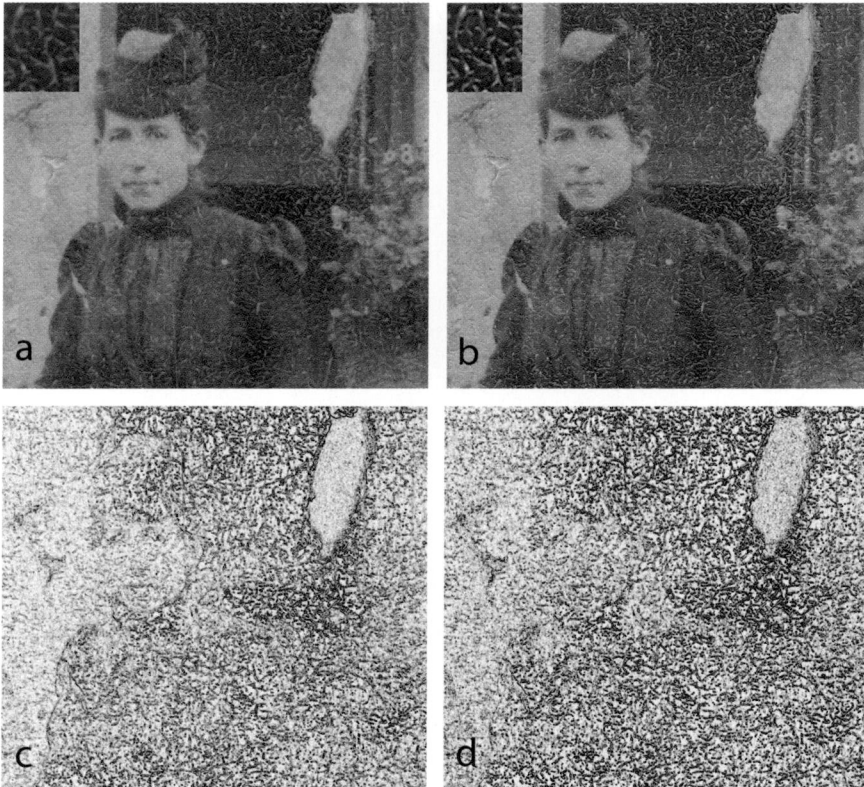

Fig. 7-15 The photograph in figure (a) is riddled with fine cracks that need to be repaired. Figure (b) shows how the cracks are accentuated by an Unsharp Mask filter, using the settings shown in Figure 7-16. This makes it easier for the Find Edges filter to pick out the cracks, as shown in figure (c). The blue channel (d) displays the cracks most clearly without including much photographic detail, so it will work best for a mask.

HOW TO ENHANCE CRACKS FOR SELECTION (continued)

is covered with very fine emulsion cracks. (The inset boxes in the upper left corners of Figures 7-15a and 7-15b show magnified views of some of those cracks.) The cracks all have well-defined edges and are very small, which make them ideal candidates for an edge-selection mask. Figure 7-15b shows what happened after I applied an Unsharp Mask (Figure 7-16) filter: The fine cracks are greatly enhanced in contrast and sharpness.

I followed this with the Find Edges filter (Figure 7-15c). Looking at the three color channels, the blue channel again did the best job of bringing out the edges of the cracks without emphasizing the edges of the photographic detail. I copied the blue channel (Figure 7-15d) and pasted it into an Alpha channel in the original photograph. In Chapter 8, Damage Control, page 284, I show you how I used this mask to almost totally eliminate the cracks and crazing in a few easy steps.

The Glowing Edges filter in Photoshop has some benefits that the Find Edges filter lacks (Figure 7-17). You can vary the edge width to encompass wider or narrower cracks; in many cases you won't even need to apply a Gaussian Blur to the results. The smoothness adjustment works more like a fine-detail finder; at lower settings it selects for smaller

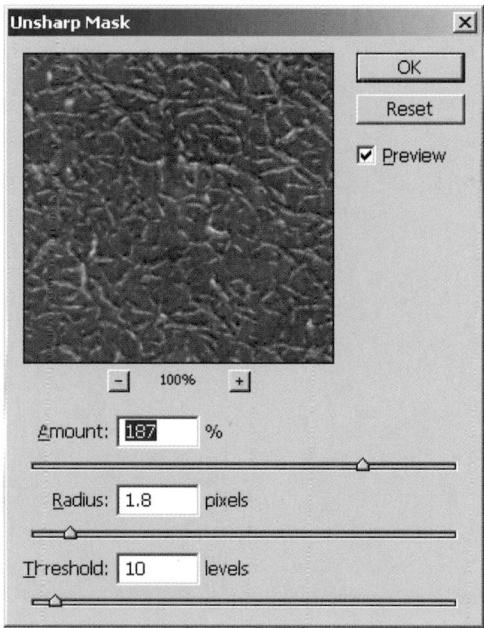

Fig. 7-16 These Unsharp Mask settings do a good job of highlighting the cracks and their edges without picking up extraneous detail in the photograph. Setting the Threshold above 0 keeps the filter from accentuating noise and low-contrast detail. This helps the filter work selectively on the cracks.

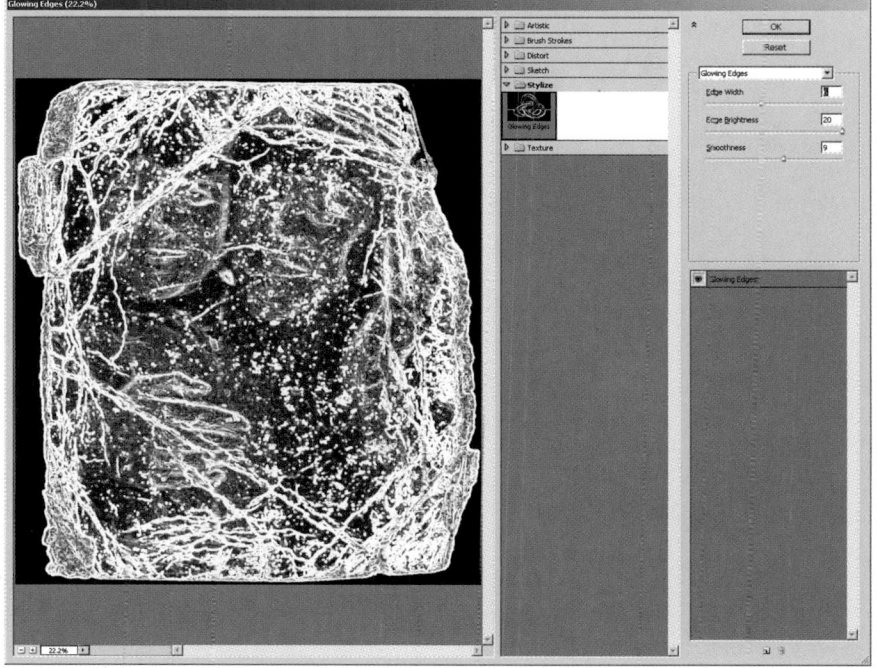

Fig. 7-17 The Glowing Edges filter has controls for Edge Width, Brightness, and Smoothness. For mask making, you'll usually leave the Brightness setting at 20, to produce maximum contrast. Adjust the Width and Smoothness sliders until the filter does a good job of selecting cracks and little else.

HOW TO ENHANCE
CRACKS FOR
SELECTION
(continued)
and sharper edges, while higher settings pick out grosser detail. You can produce a fairly sophisticated mask in a single step with this filter. Note that the Glowing Edges filter only works on 8-bit files, so you need to convert a copy of the file from 16 bits to 8 to use this.

Making Masks from Colors

Color is a great way to distinguish between different parts of a photograph that need different kinds of correction, especially if the photograph is in B&W. That's not a paradox. A B&W photograph in good condition has no color differences between parts of the photograph. It's only when you get damage like differential fading, staining, bleaching, or tarnishing that you'll see different colors in different parts of the image. Color changes are a reliable sign of damage that needs to be fixed.

I used Color differences to construct the continuous-tone mask in Figure 7-2. That mask worked so well that it gave me in one step almost complete correction of a serious tarnish problem. Here's how I did it.

HOW TO SELECT
TARNISHED PARTS OF
A PHOTOGRAPH
Figure 7-18, left, shows the original photograph, which is yellowed, faded, and tarnished. I made the adjusted scan in Figure 7-18 right by using the scan level settings shown in Figure 7-19. This gave me a much better range of tones to work with and removed most of the yellow stain. It may not be obvious in the reproduction here, but I left the image slightly yellow, just enough so that it would be easy to distinguish the bluish tarnish from the proper photographic image.

I used Asiva Selection (Figure 7-20) to build this mask, but any of several masking tools would have worked. I set the Hue range to restrict

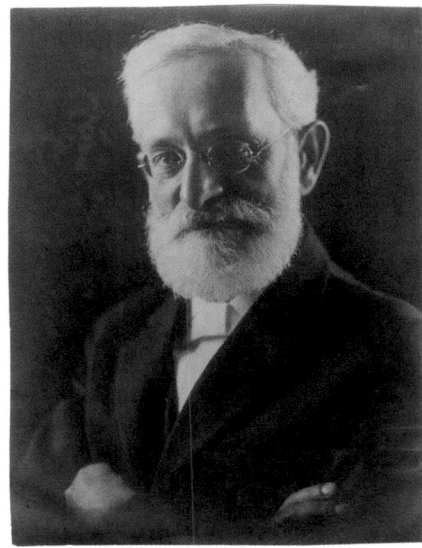
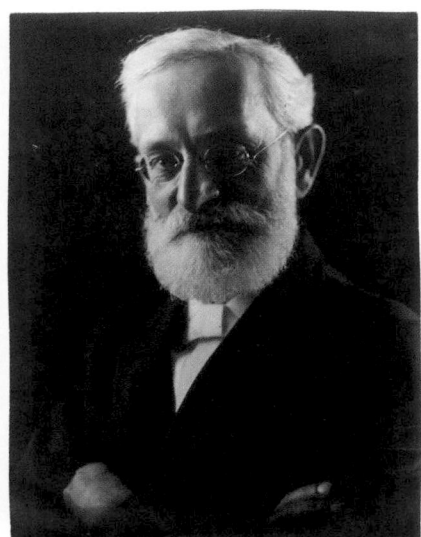

Fig. 7-18 The photograph on the left (also seen in Figure 7-2) is badly tarnished. The tarnish is lighter and bluer than the rest of the image. The scan settings in Figure 7-19 restore much of the neutrality and tonal range of the photographic image, while at the same time they accentuate the tarnish's blue color. That makes it easier to select the tarnish with a mask.

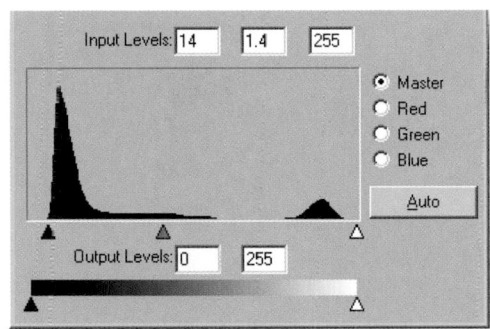

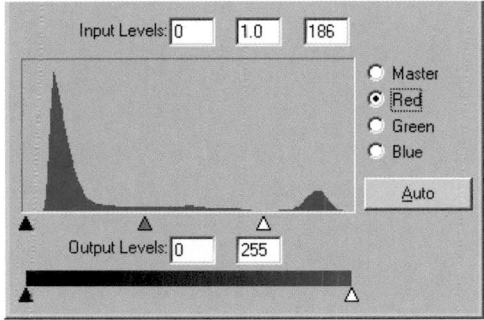

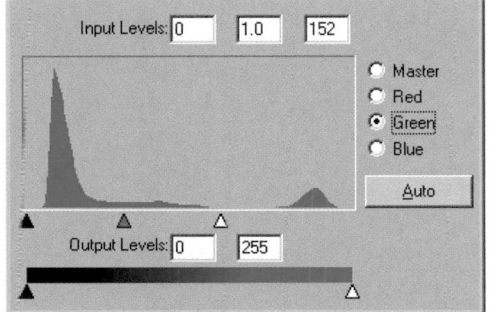

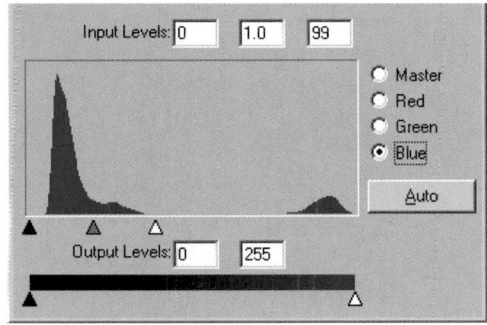

Fig. 7-19 The scan settings for Figure 7-18. The black and white sliders in each color channel are adjusted to closely bracket the highlights in the photograph while leaving the shadow tones well above 0. That leaves the true blacks in the photograph as dark grays, but it ensures good tonal separation between the dark tarnish and the darker underlying tones.

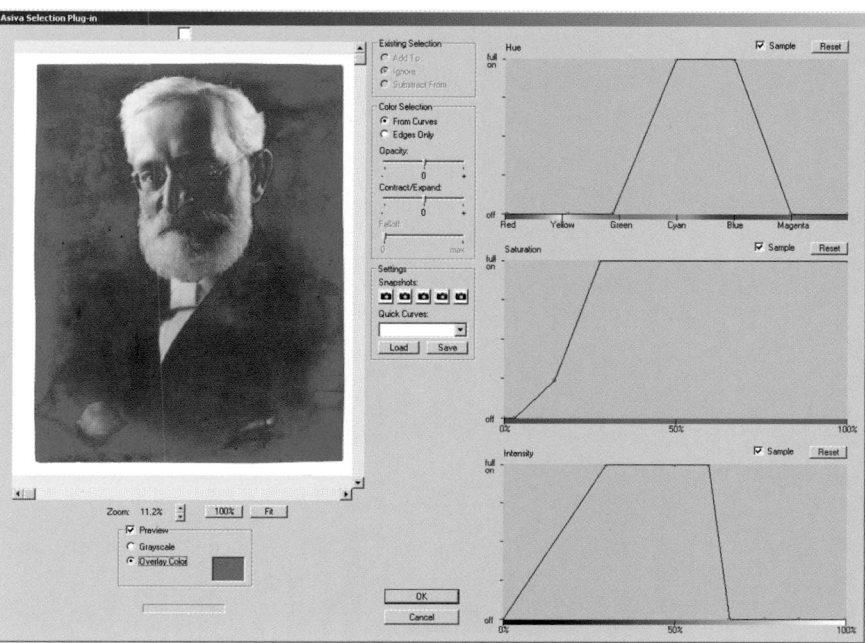

Fig. 7-20 Asiva Selection is a good tool for creating masks selected by color and tonality. The mask is shown in orange in the preview window. To select for the tarnish color, I restricted the Hue range to shades of blue. In addition, I set the Saturation slider to reject the parts of the photo that had no saturation (were near-neutral in color) and the Intensity slider to middle-dark tones because the tarnish is dark but not black. The mask this plug-in produced is shown in Figure 7-2, center.

HOW TO SELECT
TARNISHED PARTS OF
A PHOTOGRAPH
(continued)

the mask to shades of blue, which corresponded to tarnish. I adjusted the Saturation curve so that areas with very little or no saturation would be excluded from the mask. In the Value curve, I rejected the lighter tones because I could see they had very little tarnish. I also reduced the mask selection as the tones neared black because anything in the photograph that exhibited high density couldn't be badly tarnished. The orange overlay shows the areas that would be selected. This is what got me the mask in Figure 7-2.

I applied that mask to the photograph and used the curve settings in Figure 7-3 in a Curves adjustment layer. These curves moderately darkened the midtones and shadows, made them slightly more magenta, and made them much more yellow. Remarkably, this simple Curves adjustment produced the very uniform-looking photograph in Figure 7-2, right. This is *not* a B&W conversion; it is still a full-color RGB image; the curves did that good a job of correcting the tonality and color everywhere.

Exaggerating Color to Select Tarnish

Sometimes the color differences are too subtle to select for directly. Accentuate them, and they make an excellent basis for a mask. The photograph in Figure 7-21, top, has widespread, silvery tarnish. The color difference between the tarnish and the yellowed photograph is not very strong, so I couldn't make a selection mask directly. Figure 7-21,

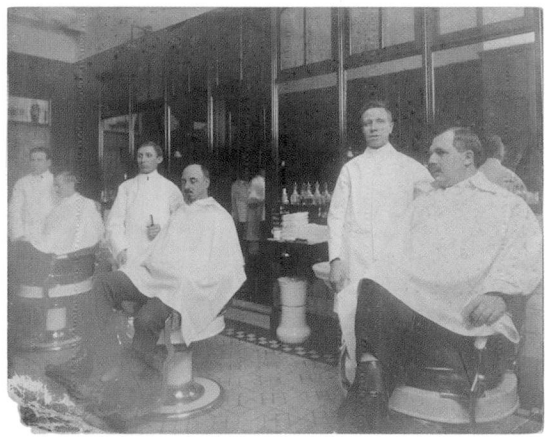

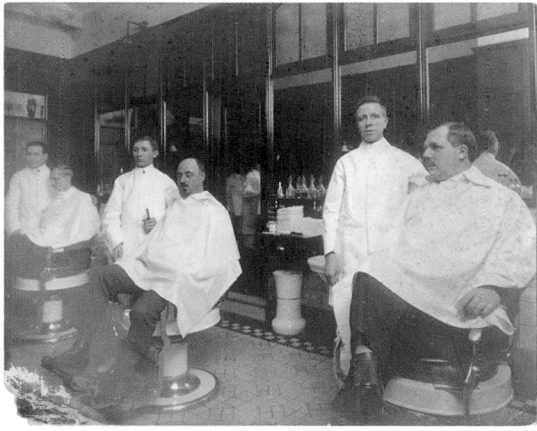

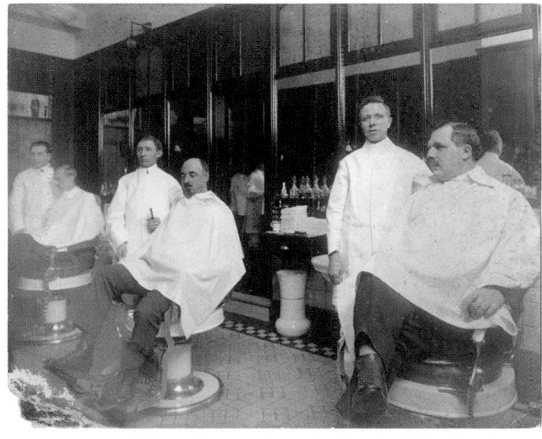

Fig. 7-21 The original photograph (top) is yellowed, faded, and tarnished. I scanned this photo using the settings in Figure 7-22 to produce the middle figure. I intentionally did not make the photographic image neutral; by leaving it warm toned, I got a more clear-cut color difference between the tarnish (which now looks bluish) and the photograph (reddish). I used that to create a tarnish-selecting mask, with which I eliminated most of the tarnish in the bottom figure.

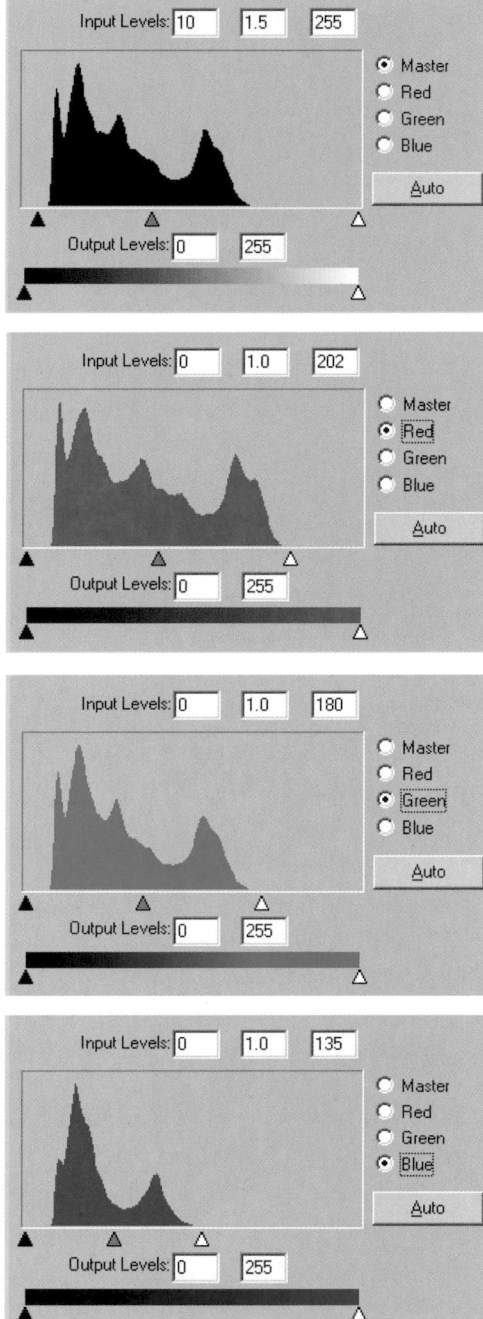

Fig. 7-22 These are the scanner Levels settings I used to create Figure 7-21, center. I let the blacks remain gray to get good tonal separation between the tarnish and the photograph. I didn't fully color-correct the photograph. Leaving the photograph reddish and the tarnish bluish makes it easier to create a selection mask.

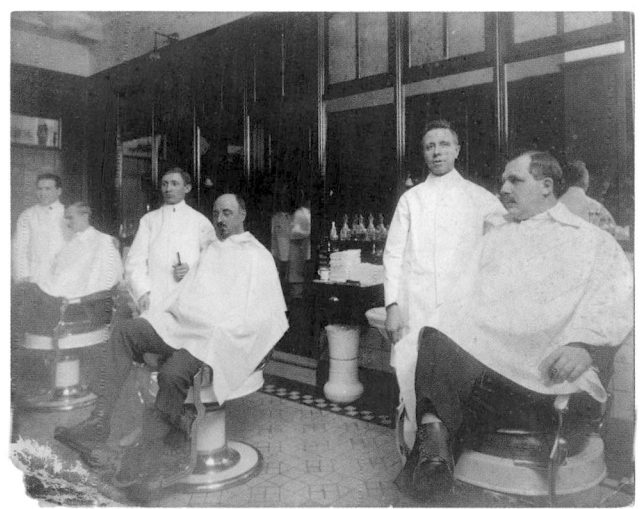

Fig. 7-23 Applying a Saturation increase of +72 points to the scan from Figure 7-21 produces this image. The color in the tarnish and the photograph are greatly exaggerated, making it very easy to see where the tarnish is. This exaggerated color makes mask-making much easier.

center, shows the scan I made with the scan settings in Figure 7-22. I increased the tonal range, whitened the whites, and made the photograph overall more neutral, but I didn't do as complete a job of scan correction as I normally would. By intent there are no tones close to black, and I left enough residual warm hue in the photograph to let me separate the tarnish by hue. In fact, I chose scan settings by trial and error to make the tarnish go bluish while leaving the photograph brown.

My next step was to enhance those colors in a copy of the scan with the Hue/Saturation control set to +72 saturation. This produced Figure 7-23. Now I had something I could sink my selection tools into. The untarnished image is reddish-orange, while the tarnish is intense blue. The color distinctions are clearly visible when you compare the red channel (Figure 7-24, top) and the blue channel (Figure 7-24, middle). I brought up the Channel Mixer (Figure 7-25), turned on the Monochrome option, and set the Blue channel slider to +200%. I slid the Red channel slider into the negative percentages to create a new B&W image that would be the difference between the red and the blue channels. At a red value of −155%, I got a mask that did a good job of highlighting most of the tarnish without including much of the undamaged photograph (Figure 7-24, bottom). I converted this image to grayscale and copied it into an Alpha channel in the original scan.

I loaded my mask as a new selection and created a Curves adjustment layer with the settings shown in Figure 7-26. That darkened most of the tarnished areas and eliminated the blue cast to produce the photograph in Figure 7-21, bottom.

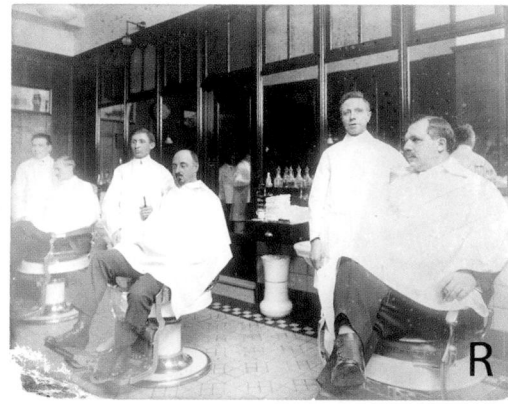

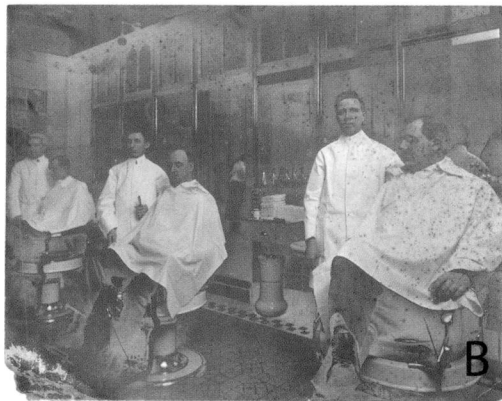

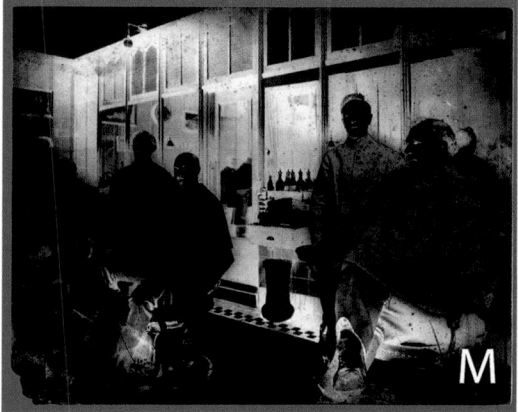

Fig. 7-24 The top two figures show the red and blue channels from Figure 7-23. The red channel shows the least tarnish, while the blue channel shows the most; this isn't surprising given the colors in the photograph. I used the Channel Mixer settings in Figure 7-25 to "subtract" the red channel from the blue channel, leaving only the tarnish behind. The bottom figure shows the resulting mask.

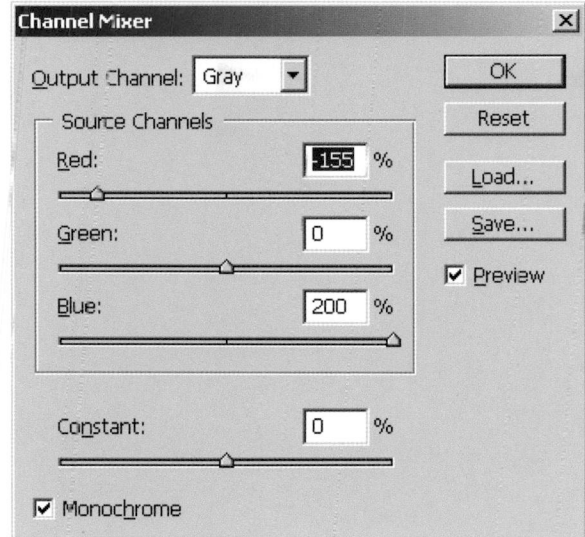

Fig. 7-25 These are the Channel Mixer settings that produce the mask in Figure 7-24, bottom. I set the Blue slider to 200% for maximum strength. I adjusted the Red slider until I got the photograph to fade out as much as possible (a setting of −155%). The Monochrome option is selected so that the output of the Mixer is a grayscale image.

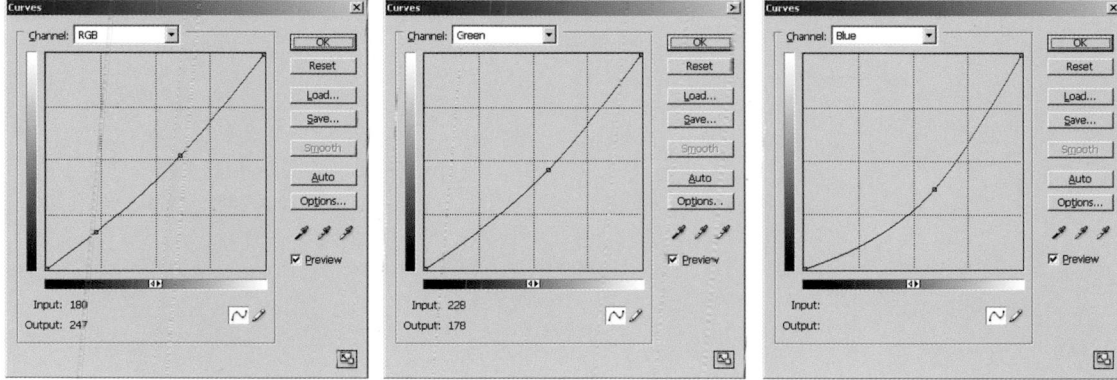

Fig. 7-26 This is the Curves adjustment I used in combination with the tarnish mask in Figure 7-24 to produce the repaired photograph at the bottom of Figure 7-21. Much like the Curves adjustment in Figure 7-3, these curves make the tarnish darker, a little more magenta, and much more yellow. That blends it in well with the background photograph.

Exaggerating Color to Select Scratches

Sometimes you can take advantage of enhanced color tricks to isolate scratches for repair. Figure 7-27 is an ideal case. This badly faded and yellowed photograph is covered with dark stains, spots, and thousands upon thousands of fine scratches. The scratches are very small and neutral in color, but they're so prevalent that they almost bury the image in places. Fortunately the damage is neutral and the image is yellow, so I can create a color-based mask that selects for the damage.

✓ HOW TO SELECT SCRATCHES AND DIRT BY COLOR

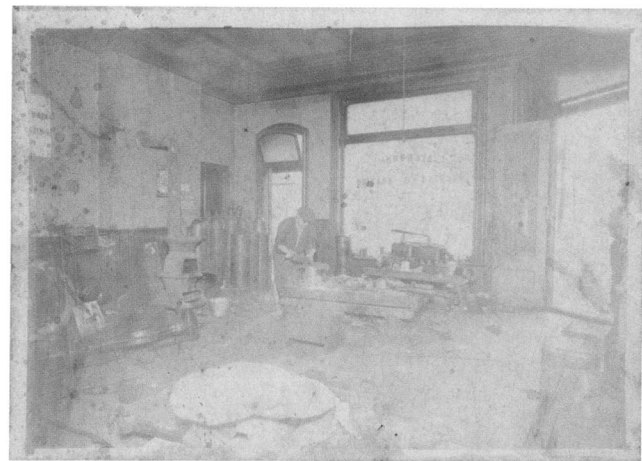

Fig. 7-27 This photograph is almost obscured by damage. It has faded very badly and is almost completely covered with fine scratches, dirt, and stains.

HOW TO SELECT SCRATCHES AND DIRT BY COLOR (continued)

The scan in Figure 7-28 has improved image contrast and color; now you can see the damage very clearly. The scan settings in Figure 7-29 produced the better, more detailed scan by expanding its tonal range and make it more neutral. The enlarged section from the center of the photograph gives you some idea of just how bad the scratches are, but even this enlargement doesn't show all the scratches.

Making the image more neutral made all the scratches distinctly blue in hue. So I started out with the same trick I used on the barbershop photograph. A saturation increase of +70 points produced Figure 7-30. Instead of creating the mask with Channel Mixer, as I did in the previous example, I used the Image Calculations tool. This tool combines two layers or channels in more complicated ways than the Channel Mixer.

Figure 7-31 shows the Calculations control panel. Just as with the barbershop photograph, I decided to use the difference between the red and the blue channels to isolate the damage. That's why I checked the Invert box next to the red channel. The tricky part to making this work is the blending mode. Photoshop has 20 different modes, most of which are difficult to describe in words and many of which have uninformative names.

What I was interested in was the subset that starts with "Overlay" and ends with "Hard Mix." What these blend modes do is accentuate the results of combining two channels. I won't just end up with the new channel that is the simple difference between the red and the blue channels; the blending mode will exaggerate that difference. Some blending modes' exaggerations are extremely useful for mask making. I haven't managed to internalize what all the blending modes do, so I don't try to visualize in my head how well a particular mode will work; I just try them all out. Very often I'm surprised.

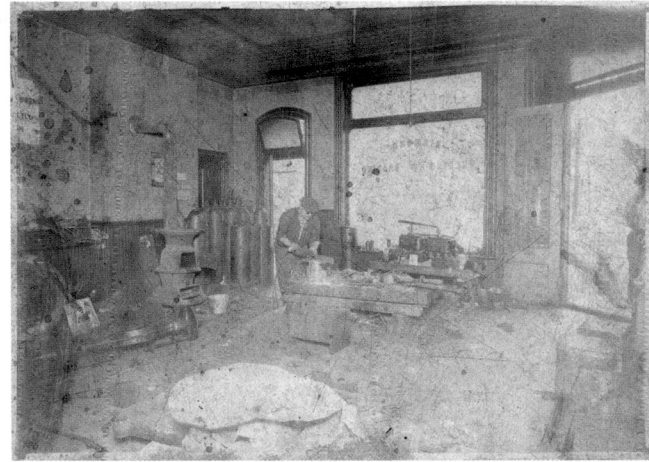

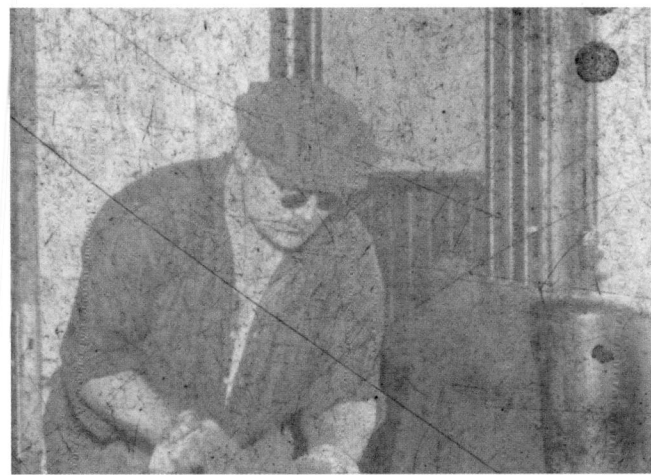

Fig. 7-28 The first step in repairing this photograph is making a good scan, using the scanner Levels settings in Figure 7-29. This scan shows that there's a great deal of detail in the photograph, hidden underneath all the garbage. The enlargement in the lower figure shows just how pervasive the dirty scratches are.

For this particular image, the Linear Light and Hard Light blending modes worked spectacularly well. Both produced masks with almost no real photographic detail in them; they're nearly perfectly isolated images of the damage. The results for those two calculations are shown in Figure 7-32. The top mask was produced by Linear Light blending, the bottom by Hard Light blending.

It's a toss-up as to which one would do the best job for repairing this photograph; both could be useful. The Linear Light blend has better contrast characteristics for a mask, with stronger differences between the scratches and the rest of the photograph. The Hard Light mask has poorer contrast, but it does a better job of suppressing photographic detail.

I chose the Linear Light mask because it needed less adjustment (Figure 7-33) to turn it into a really good mask with strong whites and

HOW TO SELECT
SCRATCHES AND
DIRT BY COLOR
(continued)

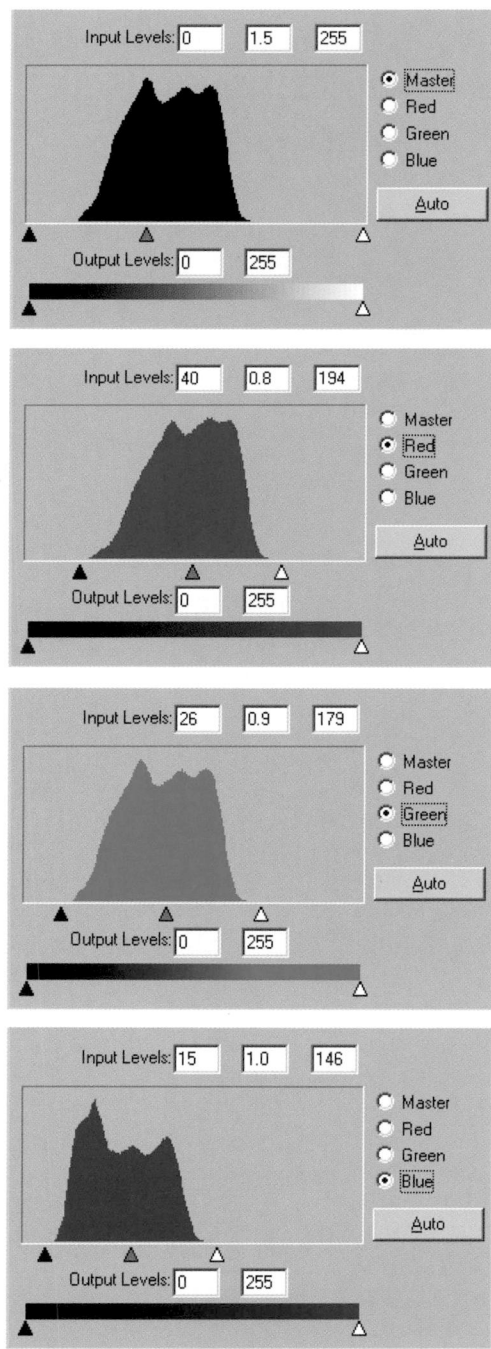

Fig. 7-29 The scanner Levels settings I used to produce Figure 7-28. As with Figure 7-21, these settings leave some residual color in the photograph, rendering it slightly yellowish. In contrast, the dirt and scratches come out blue, making them easier to select for.

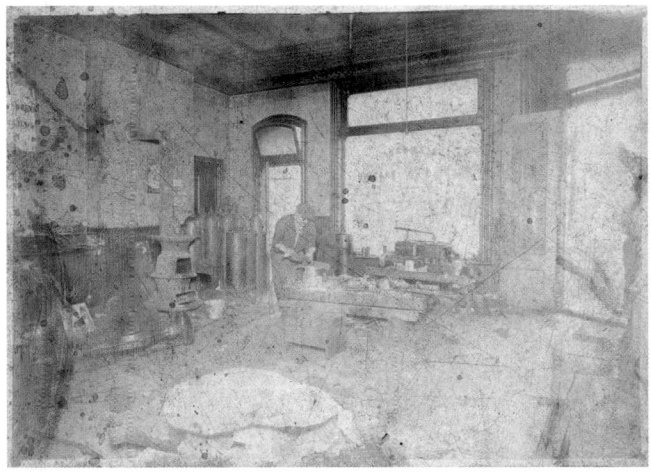

Fig. 7-30 Applying a Saturation increase of +70 points to Figure 7-28 produces this. Now the photograph and the dirt and scratches are clearly differentiated by color. This photograph gets turned into a mask in Figure 7-32.

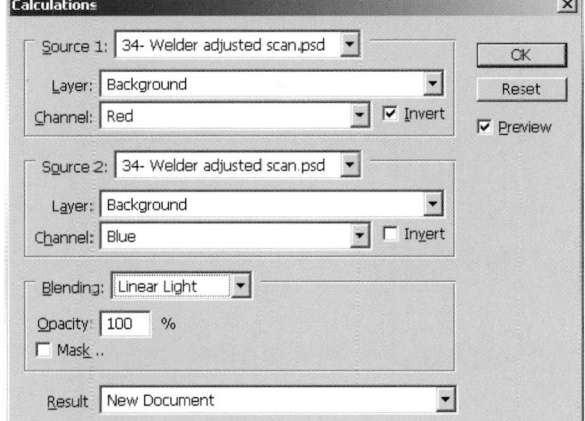

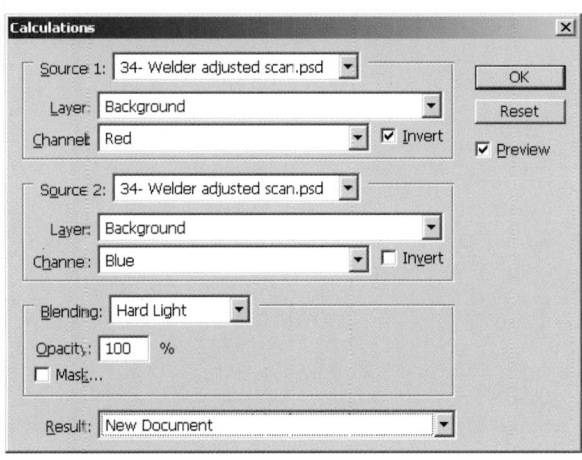

Fig. 7-31 Image Calculations works something like Channel Mixer, but it offers more complicated blending options for the channels being combined. The mask I created from Figure 7-30 involves subtracting the red channel from the blue channel because the red channel shows the damage most clearly, while the blue channel shows it hardly at all. The Linear Light (top) and Hard Light (bottom) blend modes exaggerate and enhance the differences between the two channels, producing a much stronger and more selective mask than Channel Mixer could. The results of these two blends are shown in Figure 7-32.

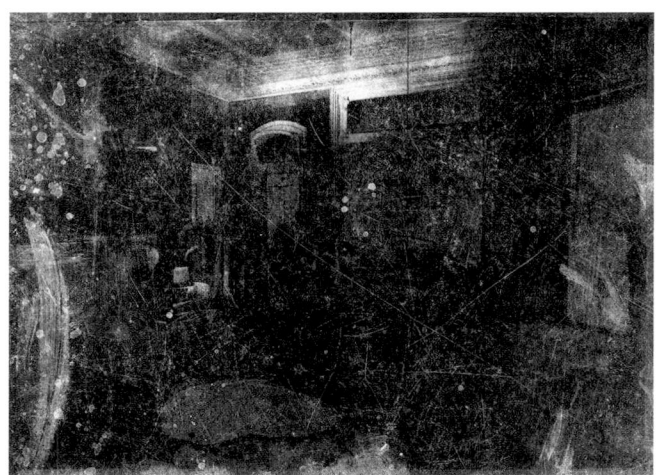

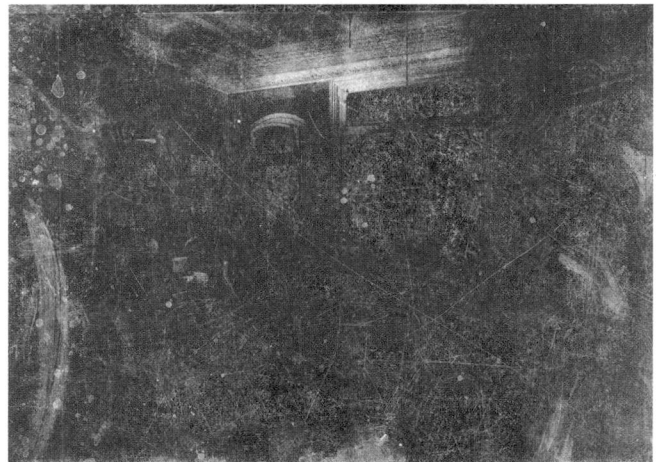

Fig. 7-32 The masks that result from Linear Light (top) and Hard Light (bottom) blending of Figure 7-30 in Image Calculations. Both of these are good damage-selection masks, but they have different strengths and weaknesses. The Linear Light mask has better contrast between the damage and the photograph, but more of the photograph is visible (selected). The Hard Light mask does a better job of rejecting the photograph, but the contrast between the damage and the photograph isn't as strong.

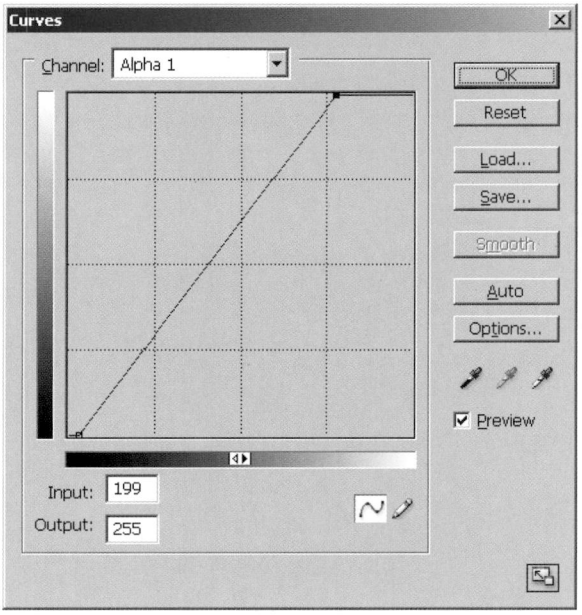

Fig. 7-33 This Curves adjustment pushes the tones in the Linear Light mask from Figure 7-32 toward stronger blacks and whites. That isolates the scratches more strongly in anticipation of their eventual correction in Chapter 8.

real blacks. In Chapter 8, Damage Control, page 276, I use this mask in combination with the original and saturation-enhanced versions of the scan to make some amazing repairs.

Exaggerating Color for Hand-Tinting Masks

Exaggerated color is a good way to prepare hand-tinted photos like the one in Figure 7-1, for masking prior to repair work. In Figure 7-34, left, I added a Hue/Saturation adjustment layer that was set to a saturation level of +75 to the original scan.

✓ HOW TO CREATE MASKS FOR HAND-TINTING PHOTOGRAPHS

I inserted a Curves layer between the original and the Hue/Saturation layer so I could adjust the color balance to make it overall more neutral. It wasn't necessary, but it let me create brighter and more distinct colors with the Hue/Saturation layer (Figure 7-34, right). I didn't do anything particularly sophisticated with the curves; I merely adjusted the end points of the individual color channels so that whites and blacks both came out modestly neutral. This was not a finely tuned color adjustment.

To create my masks, I used the Magic Wand in Contiguous mode (Figure 7-35). I started with the dress, making a few clicks in each area with the brush set to a large tolerance of 30, then narrowed down to 5 to fill in near the edges of the selections. Once I thought I had a good selection, I expanded it by 3 pixels and contracted it by 3 pixels. The reason for doing that was to fill in any "pinholes" (missing pixels) in the selected area. Finally, I feathered the selection with a radius of 2 pixels to slightly soften the edges of the affected area and make it look more like painted-on color.

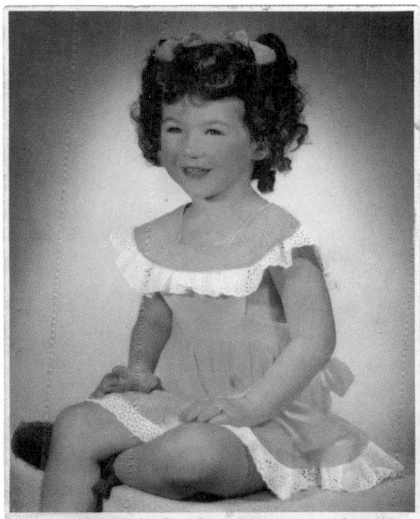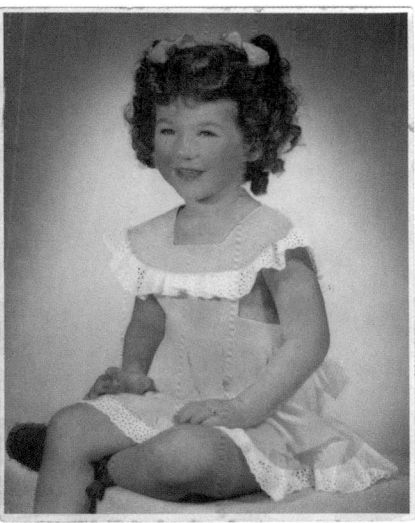

Fig. 7-34 Exaggerated color makes it easier to create masks for hand-tinted photographs. I increased the saturation of Figure 7-1 by +75 points in the photograph on the left. I used Curves to make the image more neutral overall in the photograph on the right, so that it would be easier to selected regions for hand-tinting by their colors.

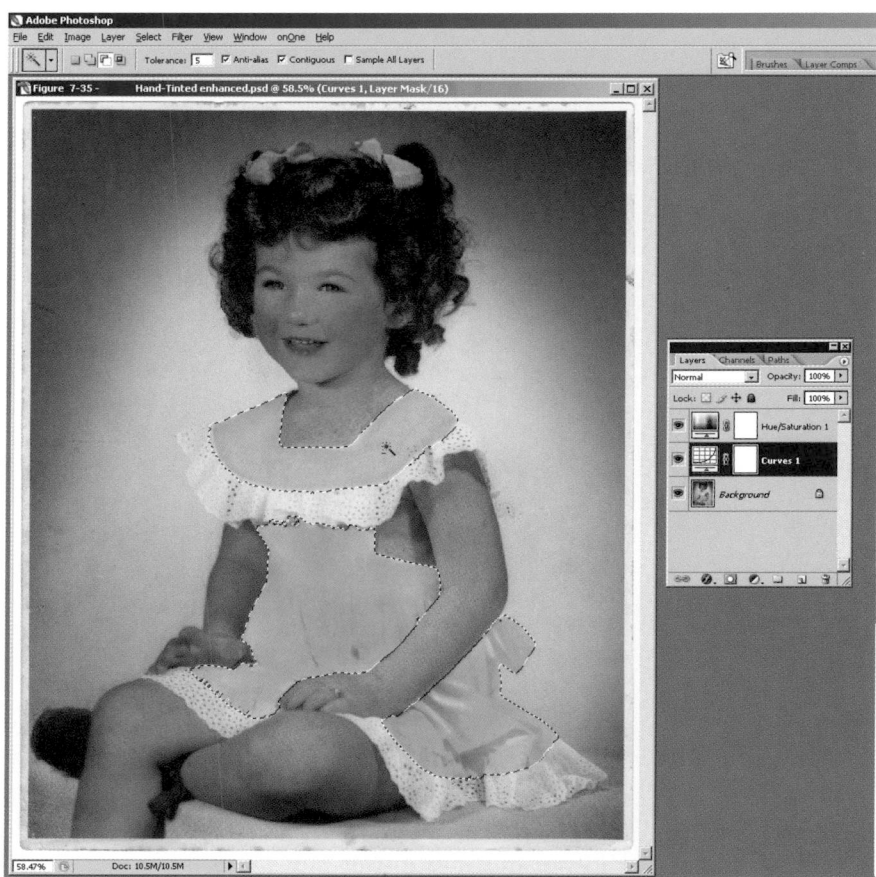

Fig. 7-35 This screenshot shows the photograph from Figure 7-34, right, with its layer stack. The Magic Wand selects just the blue of the dress to make a hand-tinting mask, shown in Figure 7-36.

HOW TO CREATE MASKS FOR HAND-TINTING PHOTOGRAPHS (continued)

I clicked Select/Save Selection and saved in a new channel that I named "dress" (Figure 7-36). Creating this mask took only a few minutes' work. Creating all the masks that I used to hand-tint this photograph in Chapter 6 took me less time than did writing this description of my methods.

Five Ways to Mask a Damaged Area

HOW TO SELECT CELLOPHANE TAPE DAMAGE FOR CORRECTION

I've described several different ways to create selection masks in this chapter. The methods aren't mutually exclusive; more often than not you can make a good mask any number of ways. In this last section, I'll show you five different methods, all of which have merits, for selecting the same area for repair.

Figure 7-37, left, shows an old, faded photograph that was taped together with cellophane tape. Brittle and brown with age, there's no way to remove the tape without destroying the photo. The photograph

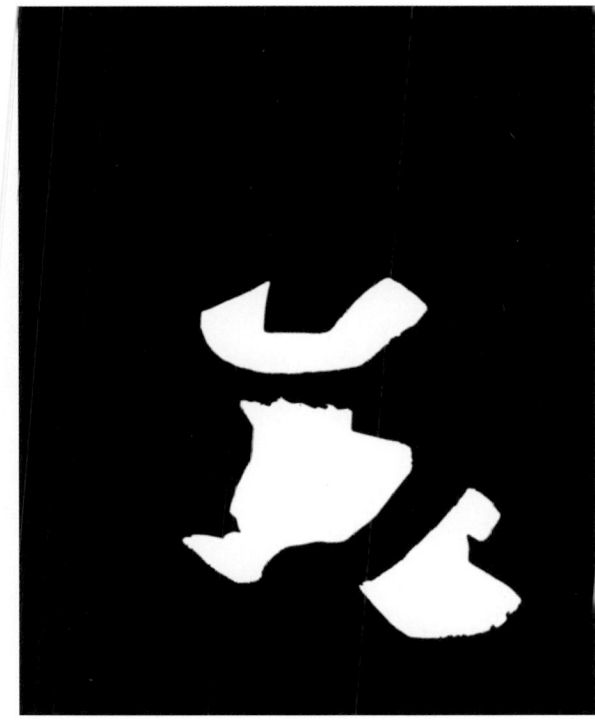

Fig. 7-36 This is the
finished hand-tinting
mask for the dress. I
expanded the selection in
Figure 7-35 by 3 pixels
and contracted by 3
pixels. That filled in any
"pinholes" in the
selection. I've feathered
the edge of that selection
by 2 pixels to soften the
border, so that the
tinting will blend better
into the photograph.

HOW TO SELECT
CELLOPHANE TAPE
DAMAGE FOR
CORRECTION
(continued)

looks very different where the tape is; to do a good restoration will require a mask that selects the taped region so that it can be repaired separately from the rest of the photograph.

My first step was to make a scan that exaggerated the difference in color between the tape and the rest of the photograph, using the settings in Figure 7-38. As you can see in Figure 7-37, right, I was able to make the photograph more neutral and contrasty without losing the distinctive orange color of the tape. That gives the masking tools a pronounced color difference to grab onto.

This is one of the rare (for me) cases where Photoshop's Color Range tool is up to the task. To make the Color Range tool's work easier, I increased the photograph's saturation by +40 before I opened the tool. I sampled three points—one bright point in the collar under the tape, one middle tone, and one dark tone on a lapel. Then I adjusted the Fuzziness slider until most of the tape (but little else) was well selected (Figure 7-39).

The color range masking tools in Picture Window did an equally good job (Figure 7-40). By itself, the range adjustments didn't completely select the tape (purple overlay on the photograph at right). They decently roughed it in, though. so I followed up by switching to the masking brush with the "Similar Pixels" setting and painted ▼

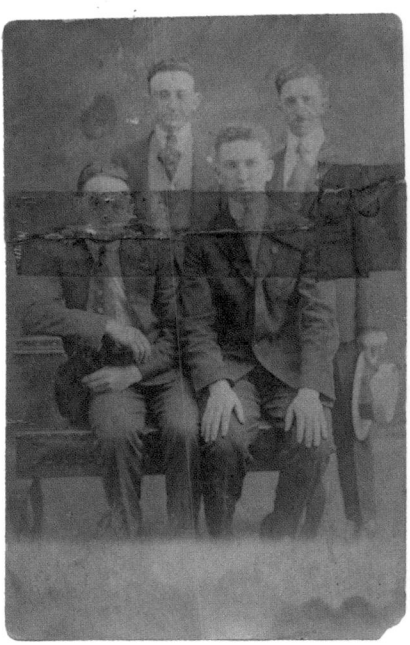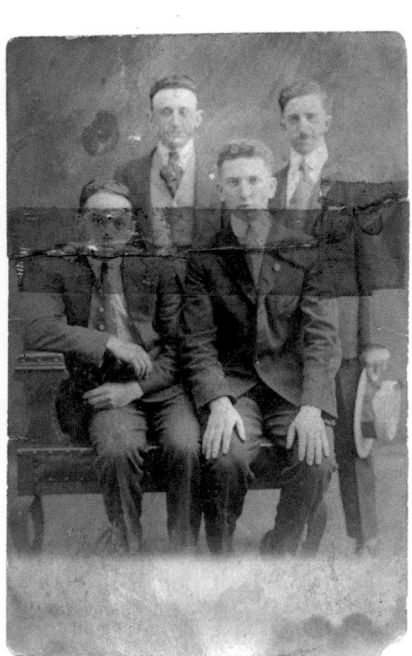

Fig. 7-37 This stained and faded photograph was taped together with cellophane tape that has turned brown with age (left). The scan made with the scanner settings from Figure 7-38 improves contrast and density. It also makes the photographic image almost neutral while leaving the tape marks orange (right). I can use that color difference to create a tape-selecting mask in several different ways.

HOW TO SELECT
CELLOPHANE TAPE
DAMAGE FOR
CORRECTION
(continued)

over the tape area. That efficiently filled in the gaps to produce the mask on the left.

The Asiva Selection plug-in produced the mask in Figure 7-41. I simply swept the eyedropper over the square piece of tape on the right of the photograph, and Asiva automatically generated the curves settings and the mask shown.

Mask Pro took a bit more work, but it produced the most complete and accurate selection of the taped area (although it selected some extraneous matter as well). After I created an 8-bit copy of the photograph for Mask Pro to work on, I used the "Keep" and "Drop" eyedropper tools to create palettes of colors that I wanted included and excluded from the selection (Figure 7-42). Then I activated the Magic Brush tool and ran it over the photograph. That produced the partial mask that you can see in green in the illustration. Satisfied that my color selections were appropriate, I applied the "Apply Everywhere" command, and Mask Pro generated the full mask shown on the right in Figure 7-42.

To make my fifth mask, I didn't use any special tools, just a simple trick. When looking at the damage to this photograph in the separate RGB channels (Figure 7-43, top row), I saw that the red channel showed the tape the least (making it a good candidate on which to do the actual restoration work), but the blue channel on the right showed it very clearly. When I increased the saturation of the photograph, this became even more pronounced. At +60 saturation, the entire taped area was

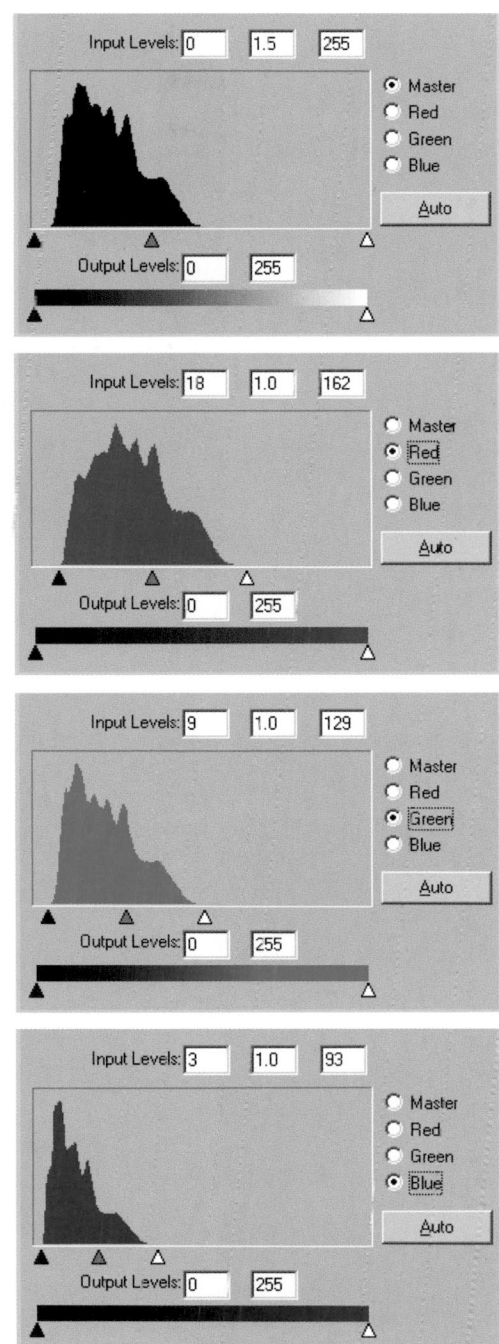

Fig. 7-38 The scanner software histograms and Levels settings for Figure 7-37. This scan improves the density and contrast of the original photograph and makes the photographic image almost neutral in color.

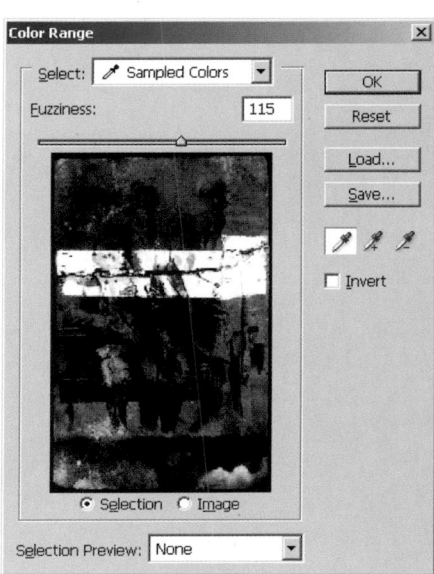

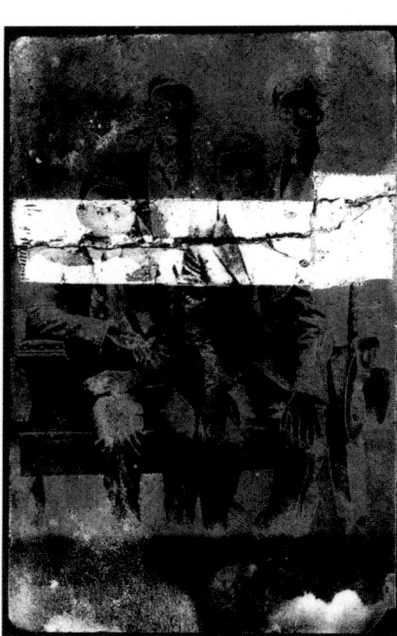

Fig. 7-39 Because there's a clear-cut difference in color between the tape and the photograph, the Color Range tool can do a pretty good job of creating a mask that selects for the tape. Before sampling the taped region, I increased the saturation of the photograph by +40 points to make the color difference even more pronounced.

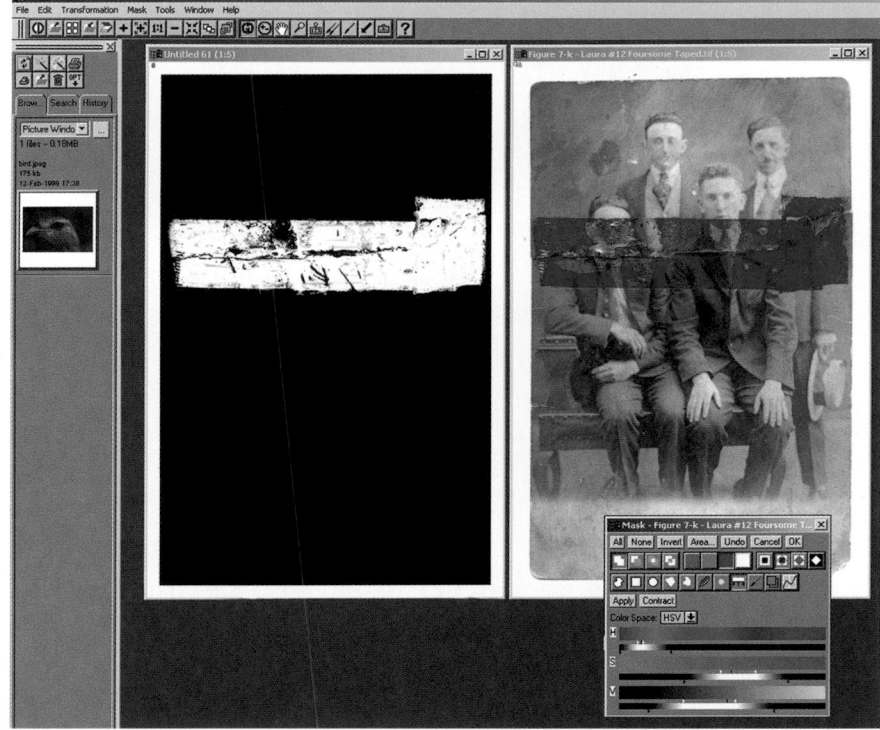

Fig. 7-40 Picture Window's Color Range masking tool selects for the tape by its distinctive hue and saturation. In this screenshot, note how I've adjusted the selection ranges on the Hue, Saturation, and Values sliders to include the tape as completely as possible while excluding the rest of the photograph. The mask on the left was created with Color Range followed by the "Similar Pixels" Brush tool.

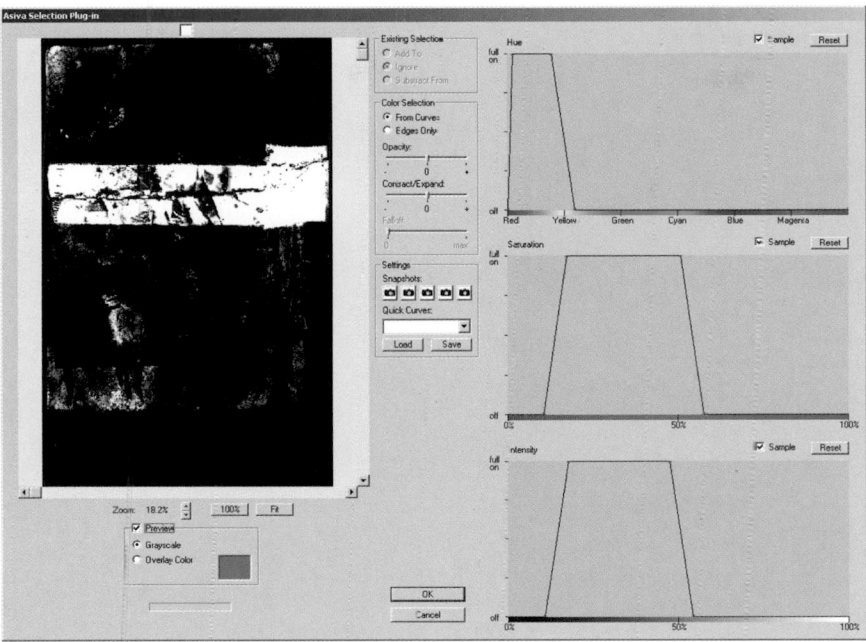

Fig. 7-41 Asiva Selection easily finds the tape in the photograph. Restricting the hues to reds and oranges and the saturation to moderate levels excludes most of the photograph while retaining the tape.

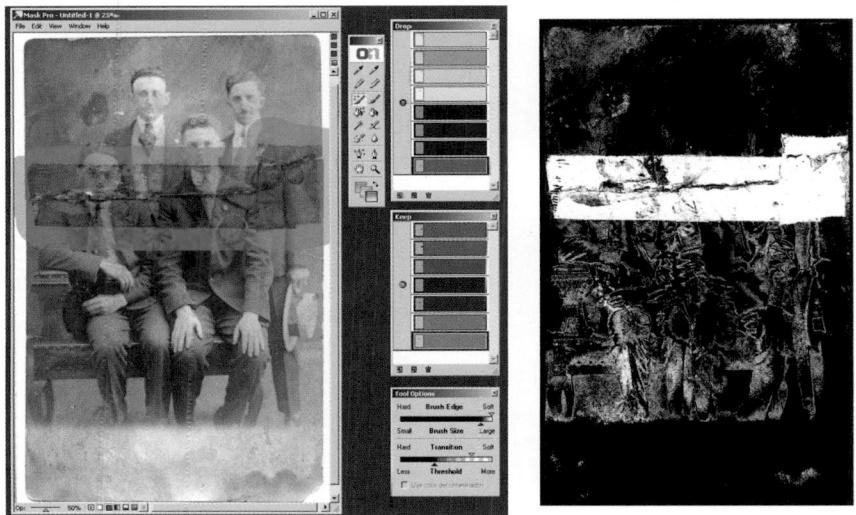

Fig. 7-42 Mask Pro is able to select the tape very completely, because its Drop and Keep sample palettes permit me to specify the tape color very completely from multiple sample points. In the window on the left, I'm using the Magic Brush with the colors from the palettes to paint in the mask. Mask Pro also includes some extraneous areas, seen in the mask on the right, but those can be erased easily with a black eraser.

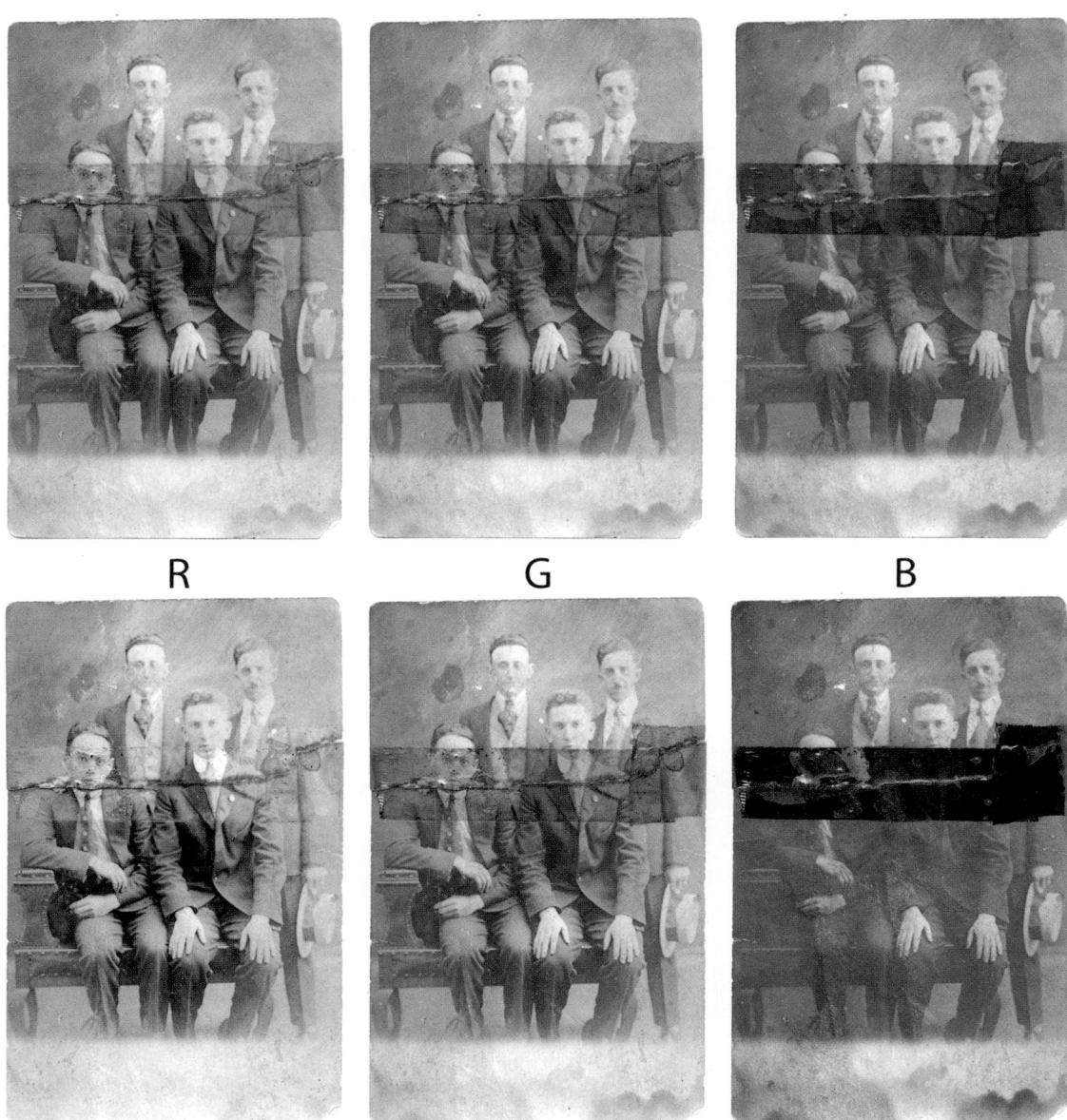

R   G   B

Fig. 7-43 The individual color channels for Figure 7-37, top row, show that the tape is most visible in the blue channel. Increasing the saturation of the photograph by +60 points exaggerates this difference and makes the taped area stand out very clearly in the blue channel (bottom row).

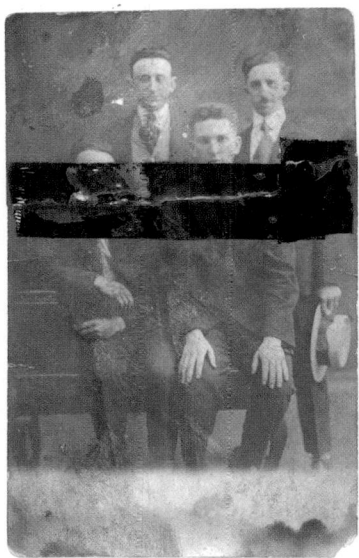 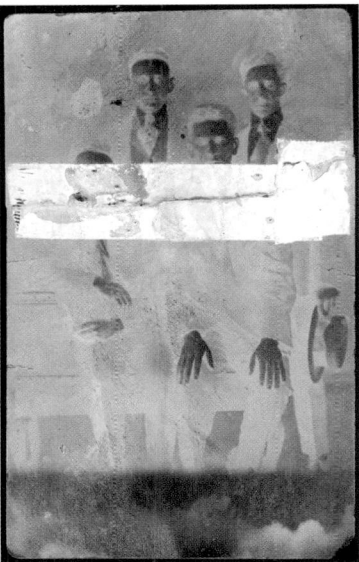 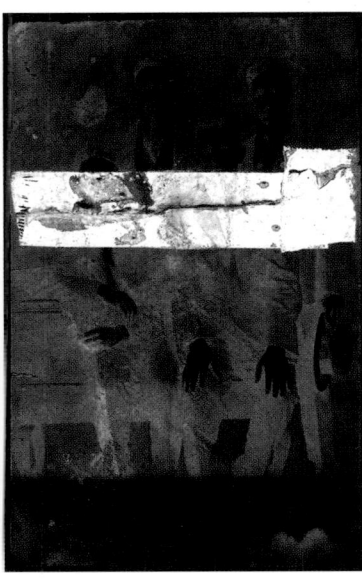

Fig. 7-44 The figure on the left is the saturated blue channel from Figure 7-43. Inverting that image produces the center figure. Applying the Curves adjustment from Figure 7-45 produces the strong, contrasty mask in the right figure.

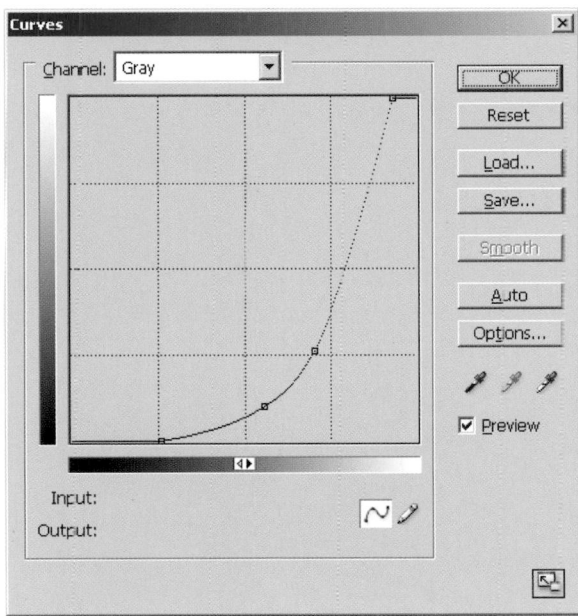

Fig. 7-45 This curve converts the middle figure in Figure 7-44 into a good, strong mask. The contrast is greatly enhanced, especially in the highlights and midtones, forcing the tones in the areas surrounding the taped region close to black.

HOW TO SELECT
CELLOPHANE TAPE
DAMAGE FOR
CORRECTION
(continued)

distinctly darker than the rest of the photograph (Figure 7-43, bottom row).

I copied the saturated blue channel into a new Alpha channel and inverted it (Figure 7-44). I applied the Curves settings in Figure 7-45 to turn that grayish image into a mask that strongly selected for the taped area.

All five masks will require some manual white and black brushwork to completely block out the areas I don't want to alter and select small parts of the tape that the mask tools missed. That's part of the beauty of a mask channel—you don't have to spend hours getting it perfect with your masking tools and software. A little manual labor can turn a pretty good mask into a perfect one.

CHAPTER 8

Damage Control

How-To's in This Chapter

How to clean up dust and scratches from a scan
How to repair a badly scratched slide
How to minimize scratches in a print with Curves
How to minimize scratches with color channels and channel mixing
How to fill in cracks in a print with a mask
How to repair cracks in stages with Median filtering
How to repair large cracks with repeated masking and filtering
How to repair a torn negative
How to remove chemical and water spots
How to eliminate tarnish and silvered-out spots
How to minimize tape stains
How to remove print surface textures
How to erase mildew spots

Every restoration job involves repairing dirt and damage. The work may be as minimal as cleaning up residual dust specks and scratches in a scan, but usually the problems are more extensive. I've restored many photographs that had very good tone and color but had suffered some kind of physical damage.

In this book I emphasize getting the computer to do as much of the work of photo restoration as I can to minimize pixel-by-pixel manual retouching. Wherever possible I use software filters, tools, and special programs to repair damage because they are faster and more efficient than manual retouching and very effective. Whether you're restoring professionally or for personal joy, you still only have so many hours a day that you can devote to photo restoration. If a bit of computer code saves you hours restoring a photograph, that is time you can spend doing something else you enjoy (even if that "something else" is restoring more photographs).

Clever code will only take you so far, though; repair work requires manual labor and there's no way around it. There are no ways to totally avoid pushing pixels around; some damage just can't be eliminated except pixel by pixel. Still, virtually all damage can be reduced with a smart application of software, making your manual repair labors less onerous.

Simple Spotting

Every scan you do will need some spotting. Scans accentuate minor scratches and other occasional defects. Even if your technique is meticulously antiseptic, you will still find bits of dirt or dust embedded in the photograph. As I explained in Chapter 4, Getting the Photo into the Computer, it's much safer to leave that dust alone than to try to remove it, so you'll have to do some cleanup work to get rid of those lingering specks and scratches.

HOW TO CLEAN UP
DUST AND
SCRATCHES FROM A
SCAN

The old copy negative in Figure 8-1 can use plenty of spotting. Most of the specks are white in the positive image (Figure 8-2), but there's a scattering of dark specks that also needs to be erased. The best and fastest way to clean a scan is to use Photoshop's Dust & Scratches filter in conjunction with the History Brush. I reserve the Clone tool or the Spot Healing Brush for only the larger flaws.

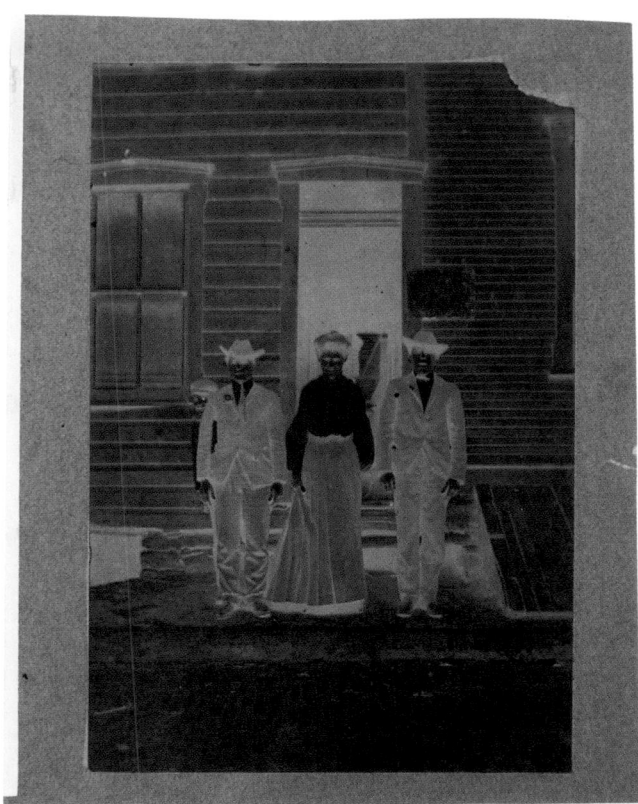

Fig. 8-1 This old copy negative has lots of dust and dirt specks that need to be cleaned up. The original photograph had dirt on it that was copied over when the negative was made. Since then the negative has acquired its own layer of grime.

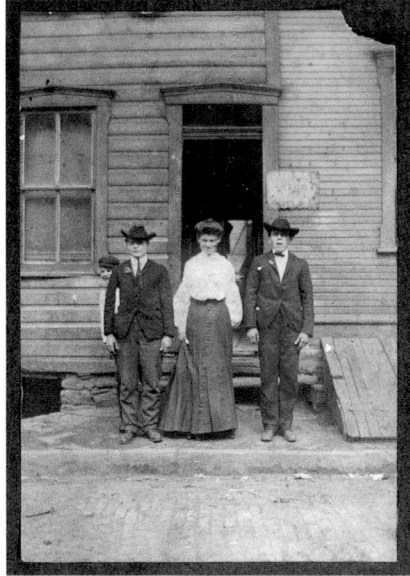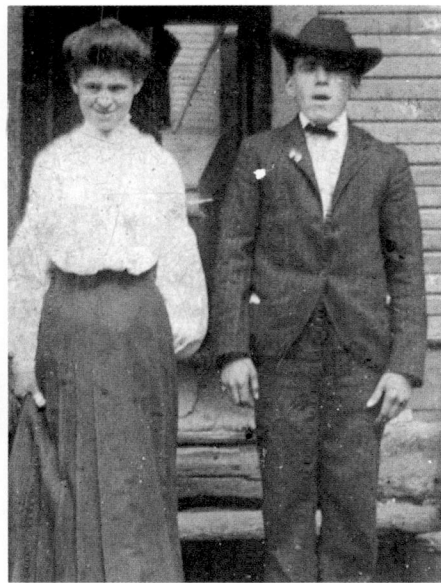

Fig. 8-2 The positive image of Figure 8-1, enlarged on the right. The tonality is pretty good, but the snowstorm of white and black specks makes clear how much cleanup needs to be done to restore this photograph.

I applied the Dust & Scratches tool using the settings shown in Figure 8-3. I used the smallest radius that I could that still eliminated almost all of the specks. The smaller you can keep the radius, the less damage it will do to the fine detail in the photograph. I raised the threshold to 15 to preserve the grain and texture of the original photograph, while still eliminating dust specks. That's important if you want your repairs to be invisible. The enlargement in Figure 8-4, top, shows what this filter did; Figure 8-4, bottom, shows what would have happened if I had applied the same filter with the threshold set to 0.

I set the History Brush to the Dust & Scratches history state and then reverted to the state just prior to that. I set the brush to Darken mode with a radius of 20 pixels. That's much, much larger than individual dust specks but small in terms of the scan, which was made at 600 ppi.

All I needed to do to clean up the white specks was to paint the brush over any part of the picture where there was dust. I didn't pick them off one by one with single mouse clicks; I used long brush strokes that took out dozens of the specks at one time. Used this way, the Dust & Scratches filter has surprisingly little effect on image detail; you can use the brush very aggressively without obliterating the photograph. If you run the brush over a sharp edge in the photograph that blurs out as the brush passes over it, just undo that brush stroke. Reset the History Brush to a smaller radius, and work it up to the edge of the boundary carefully.

Once I'd finished removing all the white specks, I changed the History Brush mode to Lighten and brushed out all the dark specks. The reason I didn't just use the brush in Normal mode to take out light and dark

HOW TO CLEAN UP DUST AND SCRATCHES FROM A SCAN (continued)

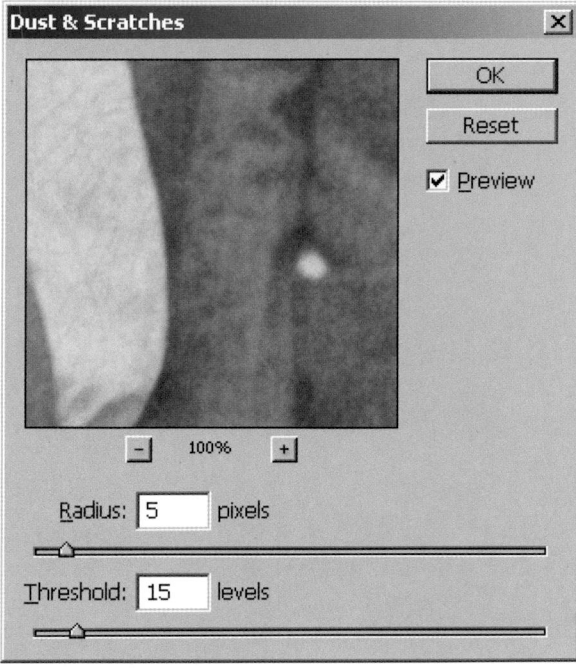

Fig. 8-3 Photoshop's Dust & Scratches filter, selectively applied with a History Brush, is the fastest and most accurate way to clean up specks manually. I set the Threshold option to 15 so that the filter preserves the grain and fine detail in the photograph (see Figure 8-4). Such a setting makes the History Brush strokes less visible.

HOW TO CLEAN UP DUST AND SCRATCHES FROM A SCAN (continued)

specks at the same time is that the Dust & Scratches filter has much less effect on photographic detail in the Lighten or Darken mode than it does in the Normal mode. That allowed me to be even more casual (translation: work faster) as I applied the brush to the photograph.

It only took a few minutes to produce Figure 8-5. All but the largest white and black spots are gone. To get rid of those, I selected the Spot Healing Brush tool with a radius of 20 pixels. For the two white spots on the jacket, I set the tool to Darken and dabbed the brush over each spot; the tool filled them in perfectly. Then I switched the tool to Lighten and eliminated the few black spots the same way.

Polishing Out the Scratches

Scratches and scuff marks can be a restoration nightmare. Sometimes they're obvious from the moment you look at the original, as with the Kodachrome slide in Figure 8-6. Often, they lurk in wait to surprise you when you enhance the tone and contrast in a badly faded photograph like that of Figure 7-28 in Chapter 7. Regardless, once scratches become evident, eliminating then with manual retouching is a very time-consuming activity.

The History Brush trick doesn't work as well on pervasive scratches and scuff marks as it does on dust specks. You'll need to increase the radius of the Dust & Scratches filter because long scratches cover more

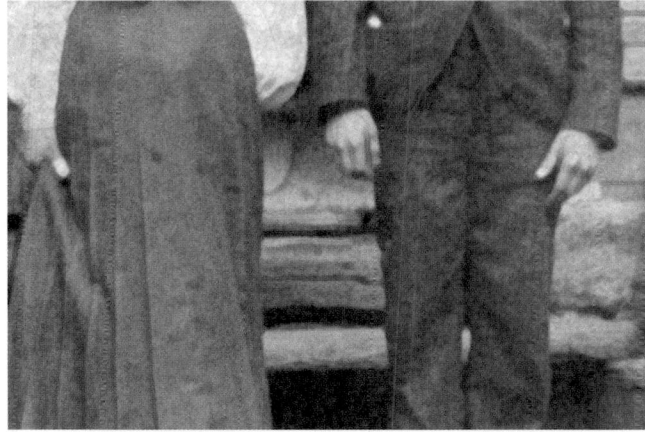

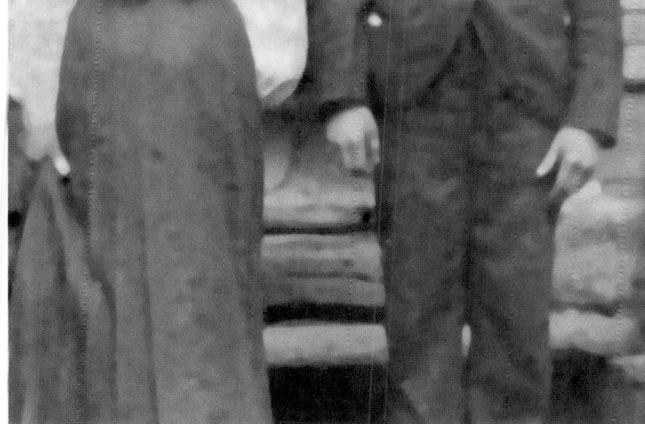

Fig. 8-4 This figure shows the effect of the Threshold setting on the behavior of the Dust & Scratches filter. With a Threshold of 15, as in Figure 8-3, there's relatively little loss of fine detail and grain in the photograph (top) although almost all the dust and dirt is filtered out. A Threshold of 0 (bottom) catches every last bit of dust and dirt, but it also destroys the fine detail and texture of the photograph.

adjacent pixels. You'll have to set the radius of the History Brush much smaller because the eye is very good at picking out even subtle brush-work artifacts when they appear as long lines. I have repaired badly scratched photographs this way, so it's not impossible, but it is assuredly a lot of work.

Your best defense is a scratch-free scan. Figure 8-7 shows enlarged portions of the Kodachrome slide of Figure 8-6 scanned normally and with DIGITAL ICE turned on. ICE couldn't remove the scratches completely because the dyes used in Kodachrome film interfere with the way the scan detects scratches. Still, it did a pretty good job and saved immense amounts of labor. This is why I so strongly recommended in the hardware chapter that you buy a film scanner that includes DIGITAL ICE. DIGITAL ICE won't work on B&W silver film, though, and the really effective version of it isn't available in flat-bed scanners. (I haven't tried it myself, but other people have reported that the version of DIGITAL ICE built into flat-bed scanners performs poorly.)

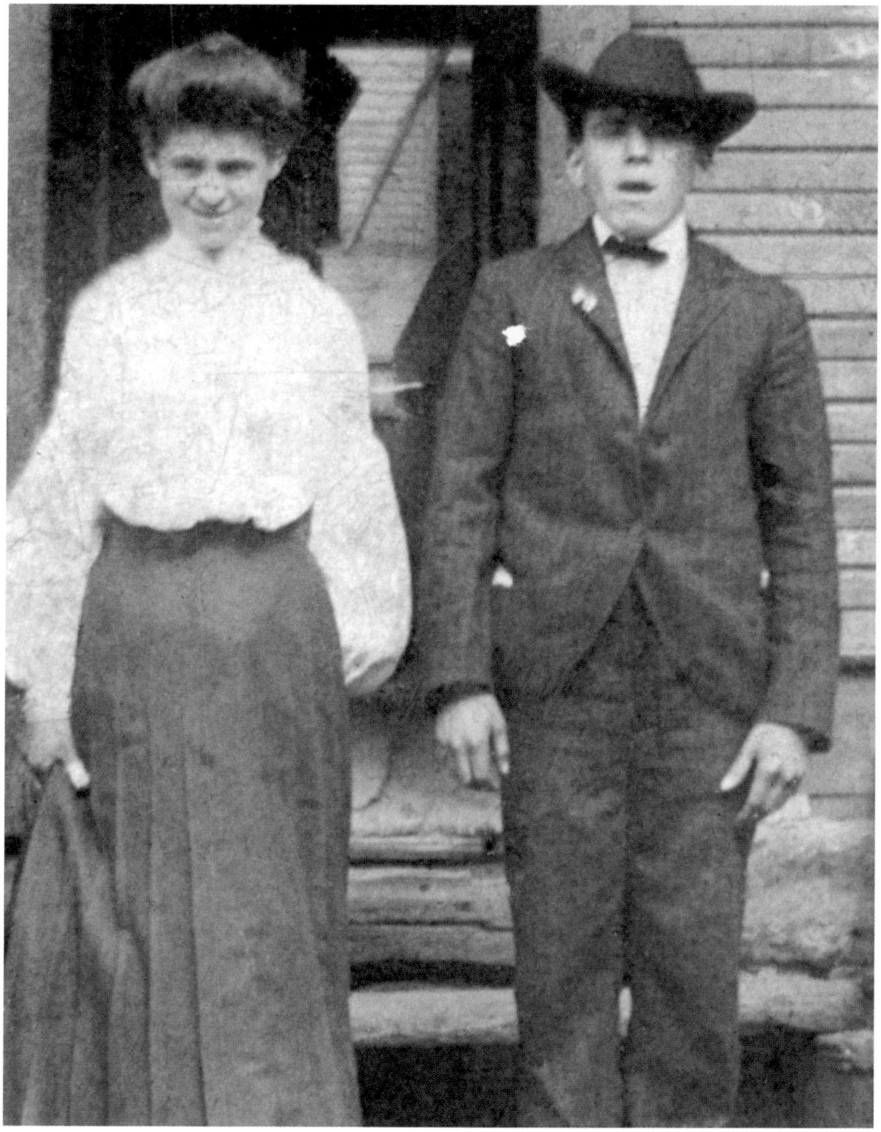

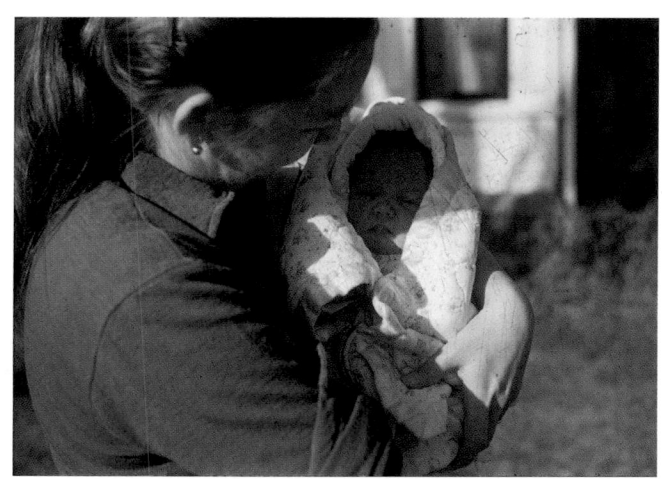

Fig. 8-5 A few minutes work with the History Brush, applying the Dust & Scratches filter, cleans up most of the garbage. A few large spots and many fine scratches remain, but this is a big improvement over Figure 8-2.

Fig. 8-6 This Kodachrome slide has color and tonality nearly as good as the day it was made, but it's very, very badly scratched.

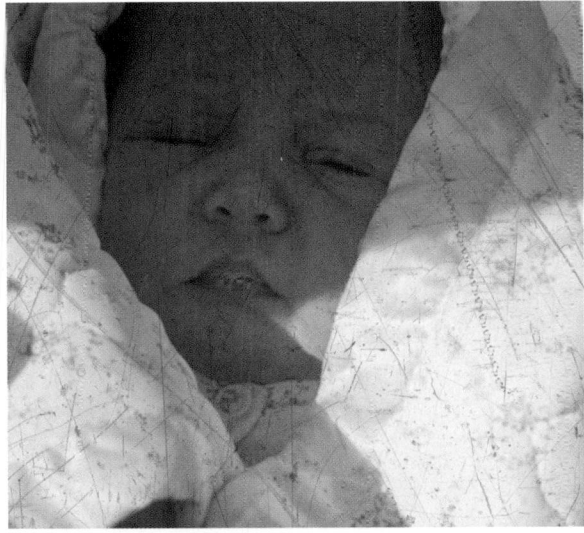

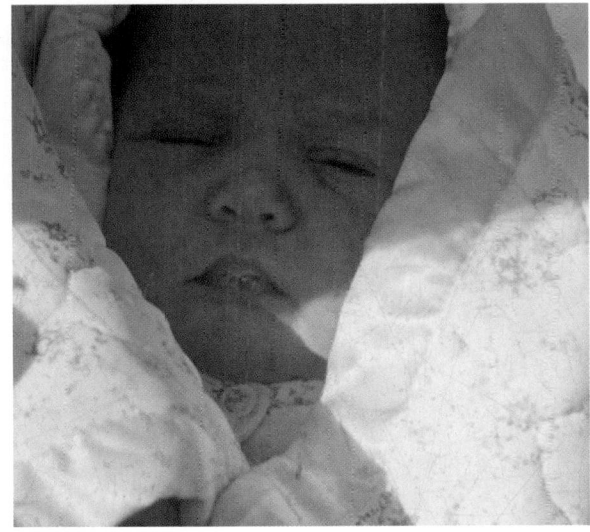

Fig. 8-7 This enlargement of Figure 8-6 shows how extensively the original slide is scratched (top). The bottom figure demonstrates what a good job DIGITAL ICE does suppressing scratches even when scanning this Kodachrome slide (with which it is less effective than with other color films).

Finding Scratches with the Find Edges Filter

So, your scan, for better or for worse, has scratches. Now what? In many cases you can obliterate them successfully with filtering if you can keep the filter from attacking the rest of the photograph. That's what I was doing manually when I used the History Brush with the Dust & Scratches filter. A good mask can make this almost automatic.

See Chapter 7, Making Masks, for many different ways to mask photographs. For the slide from Figure 8-6, I used the Find Edges filter. Figure 8-8, upper, shows what the scan looked like after applying this

✓ HOW TO REPAIR A BADLY SCRATCHED SLIDE

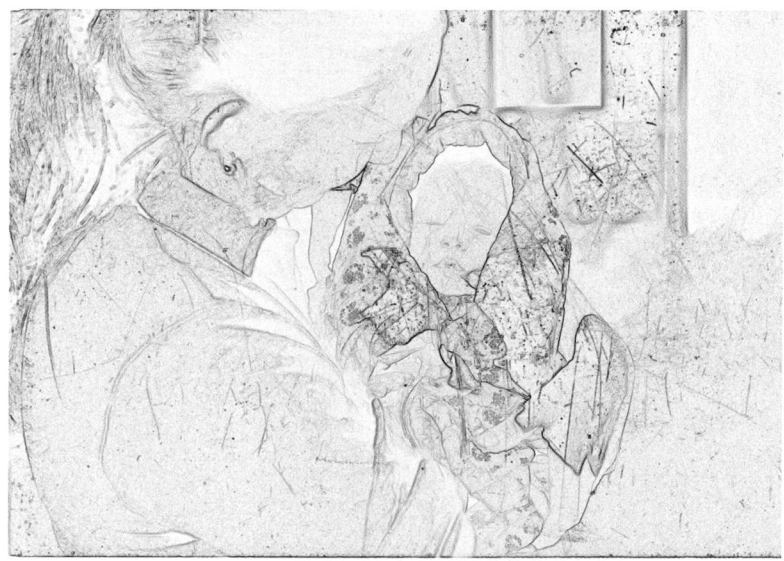

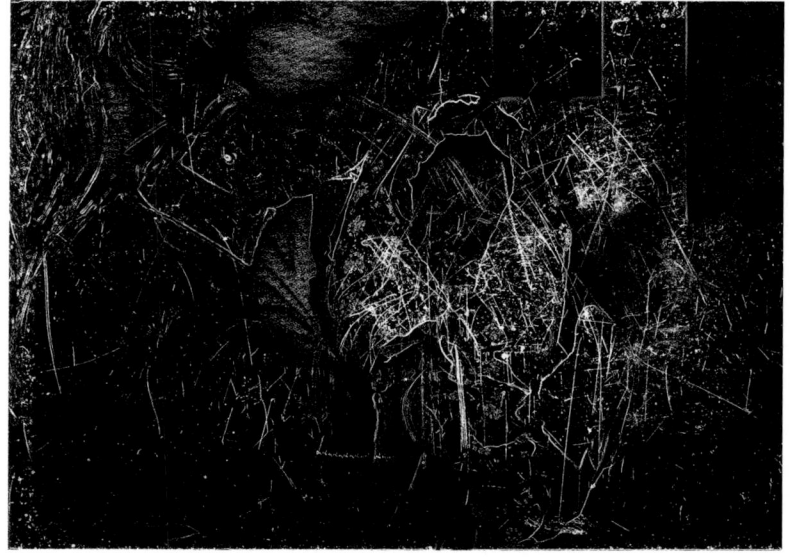

Fig. 8-8 The Find Edges filter turns Figure 8-6 into the upper figure here. Inverting that figure, converting it to grayscale, and increasing the contrast produces a good scratch-selection mask.

HOW TO REPAIR A BADLY SCRATCHED SLIDE (continued)

filter. The lower part of the figure shows the mask I created by inverting that, converting it to grayscale, and using Curves to give it the strong blacks and whites that make for a good mask.

I copied that mask into an Alpha channel in another copy of the original scan and loaded it as a selection (Figure 8-9). Applying the Dust & Scratches filter with a radius of 12 and a threshold of 0 erased a lot of the scratches. It also erased some of the fine detail; look closely at the printed flowers on the blanket and the bubbles on the baby's lips in Figure 8-10b.

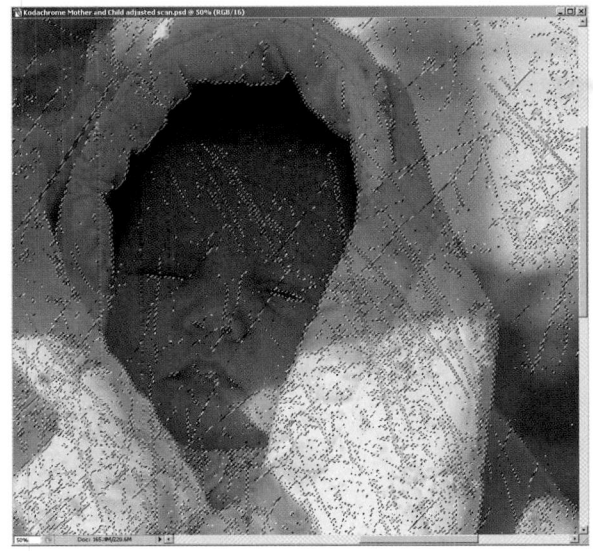

Fig. 8-9 The mask from Figure 8-8 does a pretty good job of selecting for the scratches, as this screenshot shows. Applying the Dust & Scratches filter to this produces Figure 8-10b.

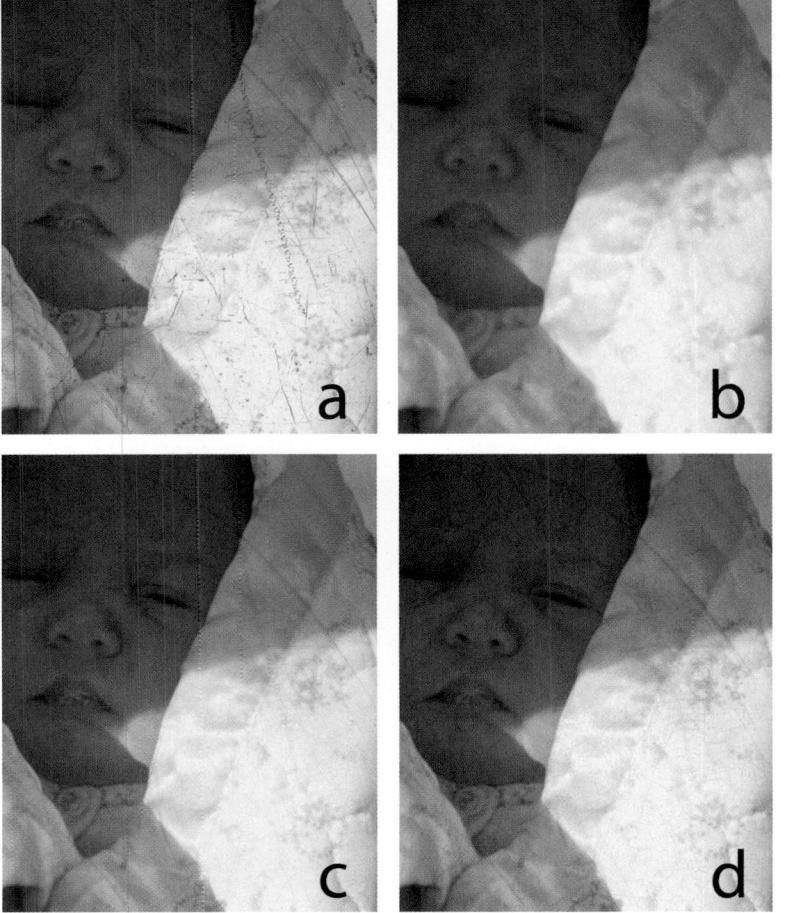

Fig. 8-10 The original scratched slide is shown in figure (a). Figure (b) results from applying a Dust & Scratches filter to the masked photograph in Figure 8-9. It has erased some fine detail, like the bubbles on the baby's lips. To restore much of that detail (c), use the Fade command set to Lighten blend after running the Dust & Scratches filter. (d) If I set the Dust & Scratches filter Threshold to 15, it doesn't do a complete job of removing the scratches, but it also doesn't erase any real photographic detail.

HOW TO REPAIR A
BADLY SCRATCHED
SLIDE (continued)

Just like the History Brush, I can apply the filter in the Lighten or Darken mode to reduce its impact on photographic detail. I did that by using the Fade command with the strength at 100% and the mode changed to Lighten (Figure 8-10c). The scratches aren't eliminated quite as well, but there's a lot less damage to photographic detail.

What do you do about that "collateral damage?" Use the History Brush! I assigned the brush to the history state just before the filter and set the brush radius to a very small value of 5 pixels. I used that to brush the unfiltered photograph back into the fine detail and edges in the photograph that had been obliterated. There wasn't a lot to brush back; the mask had ensured that the filter worked mostly on the areas that I wanted to correct.

Another way to minimize unwanted side effects is to make the corrections in gradual stages instead of trying to eliminate all of the scratches in one step. I went back to the original, masked photograph and applied the Dust & Scratches filter, but instead of setting the threshold at 0, I set it at the fairly high level of 15. Now the filter had almost no effect on the photograph at all. It missed the finer scratches, but it wiped out the darkest and worst of them (Figure 8-10d), and I had to do almost no History Brush work to restore lost details.

The DIGITAL GEM Airbrush plug-in (see Chapter 3) can sometimes help with very fine scratches. I wouldn't buy this filter solely for that, but if you've acquired it for its general retouching and "airbrush" capabilities, try it on a dirty or scratched photograph. Sometimes it can be very helpful, especially if you use it in conjunction with a selection mask or with the History Brush, so that you're only applying it to damaged areas.

Minimizing Scratches with Masks and Curves

In Chapter 7, Making Masks, page 251, I used color tools to create masks that selected for scratches and dirt and nothing else. Here's where I put them to work. I converted Figure 7-27 to grayscale, shown here as Figure 8-11a. Next I loaded the mask I created with the Linear Light blend (Figure 7-33, upper) as a selection. I applied the gray curve in Figure 8-12 to that selection. The intent was to lighten up all the dust and scratches, since they were darker than almost everything else in the photograph. Figure 8-11b shows the improvement this made to the photograph.

HOW TO MINIMIZE
SCRATCHES IN A
PRINT WITH CURVES

On the right side of Figure 8-11, I made a Curves adjustment to give these photographs a good range of tones and proper contrast. In this normal-contrast version, the original dirty photo (Figure 8-11c) looks even worse. It's very clear now that the dirt and scratches degrade much of the image. The photograph at lower right (Figure 8-11d) is remarkably clean considering how simple the masked correction was.

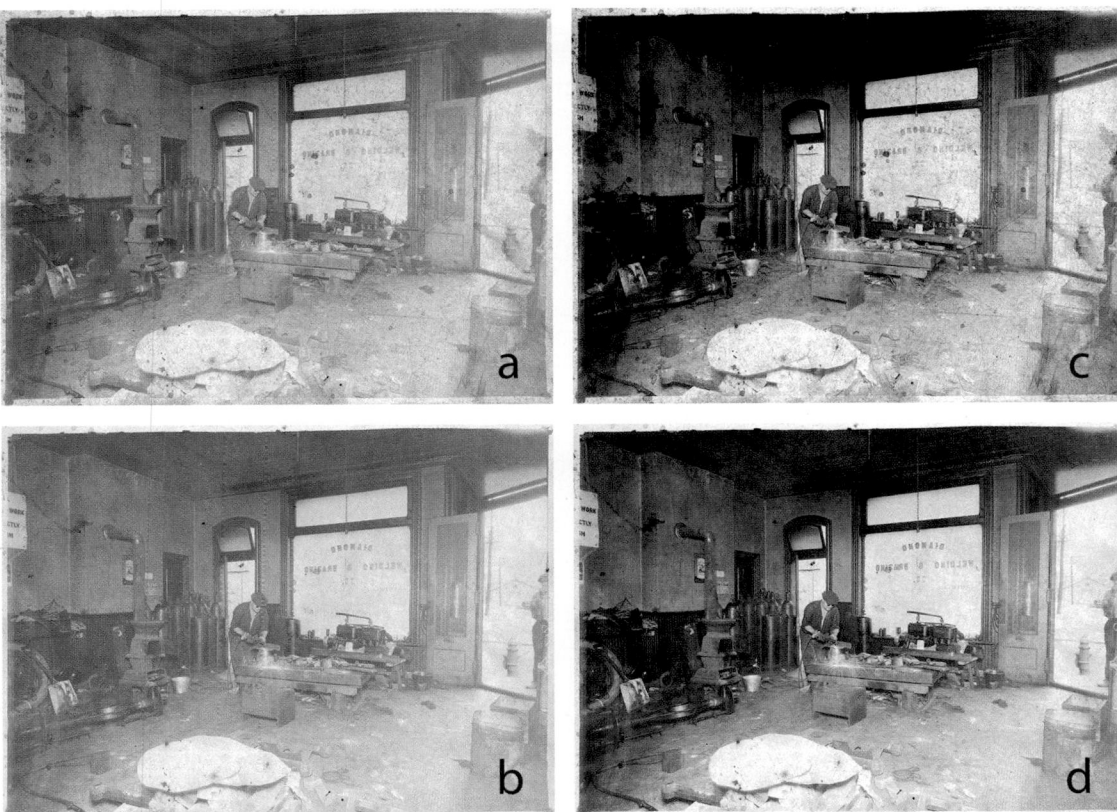

Fig. 8-11 Figure (a) is a grayscale version of the photograph in Figure 7-27. Figure (b) shows how much this photograph is improved by applying the mask from Figure 7-33, top, as a selection and making the Curves adjustment shown in Figure 8-12. That curve lightens up the dirt and scratches without altering the rest of the photograph. Figures (c) and (d) are improved-contrast versions of these photographs. They make it much clearer how well the masked Curves adjustment works.

Figure 8-13 shows an enlarged portion of Figure 8-11. The upper, uncorrected photograph shows how badly the dirt and scratches obscured the photograph. The middle illustration demonstrates how much applying that lightening curve to the mask-selected scratches improved the appearance. Using Curves like this is a very important part of doing restorations because it reduces the visible differences between damaged areas and the photograph. That makes that damage much more amenable to filtering and other software tools that can fill in the bad spots with good image data from the surrounding pixels.

It's usually impossible for a curve to make the damage completely disappear. A curve that makes the damage invisible against the middle-gray background will make it look too dark against a light part of the photograph and too light when it's over shadow tones. What you aim for is one that on average minimizes the overall visible impact of the ▼

HOW TO MINIMIZE
SCRATCHES IN A
PRINT WITH CURVES
(continued)

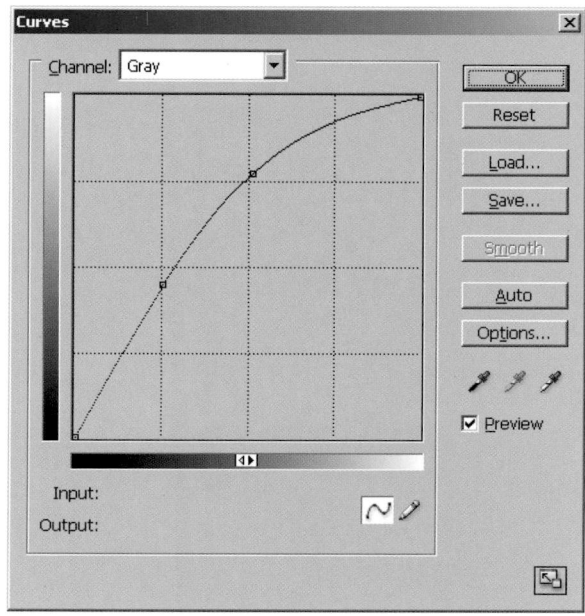

Fig. 8-12 This Curves adjustment lightens up the dirt and scratches in Figure 8-11c, making them much less visible in the photograph.

HOW TO MINIMIZE
SCRATCHES IN A
PRINT WITH CURVES
(continued)

damage, even if for some tones and for some parts of the photograph it makes it worse.

Before I applied the Curves correction, the scratches were so strong and pervasive that they would have prevented the Dust & Scratches filter from working properly. The filter would have filled in the scratches with a combination of the photograph and the dirt I was trying to eliminate. Now that the damage didn't dominate the photograph, I could apply the filter.

Applying the filter settings from Figure 8-14 produced the results you see in Figure 8-13, bottom. As I did when working on the Kodachrome slide, I used a high threshold with the filter, so that it would remove some of the scratches but none of the true photographic detail. Then I applied the filter at lower threshold settings, in combination with the History Brush, to eliminate the remaining damage.

Enhancing Color to Attack Scratches

Sometimes enhancing and exaggerating the color in a monochrome photograph actually eliminates most of the scuffs and scratches. This trick doesn't work very often, but when it does it's practically like magic. When damage has a different hue from the original photograph, the individual color channels will show more or less of that damage. In Chapter 7, page 246, I used color channels to emphasize damage to create masks. Here, I'll use color to de-emphasize the damage.

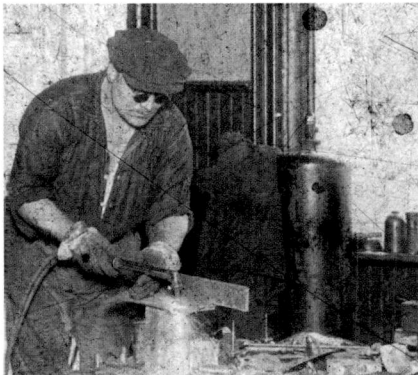

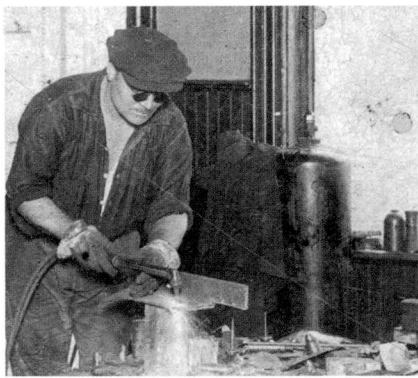

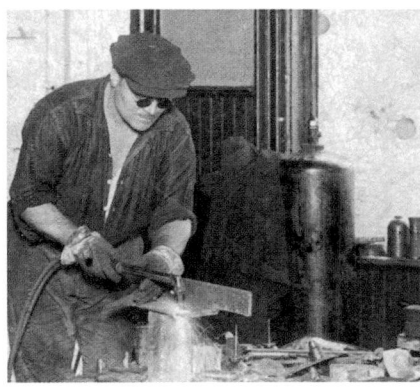

Fig. 8-13 These enlargements illustrate the benefits of masked scratch removal. The top figure is the original photograph from Figure 8-11c. The middle figure shows how much the Curves adjustment from Figure 8-12 reduces the visibility of the mask-selected scratches and dirt. I created the improved photograph on the bottom by applying the Dust & Scratches filter in Figure 8-14 to the masked photograph. Minimizing the scratches with the Curves adjustment first allows the Dust & Scratches filter to work more effectively.

In the badly scratched photograph of the welder (Figure 8-15, left), the scratches are substantially more evident in the red and green channels than in the blue channel (Figure 8-16). The photograph was a faded yellow, which meant most of the density for the photograph was in the blue channel. The scratches and scuff marks were fairly neutral in color; when I scanned the photograph to shift the image tone from yellow to more neutral, it shifted the scratches from neutral to bluish. Being blue meant they didn't have a lot of density in the blue channel. That's why

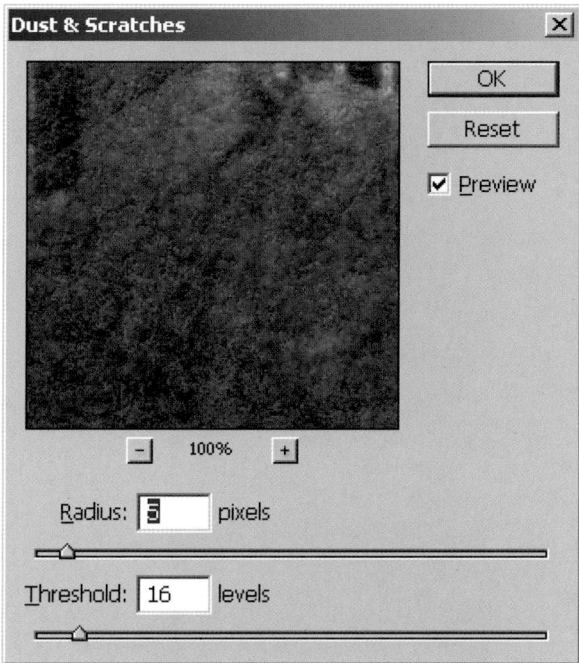

Fig. 8-14 This Dust & Scratches filter almost erases the scratches and dirt from the photograph (Figure 8-13, bottom). The high threshold value of 16 ensures that no fine photographic detail gets affected by the filter.

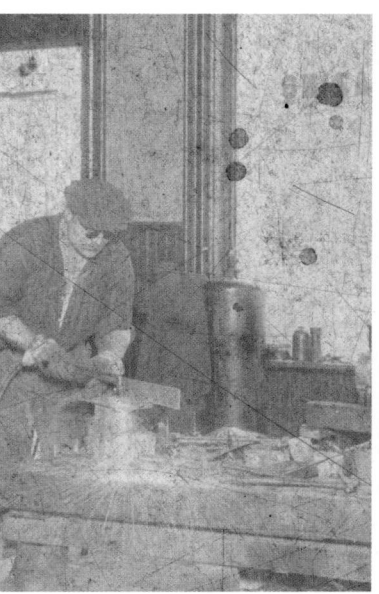 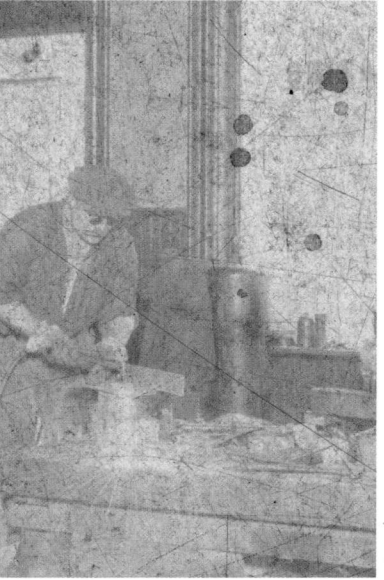

Fig. 8-15 The figure on the left is a portion of the original scan enlarged to show the dirt and scratches more clearly. On the right is that same photograph after a saturation increase of +70 points. As subsequent figures illustrate, this makes it easier to extract a clean photograph from the scan.

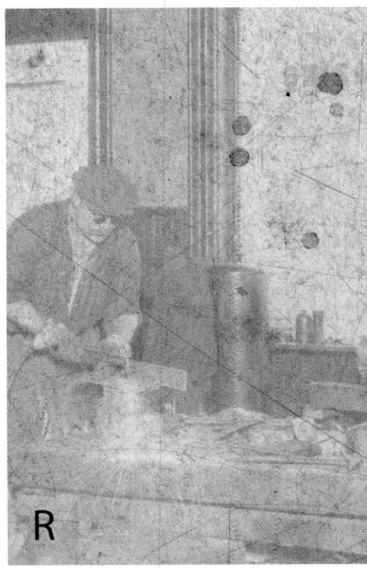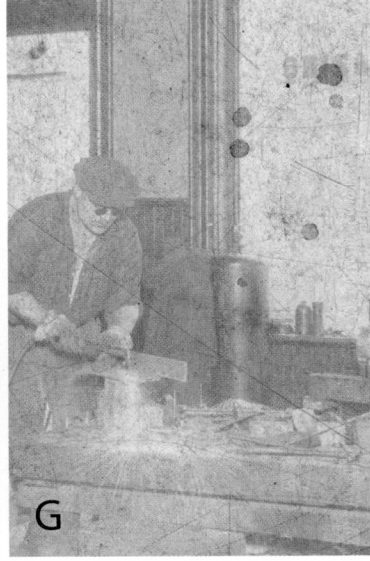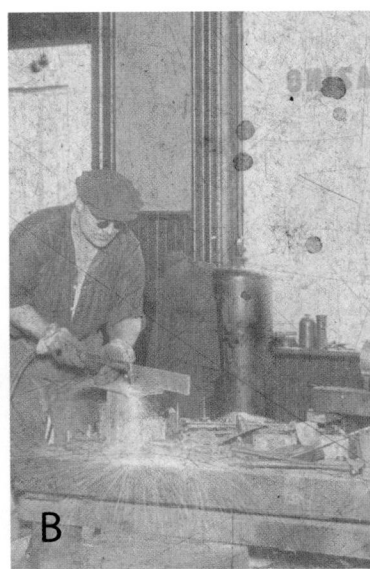

Fig. 8-16 The individual color channels from Figure 8-15, left, show that the blue-cyan dirt and scratches are most obvious in the red channel and least visible in the blue.

the blue channel in Figure 8-16 looks so much better. If I were going to use conventional techniques for eliminating the scratches, this would be the best channel to work on. I'm not; instead, I turned to the Hue/Saturation tool for further corrections (see page 304 for more on this approach).

I boosted the saturation of the photograph by +70 points (Figure 8-15, right); the individual color channels are shown in Figure 8-17. Exaggerating the saturation exaggerated those characteristics of the channels that were apparent in Figure 8-16. Now the red channel is extremely noisy with almost no image visible, while the blue channel is, remarkably, almost damage free. Even the large stains have been bleached.

Figure 8-18, left, reproduces that blue channel with the contrast and brightness adjusted for a normal-looking print. This is so much better than the original that it's hard to believe, and I achieved it with no handwork. Why did this work so well?

Look at Figure 8-15 and you'll see that saturation boost made the (false) colors in both the photograph and the scratches pretty intense. The photograph is now a very strong yellow, while the damage is blue-cyan. Strong colors always have very high densities in some channels and very low densities in others. A perfectly saturated color, like a pure red, will have no density at all in one channel (the red one). Any time you can manipulate the tones and colors in a photograph to produce a very strong color difference, you'll be able to create an image where one color channel will have a very strong rendering of the photograph and a very weak impression of the damage you're trying to fix.

✓ HOW TO MINIMIZE SCRATCHES WITH COLOR CHANNELS AND CHANNEL MIXING

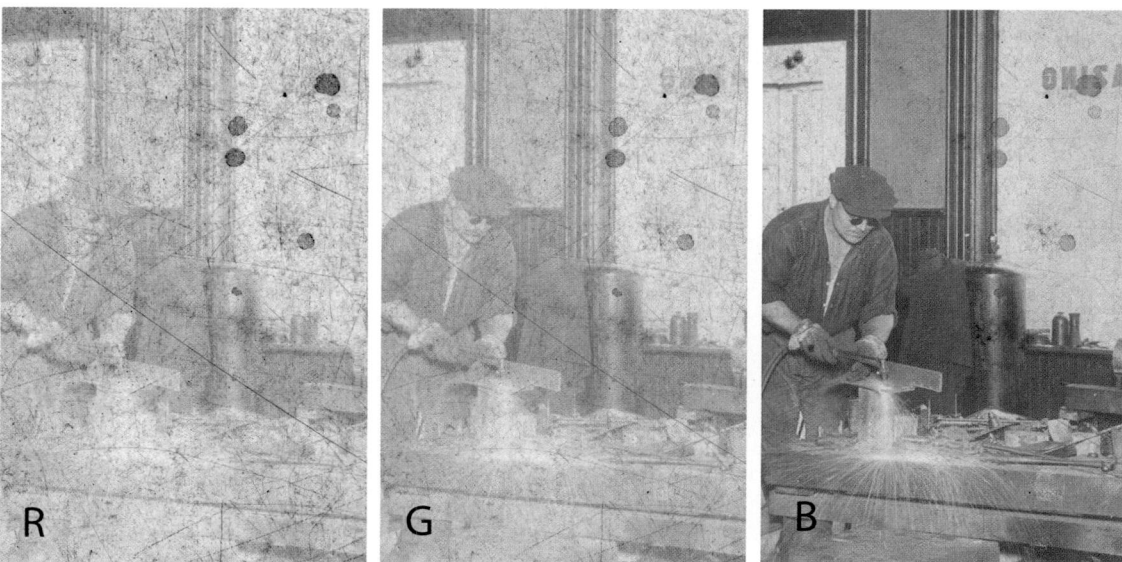

Fig. 8-17 The color channels from Figure 8-15, right, show that increasing the saturation of the photograph increases the differences between the channels. Because the color of the dirt and scratches is purer, they are even more visible in the red channel, as they are nearly eliminated from the blue channel.

HOW TO MINIMIZE
SCRATCHES WITH
COLOR CHANNELS
AND CHANNEL
MIXING (continued)

There's more I can do with this. The blue channel doesn't entirely suppress the damage, but the red channel shows almost nothing else. So, if I were to subtract some of the red channel from the blue channel, I could remove more of the damage without diminishing the photograph much. That's what the Channel Mixer settings in Figure 8-19 do. I'm subtracting one-fifth of the red channel from the blue channel. The total still adds up to about 100%, so there won't be an overall brightness change. Note that this is the counterpart to the channel mixing trick I used in Chapter 7 to create the masks that selected for the scratches and dirt. Here I'm using it to suppress, rather than enhance.

Figure 8-18, right, shows the channel-mixed photograph. It's even better than the blue channel alone, an amazing recovery for such a damaged photograph. I'm well on my way to a clean restoration.

Filling In the Cracks

Filling in cracks is similar to erasing scratches and dust specks, but it's a tougher job because cracks are fatter. A typical scratch is only a couple of pixels wide, so it doesn't take a very wide-radius filter to cover it. Small features like scratches are also easily picked up in their entirety by simple filters like Find Edges. Find Edges easily selects the edges of cracks, but selecting the interiors as well takes more cleverness.

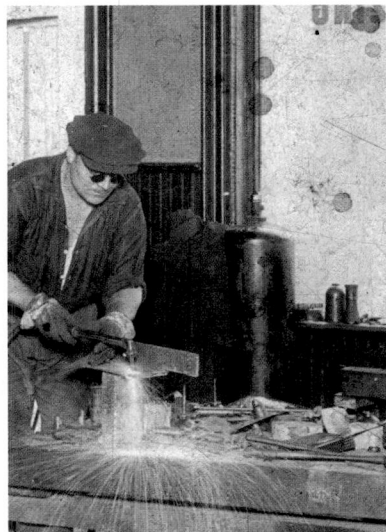 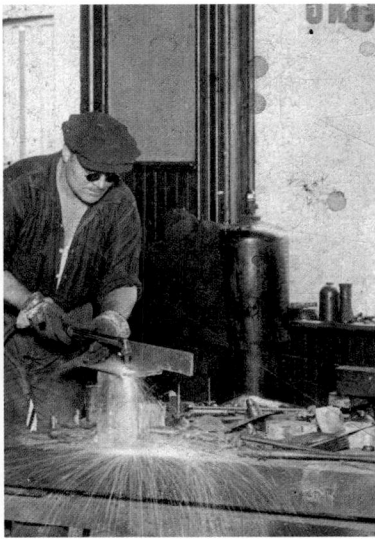

Fig. 8-18 The figure on the left portrays the saturation-increased blue channel of Figure 8-17 after I've corrected the tone and contrast. There's much less visible damage than in the original scan (Figure 8-15). The photograph on the right looks even better because I subtracted a bit of the noise-laden red channel from the blue channel, using the Channel Mixer settings from Figure 3-19.

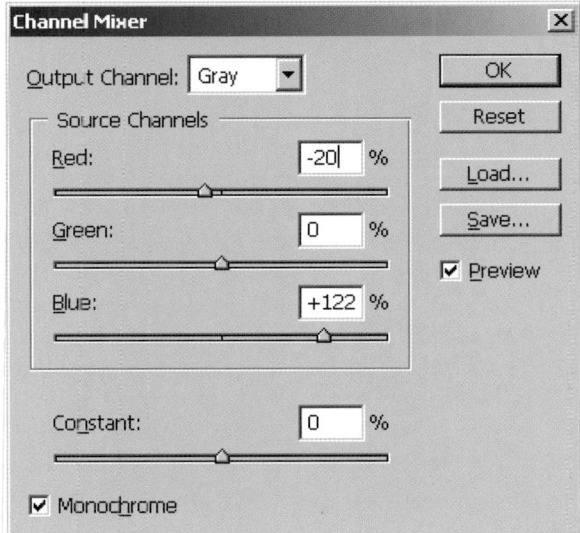

Fig. 8-19 The Channel Mixer settings here produce a grayscale image by combining the red and blue channels from Figure 8-15, right. Subtracting a small amount of the red channel from the blue channel eliminates most of the residual garbage without affecting the photographic image very much. This works because the red channel is almost entirely noise with very little image, so it doesn't subtract much from the underlying photograph.

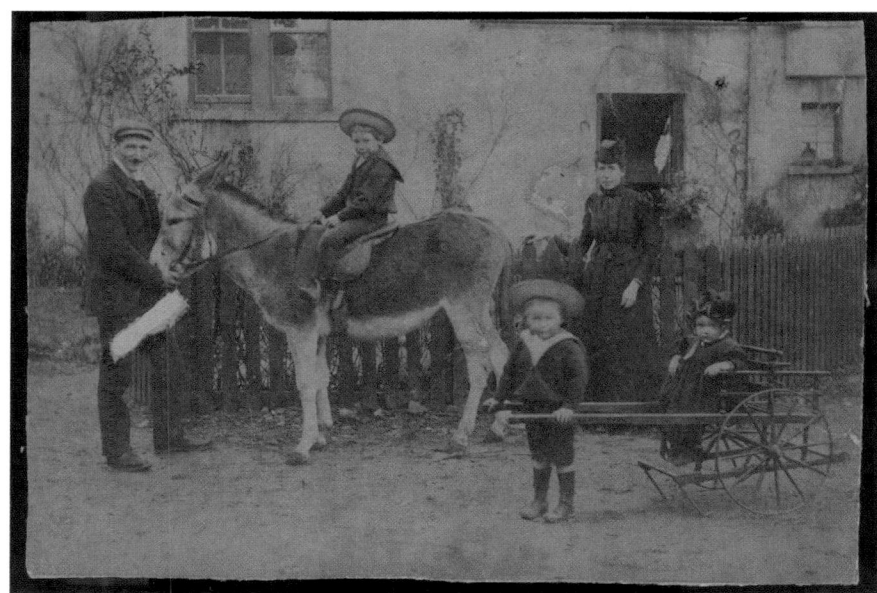

Fig. 8-20 This photograph is faded and yellowed, but its worst problem is that it is covered with a network of fine cracks, shown enlarged in Figure 7-15.

Cracks are also harder to repair because they're often not uniform in density like dust specks and scratches. They can have dark edges and light interiors, and, if the cracks are large, the interiors may be mottled or dirty. Just as when dealing with scratches and specks, you can fill in cracks with handwork, but it's harder. If you use the Dust & Scratches filter, you'll have to set it to a very wide radius, and that will increase the amount of damage to real photographic detail. That makes it harder to use the History Brush to paint in the filter, so masking becomes even more helpful.

Curve tricks like the one I used in Figure 8-13 are very useful for suppressing cracks before doing serious work on them. In part that's because cracks, being larger, occupy a greater percentage of pixels than simple scratches, so it's more important to reduce their influence on filters. Another reason is that cracks usually expose bare, white paper, which is always brighter than any other part of the photograph, so using darkening curves works everywhere in the photograph, regardless of the surrounding tones.

Removing Fine Cracks with a Mask and Median Filtering

HOW TO FILL IN CRACKS IN A PRINT WITH A MASK

In Chapter 7, Making Masks, page 242, I showed how the Unsharp Mask filter made it easier to create a crack-selection mask for a badly damaged photograph (Figure 8-20) with the Find Edges filter (Figure 7-15d). To complete that mask, I took that blue channel and inverted it (Figure 8-21b). Next I applied a Gaussian Blur of 1.2-pixel radius; this filled in the

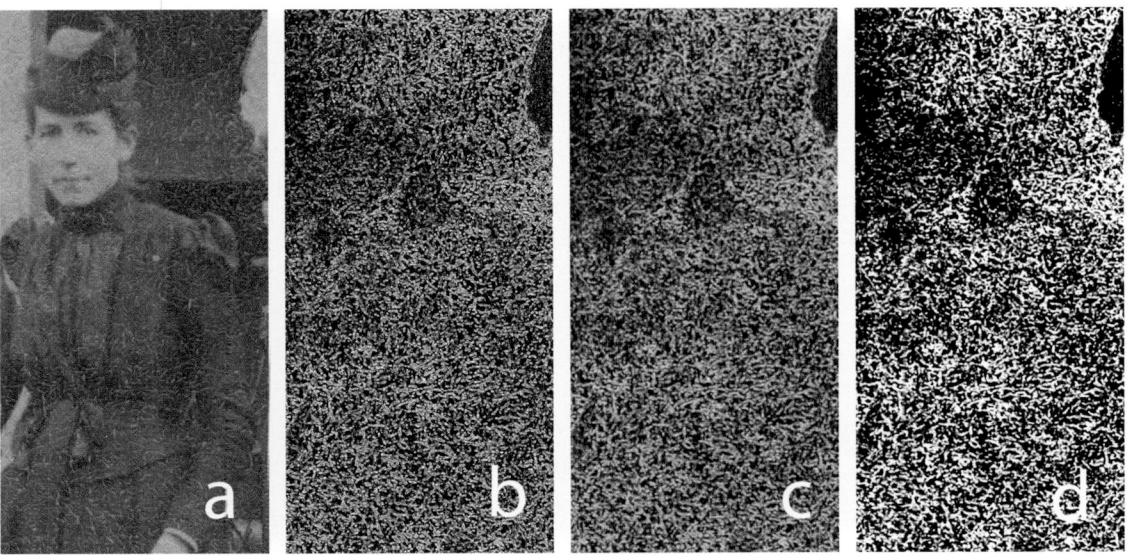

Fig. 8-21 Figure (a) shows a portion of the sharpened photograph from Figure 7-15b. Figure (b) is the inverted version of the masking image I created in Figure 7-15d. In figure (c), I blurred this mask with a Gaussian Blur of 1.2-pixel radius to fill in the crack outlines. I turned that into a strong mask (d) with good blacks and whites by applying the Curves adjustment in Figure 8-22.

outlines created by the filter, so the mask would select whole cracks and not just their perimeters (Figure 8-21c). Blurring lowered the contrast of the mask, so I applied the curve shown in Figure 8-22 to get the finished mask in Figure 8-21d.

Figure 8-23 shows an enlargement of another portion of the photograph from Figure 8-20. I repaired the cracks in that photograph in two stages. First, I loaded the mask as a selection and applied the Curves setting shown in Figure 8-24 to the cracks. That darkened them so there would be less difference between the cracks' brightness and the surrounding, undamaged photograph.

That lets me better use the Median filter to fill in the cracks. The Median filter fills a pixel with the average of the surrounding pixels. In photographs like this, where a high percentage of the pixels are in damaged areas, the average would get thrown off by those light-colored cracks. Darkening them kept them from distorting the tonal values of the filtered photograph so badly.

I applied the Median filter in Figure 8-24 to produce the photograph in Figure 8-23, right. The 6-pixel radius worked well; if I'd set the radius too small, the filter wouldn't have sampled enough good pixels to fill in the cracks adequately. If the radius were too large, the filter would sample pixels from far away, and I'd not get the average of only those colors close to the pixel being fixed.

HOW TO FILL IN CRACKS IN A PRINT WITH A MASK (continued)

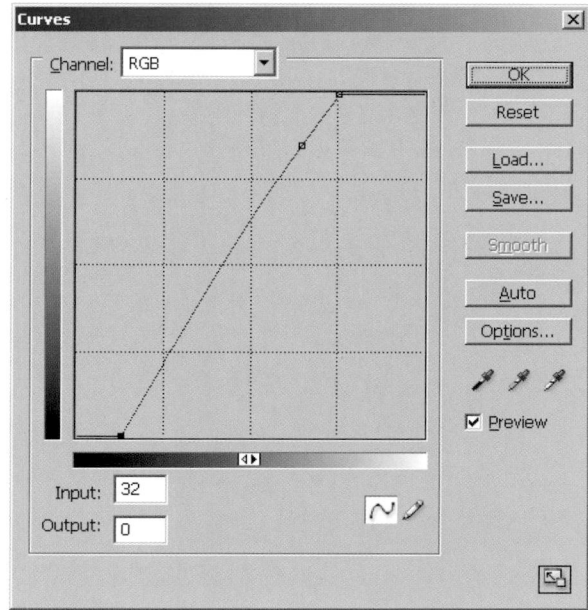

Fig. 8-22 This Curves adjustment produces a strong, contrasty mask from the image in Figure 8-21c. It both lightens and increases contrast, producing Figure 8-21d.

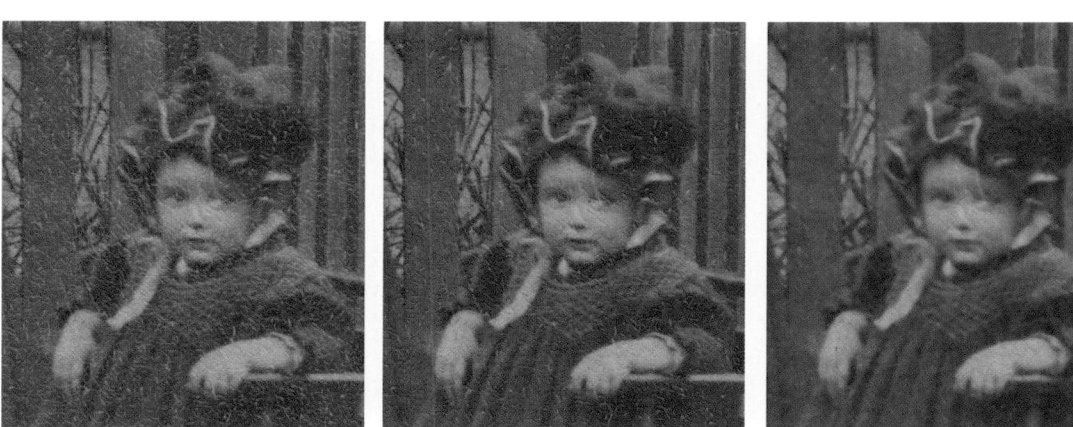

Fig. 8-23 Crack repair on this photograph is a two-stage process. On the left is an enlargement from the original photograph shown in Figure 8-20. In the center is the photograph after applying the Curves adjustment from Figure 8-24 to the masked photograph. That reduces the visibility of the cracks and gives them tones more like the surrounding photograph. This lets the Median filter in Figure 8-24 work more accurately as it fills in the cracks with surrounding tones (right).

HOW TO FILL IN
CRACKS IN A PRINT
WITH A MASK
(continued)

Figure 8-25 shows a tone and color-corrected enlargement of a portion of Figure 8-20; improving the color and contrast makes the cracks even more obvious in the unrepaired photo on the left. See how effective this combination of mask, Curves, and Median filter is at cleaning up the damage in the photograph on the right. The cracks are almost gone, and I achieved this without losing fine detail in the photograph.

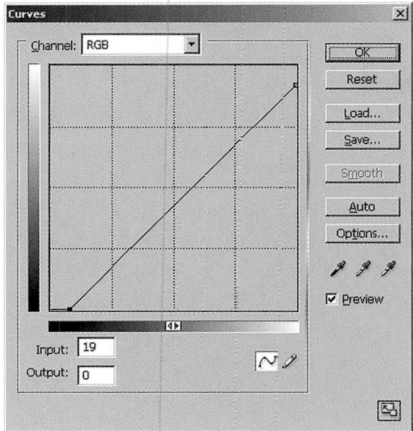

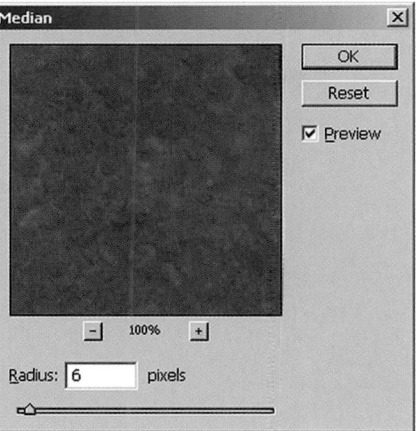

Fig. 8-24 The Curves adjustment here, applied to the masked photograph in Figure 8-23, left, darkens the white cracks in the photograph so they're closer in tone to the surrounding image. Making this adjustment lets the Median filter do a better job because the muted tones in the cracks don't throw off the average tone as much.

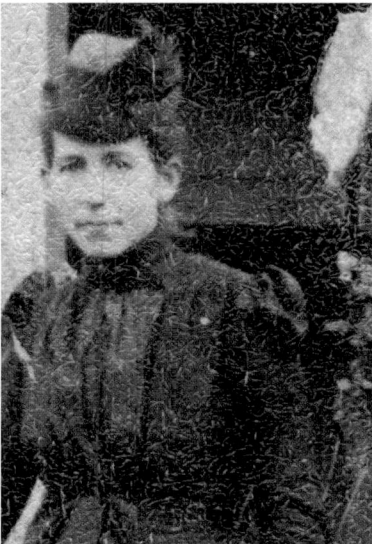

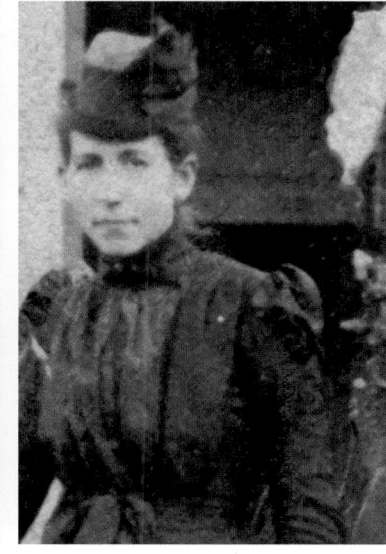

Fig. 8-25 The figure on the left is an enlargement from Figure 8-20 corrected for tone and color to produce a good B&W photograph. With the contrast improved and the stains removed, the cracking problem is glaringly obvious. The figure on the right is the result of masking for the cracks and applying the Curves adjustment and Median filter from Figure 8-24. The cracks are nearly gone, and there is almost no loss of real photographic detail.

Removing Fine Cracks in Stages with Repeated Median Filtering

The photograph in Figure 8-26 was originally very low in contrast. Making a good scan of it (see Chapter 4, page 100) meant increasing its contrast considerably. That brought out an extensive network of cracks and emulsion damage.

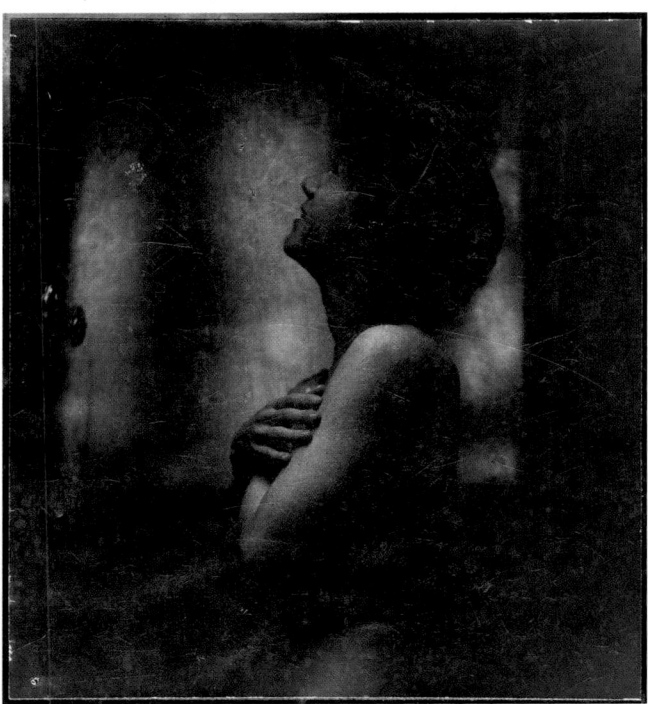

Fig. 8-26 This photograph is badly scratched and marked up. Fortunately, many scratches can be removed with proper masking and filtering.

HOW TO REPAIR CRACKS IN STAGES WITH MEDIAN FILTERING

Figure 8-27 shows the central portion of this photograph and two masks I generated using Photoshop filters. The Find Edges filter (center) produced a mask that did a good job of picking out the heaviest cracks, but it didn't create much distinction between the finest ones and the lighter background. The Glowing Edges filter (right) was a better choice for finding all the cracks; they're much more clearly emphasized, especially against the light background and skin tones.

Again, I tackled these cracks in stages. I loaded the mask selection and applied the curve in Figure 8-28, left. That subdued the cracks in the midtones and highlights, although it didn't accomplish much in the shadows (Figure 8-29b). Then I applied the Median filter with a radius of 1 to get Figure 8-29c.

I applied the Median filter three more times with the same radius, which took me to Figure 8-29d. Repeated filtering improved the picture because each pass averaged more of the good surrounding photographic image into the cracks. Had I used a large-radius filter, it would have been more aggressive at filling the cracks, but it also would have attacked real detail and caused problems with dark areas bleeding into light and vice versa. Keeping the filter radius small ensured that the filling-in was based only on neighboring tones.

I did a final Median filtering with a radius of 7 pixels (Figure 8-29e). That did a very good job of filling in all the cracks in the midtones. It

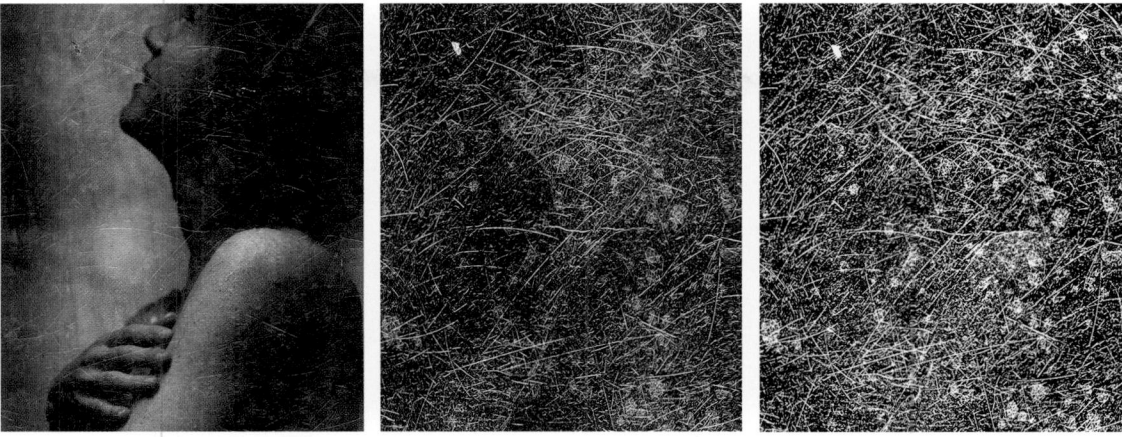

Fig. 8-27 This enlargement from Figure 8-26 shows how extensive the scratches are. Photoshop's Fine Edges filter did well at isolating the heavier cracks, but it didn't pick up the finer ones (center). The Glowing Edges filter found even the finest cracks, producing the superior mask on the right.

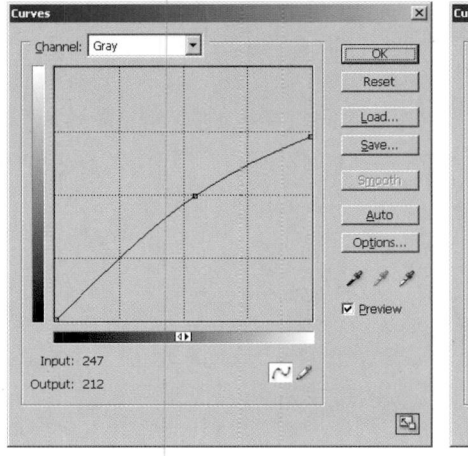
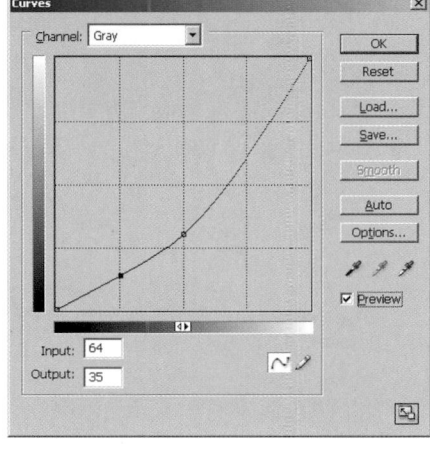

Fig. 8-28 These Curves adjustments, when applied to the masked photograph in Figure 8-29a, substantially reduce the visibility of the scratches in Figures 8-29b and 8-30b. See the main text for details.

also erased photographic detail in a couple of small places, but I restored that with the History Brush assigned to the prefilter history state. Even at this larger radius, though, the Median filter couldn't fill in the very light, closely spaced cracks in the shadows.

I went after them with a second pass. First I used the History Brush to erase the effect of the 7-pixel Median filter in the shadows (Figure 8-30a), and then I applied the curve in Figure 8-28, right. That substantially darkened the cracks in the shadows so the Median filter could work more effectively there. You can see the results in Figure 8-30b. This curve messed up the midtones and highlights, but that wasn't going to be a problem because I was planning to use the History Brush to paint in the new round of corrections only where I wanted them.

HOW TO REPAIR
CRACKS IN STAGES
WITH MEDIAN
FILTERING
(continued)

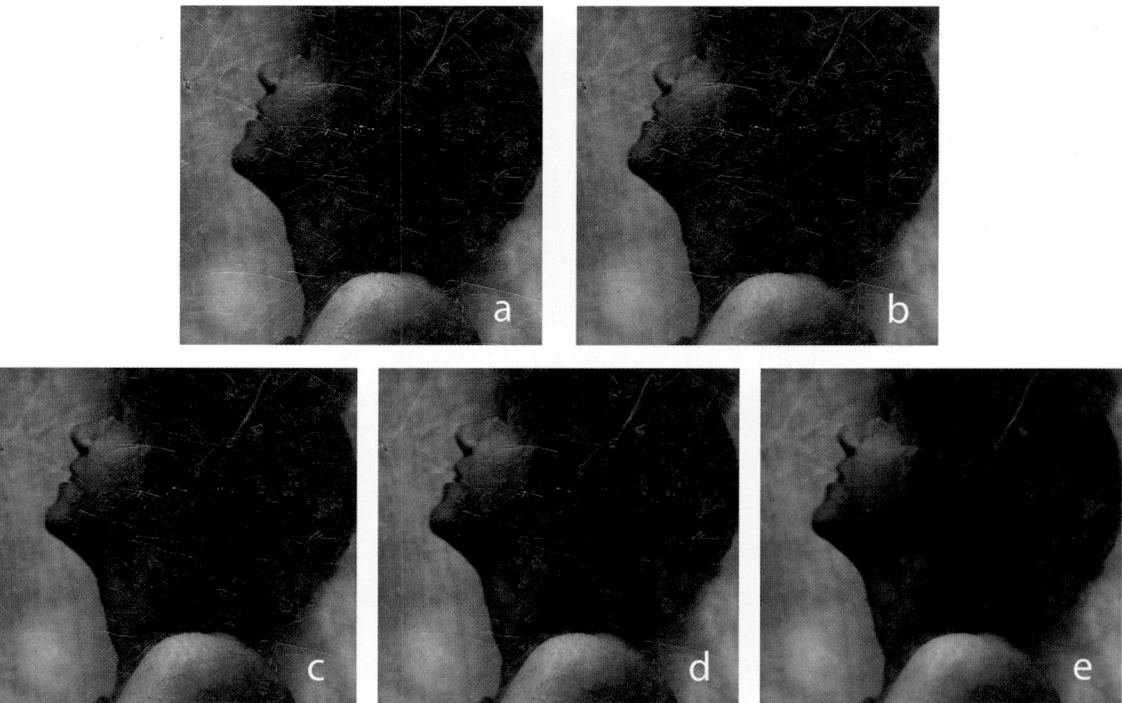

Fig. 8-29 The original photograph, in figure (a), has many white scratches defacing the image. Masking it with the mask from Figure 8-27, right, and applying the Curves adjustment from Figure 8-28, left, reduces the visibility of scratches in the midtones and highlights (figure b). Applying a Median filter with a 1-pixel radius produces figure (c); repeated applications of the Median filter generate figures (d) and (e), as described in the text.

Because I was working in the shadows where there was little image detail or difference in tones, I could use a Median filter of large radius (13 pixels) to fill in the cracks with a single pass. That produced Figure 8-30c—which looks great in the shadows but has distorted midtones and highlights. Out came the History Brush! I assigned this new Median filter history state to the brush and reverted the photograph to the state corresponding to Figure 8-30a. I used the brush to paint the Median filtration into the shadows and midtones that hadn't been properly corrected on the first pass. The result is Figure 8-30d, and Figure 8-31 shows the full before and after photographs. There's a lot of work to be done to turn this into a good photograph, mostly dodging and burning-in with layers like those I described in Chapter 5, page 160, but the majority of the fine-detail physical damage is gone.

Whittling Away at Wide Cracks

When cracks get more than several pixels wide, single-pass fill-ins are hard because it's difficult to make selections that grab the entire crack.

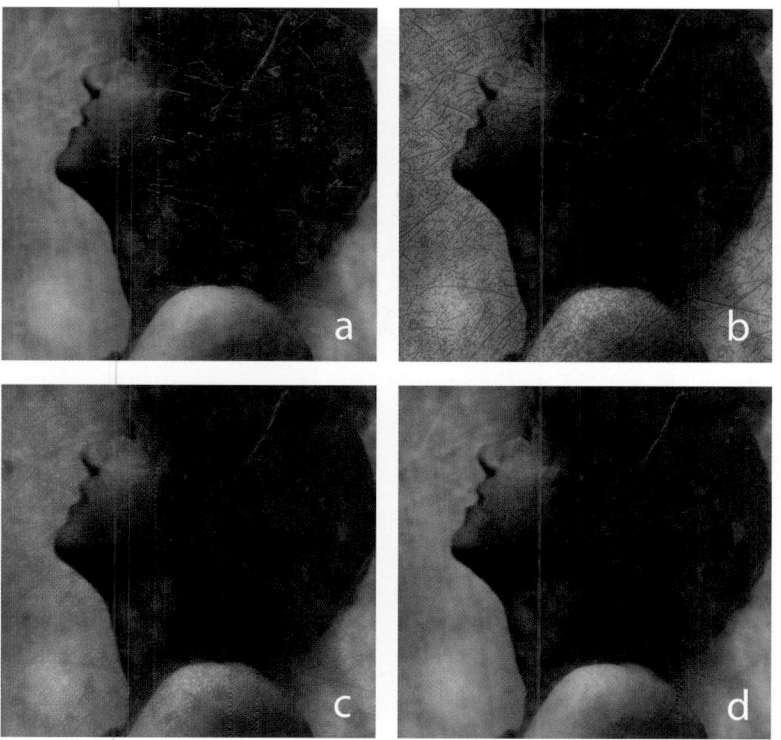

Fig. 8-30 (a) This photograph is the same as Figure 8-29b, except I used the History Brush to undo the effects of the Median filter in the shadows. (b) Applying the Curves adjustment from Figure 8-28, right, to the masked photo darkens the scratches in the shadows very effectively. Applying the Median filter then produces figure (c), which has great shadows but messed-up midtones and highlights. I assigned this state to the History Brush, reverted to Figure 8-30a, and used the Brush to paint the scratch filtering into the shadows of figure (d). The full photograph of these results is shown in Figure 8-31, right.

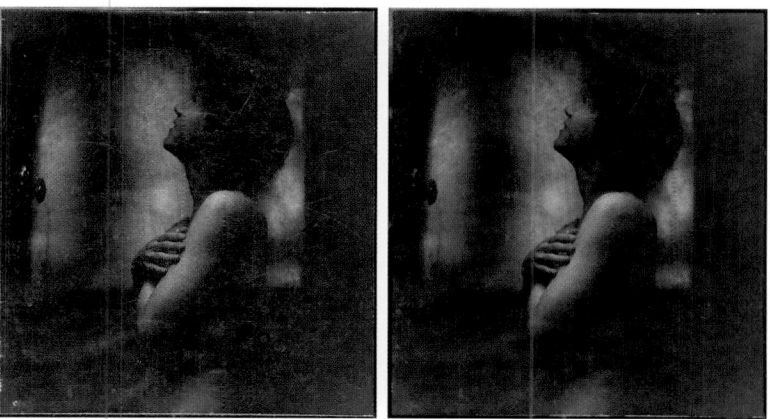

Fig. 8-31 The original photograph, left, has way too many fine scratches to make manual retouching feasible. I substantially repaired it by masking and repeated Median filtering, as shown on the right.

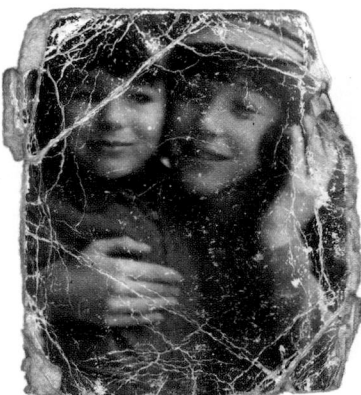 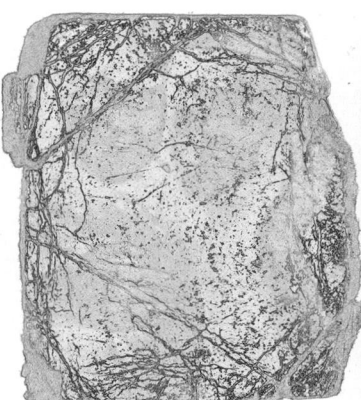 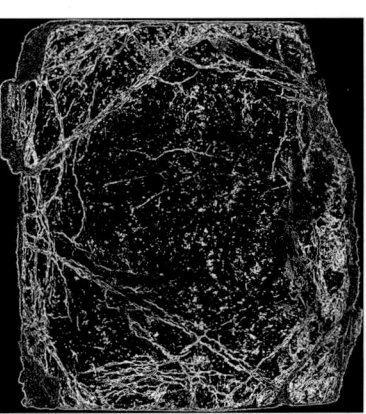

Fig. 8-32 I created a mask for this badly cracked photograph by using Photoshop's Find Edges filter. That filter (center) picks up the edges of the cracks well. The blue channel from that image, inverted and contrast enhanced, makes a good crack-selection mask (right).

Even when I succeed at this, the filters I apply will be influenced as much by the cracks as by the surrounding photograph I'm trying to fill them in with. Instead of trying to clear out the whole crack at once, I'll whittle away at it, peeling off its pixels like layers from an onion. Here's how that works.

HOW TO REPAIR LARGE CRACKS WITH REPEATED MASKING AND FILTERING

When I worked on Figure 8-32, left, in Chapter 7 (see page 240) I emphasized masking methods that would grab the damaged areas as completely as possible. Now I'm going to approach it from a different angle. I made a copy of the file and used the Find Edges filter to pick up the small specks and the edges of the large cracks (Figure 8-32, center). I copied the blue channel from that image, inverted it, and increased the contrast to make the background black and all the edges of the cracks solid white, so that it would make a good mask (Figure 8-32, right).

I loaded this mask as a selection and applied the Dust & Scratches filter shown in Figure 8-33. I set the radius on the filter large because I wanted to sample lots of surrounding pixels. I relied on the mask to limit the area that the filter affected. This eliminated most of the small cracks and specks and substantially reduced the extent of the large cracks, as you can see in Figure 8-34, left, and enlarged in Figure 8-35b.

To peel off the next layer of the cracks, I needed to create a new selection mask. First I made a copy of the cleaned-up image and aggressively sharpened it (Figure 8-35c) with the Unsharp Mask filter shown in Figure 8-36. I did that to create new sharp edges on the cracks that the Find Edges filter could grab onto. Then I made a new edge-selection mask the same way I did the first one: I applied the Find Edges filter, inverted the results, and increased the contrast so the mask had true blacks and whites. I loaded this new mask onto the photograph, used the same Dust & Scratches filter I had previously, and got the results you see in Figure 8-34, right, and Figure 8-35d.

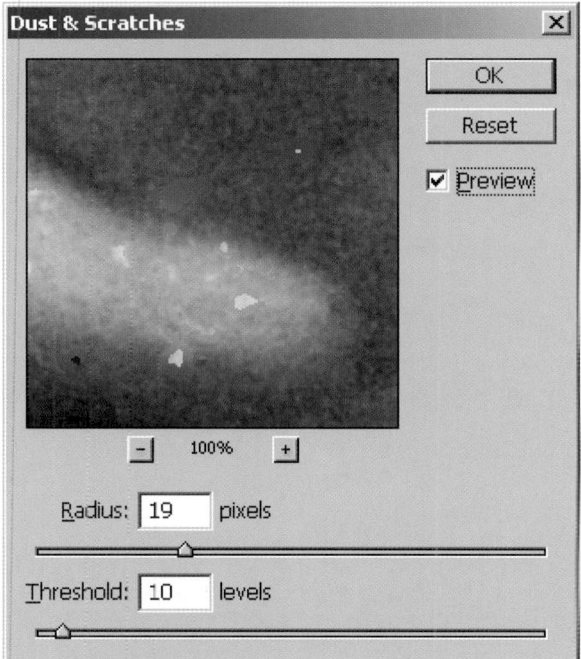

Fig. 8-33 I applied this Dust & Scratches filter to the masked photograph in Figure 8-32 to produce Figure 8-34, left. Note the large filter radius; I'm using the mask to restrict the spread of the filter's effects instead of the radius setting.

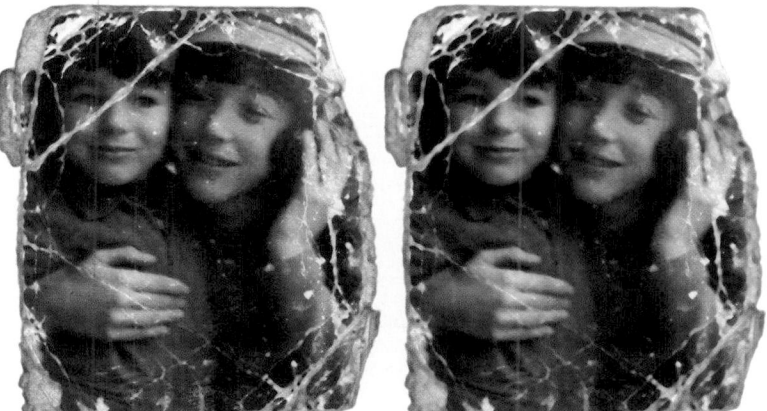

Fig. 8-34 The photograph on the left illustrates how the Dust & Scratches filter from Figure 8-33 improves Figure 8-32. The enlargements in Figure 8-35 show that the mask restricted the effect of the filter so that it whittled away at the cracks without destroying real photographic detail. Additional edge-selection masking and Dust & Scratches filtering eliminates even more of the cracks (right).

Fig. 8-35 Figure (a) shows an enlargement of Figure 8-32, left. Figure (b) shows an enlargement of Figure 8-34, left, illustrating how much damage can be cleaned up by masking plus the Dust & Scratches filter. Figure (c) is an intermediate work image I created by aggressively sharpening figure (b) with the Unsharp Mask filter settings shown in Figure 8-36. I created a new edge-selection mask from figure (c), applied it to figure (b), and ran the Dust & Scratches filter again, as shown in figure (d).

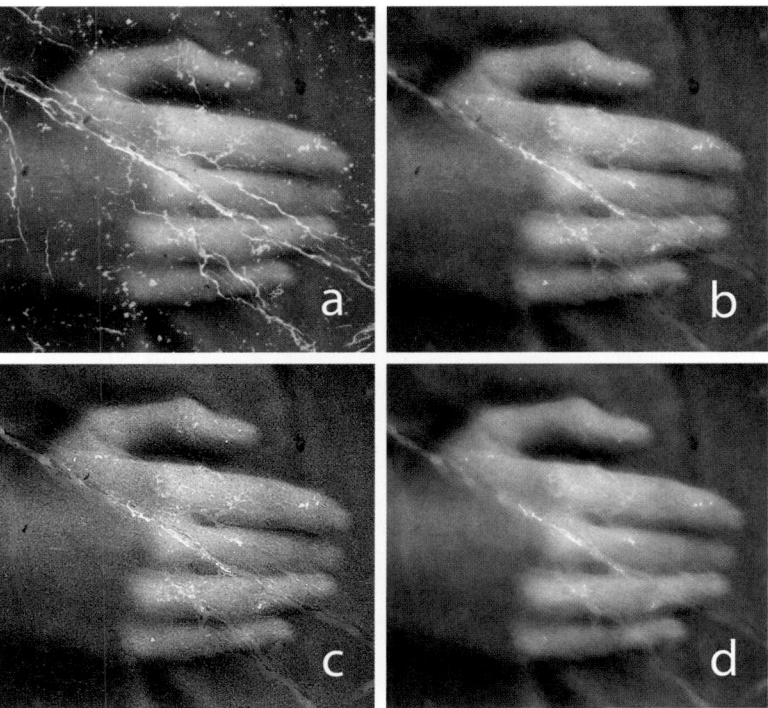

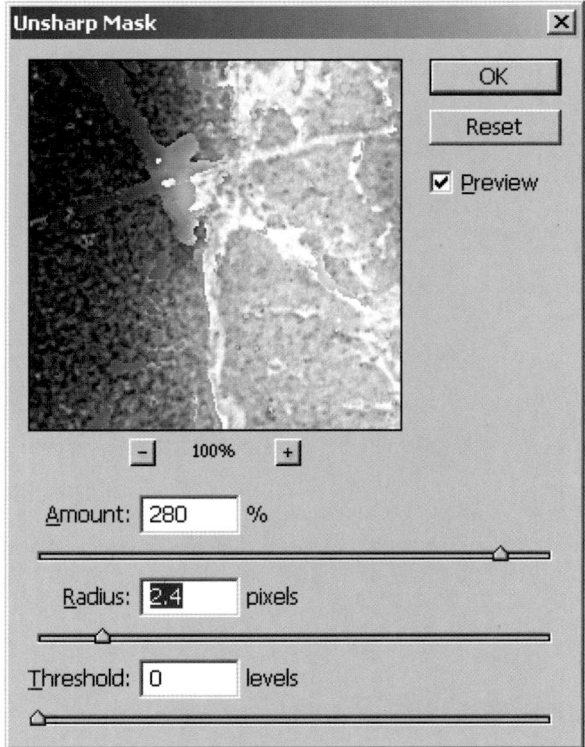

Fig. 8-36 This extremely strong Unsharp Mask filter enhances the edges of the cracks left in Figure 8-35b. This facilitates the Find Edges filter in making a new edge-selection mask from those remaining cracks.

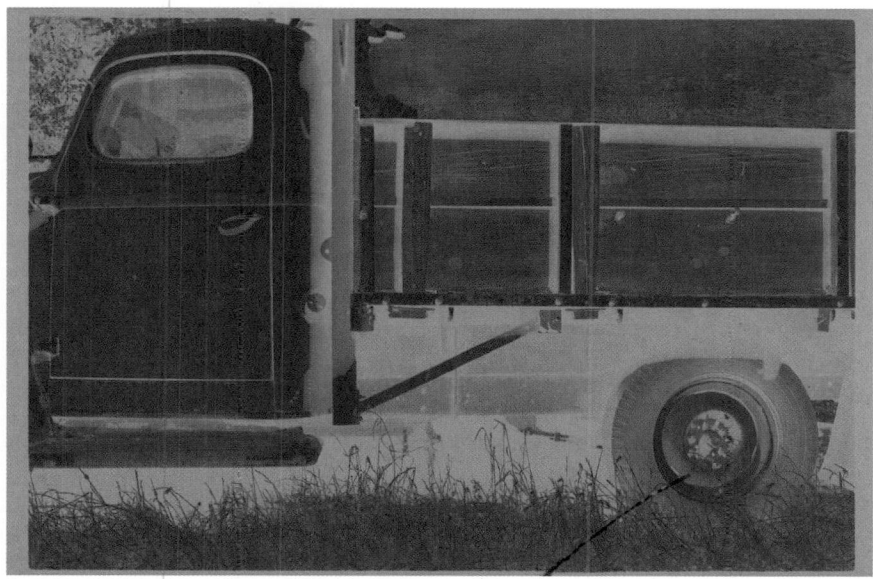

Fig. 8-37 This negative has a tear at the bottom that makes it impossible to print conventionally without a lot of print retouching.

You can run this kind of mask-and-filter cycle repeatedly until you fill in the cracks. After the second or third pass, you'll have filtered all the small cracks and only have the remnants of the largest ones left. If you do this for too many cycles, you'll start to degrade the photograph because the mask doesn't perfectly distinguish between the photograph and the damage; the filtering will "leak" into the photograph a little bit with each pass. To prevent that, I use the History Brush to paint in the later filtering passes just where I want them. Since I've already eliminated 99% of the defects, this isn't too onerous and time consuming.

HOW TO REPAIR LARGE CRACKS WITH REPEATED MASKING AND FILTERING (continued)

Paving Over Tears and Holes

Tears and small holes, while catastrophic to original photographs, are really not all that hard to repair. Clean tears, especially, produce damage that is is localized and well defined. In principle, you can repair it with nothing more than judicious use of the Clone tool, but there are lots of ways to make the job go faster.

Figure 8-37 shows a negative with a tear along its lower edge. The first tool I used to attack it was Image Doctor's Smart Fill function. (*Note:* Image Doctor only works on 8-bit files.) I circled the crack with the Lasso tool (Figure 8-38) and brought up Image Doctor. Image Doctor's default settings filled in the tear with detail extracted from neighboring undamaged areas (Figure 8-39).

If you look closely, you'll see that Image Doctor didn't get it quite right in some places, but it did a good enough job that a little spot-cloning would wipe out those artifacts. In fact, the proper way to use Image

✓ **HOW TO REPAIR A TORN NEGATIVE**

▼

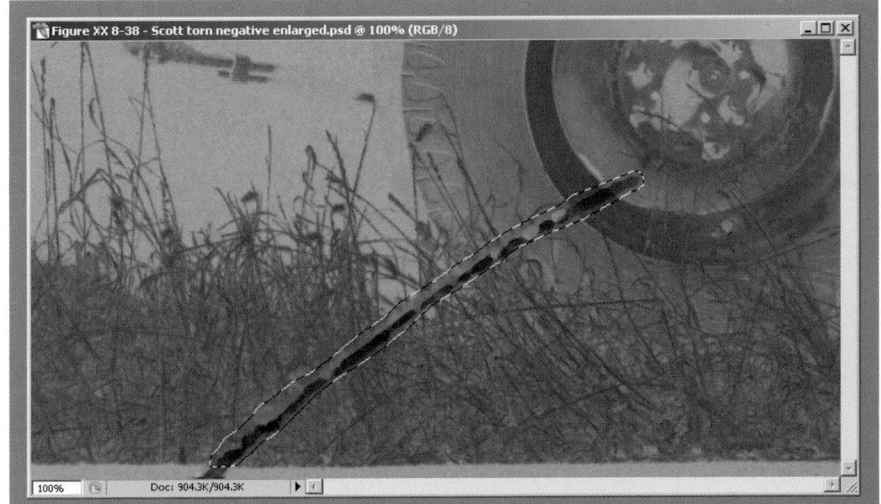

Fig. 8-38 This screenshot shows an enlargement of the tear in Figure 8-37. I've lassoed it for correction by Image Doctor.

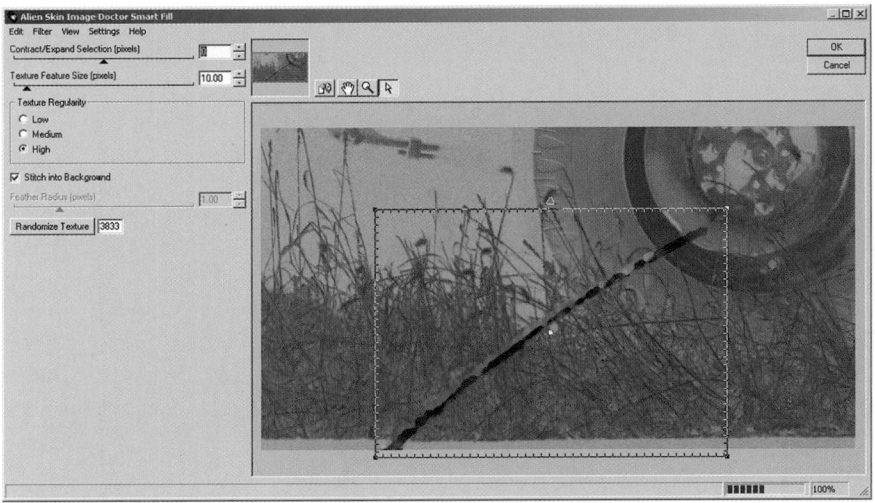

Fig. 8-39 Image Doctor's Smart Fill function samples the area around the selected crack (hatched rectangle in the top figure) and computes new detail to fill in the selection (bottom). A small amount of cloning will clean up the patches that Image Doctor got wrong.

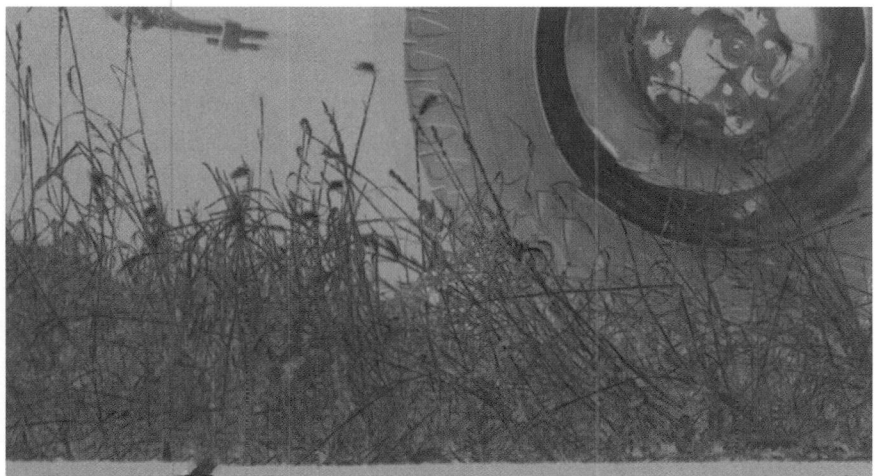

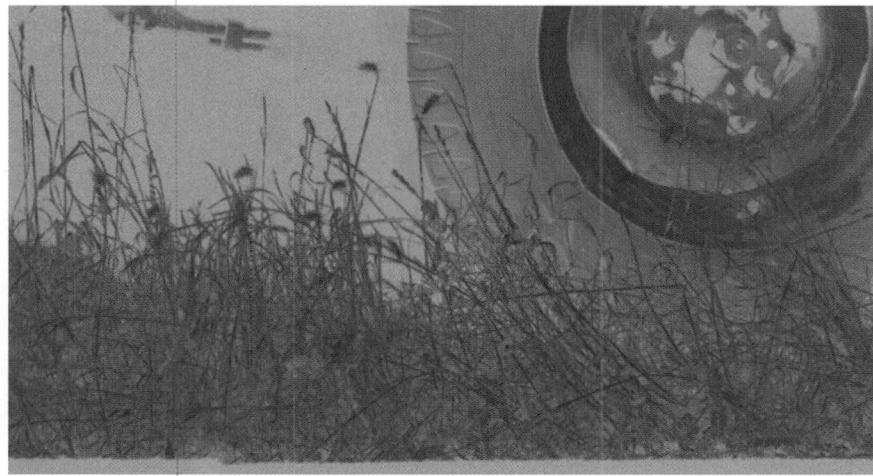

Fig. 8-40 I used Photoshop's Healing Brush to accomplish the repair in the top figure. I repaired the bottom figure with the Patch tool. Each tool has its strengths and weaknesses.

Doctor would've been to select different parts of the tear for individual correction, depending on the kind of background it was against. I did this with a single selection to show how powerful this filter is.

Some of Photoshop's built-in tools can do good jobs, too. This is not a place to use the Spot Healing Brush because it doesn't know which background textures to use to replace the tear. When there are lots of different nearby textures, as in this photograph, the brush will frequently guess wrong. The regular Healing Brush is a much better choice because you tell it what area to sample to fill in the tear. Picking a sample point adjacent to the tear worked well everywhere except along the tire, where the smooth curves were hard to reproduce. The result is shown in Figure 8-40, top.

HOW TO REPAIR A
TORN NEGATIVE
(continued)

HOW TO REPAIR A
TORN NEGATIVE
(continued)

The Patch tool will also work well on tears. Much like the Healing Brush, it lets you select what part of the photograph is going to be blended over the area you want to repair. Because the tool previews the results as you drag the selection around, it's easy to find which area and alignment work the best. For my taste, the Patch tool behaves a little too much like the Clone tool; it reproduces the sampled detail a bit too faithfully, and sharp-eyed viewers may notice repeated detail. You'll want to follow up with tools like the Clone tool and the Spot Healing Brush to "randomize" the results a bit, but the Patch tool doesn't leave too many artifacts to clean up (Figure 8-40, bottom).

Using the Spot Healing Brush

HOW TO REMOVE
CHEMICAL AND
WATER SPOTS

The Spot Healing Brush does come in handy when I'm trying to clean up isolated holes or spots. Take its name at face value; it works a lot better when you "dab" it on a bad spot than when you try to paint an extended line with it. Figure 8-41 shows a film scan of a photograph that has a bunch of chemical or water spots in the middle of it (enlargement, lower left). I removed 90% of them easily with the Spot Healing Brush.

Every so often the brush introduced an odd or inappropriate element into the photograph. Usually clicking again on the same spot or near its edge would get rid of the blemish the brush had introduced with the first click. Occasionally it made it worse. Don't sweat it; just plan on making a second pass with the cloning tool to manually repair the few blemishes that the brush couldn't take care of or created. Don't forget that you can make a history snapshot of the photo before you start in with the Spot Healing Brush, so you can use the History Brush to paint out any really bad mistakes the Spot Healing Brush makes.

Clearing the Debris

Eliminating Tarnish

Old silver photographs are prone to tarnish and bronzing—shiny or iridescent metallic-looking spots on the surface of the print, especially in the shadows. Tarnish is a vexing problem in restoration because it casts a veil over everything, but with the right techniques it is very easy to fix.

HOW TO ELIMINATE
TARNISH AND
SILVERED-OUT SPOTS

Figure 8-42, left, shows a B&W photograph that's tarnishing out. There's a bluish sheen to the blacks, and much of the print has a low-contrast, milky haze over it. The reduced contrast was easy to fix with a good scan (middle photograph); I got rid of some of the yellow in the highlights and improved the density in the shadows. It didn't get rid of the tarnish, but it did make it clearer.

The way to attack tarnish is to isolate it with a mask. I applied the Hue/Saturation settings in Figure 8-43 to exaggerate the color of the

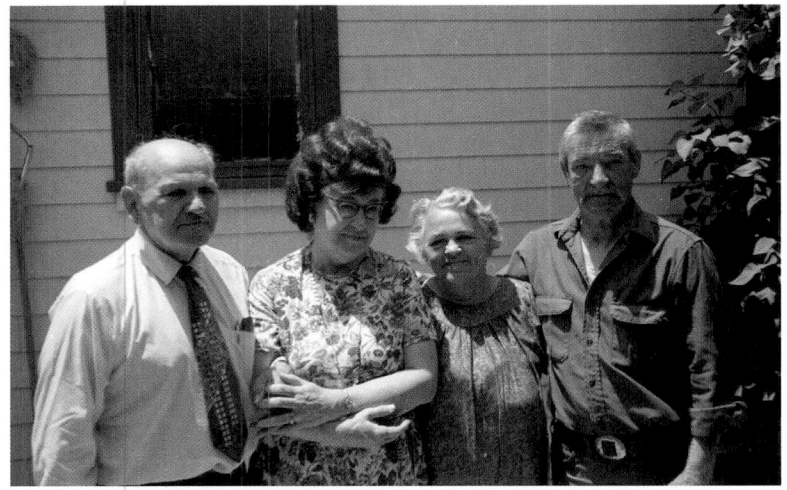

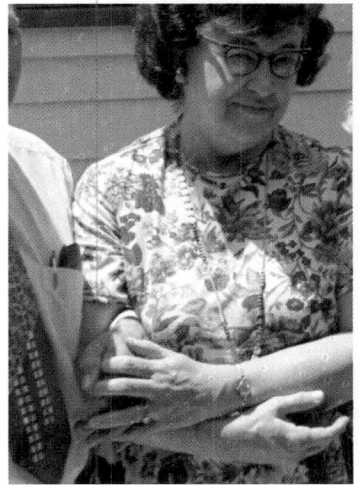 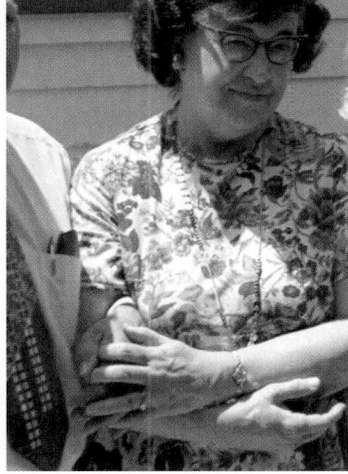

Fig. 8-41 Water spots deface this negative, seen enlarged at lower left. The Spot Healing Brush is the ideal tool for repairing this damage. It removes 90% of the spots perfectly (lower right).

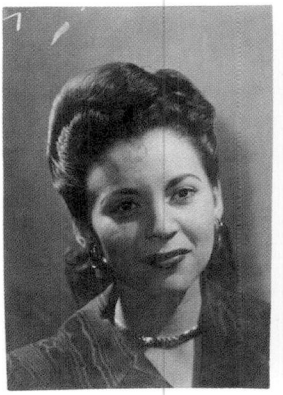 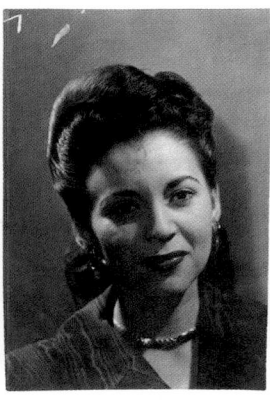 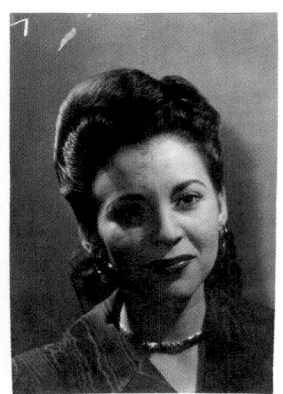

Fig. 8-42 The photograph on the left is not badly faded, but it is yellowed and severely tarnished. The middle figure shows the scan I made of this photograph that eliminated the stain and made the photographic image less yellow. This made the tarnish bluer. I accentuated the color of the tarnish with the Hue/Saturation settings in Figure 8-43 to produce the figure on the right.

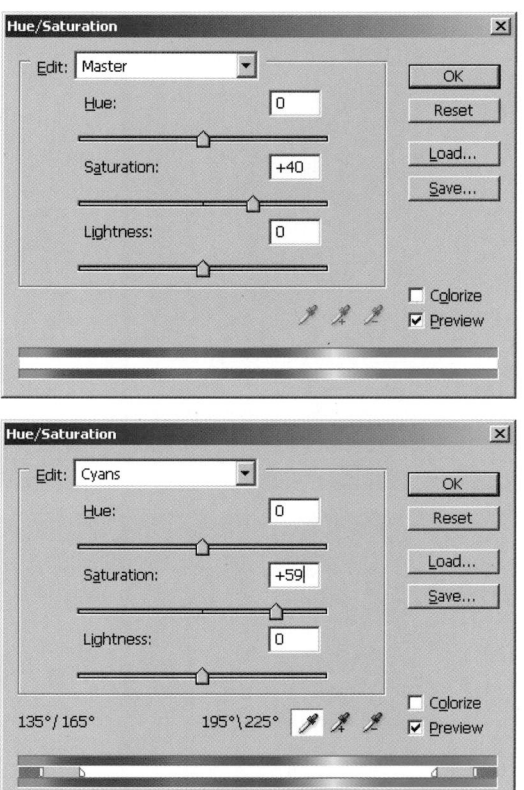

Fig. 8-43 These Hue/ Saturation settings exaggerate the color difference between the tarnish and the underlying photograph, so that it will be easier to prepare a tarnish-selecting mask. The Master adjustment of +40 points exaggerates both the slightly yellow tone of the photograph and the blue color of the tarnish. The Cyan adjustment of +59 points kicks up the saturation in the tarnish even more.

HOW TO ELIMINATE TARNISH AND SILVERED-OUT SPOTS (continued)

tarnish so that it would be easier to pick out. That produced Figure 8-42, right.

Many Photoshop tools can create a mask out of color distinctions: the Color Range selection, the Channel Mixer, or Image Calculations (see Chapter 7, Making Masks, page 252). The Asiva Selection plug-in is a favorite of mine. Figure 8-44 shows the Asiva Selection control panel with the curves I used to isolate the tarnish. The top curve restricted the selection to colors in the blue part of the spectrum, excluding undamaged parts of the photograph that were yellowish. I set the saturation curve to reject areas than had very little or no saturation, as those were untarnished. The resulting selection is shown in Figure 8-45.

I created a Curves adjustment layer with that selection. It would be just as effective to apply the curves directly to the selection, but the adjustment layer left me free to try out different curves that I could revise later. Knowing that the tarnish was greenish blue and lighter than the surrounding areas, I developed my curves by trial-and-error (Figure 8-46). The RGB curve doesn't have a big effect; it darkens the shadows some and ensures that the darkest tones really are near-black. The green

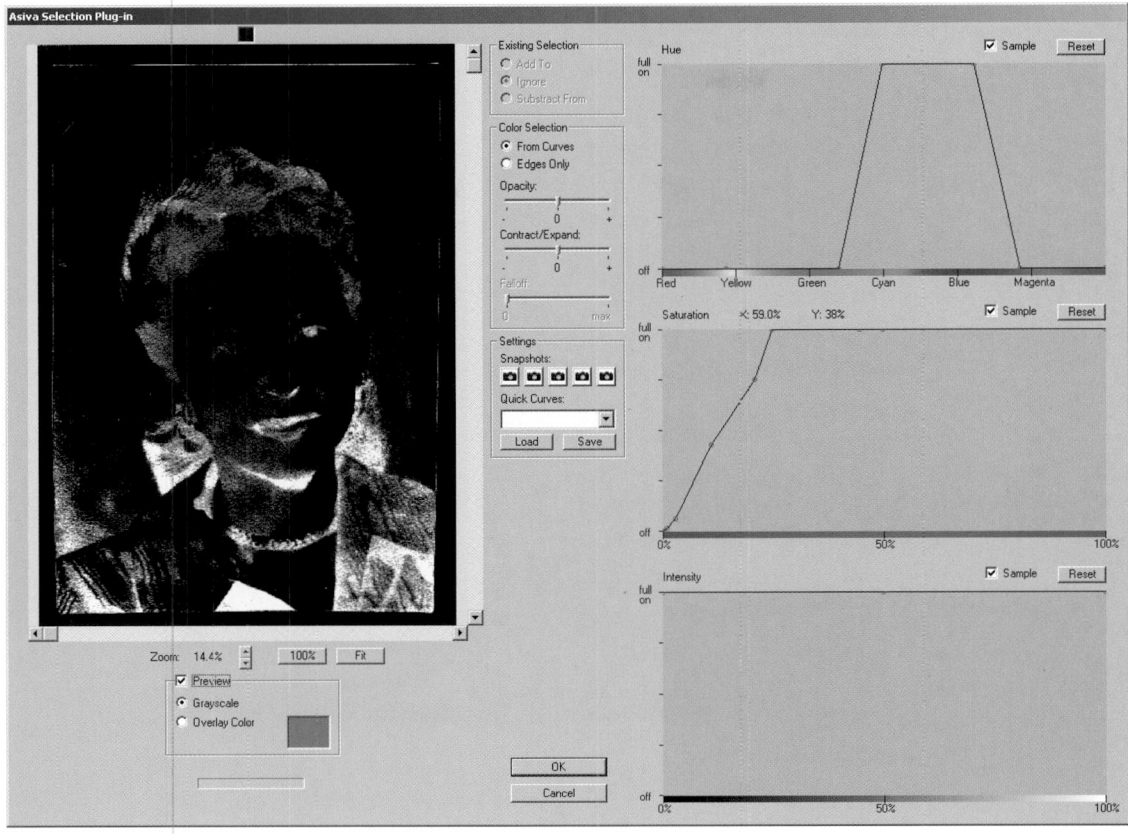

Fig. 8-44 This screenshot of the Asiva Selection plug-in at work shows the settings I used to create the tarnish-selecting mask in Figure 8-45. I restricted the range of selected colors to the blue tones characteristic of the tarnish. I also adjusted the Saturation curve to reject any tones that were not at least moderately saturated. This did a good job of isolating the tarnish for repair.

curve shifts the color substantially to the magenta, having the least effect in the highlights and the greatest effect in the shadows. The really big change occurs in the blue curve. I dragged the black point way in and added another control point, which pulled the whole curve down, so that everything except for the very whitest tones was shifted very strongly to the yellow.

The resulting photograph in Figure 8-47, left, is tarnish-free. The details in the hair and the texture of the moire silk blouse are once again rich and clear. The restoration isn't complete; there are yellow stains and marks on the surface of the print, and the paper texture is distracting, but I've fixed the worst problem. In the next section, I get rid of the stains and marks. On page 305 I subdue the annoying paper texture, which will finish up this restoration.

HOW TO ELIMINATE
TARNISH AND
SILVERED-OUT SPOTS
(continued)

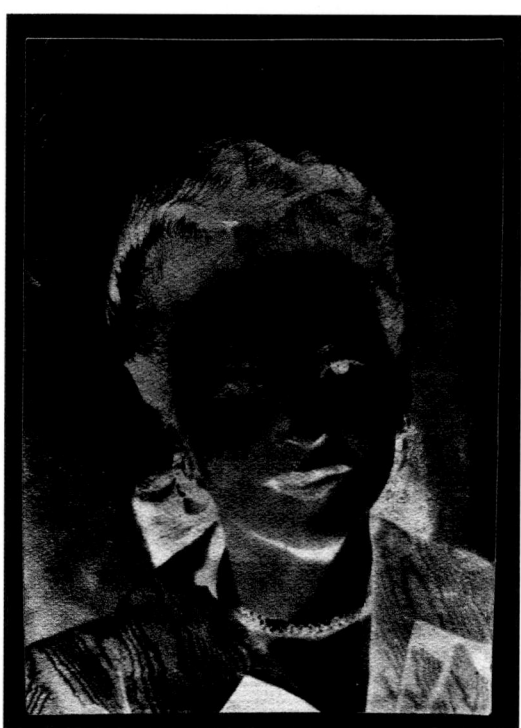

Fig. 8-45 This is the finished mask that I used to repair the photograph in Figure 8-47.

Picking the Right Color for B&W

In Chapter 7, page 244, I created masks using channels and the Channel Mixer to exploit color differences between B&W photographs and the damage inflicted on them. I took advantage of colors or combinations of colors that especially emphasized the damage over the photograph.

Those same tricks can be inverted to minimize the damage, using complementary colors. For example, damage that is especially visible in the green channel will have a strong magenta component. That means it will not be very visible in the "magenta" (red + blue) channel. I would use the green channel to build a mask from because it shows the damage so clearly. Conversely, if I wanted to suppress that damage, I would use the Channel Mixer to combine the red and blue channels and exclude the green channel.

I used the colors green and magenta merely as examples. The precise color that works best will depend on the photograph and the damage. If the damage looks reddish compared to the photograph, check out the red channel; if it looks cyan, then check out the green and blue channels. What you can usually count on when restoring a B&W photograph is that one channel will show the damage and stains on the photograph less than the other channels.

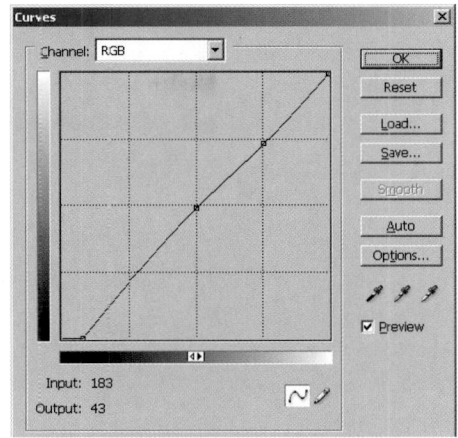

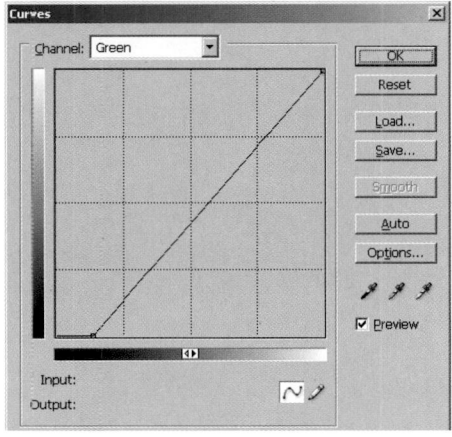

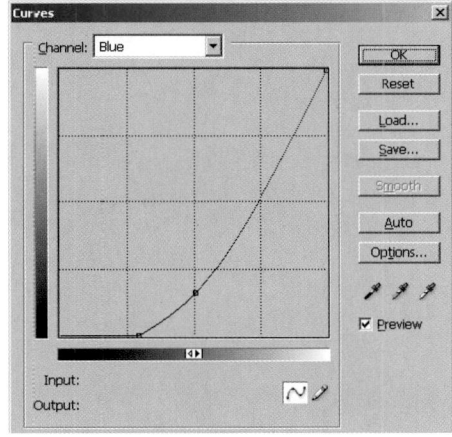

Fig. 8-46 This Curves adjustment eliminates the tarnish from Figure 8-42 when it's used in conjunction with the tarnish-selecting mask from Figure 8-45. The RGB curve slightly darkens the shadows, the green curve makes the tarnish more magenta, and the blue curve makes it much yellower. That eliminates the light blue/cyan cast that the tarnish had and makes it blend in perfectly with the photograph (Figure 8-47, left).

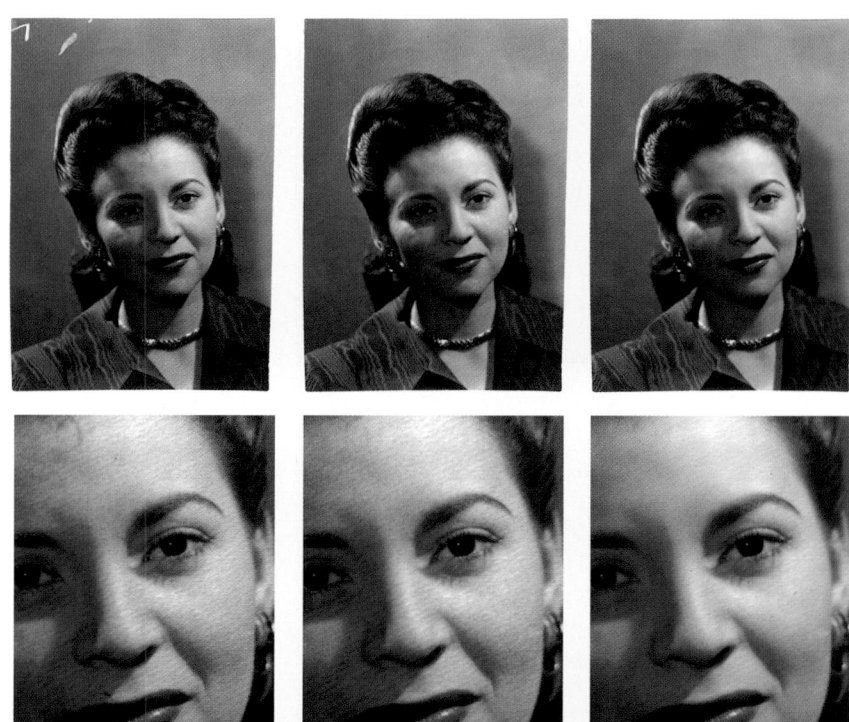

Fig. 8-47 The figure on the left shows the photograph from Figure 8-42 after tarnish repair. Tone and contrast are good, but there's some yellow-orange stain, and the paper texture is distracting. The stain is least visible in the red channel, so I copied that into the middle figure and used the Clone tool to repair the minimal amount of residual damage. The figure on the right shows the fully restored photograph after I removed the paper texture with Neat Image (Figure 8-50).

That's especially true when you've done a good scan that produces a reasonably neutral-toned photograph. Stains and other defects usually have a different color from the photograph proper. Once you've finished with the kinds of repairs that require a full-color image (like the tarnish-reducing work I did in the previous section), look at the individual color channels for the photograph and select the one that looks the cleanest for further restoration work.

In the portrait in Figure 8-47 the stains are yellow-orange in color. When I inspected each color channel, I saw that the red channel displayed hardly any of the stains. I copied that channel into a new file that is shown in the middle column of Figure 8-47. I used the Clone tool to clear out the white marks of the top and remove a couple of small dark spots from the picture; it literally took just a few minutes' work to make it look this good.

HOW TO MINIMIZE TAPE STAINS

In Chapter 7, page 258, I demonstrated several ways to mask Figure 8-48 to select the tape for repair. In preparation for that repair, I wanted to reduce the discoloration in the taped area. I did that by manipulating the Hue/Saturation control. The tape was least visible in the red channel, hardly a surprise given the color of the stain, so I went to the Channels palette and clicked off the "eyes" for the green and blue channels (Figure

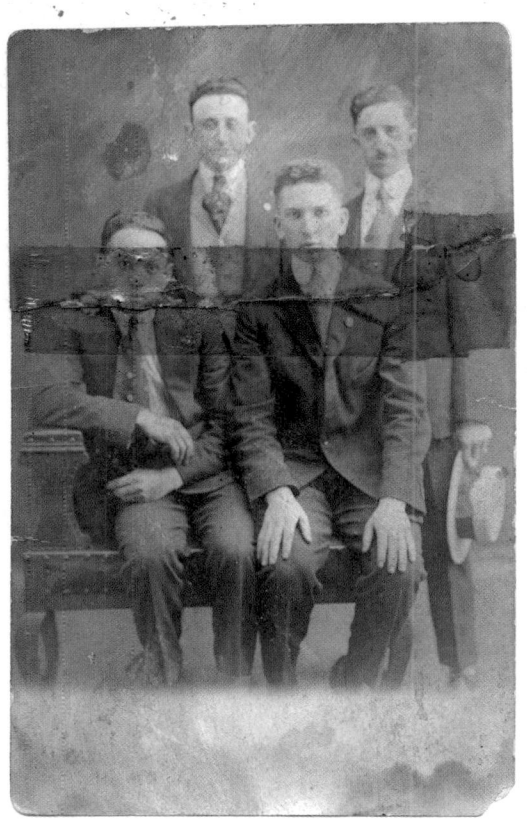

Fig. 8-48 The tape stain in this photograph has a strong red-orange color, which means that it is least visible in the red channel (see Figure 7-43).

8-49), so that I was only viewing the red channel. The RGB channel was still highlighted, so all the channels were active.

HOW TO MINIMIZE TAPE STAINS (continued)

I launched the Hue/Saturation control and began moving the Saturation slider up. That changed the intensity of the red in the tape stain and varied its appearance in the red channel. By watching how the appearance of the tape changed in the preview, I could choose the right saturation setting to minimize its impact. Normal saturation showed the tape darker than the surrounding area. Moving the saturation up to around +40 did a good job of lightening it.

Dealing with Textured Prints

Paper texture isn't really damage, because it was an intentional part of the original print. Print textures, though, usually look bad when they are reproduced on a flat-finish paper. If you want to restore an original, textured photograph to a fresh textured print, you will get a much better-looking print if you print a clean image on textured paper than if you try to print the illusion of texture. Consequently, I treat texture

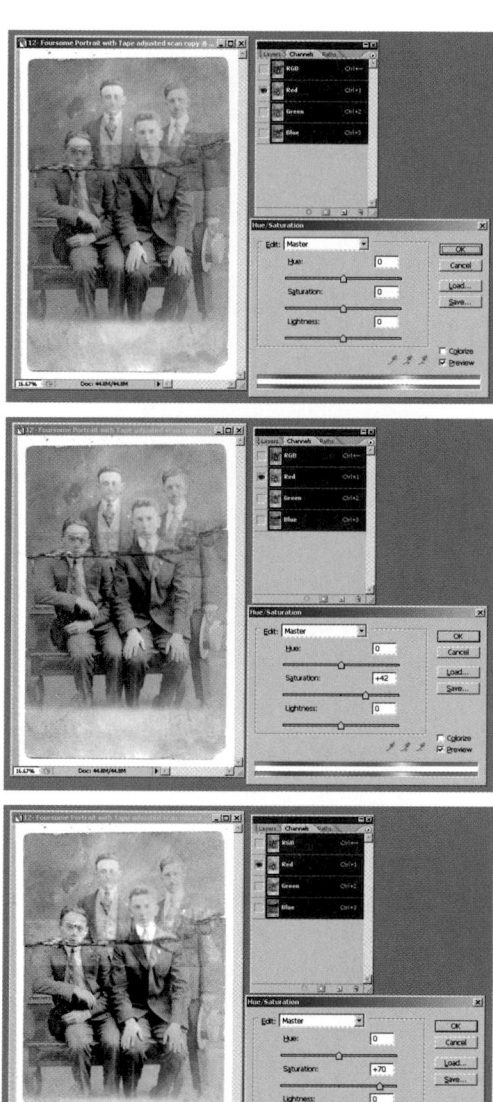

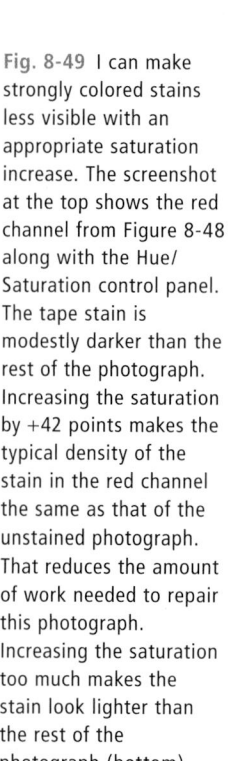

Fig. 8-49 I can make strongly colored stains less visible with an appropriate saturation increase. The screenshot at the top shows the red channel from Figure 8-48 along with the Hue/ Saturation control panel. The tape stain is modestly darker than the rest of the photograph. Increasing the saturation by +42 points makes the typical density of the stain in the red channel the same as that of the unstained photograph. That reduces the amount of work needed to repair this photograph. Increasing the saturation too much makes the stain look lighter than the rest of the photograph (bottom).

as if it were widespread damage—something I want to erase from the prints while doing as little destruction of photographic detail as possible.

Like tarnish and other surface blemishes, texture tends to get enhanced in scans. I talked in Chapter 4, Getting the Photo into the Computer, page 126, about rephotographing textured prints on a copy stand as one way to get around the paper texture problem. Here, I deal with getting rid of paper texture in scans.

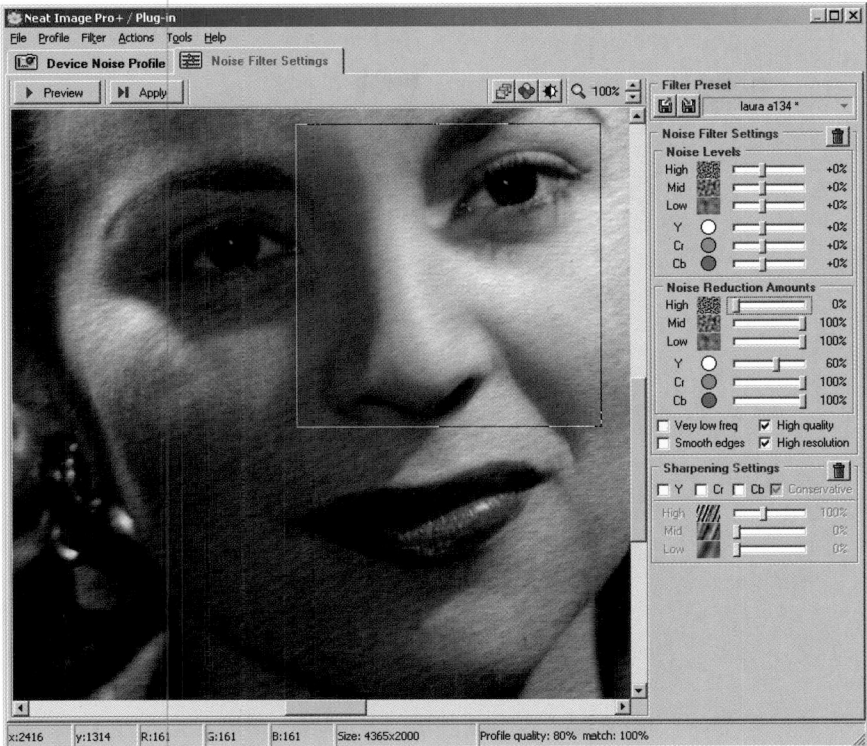

Fig. 8-50 The Neat Image plug-in for Photoshop can clean up paper texture in a scan just as well as noise. I eliminated the texture from Figure 8-47 without compromising fine photographic detail by adjusting the high-frequency Noise Reduction Amount. Turning this all the way down to 0% ensured that fine details like the eyelashes and catch lights wouldn't be filtered out. Most of the paper texture was still eliminated, resulting in a very good restoration (Figure 8-47, right).

The print in Figure 8-47 cleaned up nicely with the tarnish mask (page 302). To get rid of its texture I pulled up Neat Image, a very powerful noise reduction plug-in (see Chapter 3, Software for Restoration). Neat Image profiled a section of the background and created a filter that could cancel out the texture just as if it were noise (Figure 8-50). The filter was so effective that it completely eliminated the paper texture at its default settings, but it also softened the finest detail in the photograph.

HOW TO REMOVE PRINT SURFACE TEXTURES

I wanted to retain the fine detail. I did that by using the noise reduction sliders. I set the sliders' high-frequency Noise Reduction Amount to 0%. I left the mid- and low-frequency settings at 100%. That meant that the filter still had full effect on the coarse paper texture but left fine detail (and texture) alone.

Applying the filter produced the photograph in Figure 8-47, right. All of the image detail is still there, but almost all of the paper texture was removed. There's a very fine "tooth" to the photograph, from the high-frequency texture I allowed to get through, but it's not distracting or intrusive.

Figure 8-51 was a tougher case. This school portrait was printed on that "honeycomb" paper that was commonly used for inexpensive

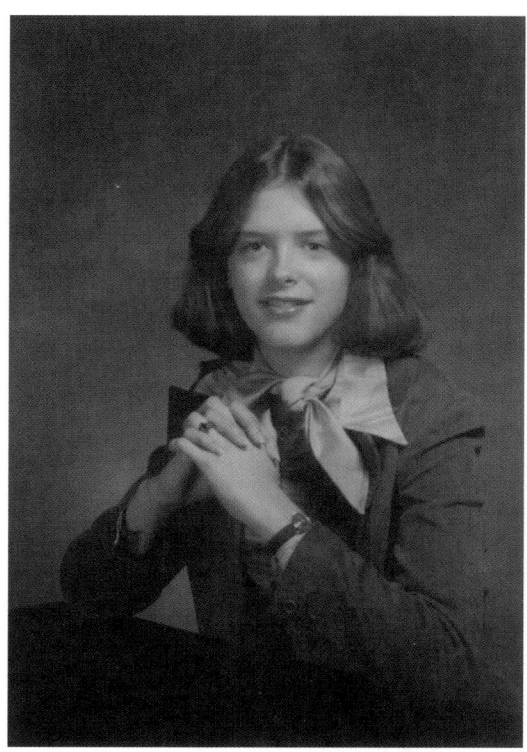

Fig. 8-51 This 30-year-old high school portrait is printed on honeycomb-textured paper. Once the color and contrast are restored, the paper texture is very intrusive because of the increased contrast (Figure 8-52, left).

HOW TO REMOVE PRINT SURFACE TEXTURES (continued)

portraits. It created some real restoration problems for me. Because this photograph wasn't very faded, overall color and tone correction was pretty easy. I made a good scan and some modest curve corrections to get the photo in Figure 8-52, left. Unfortunately, as the lower enlargement makes clear, the honeycomb texture really messed up the photograph's appearance.

I turned to Neat Image once again and, sure enough, it did great job of extracting a texture profile from a background area that completely eliminated the honeycomb. Because this texture was sharp and well defined, I couldn't turn down the high-frequency noise filtering and still remove it. In fact, I had to turn up the noise level detection for the high and mid-frequencies to successfully grab all of the pattern (Figure 8-53). I was able to turn the low-frequency noise filter and noise reduction all the way down, and that helped a little to preserve detail. Figure 8-52, center, is the result. The enlargement shows that the filter completely eliminated the paper texture and didn't blur the print detail very much—but the print wasn't that sharp to begin with. I'd like to fix that.

I turned to another favorite plug-in of mine, Focus Magic. Focus Magic restores sharpness to every part of the photograph, not just edges, so you don't want to use it on a noisy image because it will enhance the noise along with everything else. But Neat Image had done such a

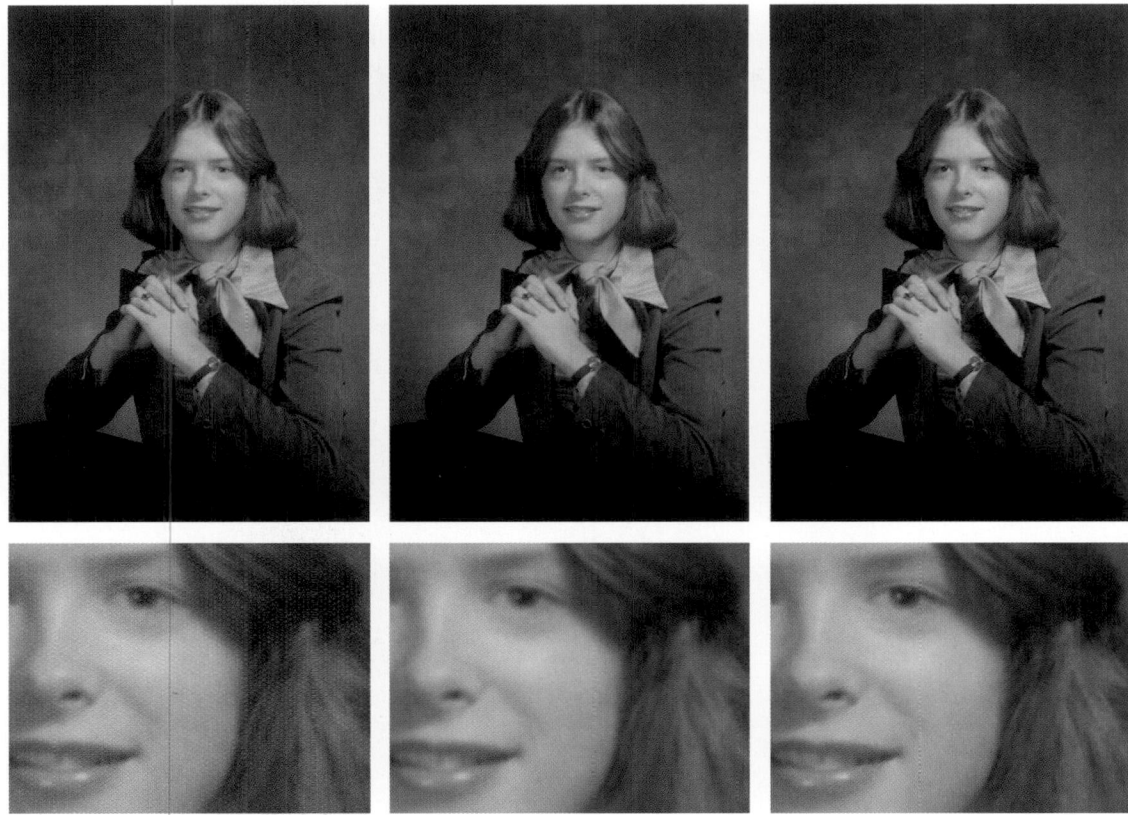

Fig. 8-52 The photograph and enlargement on the left show the color-restored version of Figure 8-51. This photograph looks great except for the annoying paper texture. Neat Image, using the settings in Figure 8-53, eliminates the paper texture entirely, but it also loses some of the fine detail in the photograph (center). Focus Magic (Figure 8-54) not only restores that lost sharpness, it actually brings out a bit more detail in the photograph than was visible in the original (right).

good job of removing the paper texture that there was little of it left for Focus Magic to exaggerate. I set the blur width to 9 pixels, as shown in Figure 8-54, and let Focus Magic do its work. The final photograph, in Figure 8-52, right, is both sharper and smoother toned than the original was.

Picture Window has a built-in tool, called "Advanced Sharpen," that works pretty well on paper texture. What makes it useful for texture removal is that it has three stages of operation: noise reduction, speck removal, and sharpening. To attack the paper texture, I used the first two operations and didn't do any sharpening.

In Figure 8-55, I applied the Advanced Sharpen tool to the school portrait. Under noise reduction, I set a blur radius of about 2.5 pixels and adjusted the noise detection sliders at the bottom of the control panel until they did a good job of picking up most of the paper texture without ▼

HOW TO REMOVE
PRINT SURFACE
TEXTURES
(continued)

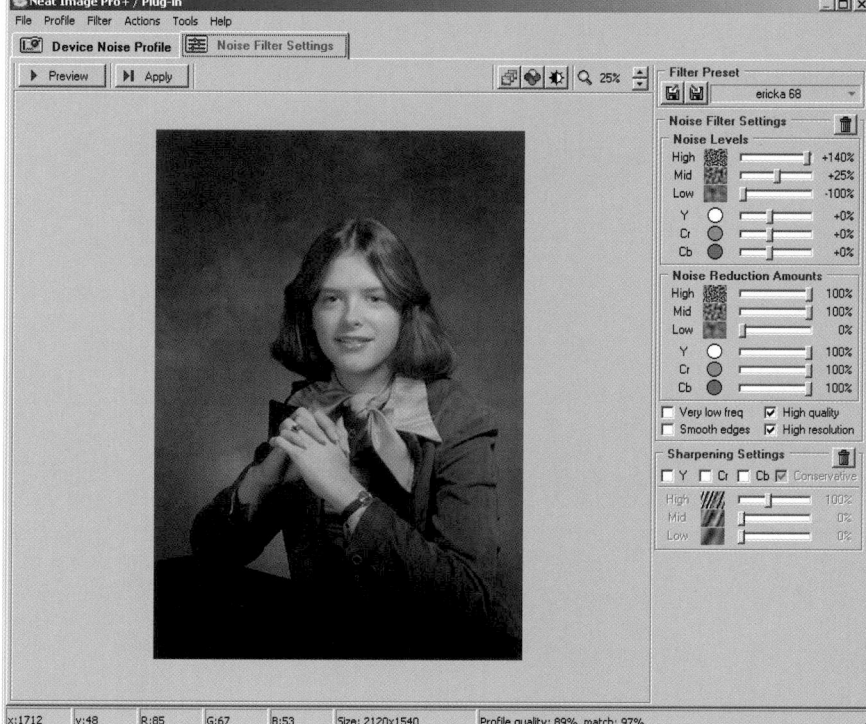

Fig. 8-53 These Neat Image settings eliminated the paper texture in Figure 8-52. The texture is very fine and sharp edged, so the high-frequency Noise Filter and Noise Reduction settings were turned up to maximum. Because the texture contains no low-frequency components, I turned that Noise Reduction setting off.

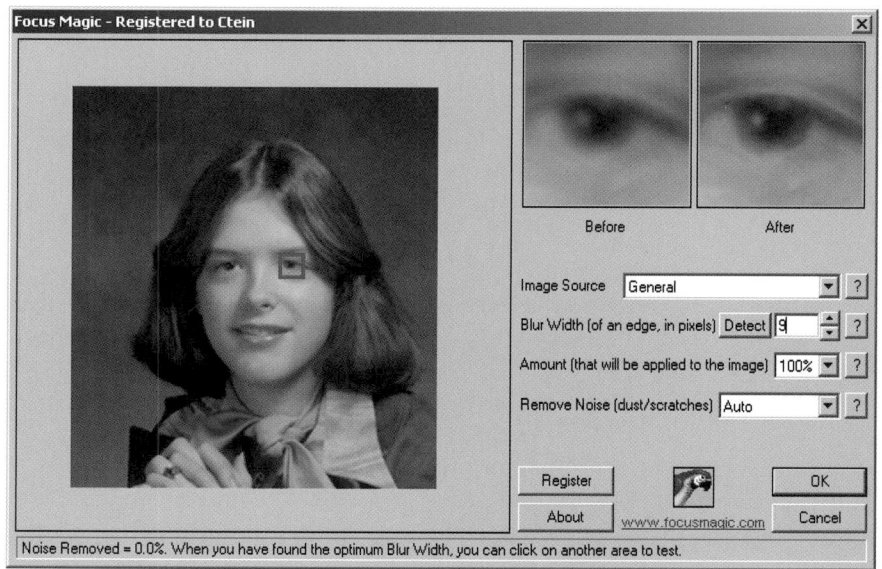

Fig. 8-54 Focus Magic effectively sharpens up the photograph in Figure 8-52, right. It did more than simply restore detail that was removed by Neat Image; it made the photograph sharper and more detailed than it was originally.

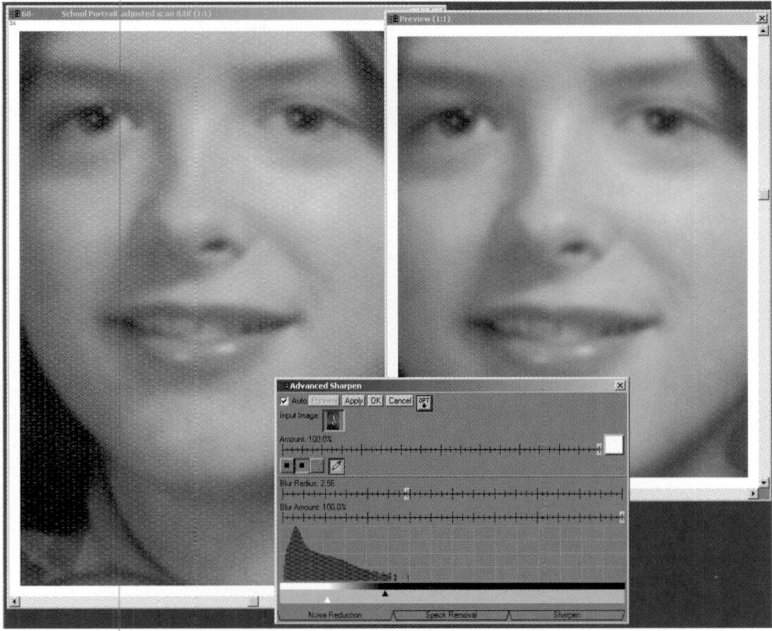

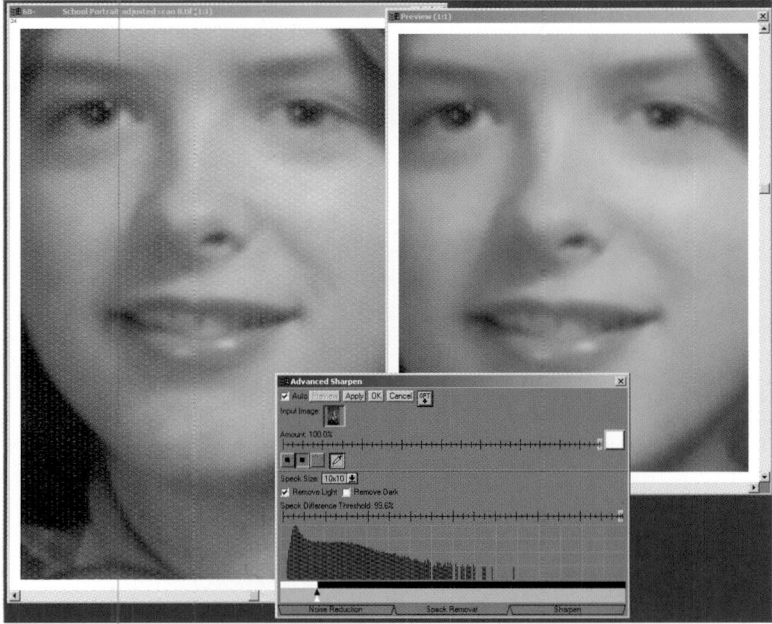

Fig. 8-55 Picture Window's Advanced Sharpen transformation includes Noise Reduction and Speck Removal tools that can minimize paper textures. In the top screenshot, I've set the Noise Reduction sliders to include most of the detail in the paper texture without compromising real photographic information too badly. That produces the results seen on the right. I can further improve that result in the Speck Removal stage by instructing the tool to remove only the light specks. That picks out the highlights from the texture that weren't eliminated by Noise Reduction.

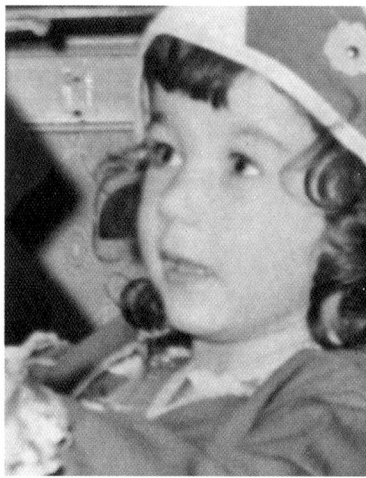 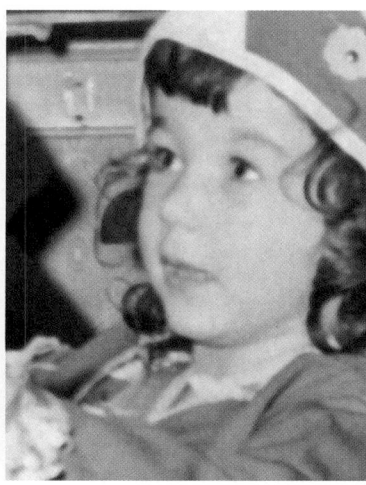 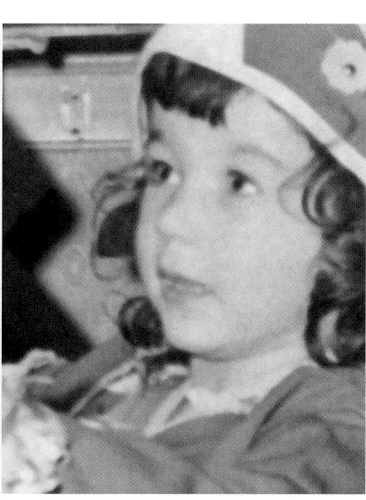

Fig. 8-56 Very fine paper texture, as in the photograph on the left, can be attacked with Photoshop's own filters. The Dust & Scratches filter, with a 2-pixel radius and a threshold of 4, produced the middle figure. The paper texture is finer than the finest detail in the photograph, so it is eliminated while photographic information isn't. Median filtering can also reduce or eliminate paper texture (right), but it has to be used very carefully to avoid blurring the photograph.

HOW TO REMOVE
PRINT SURFACE
TEXTURES
(continued)

starting to eat away at the detail in the photograph. The preview window in the upper right showed that this stage would suppress (but not entirely eliminate) the paper texture without damaging fine detail too much.

After I applied noise reduction, I advanced to the speck removal stage. Because the texture was significant, I set the speck size to 10 by 10 pixels and told the filter to remove only light specks (the highlights from the texture). I moved the threshold slider up to almost 100% so it would find low-contrast texture, and I set the detail detection histogram slider so that the filter grabbed the texture but not too much else. As you can see in the preview window, the results are not as perfect as with Neat Image, but I've eliminated most of the paper texture without compromising the detail in the photograph.

When the paper texture is finer than the image detail in the photograph, sometimes Photoshop's filters can handle it. The Dust & Scratches filter will do the job without costing you too much detail. Figure 8-56 shows before (left) and after (middle) close-ups of a textured print scan. The "after" version was generated by the Dust & Scratches filter with a radius of 2 pixels and a threshold of 4.

The Median filter does an extremely good job of suppressing fine paper texture, but it strongly attacks real image detail, too, so use it carefully. I filtered the photograph in Figure 8-56, right, with the Median filter at a radius of 2 pixels. All of the paper texture wasn't suppressed at this radius, but increasing the radius to 3 visibly blurred the photograph.

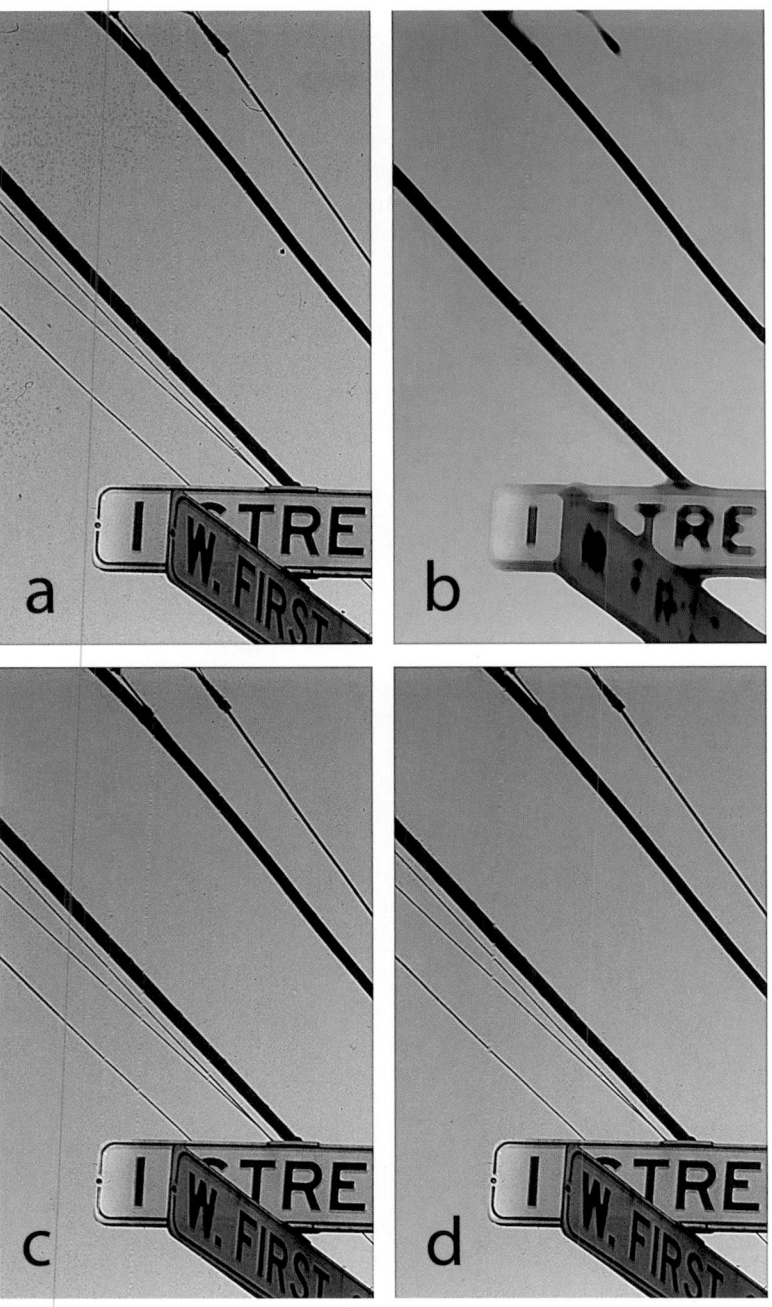

Fig. 8-57 Dark mildew specks and spots, like those afflicting the photograph in figure (a), can be filtered out in stages. A 10-pixel Median filter produced figure (b). There are broad, faint dark areas in the sky because the Median filter averaged the dark mildew into the blue sky. To get rid of those, I assigned the Median filtering to the History Brush, reverted to the previous state, and used the Brush in Lighten mode to paint over the mildew in the sky (figure c). This has no effect on the blue sky, but it lightens the mildew considerably. I applied the filter a second time and used the History Brush over the residual mildew in figure (c). The result, figure (d), is free from mildew blemishes, and the sky is restored to its natural tones.

Repairing Mildew

Mildew damage is a serious problem for original photographs. Mildew spots and filaments are composed of microorganisms that eat the photographic emulsion and grow. Mildew will expand just like bacteria in a culture dish. Photos that are starting to suffer mildew damage will only get worse, so they should get priority for treatment (or digital restoration).

Moderate mildew damage takes the form of long dark filaments or clusters of small dark spots, like closely spaced freckles. The long mildew filaments look like fine squiggly scratches in a scan, and you can treat them as you would other scratches. Because mildew spreads from single spores that take hold, the filaments grow out like the roots of a plant, so they are very close together. Throughout this and the preceding chapter, I've introduced techniques for dealing with dense networks of fine cracks, and those methods will work just as well on mildew.

Dense groups of mildew "freckles" cause many restorers problems because they aren't as well defined as the filaments and they can cover enough of a photograph to seriously distort average tonal values. That makes them harder to remove with simple filtering, and they are far too numerous to remove by cloning. Here's a trick that works well when mildew attacks a broad uniform area of the image, which is where it is most visible.

Figure 8-57a shows the corner of a slide that is developing mildew freckles. (This figure is heavily sharpened to make it easier to see the mildew spots, so ignore white halos around edges, because those are just sharpening artifacts.) The sky along the left side and upper part of the photograph is filled with numerous dark spots. You could just blur them out, but it wouldn't work well. Because the average tone including the mildew is darker, if you just blurred them out, there would be a broad dark blemish in the sky. In Figure 8-57b, I applied a Median filter with a 10-pixel radius to the photograph. The freckles were obliterated, but that faint dark blemish I warned about showed up.

HOW TO ERASE
MILDEW SPOTS

The way to fix that is to paint in the effect of the filter using the History Brush set to Lighten mode. I assigned the History Brush to the Median filter state, reverted to the previous state, and painted over the mildew with the History Brush. It lightened the mildew spots but didn't have any effect on the sky in between.

I did that on Figure 8-57c, and most of the mildew is gone. There's still a faint impression of it because the filter isn't painting in undamaged blue sky but an average of blue sky and dark mildew. The way to completely eliminate the mildew is to repeat the process. In Figure 8-57d, I applied the Median filter again and used the History Brush in Lighten mode to paint over the mildewed area a second time. This completely eliminated all evidence of the mildew and restored perfect sky color. If two passes aren't sufficient, you can repeat this Median filter lightening process as many times as needed to get a clean image.

CHAPTER 9

Tips, Tricks, and Enhancements

How-To's in This Chapter

How to scan very contrasty photographs
How to eliminate the dots from newspaper photographs
How to increase sharpness and fine detail in a photograph
How to make a photograph look like a tintype
How to combine scans to make one large photograph

Every photograph is unique, and so is every photo restoration job. Many photographs have common characteristics, though, so I've concentrated my instruction to this point on the tasks that benefit the greatest number of photographs. I've grouped those tasks into broad categories and chapters of shared purpose, like color correction.

Still, I can't ignore the inherent uniqueness that makes every restoration job an interesting and stimulating challenge, nor can you. For your part, you want to be flexible and versatile if you're going to restore photographs effectively and efficiently. For my part, I want to introduce you to a bunch of specific tricks and techniques that I've found especially useful but don't fit neatly into one of those broad categories that I laid out.

Save Time by Using Your Keyboard and Your Mouse

I've noticed that most people who work on the computer have deeply ingrained mouse and keyboard work habits. Some people are very mouse and menu oriented. When they need to save a file in Photoshop, their instinct is to go to the File menu, click on it, scroll down to Save, and click that. OK, that works, but just pressing control-S (under Windows) does exactly the same thing, and you don't have to move your mouse (or even let go of it). Not having to navigate a hierarchy of menus is a lot less disruptive to the thought processes.

Frankly, I'm more mouse oriented than not. I'm not the person to lecture you on not knowing how to play the keyboard like a virtuoso. I don't seem to be able to remember many more than six keyboard shortcuts at one time, a small fraction of the number available. But, just knowing that handful saves me a huge amount of time. I can remember that control-shift-S activates "Save As" so I can save a file with a new name, Y switches to the History Brush and S to the Clone tool when I'm retouching, and the spacebar activates the Hand tool when I'm lassoing a large area. The [and] keys expand or contract my brush; the { and } make it harder or softer. Each of these is just a tiny little time-saver, but together they add up to a lot of minutes each day.

I'm not going to prescribe which keyboard commands you should learn. Learn to pay attention to yourself. Notice when you're doing an operation repetitively. When you do, check out the menus and help files to see if there's a keyboard shortcut. Some shortcuts will show up if you move the cursor over the item and wait for a helpful little pop-up box to appear. Those are great memory-joggers (like when I forget that the Clone tool is S because the Crop tool is C).

To those of you who are already keyboard masters, don't forget to use the mouse! Double-clicking on the background brings up the Open file selection window. When you have a tool selected for use, right-clicking the mouse will bring up many useful options for it. Right-clicking on the title bar at the top of an image window brings up Duplicate, Image Size, Canvas Size, and Page Setup commands. It's much faster than scrolling through menus, and it saves having to remember more keyboard shortcuts.

While I'm talking about speeding up your Photoshop workflow, let me remind you to do two things. Go into your preferences. Set them to add central crosshairs to the brush tip cursor and assign the mouse scroll wheel to zoom the image. Little changes but big improvements.

Capturing a Long Density Range in a Scan by Stacking Images

As I've said in other chapters, some kinds of originals present real scanning problems. Old B&W films and plates can have such a high density range that a single scan can't capture it all. Transparencies that are severely faded in one channel can throw off a film scanner's exposure control and make it difficult to get good density information in all three channels from a single scan. Even with my film scanner set for maximum-density-range capture, I sometimes can't get a single scan that holds detail in both highlights and shadows.

HOW TO SCAN VERY
CONTRASTY
PHOTOGRAPHS

Picture Window's Stack Images Transformation can blend up to five images together. Photographers use it to combine bracketed exposures from a digital camera to produce one extended-range photograph. I use it to extend the dynamic range of my scanner. It's so much better than Photoshop's "Merge to HDR" operation that I never use that.

Figure 9-1 shows a badly faded slide of Richard Nixon from the early 1950s. The combination of extreme fading in the slide and very uneven

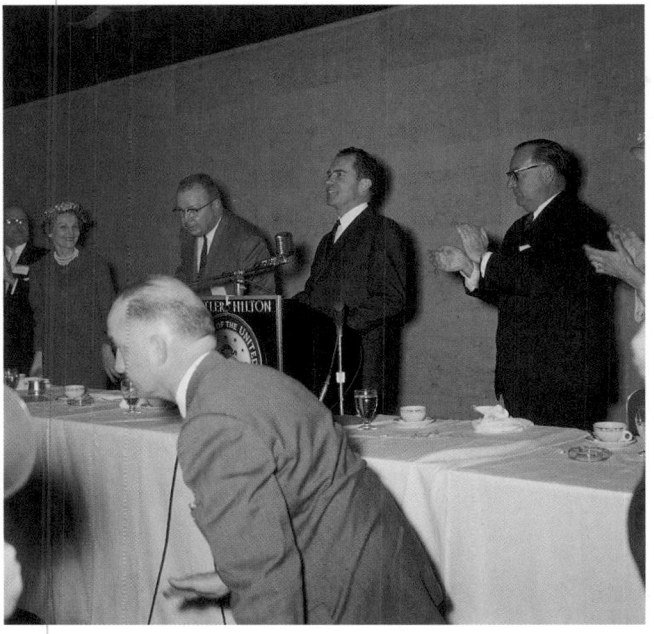

Fig. 9-1 This slide of
then-Vice President
Richard Nixon is 50 years
old. It's lost most of its
cyan dye but almost none
of its yellow. This
combination of extreme
fading and color shift
makes it difficult to make
a scan that captures the
full density range of the
slide.

lighting in the photograph made for a very difficult scan. I adjusted my
scanner's exposure settings to favor the capture of highlight, midtone,
and shadow detail in separate scans.

I saved those three scans as 16-bit TIFF files and opened them up
in Picture Window (Figure 9-2). The Stack Images Transformation
control panel is visible in the upper right. I assigned the dark TIFF file
to Image 1, the intermediate file to Image 2, and the light file to Image
3. In many cases you'll get a good result from combining just light and
dark scans.

Hit the Apply button and Stack Images creates a default blend, shown
in Figure 9-3, top. This looks like the medium-exposure TIFF file but
with substantially better highlight and shadow detail. Customizing the
blending curves is better still. Each image in the stack has its own density
mask curve. That curve controls how different tones in that image will
be blended into the mix.

Image 1 had excellent highlight detail and no shadow detail, so I
wanted the blend to make use of its highlight detail. I adjusted its curve
so that it is 0% in the shadows and 100% in the highlights. Density
Mask 2 pulled in 100% of the midtone information from the medium
scan but tapered off in the highlights and shadows. Density Mask 3 used
all of the shadow detail from Image 3, which had the most shadow
information of the three files. It used almost none of the highlight information because that was blown out in the scan.

HOW TO SCAN VERY
CONTRASTY
PHOTOGRAPHS
(continued)

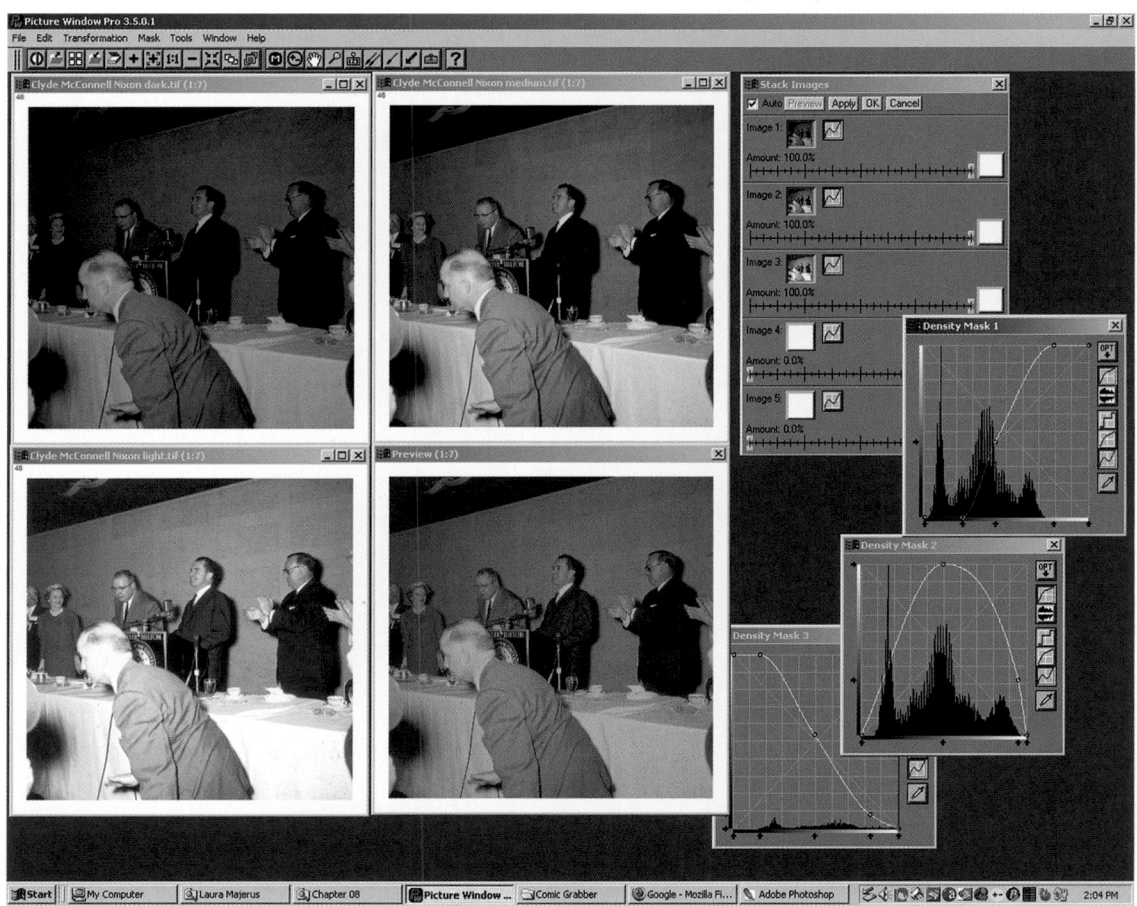

Fig. 9-2 Picture Window's Stack Image transformation is a superior tool for combining multiple scans into a single long-density-range image. This screenshot shows me combining three scans made with different exposures (upper left) into a single merged image, visible in the Preview window. At the upper right is the Stack Images control panel. Below that are the curves I created to control how the densities of the different scans get blended together. Mask 1 is for the darkest scan. I don't want to use any shadow detail from that scan, but I want all of its highlight detail. So I set the mask curve to 0% in the shadows and 100% in the highlights. The intermediate scan has good midtones but worse highlights and shadows than the other two scans, so Mask 2's curve picks up 100% of the midtones and drops off to 0% at both ends of the curve. The lightest scan has great shadow detail and no highlight detail; Mask 3 has a curve that uses 100% of the shadow detail and falls to 0% in the whites.

HOW TO SCAN VERY
CONTRASTY
PHOTOGRAPHS
(continued)

The blend preview is the lower right photograph in the quartet shown on screen; the other three are the original scan TIFF files. The finished blend is shown in Figure 9-3, bottom. It holds all of the detail that was in the original slide and substantially reduces the harsh contrast produced by the on-camera flash.

With a high-quality composite image at my disposal, good restoration became possible. Figure 9-4 shows what I achieved by applying the DIGITAL ROC plug-in to the blended image, making some Curves adjustments and doing a bit of dodging and burning-in.

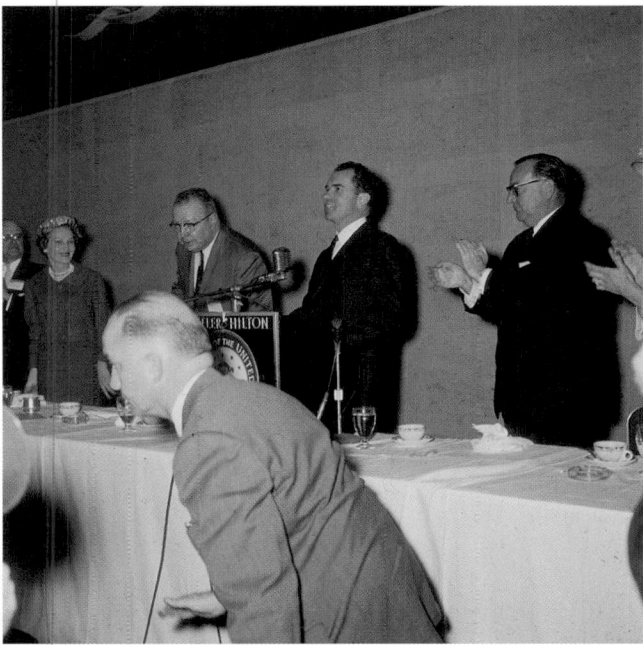

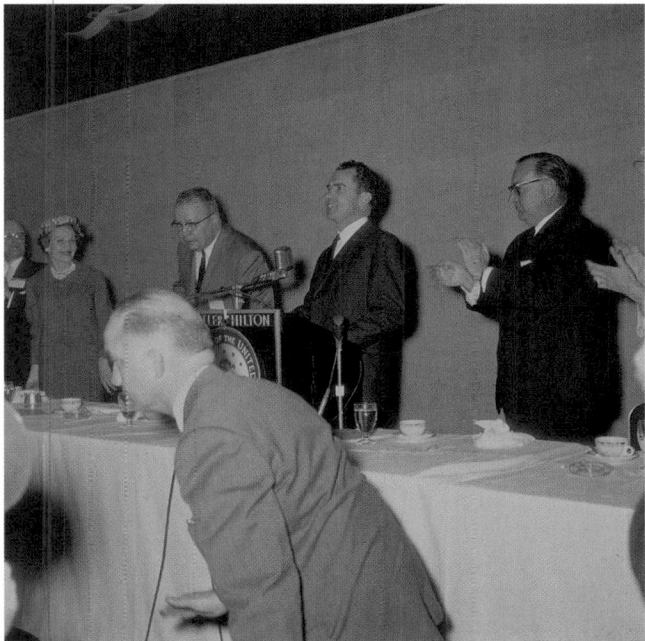

Fig. 9-3 The top figure is the best single scan I could make of the slide in Figure 9-1. It's too contrasty, with blown-out highlights and shadow detail that is too dark. The bottom figure shows the merged image I created with Stack Image in Figure 9-2. I applied color and tone corrections to produce Figure 9-4.

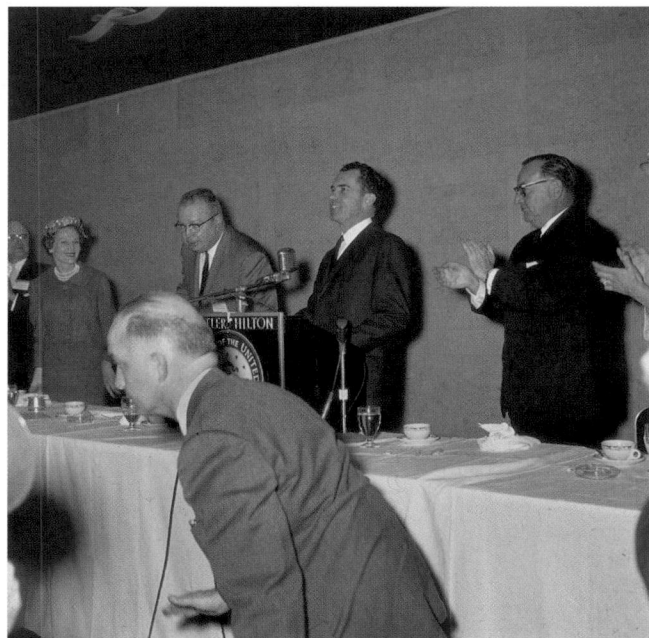

Fig. 9-4 Applying DIGITAL ROC and some Curves adjustments to Figure 9-3, bottom, gets me this photograph. The color and tones are now approximately correct, and I've retained the full range of detail that was visible in the slide.

Descreening a Halftone

Photographs in newspapers and magazines are not continuous-tone images; they are *halftones*. Halftones are made up of a fine pattern of dots that, from a distance, looks like continuous tones. In Chapter 4, Getting the Photo into the Computer, page 104, I discussed the best way to scan halftones. Now it's time to talk about how to remove the dot pattern; this is called *descreening*.

HOW TO ELIMINATE THE DOTS FROM NEWSPAPER PHOTOGRAPHS

Your scanner software probably has a descreening filter built into it. Figure 9-5 shows a halftone photograph I scanned at 1200 ppi. The greatly enlarged section on the left in Figure 9-6 shows the individual dots that make up the photograph. On the right is the scan I got when I turned that filter on. It reduced the dot pattern but didn't eliminate it entirely. We now need to turn to our software tools, which will do a better job than this.

Several different Photoshop (or Picture Window) filters can remove the halftone screen entirely, but choose wisely. Figure 9-7a shows the effect of applying the Dust & Scratches filter to the photograph. It completely eliminated the screen pattern, but it cost me some sharpness, and it made the contrast much worse. Dark areas became completely black, losing shadow detail; highlights got blown out.

Gaussian Blur worked very well (Figure 9-7b). The photograph is dot free, sharp, and has good tonal detail in both the highlights and the

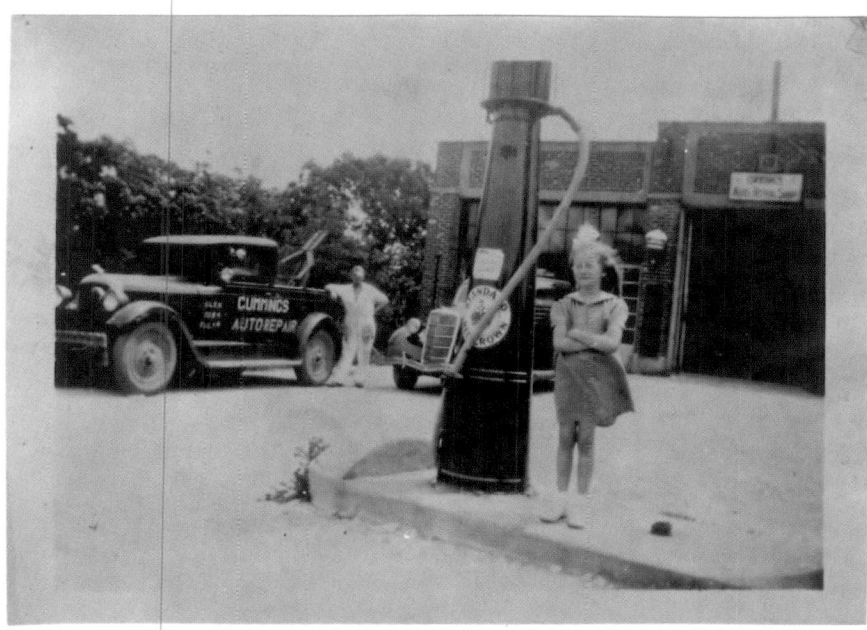

Fig. 9-5 This halftone photograph is in pretty good physical shape. It's just a little dark and has a few minor stains. The big challenge is getting rid of the halftone screen, shown enlarged in Figure 9-6.

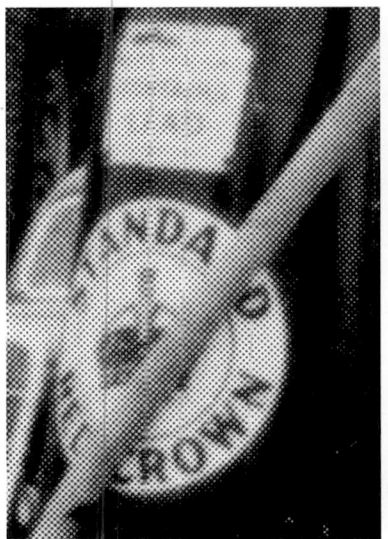
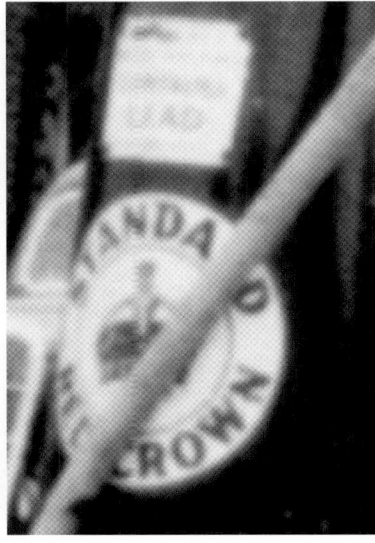

Fig. 9-6 The figure on the left is enlarged from Figure 9-5, to show the halftone dots that make up the print. One way to reduce the visibility of those dots is to turn on the Descreen option in your scanner software (right). This doesn't eliminate the dots, but it softens them. Other software tools (Figure 9-7) can eliminate them entirely.

shadows. The Box Blur (Figure 9-7c) filter does an even better job because it's a little sharper.

The Windows version of Focus Magic (see pp. 73 and 406) includes a stand-alone program (not the Photoshop plug-in component) that has a Despeckle filter. It can eliminate halftone dots while bringing out even more detail from the photograph (Figure 9-7d). Find the right "dot pitch"

HOW TO ELIMINATE THE DOTS FROM NEWSPAPER PHOTOGRAPHS (continued)

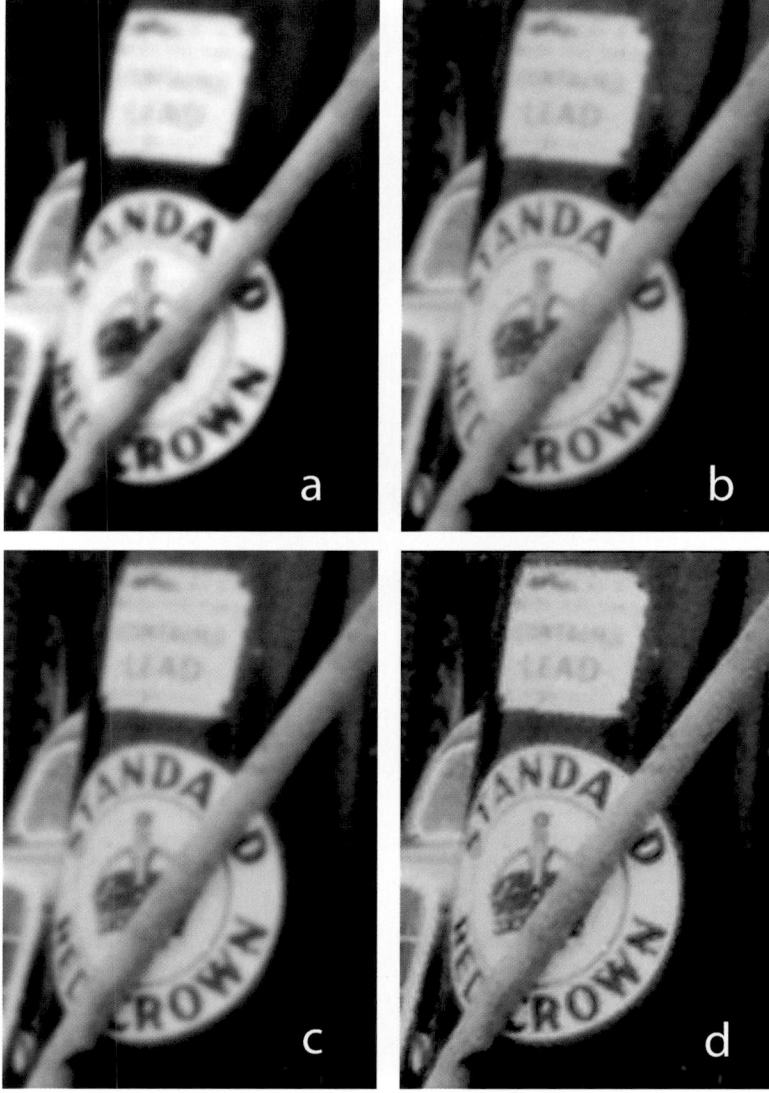

Fig. 9-7 Here are four different ways to get rid of halftone dots. Figure (a) uses the Dust & Scratches filter. That method loses sharpness and quite a bit of shadow detail. Gaussian Blur (b) works much better, and the Box Blur filter (c) better still. Both of these preserve the detail and tonality of the original photograph. Figure (d) is best of all; I created this with Focus Magic, carefully adjusting the sample radius until the dots completely disappeared.

HOW TO ELIMINATE THE DOTS FROM NEWSPAPER PHOTOGRAPHS (continued)

setting by checking the filter's preview window. Some values enhance the dot pattern; others suppress it. Correctly applied, Focus Magic reveals amazing amounts of detail. Figure 9-8 shows the entire cleaned-up, dot-free, sharpness-enhanced, and tone-corrected photograph."

Getting the Most Detail out of Your Photograph

Many photographs hold a wealth of hidden detail that can be revealed by the right tools. Good software techniques can do more than just sharpen up edges; they can bring out fine details that were invisible in

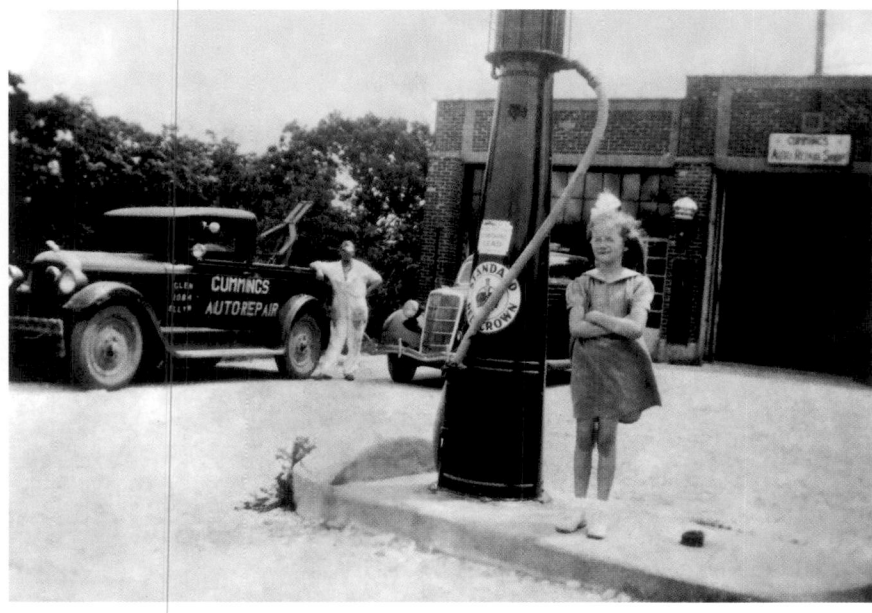

Fig. 9-8 Here's Figure 9-5, after descreening with Focus Magic, some Curves adjustments, and a bit of dodging to clean up the stains.

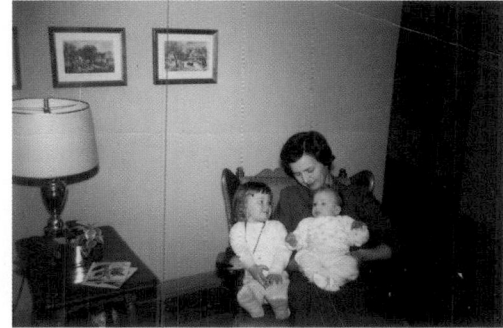
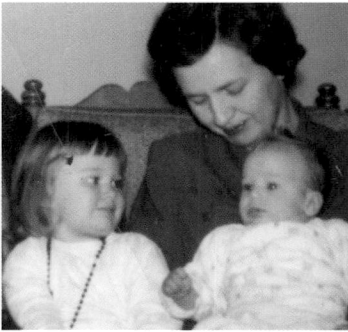

Fig. 9-9 This photograph has some physical damage, but otherwise it is in great shape. It has excellent tonality and no noise or grain. As the enlargement on the right shows, it could be sharper. There are ways to achieve that!

the original print. In some cases they can rescue unacceptably blurry photographs; in others they take an inadequately sharp photograph and improve the detail enough to let you enlarge it substantially.

The ideal candidate for detail enhancement is a photograph that has good tonality and little visual noise: no heavy texturing, visible grain, or extensive scratches or cracks. Minimal noise is important because all of these techniques enhance fine noise along with fine detail. The best of them work mostly on the photographic detail and don't enhance noise too much, but there will always be some increase. If you start out with a visually noisy original, you will not have a good-looking photograph after you've sharpened it up.

Figure 9-9 is a great candidate for detail enhancement. As the enlargement on the right shows, the photograph has some cracks and scratches and a scattering of dirt and dust, but there's no film grain, paper texture, or unevenness to the tones. The original photograph was only 2 inches by 3 inches, so I scanned it at 1200 ppi with the intention of enlarging it. I cleaned up the specks and cracks with the Dust & Scratches filter, using the settings shown in Figure 9-10. Assigning that filter to the History Brush, I painted out the flaws.

HOW TO INCREASE SHARPNESS AND FINE DETAIL IN A PHOTOGRAPH

There are several good ways to bring out detail in this photograph. A poor way is to use Photoshop's Unsharp Mask, which I did using the filter settings shown in Figure 9-10 to produce Figure 9-11a. That emphasized edges, but it didn't actually bring out any new detail.

Photoshop's new Smart Sharpen filter, with "Lens Blur" selected, does much nicer filtering than Photoshop's simpler sharpening tools. Be sure to check "More Accurate" to get the best results (Figure 9-12). Figure 9-11b shows what this filter accomplished. It's much more natural looking than the photograph created with the Unsharp Mask filter; even delicate detail in the couch and the baby's clothing was brought out. There's a slight increase in overall image noise (likely not visible in reproduction), but it's not enough to be bothersome; it just looks like very fine film grain.

Better still is Focus Magic. I applied it with a radius of 7 pixels and the Image Source set to "conventional" to produce Figure 9-11c. There is very little additional noise but a real increase in fine detail. This photograph doesn't merely look sharper, it actually is sharper.

The final enhancement tool I used was PixelGenius's PhotoKit Sharpener utilities. This large collection of automated routines provides myriad ways to sharpen a photograph with minimal increases in noise and other kinds of visual garbage. For Figure 9-11d, I used the Creative Sharpener module and ran the Super Sharpener option.

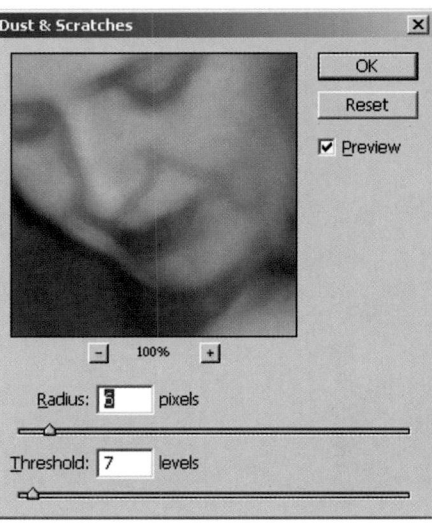 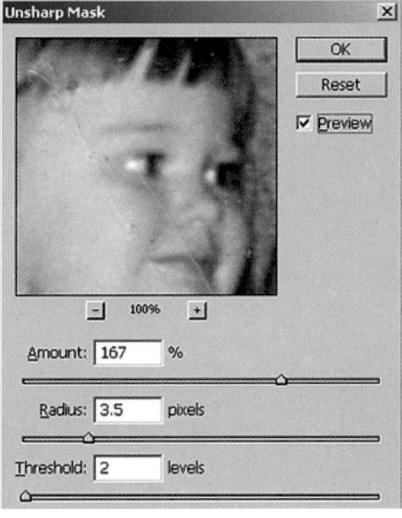

Fig. 9-10 I used the Dust & Scratches filter in conjunction with the History Brush to get rid of the dust and cracks in Figure 9-9, prepping it for sharpening. Photoshop's standard tool, Unsharp Mask (right), isn't the best choice for that (see Figure 9-11a).

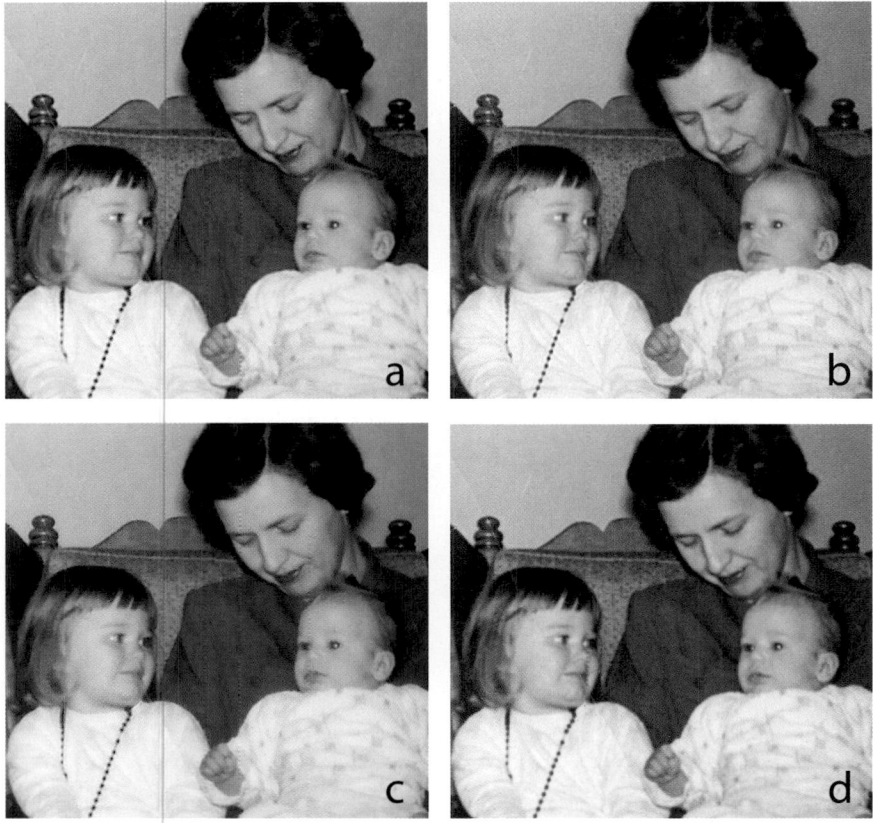

Fig. 9-11 There are different ways to sharpen up Figure 9-9. (a) The Unsharp Mask option, using the settings from Figure 9-10, doesn't really improve fine detail. It just exaggerates edges and produces the well-known "oversharpened" look. Photoshop's new Smart Sharpen filter works much better. I selected "Lens Blur" to create figure (b). It's just as sharp as figure (a), but it looks much more natural. Figure (c) is the product of Focus Magic running with a 7-pixel radius. This filter produces a real increase in fine detail and sharpness, not just the illusion of one. Last, figure (d) shows PixelGenius's PhotoKit Sharpener utilities, a collection of useful automated scripts that do sharpening in multiple layers that you can modify to suit the particular photograph.

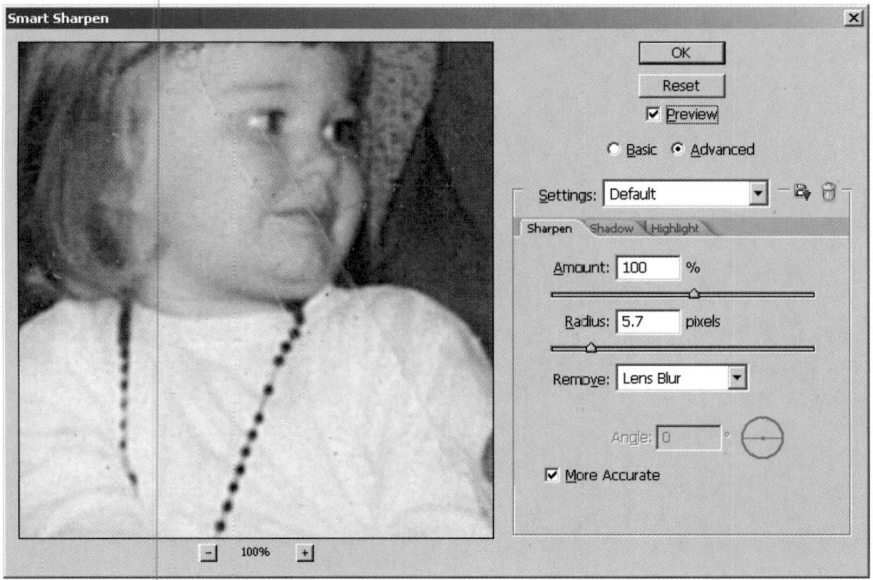

Fig. 9-12 Here are the Smart Sharpen settings I used to create Figure 9-11b. I've selected "Lens Blur" as the filter method I want to use and checked "More Accurate" because it produces better-looking results.

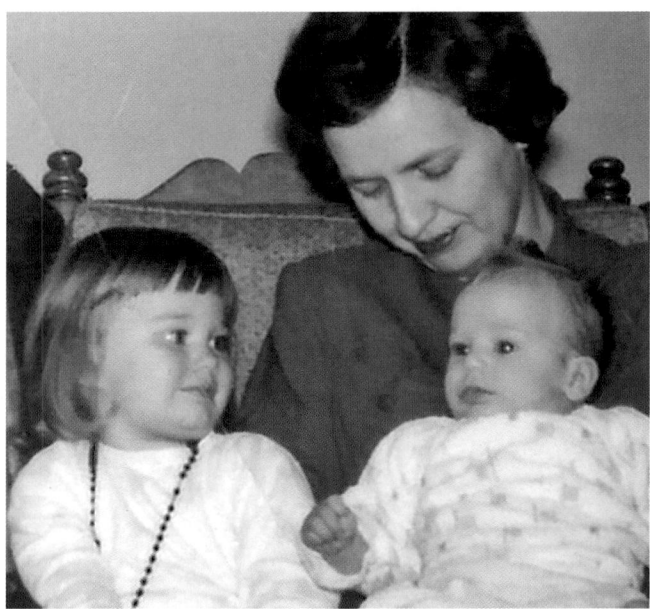

Fig. 9-13 The Shadow/ Highlight tool improves the detail in Figure 9-11c. Using this tool with the settings from Figure 9-14 makes both highlight and shadow details clearer.

HOW TO INCREASE SHARPNESS AND FINE DETAIL IN A PHOTOGRAPH (continued)

Sharpening isn't the only way to bring out detail. I created Figure 9-13 by taking the photograph I sharpened with Focus Magic and running it through the Shadow/Highlight filter using the settings shown in Figure 9-14. (See Chapter 5, Restoring Tone, page 145, for complete instructions on how to use this filter; it has a lot of different options!) This opened up shadows and tamed highlights in a fashion that made detail in those parts of the photograph much clearer. The results are not actually one bit sharper than Figure 9-11c, but the improved contrast reveals the details much more clearly.

What Do You Do with a Tintype?

Tintypes raise interesting questions about your goals in performing a restoration. Is your objective to make the photograph look the way it did originally, or to make it look like a good photograph by today's standards?

A tintype by its very nature is extremely dark. It's a B&W silver negative on a piece of black-enameled metal (usually iron). The silver image looks lighter gray than the black enamel so the photo appears as a positive. The range of tones runs not from white to black but from dark gray to black. It's not what we expect to see in modern photographs.

Figure 9-15 shows an old tintype. Figure 9-16 shows the histogram my scanner software generated for that tintype, as well as the level settings I used to make a full-range scan. You can see from the histogram

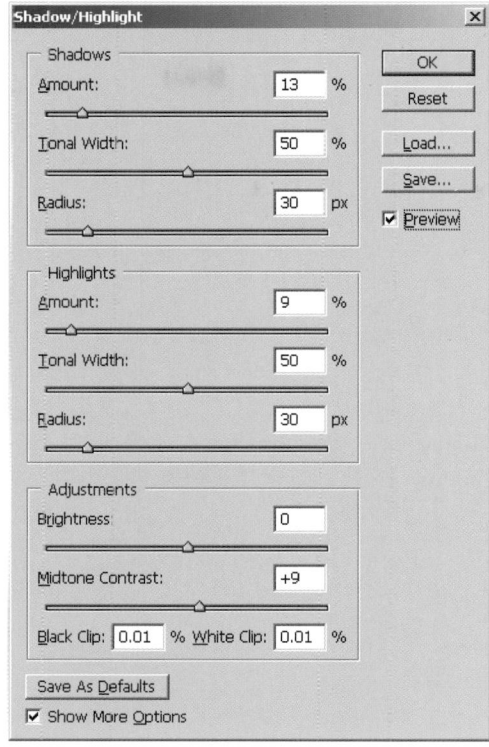

Fig. 9-14 The Shadow/ Highlight settings that produced Figure 9-13. I'm doing just a small amount of shadow enhancement but a moderate amount of highlight enhancement. I kicked up the Midtone Contrast a little bit to ensure that the photograph didn't look too flat.

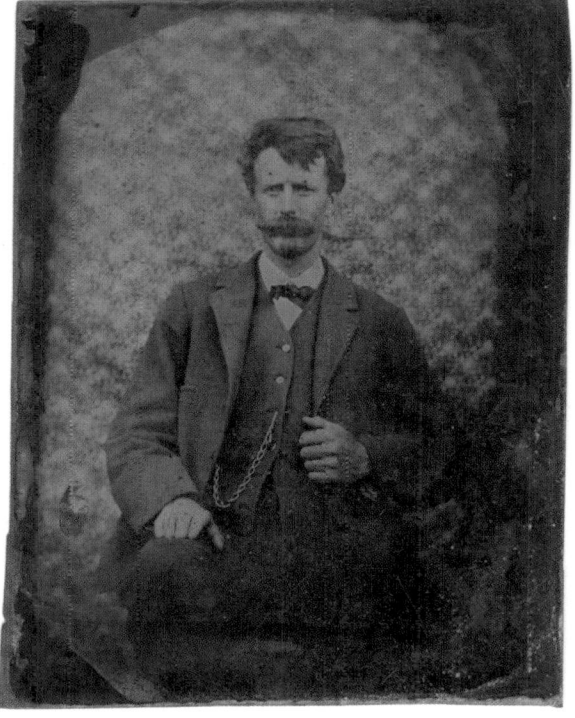

Fig. 9-15 Tintypes are naturally very dark. The "positive" image is the result of laying a dark-gray silver negative image on top of a black substrate. The scanner software histogram in Figure 9-16 shows how dark the original is.

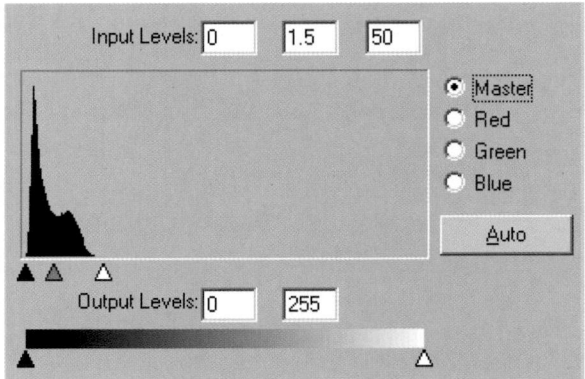

Fig. 9-16 This histogram for Figure 9-15 is typical of tintypes. All of the tones are compressed into the dark end of the scale. I've moved the scanner software Levels sliders in to bracket that narrow range in order to capture as much information as possible. It's a good idea to scan tintypes in 16-bit mode. The result is shown in Figure 9-17.

that the tintype's extremely dark; this is certainly a case in which you'd want to scan in 16-bit mode.

Figure 9-17 is the scan I made that extracted the maximum tonal information from the tintype. The red channel showed the clearest image with the least dirt and scratches, so I used it to do the partial restoration you see in Figure 9-18, left. At this point, I'm very close to having a good-looking photograph; I still have to remove some scratches and dust specks and make some final adjustments to the tones in the shadows and the background.

HOW TO MAKE A
PHOTOGRAPH LOOK
LIKE A TINTYPE

This doesn't look anything like the original tintype. It looks like a modern photograph, with modern-photograph tonality. Figure 9-18, right, shows my simulation of the tintype "look." I got that by applying the curves in Figure 9-19 to darken the restored image. So, which version is correct? That will depend on your objectives—on whether this is supposed be an aesthetically pleasing restoration or a historically accurate one.

Stitching Scans Together

Sometimes you'll want to restore a photograph that is larger than your scanner can accommodate. Scanning a photograph in sections is not difficult, but there are two problems to address when stitching sectional scans together: Some misregistration and slight differences in exposure might exist between the separate scans.

You won't want the scanner making different exposure and contrast adjustments for each section of the photograph, so turn off as much of the scanner's automatic exposure control as you can. Ideally, the exposures for all the sections should be absolutely identical. In practice, this

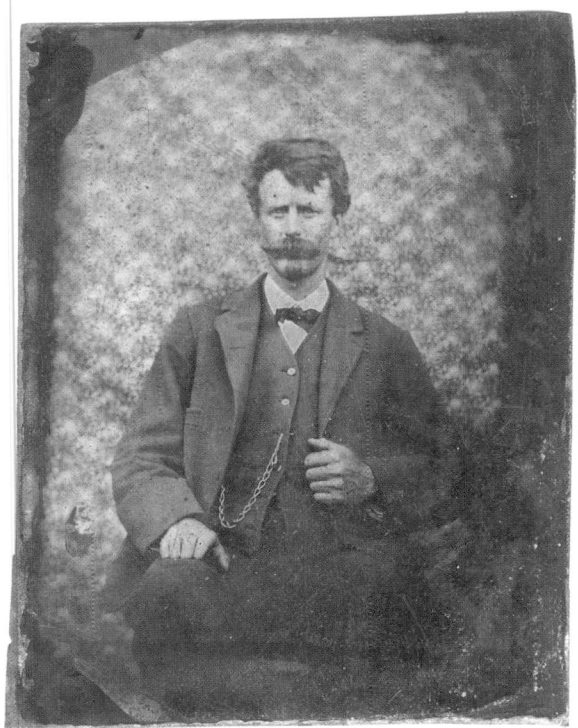

Fig. 9-17 The scan I made of Figure 9-15 using scanner settings from Figure 9-16. This doesn't look at all like a proper tintype, but it provides the maximum amount of information to work with for a restoration.

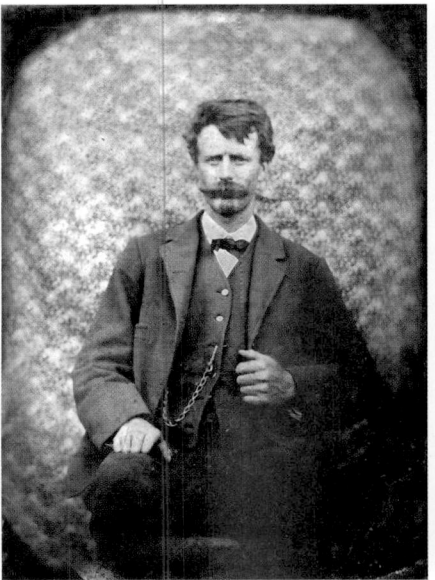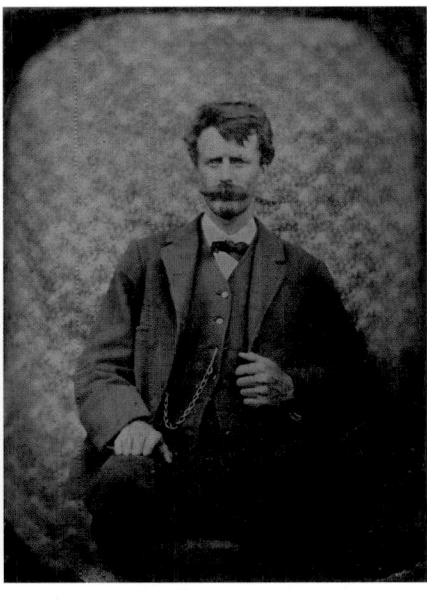

Fig. 9-18 What's the right way to restore a tintype? The figure on the left is the restoration I did from Figure 9-17, treating the image as if it were a conventional photograph. Consequently, I aimed for a photograph with good contrast and a full range of tones from black to white. On the right is the new "tintype" I created by adding a Curves adjustment layer that used the settings in Figure 9-19. This preserves the look of the original for a more historically correct restoration.

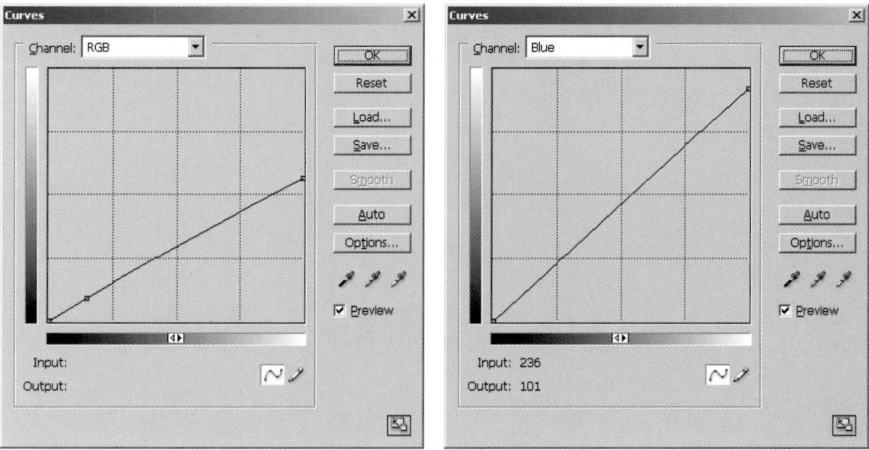

Fig. 9-19 A simple Curves adjustment turns a normal-looking photograph into one that looks like a tintype. The curve on the left darkens all the tones and lowers the contrast, so that the "whites" become grays, just as they are in a real tintype. The curve on the right adds a bit of yellow to the photograph because silver negative images are usually a little bit warm in hue. The result, shown Figure 9-18, right, is a faithful reconstruction.

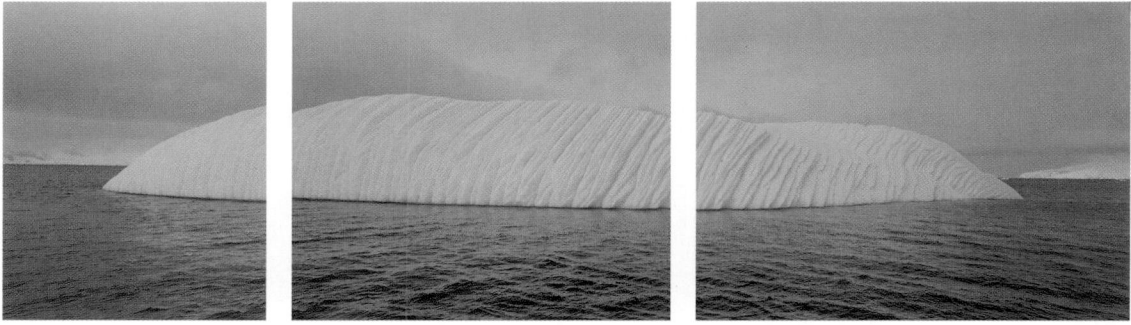

Fig. 9-20 I needed to scan this 6-cm by 17-cm negative in three sections because it was too big for my scanner. Here are the three overlapping scans I created. There is a slight color mismatch; there's also a little bit of geometric distortion. (Original photograph copyright by Stuart D. Klipper.)

doesn't always happen. The internal scanner calibration from scan to scan may not be identical. You should expect to see some slight exposure mismatches between the sections.

HOW TO COMBINE SCANS TO MAKE ONE LARGE PHOTOGRAPH

Figure 9-20 shows three sectional scans I made from a 6-cm by 17-cm negative. This magnificent photograph of an iceberg by Stuart D. Klipper had been damaged and was in need of repair. First I aligned the scans so that they'd blend seamlessly when I merged them. I copied them into separate layers of a single file and set the layer opacities to 50% so that I could see how they overlapped. Figure 9-21 shows a close-up of the overlap between the center and right-hand scans. I registered the

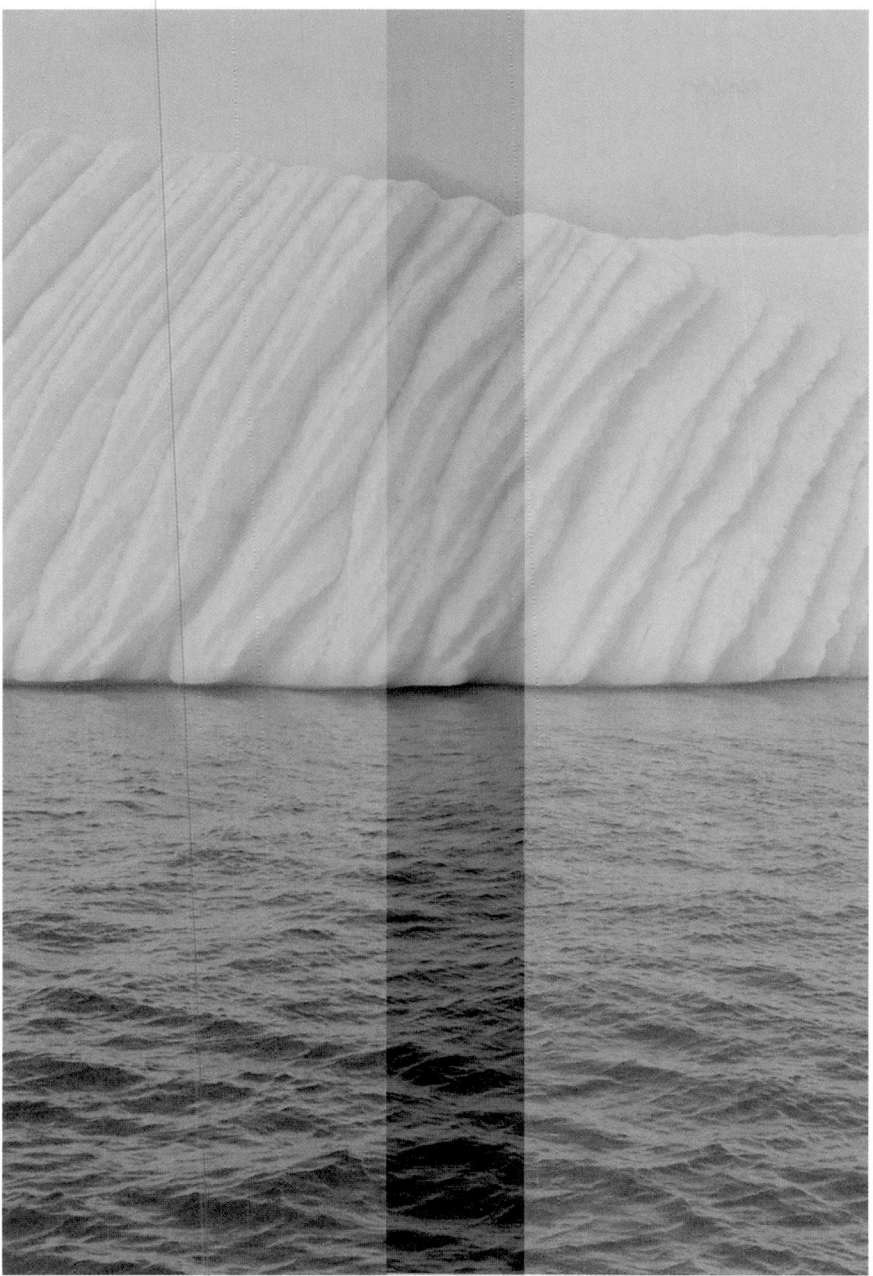

Fig. 9-21 Overlapping and aligning the middle and right-hand scans shows that they don't quite match up. The iceberg is perfectly superimposed at the top, but the wavelets at the bottom of the photo are misaligned. This is visible as a doubled image. I can fix this with Photoshop's Transform/ Warp tool (Figure 9-22).

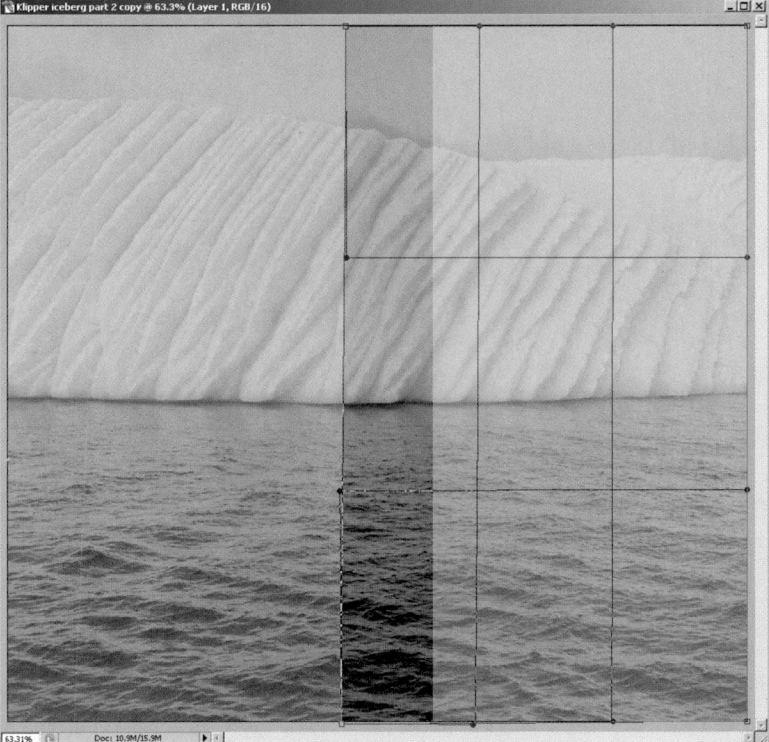

Fig. 9-22 In this screenshot of the Warp tool in action, I selected a rectangular region in the right-hand scan and created the Warp grid. By adjusting individual points in the grid, I can transform the left side of the scan so that it matches the middle scan perfectly. Warp creates a smooth transition from this bit of distortion into the rest of the rightmost scan.

HOW TO COMBINE SCANS TO MAKE ONE LARGE PHOTOGRAPH (continued)

two scans at a point at the top of the iceberg. The doubled images at the bottom of the overlap band indicate that one of the scans has a little geometric distortion.

In Photoshop, the Warp operation is the best way to fix that. It superimposes a 3-by-3 mesh on the layer (Figure 9-22). You can grab a point in the image and drag it to a new position and the rest of the layer smoothly warps to accommodate the change. Alternatively, you can manipulate control points at the corners of the mesh by their little solid-dot handles and warp the mesh that way.

If Photoshop's Warp adjustment doesn't give you enough control over the geometry of the image, turn to Picture Window, which has a much more powerful Composite Transform. You can set up to 63 control points in the Composite Transform mesh using the multipoint option. The Composite Transform does scaling, rotation, and warping all in one operation.

Once I had the three scans aligned, I set their opacities back to 100%. Now I had to match their colors. In Chapter 5, Restoring Tone, page 129, I told you about clicking on a photograph to create sample points in the Info window and to assign control points to curves (Figure 5-16). I set four sample points in the left-hand scan layer, right next to the bound-

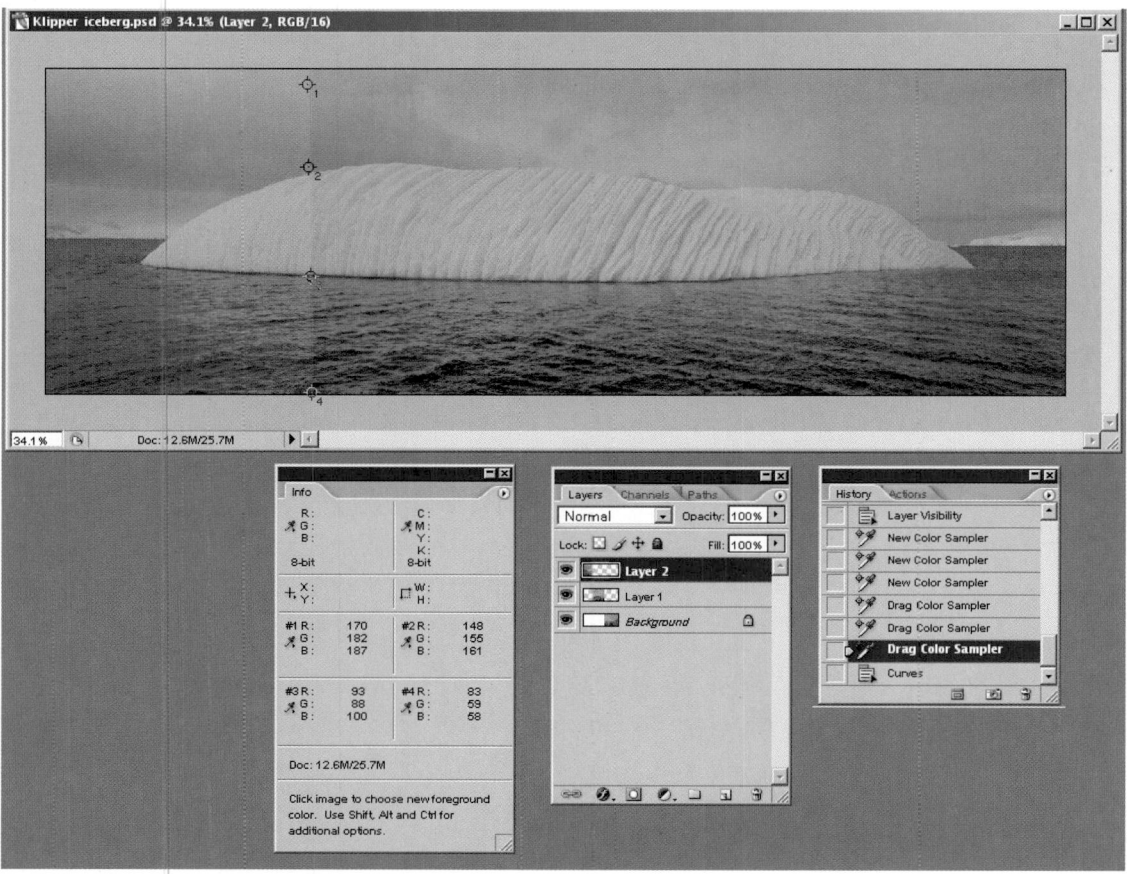

Fig. 9-23 This screenshot shows me setting up the sample points that will let me match the color between the left (Layer 2) and middle (Layer 1) scans in Figure 9-24. I set four sample points near the boundary between the scans that encompass a broad range of tones and colors.

ary with the center scan layer (Figure 9-23). All four points are actually in the region where the scans overlap; you can't see the overlap in the illustration because the upper layer opacity is 100%. That overlap's important because I use the sample points to compare the RGB values in the two layers.

I picked those points to represent a broad range of tones. The RGB values for the sample points are shown in the Info window. I made a screenshot of the Info window and pasted it into a new image window so that I could refer to the RGB values for the left-side scan layer while working on the middle scan layer. (If you don't want to clutter your computer screen with unnecessary images, you can print the screen with those RGB numbers onto a piece of paper for reference.)

I switched to the middle scan layer and launched the Curves tool. (I could have created a Curves adjustment layer associated with the scan

HOW TO COMBINE
SCANS TO MAKE
ONE LARGE
PHOTOGRAPH
(continued)

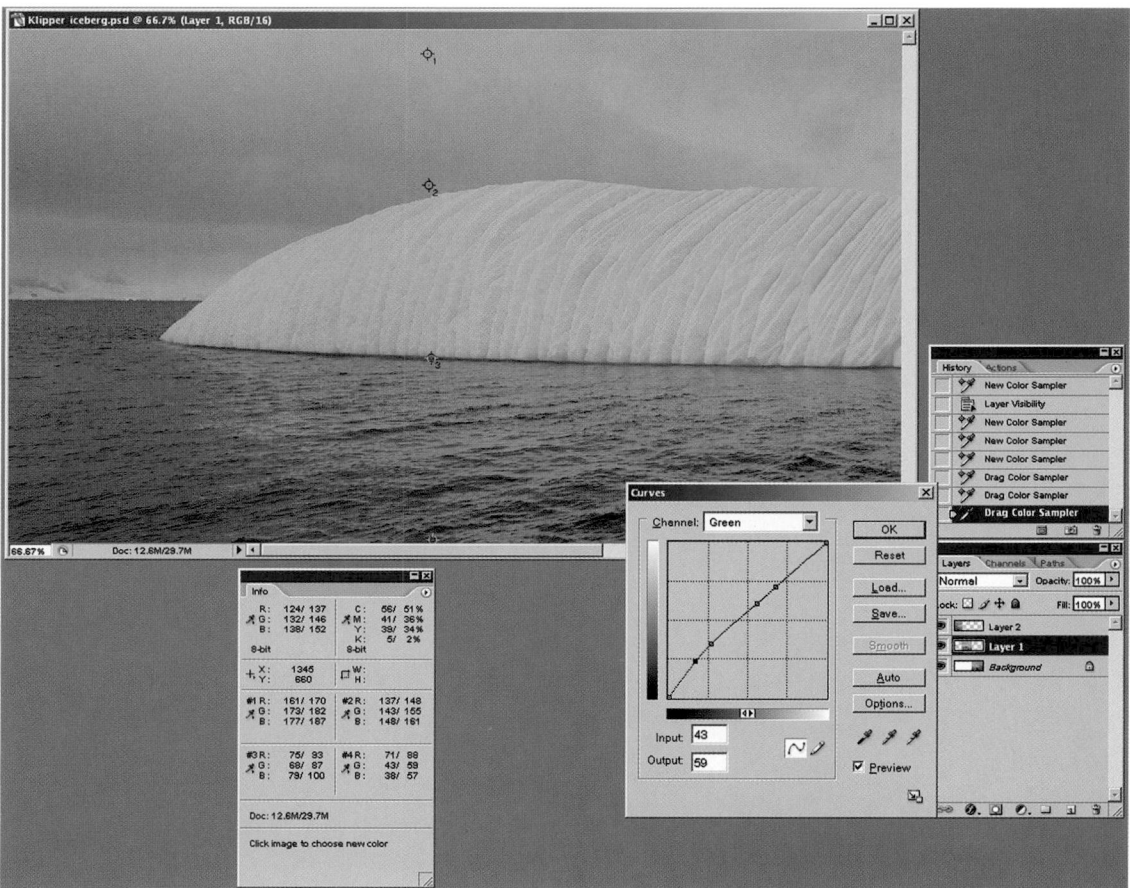

Fig. 9-24 This screenshot shows me making a Curves adjustments to the green channel of the middle scan that corrects sample point #4. Compare sample point #4's values in the Info windows in Fig. 9-23 and this figure. I've adjusted the Green curve for that point to make the two values equal (a value of 59). Doing this for all four points in all three channels produces a very good match between all the colors in the scans.

HOW TO COMBINE
SCANS TO MAKE
ONE LARGE
PHOTOGRAPH
(continued)

layer if I wanted to preserve the option of going back and readjusting the curves later.) I shift-control-clicked each of the sample points, creating four control points in the Curves window (Figure 9-24).

To match the colors between the two layers, I moved the control points in the individual curves so that their output values were the same as the ones I had recorded for the left-hand scan. For example, Figure 9-24 shows me working on sample point #4 on the green curve. That had a value of 59 in the left-hand scan, so I typed 59 into the output box for that curve point. In this manner I entered all of the sample-point RGB values for the left-hand scan into the curve control points for the center scan.

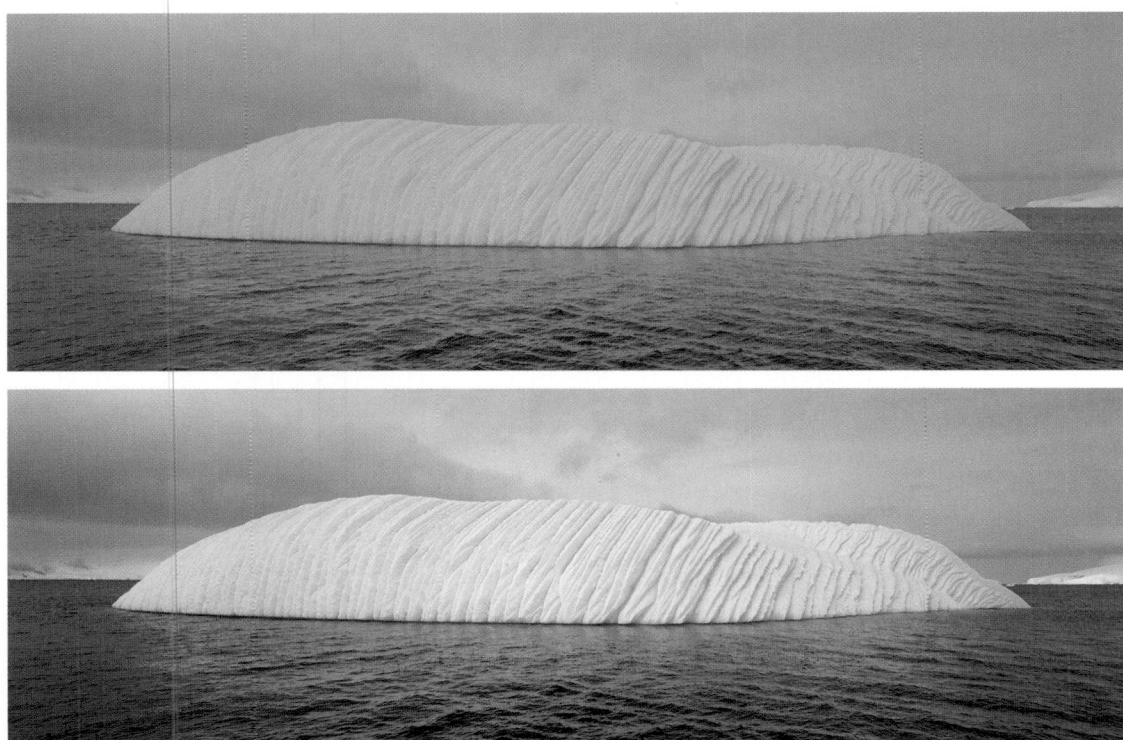

Fig. 9-25 The top figure shows the three merged scans after color matching and alignment. This appears to have been a single, seamless scan. The bottom figure shows the fully restored photograph after color and tone correction with a Curves adjustment layer. (Photograph copyright by Stuart D. Klipper.)

The two scans now blended perfectly; as long as scans don't differ too much to begin with, this four-point adjustment scheme can produce a perfect color match. I repeated this procedure for the middle and right-hand scan layers. That gave me a seamless blend between all three sections of the photo, as you can see in Figure 9-25, upper. All the file needed was overall color correction to produce a lovely, finished photograph (Figure 9-25, lower).

HOW TO COMBINE
SCANS TO MAKE
ONE LARGE
PHOTOGRAPH
(continued)

Improving the Original

Just what do I mean by "improving the original"? A recurring theme throughout this book has been my admittedly perfectionist quest to create the best possible print of a photograph. What do I think makes for a better print?

- Rich and more accurate color
- More accurate tonal rendition

- Better density range in the print

- Better and sharper detail

Many original photographs weren't all that great to begin with, even before they started to deteriorate. Your typical amateur photograph is not usually perfectly composed, perfectly exposed, perfectly in focus, and perfectly printed. Professionally made photographs may have an overall higher level of quality (although many don't), but the photographer can only do so much. Photographic films and papers don't have perfect color and tonal rendition. Even the most skilled photographers are limited by the materials with which they work.

As long as I don't need to produce a historically accurate restoration, I can't resist making little improvements. It may be sharpening up the photograph and bringing out fine detail that wasn't apparent, or perhaps correcting the color and exposure so that they're exactly right instead of merely being close to what they should be. Sometimes I'll bring out highlight and shadow detail in a previously too-contrasty photograph or eliminate excessive film grain and an annoying paper texture. I can even dodge, burn-in, and crop to improve composition.

Do not misunderstand; I am not saying the originals were bad photographs! By and large they're very good photographs. They're just not perfect photographs, and what is not perfect can often be improved, especially with the power of digital manipulation. Review the many restorations I present throughout this book, especially the complete restorations that I present in the next chapter (Chapter 10, Examples). You'll see that I often go beyond the limitations of the original to produce a better photograph than existed before. This is where the "Art" I talk about in the Introduction and Chapter 1 comes in—this is where you think like an artist and a photographer, not like a technician. Here are two examples to illustrate this.

In Chapter 3, Software for Restoration, page 61, I used a self-portrait by noted photographer Tee Corinne (Figure 9-26a) to introduce the power of the DIGITAL ROC Photoshop plug-in. It's just the kind of problem that ROC was designed to solve. Figure 9-26b is a very faithful rendition of the original photograph, and is indeed almost entirely the plug-in's doing.

Consulting with Tee on this matter, we both agreed that while this may accurately portray what the color film recorded 30 years ago, that didn't make it the best possible interpretation of this photograph. Films of that era tended to be a little contrasty and low in color saturation. The color rendition was a bit cool for Tee's taste because the portrait was photographed by bluish sky light. We agreed to improve on the original.

First I reduced the excessive contrast in the midtones to bring out more highlight and shadow detail. When I did this restoration, I used an "inverted-S" curve, as I discuss in Chapter 5, Restoring Tone, page 148, to get Figure 9-26c; today I'd probably use the Shadow/Highlight

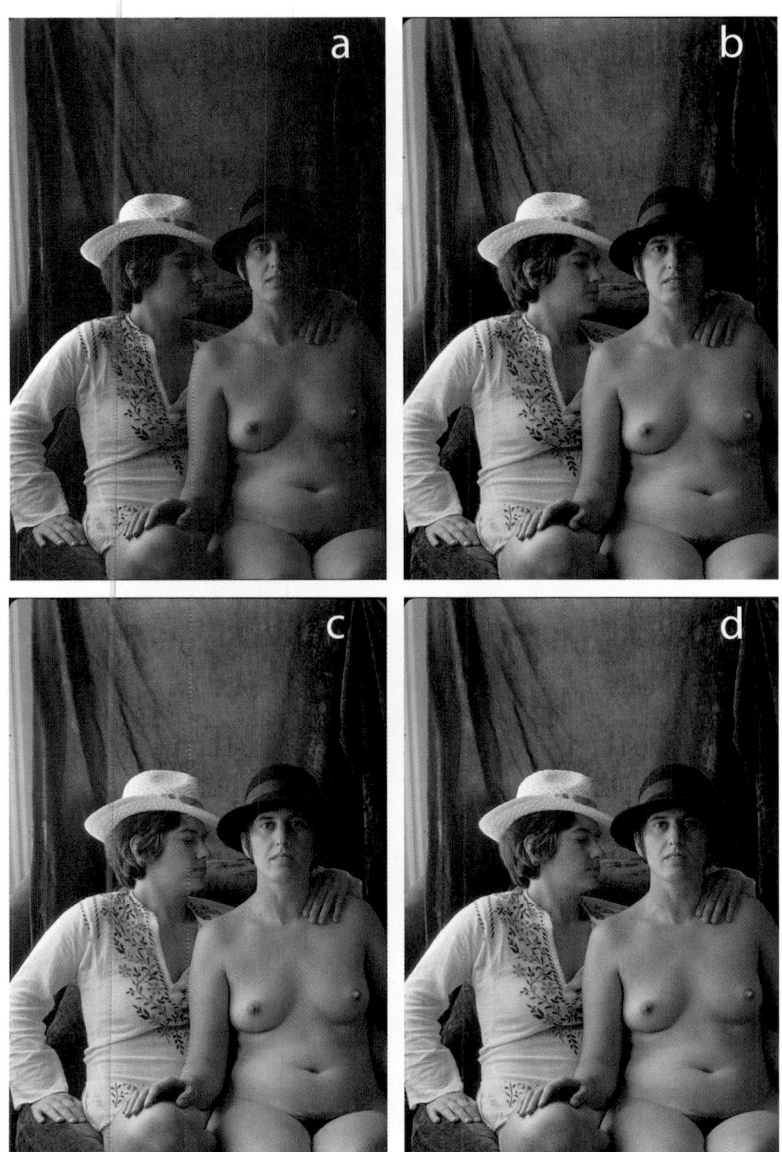

adjustment. The tonal rendition is much nicer, but lowering the midtone contrast made the saturation worse. I increased the saturation by 20 points with the Hue/Saturation adjustment and made a slight Curves adjustment to brighten the midtones a bit. That produced Figure 9-26d, which I think is a much better version of the photograph than the original. If it were my photograph, I'd probably stop here. But Tee wanted slightly warmer hues, so after a little more work with Curves, we got to Figure 9-27. That is now the final and definitive version of this

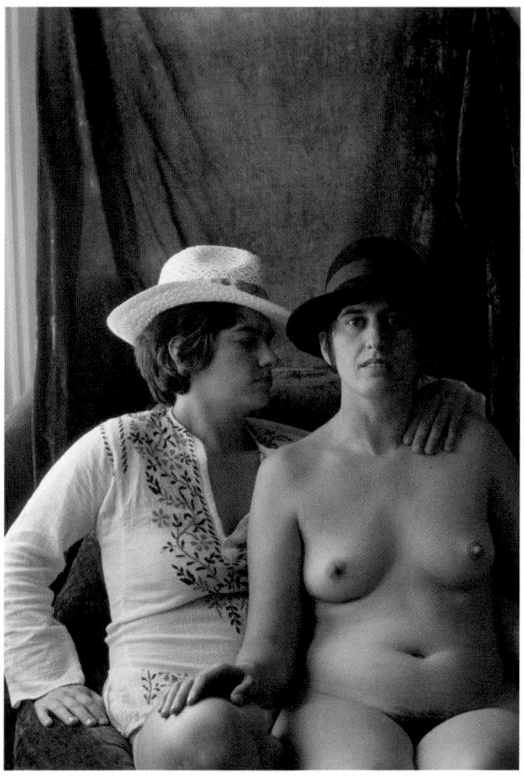

Fig. 9-27 This is the finished restoration, just as Tee and I would have it. It is a slightly warmed-up version of Figure 9-26d; a modest Curves adjustment did the trick. This looks better than the original photograph did. (Photograph copyright by Tee Corinne.)

photograph, one that Tee and I both feel is better than the original she made 30 years ago.

Figure 9-28 is the cleaned-up version of the photograph I sharpened earlier in this chapter (page 323). As a straight restoration, it's almost finished. A couple of faint folds in the paper are visible in the background, but once I erase those, it will be a pristine version of the original photograph. I think it could be a much better photograph than this!

Since I had already determined that I could sharpen and extract considerably more fine detail from the photograph, I decided to crop it to produce a much better composition (Figure 9-29). That wouldn't have been possible without the sharpening techniques I used; the original was only 2 inches by 3 inches, and it wasn't very crisp. But Focus Magic pulled up all sorts of fine detail for me, and the Shadow/Highlight adjustment brought out the details in the children's clothing and mother's hair and dress very nicely.

To finish off this photograph, I did a little dodging and burning-in, evening out the lighting on the walls so there wasn't a distracting bright spot in the upper left and dodging the mother's left side so you could better see her arm and clothing. That was it!

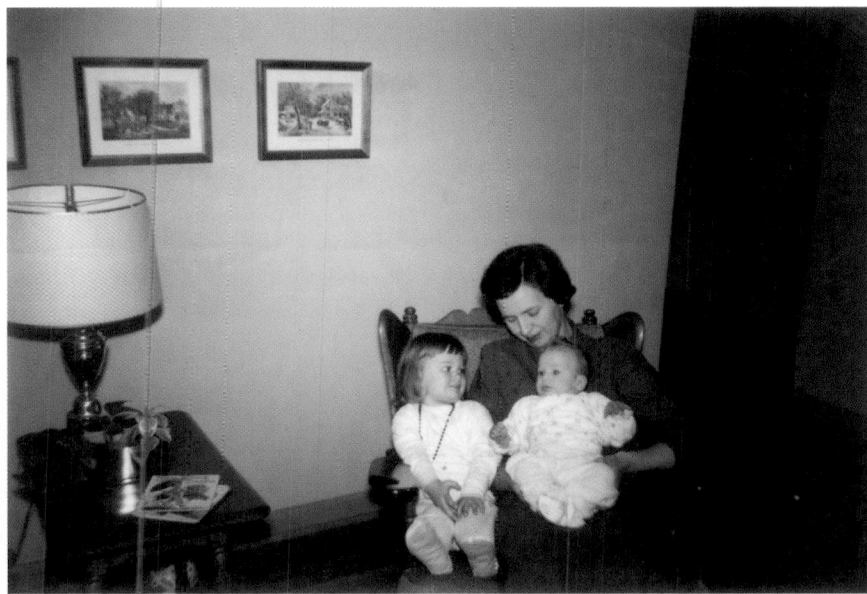

Fig. 9-28 This is the nearly restored version of Figure 9-9. It's been sharpened and cleaned up, except for a few faint folds in the paper. It's a good restoration of the original photograph, but that photograph can be improved (see Figure 9-29)!

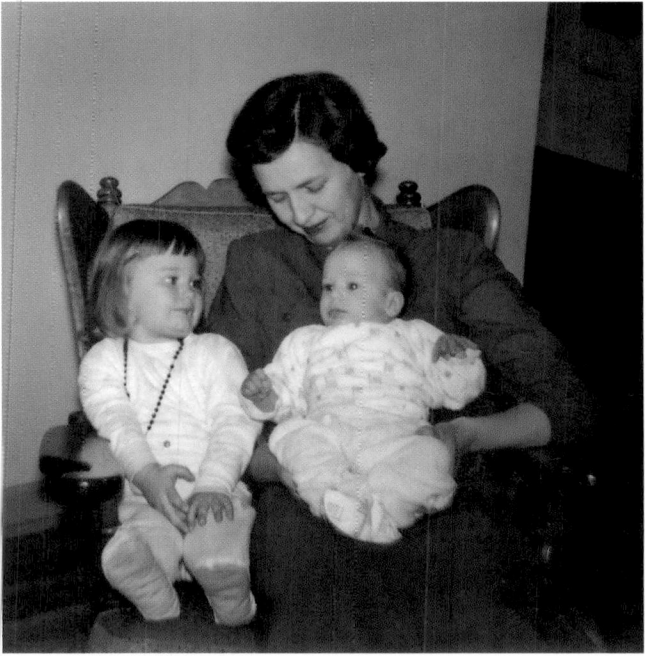

Fig. 9-29 Here's the new and improved version of Figure 9-28. I cropped away the extraneous and distracting material to produce a composition that focused on the mother and children. Next I dodged the mother's left side to even out the lighting and improve the detail. Finally, I burnt in the upper left corner to remove a hot spot on the wall. What was previously an acceptable snapshot is now a really great one. I could have eliminated the "on-flash look" in the skin tones, but I wanted to preserve the snapshot feel of the original, rather than make this look like a professionally done portrait.

I intentionally left the "on-flash look" alone. I could've retouched the faces and the clothing to get rid of the hot spots, thus making this look like a very professional photograph. I didn't because I wanted to preserve the snapshot feel of the photograph. I simply made it look like an exceptionally good one.

Up to this point in the book, I've been instructing you in myriad specific techniques for doing restorations. In the last section of this chapter, we started to pay more attention to the overall purpose and ultimate results of restoration. That's what the next chapter, Examples, is entirely about: how all these specific methodologies work together to produce complete and finished restorations.

CHAPTER 10

Examples

The examples in this chapter are case studies in restoration. Each example takes a photograph, step by step, from its original form to its fully restored glory. Within the limits of space I've left nothing out. No magic takes place behind the curtain.

As I said back in Chapter 1, what I enjoy most about doing photo restoration is going for "the best of all possible prints" from a damaged photograph. I love to take the restoration process to its limits and see just how perfect a photograph I can get. The examples in this chapter are precisely these kinds of perfectionist performances. They aren't necessarily complicated, but they are all as masterful and complete as I know how to make them.

What I want to convey in this chapter is not a set of marching orders but some understanding of how one gets from A to Z. It's about more than noting the specific tools that I use to solve each problem in the restoration. It's as much about the order in which I tackle the problems, and how I decide what path to follow to get to my goal.

This doesn't mean you have to be a perfectionist! You needn't travel all the way from A to Z to get great results; you can stop at P and have restorations that are more than good enough to make most people very happy. Chapters 5 through 9 are filled with examples that don't go to the ultimate limit of the restoration art, but they still look good.

Always remember that these are examples, not prescriptions. Give the same photograph to 10 different restorers, and they will take as many different approaches to fixing it. When you read these examples, I hope you'll sometimes find yourself thinking, "Wouldn't it have made as much sense for Ctein to address this problem this other way?" The answer is very likely "Yes!" There is never one right answer, and the more right answers you can come up, with the more tools you'll have at your disposal when you encounter a new problem.

Example 1: Repairing an Old Glass Plate

The 4-inch by 6-inch glass plate negative shown in Figure 10-1-a was made in the 1920s in Venice or Lido, Italy. It's tarnished, but otherwise

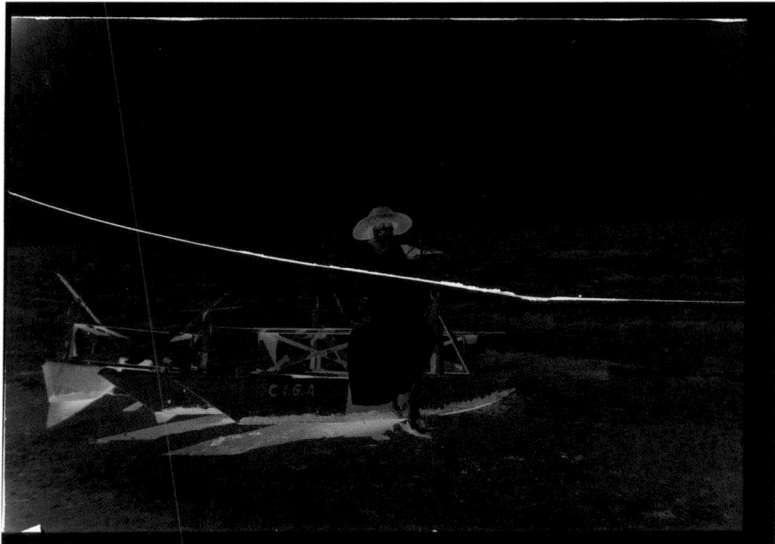

Fig. 10-1-a This glass plate negative dates from the 1920s. The silver image is in excellent condition, albeit very dense, but the plate has been broken right down the middle!

the silver image is in great shape. While the negative is very dense, typical for photographs of the time, the edges of the plate are clear and only slightly yellowed. The only thing that prevents me from printing this plate conventionally on a Grade 0 paper is that it's broken in two!

After masking off the area surrounding the image on the plate (to reduce flare, see Chapter 4, Getting the Photo into the Computer, page 113), I scanned the plate at 1200 ppi in 16-bit RGB mode. As the scanner software histogram shows (Figure 10-1-b), almost all the tonal information is concentrated in the lower 20% of the scale. The scattering of values higher than that corresponds to light leaking through the cracks and some small missing patches of emulsion.

After a couple of trial scans, I settled on a white level of 100 and a midpoint (gamma) adjustment of 2.4. That's an extreme gamma, but experiments showed that it produced a good-looking negative on the screen. I wasn't too worried about the precise curve shape because I was working in 16-bit mode. Glass plates should be scanned with the emulsion side of the plate in contact with the platen because that's where the scanner's plane of focus is. That means a scan will come out left-right reversed, so after I completed the scan I flipped the image horizontally.

Figure 10-1-c shows the resulting scan; it's much clearer than Figure 10-1-a, which shows an unadjusted scan. The histogram in Figure 10-1-d shows that I have an acceptable range of information, with no clipping of the shadow or highlight detail in the photograph.

The RGB scan is nearly 200 MB, and there's no useful color information in the photo, so I used Channel Mixer to convert the scan to gray-

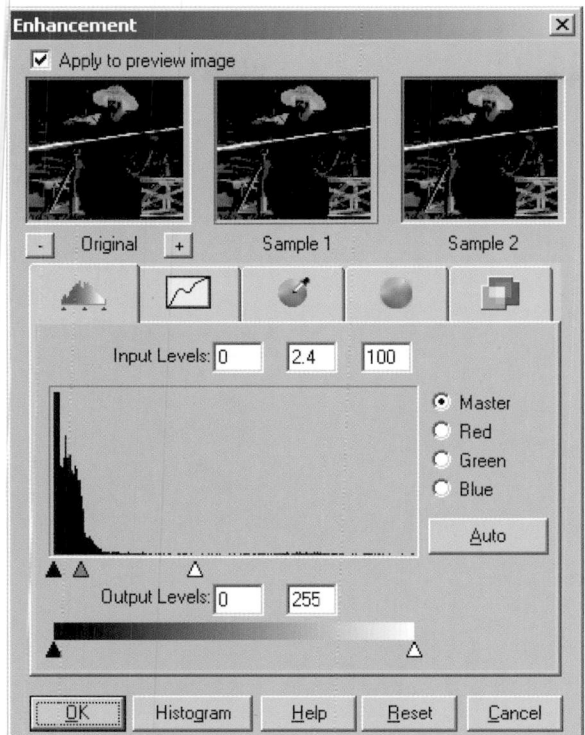

Fig. 10-1-b The scanner software histogram shows that this is a very dense negative. I moved the white slider all the way down to a value of 100 and the midtone slider to a setting of 2.4 to expand the tones in the dense parts of the negative as much as possible.

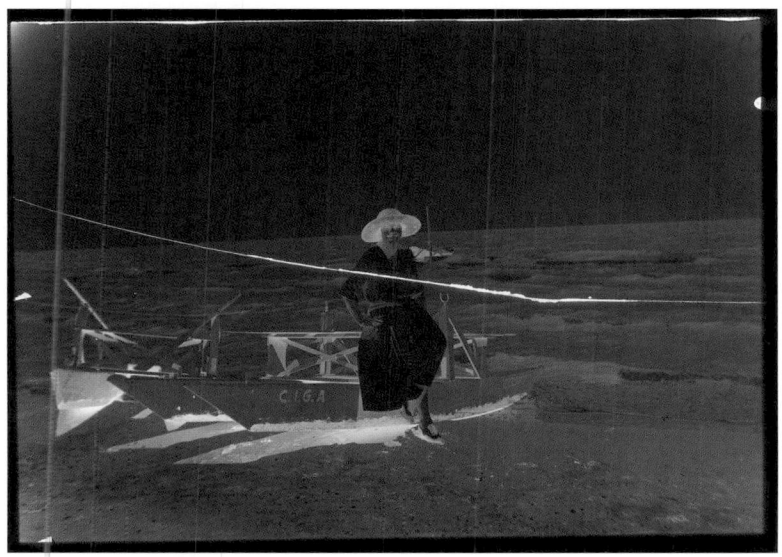

Fig. 10-1-c Scanning the glass plate with the settings shown in Figure 10-1-b produces a much-improved image. Now detail is clearly visible throughout the tonal range of the negative.

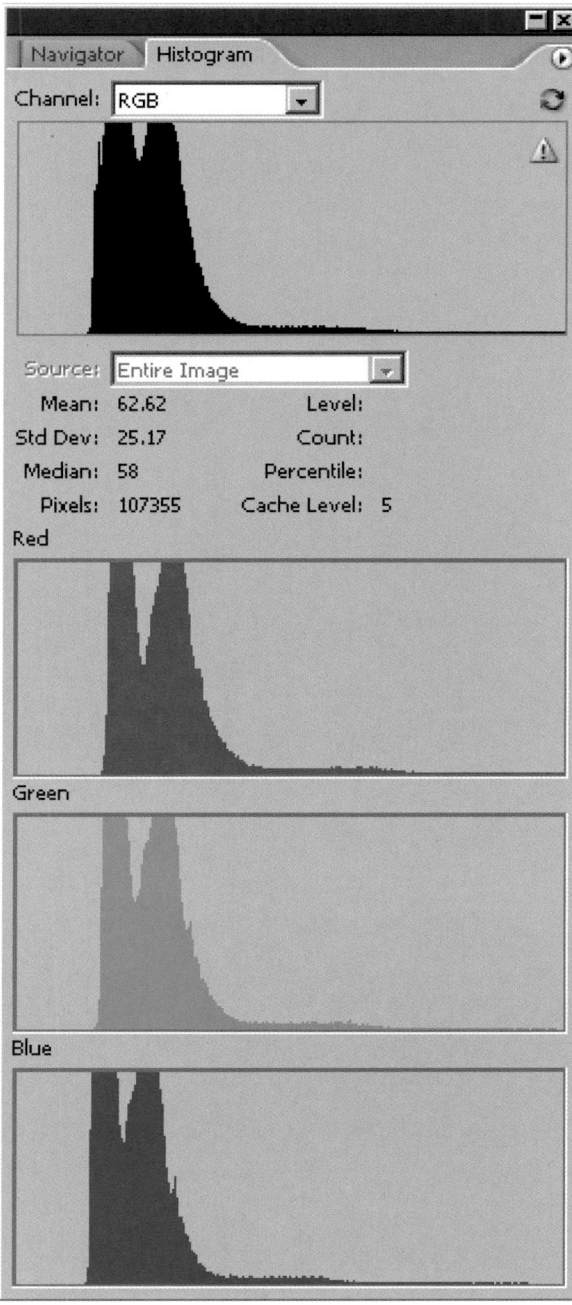

Fig. 10-1-d The histogram of the scan in Figure 10-1-c shows a considerably improved tonal range over the original. Although the range is still restricted to about one-third of the available values, there's enough data in a 16-bit scan for me to create a good finished print.

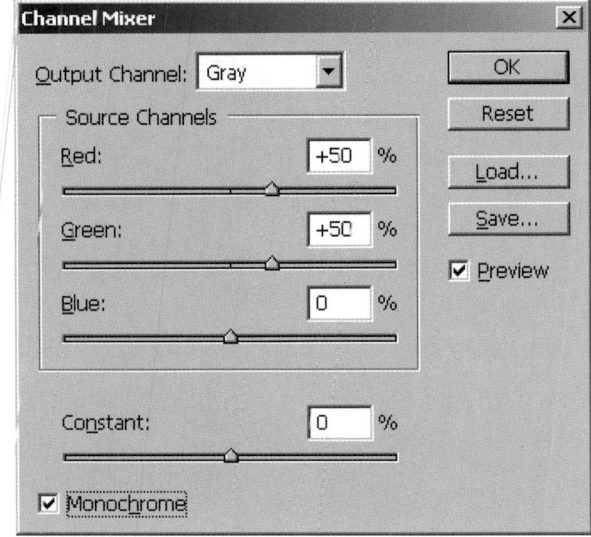

Fig. 10-1-e These are the Channel Mixer settings that convert Figured 10-1-c from RGB color to grayscale. I'm using a mix of 50% red and 50% green because these two channels have substantially less noise than the blue channel (see Figure 10-1-f), and the combination of the two produces better tonality than either of them alone.

scale to speed up further work. I used the Channel Mixer settings in Figure 10-1-e to mix equal parts of just the red and the green channels. Then I converted the RGB monochrome image to a grayscale one.

As you can see in the enlargement of the white dress and fingers in Figure 10-1-f, the blue channel is much noisier in this scan than the red and green channels, so eliminating it got me a monochrome image with better tonality and less noise than any of the individual channels. This is also a cleaner result than I would get by simply desaturating the scan or directly converting the mode to grayscale.

The two pieces of the plate were out of alignment by a few hundredths of an inch, so I created a selection around the top piece and nudged it into alignment with the bottom piece. I started by selecting the crack between the pieces. The pure white gap was easy to select using the Magic Wand tool (Figure 10-1-g). I used a broad tolerance setting of 20 with "Contiguous" checked, so that I didn't accidentally pick up any stray clear spots in the plate while grabbing as much of the crack as possible. A few clicks of the Magic Wand along the length of the crack selected it all.

I expanded that selection by 2 pixels to ensure that I had included all the glow at the edges of the crack and inverted the selection. That left me with the two pieces of the plate separately selected. Using the Lasso in subtractive mode, I circled the lower selection and eliminated it.

With the upper piece alone selected, I held down the control key, which turns the cursor into a nudging tool. I used to the arrow keys to nudge the upper piece a dozen pixels to the right and a couple of pixels down. Figure 10-1-h, right, shows the improvement in alignment.

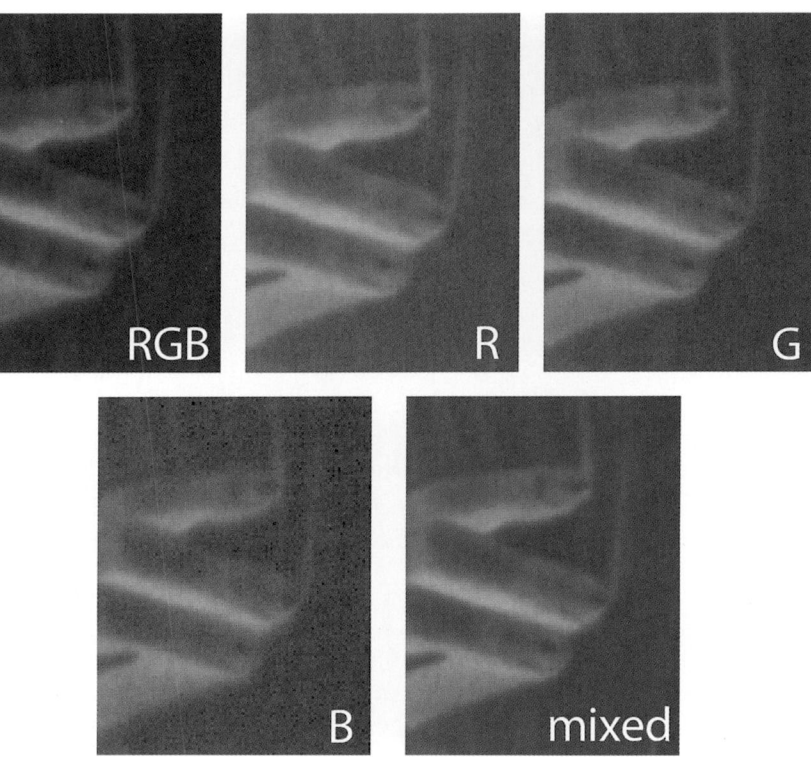

Fig. 10-1-f This enlargement of Figure 10-1-c shows how highlight detail is improved and noise reduced by using the Channel Mixer. The blue (B) channel has much worse noise than the red (R) and green (G) channels, so it gets discarded. Channel Mixer (see Figure 10-1-e) combines 50% red and 50% green channels to produce the mixed channel, lower right. This new grayscale image has better tonality and less noise than any of the individual RGB channels.

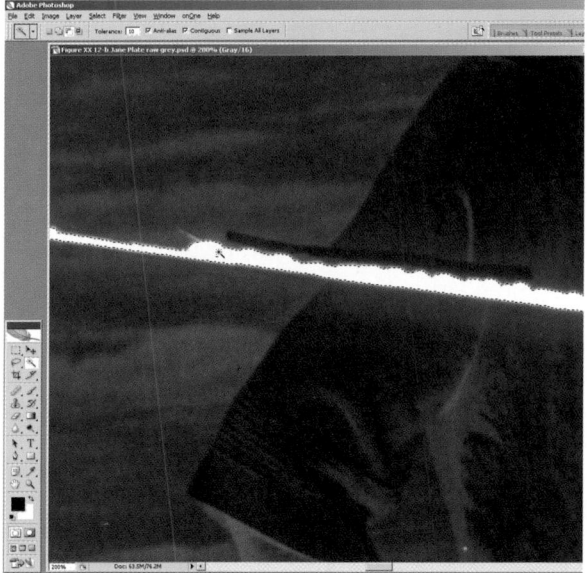

Fig. 10-1-g Selecting the crack between the plates is easy because it's pure white. I used the Magic Wand tool with a Tolerance of 20 in Contiguous mode. The selection is indicated by the dashed line in the screenshot. I expanded the selection by a couple of pixels to include the edges of the crack and inverted it to select the pieces of the glass plate and exclude the crack.

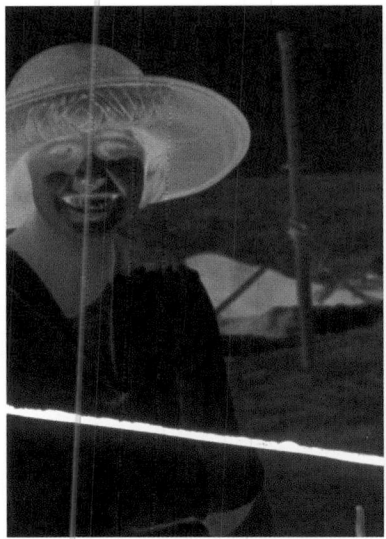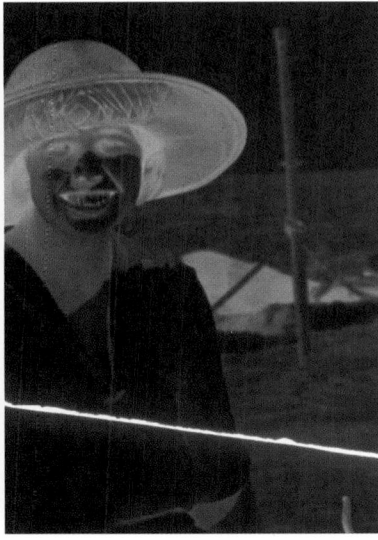

Fig. 10-1-h The figure on the left is the original scan. The two pieces of the plate are misaligned by a few hundredths of an inch. Applying the selection that I made in Figure 10-1-g to one of the pieces of the plate, I nudged the top half of the plate over until it was correctly aligned with the bottom half (right).

Because it's easier to see white spots against a dark background than vice versa, I decided to clean up the dust and scratches while the photograph was still in negative form. I used the Dust & Scratches History Brush trick from Chapter 8, Damage Control, page 268, with a 10-pixel filter radius and a threshold of 5.

Almost all of the garbage I had to clean up was lighter than the photograph, so I set the brush to Darken mode, which minimized its impact on fine detail and image grain. After working my way through the photograph and getting rid of all the light specks, I switched the brush to Lighten mode and picked off the few dark spots and scratches.

Next I inverted the image to produce a positive and cropped and rotated it to make the horizon line horizontal. That yielded Figure 10-1-i. I added a Curves adjustment layer with the settings shown in Figure 10-1-j. This approximated what a good print would ultimately look like, but it showed that there was considerable light falloff toward the edges of the plate (Figure 10-1-k). To even out the plate exposure I created a mask (Figure 10-1-l) for the Curves adjustment layer with the circular Gradient tool.

I set the foreground color to white and the background color to a gray with a luminance of 65 and drew a gradient line from the center of the image to the corner. This mask weakened the effect of the Curves adjustment layer toward the edges of the image, so that it darkened the edges less. The result, seen in Figure 10-1-m, is much more even. I can deal with the small amount of residual darkening in the corners by dodging the photograph later.

The increased contrast in the adjusted photograph revealed a new problem. The very bright light that shone through the crack during scan

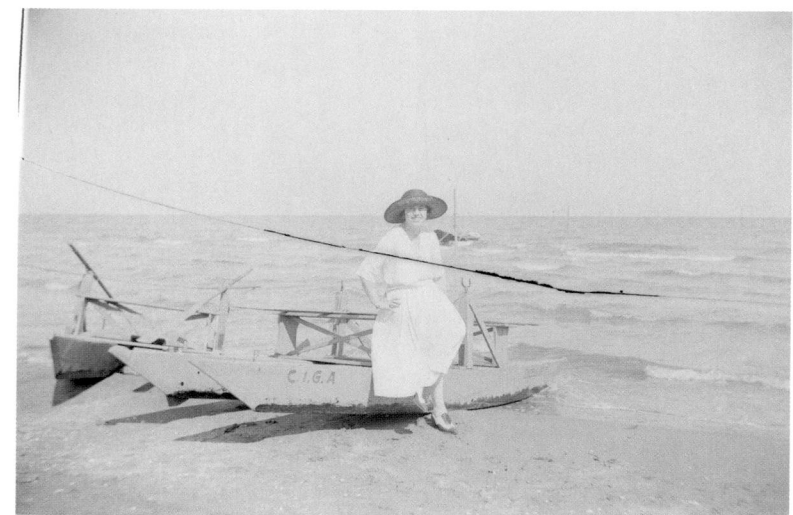

Fig. 10-1-i Now that the scan has been aligned and cleaned, I've inverted it to produce a positive image. The photograph is very pale and flat; the Curves adjustment in Figure 10-1-j will fix that.

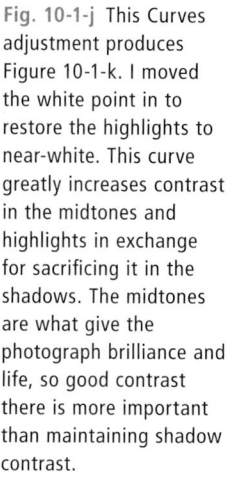

Fig. 10-1-j This Curves adjustment produces Figure 10-1-k. I moved the white point in to restore the highlights to near-white. This curve greatly increases contrast in the midtones and highlights in exchange for sacrificing it in the shadows. The midtones are what give the photograph brilliance and life, so good contrast there is more important than maintaining shadow contrast.

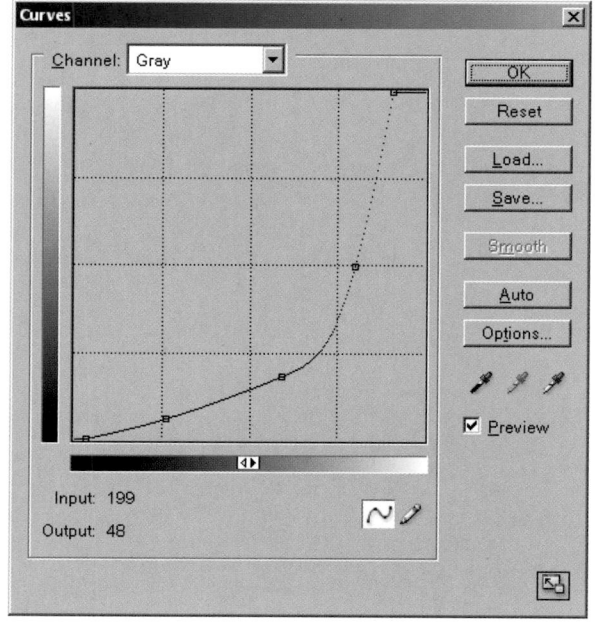

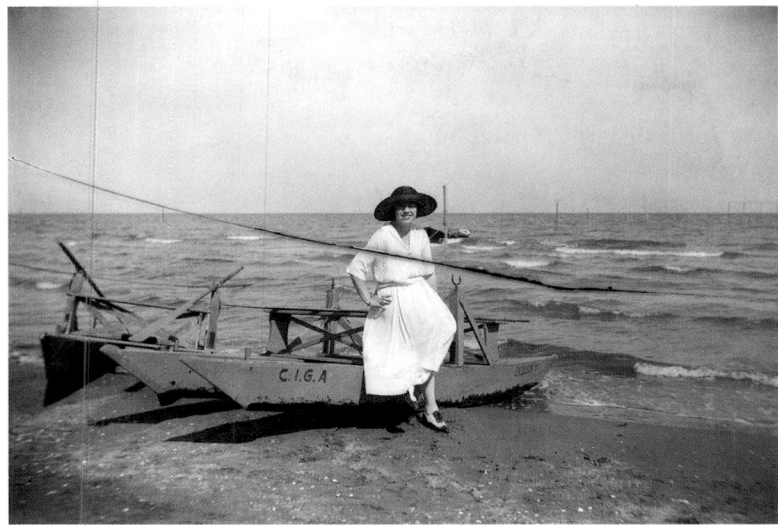

Fig. 10-1-k I applied the curve from Figure 10-1-j to Figure 10-1-i in a Curves adjustment layer. That produces very good tonal quality. Increasing the highlight contrast this much makes light falloff at the corners of the photograph very noticeable. I fixed that with an adjustment layer mask in Figures 10-1-l and 10-1-m.

Fig. 10-1-l I created this mask for the Curves adjustment layer in Figure 10-1-k using the circular Gradient tool. It fades the effect of the curve from Figure 10-1-j so that it doesn't darken the photograph as much in the corners.

had caused flare that created a dark halo around the crack in the positive image. This made the job of erasing the crack considerably more complex, so I tackled it in stages with several different tools.

The easiest step was removing the crack from the sky, where the crack was a thin line with very little halo. Since there was no sky detail other than grain, I just cloned the nearby sky into the crack to make it go away.

Next in difficulty was the ocean. There the crack was heavier and there was some evidence of a halo. There was also the blurry detail in the water to worry about. I decided first to reduce the strength of the crack.

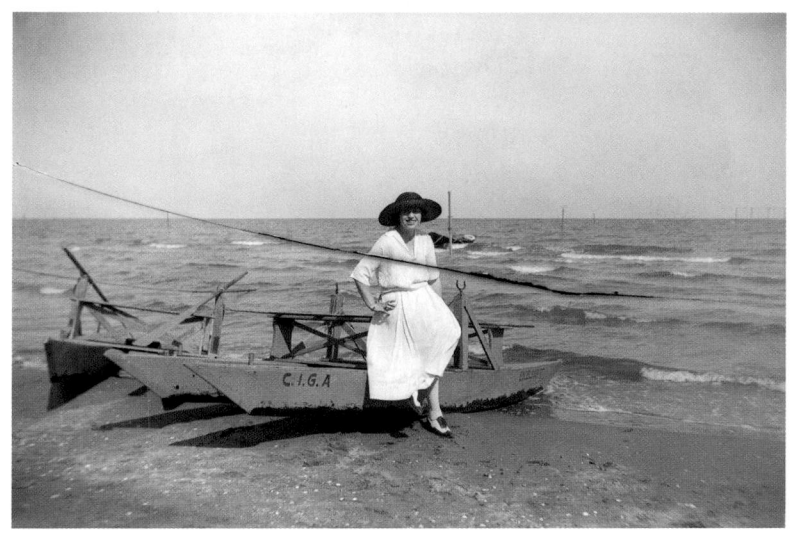

Fig. 10-1-m The masked Curves adjustment layer does a nice job of restoring proper tonality to this photograph at the same time that it evens out the lighting. The residual darkening in the corners can be cleaned up with a little bit of dodging.

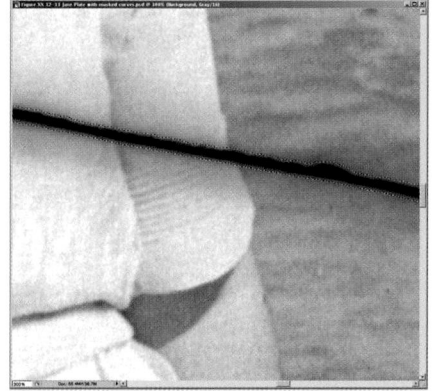

Fig. 10-1-n The first stage in repairing the crack in the plate is to select it using the Magic Wand tool. The selected area is outlined by the dotted line in this screenshot.

I selected the blackest parts of the crack with the Magic Wand, expanded the selection by 3 pixels, and feathered it by 2 pixels (Figure 10-1-n). I applied the Median filter with a radius of 85 pixels; that filled in the crack with the average brightness of the surrounding pixels (Figure 10-1-o). This made it easier to manipulate the crack in later steps.

Once I had minimized the intensity of the crack, the Spot Healing Brush in Photoshop CS2 was up to the task of erasing it from the water. I set the brush to a radius about 20% bigger than the halo with a hardness of 0. Brushing the tool along the cracks in short segments, it didn't take long to erase it.

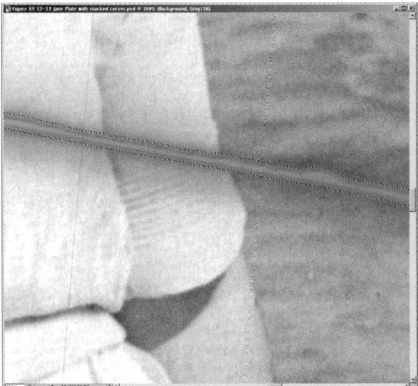

Fig. 10-1-o I applied the Median filter with a very large radius of 85 pixels to the selected crack. That filled in the selection with the average of the surrounding pixels. This makes it easier for other tools like the Spot Healing Brush to replace the selection with surrounding detail and blend it in.

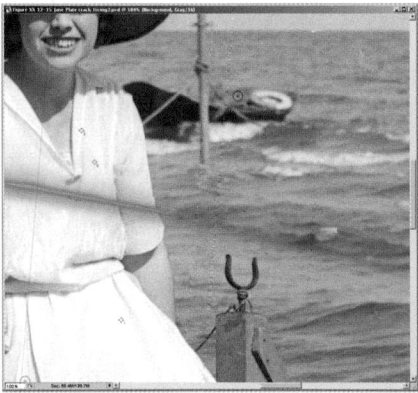

Fig. 10-1-p The Spot Healing Brush has replaced the selected crack with wave details from other parts of the ocean. All that remains of the crack over the water area is a dark smudge.

Occasionally the Spot Healing Brush produced patterns and textures that didn't merge well with the surrounding waves. Usually I could make those go away with a second pass from the brush at a different angle. If the blend still wasn't perfect, I used the cloning tool at 30% strength to blend in the boundary between the healed area and the surrounding image.

Now I was ready to tackle the residual halo where the crack had been in the ocean and the halo around the crack in the dress (Figure 10-1-p). Dealing with that required nothing fancier than the Dodge tool. I set the tool diameter to about the width of the halo, the hardness to 50%, and the strength to 7%. I ran this tool back and forth along the halo until it was mostly gone, being careful not to overdo it. Then I dropped the radius down to about a fifth of the width of the halo and carefully brushed out the residual bits, including the strong dark edge right next to the crack across the dress (Figure 10-1-q).

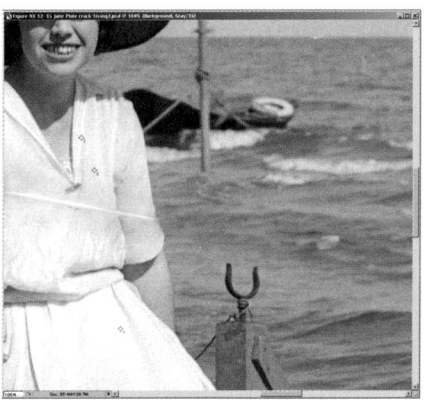

Fig. 10-1-q Dodging the dark smudge in the previous photograph completes the task of erasing the crack from the water. The Dodge tool was also effective at removing the dark halo that borders the crack over the woman's dress.

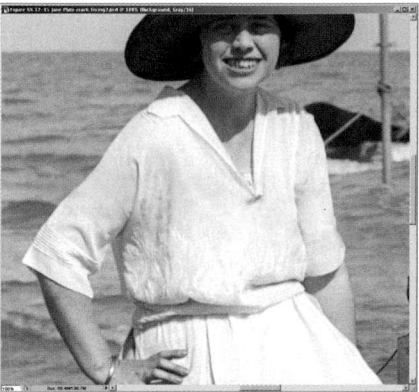

Fig. 10-1-r Now that I reduced the crack to a thin white line in Figure 10-1-q, it's a simple matter to erase it entirely from the blouse using the Clone tool.

This left a simple, narrow blank area running across the dress that I could easily fill in with the Clone tool. I made a few more light passes with the Dodge tool to remove the last traces of shadows from the repaired area, which gave me the seamless image in Figure 10-1-r.

Now I turned my attention to making the photograph look as good as possible. I used a Dodge tool of large radius to reduce the light falloff at the edges and corners of the photograph. I didn't eliminate it entirely, because a small amount of vignetting focused attention on the central subject of the photograph. I just reduced the darkening enough so that it wasn't an obvious artifact and distraction.

There was some residual garbage in the sky—light scratches, small defects in the emulsion, that sort of thing. I used the Magic Wand to select only the sky and shrank the selection by 6 pixels to ensure that I had not captured any of the foreground. Then I applied the Dust & Scratches filter with a radius of 20 and threshold of 2. Since the sky held

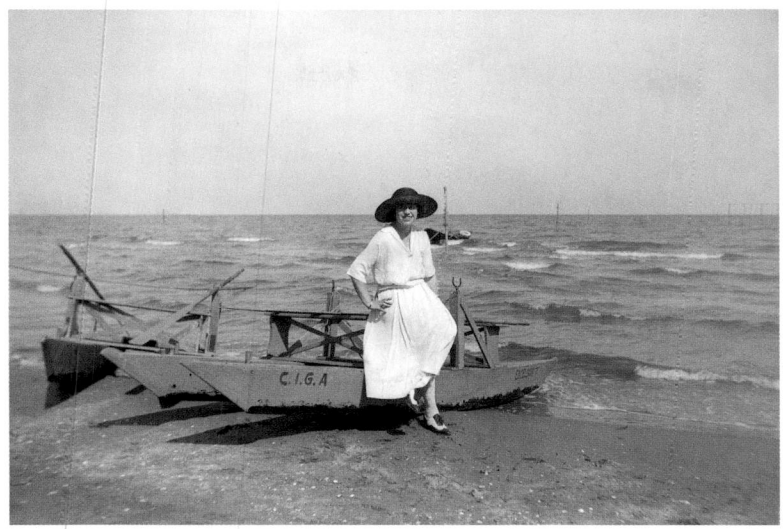

Fig. 10-1-s This photograph is fully repaired. The crack is gone, and the dust, dirt, and scratches are all cleaned up. The tonal rendition is good, and I've done some dodging and burning-in to even out the lighting a little more. Just a few more finishing touches will make it perfect.

no fine detail, the large radius didn't destroy anything except defects, and the threshold of 2 preserved enough of the grain so that there was no visible difference in texture between the filtered and unfiltered parts of the photograph.

Figure 10-1-s shows a fully repaired photograph. I saved this version as a good record of the original photograph; now I wanted to take it to the next level and come up with a good "print" of it, just as I would in the darkroom.

I used the Burn tool set to 6% and a very large radius to lightly burn in the top half of the sky and the foreground sand. That further focused the viewer's attention on the subject of the photograph. The change was very subtle, almost subliminal, but it made a big difference in the aesthetics.

Next I switched to the Dodge tool and with a brush of small radius lightened the woman's face where it was shadowed by her hat. I paid special attention to her eyes, giving them a little more dodging to bring them out and lightly dodged her hair to better separate its tones from her hat. I also lightened the shadow under her nose that fell across her upper lip and her teeth. Lastly, I dodged the right side of her face and her neck to open up the tones there.

My goal in all of this was to produce a more pleasing but still accurate rendition. I didn't cosmetically alter her appearance or eliminate the look of someone posing in the bright sun, rather I produced a rendering that was more attractive because it was more like what we would see. Figure 10-1-t shows a close-up of her face before and after these simple but important local corrections. These final adjustments produced Figure 10-1-u, a lovely and flawless photograph from a "lost" glass plate.

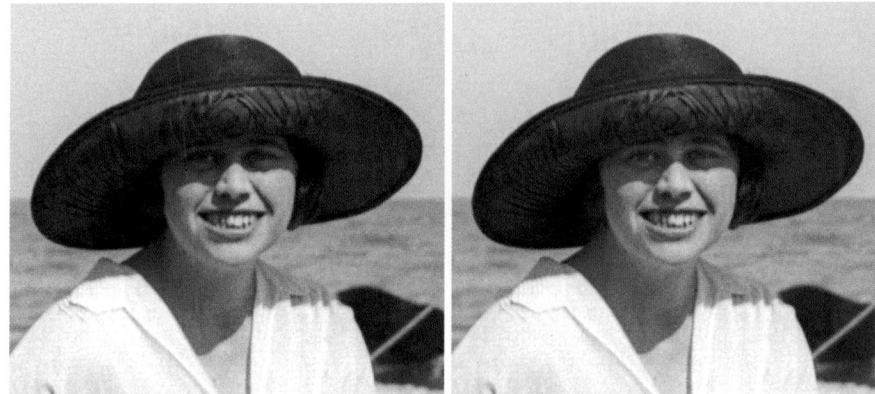

Fig. 10-1-t On the left is an enlargement of Figure 10-1-s. The direct sunlight produced a harsh photograph and buried much of the woman's face in shadow. Judicious use of the Dodge tool opens up the shadows and evens out the lighting on her face just enough to make it look more natural to our eyes. Little touches like this make the difference between a good and a great restoration.

Fig. 10-1-u The final print! Some minor adjustments to the Curves layer perk up the whites in the woman's dress and make her stand out more clearly from the background. Burning-in the sand at the bottom and dodging her face add to her sense of presence. This file makes a wonderful-looking print.

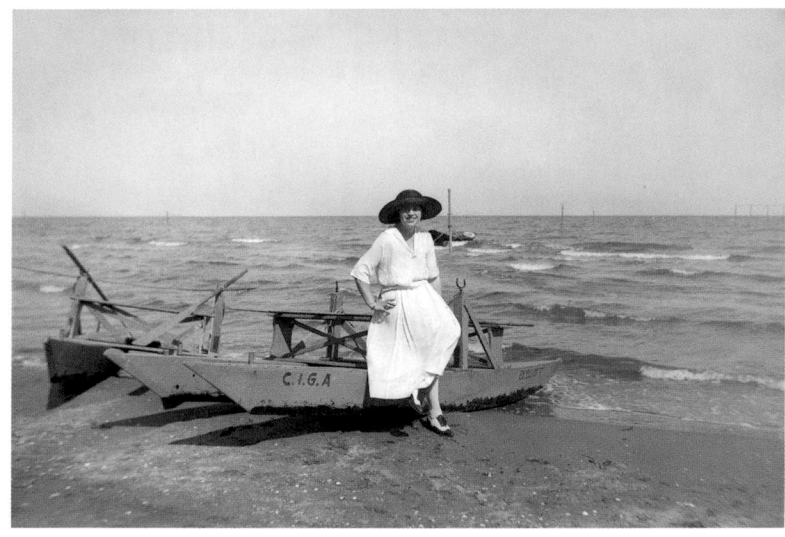

Example 2: Repairing Color with a Good Scan

Throughout this book I've emphasized the importance of getting a good scan to make your restoration job easier and better. This example is a most extreme case of that; getting the scan right got me 90% of the way to great tone and color (see also Chapter 6, Restoring Color, page 183).

The original was a 3-inch by 5-inch color snapshot made in 1966 (Figure 10-2-a). It was in very good shape for a 40-year-old color pho-

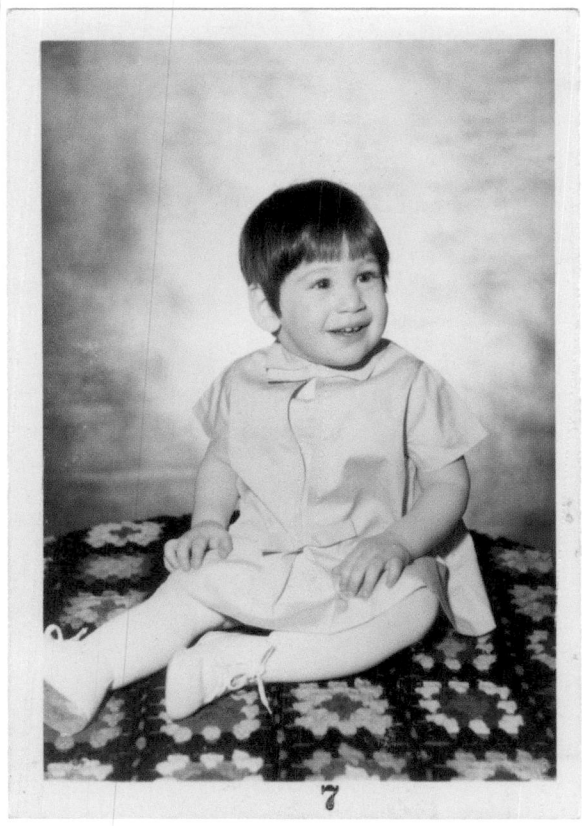

Fig. 10-2-a This mid-1960s color photograph is yellowed and significantly faded but otherwise is in very good physical condition. A careful scan can correct most of the fading.

tograph. It was little bit dirty and slightly cracked, and there were some paper fibers stuck to the surface but little physical decay. The print had a moderate amount of yellow staining and overall had faded considerably but uniformly.

I scanned the photograph on my flat-bed scanner with the Input Levels settings shown in Figure 10-2-b. I set the sliders for the black and white end points in the red, green, and blue channels so that they tightly bracketed the histograms. That wiped out the highlight stain and gave me a good range of tones from near-white to near-black. Pulling in the blue channel's "white" point far enough to eliminate the yellow stain, however, made the print come out too blue overall, so I raised the midpoint on the blue levels to make the color balance more neutral. The finished scan, in Figure 10-2-c, is an amazing improvement, just from a carefully adjusted scan!

I decided that the color was not saturated enough and the overall hue was a little bit pink for my taste. So I added a Hue/Saturation adjustment layer (Figure 10-2-d) and played around with the settings until I got

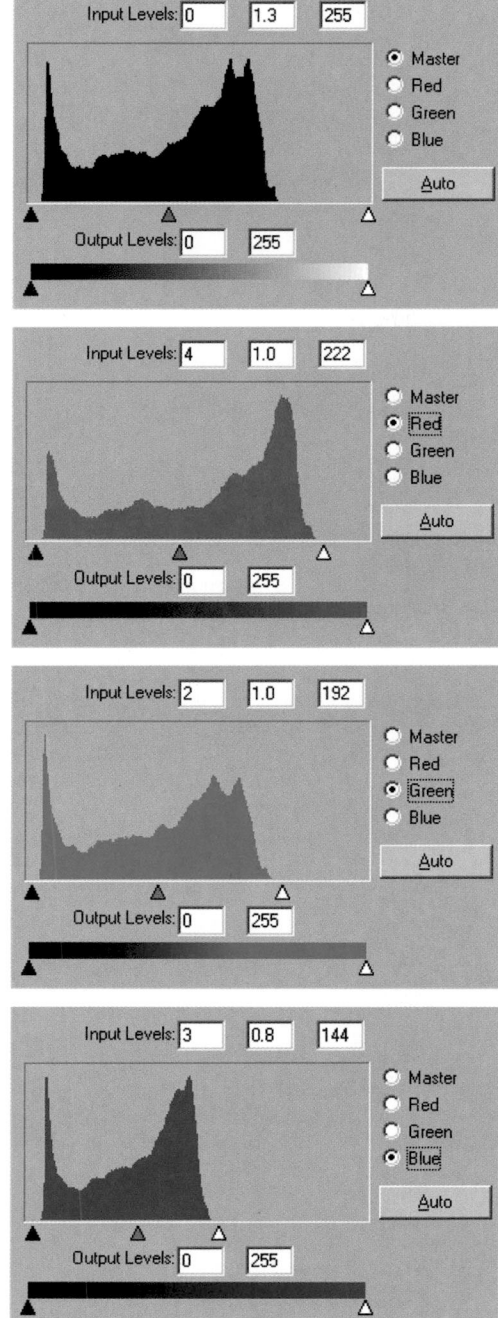

Fig. 10-2-b These are the scanner software histograms and Input Levels settings that produce Figure 10-2-c from Figure 10-2-a. I adjusted the black and white sliders to bracket the range of tones in each color channel. I also shifted the midtone slider for the blue channel to 0.8, which improved the color balance.

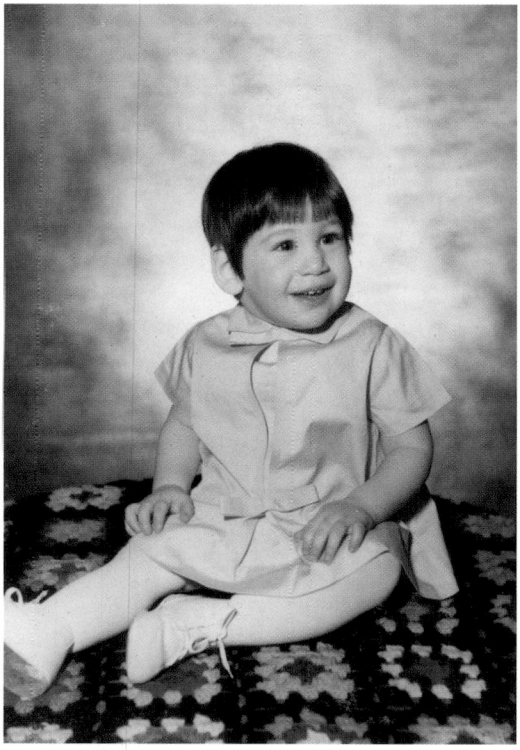

Fig. 10-2-c This corrected scan of Figure 10-2-a looks very good. It's most of the way toward having fully restored and corrected color.

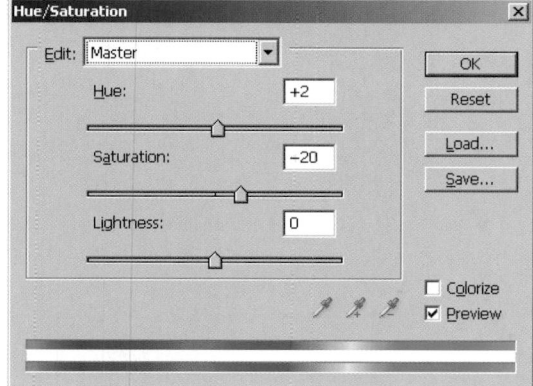

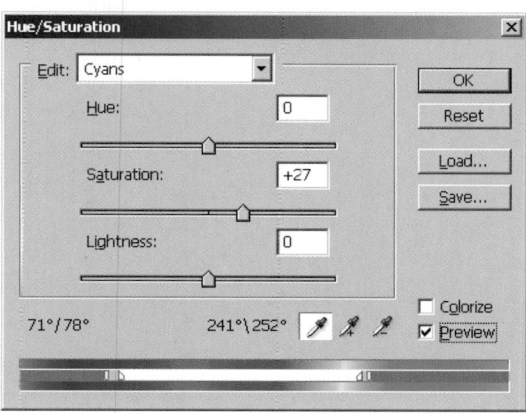

Fig. 10-2-d These Hue/ Saturation adjustments, applied in an adjustment layer, further improve the color, producing Figure 10-2-e. The Master adjustment improves the overall saturation and makes the skin tones a little less pink by shifting the Hue +2 points. The Cyans adjustment substantially increases the saturation in the greens and blues because they were very weak even in the corrected scan.

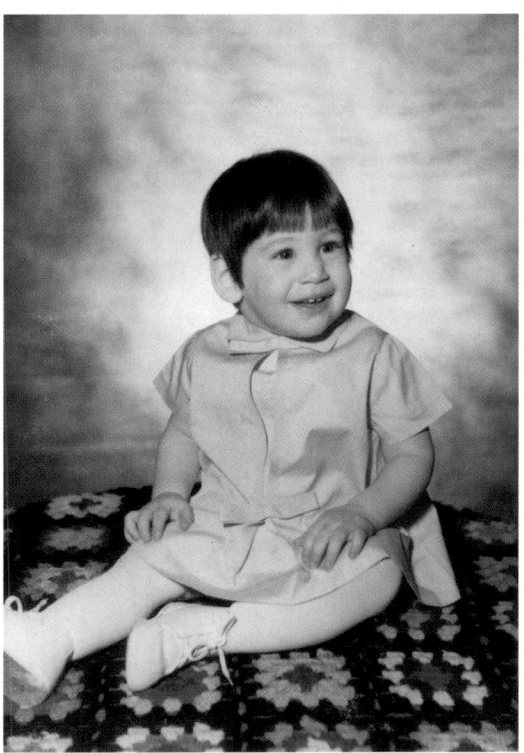

Fig. 10-2-e Improved saturation helps this photograph a lot. The color balance, though, is just a bit off—it's a little too rosy. The Curves adjustment in Figure 10-2-f fixes that.

Figure 10-2-e. The Master saturation is up 20 points, and I shifted the hue by +2 degrees, which moved the pinks and the reds a little bit toward the yellow and warmed up the print. That Hue adjustment would also move the greens and blues a little bit toward the purple, but there was so little of that in the photograph that I didn't care about them. The greens and blues, though, were still undersaturated, so I went to the Cyan channel and moved the spectrum sliders at the bottom so that all colors from green through blue were selected. Then I increased the saturation by 27 points. This pumped up the colors in the quilt and added a bit more variation to the background (Figure 10-2-e).

I didn't have to use an adjustment layer for this, by the way. It made it easier for me to fiddle around with the Hue/Saturation settings to figure out what I wanted.

The color was almost there, but it was a bit too rosy for me. Moving the eyedropper around the picture confirmed that impression; even the white shoes had red values that were substantially too high (meaning there wasn't enough cyan in the image). So I launched the Curves tool, pulled up the red channel, and made the single-point adjustment you see in Figure 10-2-f. That tempered the rosiness a bit to give me the very natural color you see in Figure 10-2-g.

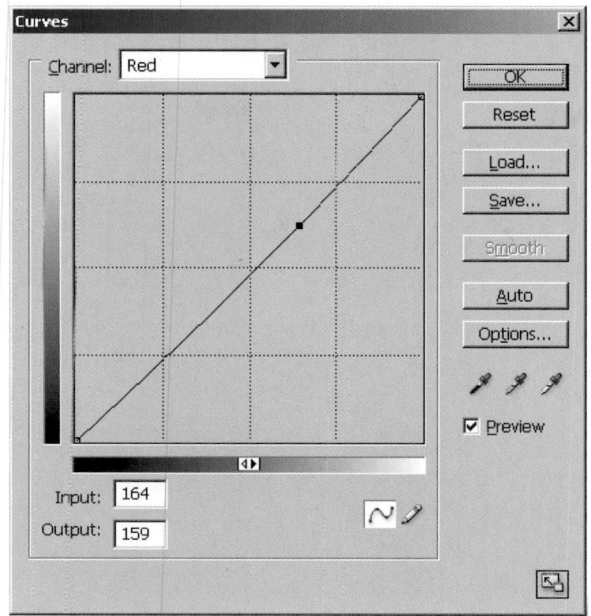

Fig. 10-2-f This single-point Curves adjustment gets rid of the excess pink from Figure 10-2-e, as shown in Figure 10-2-g.

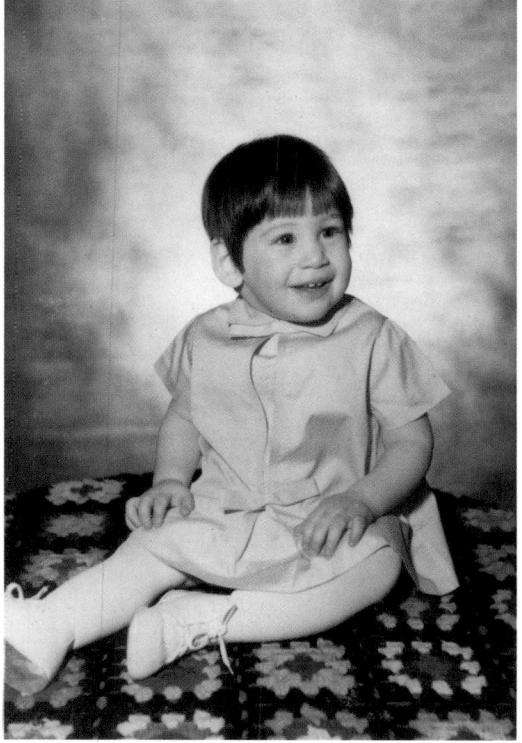

Fig. 10-2-g This photograph has excellent color. The Curves adjustment from Figure 10-2-f makes the whites neutral and gives the tot a natural, childlike complexion. Everything is done except a small amount of damage repair and detail enhancement.

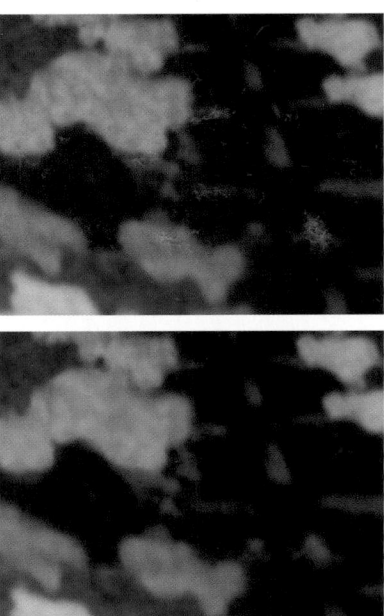

Fig. 10-2-h This enlargement from Figure 10-2-g shows the white paper fibers that are stuck to the print (top). It took very little work to clean them up with the Dust & Scratches filter. I just assigned the filter to the History Brush, reverted to the previous History State, and brushed out the clumps of fibers. The result is shown in the bottom figure.

The next-to-last thing I had to do was clean up the garbage. I used my favorite tool for that, the Dust & Scratches filter applied via the History Brush. I set the filter for a radius of 10 pixels with a threshold of 4. That aggressively wiped out all of the dust and dirt and most of the paper fibers. Setting the History Brush to that state, I painted the filter over the background. I could use a very large-radius brush because the background was out of focus and the filter had no effect on it except for correcting the damage.

Cleaning up the child and the quilt required the usual small-radius brush so that I didn't accidentally wipe out real details, but since the background constituted more than half of the photograph, I spent relatively little time on cleanup. Figure 10-2-h is an enlarged section of the photograph that shows what the dirt and paper fibers looked like before and after cleaning up with the Dust & Scratches filter brush. The filter didn't erase larger fiber clumps, but it wasn't much work to obliterate those using the Clone tool.

This file was ready to archive and print out at its original size, but I decided to add one last refinement—enlargement. When I saw what a high-quality, clean scan I could get from this photograph, I decided to scan it at 1200 ppi instead of the 600 ppi that would've been more appropriate. The 1200-ppi scan didn't hold more image detail than a 600-ppi scan would; there wasn't any finer detail to be captured. What it did was capture four times as many pixels for Focus Magic to chew on (Figure 10-2-i).

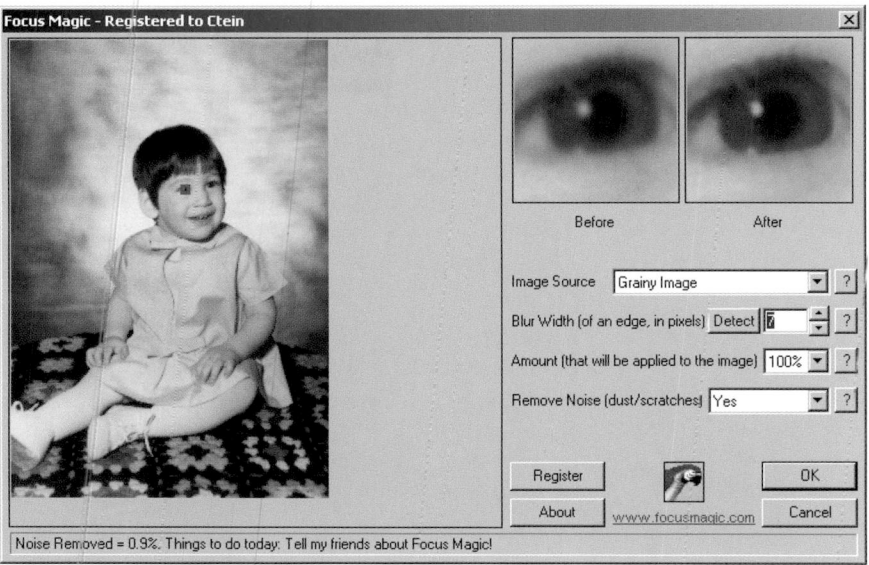

Fig. 10-2-i Focus Magic can improve the sharpness of this photograph to make it even better than that of the original print. Setting the source for Grainy Image minimizes enhancement of noise and film grain. That's important in this photograph because I want the child's skin to remain baby smooth.

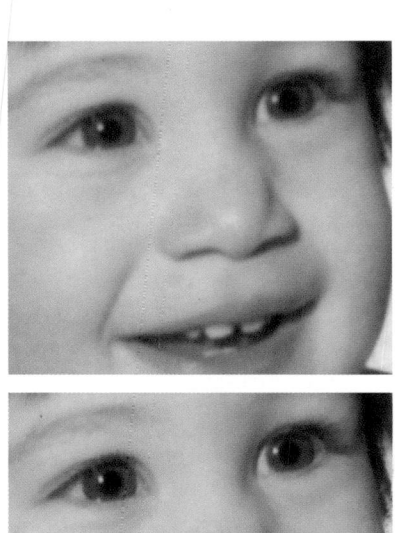

Fig. 10-2-j This enlargement from Figure 10-2-h shows the photograph before (top) and after (bottom) running the Focus Magic filter from Figure 10-2-i. See how much better the detail in the eyes and mouth is! This photograph can be enlarged 50% to 100% when it's printed out, and it will still look nice and sharp.

I set the Focus Magic image source to "Grainy Image" because that minimizes the filter's sharpening of fine grain and noise. I didn't want to exaggerate textures in that smooth baby skin. I turned on "Remove Noise" just in case there were some dirt specks I missed, set the Blur Width to 7 pixels, and let the filter run. What a difference that filter made (Figure 10-2-j)! Now the photograph is sharp enough to take up to 6 inches by 10 inches and still stand up to close inspection.

Example 3: Mother and Child—A "Legacy" Restoration Job

In this example, the original photograph (Figure 10-3-a) was made by a chain department store's portrait studio over 20 years ago. Poorly processed and taped into a cheap cardboard matte, the print hung on the family home wall for two decades. Consequently, it had faded something terrible. Although it looks like a nearly monochrome red image, there was enough color information left to do an excellent digital restoration.

When I started doing professional-quality restoration in 1998, this was the first job I ever did. The computer was slow with little memory, I could only work with 8-bit files, and all the work was done under Photoshop 4. That meant no adjustment layers, no History States, no Healing Brushes, and no clever third-party plug-ins. That's why I'm

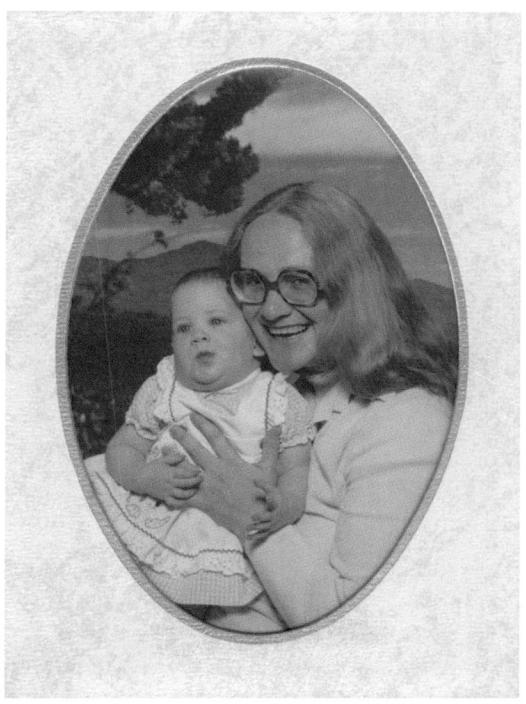

Fig. 10-3-a This is a chain-department-store portrait made in the 1970s. It hung on a wall in this oval matte for 20 years before I received it for restoration.

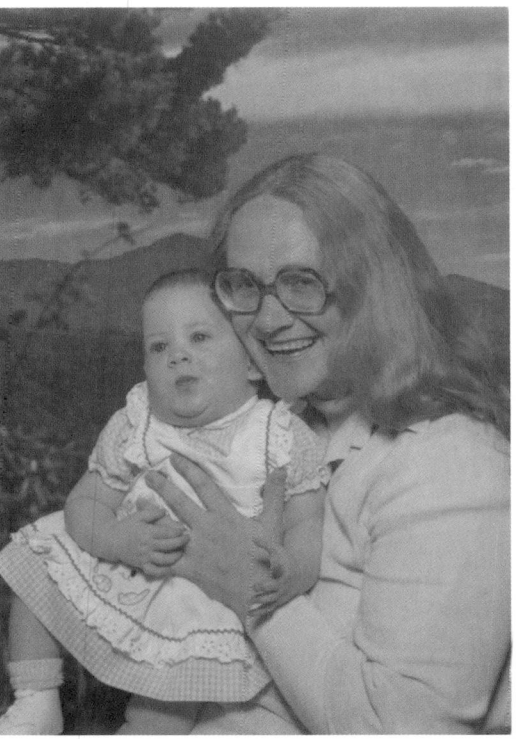

Fig. 10-3-b Removing the matte reveals that the photograph has faded unevenly. Where it was struck by light, the fading is more severe.

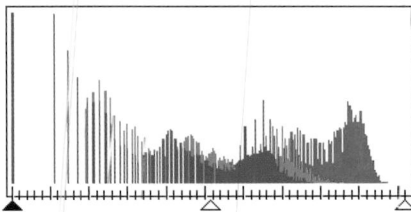 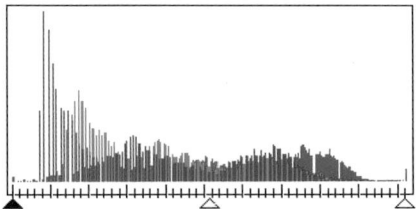

Fig. 10-3-c The scanner software histogram on the left, for Figure 10-3-b, illustrates the severe color shift in this photograph. The blue channel hasn't faded much, but the green channel has lost considerable shadow density, and the red channel barely spans the upper half of the histogram range. The histogram on the right shows the improvements possible with the adjusted scan of Figure 10-3-d; now all three color channels have data that spans most of the range of values.

including it in this book. The methods and tools I used to restore this photograph are available in just about any image processing program; this is as close to "generic" technique as you can get.

Figure 10-3-b shows an uncorrected scan of the unmounted print. There was almost no information in the red channel below middle gray, and the green channel showed considerable loss, as can be seen in the scanner software's histogram (Figure 10-3-c, left). The cyan dye image had faded the most, plus there was some dye loss in the magenta. Stain-

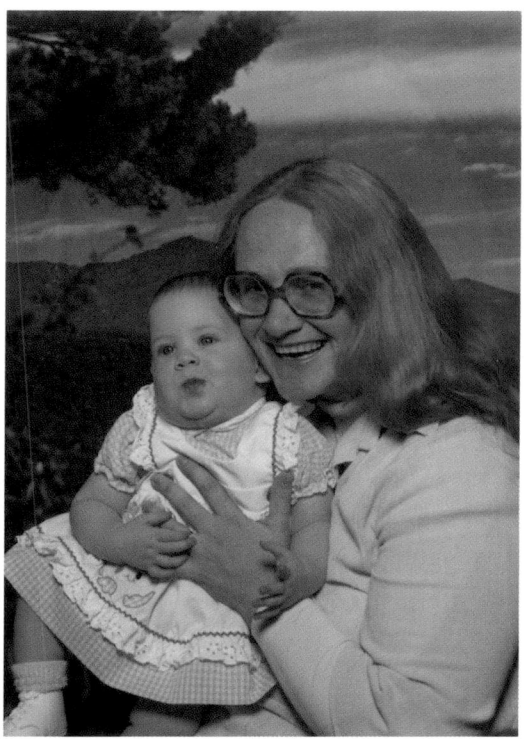

Fig. 10-3-d The adjusted scan has considerably better tone and a wider range of colors than the original photograph. The outline of the oval matte is very obvious; that's what needs to be fixed first.

ing had given the print an overall orange cast as well. I adjusted the scanner level sliders, expanding the red and green ranges to compensate for the dye loss and setting the white points for the green and blue ranges to compensate for the yellow-magenta stain. There was now a much better overlap between the three color channels, and the red data was spread out enough to give a decent range of tones to work with (Figure 10-3-c, right), indicating that I'd get a much more neutral overall color rendition in the scan (Figure 10-3-d).

The part of the photograph hidden by the cardboard matte had faded differently from the central oval exposed to light. In preparation for eliminating that difference, I created an oval mask (Figure 10-3-e) that precisely matched the outline of the faded area in the photograph. The Elliptical Marquee tool created a selection that approximately fit the oval. I saved that selection in its own channel and made it visible as an overlay on top of the photograph. I used white and black Brush and Pencil tools to refine the edge of the mask so that it exactly matched the oval area in the photograph.

After selecting the central oval area, I pulled up the Curves tool and created customized red, green, and blue curves to correct the differential fading. To begin with, I picked adjacent near-black areas in the tree on either side of the oval boundary and added adjustment points to the

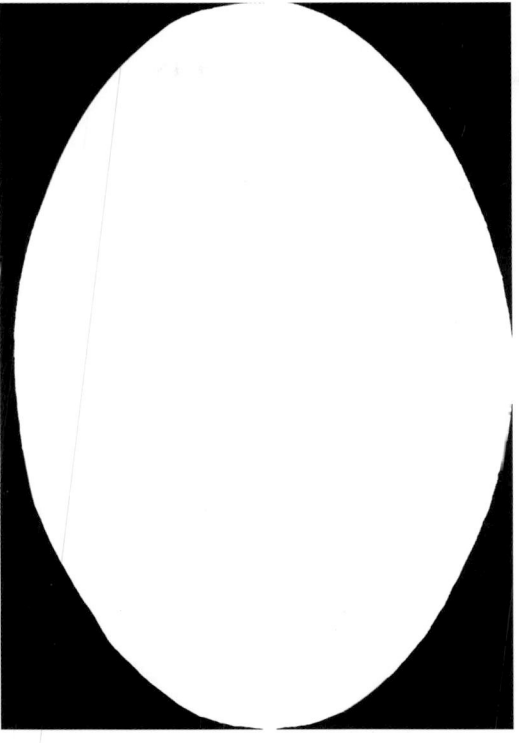

Fig. 10-3-e I created an oval matte using the Elliptical Marquee tool in Photoshop. The oval matte cutout isn't a perfect ellipse, so I painted along the edge of the mask with a hard-edged brush, using white and black tones, until I had an outline that precisely matched the cardboard matte.

individual curves corresponding to the values in the area inside the oval. I lowered those adjustment points until the areas inside and outside the boundary matched.

Next I picked a dark midtone area in the mountains in the backdrop and added adjustment points to the three color curves corresponding to the values there. I raised or lowered those points until the mountain tones matched.

I added adjustment points for an area in the sky, in the light sweater, and finally in the clouds. At each stage I adjusted only those points corresponding to the target areas to bring those areas into a good match on both sides of the oval. In this manner I worked my way up the tone scale from black to white to produce a complicated custom curve set (Figure 10-3-f) that would bring all the tones and colors together. The faded oval area was almost completely invisible in the resulting photograph in Figure 10-3-g. Now I had a uniformly degraded photograph to work with, and I could start correcting the overall tone and color.

Figure 10-3-g was dark, red, and lacked saturation. I improved the brightness and got rid of most of the red cast with the curves in Figure 10-3-h. The green curve adjustments made the shadows more neutral without affecting the middle and highlight tones. Dropping the midtone

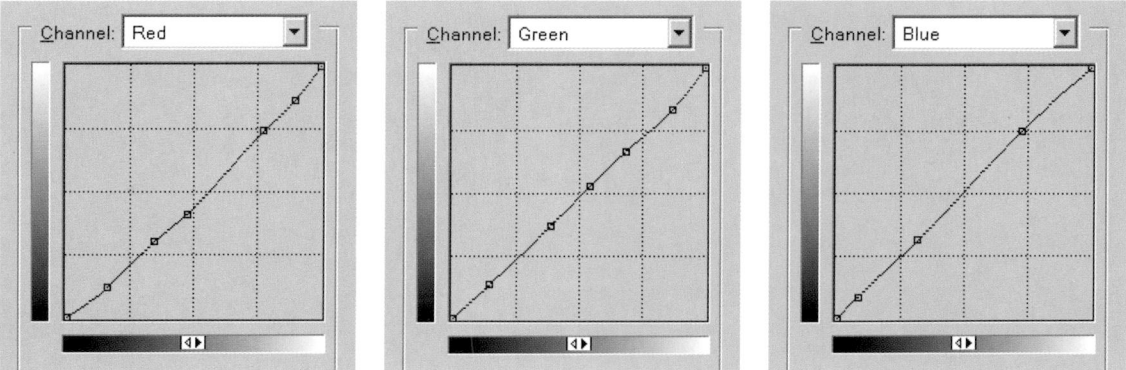

Fig. 10-3-f This is the Curves adjustment I made to Figure 10-3-d, masked with the oval mask from Figure 10-3-e. It makes the tones inside and outside of the masked area match nearly perfectly (Figure 10-3-g).

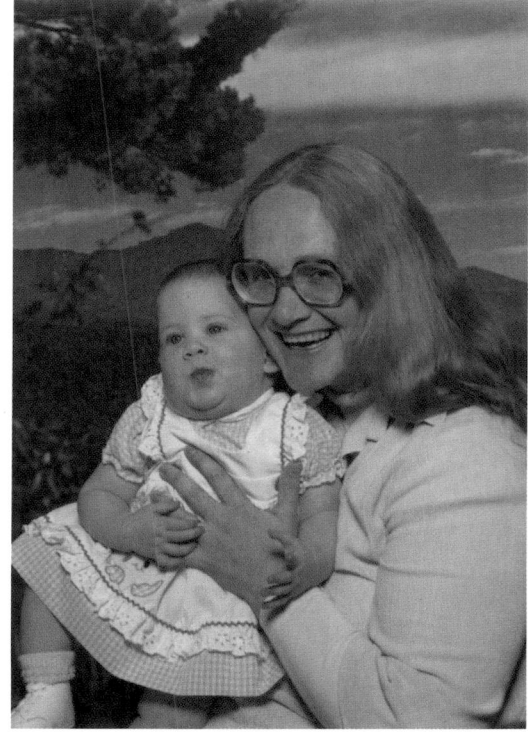

Fig. 10-3-g After the masked Curves correction from Figure 10-3-f, this photograph is uniform enough in appearance for me to begin serious color and tone restoration.

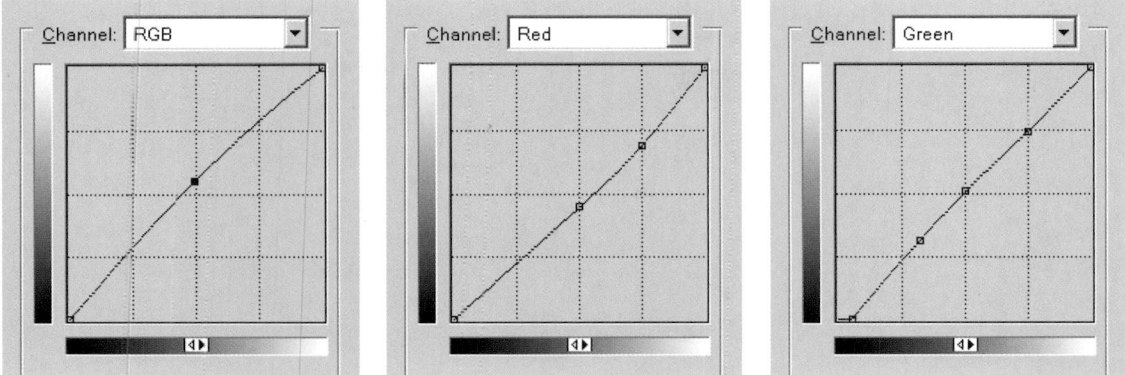

Fig. 10-3-h I made this Curves adjustment to produce Figure 10-3-i. The RGB curve lightens the photograph, while the red curve adds cyan to eliminate the reddish cast. The green curve makes the shadows more neutral by eliminating a green bias in the darker tones.

and higher red values and raising the midpoint in the RGB curve substantially improved the picture.

I followed that change with a saturation boost of 36 points to get Figure 10-3-i, which has fair overall color balance for the mother and child, but serious problems remained. The background looks far too brown. The clothing and highlights are dull and gray. The average skin tone is correct, but it's blotchy and harsh. From this point on, I worked on the photograph piecemeal, using masks. I decided to attack the background problem first.

I carefully traced around the mother and child with the Lasso tool to create the mask shown in Figure 10-3-j. I inverted that mask and applied it to the photograph to select the background. I used the Curves and Hue/Saturation tools on the background to reduce the amount of red, increase the overall contrast, and improve the saturation. I fine-tuned color curves to make the clouds neutral, the sky blue, and the foliage dark green to black (Figure 10-3-k). Then I increased the saturation by 20 points, which got me to Figure 10-3-l.

Streaks, blotches, and other defects such as surface cracks became all too visible after so much enhancement. I had to do a large amount of touch-up work with the Clone, Dodge, and Burn tools to correct the color and tone artifacts. I used the Clone tool to remove the most obvious of the cracks. I followed that with a 1.5-pixel-radius Gaussian Blur to the background to subdue noise and cracks in the background.

Having finished with the background, I deleted the selection and made some minor adjustments to the color and contrast to make the picture a bit more snappy. Next I focused my attention on the mother and child. The most evident flaw was the harsh and blotchy skin tones. Figure 10-3-m shows a full-color close-up of the faces along with the

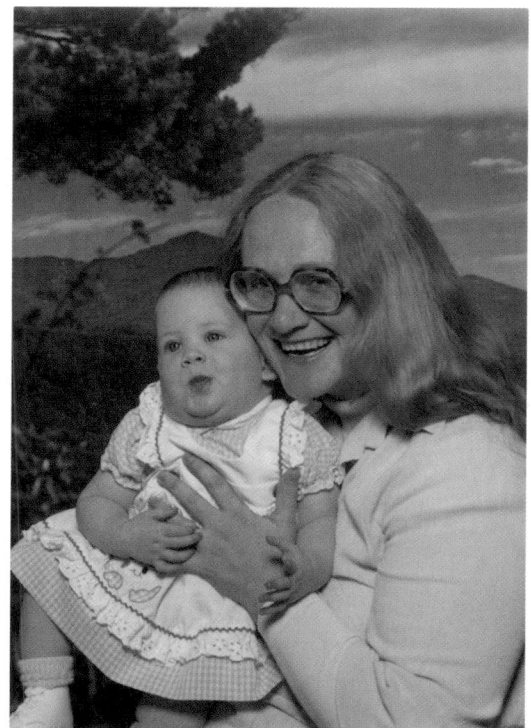

Fig. 10-3-i As a result of the Curves adjustment from Figure 10-3-h and a 36-point increase in contrast, the mother and daughter are looking pretty good, but the background is definitely off-color. It's time for another mask, so that I can work on the two regions of the photograph separately.

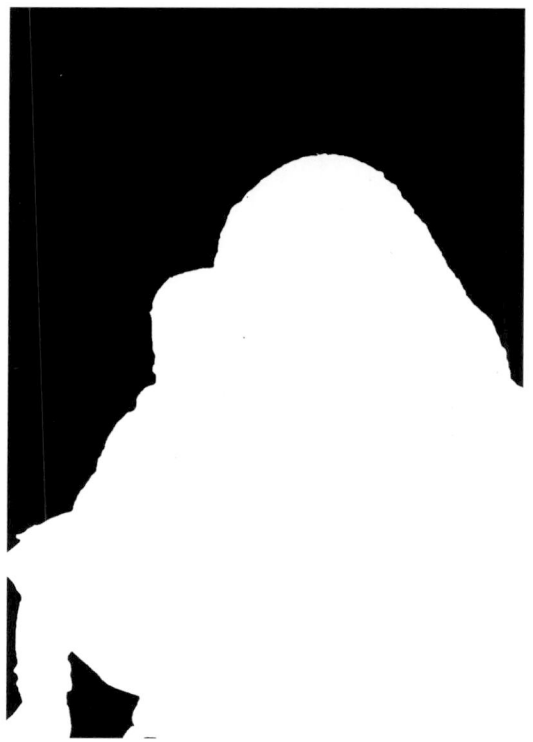

Fig. 10-3-j I drew this mask by hand, using the Lasso tool to carefully follow the outline of the mother and child. It lets me perform separate corrections on the background and the people. I applied it to Figure 10-3-i and inverted it to select the background.

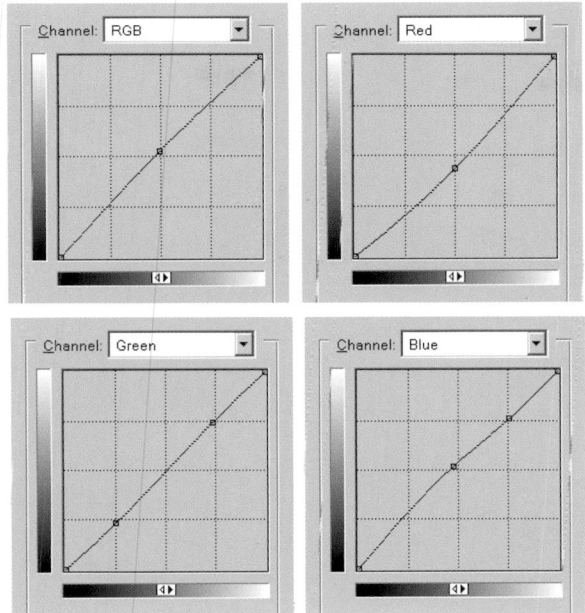

Fig. 10-3-k This is the Curves adjustment I used to correct the background. I applied this adjustment, using the mask in Figure 10-3-j, to produce Figure 10-3-l. These curves lighten the background slightly and make it substantially bluer and more cyan. The green curve eliminates some color crossover, making the shadows less green and highlights less pink, as shown in Figure 10-3-l.

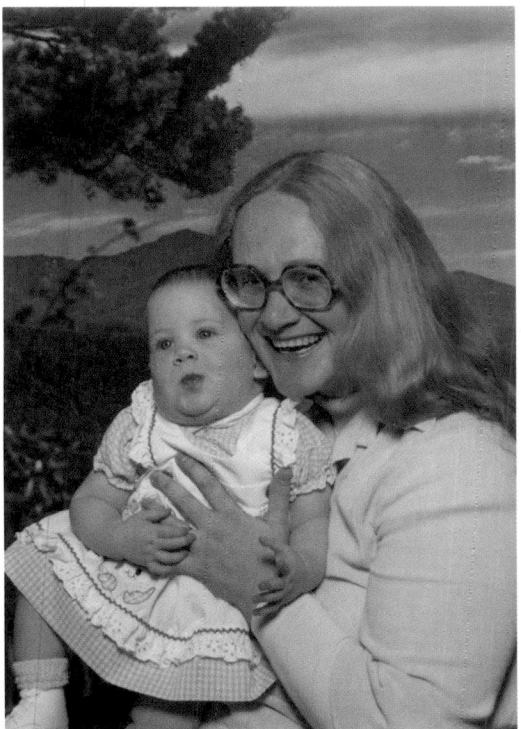

Fig. 10-3-l The masked Curves adjustment from Figure 10-3-k, plus a saturation boost of 20 points, improved the background a lot. The sky in the backdrop is now a shade of blue instead of muddy green, the clouds are closer to neutral, and the tree branch is more green than brown.

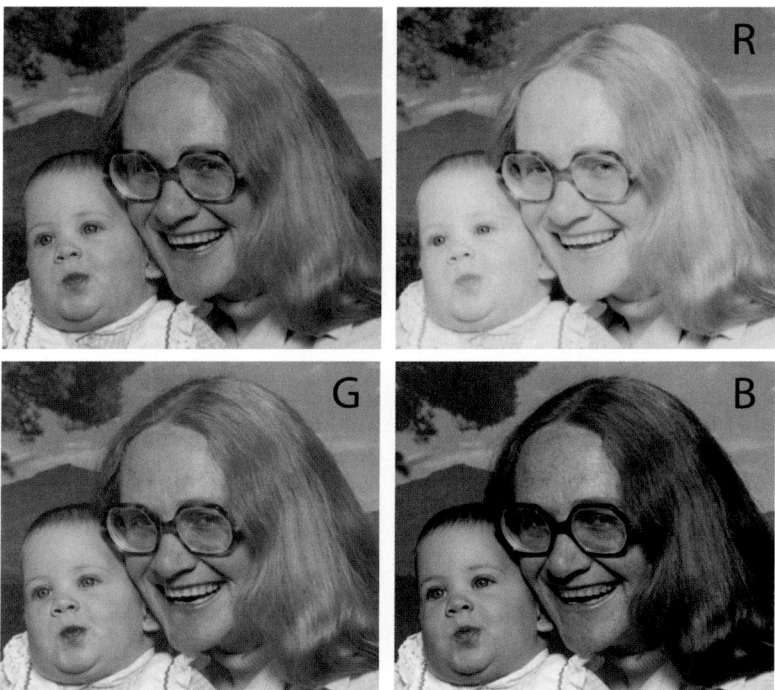

Fig. 10-3-m This close-up of the faces shows the need for some skin tone corrections. The skin color is uneven and blotchy. The individual color channels indicate that the problem is not with the red channel, which has smooth and even tones, but with the green and blue channels. The green channel is a particular problem because it has too much midtone contrast; that's what makes the skin color vary from flushed to sallow.

individual red, green, and blue channels. The green channel (lower left) made it clear that most of the problem was due to excessive contrast in the magenta. That exaggerated modest variations in the rosiness of the skin tones such that they ended up with sallow and flushed complexions.

To fix this, I traced out a new mask with the Lasso tool, shown in Figure 10-3-n, to let me work on skin tones and nothing else. I created a set of curves (Figure 10-3-o) to correct the blotchiness. The green curve left most tones unchanged, but it reduced the contrast in the green values between about 120 and 170, which corresponded to the range of values in the face. To a lesser degree, the blue curve lowered the contrast of the yellows, eliminating the sallow quality in the shadows and making the highlights less pink. A very slight raising of the midpoint of the RGB curve lightened the skin tones overall.

This was all it took to produce a much improved complexion for both mother and baby (Figure 10-3-p). There were still some yellow and pink blotches, especially in the shadows. I eliminated them by grabbing a good average skin color with the eyedropper and using the airbrush tool set to Color at a few percent strength to spray in that hue without altering the brightness in those areas. I also used the airbrush set to Darken to mute the highlights on the faces.

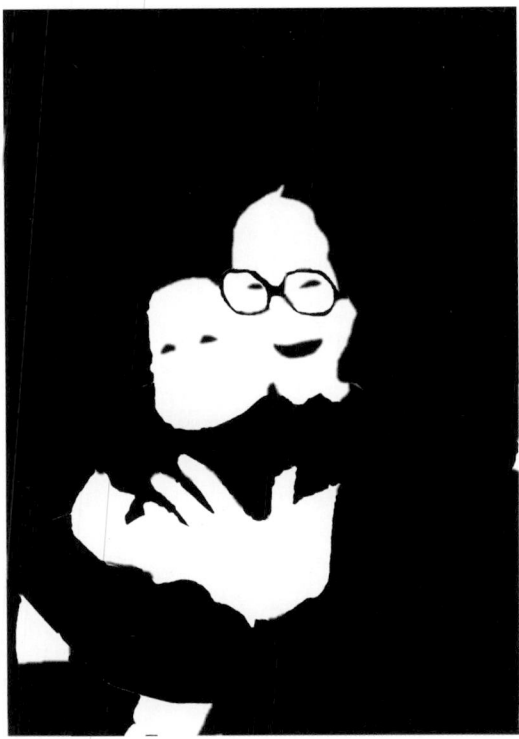

Fig. 10-3-n This mask, hand-drawn with the Lasso tool, allows me to correct the skin tones in Figure 10-3-l without altering the rest of the photograph.

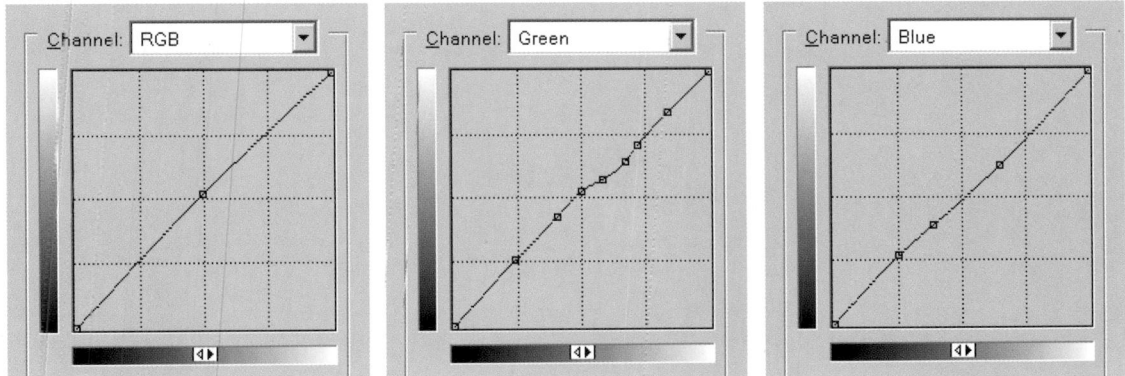

Fig. 10-3-o This Curves adjustment, applied through the mask from Figure 10-3-n, eliminates the blotchy skin tones (see Figure 10-3-p). The RGB curve lightens the skin tones slightly. The major correction is to the green curve, which substantially lowers contrast in the range of the magenta tones shown in the face. The blue curve adds a bit of yellow to the highlights, so they're less pink, and subtracts a little from the shadows, making them less brown.

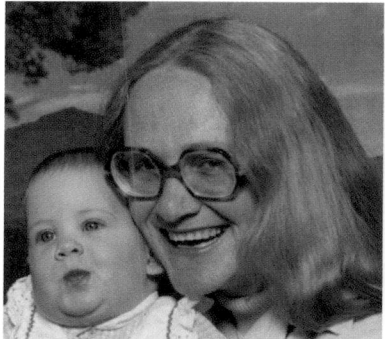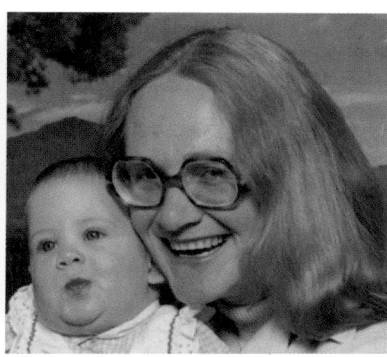

Fig. 10-3-p The enlargement on the left is from Figure 10-3-l before correction. The enlargement on the right shows the effect of the Curves adjustment from Figure 10-3-o. It really improves the skin color.

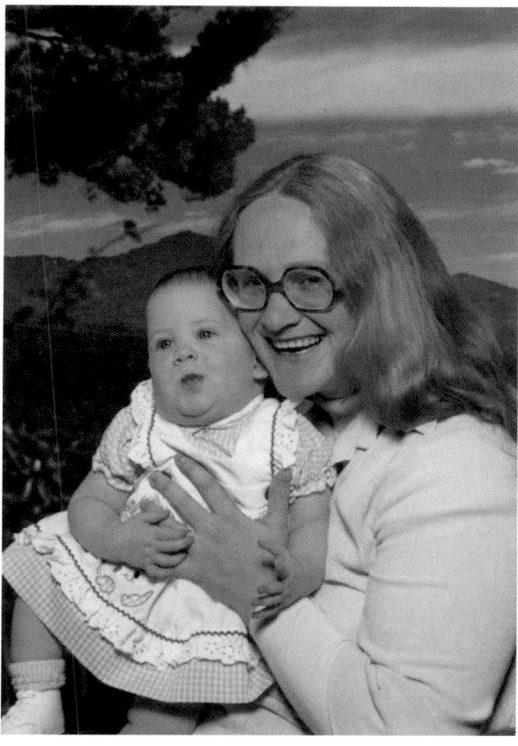

Fig. 10-3-q Here's the final restoration, after some final local color adjustments, dodging and burning-in, a little bit of airbrushing to get rid of the worst hot spots on the skin, and a thorough cleaning up of dirt, cracks, and minor physical damage. Yes, that flaming red hair is correctly colored . . . and natural, to boot!

I corrected the slightly flat and bluish highlights in the clothing by applying the foreground mask and kicking up the RGB highlight value in the Curves tool while dropping the blue highlight value a notch. I switched to the background and slightly darkened it to bring it into better compositional balance with the subjects.

The color was now almost on target except for two items—the woman's hair and her teeth. She's a brilliant redhead, not the reddish blond in the photo. I fixed that with the Burn tool set to a value of 10%

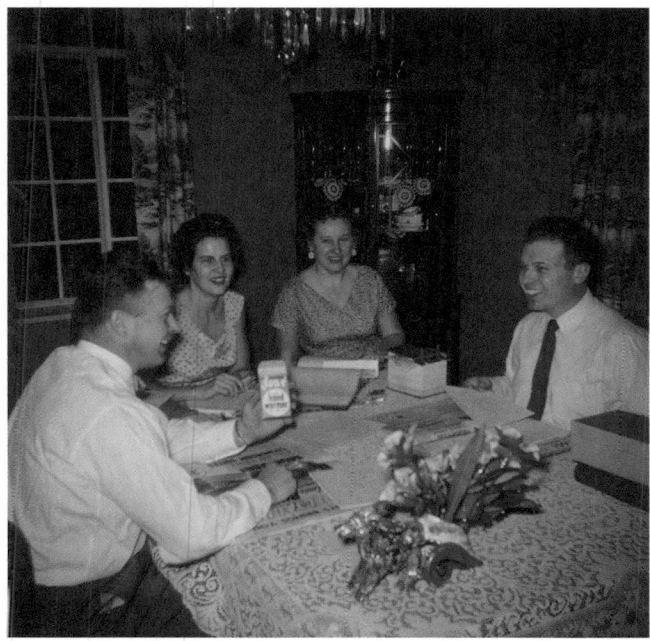

Fig. 10-4-a This is a 50-year-old Ektachrome (E-1) slide. It's lost a great deal of cyan dye and has developed an overall red stain. In addition, it has a bad case of the "measles"—there are yellowish spots all over the background.

for the midtones. In the channels palette I made the green channel the only active one (but left all the channels visible, so I could judge the full-color photograph) and gave the hair a couple of passes with the Burn tool. The results were perfect!

As for her teeth, which were excessively dark and yellow in the restored photograph, I first dodged them lightly overall and then dodged only the blue channel to remove some of the yellowish cast.

The final cleanup wasn't difficult, but it was very time consuming. I went over the picture at 100% magnification using the Clone, Dodge, and Burn tools to eliminate any blotches, scratches, dust specks, and artifacts along the boundary between the oval area and the surrounding area that my initial adjustments missed. The finished restoration (Figure 10-3-q) is impressive, especially considering that very little of what I did was an arbitrary application of tone and color to the image—95% of what you see truly was a restoration from data contained in the original print.

Example 4: A Faded E-1 Slide

The 1950s medium-format Ektachrome slide shown in Figure 10-4-a is very badly faded. Process E-1 slide films have proven very unstable. This slide has lost about two-thirds of its cyan dye; the maximum density of the cyan image is only 1.0 density units—a terribly low number!

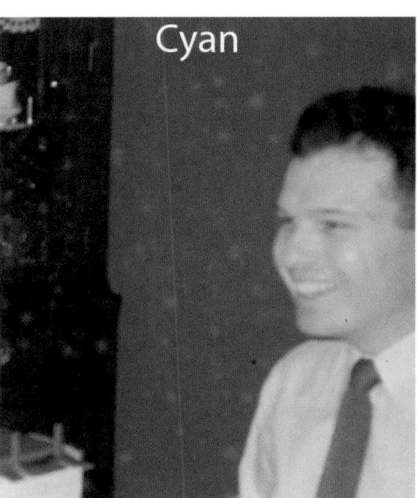 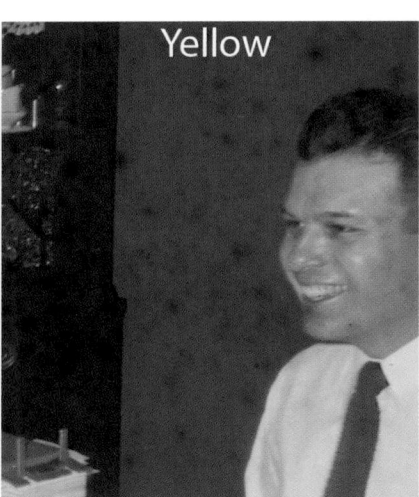

Fig. 10-4-b
Enlargements of the red (cyan dye image) and blue (yellow dye image) channels from Figure 10-4-a show the "measles." The spots are missing cyan dye and have excess amounts of yellow dye, making them a lighter orange-yellow in the photograph.

To make matters worse, the slide is pockmarked with orange-speckle "measles" damage (Figure 10-4-b), regions where the cyan dye image has faded even more and serious yellow stain has occurred. And if that were not enough, the amateur camera and flash that made this photograph produced severe vignetting and chromatic aberration (color fringing).

Right out of the gate, I ran into another obstacle: making a good scan was going to be extremely difficult. This is exactly the kind of slide I warned about back in Chapter 4, Getting the Photo into the Computer, page 119. There's so much density loss in one dye layer that it makes it very difficult for the scanner to collect good tonal information from all the dye layers. The magenta dye layer is nearly intact, with the result that scans that produced acceptable cyan information completely wiped out the magenta midtone and shadow detail (Figure 10-4-c). Without magenta tonal separation, it would be impossible to accurately restore color in the midtones and shadows.

One way to acquire the whole density range would be to make several scans at different exposures and combine them using Picture Window's Stack Images Transformation, as I illustrated in Figure 4-31. Chapter 9, Tips, Tricks, and Enhancements, page 316, tells you how to do this. For this particular restoration job, though, I solved my problem with the scanner's built-in DIGITAL ROC software. Actually, I ran the full DIGITAL ICE[3] suite to clean up dirt and scratches and suppress film grain, but ROC was the essential tool. DIGITAL ROC in the scanner has access to the raw scanner data, so it can make use of all that raw shadow information that a straight scan has trouble retaining (Figure 10-4-d). ROC substantially corrected the color but the high magenta densities cost me some shadow detail and made the image a little noisy, so I made

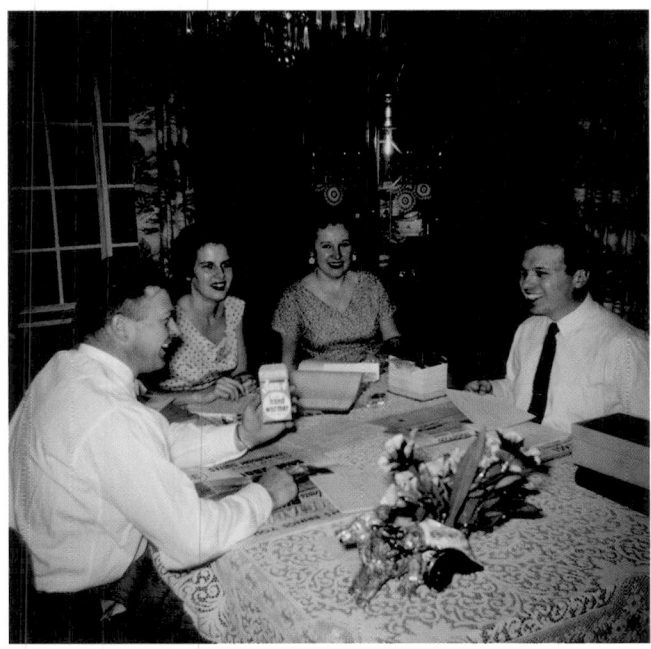

Fig. 10-4-c The magenta dye image makes it tough to scan this slide; it has so much density in the shadow areas—especially compared to the cyan and yellow dye images—that a normal scan cannot capture all three layers successfully. A scan that records the other two dye layers correctly completely blocks up the shadows in the magenta layer, as pictured here.

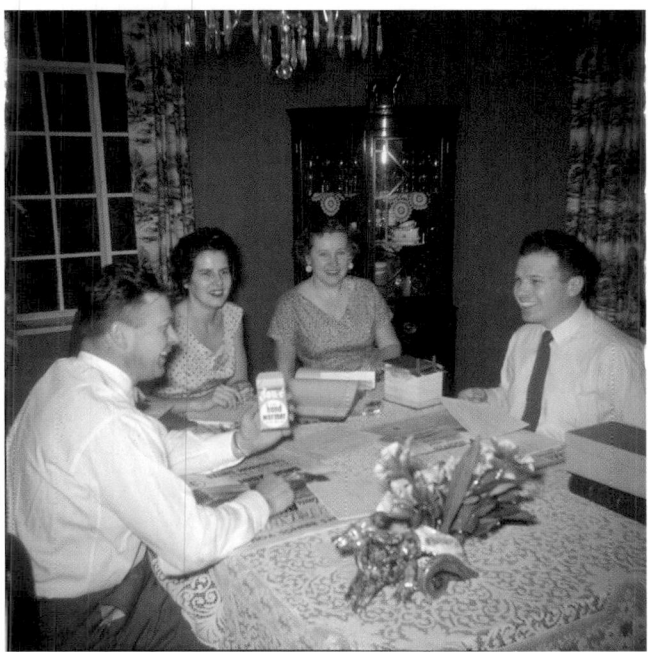

Fig. 10-4-d DIGITAL ROC to the rescue! ROC normalizes the densities in all three dye images as it does its color analysis and correction. It pulls in much better shadow detail in all the channels that any straight scan would.

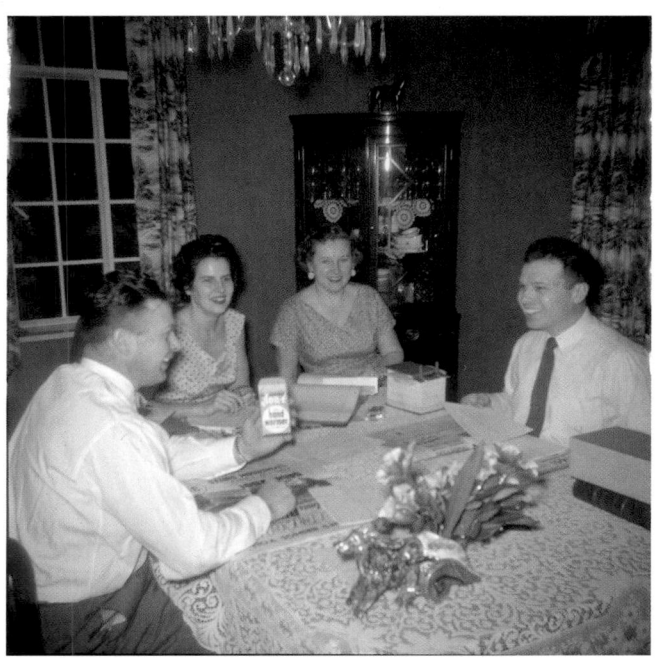

Fig. 10-4-e Scanning with 16× sampling does an even better job in the shadows. Compare the detail in the cabinet in the background in this photo with the one in Figure 10-4-d. More detail's visible here, and it has less noise. The color produced by ROC in the single-sampled scan, though, is better than in the 16× scan. Combining the two scans in layers gets me the best of both (see Figure 10-4-f).

a new scan with 16× multiple sampling turned on. In this mode the scanner makes 16 measurements of each pixel instead of one, which substantially reduces noise and extracts more shadow detail, but also greatly increases scan time.

The shadow tones were substantially improved (Figure 10-4-e), but strangely ROC did not do as good a job of color restoration as it did with a single-sampled scan. The easiest way to fix this was to combine the best of both. I made a layered file with the 16×-sampled scan as the background layer and the single-sampled scan as Layer 1 and set the blend mode for Layer 1 to Color. That produced an image combining the luminance values from the 16× scan with the color values from the single-sampled scan (Figure 10-4-f). I flattened that file to reduce bulk and saved it.

Before correcting the chromatic aberration, I cleaned up the dust and scratches. If I corrected the chromatic aberration first, the point-light specks would be converted to colored smears that would be harder to get rid of, as illustrated in an earlier chapter (Figure 6-51). To clean up the scan, I used my usual method of applying the Dust & Scratches filter, assigning this to the History Brush, reverting to the previous state, and painting over the defects with the brush (Chapter 8, page 268).

I saved the retouched file as a TIFF file so that I could import it into Picture Window, whose Chromatic Aberration correction tool is much better than Photoshop's (Chapter 6, page 220). The control window is

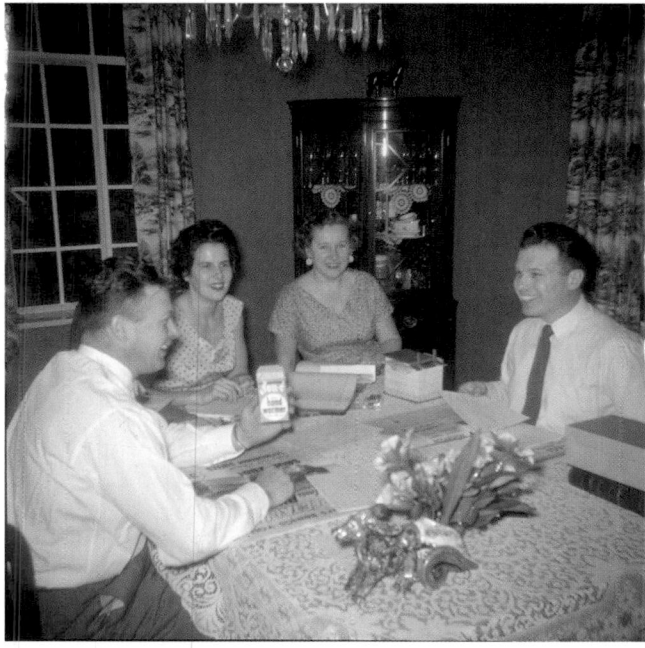

Fig. 10-4-f To create this photograph, I copied the single-sampled scan into a background layer in a new file. I copied the 16× scan into Layer 1 and set the blend mode to Color. That merged the color rendition of Figure 10-4-d with the tonality of Figure 10-4-e, producing this result, which is superior to both.

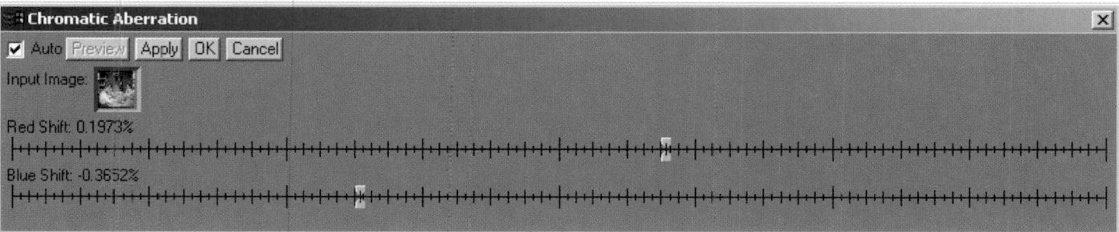

Fig. 10-4-g Picture Window has a better tool for fixing chromatic aberration than Photoshop. The resizable Chromatic Aberration control window lets me make much finer adjustments to correct color fringing. The result of this fix is shown in Figure 10-4-h.

resizable (Figure 10-4-g), so I stretched it out horizontally to give me much finer control. I saved the corrected TIFF file (Figure 10-4-h) and returned to Photoshop.

I decided not to fix the vignetting with the vignetting correction available in Photoshop's Lens Distortion filter, because the edges were not just darker but also more green-cyan. I wanted to correct both the tone and color, so the right solution was a Curves adjustment layer (Figure 10-4-i) with a radial gradient mask to restrict the effects to the periphery. I modified the mask a bit with a black airbrush in the lower

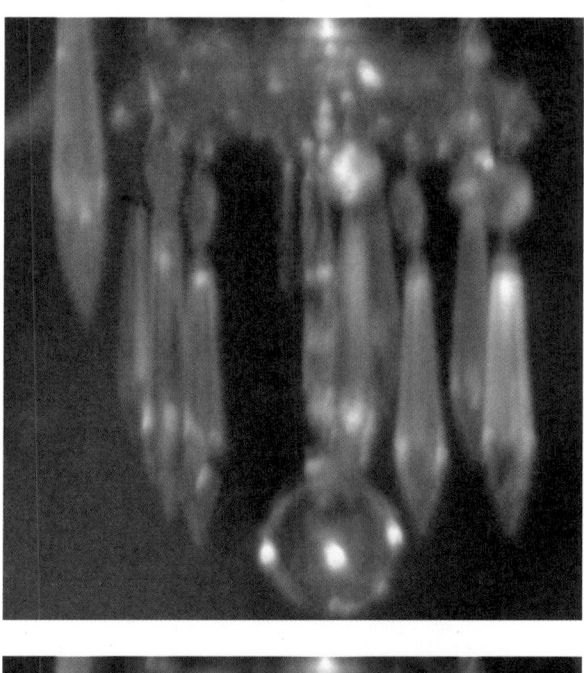

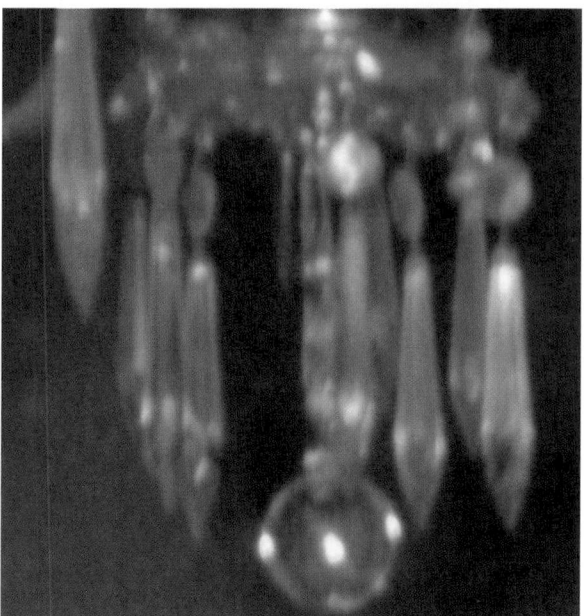

Fig. 10-4-h This enlargement of the chandelier from Figure 10-4-f shows how Picture Window's Chromatic Aberration tool gets rid of the color fringing. The upper figure is the photograph before correction; the bottom one is the same photograph after I've removed the chromatic aberration.

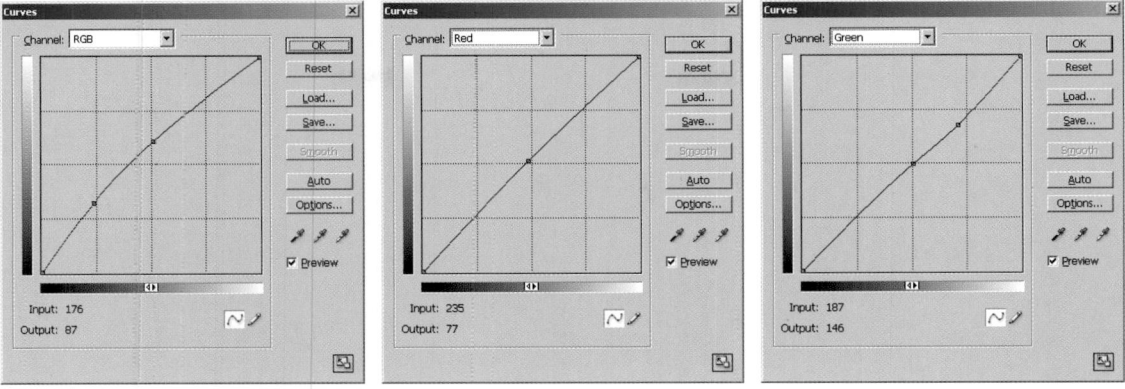

Fig. 10-4-i A Curves adjustment layer containing the mask in Figure 10-4-j corrects the vignetting that's visible in Figure 10-4-f. It also removes the slight greenish tinge from the darker edges of the photograph.

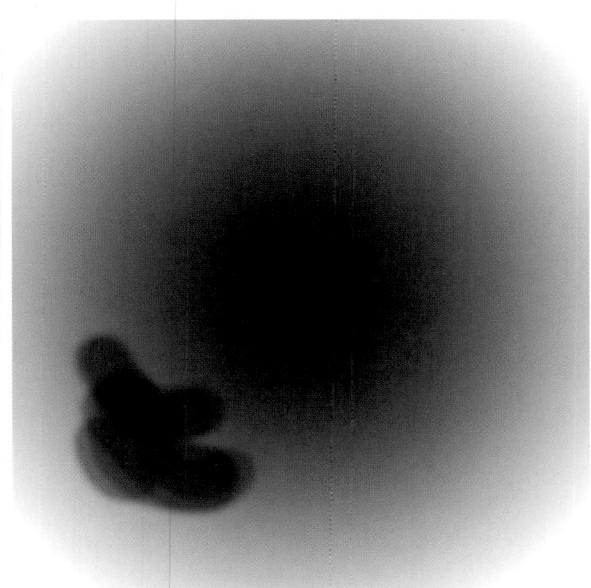

Fig. 10-4-j This is the mask I used in the Curves adjustment layer that contained the curves from Figure 10-4-i. The main component of the mask is a circular gradient running from black at the center to white in the corners. The dark splotch in the lower left portion of the mask corresponds to the bright white shirt in the photograph. I didn't want that shirt to get any lighter, so I blocked the effect of the Curves adjustment there.

left portion so that the white shirt wouldn't be further lightened (Figure 10-4-j).

Next I darkened the foreground to reduce the uneven flash illumination, using another Curves adjustment layer (Figure 10-4-k) with the mask in Figure 10-4-l. A bit of highlight burning-in on the white shirt in the foreground and some cloning work along the edges to clean them up took me to Figure 10-4-m.

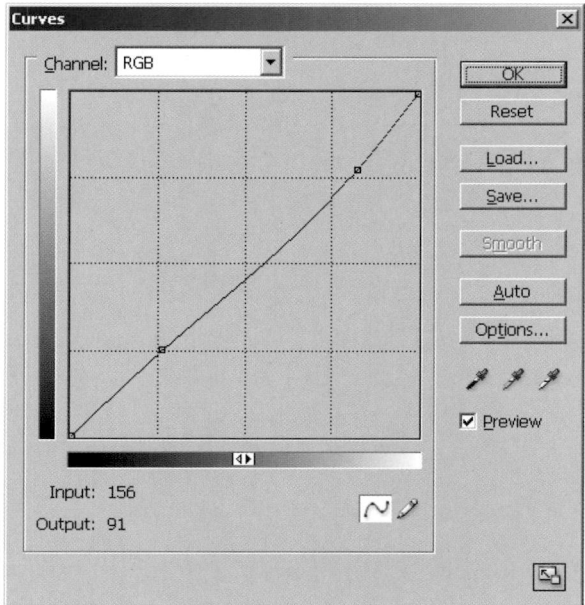

Fig. 10-4-k This Curves adjustment burns in the foreground of the photograph, which was brightly illuminated by the on-camera flash that made the photograph. I used this curve in an adjustment layer with the mask from Figure 10-4-l.

Fig. 10-4-l The mask for the foreground burn-in layer that evens out the illumination in the photograph by eliminating the hot spot on the tablecloth and the planter.

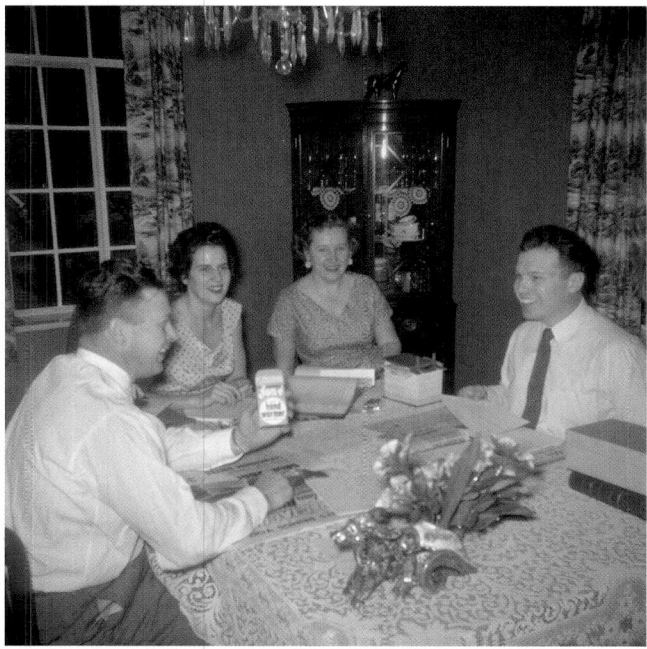

Fig. 10-4-m This is how the photograph looks after correcting the vignetting and the bright foreground with two Curves adjustment layers. Compare it to Figure 10-4-f; the lighting looks much better in this photograph.

It was time to deal with the orange-speckle problem. I wanted to create a mask that would select for them to avoid having to deal with each and every speckle individually. Since each speckle was minus cyan and plus yellow, I started by subtracting the blue channel from the red channel. I made a copy of the full-color image and used the Channel Mixer with the settings shown in Figure 10-4-n to subtract the channels and double the contrast.

This did a pretty good job of grabbing the speckles, although it retained some image detail. I made a Levels adjustment on that image to bring the speckles up to white and pushed everything else as close to black as I could without clipping off too many of the speckles (Figure 10-4-o). I copied that grayscale image into a new channel in the original file for use as a mask.

I loaded this mask as a selection and created a new Curves adjustment layer. I adjusted the red and blue curves to make as many of the speckles as possible blend into the background (Figure 10-4-p). This was highly successful, but some speckles were missed, and other parts of the image that were retained by the mask were slightly altered.

I fixed that by retouching the layer's mask. Using a white airbrush set to about 20% opacity I spotted out the few unrepaired speckles by adding gray and white dots to the mask. Switching the brush to black, I filled in the parts of the mask that erroneously selected real image detail, switching back and forth between viewing the mask and viewing

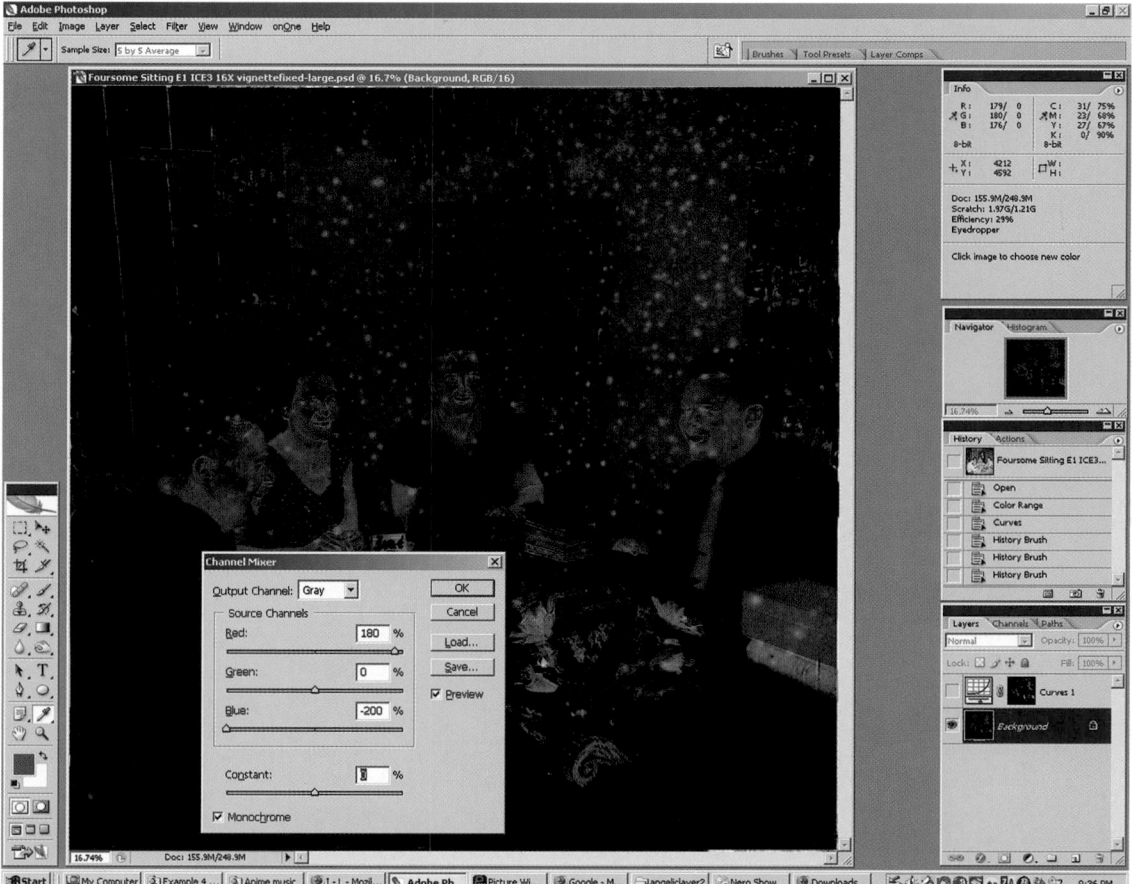

Fig. 10-4-n I used Channel Mixer to create a mask that selected for the "measles." Since the measles are light in the red channel and dark in the blue, relative to the rest of the photograph (see Figure 10-4-b), I set the blue channel to –200% and adjusted the red channel until I got maximum contrast between the measles and the rest of the photograph (180%). That created the low-contrast mask in the background of this screenshot.

the photograph to catch areas I had missed. It took me over an hour to get to the finished mask in Figure 10-4-q, which is much less time than it would have taken to attack all the speckles by hand. Figure 10-4-r shows an enlarged portion of the photograph before and after speckle elimination.

Now we're on the home stretch of the damage repair. There are some yellow stains in the man's shirt in the foreground and some cyan stains on the other man's left shoulder. I eliminated those easily by using the Clone tool set to Color mode to clone the color from the neutral part of the shirt over the stains. They disappeared entirely.

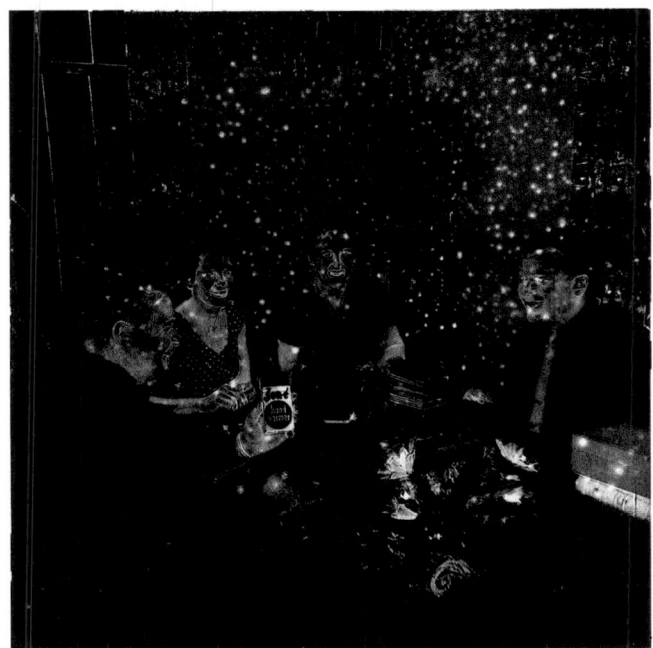

Fig. 10-4-o I used a Levels adjustment to greatly increase the contrast of the mask, making the majority of measles pure white and most of the rest of the photograph solid black.

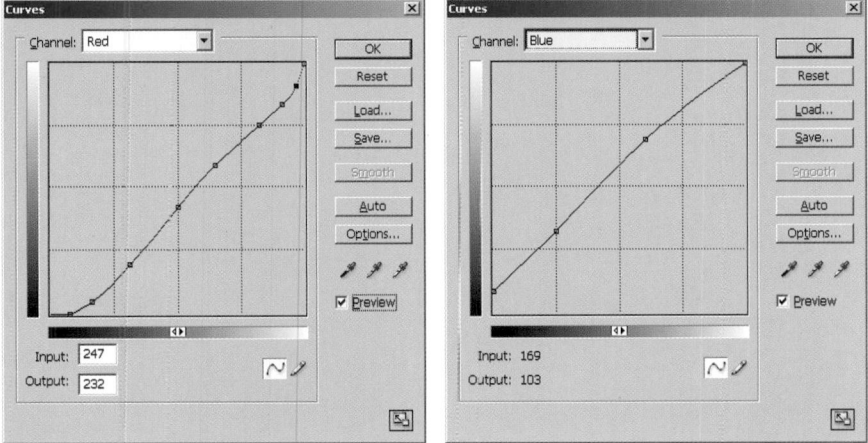

Fig. 10-4-p To attack the measles, I used these curves in a Curves adjustment layer that was masked with Figure 10-4-o. The red curve increases the amount of cyan in the measles, while the blue curve reduces the amount of yellow. I adjusted the curves by eye to eliminate as many speckles as possible. It did not do a perfect job; a few measles slipped past the adjustments, and some other parts of the image were affected.

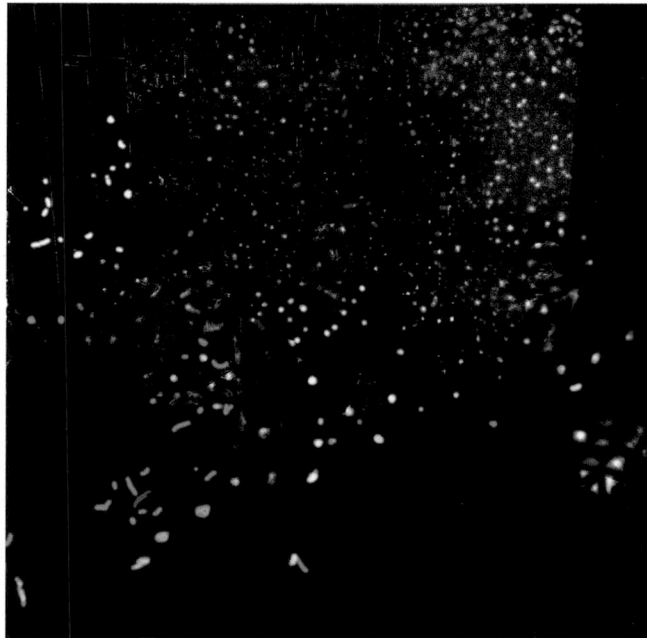

Fig. 10-4-q I hand-retouched the mask with white and black brushes to completely block out the photographic image and to pick up a few speckles that the Channel Mixer mask missed. This mask got rid of the measles most effectively (see Figure 10-4-r).

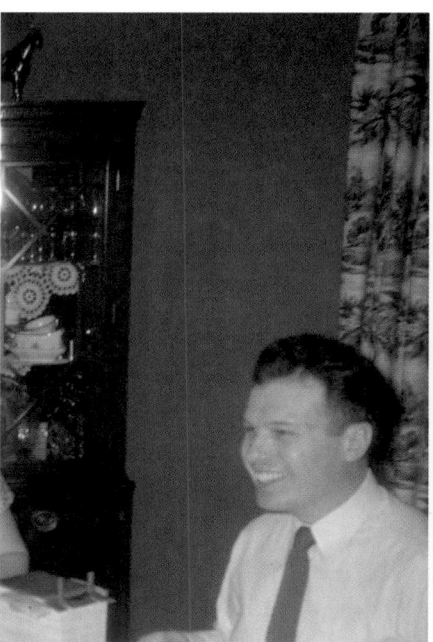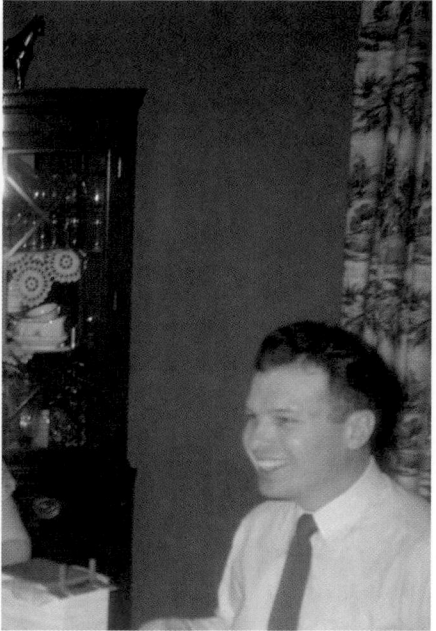

Fig. 10-4-r Before and after measles eradication! The figure on the left is enlarged from Figure 10-4-m. The figure on the right shows how well the Curves adjustment layer erased the measles entirely. Now that the photograph's been cleaned up, it's time to make the final tone and color adjustments.

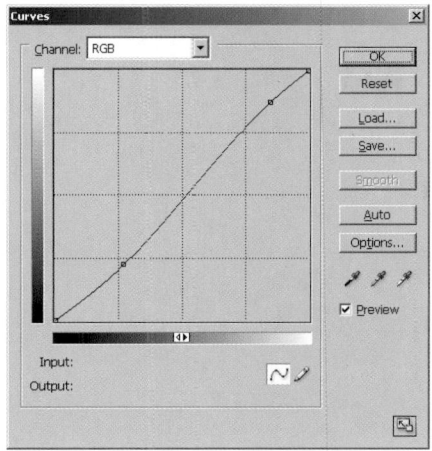 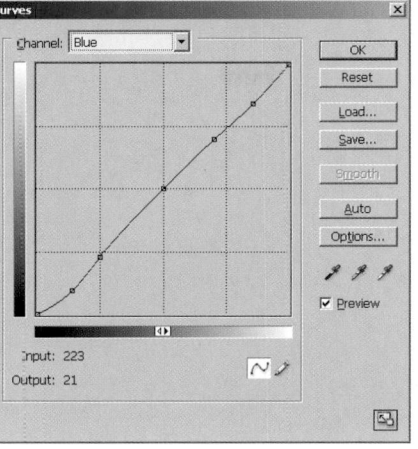

Fig. 10-4-s The RGB curve, a modest S-shaped curve, gives the midtones a little more brilliance and darkens the photograph slightly. The blue curve leaves the midtones alone but removes a small amount of blue color cast in the highlights and shadows (see Figure 10-4-t).

The burgundy wall in the background needed a little bit of cleanup to eliminate scan noise and slight tonal irregularities that were left behind by the orange-speckle elimination. Because the wall was distinctively colored, I could easily select for it using the Magic Wand with only a little bit of Lasso work to eliminate spurious selections in the curtain and china cabinet. I shrank that selection by 15 pixels and feathered it by 10. That was to avoid a sharp demarcation line between the selected area and the rest of the picture. Applying the Dust & Scratches filter with a radius of 50 pixels and a threshold of 5 cleaned up the wall very nicely.

Having completely cleaned up the damage, it was time for me to refine the tone and color. The photograph was dull and desaturated, problems easily fixed with a Curves adjustment layer that increased the midrange contrast (Figure 10-4-s). I also used this layer to refine the color in the highlights and shadows.

The skin tones still lacked a certain richness, so I increased saturation by 14 points and assigned that change to the History Brush. I reverted to the previous state and painted in the increased saturation on the folks' skin to get Figure 10-4-t.

Next I zoomed in on the faces and did a little cosmetic work. On-camera flash tends to blow out the highlights in a face and often produces sallow, even cyanotic, skin tones, depending on just how the light reflects off the skin. The two women look distinctly jaundiced, and the five-o'clock shadow on the man in the foreground had an unhealthy greenish cast. Hair highlights were also unrealistically blue.

I fixed all of this with the Burn tool set to an exposure of 5% for the midtones. First I switched to the green channel and brushed a bit of "blush" into the skin tones that were especially sallow. That also took care of the green five-o'clock shadow. Then I switched to the blue

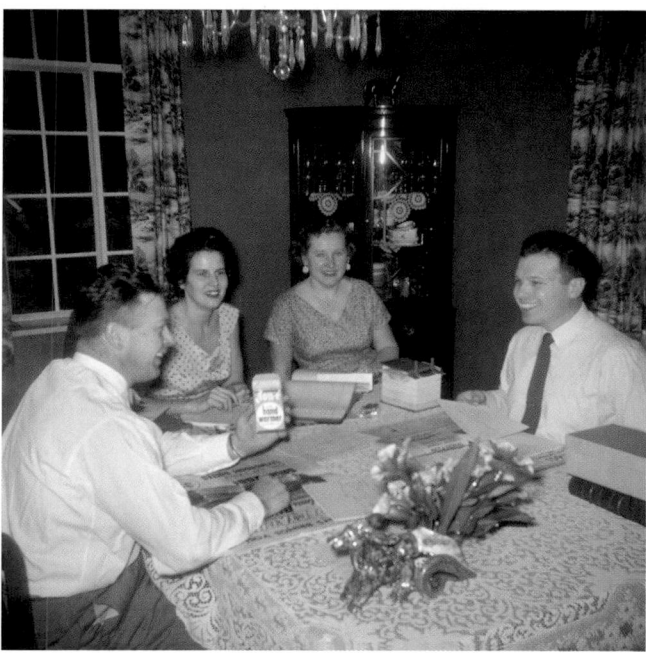

Fig. 10-4-t This is how Figure 10-4-m looks after I've cleaned up the yellow stains and made the Curves adjustment from Figure 10-4-s. The colors look better, and the faces no longer look flat and pasty.

channel and ran the Burn tool over skin tones that were too pink and over the hair.

The trick is to not overdo this. I didn't want to wipe out the variations in tone and color, which would have made the faces look unnaturally flat. The objective was to narrow the range of colors and center all of them around a healthy look.

As a finishing touch on the faces, I used the Brush tool set at 5% strength to carefully brush some tone into the strong highlights on the faces. I used the eyedropper to sample the tones near the areas I wanted to soften. Just as with burning-in, it's important not to overdo this. A little bit goes a long way. Figure 10-4-u shows how much these little adjustments improved the people's appearance.

My very last action was to burn in the highlights and the midtones in the foreground by about 10%. This kept those broad light areas from dominating the picture so much, and it focused attention better on the people. The result is in Figure 10-4-v.

Example 5: Reassembling an Astronomical Glass Plate

I made the photograph shown in Figure 10-5-a, my first astrophotograph, back in high school in 1966. Back then all serious astrophotography was done on special glass plates that were only about half the thickness of the old pictorial photography glass plates. Twenty years ago

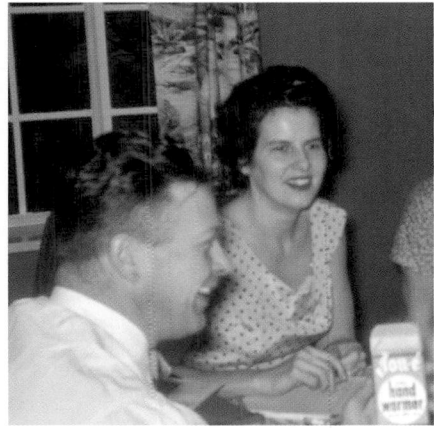 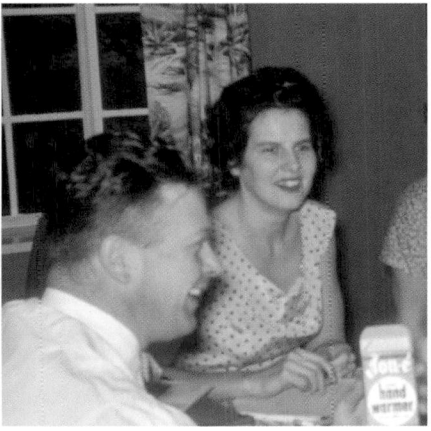

Fig. 10-4-u The enlargement from Figure 10-4-t, on the left, shows some unattractive hot spots on the faces, and the skin colors are slightly blotchy. The figure on the right shows the improved faces after a little retouching work with the Burn and Brush tools, as described in the main text.

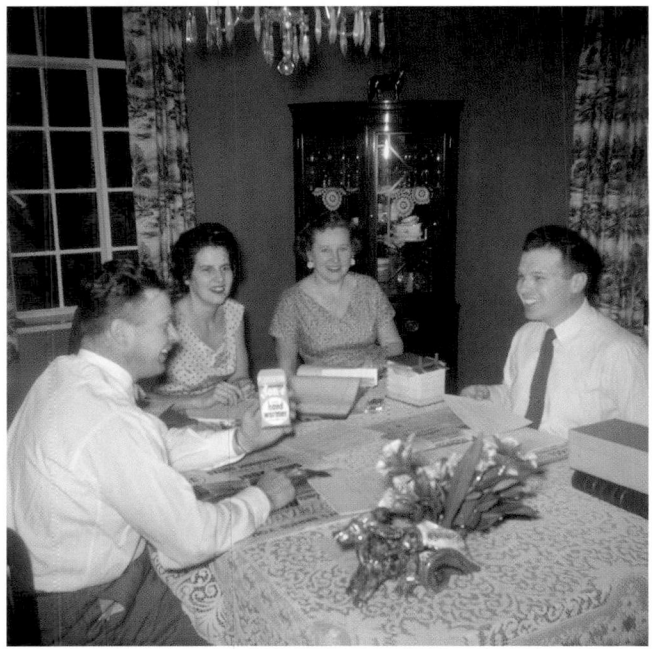

Fig. 10-4-v Here's the finished restoration. The color looks good and natural, there's plenty of highlight and shadow detail, and I've attractively softened the harsh lighting of the original photograph. Plus, all the measles are gone!

my photograph got broken into eight fragments during a move. Now it's time to fix it.

Fortunately, all the breaks in the plate were very clean, so I was able to reassemble the pieces on the platen of the scanner in positions very close to where they should be in the repaired photograph. Unlike the antique glass plate in Example 1, this was an easy scan with no unusually high densities, so I didn't bother masking off the edges of the plate.

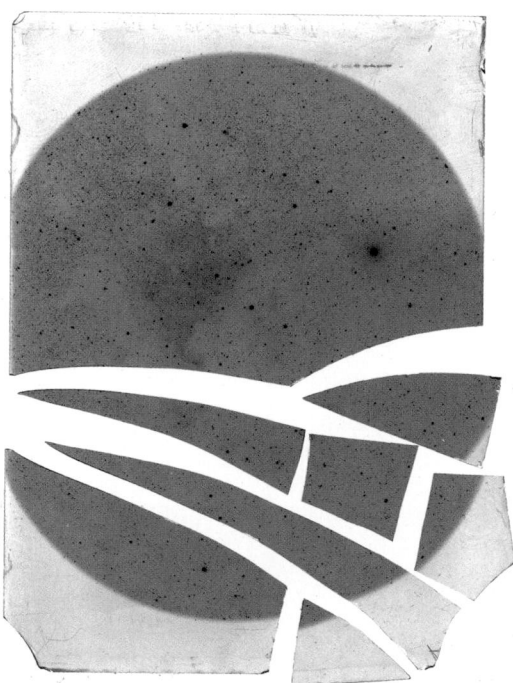

Fig. 10-5-a I made this photograph of the North America Nebula 40 years ago on a glass plate. It got broken in a move about 20 years ago. I'm glad I saved the pieces, because now I can repair it digitally.

My plate recorded a lot of sky glow in the "black" parts of the sky, so I adjusted the levels in the scanner software and the gamma to lighten up the scan (Figure 10-5-b). I also made some modest adjustments to the curves to open up the tones a bit more. None of this was strictly necessary, and a straight 16-bit scan would have been entirely adequate, but it never hurts to improve things early on.

I scanned the plate in 16-bit RGB mode at a resolution of 1200 ppi. In Photoshop, I flipped it left to right and used the Channel Mixer (Figure 10-5-c) to blend all three channels into a monochrome image and converted it to the grayscale file you see in Figure 10-5-d.

My next task was to reassemble all the fragments into as perfect a fit as possible before repairing the cracks. Because of my careful scan, there were almost no gaps between the fragments. The best tool for outlining each fragment as a selection was the Magnetic Lasso tool. Beginning at the lower right corner of the plate, I pinned the Lasso to the start of the edge of the long shard and dragged it along the crack, setting curve points as I went. When I finished selecting this long, thin knife-shaped fragment, shown against the pink mask overlay in Figure 10-5-e, I saved that selection as a mask in a new channel (Mask 1 in Figure 10-5-f).

Next, I used the Magnetic Lasso tool to pick out the horizontal crack that bisected the plate, selecting for the two fragments in the top portion

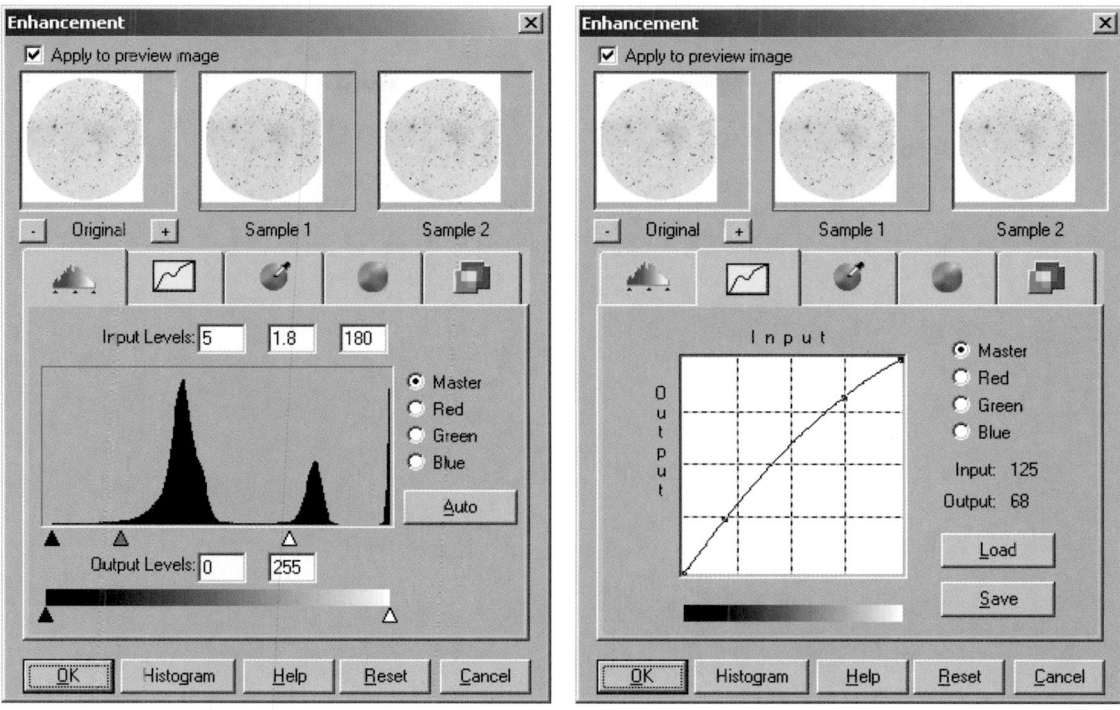

Fig. 10-5-b These are the scanner settings I used to produce Figure 10-5-d. They remove the overall fog and stain from the plate and increase the contrast in the dense parts of the negative, which correspond to the real astronomical details.

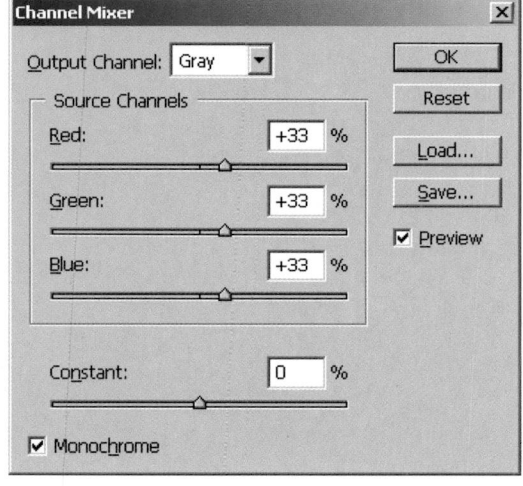

Fig. 10-5-c These Channel Mixer settings combine equal amounts of the RGB components of the scan to produce a grayscale image (Figure 10-5-d). This gives me maximum tonal information with minimum noise for this photograph.

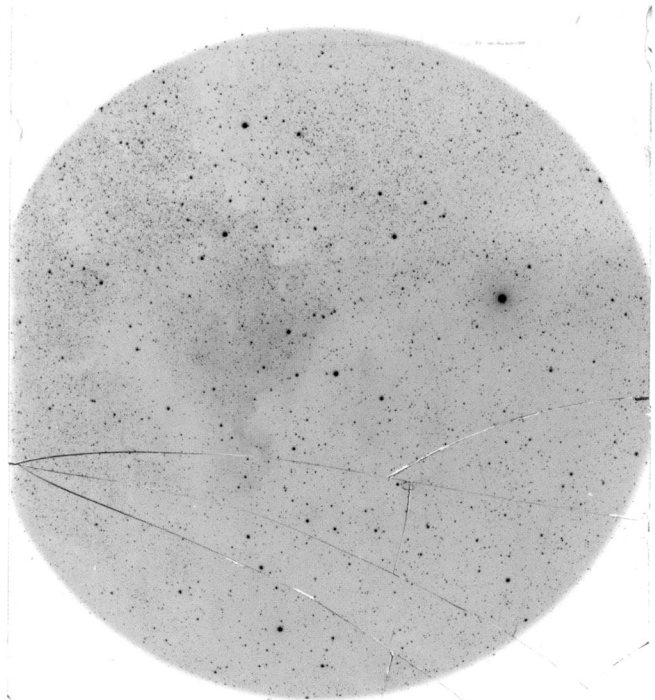

Fig. 10-5-d The adjusted scan of Figure 10-5-a, converted to grayscale. I positioned the shards of glass in approximate alignment on the scanner platen before making the scan. I'm going to have to digitally move them around like pieces of a puzzle to get the alignment perfect.

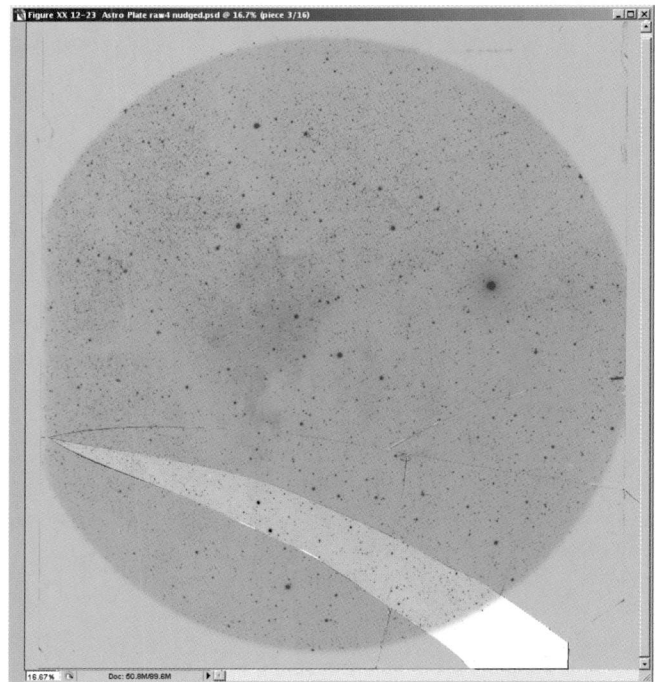

Fig. 10-5-e I use masks to isolate each fragment of the plate, so that I can nudge it into the exactly the right position. I made the mask, shown here as a pink overlay on the photograph, using the Magnetic Lasso tool to trace the boundary of this shard.

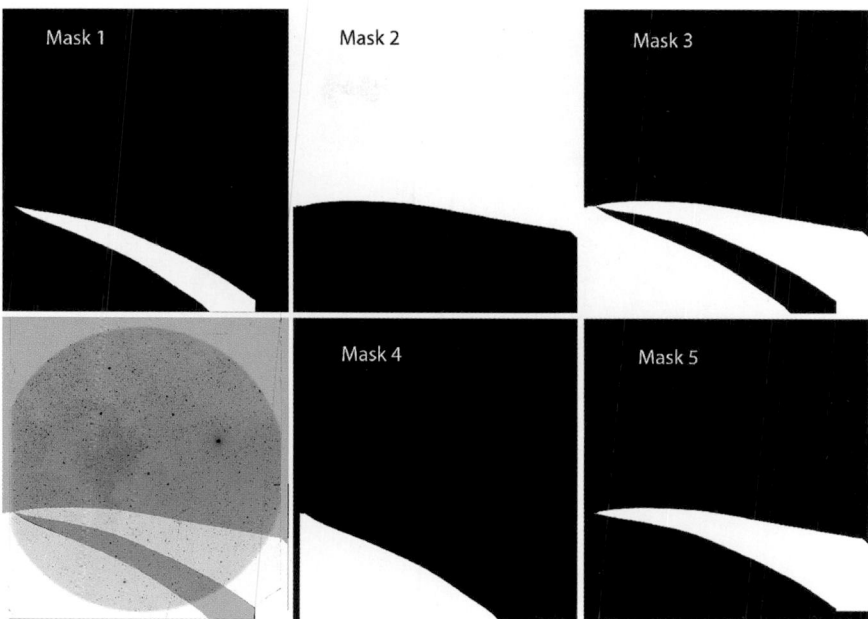

Fig. 10-5-f Mask 1 is the mask I created in Figure 10-5-e. I made Mask 2 by tracing the long horizontal crack with the Magnetic Lasso tool. Inverting Mask 2 and subtracting Mask 1 from it, using the Load Selection dialog, produced Mask 3, shown superimposed on the original photograph at the lower left. It selects two areas of the plate, each of which contains two fragments. I isolated those areas with the Lasso tool and saved them as Masks 4 and 5. I subdivided those masks using the Magnetic Lasso tool to give me four more masks (not pictured) for those individual fragments of the plate.

of the plate. I saved that mask in another channel (Mask 2, Figure 10-5-f).

I can combine masks in a variety of ways, so I can isolate some pieces of the plate without having to retrace their edges by adding and subtracting masks. For example, I loaded the first mask and inverted it; that selected everything but the thin knife-shaped shard. Using the Load Selection dialog, I inverted the second mask and added it to the selection I'd already made.

That composite selection I made subtracted out the knife-shaped shard and everything in the top of the plate (Mask 3, Figure 10-5-f). It neatly selected two areas, each containing two fragments, as you can see in Figure 10-5-f, lower left, where I've overlaid this selection on the original scan. Using the regular Lasso tool, I selected each of those areas in turn and saved them as separate masks (Figure 10-5-f, Masks 4 and 5). Now the plate was subdivided into sections containing one or two fragments. I used the Magnetic Lasso tool to select each individual fragment out of those masks. I used the large unbroken top half of the plate

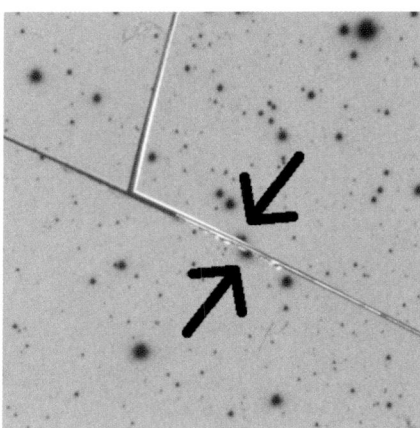 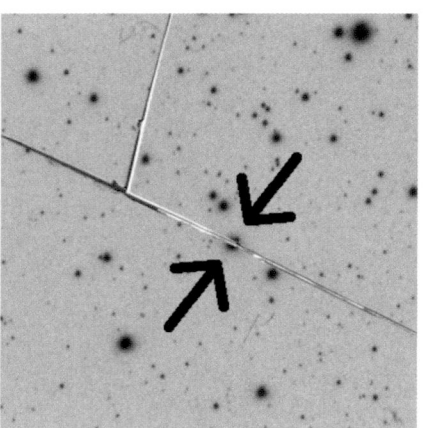

Fig. 10-5-g To find the correct alignment of the pieces of the plate, I looked for star images that straddled a crack and used them to match the two fragments. The arrows here point to the halves of such a star image in the unaligned (left) and aligned (right) images.

as a fixed base, loading the masks that selected the fragments that bordered that half and nudging them into alignment with it. I looked along the cracks for the occasional star image that straddled a crack (Figure 10-5-g). Those images worked like registration marks to let me guide the pieces into pixel-perfect alignment with each other. (*An aside:* If I were trying to preserve this as a scientific record, rather than just a nice picture, I would skip the whole next step of eliminating the cracks because that would erase real stars.)

Having "repaired" the plate, I erased the cracks themselves. The Median filter was ideal for this purpose because there was little or no detail along cracks that needed to be preserved, and the background was very uniform in average density. I set the filter with a wide radius (Figure 10-5-h) to completely obliterate the cracks.

I assigned the Median filter History state to the History Brush and reverted to the history state just before I applied the filter. That undid the global effect of the filter, so that I could use the History Brush to paint over the cracks

I attacked the cracks in two passes. The cracks themselves scanned as dark, but associated with them were clear parts where the emulsion of the plate had broken away. Those areas were all very small and whiter than the image and had no useful information, so I quickly painted them in with a large-radius History Brush set to Darken.

I zoomed in to 100% on the screen image and set the History Brush back to Normal with a radius of 5 pixels and 50% hardness. At that magnification, the cracks were long, shallow arcs for the most part. That permitted me to use shift-clicking to quickly select lengths of the crack and cover them over. I clicked the brush on the crack, moved the brush down the crack a short distance that corresponded to a "straight" segment, and shift-clicked the brush. The brush painted a straight line

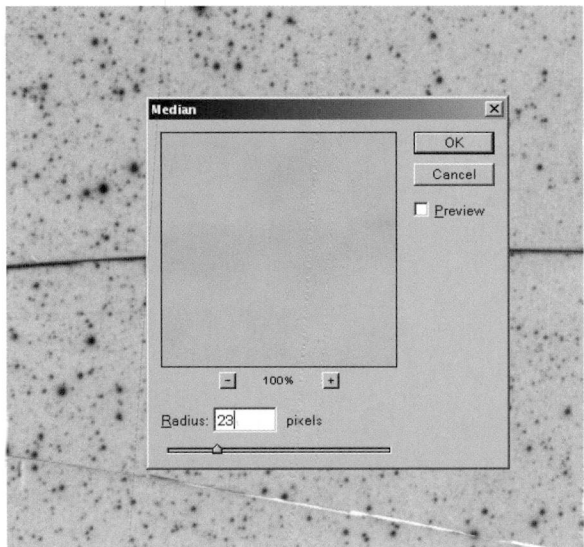

Fig. 10-5-h The Median filter, set to a wide radius, is a good way to erase the cracks. Here I've superimposed the Median filter preview on the corresponding area of the image. Observe how the dark horizontal crack's turned into an almost-invisible faint shadow. Painting in this filter with the History Brush eliminates cracks efficiently.

of Median filtering that nicely obliterated the short segment of the crack. I shift-clicked my way along the crack in short jumps, wiping whole sections with a single mouse-click. This was much faster and more accurate than manually painting along the length of the crack.

While I was at it, I used the Median filter History Brush to wipe out the scratches and dirt specks as well. Once the photograph was clean and crack-free, I cropped it and inverted the tones so that I could start working on it as a positive (Figure 10-5-i).

I used the eyedropper to spot-check the values in the darkest parts of the sky over the field of view. Near the center of the plate the blackest areas had a value of 88; this fell off radially to a value of 78 at the perimeter. I created a Curves adjustment layer to make the blacks darker and to even out the exposure.

First I created the adjustment layer with the curve settings shown in Figure 10-5-j. That layer dropped the values for the blacks by about 60 points. I wanted to darken the blacks at the perimeter about 10 points less than at the center to even out the exposure. That's five-sixths as much of a change at the edges as at the center.

To achieve this I added a radial gradient mask to the layer. I set the foreground color to 100% white, the background color to 85% (five-sixths) white, set the starting point of the gradient at the center of the circular image, and drew a gradient line out to just beyond the edge of the field of view. That produced the mask shown in Figure 10-5-k, which reduced the effect of the layer by just the right amount to give me a uniform exposure over the entire plate (Figure 10-5-l).

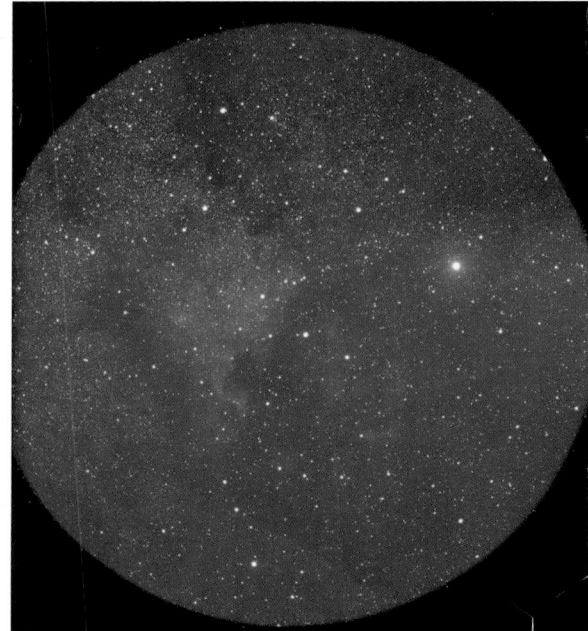

Fig. 10-5-i Here's the plate, repaired, cleaned up, and inverted to make a positive image. Now it's time to improve the tonality and clean up residual artifacts left from the repair job.

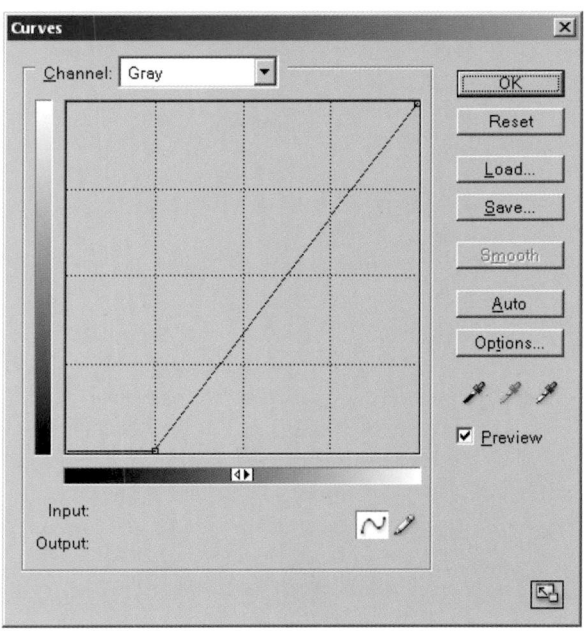

Fig. 10-5-j This Curves adjustment takes the sky background down to a dark charcoal gray in Figure 10-5-l. I used it in conjunction with the mask in Figure 10-5-k to even out the light falloff at the edges of the image.

Fig. 10-5-k This faint circular gradient mask, used in a Curves adjustment layer with the curve from Figure 10-5-j, produces the uniform and good-looking photograph in Figure 10-5-l.

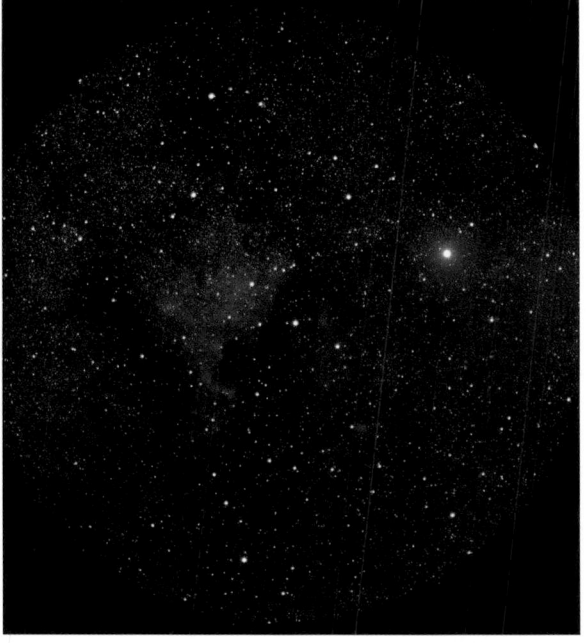

Fig. 10-5-l Here's the photograph corrected with a Curves adjustment layer using the curve from Figure 10-5-j and the mask from Figure 10-5-k.

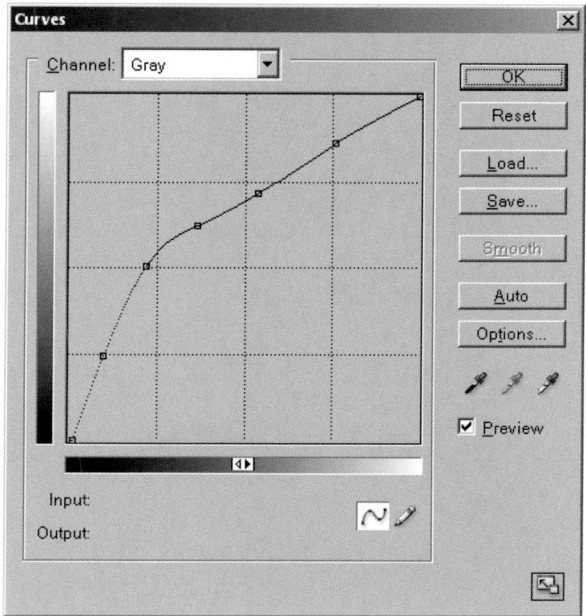

Fig. 10-5-m This Curves adjustment enhances contrast in the shadows, bringing out faint nebulae and detail in Figure 10-5-q.

I added a second Curves adjustment layer (Figure 10-5-m) that made the blacks a little richer and greatly boosted the contrast in the shadows to bring out the faint nebulosity without sacrificing detail in the star images. From an overall pictorial point of view this looks great, but the heavy contrast boost made it clear that more work was needed to blend the erased cracks into the image. Figure 10-5-n shows a particularly bad section that I selected with the Lasso tool for correction.

Image Doctor is very good at dealing with this type of problem. Its Smart Fill function does a better job of synthesizing complicated random-looking textures than the Spot Healing Brush in Photoshop or manual cloning and blending. Image Doctor only works on 8-bit images, though, which is the reason I didn't apply it earlier. I wanted to do as much tonal correction as I could to the photograph before reducing the bit depth from 16 to 8 bits.

After converting the photograph to 8 bits, I applied Image Doctor's Smart Fill to the area I selected (Figure 10-5-o). That produced almost the effect I wanted (Figure 10-5-p), but some areas that should have been filled with faint nebulae were filled with darker sky areas.

I corrected that using the History Brush. I assigned the Smart Fill operation to the brush, and reverted to the previous history state. I set the brush to 100% strength and Lighten and painted over the selected area. That laid down the random star images that Smart Fill had created for me. Then I switched the brush to Normal and 40% strength and

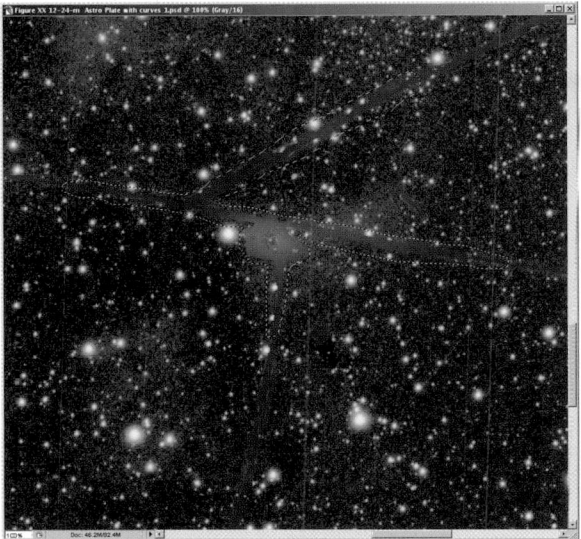

Fig. 10-5-n This screenshot shows an enlargement of the plate where four shards come together and some of the emulsion was flaked off (down and to the right of center in Figure 10-5-d). Here, the Median filter created a blur that has a distinctly different look and texture from the surrounding star field. I selected that region with the Lasso tool for repair by Image Doctor.

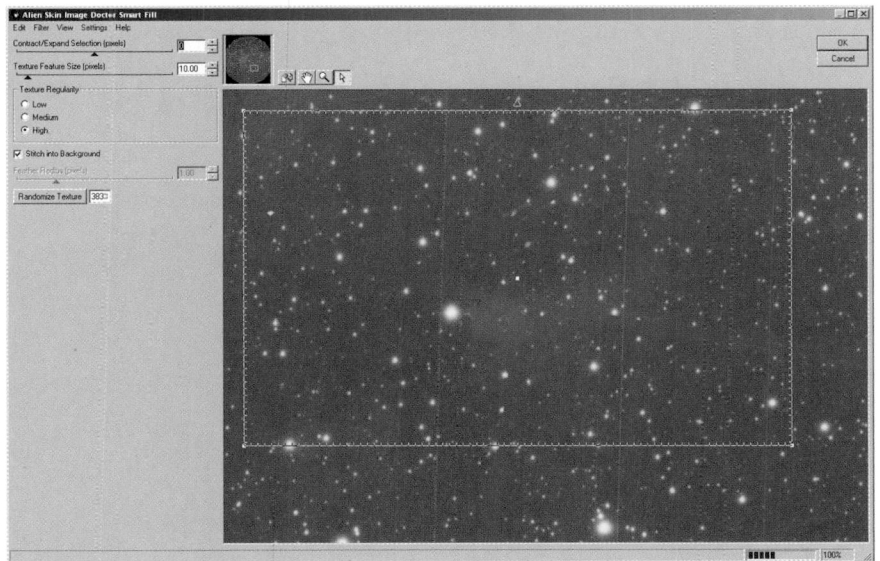

Fig. 10-5-o Image Doctor analyzes the star field inside the rectangular region that bounds the selection in Figure 10-5-n. It synthesizes texture and detail from that information to fill in the selection area (Figure 10-5-p).

started painting in the crack, applying more strokes of the brush to the darker areas and fewer to those where I wanted to retain more of the nebula's glow. That did an almost perfect job (Figure 10-5-q). In this manner I was able to work over all the obvious cracks and blend them almost invisibly into the background. The finished photograph is shown in Figure 10-5-r.

Fig. 10-5-p Here's the repair job that Image Doctor did. I left the dotted selection line on to make it easier to see the repaired region. Note that the stars and nebulae that fill the repaired area are not real. They're inventions of Image Doctor. This kind of repair would not be acceptable if the restoration were meant to have historical or scientific value.

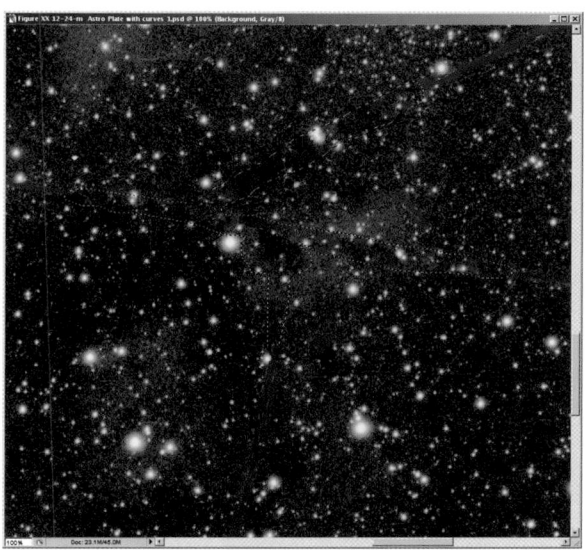

Fig. 10-5-q Image Doctor didn't produce precisely the effect I wanted in Figure 10-5-p, so I assigned that result to the History Brush and reverted to the previous state. I used the Brush in Lighten and Darken modes to paint in Image Doctor's corrections with just the strength needed to make it blend into the surrounding image.

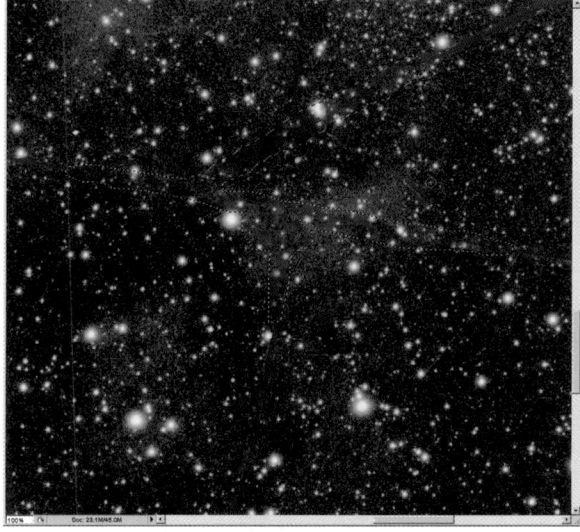

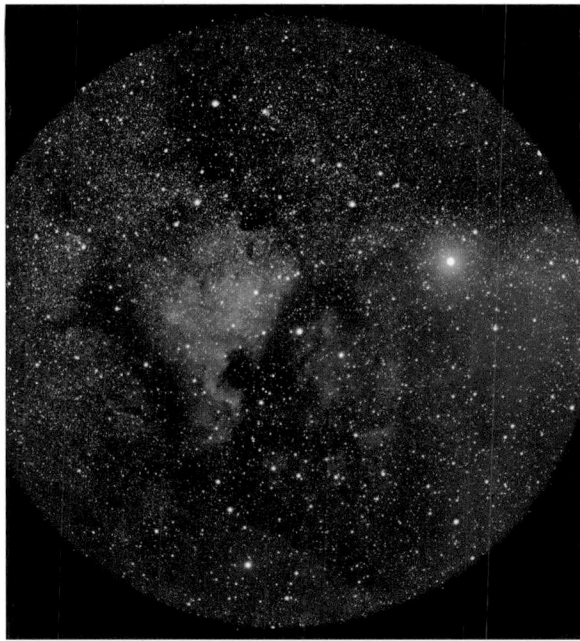

Fig. 10-5-r The finished photograph, after the Curves adjustment from Figure 10-5-m. I not only completely repaired the cracks, but with the assistance of Photoshop's tonal-control tools, I made a photograph that looks better than the original print I had made from the unbroken plate in the darkroom.

Example 6: A Rare and Historic Old Polaroid

I made (I've never liked the phrase "taking" pictures—I don't take'em, I make'em.) this Polaroid photograph (Figure 10-6-a) as a teenager more than 40 years ago. What makes it historically interesting is that it's a portrait of the world-famous physicist, Dr. Richard P. Feynman. What makes it rare is that it shows him with a mustache, a short-lived "look" for the brilliant scientist. For those reasons, I wanted to make minimal changes to this photograph when I restored it. I did not want to obscure or alter some detail that might be of importance to a future viewer.

Where the lacquer didn't sufficiently protect the silver from oxidation, the Polaroid had turned yellowish, but that hadn't gotten so bad yet that it substantially altered densities. Since the blue channel didn't provide any detail that wasn't in the red and green channels and it was the one that showed the color shift most strongly, I used the Channel Mixer to combine equal parts of the red and green channels to make a new monochrome image, just as I did in Example 1 (Figure 10-1-d).

Next I cleaned up the white spots, which were places where the Polaroid image hadn't transferred to the receiving sheet when it was made. I did that using the Dust & Scratches filter, set to a radius of 7 and a threshold of 12, and assigned to the History Brush. The reason I

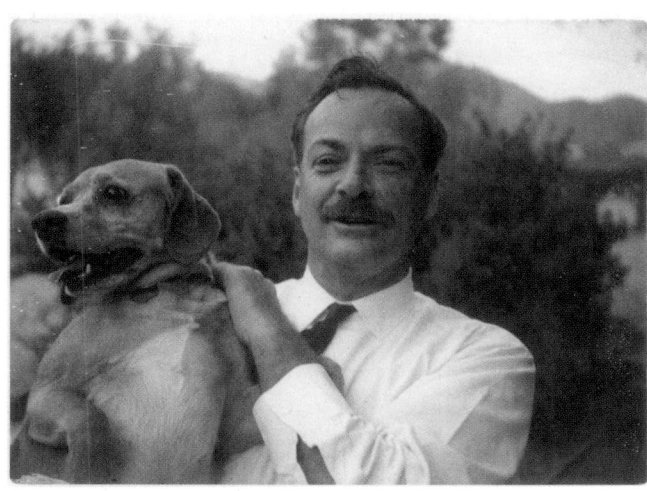

Fig. 10-6-a This 40-year-old Polaroid photograph of Dr. Richard P. Feynman sporting a mustache was made by the author as a teenager. It has faded and needs restoration, but because it has historical value I want to alter the image as little as possible.

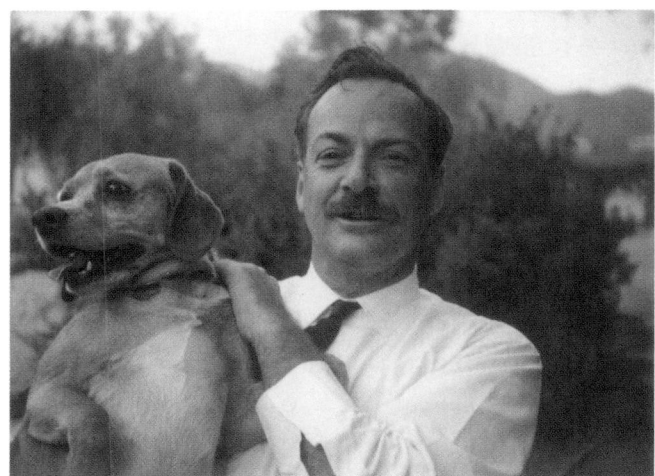

Fig. 10-6-b This grayscale scan is a mix of 50% red and 50% green channels. It has good tones, but it lacks contrast, as shown by the histogram in Figure 10-6-c.

used that high threshold was to make sure that the Dust & Scratches filter wouldn't alter any of the grain in the photograph.

I used the History Brush in Darken mode to paint out the white specks. The background was out of focus, and the filter hadn't changed any of the grain in the photograph, which allowed me to use a very-large-radius brush to eliminate all white specks in the background with only a few strokes. There was no fine image detail there that I had to be worried about obliterating.

Now I had a pretty clean photograph (Figure 10-6-b), but the contrast was flat, and it didn't have good blacks. The histogram in Figure 10-6-c,

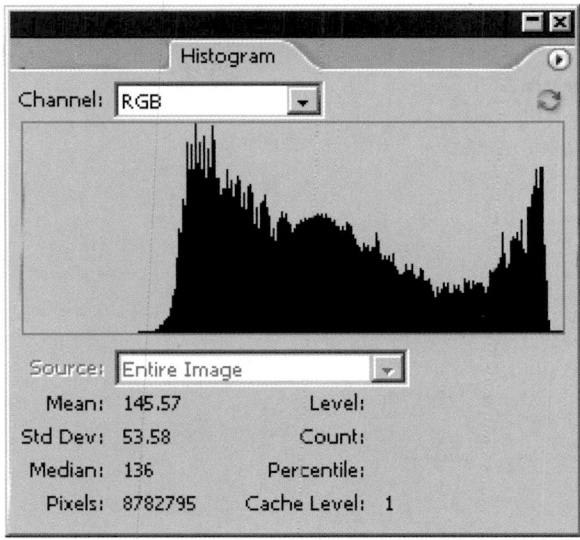

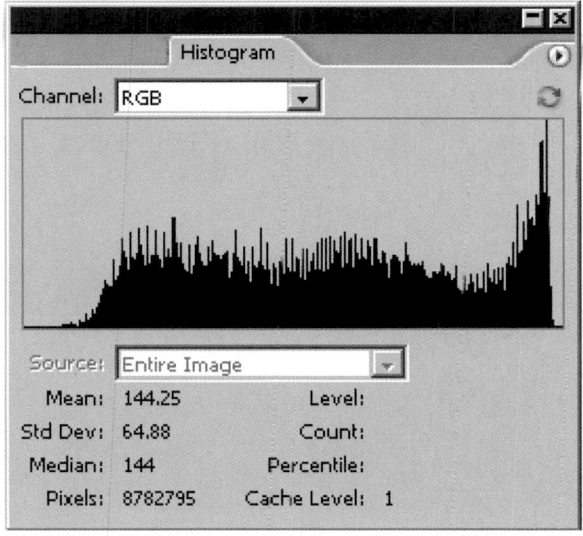

Fig. 10-6-c The top histogram, for Figure 10-6-b, shows that the whites are pretty good, but the blacks are substantially lacking in density. That leads to the correction curve in Figure 10-6-d. Applying this curve produces Figure 10-6-e, whose histogram is shown in the lower figure here.

top, showed that I wasn't using the lower 25% of the tonal range effectively, so I applied the curves in Figure 10-6-d. The adjusted photograph (Figure 10-6-e) looked a lot better, with the histogram in Figure 10-6-c, bottom. That's a much better distribution of tones.

Overall, though, I felt the photograph was a bit harsh; and had that "amateur look" characterized by poor tonal separation in the highlights and shadows. The shirt in particular looked blown out. It was time to use Photoshop's Shadow/Highlight adjustments (Figure 10-6-f; see

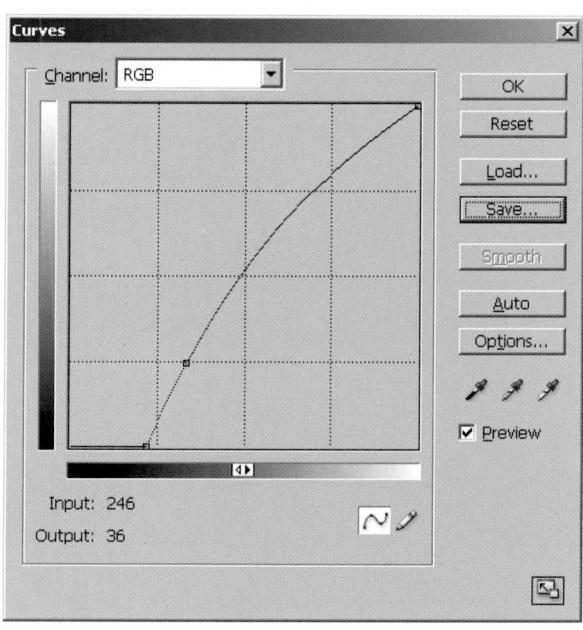

Fig. 10-6-d In this Curves adjustment, I've pulled the black point way in to improve the tonal range in the photograph. I bowed the curve upward to maintain midtones at the same level because they looked good in Figure 10-6-b. The result is Figure 10-6-e.

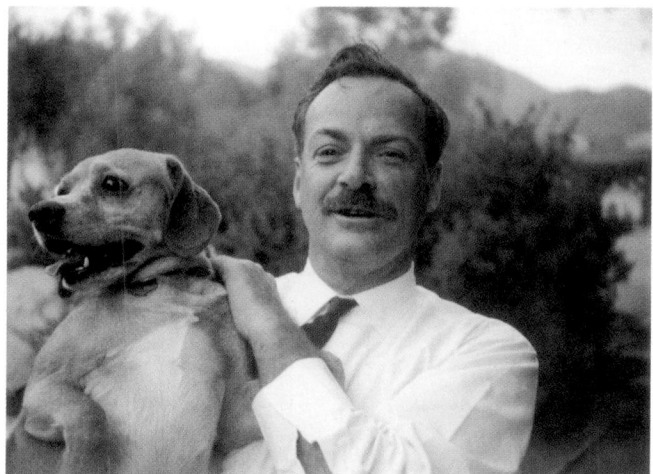

Fig. 10-6-e The tonality is considerably improved, but I'd like the detail in the highlights and shadows to be a bit better. I can enhance this with the Shadow/ Highlight adjustment (Figure 10-6-f).

Chapter 5, Restoring Tone, page 145, for a full explanation of how to use this tool). I set the Shadow Amount at 24% and the Tonal Width to 16%, to restrict the change to the deepest shadows. I added just a bit of highlight correction—only 5% over a Tonal Width of 29%—but even that small amount made a big difference in the results, as you can see in Figure 10-6-g. Shadows are opened up, there's much more detail

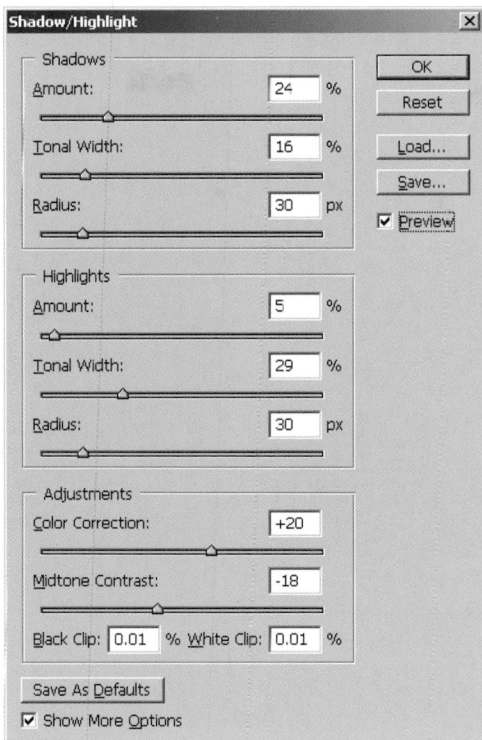

Fig. 10-6-f This Shadow/Highlight adjustment produces Figure 10-6-g. I applied a substantial amount of shadow adjustment, but I kept the tonal width small, so only the darker shadows were affected. I added in a little bit of highlight adjustment to improve detail in the shirt and dropped the midtone contrast substantially to give the photograph a more pleasing, linear tonal scale overall.

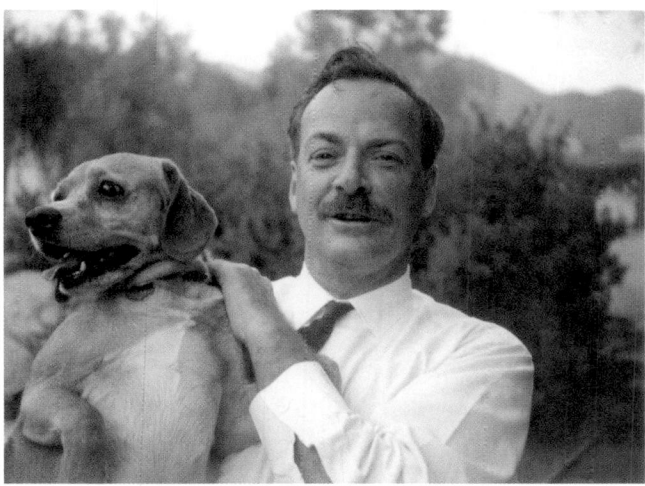

Fig. 10-6-g The improvements produced by the Shadow/Highlight adjustment in Figure 10-6-f are subtle, but they make the photograph look noticeably better than Figure 10-6-e. Highlight and shadow detail are definitely improved.

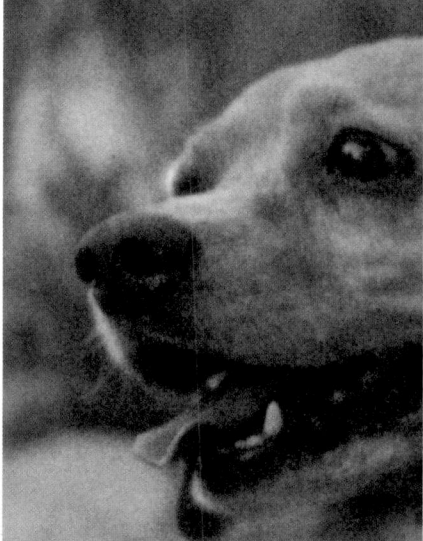 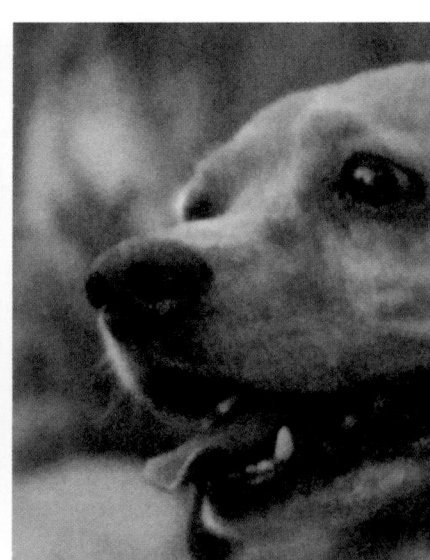

Fig. 10-6-h The tone- and contrast-enhanced photograph is fairly grainy, as can be seen in the left figure. I used DIGITAL GEM to suppress the grain without sacrificing fine detail (right).

visible in the shirt, and the overall tonality looks a lot smoother and more professional.

I could have stopped at this point, but I wanted to see if I could suppress the grain in the photograph a bit. This was a small (less than 3 inches long) photograph made on Polaroid 3000 speed film. Consequently the photograph was grainy to begin with, and correcting and enhancing the contrast only accentuated that (Figure 10-6-h, left).

Because of the historical value of the photograph, I didn't want to do any grain reduction that would reduce image detail in the slightest. After experimenting with the blurring and noise reduction filters in Photoshop and Picture Window, I concluded that the best way to suppress the grain without destroying any detail was with a third-party plug-in. Two that did a good job on this photo were PixelGenius's PhotoKit Sharpener edge-protected smoothing brush and Kodak's DIGITAL GEM (Figure 10-6-i), discussed in Chapter 3, Software for Restoration.

I went with GEM. The settings were the default ones except for blending, which I reduced to 55%. (I could have accomplished the same thing by applying the filter at full strength and fading it back to 55% afterward.) This softened the grain without compromising image detail (Figure 10-6-h, right).

As the finishing touch, I burned in the sky and the background along the right edge with a 5% highlight burn. That darkened those areas just enough to direct the focus of attention onto Dr. Feynman (Figure 10-6-j). A subtle change, but one that substantially improved the composition for me without compromising its accuracy.

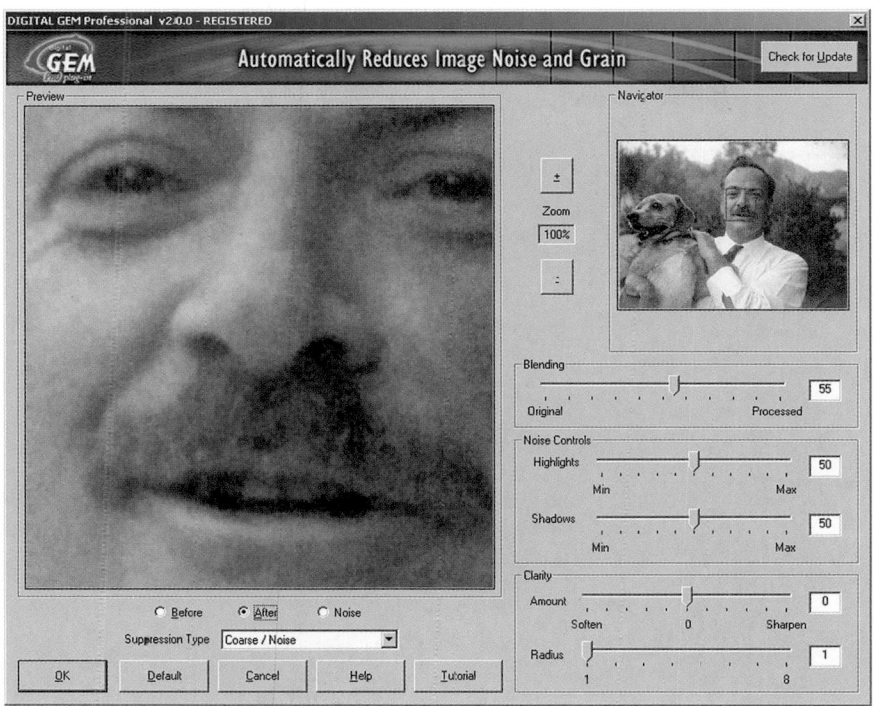

Fig. 10-6-i The DIGITAL GEM plug-in, shown in this screenshot, substantially softens the grain without destroying fine detail.

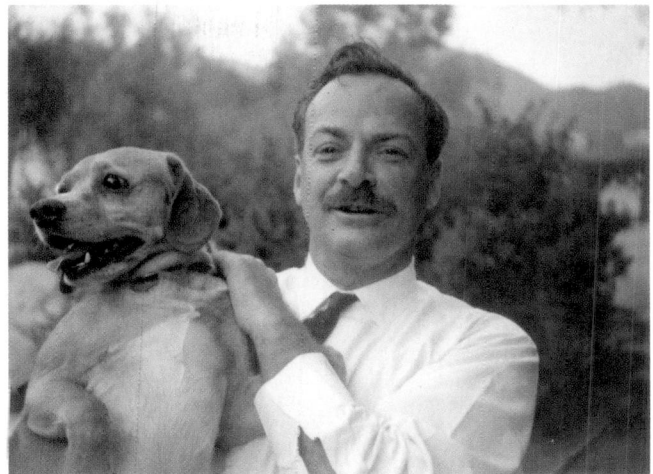

Fig. 10-6-j This fully restored photograph looks much better than the original Polaroid print in Figure 10-6-a, and I achieved these improvements without changing any important details in the photograph. The restoration looks much better than the original, but it is still historically accurate.

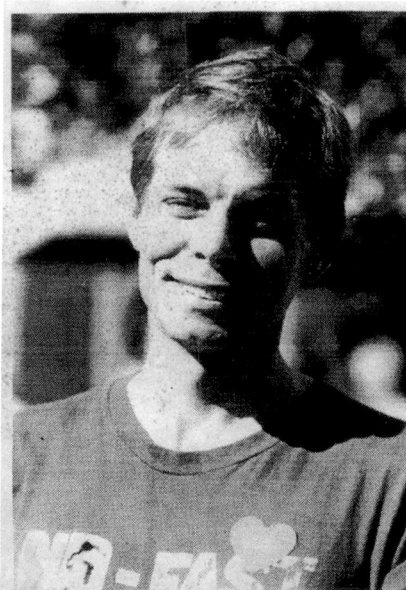 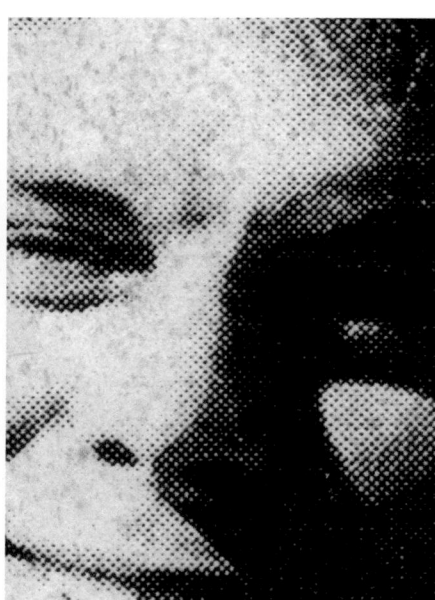

Fig. 10-7-a Photocopies of photographs can be restored! This memorial photograph from a color snapshot was screened and poorly photocopied onto nonarchival paper. After less than a decade, lots of dark spots have appeared.

Example 7: Fixing a Photocopied Halftone

The photograph in Figure 10-7-a is a clipping from a memorial service pamphlet that was printed in the late 1990s. It was not very good to begin with; the original photograph, presumably a color snapshot, was screened and poorly photocopied for the leaflet. During its short life it's gotten much worse, because the nonarchival paper started developing brown spots and freckles, which are easily seen in the enlargement on the right.

The first restoring step was to get rid of the halftone screen. I turned to the Focus Magic stand-alone program, which includes a Despeckle filter for eliminating halftone dots (see Chapter 9, page 321). Figure 10-7-b, top, shows the Focus Magic control panel. I selected a dot pitch of 17 pixels, which closely matched the spacing between halftone dots. Running the program produced the result shown in Figure 10-7-b, bottom.

The original halftone screen has been replaced by a low-contrast secondary pattern with a spacing of 8 pixels. I ran the program again with the settings shown in Figure 10-7-c and got a nearly dot-free result. The descreened photograph, converted to grayscale, is shown in Figure 10-7-d; compare it to Figure 10-7-a.

Next I went after the horizontal photocopy "scan lines" that are visible throughout the photograph. I created a Curves adjustment layer to use as a burn-in layer (see Chapter 5, page 160) with the curve shown

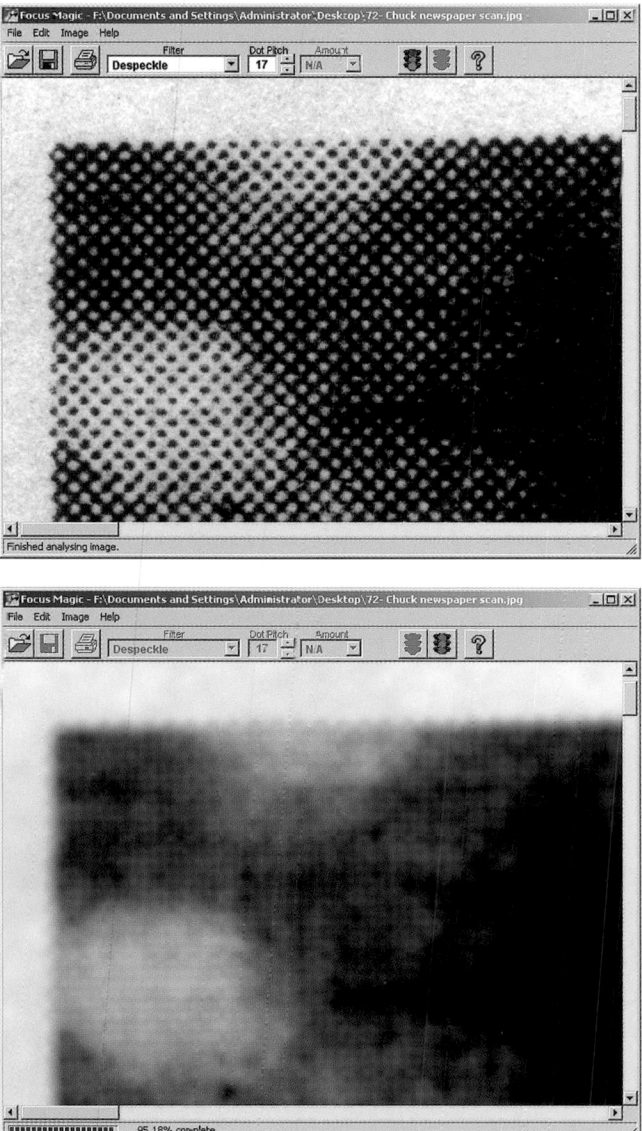

Fig. 10-7-b Focus Magic's stand-alone application is a good tool for eliminating halftone screens. The top figure shows the Focus Magic control panel previewing the upper corner of the photocopy before descreening. The bottom figure shows the photocopy after it's been "despeckled" with a 17-pixel radius. There's still some residual screen pattern.

in Figure 10-7-e. I filled in the mask channel for that layer with black and used a white brush to paint over the scan lines, darkening them until they blended into the surroundings. The finished burn-in mask is on the right in Figure 10-7-e. Figure 10-7-f shows an enlarged section of the photograph before and after burning-in, so you can see in detail how the mask worked to subdue the lines.

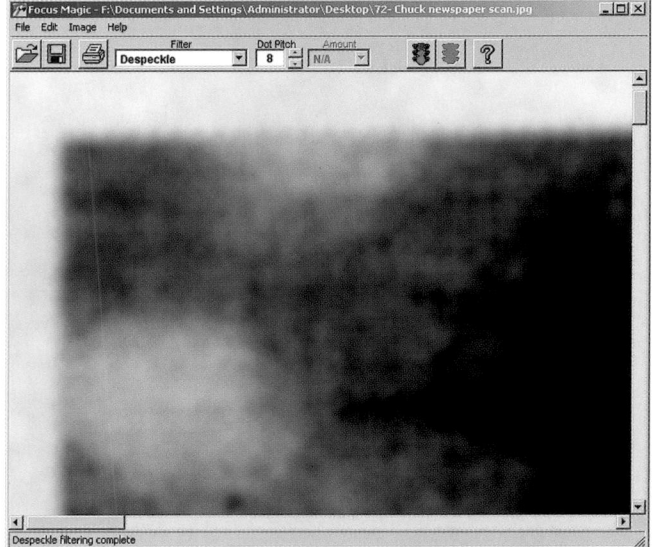

Fig. 10-7-c A second pass with Focus Magic, using an 8-pixel radius, completely removes the screen pattern. Figure 10-7-d shows the results.

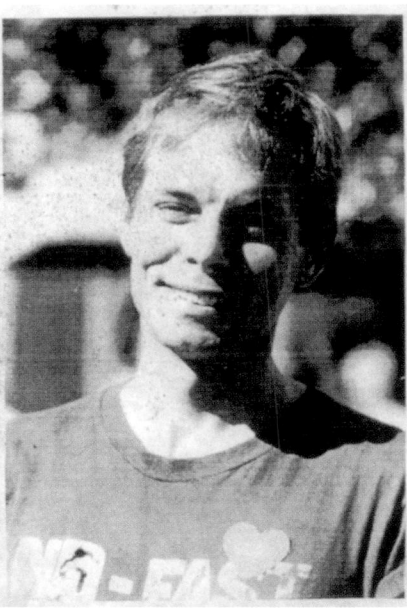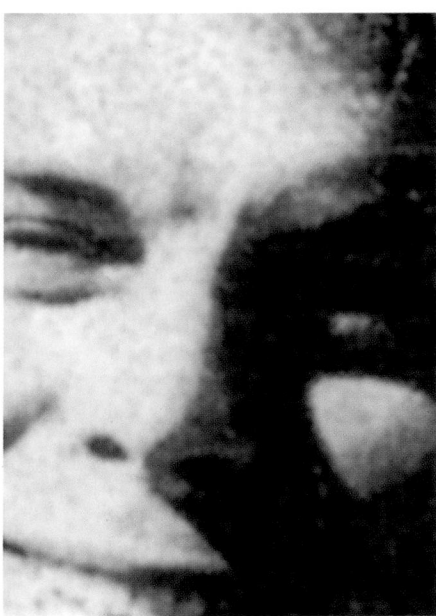

Fig. 10-7-d This is what Figure 10-7-a looks like after being descreened with Focus Magic and converted to grayscale. The photograph is almost as sharp as the original photocopy, but that annoying screen pattern is entirely gone. Copier "scan lines" mar the photograph, though.

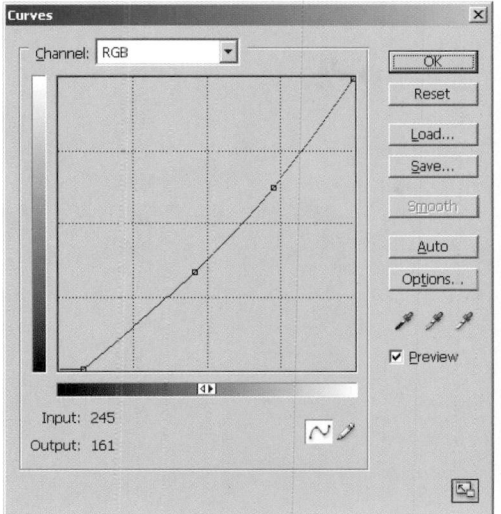

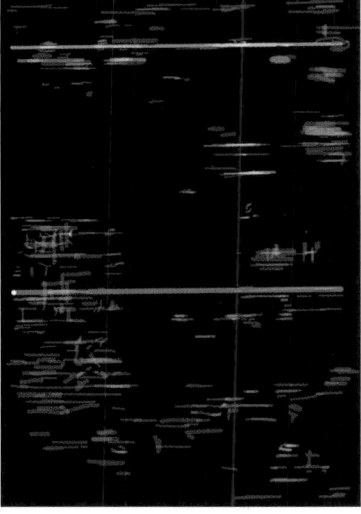

Fig. 10-7-e A burn-in Curves adjustment layer can get rid of scan lines like those in Figure 10-7-d. The burn-in curve that I used is shown on the left. After I brushed out all the scan lines, the finished mask for that adjustment layer looked like the right figure.

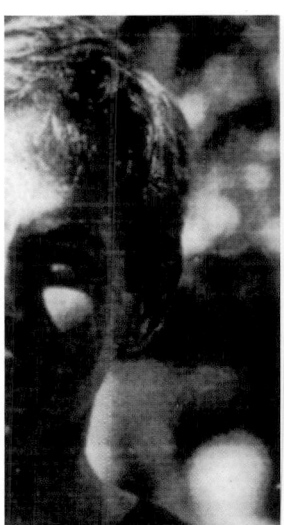

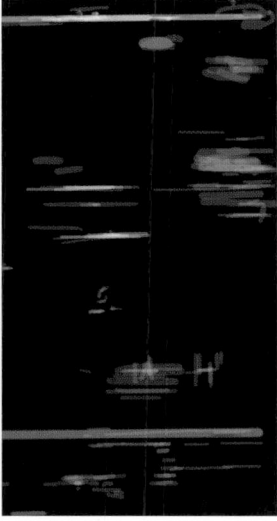

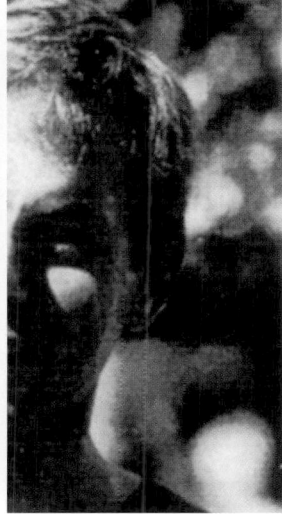

Fig. 10-7-f This enlargement shows how well the burn-in adjustment layer in Figure 10-7-b cleaned up the photograph in Figure 10-7-d. On the left is a section of that photograph before burning-in. In the center is the corresponding section of burn-in mask from the adjustment layer. On the right is the cleaned-up photograph.

I added another Curves adjustment layer to reduce the contrast of the spots in the photograph. The Color Range selection tool created a mask that selected only the light areas of the photograph (Figure 10-7-g, right). That layer's curve lightens and reduces the contrast in the middle-light tones to almost nothing. If there were any middle-light detail in the photograph, it would be completely suppressed by this curve. Since there isn't, it has almost no effect on the photograph proper, but it substantially subdued the spots.

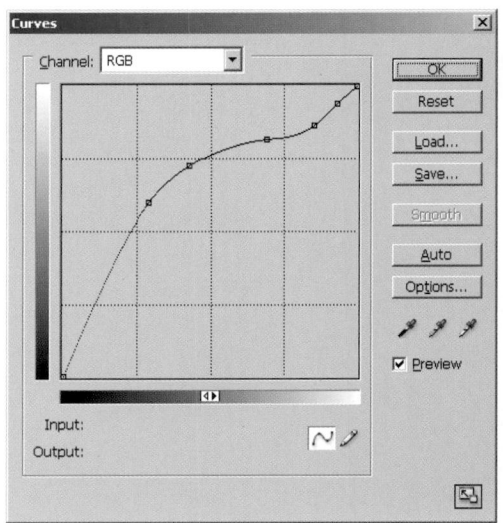 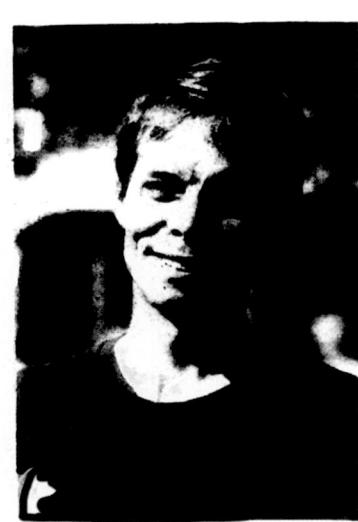

Fig. 10-7-g This Curves adjustment layer suppresses the dark "freckles" marring the paper by dropping the contrast in the middle highlights to nearly zero. The mask on the right, created with the Color Range selection tool, limits the effect of this curve to the highlight areas of the photograph.

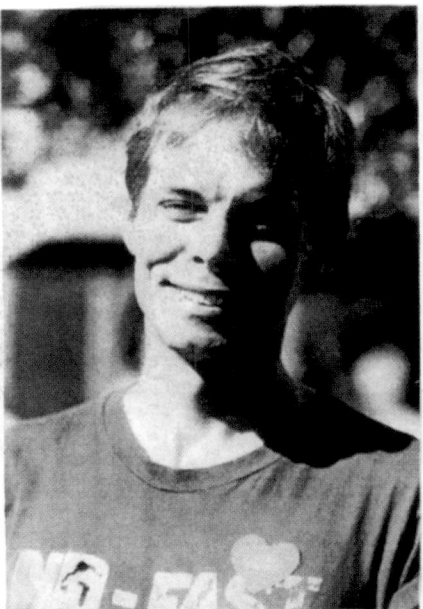 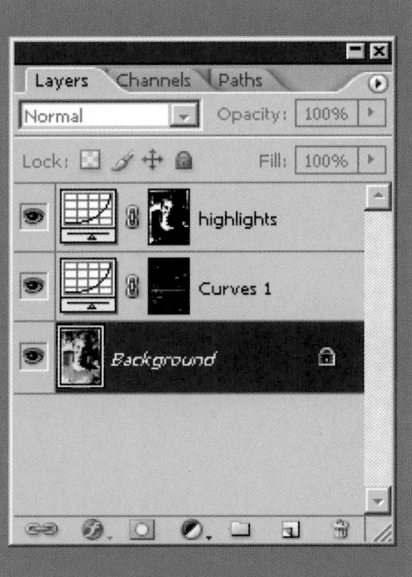

Fig. 10-7-h The photocopy after I've eliminated the scan lines and suppressed the freckles. The Curves 1 layer in the layer stack holds the burning-in that gets rid of the scan lines (see Figure 10-7-d). The highlights layer reduces the appearance of the freckles (see Figure 10-7-g).

Figure 10-7-h shows the result, with the layer stack on the right. Freckles are only visible in the light, featureless parts of the photograph, so I attacked them aggressively. I ran the Dust & Scratches filter with a zero-threshold and a 30-pixel radius. I assigned that filter to the History Brush, reverted to the previous history state, and painted over the blank, light parts of the photograph with the brush to erase the freckles.

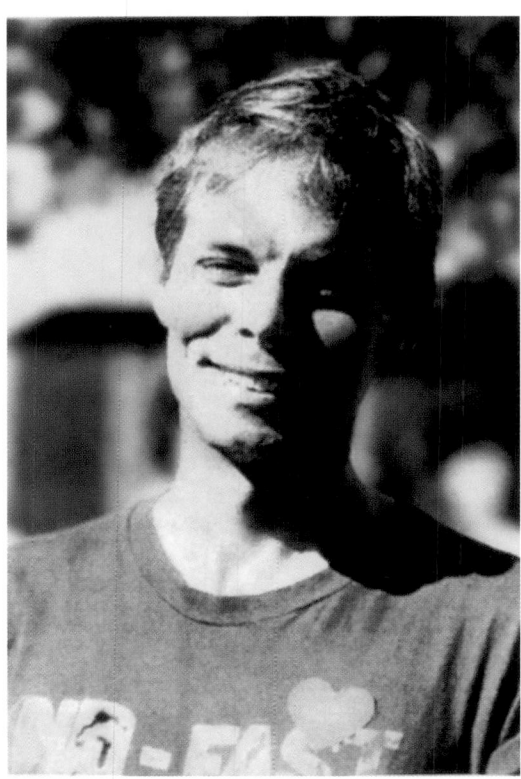

Fig. 10-7-i In Figure 10-7-h, I used the Dust & Scratches filter with the History Brush to eliminate the freckles from the highlights. Then I used a 35-pixel Gaussian Blur filter with the History Brush to smooth out the background and make it less distracting. Just a bit more cleanup and a little tone correction, and this restoration will be complete.

I didn't like the distracting background, so I ran the Gaussian Blur filter with a 35-pixel radius, assigned it to the History Brush, and painted over the background. Those two operations got me to Figure 10-7-i, which looks pretty nice!

The last major thing I did to finish up the photograph was to enhance the detail and contrast to the highlights. I created another Curves adjustment layer with the curve in Figure 10-7-j. That curve leaves everything but the lightest tones untouched (see Chapter 5, Restoring Tone, page 148). It drastically increases the contrast in the tones with values above 200, darkening the lower values, lightening the higher values, and taking the lightest values up to almost pure white.

As a finishing touch, I lightly burned in the line of the jaw and curve of the cheek to define the face better. The final result is shown in Figure 10-7-k. I don't claim that this is a gorgeous photograph, but it is astonishingly better than what I started with. It should come as no surprise that it made the owner of the clipping incredibly happy.

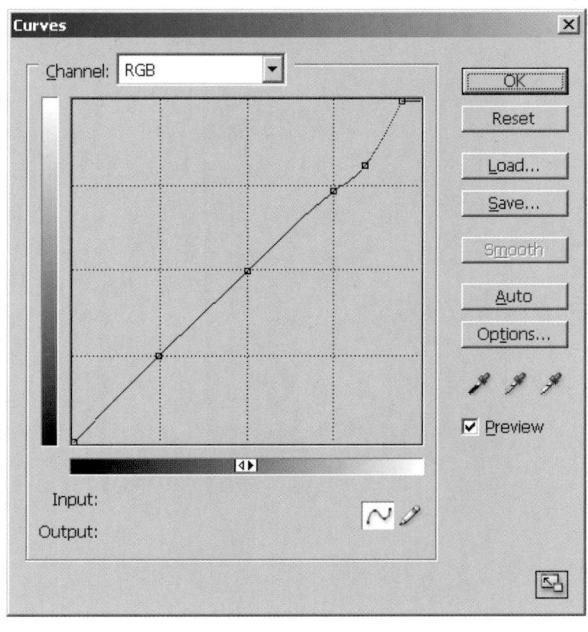

Fig. 10-7-j This Curves adjustment boosts the contrast in the highlights, helping to emphasize what little detail is present there. It also cleans up the whites, making them close to pure white instead of dingy gray, as shown in Figure 10-7-k.

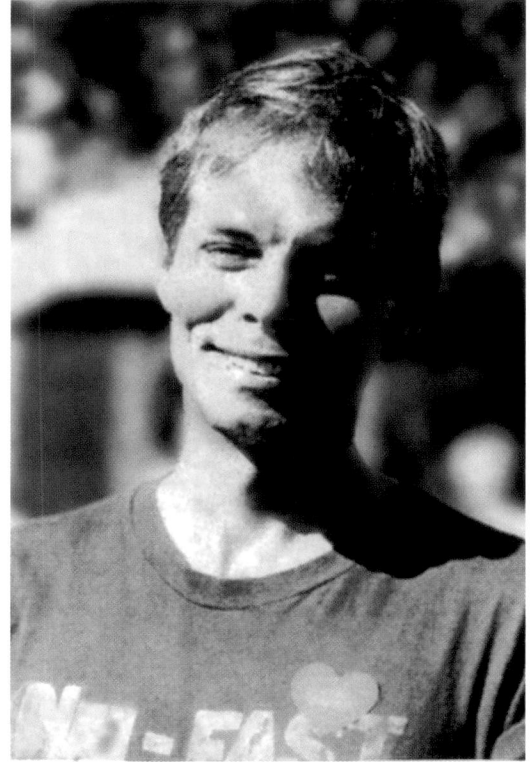

Fig. 10-7-k The finished restoration. After applying the curve from Figure 10-7-j, I did a little bit of burning-in along the jaw line and the cheek to bring out some modeling in the face. Compare this to the original in Figure 10-7-a; it's an immense improvement!

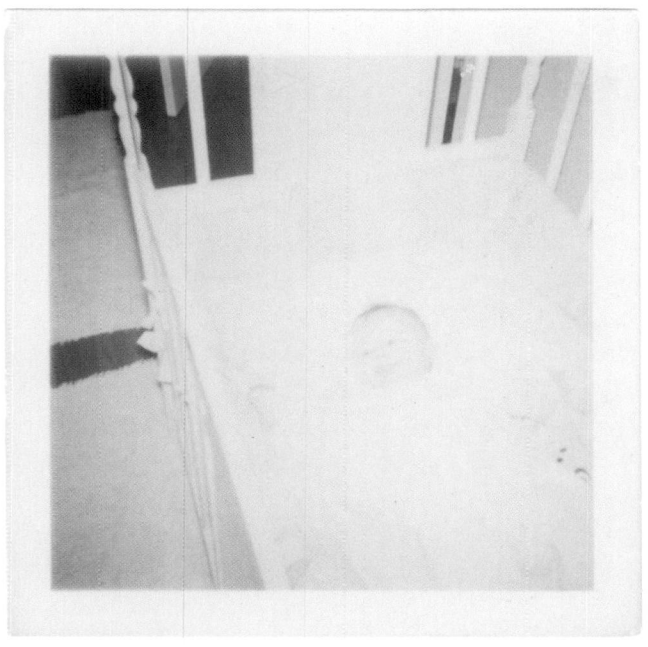

Fig. 10-8-a It's hard to believe there's anything worth rescuing in this 1950s color snapshot. Hardly any detail is visible except in the shadows.

Example 8: Restoring an Almost-Blank Photo

Back in Chapter 5, Restoring Tone, on page 167, I introduced you to Figure 10-8-a, the most badly faded photograph I've restored to date. I showed you how a careful scan combined with DIGITAL ROC could restore some semblance of color and detail to the photograph (Figure 10-8-b).

This photograph is still extremely pale, so I added the Curves adjustment layer shown in Figure 10-8-c. The curve greatly darkens the photograph and increases the contrast in the highlights and midtones by a factor of three. I incorporated a radial gradient mask in the layer to eliminate light falloff in the original photograph. That falloff wasn't apparent until I applied the Curves correction, but as Figure 10-8-d, left, shows, it was there just waiting to come out. The gradient mask neatly eliminated most of it; I left some falloff to focus attention on the baby.

Now that I could more clearly see the photograph, not to mention the dirt and scratches, I cleaned it up with my usual technique. I applied the Dust & Scratches filter with a radius of 11 pixels and a threshold of 8, assigned that filter to the History Brush, and reverted to the previous History state. I set the Brush to Lighten mode and cleaned up the photograph. The Clone tool picked off the few blemishes that the History Brush missed.

Figure 10-8-e, left, shows what the photograph looked like after I'd cleaned it. It's apparent that the color is a little uneven; it's hard to make

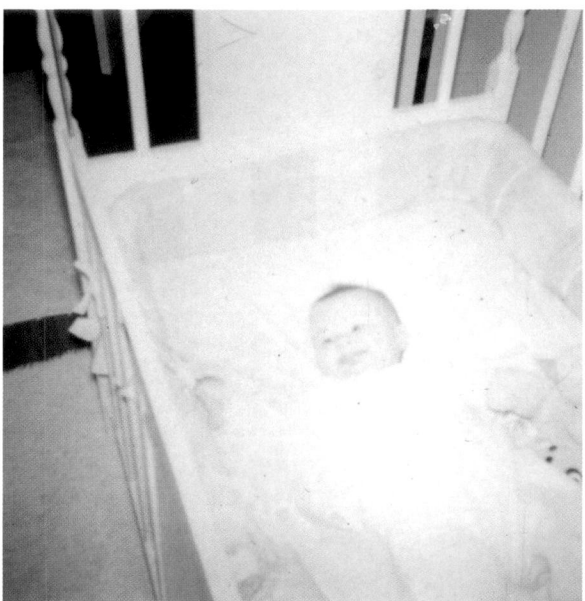

Fig. 10-8-b A careful scan and DIGITAL ROC make a big difference. Now there's color and detail in the baby and crib. It's faint, to be sure, but it's something to work with.

Fig. 10-8-c A Curves adjustment layer turns Figure 10-8-b into Figure 10-8-d. This RGB curve darkens the photograph and greatly increases contrast and detail in the highlights. The radial gradient mask for the layer evens out the exposure, eliminating the vignetting at the corners of the photograph.

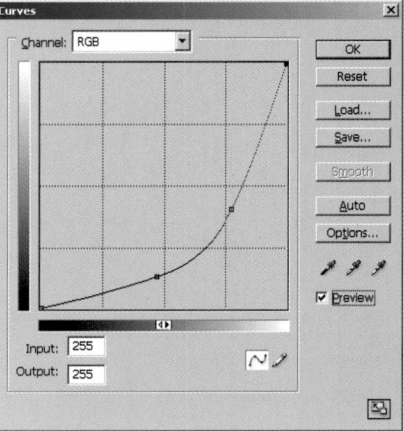

out, so I added a Hue/Saturation layer set to +50 points. That amplified the color differences, producing the figure on the right. Now the pattern of red and green mottling is very clear.

I went after that with a couple of Curves adjustment layers. These work like the dodging and burning-in adjustment layers I introduced in Chapter 5, page 160, except that here I'm using them to correct color instead of tonality.

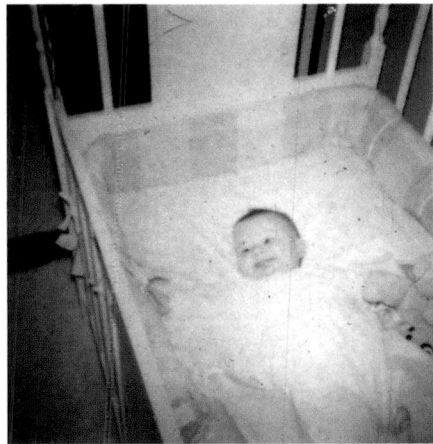 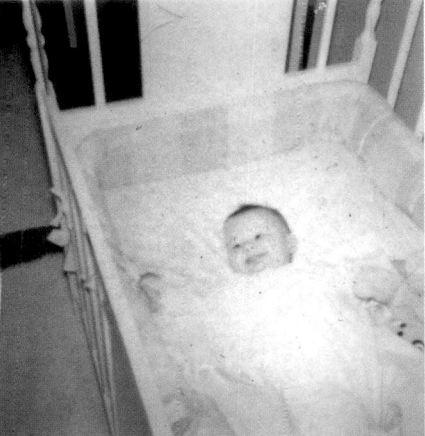

Fig. 10-8-d Here's Figure 10-8-b after applying the Curves adjustment layer from Figure 10-8-c. The photo on the left shows the effect of the RGB curve before I added the gradient mask; the photograph has serious light falloff at the edges. The mask evens out the lighting in the photograph (right).

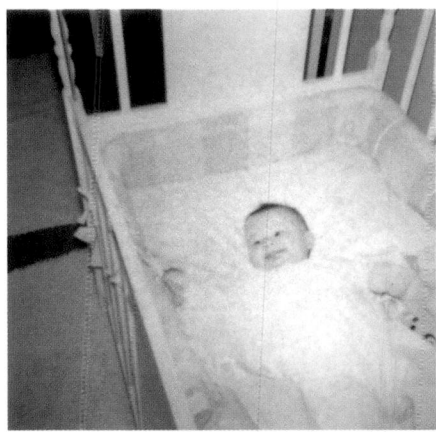 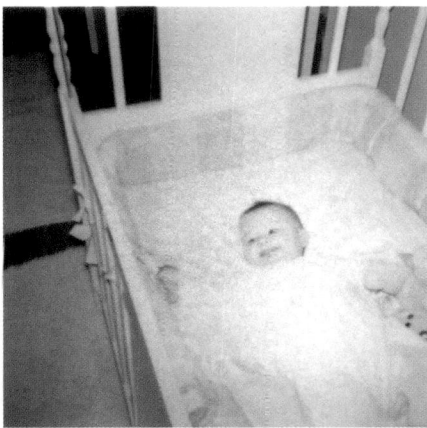

Fig. 10-8-e The Dust & Scratches filter, used in conjunction with the History Brush, cleans up Figure 10-8-d very nicely. The photograph on the left has normal saturation. I added a Hue/Saturation adjustment layer with +50 points saturation to the photo on the right. This makes it easier to see the color blotches while I correct them with some adjustment layers.

First, I tackled the reddish tinge around the perimeter of the photograph with the curves in Figure 10-8-f. The green and blue curves shift the color toward the greenish-cyan, the complement of the color cast that I want to remove from the photograph. I filled in the mask channel for that layer with black, set the Brush tool to white, and painted out the unwanted tint. Just as in Chapter 5, I ignored what was actually happening in the mask channel; I only paid attention to the color in the photograph. The enhanced saturation produced by the Hue/Saturation layer worked like a kind of a magnifying glass for color; it was really easy to see subtle differences in the tint and paint them away. The finished mask is shown on the right.

Next, I went after the greenish-yellow splotches in the center of the photograph with the Curves adjustment layer in Figure 10-8-g. The red

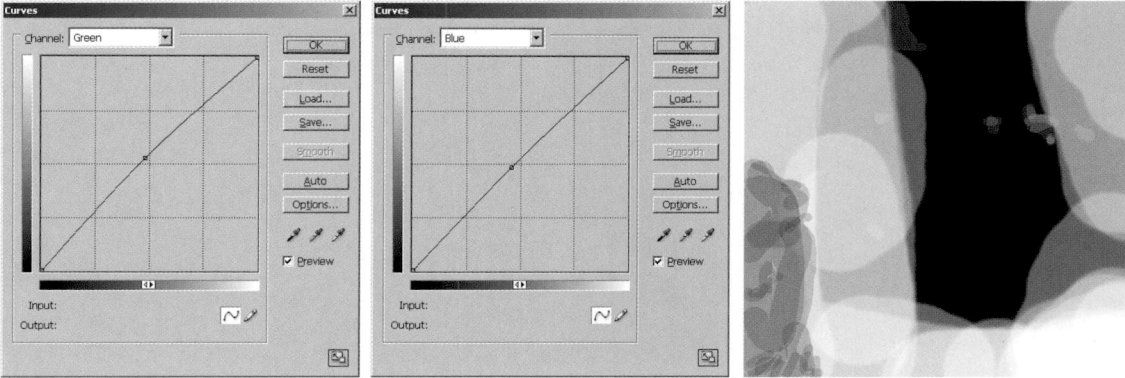

Fig. 10-8-f This Curves adjustment layer eliminates the reddish tinge around the periphery of the photograph. The green and blue curves shift the hue away from red. I hand-painted the mask on the right the same way I created burn-in layers in Chapter 5. The mask restricts the curves' effects to just those parts of the photograph I need to erase the unwanted red from.

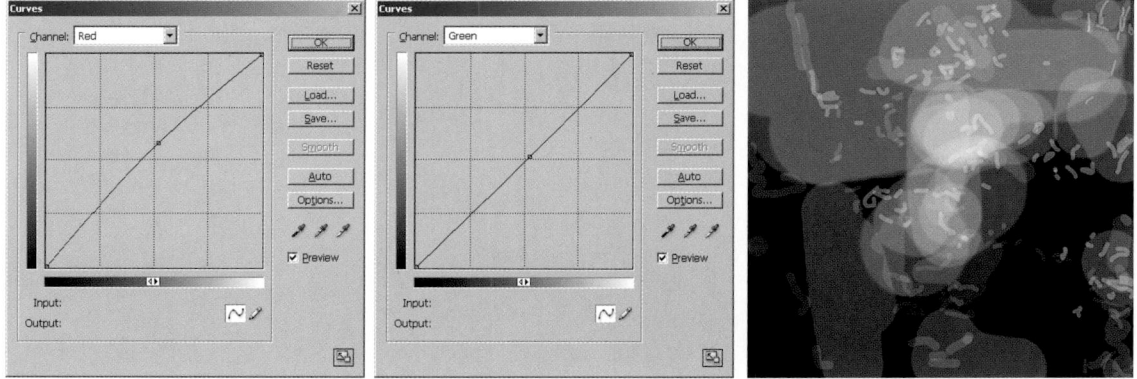

Fig. 10-8-g A second hand-painted Curves adjustment layer eliminates most of the green-yellow spots. The red and blue curves shift the color toward neutral. Figure 10-8-h shows the results.

and green curves shift the color toward red-magenta to cancel the color of the splotches. I painted in the mask channel wherever I saw that greenish-yellow tinge in the photograph until most of it was eliminated.

After I finished getting rid of the color mottle, I discarded the Hue/Saturation layer. The photograph that this color retouching produced, shown in Figure 10-8-h, has pretty good overall color balance but the saturation is very low. Also, there's a lot of grain and noise in the photograph, as is evident in the enlargement. Tackling that noise was my next challenge.

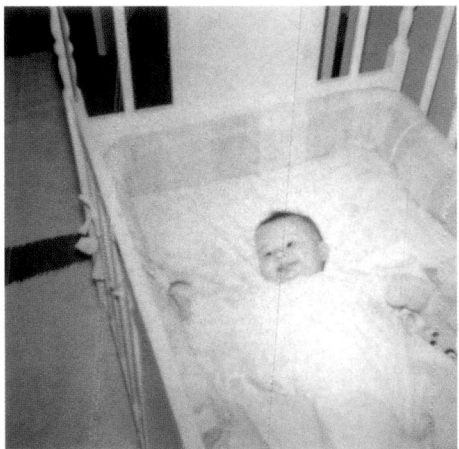
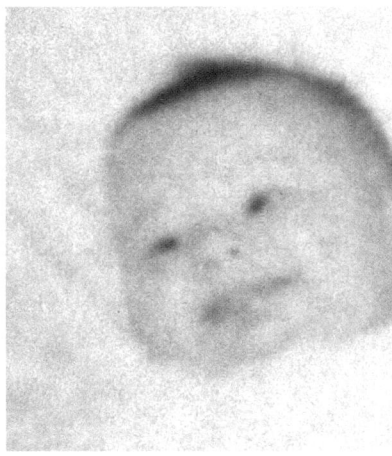

Fig. 10-8-h The two Curves adjustment layers in Figures 10-8-f and 10-8-g did a good job of eliminating the large areas of uneven color. As the enlargement on the right shows, though, there is still a lot of grain and color noise, especially cyan, in this photograph.

I turned to the Neat Image Pro+ plug-in (Figure 10-8-i). I selected an area on the back of the crib (gray square) and let Auto Profile compute the noise signature for the photograph. Then I ran Auto Fine-Tune to fine-tune the noise profile using the whole image. I applied that profile with the default filter settings to get Figure 10-8-j. The fine noise is gone, and the photograph looks a lot cleaner. The most distracting problem is an overall pattern of fine, slightly dark and bluish marks that obscure the delicate, light tones in the photograph. There's no way to filter those out; it's time for handwork.

The dark marks are very hard to see clearly, so I added a new Curves adjustment layer (Figure 10-8-k) to the photograph that greatly increases its contrast and darkness. Now the defects stand out, permitting me to retouch them the same way I corrected the large pink and green areas in the photograph. I created a dodging adjustment layer with the curves shown in Figure 10-8-l. The RGB curve lightens up the tones. Since the dark spots are, on average, a little cooler in color than the rest of the photograph, I also adjusted the red curve to remove a small amount of cyan. I filled in the mask channel with black and went to work with the white Brush tool set to an opacity of 20%.

It took me about 45 minutes to clean up the photograph, producing the mask in Figure 10-8-l, right. While doing this work, I noticed that there were some pink-green color variations that I hadn't completely cleaned up in Figure 10-8-h. I went back to the Curves adjustment layers that dealt with that and did a little more fine work on their masks. Adjustment layers are great that way; you're not locked into one set of corrections. You can modify or improve on them at any time.

The result of all that work is shown in Figure 10-8-m, left. The contrast-enhancing layer is still in place. The photograph doesn't look perfect; there's some residual tonal noise and variation visible in the

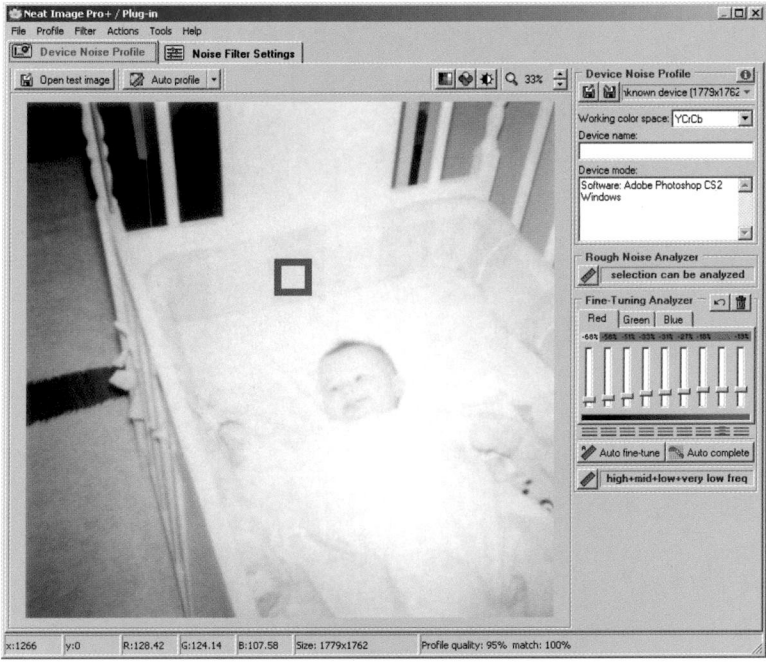

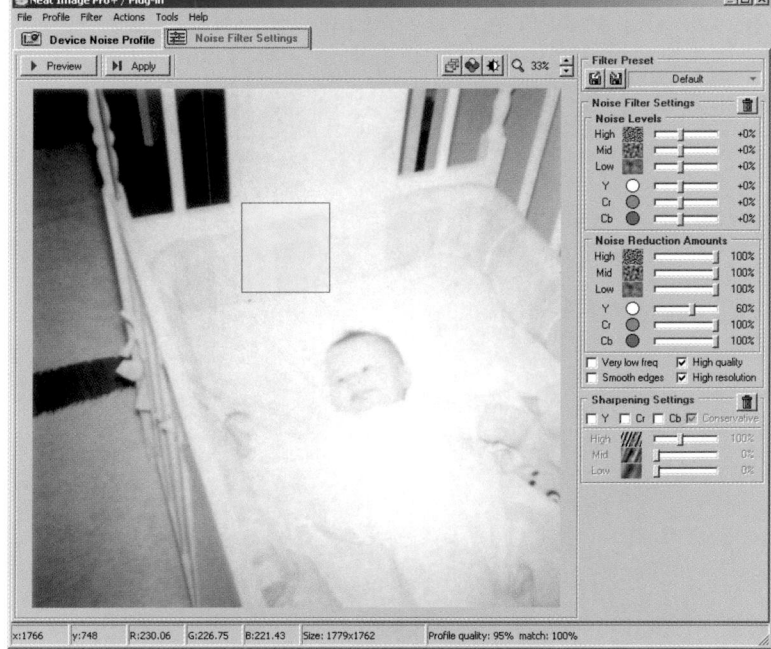

Fig. 10-8-i Neat Image is a great tool for fixing difficult noise problems. In the first control panel (top), I selected an area on the back of the crib to analyze for noise and grain, and ran Auto Profile and Auto Fine-Tune to create a noise profile for the photograph. In the second Control Panel (bottom), I applied that noise profile with the default filter settings shown on the right.

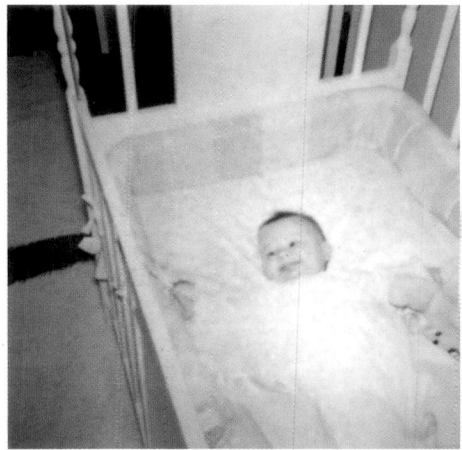
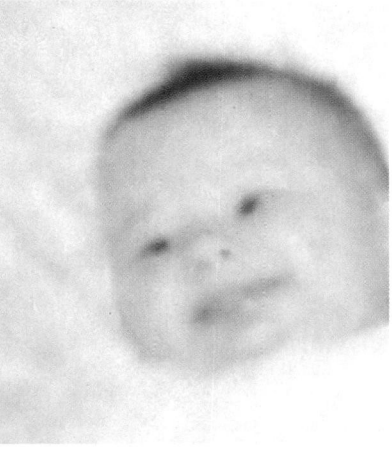

Fig. 10-8-j Here's Figure 10-8-h after Neat Image has finished with it. The grain pattern is completely gone, and the color noise is greatly reduced.

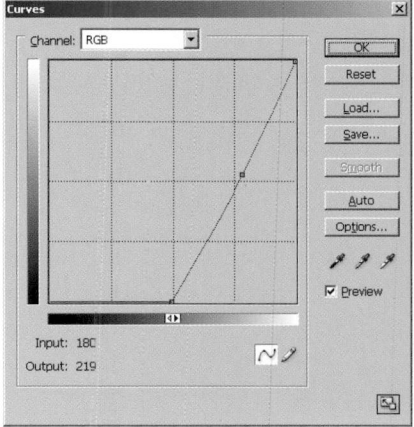
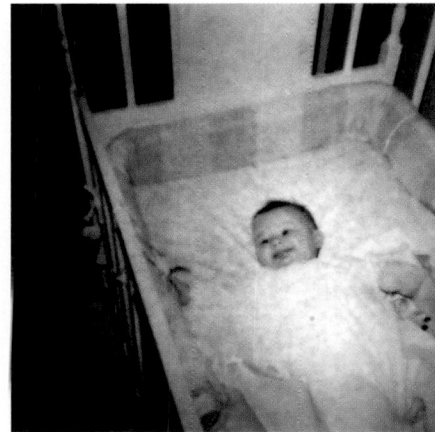

Fig. 10-8-k I added a Curves adjustment layer with the RGB curve on the left to the photograph, to exaggerate highlight contrast. This makes it easier to see the tone and color variations that I want to retouch out of the photograph.

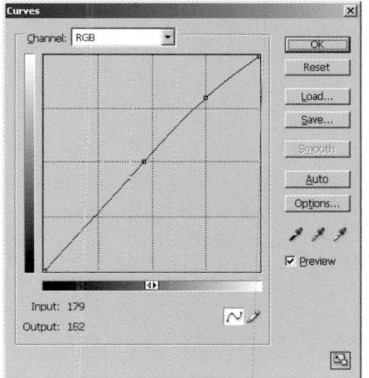
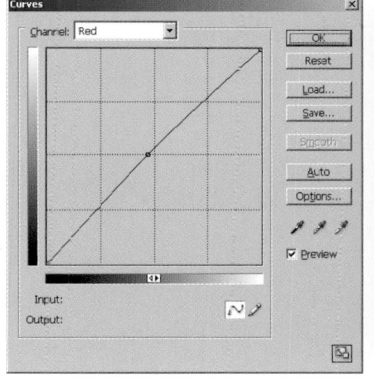
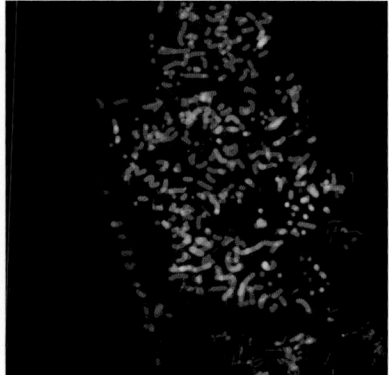

Fig. 10-8-l This Curves adjustment layer eliminates the pattern of faint dark spots that obscure the photograph in Figure 10-8-j. The curves lighten and slightly redden the parts of the photograph that the mask (right) allows to be affected. I hand-painted this mask to clear out those dark spots, producing Figure 10-8-m.

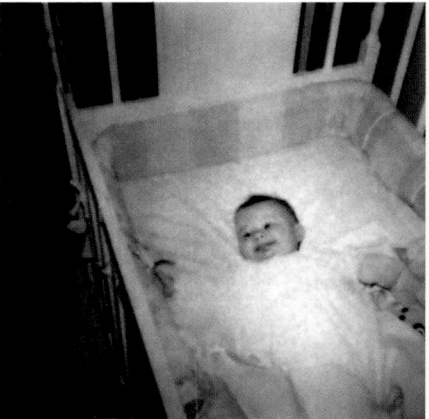
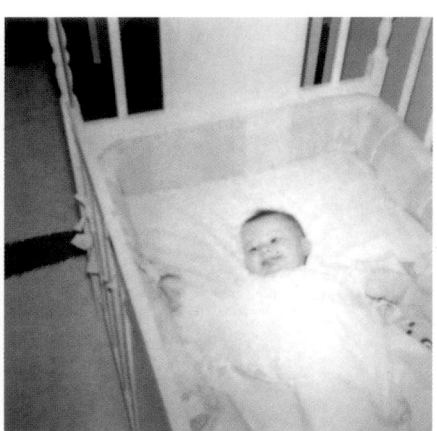

Fig. 10-8-m On the left is the retouched photograph, using the dodging adjustment layer from Figure 10-8-l. The contrast-exaggerating layer is still in place. Deleting that layer yields the figure on the right; compare this to Figure 10-8-j.

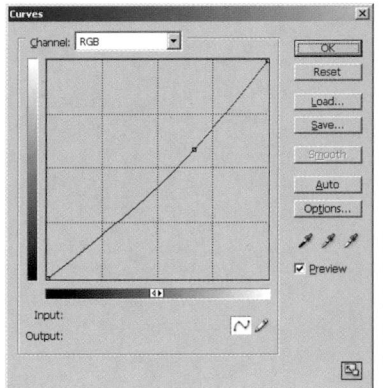
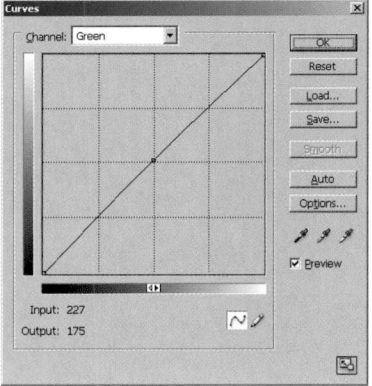
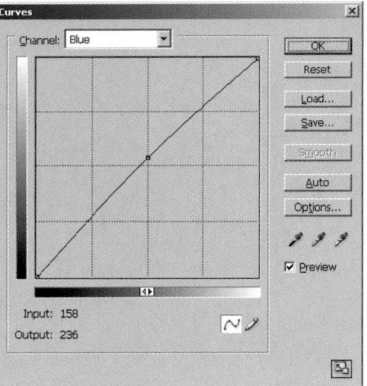

Fig. 10-8-n This Curves adjustment layer makes the final tone and color corrections to the photograph. The RGB curve darkens the photo a little and improves highlight detail, while the green and blue curves correct the color balance by removing a little yellow-orange cast.

photograph. But that's only visible because of the enhancing layer. As soon as I strip that off (right), the photograph looks nicely uniform and even. Compare this to Figure 10-8-j.

I finally have a clean photograph, and I'm on the home stretch. I'm ready to make the final tone and color adjustments to this photograph. I created a new Curves adjustment layer with the curves shown in Figure 10-8-n. The RGB curve darkens the photo a bit and increases contrast in the highlights. The green and blue curves remove a little bit of excess yellow-orange color and make the photo more neutral overall.

I felt the baby's face still lacked healthy color, so my final correction was to add the Hue/Saturation adjustment layer shown in Figure 10-8-o.

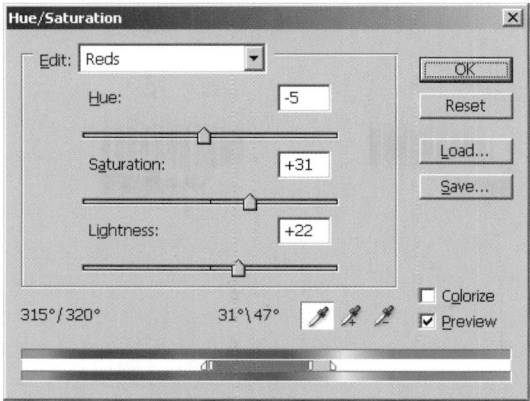

Fig. 10-8-o This Hue/Saturation adjustment layer improves the color in the baby's skin, making it lighter, pinker, and more saturated. The hand-painted mask prevents the rest of the photograph from being altered by this layer.

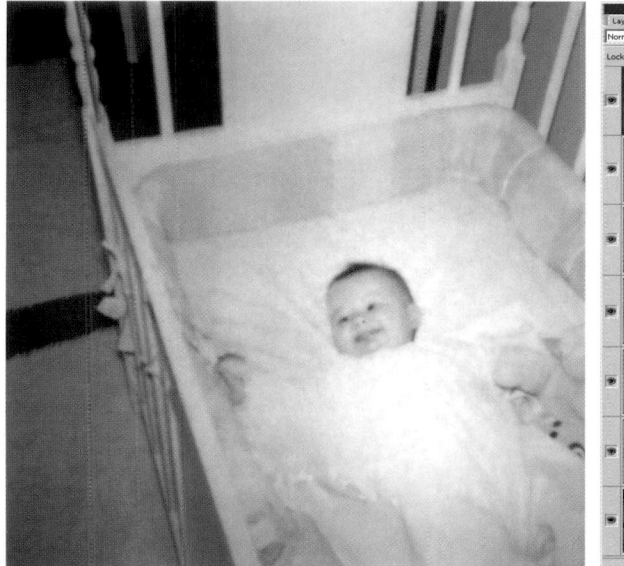

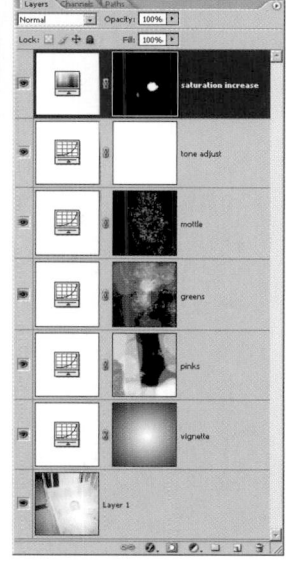

Fig. 10-8-p The finished restoration is an amazing improvement over Figure 10-8-a. It shows details I didn't even realize existed before I started the restoration. On the right is the layers stack that makes up this extraordinary reconstruction.

I corrected the reds, shifting the hue by –5 points, which made the skin tones a little pinker. I increased the saturation by 31 points and lightened the color by 22 points. That gave me nice baby skin tones. To restrict the effect of this layer to just the baby, I hand-painted the mask shown in the lower part of the figure.

The finished photograph is shown in Figure 10-8-p, along with its layer stack. It truly amazes me how much photographic information turned out to be buried in Figure 10-8-a. I never guessed I'd be able to do this much with that photograph when I first looked at the nearly blank square of paper.

CHAPTER 11

Printing Tips

Choosing the Right Printer

In case you're looking here to see what printer I recommend, let me repeat what I said back in Chapter 2: There is no one printer I'd recommend. Every high-end consumer and low-end professional printer produces really good prints these days. Several hundred bucks gets you a printer that will produce excellent photographs.

What you want to do determines your choice of printer. Are you going to want to make prints bigger than $8\frac{1}{2}$ inches by 11 inches? Do you prefer glossy, semigloss, or matte paper? Will a high percentage of your printing be B&W? Is print speed important to you? If you're thinking about starting up a full-service restoration business, the answers to the above questions will be "Yes," "All of these," "Yes," and "Yes." If it's relatively recent personal family photos you'll be restoring, the answers are more likely to be "No," "Whatever," "No," and "No."

Indeed, I have my personal favorites among printers (see Chapter 2, page 47) but I want to emphasize that those are my *personal* favorites. I'm suppressing my penchant for laying down The Word because I really think this has to be your decision, not mine.

Choosing Your Print Media for Permanence

Ideally we would like the prints of our restorations to be permanent. After all, impermanent film and prints forced us into restoration in the first place. A digital file can be printed out again and again, but that doesn't make permanent prints any less desirable. Having to go back and reprint your earlier work is a waste of your time and your money and, if you're performing restorations for others, not at all good for your reputation. Better to get it right the first time.

In the world of digital print permanence, there's good news and there's bad news. The good news is that pretty much any current printer on the market will produce permanent prints (we hope, and I'll get back to that). Epson, HP, Canon—they're all good. Oh yes, people argue about the different longevity numbers for the different makes and models and print media, but all the numbers look very, very good. The most reliable source for longevity data is still Henry Wilhelm's website (http://www. wilhelm-research.com). Henry won't be right 100% of the time; no one in the conservation business is. But in my experience Henry is right more often than anybody else, and his objectivity is unimpeachable and impeccable. He doesn't favor one manufacturer or medium over another, and his life's goal is to provide us with the best, most accurate, and most objective information on print permanence that he can.

Even less-permanent digital prints today get display ratings of half a century, far better than that of conventional color photographs from the 1980s. The best test out as having display lives of centuries. In the dark, in storage boxes or albums, the print life will be even better, according to the tests.

That's the good news. The bad news is that none of these new digital print materials have been around long enough for us to be positive that the accelerated tests are good predictors of print life under normal conditions. Not that we really have any choice in the matter if we're doing digital restoration, but it's worth being a little cautious in our choices.

I always use the printer manufacturer's recommended inks and papers. Mixing and matching inks and papers may get you the "look" you want, but more often than not it compromises print permanence. Some combinations of third-party papers and inks perform just as well or even better than the printer manufacturer's materials, but most don't; many perform much worse.

If you're going the third-party ink route, look for the folks who sell complete, quality inking systems, like Piezography. You're much less likely to get burned by them. Beware of the folks who just want to sell you replacement cartridges for your existing inks that are supposed to be as good as the manufacturers' inks while costing a fraction of the price. These third-party inks are usually bad news in the permanence department. Henry has some data about third-party materials on his website, but it's impossible to test every combination of materials out there. Do not trust the manufacturers of third-party inks and papers to tell you how they will perform; few of them run good longevity tests, and they all have a vested interest in selling you their product.

Beware of extreme bargains. By careful shopping around I can get OEM ink for 25% to 30% less than list price. If you see someone offering ink for your printer at one-half or one-third of list price, read the fine print; it will almost always turn out to be third-party ink that is "compatible" with your printer. That means it won't hurt your printer (no matter what some printer manufacturers claim), but don't expect good print life.

While I'm on the subject of longevity, I'd like to warn you against a common practice of digital photographers who are looking for the most permanent prints. Don't try to test your prints' display life by sticking prints in your window and exposing them to bright daylight and sunlight. This is a pointless exercise unless you're actually planning on displaying your prints that way. Indoor illumination is 100 times less intense and much less actinic than direct sunlight; the way prints react to direct sunlight is no predictor of how they will react under normal indoor lighting. It's not even a good relative measure. In some cases Paper A will fade much more quickly than Paper B in direct sunlight, but under normal light levels, Paper B will turn out to fade faster than Paper A.

Profiling the Printer

Anyone who does digital printing pretty quickly discovers that what you see on the monitor screen isn't exactly what you'll get in the print. Some of the discrepancies are due to inherent differences between the two forms of output. Monitors, which display colors as combinations of red, green, and blue light, portray a different color range than printers, which generate tones and colors as combinations of cyan, magenta, yellow, and black inks. There are colors that can be seen in a monitor's RGB space that simply can't be printed; it's a physical impossibility. Even six- and eight-color printers don't match the range of colors that you see on a display.

Slide photographers have known for years that a projected slide looks more brilliant than a print of the same photograph. Similarly, whites on a display look brighter than on paper because our eyes see the luminous display as being the brightest object in the field of view. In a print, other objects in our field of vision compete with the print for the sensation of pure white.

Within these limits, though, we would like the tones and colors in the print to be as close as possible to what we see on the monitor. For that we need a translation program that converts RGB data (what you see) to the right CMYK data (what you print). That's where the printer profile comes in. The profile is a set of instructions that correct the color and tonal values in the output data when that data is sent to the printer. Printer profiles don't affect what you see on the monitor or change anything in the image data. They only translate that data as it goes to the printer.

The profile minimizes the color errors produced by your printer. For example, suppose the printer produces greens that are too yellow and too dark. A printer profile will correct for that by adjusting greens to be lighter and bluer before passing that information on to the printer. The changes the profile makes to the data counterbalance the errors of the printer, so the printer produces a green that looks much more like what you saw on your monitor.

Because every printer needs corrections like this to match what's on the display, why isn't that correction just built into the computer

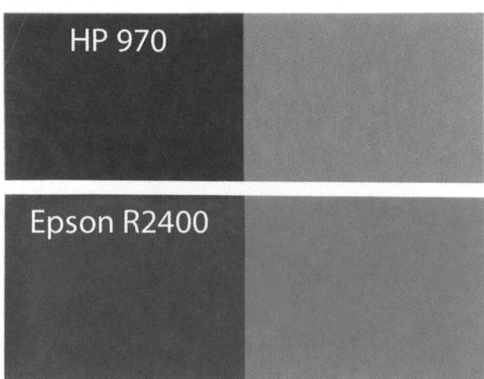

Fig. 11-1 Different inkjet printers use different inks, so inevitably they portray colors differently. The patches on the left are 100% reds (maximum amounts of magenta and yellow ink) produced by an HP 970 and an Epson R2400 printer. The patches on the right are 50% reds.

software so that we don't have to worry about it? The answer is that no two printers produce the same kinds of errors, and so no one universal set of corrections will fix things. That's inherent in the nature of printers. Let's look at an example that I hope will make this clear.

Imagine that you want to print out pure red on your printer. On the monitor, that's the red that would correspond to the RGB values of (255, 0, 0). On your printer, that maximum pure red corresponds to 100% magenta and yellow dyes and no cyan or black dye. Logically, a 50% red with RGB values of (255, 128, 128) should be half-strength magenta and yellow inks.

I printed out those 100% and 50% reds on my 6-year-old HP DeskJet 970 and a state-of-the-art Epson Stylus R2400 (Figure 11-1). The former is a four-color dye printer; the latter is an eight-color pigment printer. The reds on the two printers don't look anything alike. That's a good thing; it shows that printers are getting better. The much newer Epson printer produces much richer color than the HP printer does.

So, how do we get consistent and accurate reds? The printer and ink manufacturers can't do it. Not unless they all agreed to use exactly the same inks and papers, to lay them down exactly the same way, and to never, ever make improvements on the print quality. No one has yet invented the perfect printer and inks; there's still reason to improve the purity of color and to make the inks richer and more saturated. Manufacturers are not going to stop doing so any time soon. Instead, we turn to software to solve the problem: printer-specific profiles that are designed to correct the differences that are particular to your printer.

Figure 11-2 was printed out using custom profiles for my two printers that were created by Cathy's Profiles (see below). The reds don't match perfectly between the two printers—the Epson printer is always going to produce purer and richer colors—but they're close to each other, and they're both producing colors that are close to the correct shades of red. That is the whole point of color management: to get consistency and accuracy.

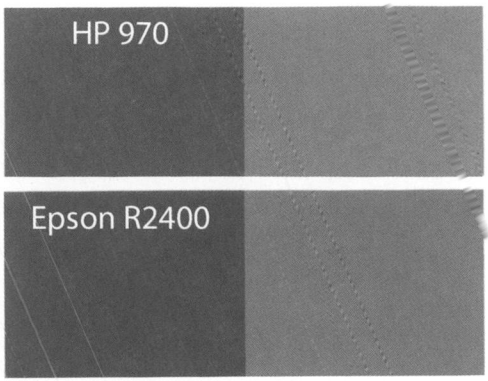

Fig. 11-2 The same 100% and 50% reds from Figure 11-1 look very different after they've been corrected by custom color profiles for each printer. The two printers produce much more similar (and more accurate) results after profiling.

Unless your printer is more than a few years old, you are already using a profile, even if you don't know it. Uncorrected output from a printer (Figure 11-3) is always a far cry from what you see on the monitor. The reason that current printers produce pretty good color right out of the box is because the printer driver that the manufacturer supplied with the printer includes a profile for that printer.

In that case, why do we need to worry about a custom profile at all? The reason is that the "canned" profile the printer manufacturer provides is correct for an average printer of that make, but every individual printer behaves differently. A custom profile, created for your own printer and ink and paper combinations, will correct your printer's unique errors and produce an even more accurate rendering.

Printer profiles are specific for each printer/paper/ink/operating system combination. Ideally one wants a profile for every combination, but a good custom profile often works better with several papers than the canned profile the printer manufacturer provides. Changing to a different brand of ink or a different operating system almost always means you'll need a new profile.

On the positive side, though, printers don't drift as monitors do. Once you've settled on a particular printer, paper, and ink combination, your profile should be good for the life of that printer.

I once asked both Jonathan Sachs (author of the Profile Mechanic and Picture Window programs) and Michael Reichmann (owner of http://www.luminous-landscape.com) what package I should buy to make printer profiles. Both recommended that I not do it myself and instead go to an outside service such as Cathy's Profiles (http://www.cathysprofile.com). They told me that I would not be able to produce results as good unless I was willing to spend several thousand dollars on a real spectrophotometer. They both know how good my "lab skills" are; they wouldn't be saying this without reason.

Even an inexpensive printer profiling package costs several hundred dollars. A custom profile from Cathy costs $40. I'd have to purchase

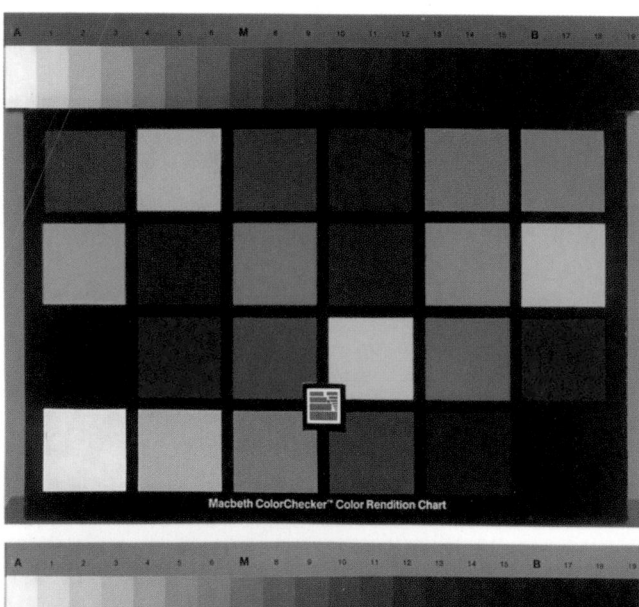

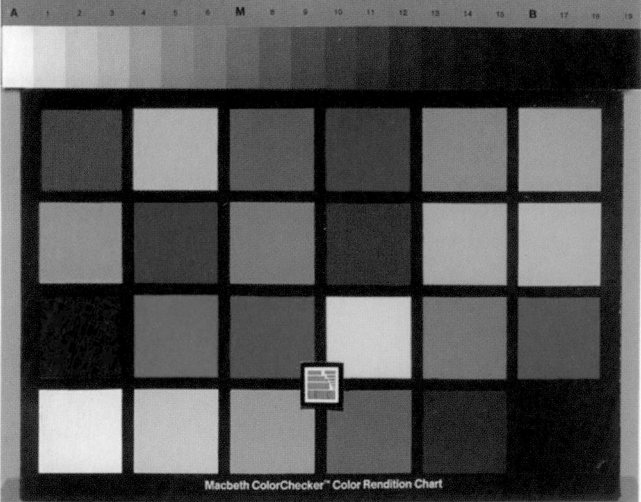

Fig. 11-3 The top print comes from an Epson R2400 printer running with no profiles enabled. The bottom print was made using a custom color profile for this printer. The profile makes the Macbeth chart and Kodak grayscale look very close to how they appear on the computer monitor.

seven or eight profiles before it would cost me as much as one of the cheap (and inferior) home-profiling packages.

The Cathy's Profiles website has clear and straightforward instructions. You print out some standard test charts on your printer and mail them to her. About a week after she receives the test prints she e-mails you your profile. I've found Cathy's custom profile to be consistently better than the printer manufacturer's profile. In some cases the differences were very subtle, in others they were dramatic.

It's important that the test prints be made with printer color management turned off, or, failing that, the printer color settings need to be exactly the same as they will be when you use the profile. Every printer's interface and driver is different, and some of the printer software makes it difficult to figure out how to do this, especially under Windows. Sometimes it takes a bit of work to figure out the right settings to produce proper test prints. This is not the fault of Cathy's Profile service; you would run into the same predicament doing your own profiles. If you have any doubts or questions about how to set up your printer, be sure to ask Cathy for advice.

Get a custom profile made sooner rather than later. A good profile means fewer test prints because you can better evaluate what the print will look like on a monitor. Besides saving you time and money from reduced wastage, starting off your printing with a custom profile means you won't have to go back and revise earlier works. My Epson 2200 printer produced decent color out of the box, and I wasn't sure that a custom profile would improve on it. But the Epson printer tended to reproduce dark greens, which appear frequently in my landscapes, as a duller olive green. I took that into account in my work, adjusting the color values and saturation in my files to produce the best possible looking prints. This adjustment meant that, as seen on the monitor, greens were somewhat exaggerated and more brilliant in the shadows, but this ensured than they printed out exactly the way I wanted.

A custom profile from Cathy substantially reduced my Epson 2200's color distortion and produced more accurate overall color saturation. I had to go back and revise a portfolio of two dozen photographs that I had just finished to take into account the difference in printer behavior The improved results were worth it, but I kicked myself for not having gotten a custom profile a few months earlier.

Toning the B&W Print

As often as not, you'll want to "tone" your B&W restorations before printing them out. Many old photographs were never neutral in color. Some processes naturally produced brown or sepia-toned prints, cyano-types were a strong blue-cyan color, and gold toning could produce a purplish hue. When making modern silver-gelatin prints, photographers and studios often used warm-tone papers and chemicals to produce a print on the warm side of neutral. Even when the original pristine print was completely neutral in color, people have an expectation that old photographs have an antique, brownish look to them. *Care and Identification of 19th-Century Photographic Prints*, which I recommended in the Introduction, is a good guide to original print tone and color.

Several different techniques can be used to tone digital prints. If you're fortunate enough to be printing on one of the new-generation Epson printers that use the Ultrachrome K3 inks, the printer control panel has an option called "Advanced B&W Photo," which works so well that I don't usually bother with other toning controls.

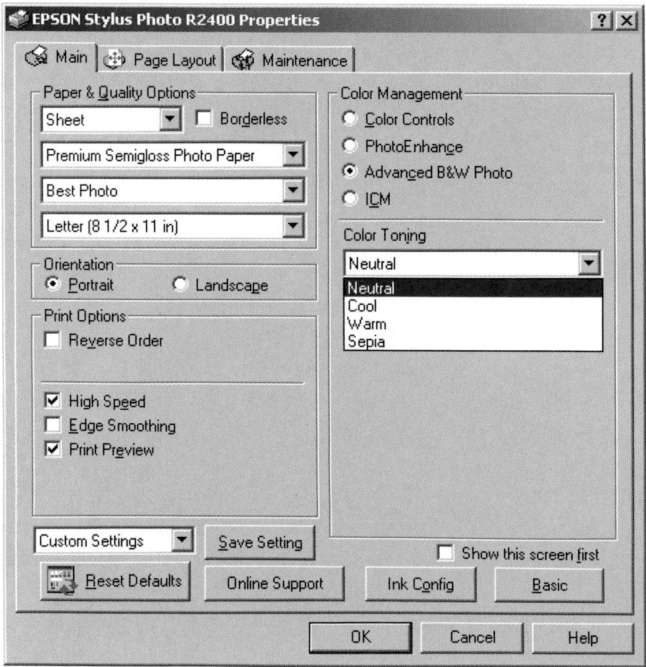

Fig. 11-4 Epson printers using the Ultrachrome K3 inks offer excellent B&W print control through the Advanced B&W Photo option. There are preset color tones for Neutral, Cool, Warm, and Sepia, but the real power lies in the Advanced B&W Photo options, shown in Figure 11-5.

The Color Toning drop-down menu (Figure 11-4) offers Neutral, Cool, Warm, and Sepia tones. Make your choice and click the Settings button to bring up the Advanced B&W Photo control panel with a color selection wheel (Figure 11-5). You can reposition a setting point in the color wheel to choose exactly the overall hue you want for the print and move it closer to or further from the neutral center points to vary the strength of the tone. There are sliders to fine-tune brightness, contrast, the strength of toning in the shadows, and the strength of toning in the highlights, selectively. The Preview window makes using these controls intuitive, and the results look wonderful. The toning has no undesirable color crossover nor artificial look to it.

If you intend to do strictly B&W printing, a third-party monochrome inking system like Piezography will solve your toning problems; the software drivers that accompany these ink sets include the controls you need to precisely refine the color of your prints. You can also find a huge amount of online expertise among the user groups and forums devoted to the various systems.

There are also great ways to tone prints that don't depend on special ink sets or printer models. Picture Window has the Tint transformation option. This will produce a monochrome, toned version of any original, B&W or color (Figure 11-6). It is simple to use; launching the transformation opens a control panel with a slider that controls the strength of the effects and a grayscale at the bottom. Shift-clicking on the grayscale

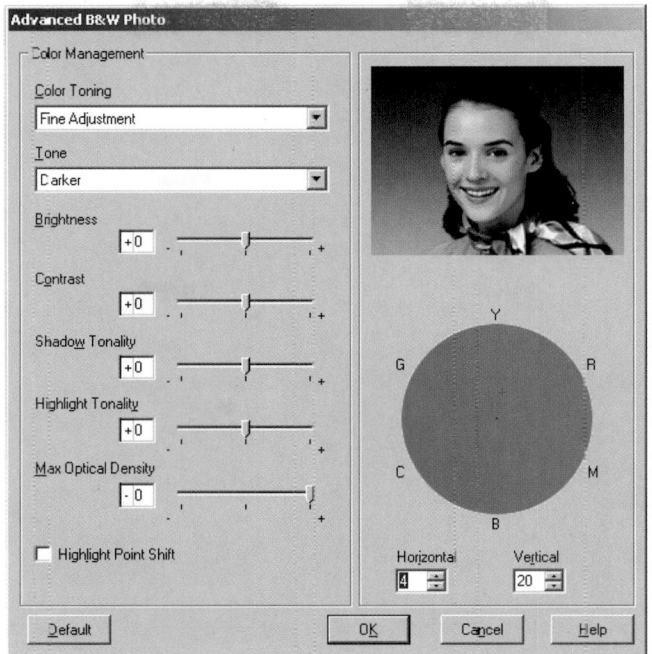

Fig. 11-5 Epson's Advanced B&W Photo options let you precisely adjust print density, contrast, and color in the printer controls. The color wheel at right lets you pick just what tone you want the print to have and how neutral or saturated it will be. Prints come out perfectly monochrome, with no sign of color crossover. This is a great advance in out-of-the-box B&W printing.

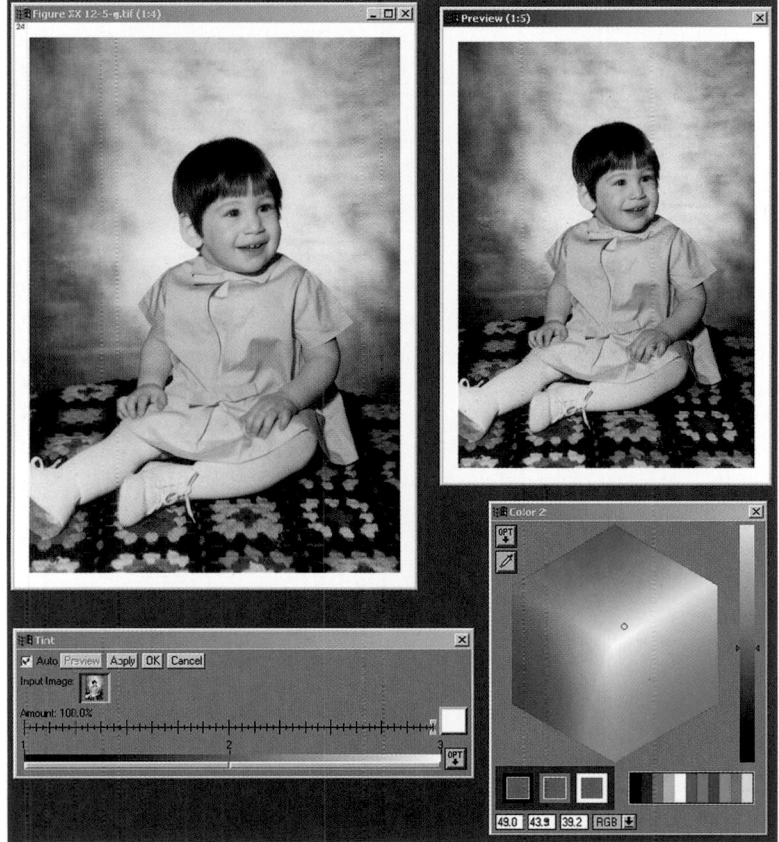

Fig. 11-6 Picture Window's Gray/Tint transformation is an excellent and simple-to-use way of producing monochrome prints from any original, B&W or color. Set a control point slider, and use the color picker wheel to adjust the color and density of that point. The whole picture will be toned uniformly, as can be seen in the Preview window at top right.

Fig. 11-7 You can set multiple tint points in the Tint transformation option to produce more complex toning effects. Here, I've set Point 2 one-third of the way up the tonal scale and a Point 3 two-thirds of the way. I've assigned them different hues to simulate selenium split-toning. For this illustration shot I exaggerated the toning to make it more visible in the reproduction by giving Point 2 a very strong red-brown color and Point 3 a visibly bluish cast. Because these colors are adjustable, along with the total amount of tinting applied via the percentage slider in the control panel, you can produce toning effects as intense or subtle as you like.

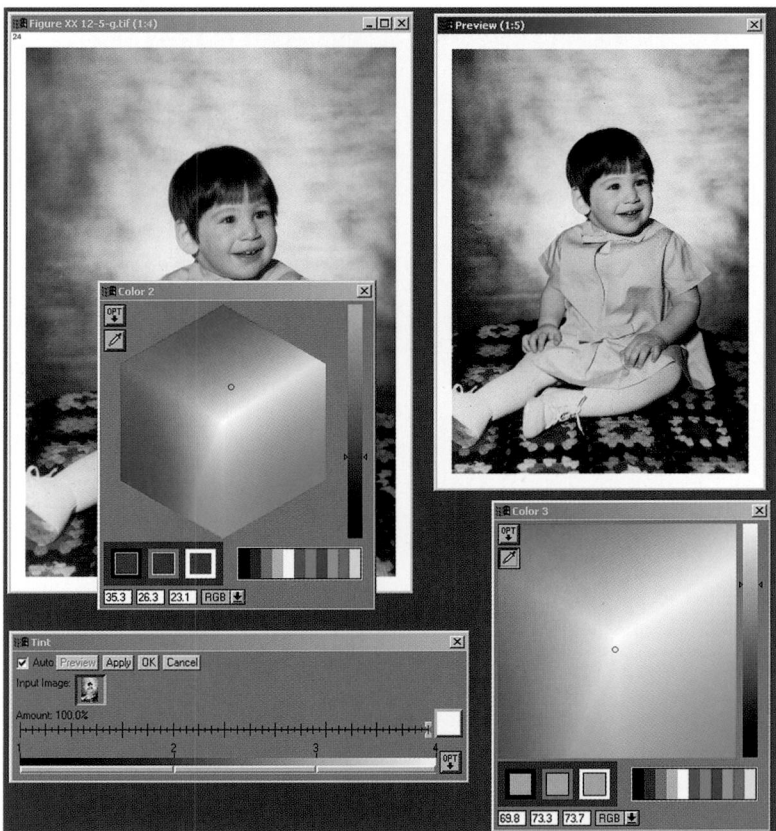

adds control points to it. Double-clicking on the number above a point opens up the color picture window, and you can assign a hue to the grayscale at that numbered point. For simple toning jobs, you'll probably just assign one point in the middle of the curve, pick a color for it, and be very satisfied. Once you've decided on the color, you can slide that control point to the left or right to change the distribution of tones (it works a lot like the midpoint slider in the Levels tool). All the time the Preview window shows you how your choices will affect the photograph.

You can simulate more complicated toning, such as split toning (Figure 11-7) or other kinds of combination toning that render different values with different hues. Add two or more control points to the grayscale, assign them individual colors, and reposition them to refine the tonality of the print. It's that easy.

Photoshop's option for toning monochrome images is not as intuitive. You can tone by adding midpoints to curves and adjusting them up and down. This is a good place to use the gray eyedropper tool (Figure 11-8).

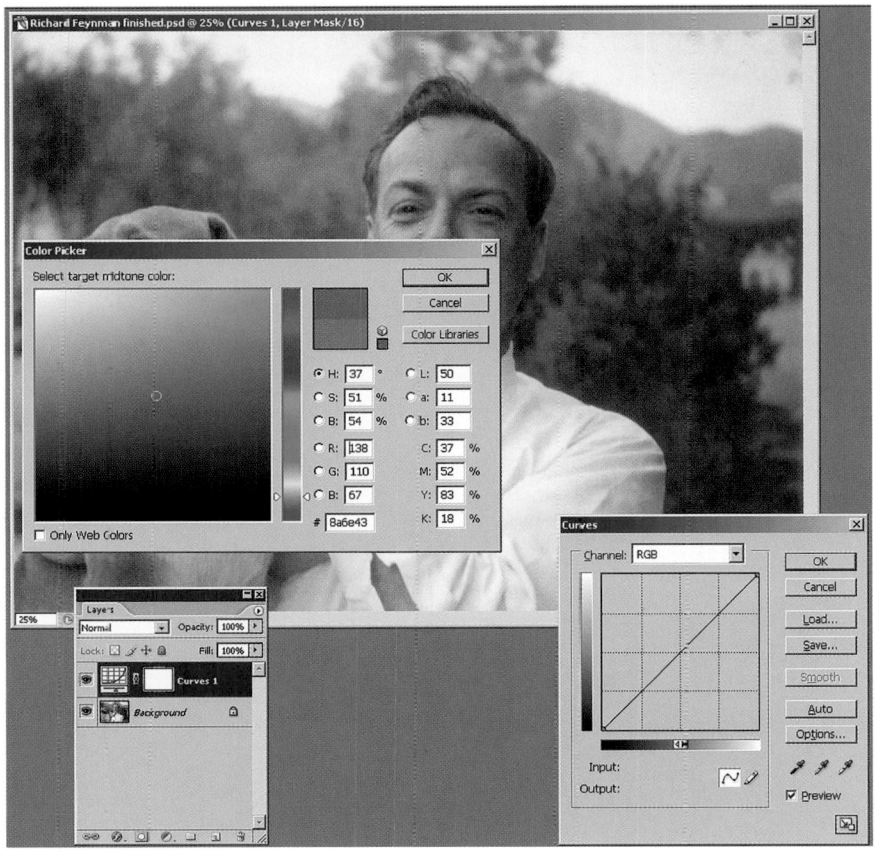

Fig. 11-8 You can apply tints to B&W photographs in Photoshop using a Curves adjustment layer, as this screenshot illustrates. First select the tone you desire by double-clicking the midtone eyedropper in the Curves control panel and choosing the target color in the Color Picker. That assigns a custom color to that eyedropper. When you click that eyedropper on a midtone in the photograph, you'll get a set of curves like those in Figure 11-9 and a tinted photograph like that in Figure 11-10.

Double-click that tool to open up the color picture window, assign the hue you want to the eyedropper, and then click with the eyedropper on a gray area of the photograph (it doesn't have to be a perfect midtone). That sets midpoint values on the curves to create the hue you want (Figure 11-9).

It's best to do this in an adjustment layer and merge the change into the original image by setting the blend mode to Color, which alters the hue of the image without altering the values. This also lets you use the opacity slider to vary the strength of the toning (Figure 11-10). If you also want to alter brightness, create another Curves adjustment layer, set its blend mode to Luminosity, and make your tonal adjustments there. This is a good method to use if you want to keep your images in 16-bit form and be able to manipulate them later.

For really sophisticated monochrome hue control in Photoshop look to Duotone mode. In graphic arts, *duotones* are photographs printed with two printing plates and two inks. Commonly, one ink is black and the other tinted, to give the printed image a bit of color. There is also tritone

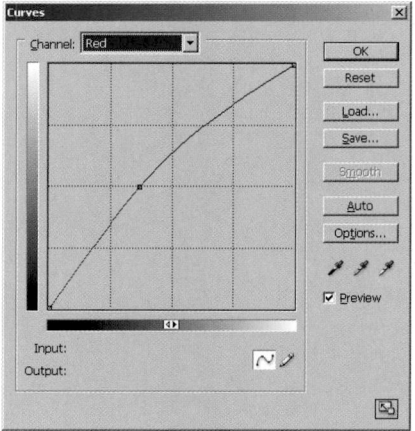

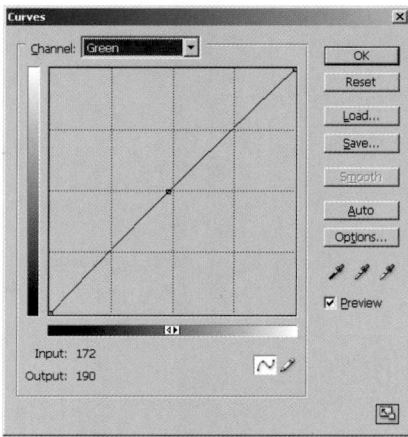

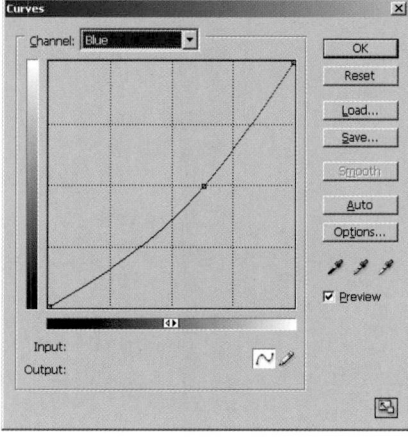

Fig. 11-9 These are the curves that the midtone eyedropper produced for Figure 11-8 when I set the midtone eyedropper to a brown hue with the Color Picker and clicked the eyedropper on the photograph. I applied these curves in the Curves adjustment layer in Figure 11-10.

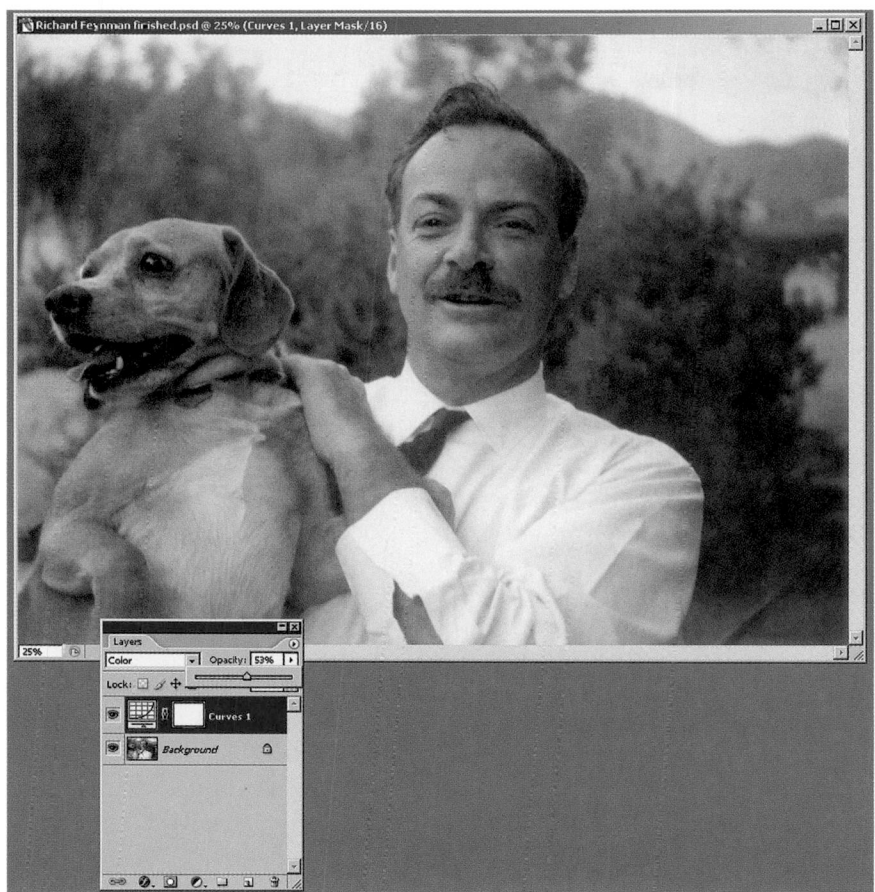

Fig. 11-10 Once you've created a tinting Curves adjustment layer, you can control the strength of the tint by changing the opacity. I've dialed it back to 53% in this screenshot, which is the right level to make the image look like a brown-tone photograph. Notice that the blend mode has been set to Color, so the Curves adjustment only alters tint and not brightness or darkness.

and quadtone printing, involving three and four inks, respectively. Duotone mode in Photoshop creates those same effects on your computer printer.

Duotone mode, however, has a couple of disadvantages. The first is that you'll be throwing away your 16-bit data. You must convert the photograph to 8-bit grayscale mode before you'll be able to convert it to duotone. You should never convert your only copy of a restoration to duotone; instead, duplicate that file and use that to create a duotone for your output.

The other disadvantage is that duotone printing is not something with which most photographers are familiar. One has to climb something of a learning curve to get any good at it. Fortunately, Photoshop comes with a bunch of predefined duotone settings that you can load and manipulate until you get the hang of creating your own.

As soon as you click on Duotone mode, the duotone interface opens up. Initially it looks like Figure 11-11. This is just ordinary B&W printing

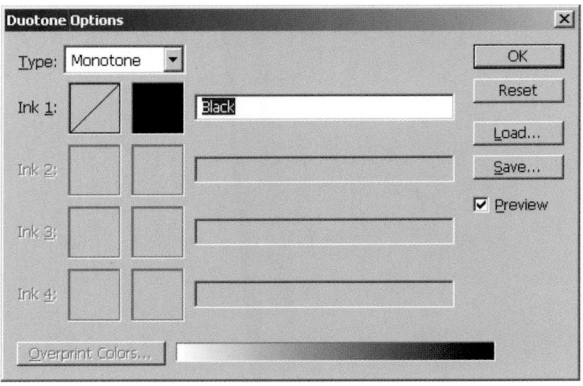

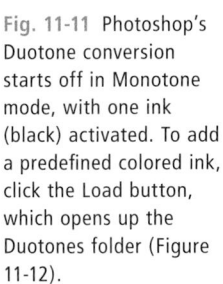

Fig. 11-11 Photoshop's Duotone conversion starts off in Monotone mode, with one ink (black) activated. To add a predefined colored ink, click the Load button, which opens up the Duotones folder (Figure 11-12).

with a single ink. The Type drop-down menu indicates monotone: Only Ink 1 is active. You'll also see what looks like an empty box with a diagonal line through it: that's actually a button that activates a Curves tool for that ink. It works just like the Curves tools you use for adjusting image values. Next to it is a solid black square button. This indicates the color of the ink—clicking on it opens up the Color Picker and gives you access to the color libraries, so you can select the color of ink you desire. Unless you're trying to print out a cyanotype, you're always going to want Ink 1 to be black.

To get to duotones (and tritones and quadtones), you could go to the Type drop-down menu and select the mode you want, but that's not what I recommend if you're new to duotones. Instead, click the Load button on the right. Open up the Duotones folder; inside it you'll find a folder named PANTONE(R), which contains many preset duotone settings (Figure 11-12).

Don't worry about all the numbers and percentages, just focus on the name of the color. Pick one that seems appropriate to the hue you want to apply to the print. For example, Burgundy is a good choice if you're trying to emulate strong selenium tone. Double-click your selection to load it, and the Preview window will show you how the photograph has changed (Figure 11-13). If you don't like the color you loaded, click Load and choose a different setting. Don't worry about how strong the tint is; you get to adjust that later.

If you can't find exactly the hue you want among the preset offerings, click the square ink color button to the left of the ink's name to bring up a color library with all the other inks the Pantone set offers. Move the slider up and down the rainbow bar, and wherever you stop a selection of inks in that hue appears next to it. Single-click one of those inks, and the preview instantly changes (Figure 11-14). Double-click on it, and that selection gets applied back to the main duotone window. If you don't like any of the Pantone colors, click the Book drop-down menu to bring up a list of other color books from which to choose. If you don't

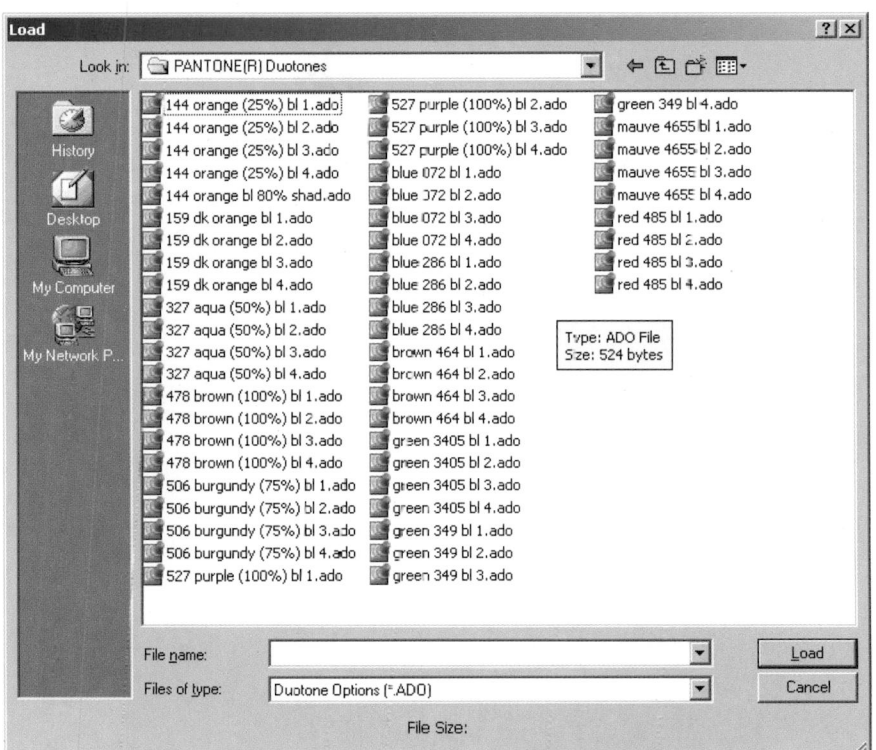

Fig. 11-12 You can find many colored-ink choices in the PANTONE(R) Duotones folder. Select a color name that sounds appropriate to the tint you want to give your photograph, and double-click it to load the ink into the Duotone Options control panel.

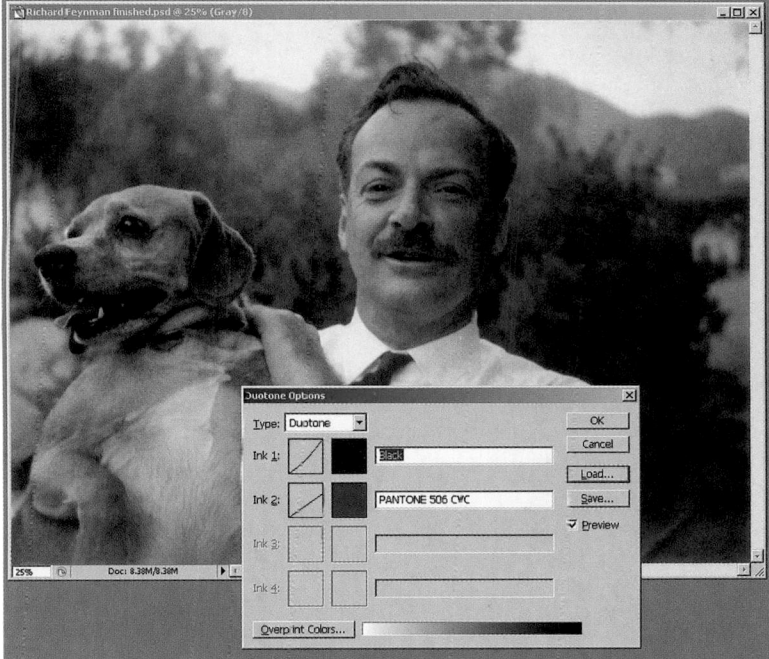

Fig. 11-13 The Duotone Options control panel shows which inks you've selected and previews what the final print color will look like. You can bring up controls to change the color or intensity of the hue by clicking the square buttons to the left of the ink's name.

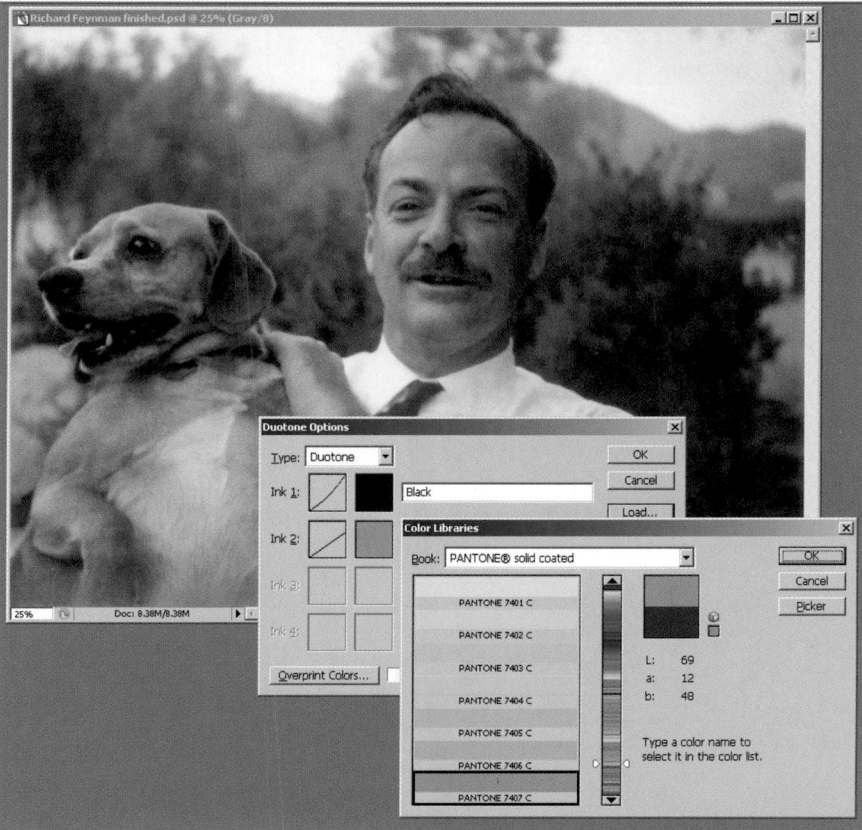

Fig. 11-14 If you want to change or customize the color of the duotone ink, clicking the colored square next to the ink's name opens up the Color Libraries, which contain thousands of individual ink colors you can choose among. Move the slider up and down the rainbow-hued scale to pick a subset of inks to examine. A new ink choice is reflected in the Duotone Options control panel and in the preview image.

want to use one of the books of prepackaged colors, click the Picker button to the right to open the traditional Photoshop color picker within which you can assign your color.

Once you've waded through all of the color choices and picked Ink 2, you'll be back in the Options window. The tinted effect will usually be too strong, looking less like you toned the photograph than hand-colored it, as in Figure 11-13. To fix that, turn to the Curve buttons next to the inks.

What a curve tells us here is how much of an ink will be applied to each value in the photograph. The higher the curve, the more ink that will be applied. So, for example, grabbing the midpoint of the Ink 2 curve and dragging it downward decreases the amount of colored ink that would be printed (Figure 11-15). That reduces the tint and also lightens the print. If you don't want to lighten the print, you need to add more black ink to compensate for the colored ink you removed. Close the curve for Ink 2, open the curve for Ink 1 (Figure 11-16), and drag

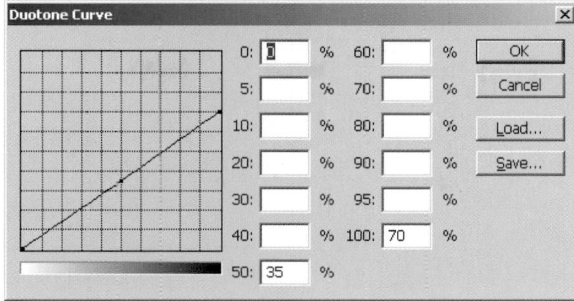

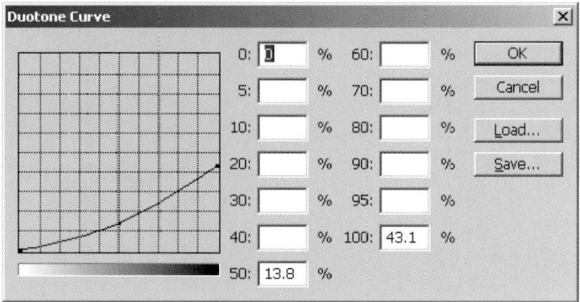

Fig. 11-15 The Curves button in the Duotone Options control panel lets you control how much of each ink is applied to each density. The top figure shows the default amount of burgundy ink being applied in Figure 11-13. To reduce the intensity of the color, I dragged the curve down, as shown in the lower figure. That decreases the amount of colored ink in the photograph, making the image lighter as well as more neutral. To keep the densities the same, I'll need to increase the amount of black ink (see Figure 11-16).

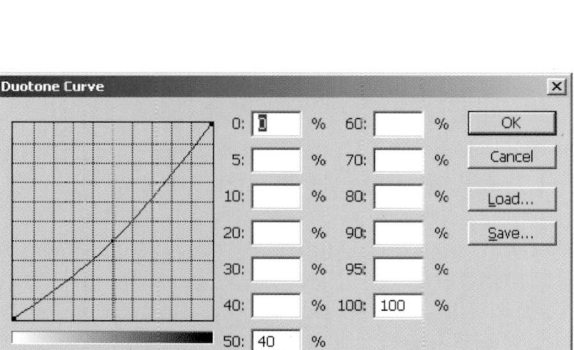

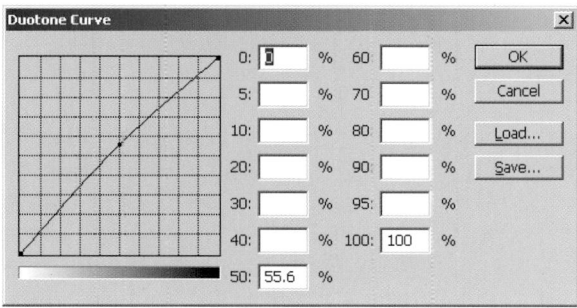

Fig. 11-16 Here are the changes I made to the black ink for Figure 11-13. The default curve is at the top. Raising the midpoint (bottom figure) increases the amount of black ink used to compensate for the reduction in burgundy ink. That keeps the photograph at its original density, as shown in Figure 11-17.

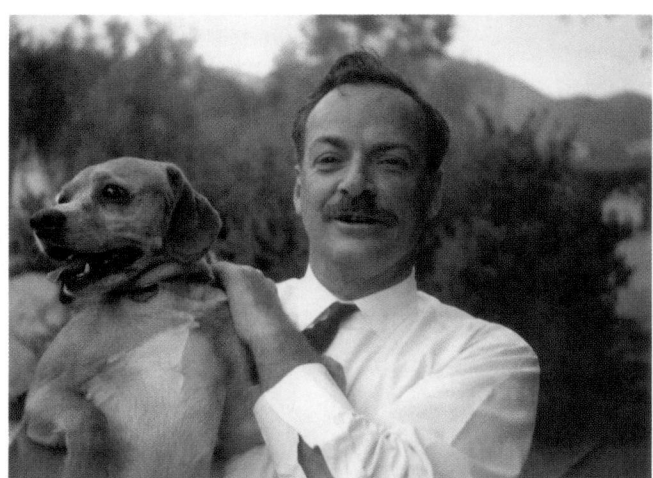

Fig. 11-17 This finished duotone is reminiscent of a strongly selenium-toned B&W darkroom print.

the midpoint of the curve up until the brightness of the print looks appropriate (Figure 11-17).

If you're thinking to yourself that this is rather complicated, that's OK. It *is* complicated, which is why I've spent so much time explaining how to use this one tool in Photoshop. The duotone controls are much appreciated by B&W photographers who want to be able to have complete and precise control over the color and tonality of their prints. Honestly, it's a bit of overkill for our needs, but it's what Photoshop offers us. If duotone is your cup of tea, you'll have to experiment with it for some time before you master it. Don't even think about tackling tritone or quadtone effects until you get the hang of duotone.

Probably the easiest way to do toning in Photoshop without messing up the original image is to use the PixelGenius PhotoKit plug-in that I described in Chapter 3 on page 81. PixelGenius PhotoKit has a B&W Toning Set (Figure 11-18) that includes scripts for a variety of standard tonings. The quality of the results is aesthetically excellent, fully as good as you'd expect from color adjustments created by some of the top gurus in the Photoshop world. I doubt that you could create better-looking toning than this yourself; I know that I certainly couldn't.

PixelGenius PhotoKit works just as well with 16-bit as 8-bit files. Its effects are applied as new layers on top of the original photograph (Figure 11-19), so the source photograph, whether it's B&W or color, remains unaltered at the bottom of the layer stack. Each toning is applied in a new layer, so you can create a whole bunch of toning variations through repeated applications of PixelGenius PhotoKit and decide which one you like best later (or keep them all, as I did in this case).

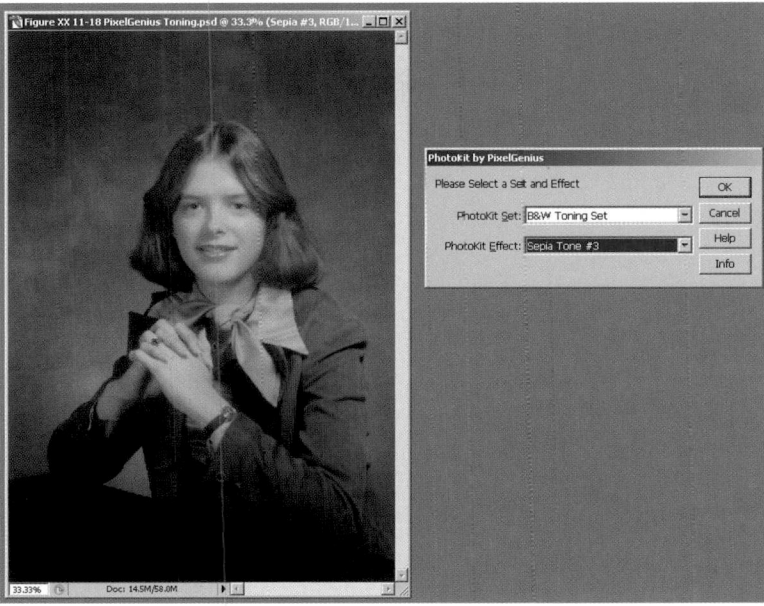

Fig. 11-18 The PixelGenius PhotoKit plug-in, accessed via Photoshop's Automate menu, is a great third-party solution to the problem of making beautifully toned B&W prints. PixelGenius PhotoKit works on 8- or 16-bit color or B&W originals.

Display and Storage Conditions for Maximum Print Longevity

The rules for caring for digital prints aren't all that much different from the ones you'd follow for conventional color photographic prints. Broadly put, there are prints you have on display and prints you have stored away. In either situation, the important guiding principle is the same one that doctors follow: "First, do no harm." That means avoiding bad practices and display or storage conditions that shorten print life.

Prints on display should be framed under glass or acrylic. This keeps dirt and grime away from the print. Even ordinary framing glass markedly extends print life by filtering out some of the UV light that would otherwise attack the inks.

If possible, put a spacer matte between the print and the glass, so the surface of the print does not directly touch the glass. Use unbuffered, acid-free archival matte board for the spacer. Avoid buffered boards; many dyes and coloring agents don't like the slightly alkaline environments the buffer creates and deteriorate more quickly in those conditions.

Also avoid wooden frames. Wood contains compounds called lignins that break down over time and release chemicals such as peroxides that can oxidize the colors in prints. The "gas fading" problem of several years back that caused some Epson inkjet prints to fade in days was an oxidation problem.

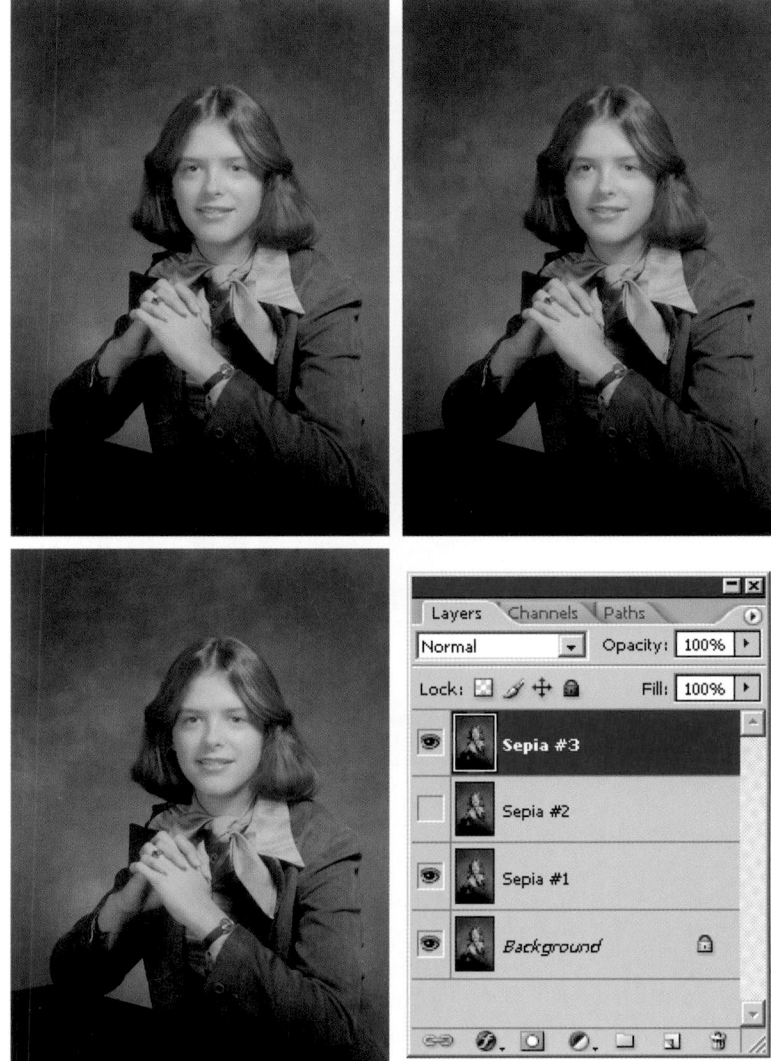

Fig. 11-19 I produced three toned variations of the color photograph in Figure 11-18 just by selecting the degree of Sepia Tone I wanted from PixelGenius PhotoKit's drop-down menu and clicking OK. PixelGenius PhotoKit creates a new layer for each effect, so I could preserve all three strengths of sepia toning (portrayed here). My original photograph is intact in the background layer, as the layer stack shows.

Considerable argument surrounds whether lacquers and laminates are good ideas. In the short term, lacquer and lamination certainly prevent damaging chemicals, moisture, and some amount of UV from getting to the print surface. The vexing question is what happens in the long term. Many conventional color photographs have had their lives drastically shortened by lacquers made by some of the best companies in the business specifically for the purpose of protecting said photos.

Solvents and plastics in the lacquers and adhesives in the laminates concern me. This may be unwarranted paranoia on my part, but I am

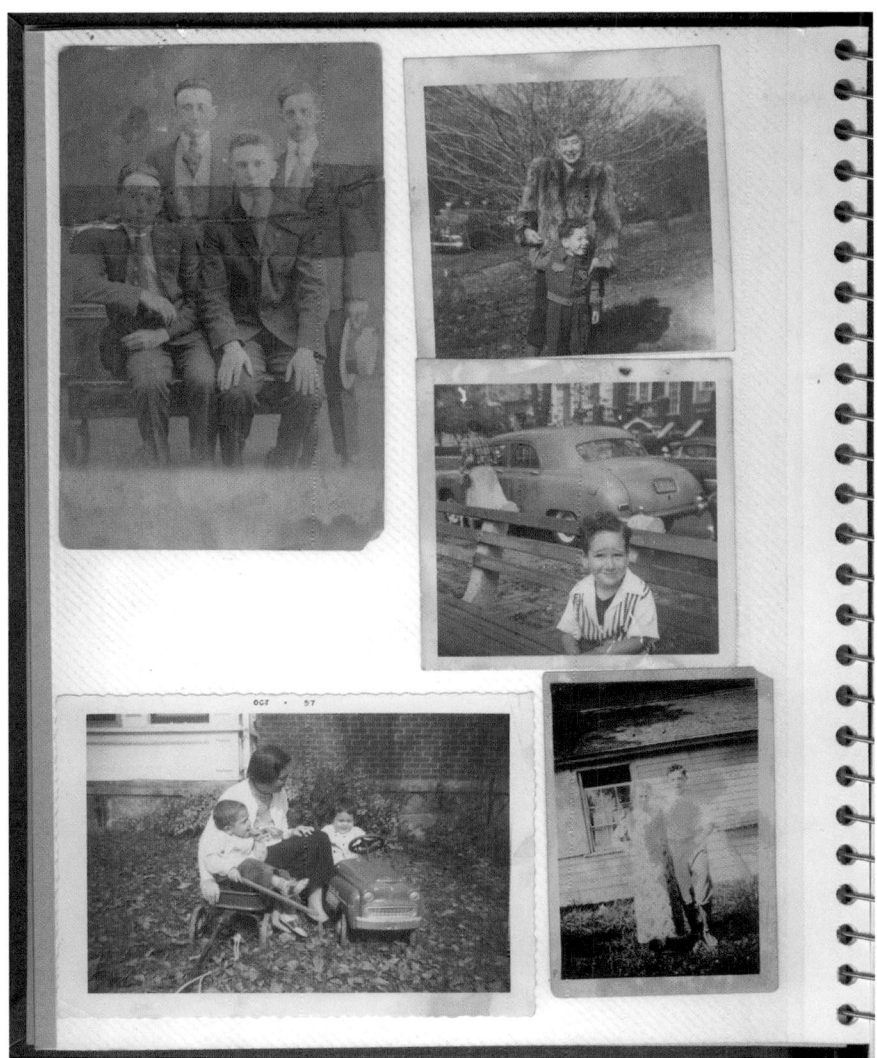

Fig. 11-20 Under no circumstances should you store your photographs, conventional or digital, in an album like this! These "magic" photo albums, with their sticky pages, do more than just damage photographs. The glue hardens with time, so it becomes impossible to remove the photograph from the album that is ruining it.

inclined to avoid them. There's no good way to run accelerated tests on how these compounds interact with the prints; only time will tell whether, over the long run, they enhance or diminish print life.

For prints that are stored away in albums or boxes, I have a different set of admonitions. If you sleeve individual prints, use Mylar or polyethylene sleeves. Beware of vinyl, which will destroy prints in short order. Even acetate sleeves are not good for long-term preservation; the plastic gradually breaks down and releases acetic acid. It's a slow process, but we are trying to think in time spans of several decades or more.

Avoid "magic" photo albums at all costs! Those are the ones with the sticky pages that have plastics overleaves. You peel back the overleaf and position the picture where you want it on the page. The releasable adhesive holds the photo in place, and the overleaf protects it. That's the theory, but it's not the reality of it.

The truth is that those albums contain all sorts of nasty compounds that will wreak havoc on your prints (Figure 11-20). The adhesive isn't close to being archival and furthermore may harden and permanently bond to the print over time. Should that happen, when problems start to appear there will be no way of removing the print from the album that won't destroy the print.

Companies like Light Impressions make storage boxes and albums suitable for digital prints. As with matte board, what you're looking for are unbuffered, acid-free materials.

Ultimately, the saving grace of digital restoration and printing is that it's relatively easy to turn out a replacement print that looks just as good as the original one, as long as the digital file has been properly archived (see the next chapter). "Relatively easy," though, is not the same as "no trouble at all." It will cost you some time and expense to turn out that replacement print, and you may need to make some tone and color adjustments to the digital file to get the new print to look just like the old one did. The best option is to avoid all of that by properly caring for the original print—reprinting is your fallback solution, not your best one.

CHAPTER 12

Archiving and Permanence

The Special Needs of Digital Storage

Once you have successfully restored a photograph, you'll need to preserve that restoration. That digital file is no less important and valuable than the original, deteriorated photograph. In the future it is likely to be the only good or even usable rendition of that image.

We need to think about the long term. The photographs you are restoring range from several decades to more than a century old. If you're taking photographic preservation and restoration seriously, you have to be thinking on the same timescale for your archives. It's not about whether the restored photographs will be viewable 5 years from now, but whether they will be accessible 50 or 100 years from now.

The foremost misconception newcomers to the field have about digital photographs (including digital restorations) is that archiving presents no problems because digital files can be copied perfectly. That is an important difference between physical and electronic photographs: Physical photographs can only be duplicated with some loss of fidelity, whereas those digital 1s and 0s can be replicated indefinitely into the future. But there are caveats. Your digital restorations are theoretically immortal, but you'll realize that permanence only if you follow good preservation techniques and maintain ongoing vigilance for deterioration.

Successful archiving means:

- Keeping digital photographs intact

- Being able to read the data

- Understanding the data

- Lastly, being able to find the data!

This final item is not a problem that is unique to digital files; any archive needs a good filing system. I'm limiting this discussion to problems unique to digital archiving, but I want you to remember that the biggest library in the world is useless if you don't have a good way to find the book you need.

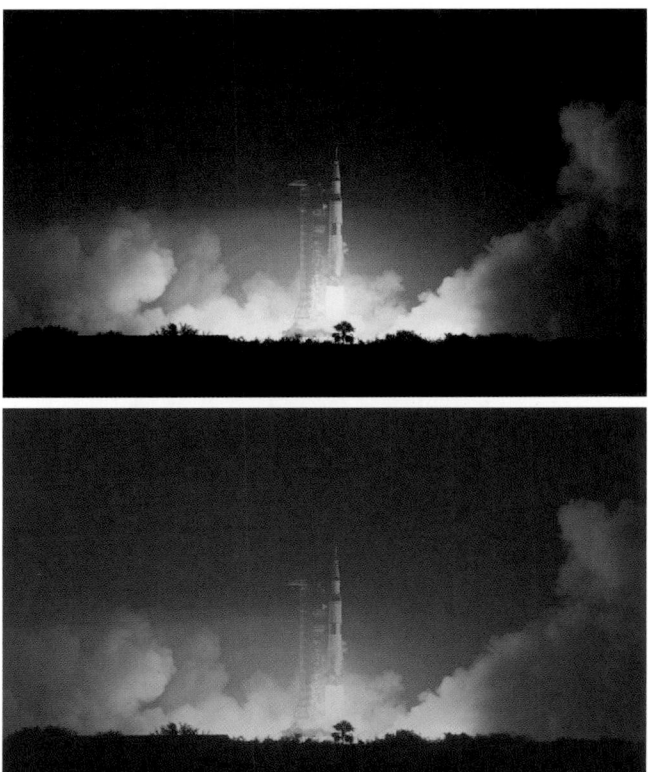

Fig. 12-1 Film-based photographs, like the top figure, start deteriorating from the day they're made, but they usually do so in a gradual and predictable way (bottom). This photo developed a pink highlight stain and lost magenta and cyan image density. When deterioration is not too advanced, restoration is feasible—that's the whole point of this book.

In the remainder of this chapter, I'll talk about the best media for storing your images, suitable data formats for storing them, and how to minimize your chances of losing your files. Before getting into the details, I'd like to explain why this attention to technical minutiae is necessary. It's time to get physical.

In a Material World

There's a widespread and mistaken belief that digital files don't undergo deterioration as film does (Figure 12-1). Digital data may theoretically be immortal, but the real world is not quite so cooperative. Have you ever had a floppy or a CD become unreadable, a hard disk crash, or a backup tape behave unreliably? Digital data obviously isn't impervious.

In truth, the digital restoration, both the print and electronic file, can prove less permanent than the original film-based photograph. While digital print deterioration will be immediately visible, just as it is with silver-based photographs, electronic file deterioration won't be. You may see no outward signs that the storage medium (or the data it con-

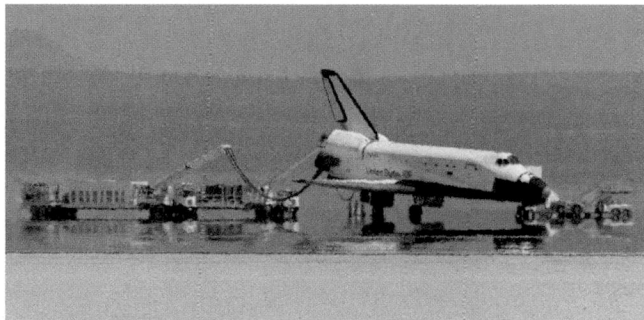

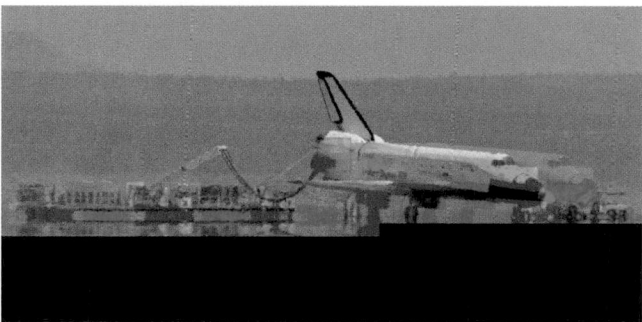

Fig. 12-2 Digital files will show no deterioration initially (top), but beyond a certain point, information will disappear suddenly and often irreversibly. This JPEG (bottom) had some bytes corrupted midfile. This is currently not a recoverable loss.

tains) has deteriorated until you attempt to open the file and it looks like Figure 12-2—at that point, it's a bit too late.

Digital photographs are binary data: strings of 1s and 0s assembled into bytes, pixels, and finally photographs. One ought not mistake a 1 for a 0, but in the real world it happens. We've all had the experience of finding that we can't read a phone number we wrote down because it became smudged or smeared. Numbers may be fixed and immutable, but their physical manifestations aren't. Even communicating those digits you are sure of may fail. Think about how difficult it can be to tell someone your phone number during a noisy party. These are problems that data is heir to.

No existing storage medium actually records 1s and 0s in digital form; they're recorded as analog signals that are interpreted digitally. Even old-fashioned punched tape and cards are analog signals. It might seem that there is nothing more unambiguous than a hole, but think back to Florida in November 2000 to realize that there can be malformed punch holes in cards that both machines and human beings have trouble interpreting correctly and unambiguously.

Similarly, magnetic regions on tape or disk and data pits on CDs vary in size and intensity. Recordable CDs, for example, store data in small regions whose reflectivity differs from that of the surrounding medium. A laser beam in the CD player scans the CD and measures the reflectivity of the disk, point by point. When this analog measurement changes by

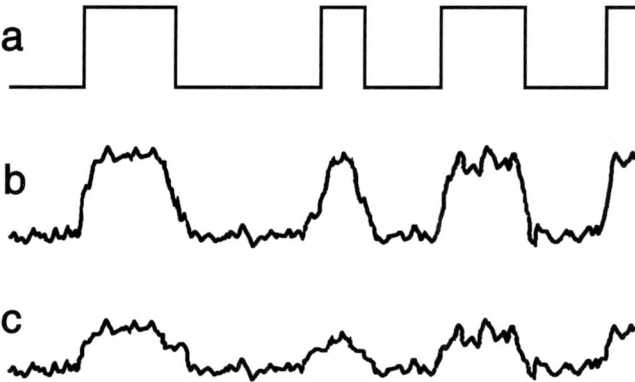

Fig. 12-3 (a) This is how we imagine a digital signal to be: a clear and unambiguous string of 1s and 0s. (b) This is what a digital signal really looks like. (c) As the storage medium degrades, the signal strength weakens (and the noise may increase). The more the signal deviates from the imaginary ideal, the greater the chance that it will be misinterpreted by the computer. Serious and uncorrectable numbers of errors become inevitable.

more than a certain amount, the electronics in the CD reader interpret it as data and convert it to 1s and 0s.

So, our precise 1s and 0s don't have a physical presence; we extract them from recordings that are actually analog. Ideally, we imagine a digital signal to look much like Figure 12-3a, with nice sharply defined pulses. Anyone can readily see that this signal starts out with a long pulse, a short pulse, and another long pulse. If I tell you that a long pulse is supposed to represent a 1 and a short pulse a 0, we'd all agree to read this as "101." That's the theory, anyway. In reality, square waves with perfectly sharp sides and flat full-strength tops don't exist. The random vagaries of the real world and normal electronic noise make digital signals look more like the jagged and rounded peaks in Figure 12-3b.

Here's what's magic about digital processing. As long as the underlying signal is strong enough and the noise isn't too bad, we can figure out which jagged pulses are really 1s and which are 0s. Digital electronics don't merely reproduce the noisy signal of Figure 12-3b, they correctly interpret it and report it as "101." At each and every stage of digital data processing, the electronics take that noisy signal and push it back to being as close to perfect binary data as it can.

This is why we can make perfect copies of digital files ad infinitum and run bits of data back and forth a million times through the innards of our computers without losing any of them. It's not that the digital data is inviolate, it's that at every stage we can almost always restore the digital signal to its original form.

Picking Up the Pieces

Occasionally data is lost. A hill or valley in the signal may be unusually shallow, or there may be noise spikes. When these things happen, sometimes a 1 gets misinterpreted as a 0 or vice versa. When you're moving around trillions of bits, it's really important to catch all of those errors. That's done by adding error-controlling data to the original information. We can design elaborate error correction schemes that will tell us when bits are misinterpreted and even correct multiple-bit errors.

The most extreme form of error correction exists in ordinary CD and DVD disks. Bits of dust and scratches can obliterate hundreds of bits of data. The disks' data formats use an incredibly complex error correction scheme that can restore dozens upon dozens of errors flawlessly. Most people don't realize it, but almost every time they read data from a disk, there are errors that get fixed invisibly by error correction techniques. Error correction is a necessity; without it all large data files would become corrupted. So why doesn't that make it all OK forever?

It's Just a Matter of Time

All storage media degrade. The dye layer in a recordable CD that actually holds the data gradually fades, just as the dyes in color films do. Random thermal motion of the molecules will gradually demagnetize the domains in magnetic storage. As the dye fades and the domains demagnetize, the signal the playback drive reads gets weaker and weaker. Degradation begins the moment you record data and continues unabated until you re-record that data. Hardware ages, too. CD players can get dirty or go out of alignment after prolonged use.

These are gradual processes that reduce the signal and increase the noise. As the quality of the signal goes down, the error rate goes up. Our archiving problem is that this is all invisible to us, as long as error correction codes catch and fix all those errors. When the error rate becomes greater than the correction code can handle, though, the computer system starts reporting that it can't successfully read a file, or it may not even mount a disk at all. From our perspective something has suddenly gone wrong, but it was really a gradual deterioration that was hidden from us until the computer could no longer cope with it. One day, you find that uncorrectable errors have "suddenly" popped up (Figure 12-3c).

CD/DVD Diagnostic (http://www.infinadyne.com) is a Windows-only program that will test CDs and DVDs for read errors, to let you catch them going bad before they become unreadable. It also includes data recovery utilities to help you recover files from bad CDs. CD/DVD Diagnostic (with a 14-day trial download) isn't as thorough or capable as hardware diagnostic systems, but it's about as good as it gets for a home system, and it's a heck of a lot better than just spot-checking your CDs every year or so.

Magnetic media are different. Unlike the dye layers in a CD or DVD, the magnetic recording layer in a hard drive is not likely to physically degrade—it's just that the signal will get weaker over time. That means you can very simply restore magnetic data to its original pristine state by copying it off the drive and writing it back to the drive. That resets the clock on deterioration. By periodically refreshing your magnetic media, you can maintain the files indefinitely (until the drive fails physically). Which brings me to my next topic: What are the good storage media?

All Storage Is Not Created Equal

Archiving film images is simple. Buy a deep freezer, package the photographs in airtight polyethylene bags, stick them in the freezer, and ignore them. They'll still be good a couple of hundred years from now, assuming someone pays the electric bill. Digital archiving requires an ongoing maintenance plan that allows for the time and expense of periodically re-recording the data. This is where many newcomers mess up. Their strategy is "back up and forget." Down the road this will most certainly cause them grief.

As I've just explained, digital storage usually seems perfect until it is suddenly not. It is most important that we periodically copy old stored data before we actually see bad bits. Also, we need to periodically spot-check our older records, or run a program such as CD/DVD Diagnostic, so that we don't get caught short by degrading data.

We want to keep the need for maintenance to a minimum, not only to save time and money, but to reduce the chances of getting caught by surprise. To some extent that means predicting the future, and we're all prone to make mistakes that way. Figure 12-4 shows a variety of media I own that are no longer readable for one or more of the reasons I'm about to present.

Analog tape is right out. The failure rate for those formats is appalling; look at how often things like QIC-80/Travan backup tapes go bad. The media all come with "lifetime warranties," but that doesn't seem to prevent tape data from going south in a matter of months to years. It's cheap storage, but you'll be lucky if anything is readable in 10 years. Digital tape is better, but it's costly, and tape is still physically fragile.

Flexible magnetic disks are also a very poor choice. Whether they're ordinary floppies or high-density media like Zip disks or Superdisks, they have poor reliability for archiving. They're also not particularly cheap, and it isn't that hard to run up many gigabytes each year of digital image files. Except for their convenience for swapping small files between friends and computers, these media are obsolete: CDs are faster, cheaper, more reliable, and better if you have to move files of any size.

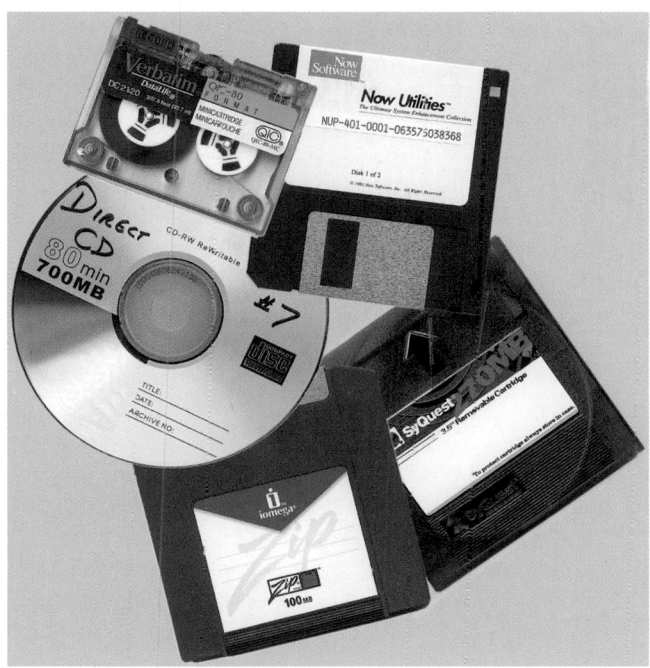

Fig. 12-4 Are you unintentionally committing your photographs to a graveyard of lost data? All of these media hold data of mine that is now unreadable for one reason or another.

Recordable DVDs have great storage capacity, but they are currently less certain tools for archiving because we have less data on their long-term permanence. That uncertainty will certainly be reduced with time, but at the moment I'm not entirely comfortable with using them for archiving. Today, I would definitely avoid dual-layer DVD disks. The way these disks get double the capacity of conventional DVDs is by having a second data layer underneath the outer layer. The outer layer is semi-transparent, so the underlying one can be seen through it. Therein lies the potential problem; the signal that comes back from a dual-layer DVD can't be as strong as that from a single-layer DVD. A weaker signal means that when the disk deteriorates, the data will reach the point of unreadability sooner than it will for a single-layer DVD.

It may turn out this is not a practical problem; maybe we will find that single-layer DVDs are good for 150 years, and the dual layer ones for a "mere" 75. Maybe not, though. As long as the durability of all these media is still under investigation, sacrificing any data life for a modest 2× increase in storage capacity seems very imprudent. It's also not currently cost effective.

It does seem that most drives will support DVD+ and DVD– formats in perpetuity, so we dodged that obsolete-format bullet, but in the future there may be other format-compatibility issues. The "blue" DVD format wars have yet to be settled, and there's no guarantee we won't wind up with one format declining into insignificance (and that means obsolescence).

Removable drive cartridges have good capacities, but unless they are entirely self-contained (sealed units that include the read heads), they're not reliable enough for serious archiving. That precludes using the traditional Syquest/Orb/Iomega varieties of cartridges.

Even sealed cartridge units are unacceptable if they require proprietary hardware support like special cradles or readers (or software drivers). You can be pretty certain that the company making these devices now will not be making nor supporting that model in 20 years; there's a pretty good chance the company won't even be in business. More on this in a few pages; it's the big problem with these formats.

On the other hand, conventional hard drives, whether internal or external, are excellent for archiving. The external ones are best of all because it's easy to have multiple archives (you should always have two copies of anything you really care about) and to add capacity by buying more drives. Hard drives are extremely reliable these days, and data recovery is possible from even heavily damaged platters, although it's pricey. The odds of you losing everything on a hard drive are quite small. The odds of you losing anything that's been duplicated on two hard drives is insignificant.

Hard-drive data degrades slowly, but it is easy to refresh the data by reading it off of the drive and writing it back. It costs about $0.50/gigabyte to maintain duplicate external hard-drive archives as of mid-2006, and prices are dropping daily. That's a penny an image for archiving 20-MB image files, and the process of archiving is as fast and painless as copying files from one hard drive to another. In fact, no other storage device is faster.

If you expect to be amassing large amounts of data, a removable hard-drive "bay" or "drawer" is definitely the route for you. See Chapter 2, Hardware for Restoration (page 40), for further information on this option. Hard-drive bays have several advantages. Your storage capabilities are unlimited; every time you need more storage, just buy another hard drive and tray. Regular internal hard-drive storage is half the cost or less of a prepackaged external hard drive. Even when you add in the cost of a tray, it is still a lot less money per gigabyte than an external hard drive. Removable hard-drive trays are ideal when you want to maintain duplicate archives, especially if you want keep one off site.

CD-R is another good storage medium. Its biggest limitation is the storage capacity; these days 700 MB doesn't seem like all that much. In all other respects it's a winner. High-quality blanks are a little expensive per megabyte than hard-drive storage, but you don't have to invest in 100+ gigabytes at one time. It's easy to make duplicate archives that you can keep off site in case of fire, theft, or other disaster. High-quality blanks should have a data storage life of decades. I recommend Kodak Preservation Gold CDs. Best of all, CD-Rs are permanent; you can't accidentally write over an existing file.

One caution about archiving to CDs. Use standard CD authoring software like Nero or Easy CD Creator for PCs or Toast for Macs. Do *not* use programs that let you "drag and drop" files on your CDs just as if they were floppy disks or hard drives (for example, Direct CD). Disks written in "drag-and-drop" formats can only be read on computers that have special software that can interpret these formats. Such software may not be available in the future. Furthermore, this format turns out to be nowhere near as robust as the normal data format. I and other people have had "direct" CDs become unreliable or entirely unreadable on a short timescale, while conventionally authored CDs have held up just fine.

I don't recommend using online storage for your archive, even though the companies offering the services provide extremely reliable storage. First of all, it's not very feasible when you are generating hundreds of megabytes or even gigabytes of data. Even with a high-speed connection, you're talking about hours to upload your files and then read them back to confirm that they arrived intact.

Furthermore, storing your data with online services has the same problem that archiving on proprietary cartridges does: When the company disappears (and all companies do sooner or later), so may your prospects for retrieving your data.

Can You Hear Me Now?

One of the things that makes digital storage so problematical is that different brands of media have very different levels of reliability and durability. People have long known that about magnetic tape, but it's just as true of floppy disks and CDs (these days the reliability of hard drives is so high that this isn't really an issue). Some particularly bad CD blanks have lasted for as little as a few years before starting to develop read errors, even though they were supposed to last for decades. This is why I am distrustful of DVD blanks, especially double-sided ones, for archiving until we get more real-world data. I don't know that they have problems, but I don't know that they don't, either.

Folks get into long arguments about how long different media will last; there's even the possibility that all the cautions I've given you aren't necessary. It's prudent to take the precautions because "better safe than sorry" are the watchwords of good archiving. I admit that it may turn out that CDs and other media really will last many decades as the manufacturers claim. Still, when it comes to archiving my work, I'd rather err on the side of caution and hope that will let me avoid unpleasant repercussions years from now.

What we can be certain of, though, is that data formats will change and old formats and media will become obsolete. Over time measured in decades the problems of data deterioration pale compared to those of equipment obsolescence. In the year 2050 your highest quality Zip disks may still be readable (although I doubt it), but it's absolutely certain that Zip drives will be obsolete by then. It's not much use having perfect media if you don't have any way to read it.

Don't be on the cutting edge of the technology. You don't want to be one of the trendsetters; you want to be one of the teeming masses that follow. Security and survival lie in numbers. The more popular and standardized a format is, the more likely you'll be able to read it in the future. It's still not hard nor expensive to get drives that read 5¼-inch floppies although, by today's standards, relatively few people ever used them and relatively little data is stored that way. There's a hundred times as much data stored on 3½-inch floppies and the drives will certainly be available for a long time. There's a million times more data archived onto CDs, in both private individuals' and major institutions' collections, than on floppies. Devices that can read CDs will be around for a very long time. IDE and SCSI hard-drive interfaces will also endure. There's so much data stored on such drives that the demand for hardware that can read them will exist long after the data formats and media have been superseded by better ones.

Make sure your storage format is supported by more than one manufacturer. That's the biggest thing that's wrong with proprietary formats and the main reason why most of the removable cartridges on the market—reliability concerns aside—are unacceptable. They are only readable with the manufacturer's hardware, and third-party support is minimal.

This problem isn't limited to cartridges. Many Macintosh users were left with stranded data when Apple abruptly stopped supporting 800-KB Mac-format floppy disks. In most cases one could transfer data or programs to 1.4-MB floppies or network the data between machines, but I have at least one copy-protected, key-disk program that even Steve Wozniak couldn't tell me how to port over to a newer PowerBook.

Babel Fish

Assuming you've passed the hurdles of safely recording and retrieving your data, can you figure out what it means? You need software that can interpret the format you used. That means staying away from proprietary file formats as much as possible and using the most popular ones, the same way you did when choosing the physical storage format. Bit-mapped formats like BMP and uncompressed TIFF are almost universally readable. TIFF is excellent because it can save both 8-bit and 16-bit images. That means you can save your finished restorations with maximum fidelity. The 16-bit uncompressed TIFF format is widely supported and can be read by lots of different programs perfectly. TIFF also lets you store your color profile with the file.

These uncompressed formats provide some measure of protection against data deterioration; if you lose some bits, only the pixels containing those bits are affected. With the right software you can reconstruct the rest of the image entirely intact, and the formats are simple enough that such software is easy to write. That means it will be available for all sorts of different platforms for many years.

Compressed formats are less physically robust: the encoding schemes that shrink the file size make it so that each data byte affects many pixels. A bad byte in a JPEG file can prevent the entire remainder of the image from loading correctly, much as in Figure 12-2. JPEG (at very low compression ratios of, say, 1 : 2 or 1 : 3) is still a good archiving format for 8-bit data because JPEG readers will be available on just about every platform for the foreseeable future.

Compressed TIFF is also a good format as long as you use one of the most popular programs, like Photoshop, to do the compressing. There are literally dozens of different TIFF variants, some of which are so obscure and little used that future support for them is dubious. Translator software like GraphicConverter (for Macs) and DeBabelizer can overcome many of the format hurdles you'll encounter, but why create unnecessary potential problems for yourself?

Don't use Photoshop PSD in preference to TIFF. Even today not all software can read all PSD files because Adobe has modified the format over the different versions of Photoshop. Who knows what PSD will look like in 20 years, when Photoshop 15 comes out? If you need to preserve a PSD file because it includes layers or other special Photoshop effects, save a flattened TIFF or JPEG version of the photograph, too—just in case.

Final Words

Safely archiving digital photographs is a more demanding task than many realize, but it's not unbearable. Once you've set yourself up well, it won't even feel particularly inconvenient. It only takes a little care and forethought to save your work so that you and your descendants can actually be sure of retrieving it later.

Even in the case of a catastrophe, your archives can probably still be resurrected. Many companies are in the business of retrieving data from storage media that seemed hopelessly damaged. For example, Drive Savers (http://www.drivesavers.com) can successfully recover data from hard drives that have been drowned, burnt, and crushed. Data recovery services aren't cheap, but at least recovery is possible.

But, if you do your archiving correctly from the start, you'll probably never be faced with one of those data recovery bills. Here's the short version of what you need to do:

1. Save your files in a common, nonproprietary format. The 16-bit uncompressed TIFF format is ideal, but compressed TIFF is acceptable. For 8-bit color, JPEG at very low compression ratios is also acceptable. All of these formats should remain readable for a very long time.

2. Save your files on media that is durable, in common use, and not likely to be affected by a particular company going out of business or changing its technology. CDs and removable hard drives are ideal. Make a schedule for periodically checking the archived files to make sure that deterioration isn't setting in, and plan to duplicate them on a regular schedule before you see any signs of trouble.

3. For the best security against loss, make two copies of each file and keep one copy off-site. That way, if a disaster hits your home or office, you won't lose your photographs.

4. Finally, have an easily read catalog of what is stored in your archives. A photographic database program is fine for maintaining your archives and making it easy to find files when you need to work on them, but don't expect that database to be readable a few decades from now. Extract all of the catalog information and save it as a simple text file or Word document or convert it into an Acrobat PDF file. All of those formats will be readable for very long time; your proprietary cataloging program's format is not likely to be. Save a copy of this catalog document on each archived storage disk. Safe and sane archiving is neither difficult nor especially much work. A bit of planning now will surely save you a lot of grief years from now.

Index